ALCOHOL USE DISORDERS

ALCOHOL USE DISORDERS

*A Developmental Science Approach
to Etiology*

EDITED BY

HIRAM E. FITZGERALD

AND

LEON I. PUTTLER

OXFORD
UNIVERSITY PRESS

OXFORD
UNIVERSITY PRESS

Oxford University Press is a department of the University of Oxford. It furthers
the University's objective of excellence in research, scholarship, and education
by publishing worldwide. Oxford is a registered trade mark of Oxford University
Press in the UK and certain other countries.

Published in the United States of America by Oxford University Press
198 Madison Avenue, New York, NY 10016, United States of America.

© Oxford University Press 2018

Library of Congress Cataloging-in-Publication Data
Names: Fitzgerald, Hiram E., editor. | Puttler, Leon I., editor.
Title: Alcohol use disorders : a developmental science approach to etiology /
edited by Hiram E. Fitzgerald and Leon I. Puttler.
Description: Oxford ; New York : Oxford University Press, [2018] |
Includes bibliographical references and index.
Identifiers: LCCN 2017040487 (print) | LCCN 2017040862 (ebook) |
ISBN 9780190676018 (updf) | ISBN 9780190676025 (epub) | ISBN 9780190676001 (hardback)
Subjects: LCSH: Alcoholism. | Developmental psychology. | BISAC: PSYCHOLOGY /
Developmental / General. | PSYCHOLOGY / Clinical Psychology.
Classification: LCC RC565 (ebook) | LCC RC565 .A4445 2018 (print) | DDC 616.89—dc23
LC record available at https://lccn.loc.gov/2017040487

1 3 5 7 9 8 6 4 2

Printed by Sheridan Books, Inc., United States of America

Contents

Preface

Alcohol and other substance use addictions are a major public health issue worldwide. Historically, the study of these addictions focused on adults, discussing the origins of alcohol use disorders (AUDs) as emergent in adolescence but paying little attention to developmental issues related to the etiology or progression of the problems. Starting with seminal publications in the mid-1970s, Robert Zucker helped pioneer the movement to help us understand that the etiologic processes that heighten risk or resilience factors for these problems involve a multilevel consideration of biological, psychological, and social factors that involve a great deal of heterogeneity over the life course. The impetus for the current volume stems from a celebration held on April 29, 2015, at the University of Michigan honoring Zucker's long, productive, and distinguished research career and his many contributions to the field of addictions. Some of the material in this book was presented that day, with additional information and contributors added to help readers learn where we are today in our understanding of the development of addictions.

Chapters in this volume reflect, to one degree or another, eight critical aspects of contemporary research attempting to understand the etiologic processes that heighten risk or resilience factors for substance use disorders: (1) a focus on systemic frameworks for understanding developmental process, (2) the heterogeneity of developmental pathways,

(3) the role of genes and epigenetic–experience transactions in risk and resilience, (4) risk cumulative/cascade models of the effects of exposure to adverse childhood experiences, (5) negotiating developmental transitional periods, (6) neurobiological embodiment of adverse childhood experiences, (7) links between AUD and tobacco addictive behaviors, and (8) longitudinal studies and data analysis within and between studies. These themes were implicit in Zucker's work and that of other investigators who helped to solidify the longitudinal research framework for studying the dynamics of AUD over various segments of the life course. Notable among these investigators are Laurie Chassin (Arizona State University), Kenneth Sher (University of Missouri), Kenneth Leonard and Rina Eiden (University of Buffalo), Kim Fromme (University of Texas at Austin), and John Donovan (University of Pittsburgh), each of whom is a contributor to this volume.

Contemporary understanding of addictions benefits from 30 years of longitudinal studies, one of which is the Michigan Longitudinal Study (MLS) developed by Robert Zucker and his colleague, Hiram Fitzgerald (co-editor of this volume). This study began in the mid-1980s with a grant from the National Institute of Alcoholism and Alcohol Abuse, with data collection and analyses continuing through the present. The MLS and other longitudinal studies in this area were specifically designed to assess pre-onset origins of problems, predictors of onset, and outcomes through early adulthood. The overriding theme of the current volume is that the origins and expression of addiction are best understood within the context of developmental processes and dynamic systems organization and change. Such dynamic systems give rise to diverse or heterogeneous pathways that are characterized by multifinality and equifinality due to the exchanges among genes, epigenetic processes, and the complexities of the individual organism's experiential world. For some individuals, these dynamic processes lead to risk cumulative or cascade effects that embody adverse childhood experiences that exacerbate risk; predict early onset of drinking, smoking, or other substance use; and often lead to a substance use disorder (SUD) during the transitions to adolescence and emergent adulthood. In other cases, protective factors within or outside of the individual's immediate family enable embodiment of normative stress regulatory systems and neural networks that support resilience and prevention of SUDs.

Hiram E. Fitzgerald
Leon I. Puttler
2017

Acknowledgments

We extend deep thanks to each of the authors for sharing their important findings and insights about AUD. Understanding the dynamics and developmental issues related to AUD is important for researchers, clinicians, national and international policy makers, as well as the general public so that we may prevent the serious consequences of AUDS. We are indebted to our editor at Oxford University Press, Andrea Zekus, and our production editor, Issac D Priyakumar, for their guidance and persistent encouragement that kept us from straying too far from established time lines and production schedules. A special note of gratitude to Daniel Hays for his absolutely fabulous copy editing, and to Michigan State University students Alyssa Bedaine, Kaitlyn Lumpkin, Allison Rochon, and Julia Gabrysh for their help in assembling the index. Foremost, we extend our thanks to our colleague Robert Zucker for his 30-year leadership of the Michigan Longitudinal Study of children at risk for alcoholism and co-active psychopathology. Nearly forty years ago, Zucker published the first of many papers that provided a framework for considering alcohol use disorders as emergent, with heterogeneous developmental pathways. Notably, his work stimulated a shift in understanding AUD as an adolescent-onset disorder to one that reflects dynamic systemic processes, many of which have origins in the events of infancy and early childhood. The articles in this anthology collectively draw attention to these processes and to the heterogeneous life course events that are critical aspects of the developmental psychopathology of AUD.

About the Editors

Hiram E. Fitzgerald is University Distinguished Professor in the Department of Psychology and Associate Provost for University Outreach and Engagement at Michigan State University. His major areas of research include the study of infant and family development in community contexts, the impact of fathers on early child development, 0–5 age boys and risk, the etiology of alcoholism, implementation of systemic community models of organizational process and change, and broad issues related to the scholarship of engagement. He is a member of the Native Children's Research Exchange, the Tribal Research Center for American Indian/Alaska Native Early Childhood Education, and the national advisory board for the University of Nebraska Buffett Early Childhood Institute. He has published more than 400 journal articles, chapters, books, and technical reports. He has received numerous awards, including the ZERO TO THREE Dolley Madison Award for Outstanding Lifetime Contributions to the Development and Well Being of Very Young Children. He is a Fellow of the Association of Psychological Science and of five divisions of the American Psychological Association.

Leon I. Puttler is a clinical psychologist working in the Department of Psychiatry at the University of Michigan. His is Project Director of the Michigan Longitudinal Study, for which he has worked for 22 years. He received his PhD in 1996 from Michigan State University. Current research interests include the development of addictions with an emphasis on risk factors associated with its development, resilience in deviating from expected pathways, and the effects of recovery status of parental alcohol problems on the functioning of children and their parents; child sexual abuse; and psychotherapy with children, adults, couples, and families. In addition to his work as a psychologist, he is also an elected local official as a Trustee in Bath Charter Township, Michigan.

About the Contributors

Deepti Agarwal is a doctoral student in Health Behavior and Health Education in the Department of Kinesiology and Health Education at The University of Texas at Austin. She earned undergraduate and graduate degrees in English literature from the University of Delhi. Her involvement with Teach India and the World Health Organization in India inspired her to pursue a career in improving the health outcomes of disparate populations. Thereafter, she earned an MSSW in social work from The University of Texas at Austin before entering the PhD program in Health Behavior and Health Education. Her research interests and goals are to decrease risky health behavior, particularly tobacco use among young adults.

James R. Ashenhurst contributed his chapter while he was a Postdoctoral Fellow in the Department of Psychology at The University of Texas at Austin. After completing a bachelor's degree in psychology from Princeton University, he received his PhD in neuroscience from the University of California, Los Angeles. His dissertation work focused on direct translational (both animal and human) research on decision-making and genetics in the context of alcohol dependence. His areas of interest include pharmacogenetics, impulsivity, behavior genetics, personality, and the neuroscience of substance use disorders and motivated behavior. He is currently a product scientist at 23andMe, Inc., in Mountain View, California, where he is helping to make US Food and Drug Administration-approved direct-to-consumer genomic interpretation a reality.

Guadalupe A. Bacio is Assistant Professor in the Departments of Psychology and Intercollegiate Chicana/o–Latina/o Studies at Pomona College. She received her PhD in clinical psychology from the University of California, Los Angeles. She is a member of the Research Society on Alcoholism, the Society for Prevention Research, and the National Hispanic Network on Drug Abuse. She currently directs the Cultural contExts, adolesceNt healTh behavioRs, & develOpment (CENTRO) Research Lab at Pomona College. The overarching goal of her program of research is to help eliminate disparities in patterns and consequences of alcohol and drug use encountered by ethnic minority adolescents of different immigrant generations. To this end, her research focuses on (1) understanding factors in the etiology and development of alcohol and drug use among these groups, (2) identifying mechanisms that generate and maintain these disparities that can be targeted through prevention/intervention efforts, and (3) examining the effectiveness of adolescent alcohol intervention programs in addressing these groups' needs.

Kelly Birch is an undergraduate honors student at the University of San Diego studying behavioral neuroscience and chemistry. After graduation, she will pursue a doctorate in clinical psychology with a concentration in neuropsychology. She hopes to eventually work in the assessment and treatment of traumatic brain injury.

Sandra A. Brown is Vice Chancellor for Research and a Distinguished Professor of Psychology and Psychiatry at the University of California, San Diego. She is internationally recognized for her developmentally focused alcohol and drug intervention research. Her primary research focuses on the impact of alcohol and other drugs on human development and clinical course for substance abuse factors influencing transitions out of alcohol and drug problems. Her research yielded pioneering information on adolescent addiction, relapse among youth, and long-term outcomes of youth who have experienced alcohol and drug problems. She is the past President of Division 50 (Addictions) of the American Psychological Association, is on the executive board of numerous scientific organizations, and has more than 35 grants and 350 publications. She is involved in addiction prevention and intervention at the regional, state, and national levels and helped lead the National Institute of Alcoholism and Alcohol Abuse's (NIAAA) effort to establish national screening and early intervention guidelines for youth. She currently directs the National Consortium on Alcohol and Neurodevelopment in Adolescence (NCANDA).

Ty Brumback is an Addictions Fellow at the VA San Diego Healthcare System and in the Department of Psychiatry at the University of California, San Diego. His research examines the relationships among neurocognition, brain function, and risky behaviors, specifically alcohol and other drug use, in adolescents and young adults. He received his PhD in clinical psychology from the University of South Florida in 2013.

Anne Buu is Associate Professor in the Department of Epidemiology and Biostatistics at Indiana University–Bloomington. She is a biostatistician and a developmental psychologist. She received a PhD in statistics from the University of Florida and a PhD in educational psychology from Indiana University–Bloomington. Before joining the faculty of Indiana University, she was a research faculty member at the University of North Carolina at Chapel Hill and the University of Michigan. Her research interests include longitudinal data analysis, health communication, bioinformatics, and substance abuse prevention. She is the recipient of a Research Scientist Development Award from the NIAAA. She is the principal investigator of two 5-year methodology projects funded by the National Institutes of Health (NIH). She has also served as a study statistician for several longitudinal projects funded by the NIH, such as the Michigan Longitudinal Study and the Flint Adolescent Study.

Laurie Chassin is Regents Professor of Psychology at Arizona State University. Her research interests are in developmental psychopathology and intergenerational transmission of substance use disorders and in life course trajectories and etiological processes underlying cigarette smoking. She is a principal investigator of NIH-funded longitudinal studies of cigarette smoking and alcohol use. She received her PhD in clinical psychology from Teachers College Columbia University, postdoctoral training in sociology and mental health from Indiana University–Bloomington, and a BA in psychology from Brown University.

Dante Cicchetti is McKnight Presidential Chair and William Harris Professor of Child Psychology at the University of Minnesota (2005–present). After receiving his PhD in clinical psychology and child development from the University of Minnesota in 1977, he joined the faculty at Harvard University, where he was subsequently Assistant Professor (1977–1982) and Norman Tishman Associate Professor of Psychology and Social Relations (1983–1985). In 1985, he moved to the University of Rochester, where he served as Director of Mt. Hope Family Center for 20 years. He has published more than 500 articles, books, and journal special issues that have had a far-reaching impact on developmental theory as well as on science, policy, and practice related to developmental psychopathology, child maltreatment, depression, and developmental disabilities, as well as numerous domains of normal development. He founded the journal *Development and Psychopathology* and is in his 27th year as editor. He has received four honors from the Developmental Division of the American Psychological Association (APA): the Boyd McCandless Award, the G. Stanley Hall Award; the Urie Bronfenbrenner Award, and the Mentor Award in Developmental Psychology. He was honored with the Society for Research in Child Development's Distinguished Scientific Contributions to Child Development Award and the

AAAS Fellow Award by the American Association for the Advancement of Science. He is the recipient of the 2012 Klaus J. Jacobs Research Prize and received the 2014 James Cattell Award from the Association for Psychological Science.

James A. Cranford is Research Assistant Professor in the Addiction Research Center at the University of Michigan. He received his PhD in social and personality psychology from the University at Albany, State University of New York, and completed postdoctoral fellowships in the Department of Psychology at New York University and in the Addiction Research Center at the University of Michigan. He is a member of the Association for Psychological Science, the Society for Personality and Social Psychology, and the Research Society on Alcoholism. His research focuses on (1) the marital and family context of substance use and substance use disorders; (2) mechanisms of behavior change in substance use disorders; and (3) application of intensive longitudinal methods to studies of stress, social interaction, and substance use.

John E. Donovan is Professor of Psychiatry and Epidemiology at the University of Pittsburgh. He received his doctorate in personality and social psychology in 1977 from the University of Colorado at Boulder. He stayed on there as a Research Associate from 1977 to 1992, working with Dr. Richard Jessor on studies testing and expanding problem behavior theory in community, state, and national samples of adolescents and young adults. In 1992, he was recruited by the University of Pittsburgh to serve as Scientific Director of the Pittsburgh Adolescent Alcohol Research Center until 1997. Since 2000, he has directed the Tween to Teen Project, a 16-wave longitudinal study of 8- and 10-year-olds and their families to ages 21–23 years that has focused on describing the developmental course of involvement with alcohol, examining the antecedent risk factors for the initiation and escalation of drinking and problem drinking, and determining the young adult outcomes of early alcohol involvement.

Rina D. Eiden is Senior Research Scientist at the Research Institute on Addictions, State University of New York at Buffalo, and Adjunct Faculty in the Departments of Pediatrics and Psychology. For more than two decades, she has been conducting research with families who have been impacted by parental substance abuse, using prospective designs beginning in pregnancy or early infancy. The goal of these studies broadly has been to examine when and under what circumstances children of substance-using parents exhibit patterns of maladjustment, what factors lead to resilience in the context of high parental and comorbid family risks, and ideal timing of preventive interventions with these families. She received her PhD in applied developmental psychology from the University of Maryland in 1992 and completed a postdoctoral fellowship on children of substance-using parents at the Research Institute on Addictions.

Catharine E. Fairbairn is Assistant Professor in the Psychology Department at the University of Illinois at Urbana–Champaign. She graduated in 2015 from the University of Pittsburgh with a PhD in clinical/health psychology and completed her clinical internship at the Ann Arbor VA. In addition to her training at the University of Pittsburgh, she has conducted research at Columbia's New York State Psychiatric Institute and the University of Pennsylvania's Treatment Research Center, and she has completed a fellowship in quantitative methods in the University of Oslo's Department of Biostatistics. She is a recipient of the National Science Foundation's Graduate Research Fellowship and also the National Science Foundation's Graduate Research Opportunities Worldwide Grant, and she received the Society for the Science of Clinical Psychology's Outstanding Student Researcher Award. Her research focuses on alcohol's rewarding effects within the context of social interaction, with the aim of understanding the basic social processes that might underlie alcohol use disorder.

Kim Fromme is Professor of Clinical Psychology at The University of Texas at Austin, where she has been on faculty since 1993. She received her PhD in clinical psychology from the University of Washington and completed her internship at the Palo Alto VA Medical Center before taking her first faculty position at the University of Delaware. Her program of research is based on a broad conceptual model that includes individual, social, environmental, and developmental factors in an effort to understand and prevent alcohol abuse and other behavioral risks. Using survey research, experimental designs, and randomized clinical trials, her research has identified critical etiological factors that may then be effectively changed to prevent hazardous drinking patterns and their negative consequences. Her current research combines 10 years of longitudinal behavioral data with genetic analyses to examine the mechanisms through which genetic and environmental factors influence changes in alcohol use and other externalizing behaviors during emerging adulthood.

Maleeha Haroon is a doctoral candidate in the Clinical Psychology program at the University of North Carolina at Chapel Hill. She received her BS in human development from Cornell University and completed a 2-year post-baccalaureate research fellowship at the National Institute on Drug Abuse. Her research interests concern the developmental processes underlying individual trajectories of substance use and abuse. Specifically, she is currently examining how early experience with drug use may change cognitions about use and how these changes may influence future patterns of use. Furthermore, she would like to explore how environmental contexts such as the peer group may moderate the effects of these early experiences on cognitions about use. In the future, she would like to explore how the results of such research could inform intervention efforts targeting adolescent cognitions about drug use as well as risk behaviors more broadly.

Sarah Harrison is an undergraduate honors student in behavioral neuroscience at the University of San Diego. Following graduation, she will pursue graduate training in neuroscience research focusing on the military veterans' community. She hopes to engage in advanced studies on neurodegenerative diseases and the interaction between neuroscience and genetics.

Mary M. Heitzeg is Assistant Professor in the Substance Abuse Section of the Department of Psychiatry and the Addiction Research Center at the University of Michigan. She received her PhD in biological psychology from the University of Michigan and completed her postdoctoral training in the Addiction Research Center. Her primary research focus is on developmental neuroimaging targeted at investigating genetic and behavioral risk factors for substance abuse. She has developed a program of research using longitudinal neuroimaging to investigate two related themes relevant to adolescent substance use: (1) how early individual differences in brain function relate to susceptibility to alcohol and other drug problems and (2) the effects of substance use on

the developing brain and how substance use impacts risk trajectories. She incorporates genetic information into these analyses, whereby systems-level syntheses can be accomplished by examining relationships across genetics, neural circuitry, and behavior.

Brian M. Hicks is Associate Professor in the Department of Psychiatry at the University of Michigan. The focus of his research has been to examine the interplay among genetic, environmental, and developmental influences on substance use, antisocial behavior and psychopathy, and personality. His work is supported by grants from the National Institute on Drug Abuse (NIDA) and the NIAAA. His research has also been recognized with early career contribution awards from the Behavior Genetics Association, the Society for Research in Psychopathology, and the Society for the Scientific Study of Psychopathy, and also by a Research Faculty Award from the University of Michigan.

Andrea M. Hussong directs the Center for Developmental Science and is Professor of Clinical Psychology at the University of North Carolina at Chapel Hill. Prior to joining the faculty, she completed a BA at Indiana University, a doctorate at Arizona State University, and a postdoctoral fellowship at the Center for Developmental Science at the University of North Carolina at Chapel Hill. Her research primarily concerns the developmental processes underlying substance use and later addiction, particularly among children of alcoholic parents. This work includes the study of an internalizing pathway to substance use and disorder posited to emerge during the first three decades of life and to encompass risk for substance use associated with a core deficit in emotion regulation. She pairs this substantive work with an interest in advanced developmental methodology and co-developed integrative data analysis as a means to study developmental processes by combining multiple independent studies in a single analysis.

Michael Ichiyama is Chair of the Department of Psychological Sciences at the University of San Diego. After receiving his PhD in psychology from the University of Cincinnati, he served as a research fellow in the Department of Psychiatry Alcohol Research Center at the University of Michigan from 1993 to 1995, where he worked under the mentorship of Dr. Robert Zucker. His research has focused on the investigation of risk factors related to heavy drinking and alcohol-related problems among university students and the study of social and cultural influences on the self-concept. He was the principal investigator on an NIH–NIAAA research grant, "University of San Diego Freshmen Research Initiative," which evaluated a parent-based intervention for the prevention of problem drinking in matriculating college freshmen. His peer-reviewed work has appeared in the *Journal of Studies on Alcohol and Drugs*, the *Journal of Consulting and Clinical Psychology*, *Social Psychology Quarterly*, and the *Journal of Cross-Cultural Psychology*.

Justin Jager is Assistant Professor in the T. Denny Sanford School of Social and Family Dynamics at Arizona State University. While focusing primarily on family, peer, as well as historical contexts, his research is devoted to unpacking how complex person–context interactions inform development across adolescence and the transition to adulthood. In terms of developmental outcomes, his research focuses primarily on substance use, risky behavior, mental health, and academic achievement. He received his doctorate in developmental psychology from the University of Michigan, postdoctoral training within the Intramural Research Program of the NIH, National Institute of Child Health and Human Development (NICHD), and a BA in psychology from Calvin College.

Matthew Lee is a Research Assistant Professor of Psychological Sciences at the University of Missouri at Columbia. Dr. Lee received a PhD from Arizona State University and post-doctoral training from the University of Missouri at Columbia, with training emphasizing clinical, developmental, and quantitative aspects of psychological research. His primary substantive interests are in the developmental psychopathology of alcohol use and disorder, with methodological interests in quantitative techniques for longitudinal data analysis. His research has focused primarily on understanding the normative reductions in problem drinking that occur in young adulthood (i.e., "maturing out"). Supported by an NIH K99/R00 "Pathway to Independence" award, Dr. Lee's research agenda has recently broadened toward investigation of desistance from problem drinking across the adult lifespan. Objective of this work include characterizing patterns and mechanisms of desistance, in

part toward understanding how they may vary across different developmental stages of the lifespan.

Kenneth E. Leonard is Director of the Research Institute on Addictions and Research Professor in Psychiatry at the University at Buffalo Medical School. He received his PhD in clinical psychology from Kent State University in 1981 and postdoctoral training in psychiatric/alcohol epidemiology at the Western Psychiatric Institute and Clinic at the University of Pittsburgh. He is a Fellow in Divisions 50 (Addictions) and 28 (Psychopharmacology and Substance Abuse) in the American Psychological Association, and he is a former President of Division 50. His research interests have been centered on the interpersonal and familial influences on substance abuse, as well as the influence of substance abuse on interpersonal and family processes. He is internationally recognized for his research on substance abuse and intimate partner violence, but he has also studied the impact of alcoholism on child development and the role of marital/family processes in the prevention and treatment of substance abuse.

Ash Levitt is Senior Research Scientist at the Research Institute on Addictions at the University at Buffalo. He received his PhD in social psychology from the University of Missouri in 2010 and postdoctoral training at the Research Institute on Addictions. His research primarily focuses on the antecedents and consequences of alcohol use processes in romantic relationships. In particular, he examines relationship-specific factors that can help explain when, how, and for whom relationship alcohol use might be adaptive or maladaptive. These factors include relationship-specific drinking contexts (e.g., drinking with one's partner), alcohol expectancies (e.g., intimacy enhancement), and drinking motives (e.g., to cope with a stressful relationship problem). His current research examines motivational factors surrounding momentary alcohol use processes in romantic relationships.

Runze Li is Verne M. Willaman Professor of Statistics at The Pennsylvania State University. His statistical expertise includes analysis of intensive longitudinal data, variable selection for high-dimensional data, and feature screening for ultrahigh-dimensional data. He has built strong and productive collaborations with several more applied scientists and has guided the application of his methods to data on drug abuse. He has published more than 100 papers in the finest statistical methodological and theoretical journals, including *Journal of American Statistical Association* (JASA) and *Annals of Statistics* (AOS), and top-tier journals in disciplines beyond statistics, such as *Psychological Methods, Drug and Alcohol Dependence,* and *Nicotine and Tobacco Research.* He was the recipient of an National Science Foundation Career Award in 2004. He is a Fellow of the Institute of Mathematical Statistics and a Fellow of the American Statistical Association. He has served as co-editor of *AOS* since 2013 and associate editor of *JASA* since 2006.

Andrew Littlefield is an Assistant Professor at Texas Tech University. His research interests include the development of substance use disorders with a particular focus on factors that contribute to alcohol disorders among emerging adults. He is also interested in the implementation of advanced statistical methods in order to address substantive research questions. He is a principal investigator of SAMHSA-funded project which involves implementing a SBIRT model among medical professionals serving in west Texas. He received a PhD in clinical psychology from the University of Missouri and completed his clinical internship at the University of Mississippi Medical Center.

Alexandra Loukas is the Barbie M. and Gary L. Coleman Professor in Education in the Department and Kinesiology and Health Education at the University of Texas at Austin. She earned her PhD in developmental psychology from Michigan State University in 1997, under the mentorship of Hiram E. Fitzgerald and Robert A. Zucker. The focus of her research is on adolescent and young adult health, particularly problem behavior development and tobacco use and cessation. She has a special interest in examining how factors from multiple ecological levels (e.g., family, school, and culture) interact to protect adolescents and young adults from negative health outcomes.

Jonathan T. Macy is Assistant Professor of Applied Health Science in the School of Public Health at Indiana University–Bloomington. His research interests include tobacco control policy, smoking cessation, adolescent smoking prevention, and implicit attitudes toward smoking. He is principal investigator on a study testing contingency management as a strategy to reduce smoking among pregnant women and co-investigator on an NIH-funded 35-year longitudinal study of smoking attitudes and behaviors. He received his PhD in health behavior from Indiana University, an MPH in international health from Emory University, and a BA in economics from DePauw University.

Julie Maslowsky is Assistant Professor of Health Behavior and Health Education in the Department of Kinesiology and Health Education at the University of Texas at Austin. She received her PhD in developmental psychology from the University of Michigan and completed postdoctoral training in population health with the Robert Wood Johnson Foundation Health & Society Scholars. Her research focuses on the epidemiology and etiology of adolescent health behavior.

Eun-Young Mun joined the Center of Alcohol Studies at Rutgers University in 2006 after 4 years on the faculty of the University of Alabama at Birmingham. She holds a joint appointment in the Department of Clinical Psychology, Graduate School of Applied and Professional Psychology, and is a Graduate Faculty member in the Department of Psychology. She has researched developmental processes through which one's risk for the development of alcohol problems is maintained, intensified, or ameliorated throughout the lifespan using longitudinal, experimental, and intervention data. She is particularly interested in adolescents and young adults going through life transitions because these transitional points may provide better opportunities for change. In recent years, she has focused on (1) examining the magnitude and consistency of the intervention effect of brief motivational interventions for college students and (2) discovering subgroups via analyzing individual participant-level data from multiple studies in integrative analyses.

Joel T. Nigg directs the ADHD Program and the Division of Psychology and is Professor of Psychiatry and Behavioral Neuroscience at Oregon Health & Science University. Prior to joining the faculty there, he obtained a PhD in clinical psychology from the University of California at Berkeley and was Director of Clinical Training in the Department of Psychology at Michigan State University. His research examines the neuropsychological, physiological, cognitive, genetic, and neural contributors to the development of attention and impulsivity and their disorders, particularly as expressed in attention-deficit/hyperactivity disorder (ADHD). ADHD is a major risk factor for substance use disorders. He therefore also works on the role of executive functioning, temperament, personality, and self-regulation in risk for alcoholism and addiction, in collaboration with the University of Michigan–Michigan State University Family Study. He has a particular interest in the intersection of cognitive and emotional regulation in developmental psychopathology.

Igor Ponomarev is Assistant Professor at the Waggoner Center for Alcohol and Addiction Research and the College of Pharmacy at the University of Texas at Austin. His current research focuses on the interplay between genetic, epigenetic, and environmental factors in controlling brain gene expression and behavioral abnormalities in models of alcohol use disorder. His lab applies systems approaches to data analysis to provide an integrated view of brain changes associated with alcohol-related neuroplasticity and neuropathology. He received his PhD in behavioral neuroscience from Oregon Health & Science University and postdoctoral training in molecular biology and bioinformatics from the University of Texas at Austin.

Clark C. Presson is Professor of Psychology at Arizona State University. His research interests include the development of spatial knowledge and reasoning, the use of spatial symbols, applications of cognitive development to child and adolescent health psychology, and processes of initiation of cigarette smoking. He is a principal investigator on an NIH-funded 35-year longitudinal study of smoking attitudes and behaviors. He received his PhD in developmental psychology from Columbia University Teachers College, postdoctoral training in clinical psychology at Arizona State University, and a BA in psychology from Pomona College.

Anne E. Ray joined the Center of Alcohol Studies in 2011 after completing her PhD in biobehavioral health at The Pennsylvania State University. Her research is broadly focused on the etiology and prevention of high-risk substance use among adolescent and emerging adult populations. She is particularly interested in the role of self-regulated drinking behaviors, actions that can be protective or risky in nature and capture a stylistic element of drinking (i.e., pacing drinks, setting limits, and playing drinking games), in the experience of alcohol-related harm, and how prevention efforts can be improved through increased emphasis on these behaviors. She is actively involved in Project INTEGRATE, an integrative data analysis study that utilizes individual participant-level data from 24 brief motivational interventions (BMIs) to reduce risky drinking in college student samples. Specifically, she has focused on the examination of variation in BMI content and how differences in content are related to drinking outcomes. She is also involved in several program evaluation efforts within the Education & Training Division at the Center of Alcohol Studies.

Fred A. Rogosch is Director of Research at Mt. Hope Family Center, a research and clinical institute at the University of Rochester, and Associate Professor in the Department of Clinical and Social Sciences in Psychology at the University of Rochester. He obtained his PhD in clinical psychology from Michigan State University and completed a postdoctoral fellowship in prevention science and child mental health at Arizona State University. His research focuses on the area of developmental psychopathology, with a special emphasis on studying developmental processes from infancy into emerging adulthood in children exposed to adversity, particularly child maltreatment and early trauma, and maternal major depressive disorder. His research incorporates influences at multiple levels of psychological and biological analysis in understanding emergent psychopathology and maladaptation, as well as resilience, in chronically stressed children and families. Evaluation of early interventions to prevent maladaptive developmental trajectories in development also is a primary interest.

W. Andrew Rothenberg is a doctoral candidate in the Clinical Psychology Program at the University of North Carolina at Chapel Hill. Prior to entering the Clinical Psychology Program, he completed a BA as a Roy H. Park Scholar at North Carolina State University. His primary research interests concern the developmental processes that underlie continuity in maladaptive parenting and family conflict across generations. This work includes the identification of mediating pathways and contextual risk factors (e.g., familial substance misuse) that increase the likelihood that deleterious parenting and family environments persist across generations. He pairs these research interests with an interest in the development, implementation, and dissemination of evidence-based interventions for families experiencing coercive cycles of conflict.

Gabriel L. Schlomer is Assistant Professor in the Division of Educational Psychology and Methodology at the University at Albany, State University of New York. He received his PhD in family studies and human development from the University of Arizona, where he gained expertise in evolutionary theoretical approaches to studying children and families. Following his PhD, he completed postdoctoral work at The Pennsylvania State University as part of both the Biobehavioral Health and Human Development and Family Studies departments, where he gained additional training in molecular genetics and gene-by-environment interaction (G×E) research. His current research interests center on gene–environment interplay, including G×E interactions, epigenetic modifications, and evaluating conditional adaptation. His research focuses on evaluating genetic and environmental effects, and their co-action, on externalizing behavior problems in adolescents, including substance use, aggression/delinquency, and risky sexual behavior.

John Schulenberg is Professor, Department of Psychology, and Research Professor, Institute for Social Research, at the University of Michigan. He has published widely on several topics concerning adolescence and the transition to adulthood, focusing on how developmental tasks and transitions relate to health risks and adjustment difficulties. His current research is on the etiology and epidemiology of substance use and psychopathology, focusing on risk factors, course, comorbidity, and consequences during adolescence and the transition to adulthood. He is co-principal investigator of the NIDA-funded national Monitoring the Future study concerning substance use and psychosocial development across adolescence and adulthood. His work has been funded by NIDA, NIAAA, NICHD, the National Institute of Mental Health, the National Science Foundation,

and the Robert Wood Johnson Foundation. For these and other institutes and foundations (including the Institute of Medicine), he has served on numerous advisory and review committees. He is a Fellow of the APA and President of the Society for Research on Adolescence.

Kenneth J. Sher is Curators' Distinguished Professor at the University of Missouri. He received his BA from Antioch College (1975) and his PhD in clinical psychology from Indiana University (1980). His research focuses on etiological processes in the development of alcohol dependence, factors that affect the course of drinking and alcohol use disorders across the lifespan, psychopharmacology of alcohol, and nosology. He is a Fellow of the APA, the Association for Psychological Science, and the American Association for the Advancement of Science. His research contributions have been recognized by professional societies (e.g., the Research Society on Alcoholism and the APA), the National Institutes of Health, the University of Missouri, and Indiana University. He is currently associate editor of *Clinical Psychological Science* and field editor of *Alcoholism: Clinical and Experimental Research* and has previously served as associate editor of *Psychological Bulletin* and the *Journal of Abnormal Psychology*.

Steven J. Sherman was trained as an experimental social psychologist. He received his PhD from the University of Michigan in 1967, working primarily with Robert Zajonc. Since then, he has been at Indiana University, where he is current Chancellor's Professor. Sherman has published empirical and theoretical papers in many areas of social/cognitive psychology, including the relations between attitudes and behavior, mispredictions of future behavior, effects of imagining and explaining the future, false consensus effect, a feature-matching model of preferences, counterfactual thinking, language and thinking, metaphors, and psychology and the law. He has also applied his experience in experimental psychology to an understanding of an important real-world problem—cigarette smoking. For more than 35 years, he was involved in the longest longitudinal study of the social psychological factors that help to understand smoking initiation and cessation.

Ruth K. Smith is a doctoral candidate in the Clinical Psychology program at the University of North

Carolina at Chapel Hill. She completed a Bachelor of Science in psychobiology at La Sierra University. Prior to her doctoral studies, she conducted longitudinal work as part of a research team at the University of Maryland College Park, where she investigated factors that contribute to adolescent engagement in risky sexual and drug use practices. Her research interests include risk and protective factors that contribute to youth resiliency and maladjustment. Specifically, her focus lies in examining the interplay between developmental transitions, life stressors, and familial influences that contribute to the development of emotion regulation, substance use, and other forms of psychopathology. Furthermore, she has interest in investigating how advanced quantitative methods can improve the measurement of substance use and disorder and thus inform prevention programming within this line of research.

Kayla Swart is the laboratory manager for the Department of Psychological Sciences at the University of San Diego. She received her undergraduate degree in neuroscience from Davidson College. She plans to pursue graduate research training focusing on the areas of neuroplasticity and neuroprotection.

Elisa M. Trucco is Assistant Professor in the Department of Psychology and an affiliate of the Center for Children and Families at Florida International University. She received her undergraduate degree from the University of Pennsylvania and her doctorate from the University at Buffalo, State University of New York. She completed her clinical internship at Yale University, School of Medicine. She also completed two postdoctoral T32 fellowships through the University of Michigan and is a licensed Clinical Psychologist in Michigan and Florida. Her program of research is grounded in developmental psychopathology and social ecological perspectives. Her work involves delineating risk and protective factors for the development of adolescent problem behavior and substance use across multiple levels of analysis, including biological factors (genetics and neurobiology), social contexts (peers, parents, and neighborhoods), and individual characteristics

(temperament and personality). The aim of her programmatic work is to improve existing substance prevention programs for youth.

Annie Wescott is Executive Assistant and Library Sciences Liaison for the Department of Psychological Sciences at the University of San Diego. Following her BA in interdisciplinary studies from Southern Oregon University, she received her master's degree in library and information science from the University of Washington.

Maria M. Wong is Director of the Development and Resilience Lab in the Psychology Department at Idaho State University. She is interested in examining risk and protective factors that affect important developmental outcomes such as substance use, suicidal behavior, and resilience. Her current work focuses on understanding how sleep and self-regulation (control of affect, behavior, and cognitive processes) affect health and behavior. Her research projects have been funded by the National Institute of Health. Her work has been cited by National Public Radio, *TIME Magazine*, BBC, CNN, NBC, Reuters, and the Associated Press.

Robert A. Zucker is a Professor in Psychiatry and Psychology at the University of Michigan, Director Emeritus of the UM Addiction Research Center and the Department of Psychiatry Substance Abuse Program. His major career focus has been the lifespan etiology and course of alcohol and other drug involvement, and the development of screening, early identification, and early intervention programming for high-risk populations. He has been one of the major contributors to the understanding of alcoholism as a developmental disorder and has been involved in the translational ramifications of this work as a member a number of NIH action committees to identify and screen for early substance abuse, and as the director of an NIH supported program to develop substance abuse research infrastructure in Eastern Europe. He is author of over 300 publications, editor/author of 11 books, and a recipient of the Research Society on Alcoholism's Distinguished Researcher Award. He is past-President of the Society on Addiction Psychology.

PART I

ALCOHOL USE DISORDERS

Perspectives from Developmental Psychopathology and Developmental Science

In the 21st century, scientists, clinicians, and practitioners share the conclusion that the development and expression of psychopathology is a dynamic process that is influenced synergistically by the individual's genetic, epigenetic, and life course experiences (Oken, Chamine, & Wakeland, 2015). When life course events include exposure to, and the accumulation of, adverse childhood experiences, the stage is set for the organization of negative life course pathways, including those that may express addictive behaviors. Conversely, positive life course events set the stage for the organization of positive life course pathways. We refer to "setting the stage" because life course events frequently challenge emergent developmental pathways and just as in dramatic plays, the plays of life can change, sometimes dramatically, from one day to the next and certainly from one age prior to another. In fact, one can easily argue that from the moment of conception until death, each individual's life consists of balancing risk and resilience factors, sometimes moment to moment but clearly from one developmental period to the next. Exposure to risk and resilience factors therefore can be conceptualized as one's varying position on the continuum over the life course. Figure P.1 illustrates the risk–resilience continuum with respect to critical factors affecting development of substance use disorders (SUDs) from conception to the end of emergent adulthood.

Eight recurrent themes concerning etiologic processes that heighten risk or resilience factors for the emergence of an SUD, and alcohol use disorders

(AUDs) in particular, are referenced throughout the chapters of this volume. In fact, these themes simultaneously serve as summative conclusions about the etiology of SUD/AUD from a developmental science framework. The eight themes reflect etiologic origins of AUD in genetics and epigenetics, and they also focus on heterogeneity, developmental phases, organizational processes, and the critical role of experience as core to understanding AUD pathways. The foundational themes are as follows:

- Systemic theories and methods are necessary for understanding AUD etiology.
- Genes and epigenetic experiences influence pathways of AUD throughout life.
- AUD is a heterogeneous biopsychosocial addictive behavior.
- Cumulative adverse childhood experiences exacerbate risk for AUD expression.
- Neurobiological embodiment of adverse childhood experiences impacts AUD.
- Transitions between developmental periods impact etiologic pathways.
- Tobacco addiction often is a gateway to AUD and other drugs.
- Longitudinal research designs are essential for tracking developmental changes on the risk–resilience continuum related to AUD.

In Chapter 1, Puttler, Zucker, and Fitzgerald draw attention to the complexity of the etiology of one of the most pervasive and destructive forms of psychopathology, namely alcoholism in general and antisocial

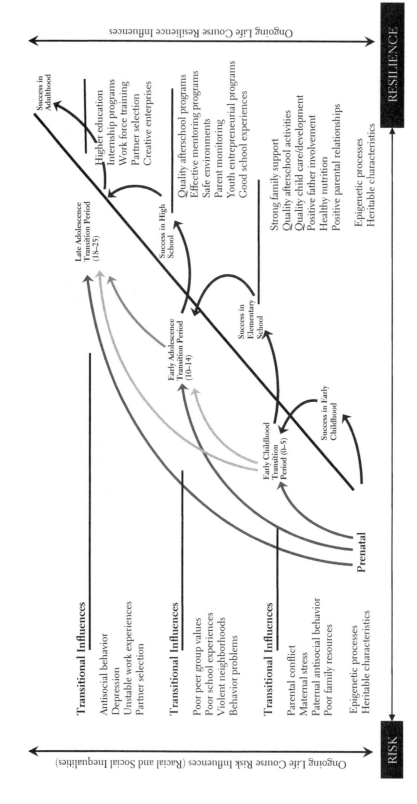

FIGURE P.1 Transitional periods: Dynamic factors affecting positioning on the risk–resilience continuum from conception to adulthood.

Source: Adapted with permission from Fitzgerald, H. E. (2010). Birth to work: A community driven framework for systems change. *The Engaged Scholar, 5,* 20–21.

alcoholism in particular. They indicate that the natural complexity of developing and organizing systems is best understood by comparable scientific approaches. These approaches include emphasis on models driven by developmental systems theories—organizational, transdisciplinary, and social–ecological sources of variation using longitudinal research designs to enable assessment of change and stability across transitional periods and within and between developmental pathways. Indeed, developmental science focuses on the organization of behavior within the context of emergent, epigenetic, systemic, constructive, and dynamic processes embedded within a bioecological framework (Fitzgerald, Davies, Zucker, & Klinger, 1994; Fitzgerald, Zucker, & Yang, 1995; Kanherkar, Bhatia-Dey, & Csoka, 2014).

Dynamic systems models give rise to diverse or heterogeneous pathways that are characterized by multifinality and equifinality due to the exchanges among genes, epigenetic processes, and the complexities of the individual organism's experiential world. Equifinality refers to obtaining the same outcome despite variation in initial conditions and in developmental pathways. Multifinality refers to achieving different outcomes even though the initial conditions were extremely similar, as were the developmental pathways. For example, 70% of children of alcoholics do not develop AUD, whereas 5% of children of non-alcoholics do develop AUD. Why is this the case? Diversity of pathways and dynamic developmental process mean that over the life course each individual resides somewhere on the risk–resilience continuum (Fitzgerald & Simon, 2012). Where one resides on the continuum will change because of life experiences, aging, health, and so on. Although both risk and resilience factors can accumulate over time, greater research attention is given to the accumulation of risk, particularly with regard to the accumulation of adverse childhood experiences. According to Child Trends, 11% of all children (birth to age 17 years) are persistently exposed to three or more adverse experiences, including family alcohol/drug problems and mental health problems (Golding & Fitzgerald, 2017). Puttler et al. focus on the adverse childhood factors that provide early evidence of psychopathology and organize pathways that lead to early onset smoking, alcohol consumption, or other types of psychopathology.

In Chapter 2, Cicchetti and Rogosch continue this theme, noting that child maltreatment indicates that caregivers fail to provide the just expectable experiences necessary to promote positive development. Child maltreatment contributes to epigenetic changes as children adapt to stress and emotional damage that exacerbates the likelihood of failure and disruption in the successful resolution of major developmental tasks of infancy and childhood. As noted by Cicchetti and Rogosch, repeated disruptions compromise the positive organization of diverse developmental systems, thereby increasing the probability of maladaptation, psychopathology, and substance abuse, as negative transactions between the child and the environment ensue. Cicchetti and Rogosch's cascade model of child maltreatment predicts risk for externalizing and internalizing problems and poor social competence in children (Hosseinichimeh, Rahmandad, & Wittenborn, 2015; Oken et al., 2015). Moreover, if maltreatment persists, stability in behavioral symptomatology increases and exacerbates risk for the emergence of SUD. In short, child maltreatment embeds the child on the risk edge of the risk–resilience continuum. The good news from epigenetics is that with effective intervention and treatment, many maltreated children can be assisted to move toward resilience.

In Chapter 3, Hussong, Rothenberg, Smith, and Haroon discuss pathways that increase risk for internalizing and externalizing behavior problems—two significant components of pathways leading to SUD or other forms of psychopathology. According to the authors, the externalizing pathway includes a core deficit in behavioral control and risky behavior that persists over the life course. Emotion regulation is a core symptom within internalizing disorders, as are social skills deficits and cognitions or expectancies that are related to drinking as a coping mechanism. Hussong et al. advocate for the development of interventions aimed at identifying more precisely precursors of risk for AUD and for generation of effective interventions preventing early childhood experiences that lead to AUD. Critical to such efforts is more research to determine how externalizing and internalizing pathways interact within and between individuals.

REFERENCES

Fitzgerald, H. E., Davies, W. H., Zucker, R. A., & Klinger, M. (1994). Developmental systems theory and substance abuse: A conceptual and methodological framework for analyzing patterns of variation in families. In L. L'Abate (Ed.), *Handbook of developmental family psychology and psychopathology* (pp. 353–372). New York, NY: Wiley.

Fitzgerald, H. E., & Simon, L. A. K. (2012). The world grant ideal and engagement scholarship. *Journal of Higher Education Outreach and Engagement*, 16(3), 33–55.

Fitzgerald, H. E., Zucker, R. A., & Yang, H.-Y. (1995). Developmental systems theory and alcoholism: Analyzing patterns of variation in high-risk families. *Psychology of Addictive Behavior*, 9, 8–22.

Golding, P., & Fitzgerald, H. E. (2017). Psychology of boys at risk: Indicators from 0–5. *Infant Mental Health Journal*, 38, 5–14.

Hosseinichimeh, N., Rahmandad, H., & Wittenborn, A. R. (2015). Modeling the hypothalamic–pituitary–adrenal axis: A review and extension. *Mathematical Biosciences*, 268, 52–65.

Kanherkar, R. R., Bhatia-Dey, N., & Csoka, A. B. (2014). Epigenetics across the human lifespan. *Frontiers in Cell and Developmental Biology*, 2, 1–19.

Oken, B. S., Chamine, I., & Wakeland, W. (2015). A systems approach to stress, stressors, and resilience in humans. *Behavioural Brain Research*, 282, 144–154.

Developmental Science, Alcohol Use Disorders, and the Risk–Resilience Continuum

Leon I. Puttler

Robert A. Zucker

Hiram E. Fitzgerald

CASE STUDY

Joe Smith[1] died of an accidental overdose from drugs at age 29 years while staying with his mother and stepfather, who found him lifeless in his childhood bedroom. After serving in Iraq for 15 months, Joe had been suffering from post-traumatic stress disorder (PTSD) and depression for 8 years before his death. This symptomatic burden continued intermittently since his return to the United States. But this tragic story began well before Joe's time in the military.

Joe's Parents

Joe was the youngest of three children born to parents with a long history of their own problems, not the least of which was significant substance abuse. His mother, Sarah, is the second oldest of four children. She had an extensive history of antisocial behavior in her teens, including regularly skipping school, running away from home, and stealing. Sarah met Joe's father, Steven, and had two daughters with him at age 15 years (Amber) and age 16 years (Tricia). She was placed into foster care after the birth of her second child, and then she married Joe's father at age 17 years. Another son was born when Sarah was 20 years old (Alex), and then Joe was born when she was 22 years old.

Sarah started consuming alcohol at age 13 years, but she never drank very much over her life other than a brief period after divorcing Steven. She started smoking regularly at age 14 years and continued to do so into her late 40s when she was last interviewed. Most prominent was her extensive use of drugs. Although Sarah had her first experience with drugs at age 14 years, this was just minor experimentation. It was not until age 25 years that she started using drugs extensively, along with her husband, in part to try to be closer with him. At that time, Sarah used almost every category of drugs, including marijuana, amphetamines, barbiturates, cocaine (and crack), heroin, and other opioids. She quit her drug use after separating from her husband at age 26 years. Sarah has a long history as an adult of suffering from physiological problems (including hepatitis, which she contracted from needle usage with her heroin use), depression, and compulsive behavior. Her physical symptoms were so severe she was unable to work for many years.

Steven was the youngest of four children. His parents divorced when he was 10 years old, and he was later reportedly abused by his stepfather. He experienced traumatic events as a child leading to PTSD (being burned at age 9 years, leading to the need for several skin grafts, and witnessing a drive-by shooting during which several children were killed). Steven also had a long history of antisocial behavior as a child/adolescent, including skipping school and fighting. He was arrested several times, with the first time being at age 12 years. He started smoking regularly at age 7 years and continued throughout his adult life. Steven had his first alcoholic drink at age 6 years, with problematic usage taking place by the time he was 16 years old. Drug use was extensive starting at age 12 years, including use of marijuana, amphetamines, barbiturates, tranquilizers, cocaine, heroin, and other opioids. Steven began dealing drugs at age 15 years. He also had a history of depression, with the most severe occurrence at age 27 years after his brother committed suicide.

We do not know much about the early history of Sarah and Steven's relationship. As mentioned previously, in their mid-20s they were abusing substances together. Their relationship at that time was also quite abusive, with Steven being very physical, even knocking out Sarah one time with a hard wood object. Child Protective Services (CPS) was involved with the family, with the children being removed from the home on occasion. Steven was also engaging in other criminal behavior during this time period, including robbing drug stores. Eventually, Sarah separated from him, but he continued to stalk her. Steven was eventually arrested for possession of drugs (other arrests occurred previously), and he spent 6 years in prison. During the time Steven was in prison, Sarah divorced him (Joe was 4 years old at the time). She moved to another state with her three younger children (the oldest, Amber, was raised by Sarah's mother and had little contact with Sarah during her upbringing). She was involved with another man (actually an adult relative) who was not good for her, nor her family. As well as having sex with Sarah, he sexually abused Tricia. It is not clear if he sexually abused the boys, but that is a possibility. Sarah had significant problems with Tricia and Alex regarding their behavior (described briefly later). She then met another man, whom she married and to whom she is currently married. He became a stable force in her life and those of her children. However, it was a difficult position for him to be in because all the children were already exhibiting serious problems. Sarah continued to have significant health problems and depression into her 40s, but all substance use other than cigarettes ended in her mid-20s.

Meantime, even during his prison time, Steven continued to abuse substances. He experienced more traumatic events (witnessing four other prisoners killed in a stabbing incident), and his depression continued, with some mania symptoms beginning as well. He had some, but little, contact with his children in later years. We were not able to locate him in subsequent years and thus do not know many details of his later life. However, we were informed when working with his children that he eventually died of a drug overdose at age 35 years.

Joe's Older Sister and Brother

Tricia has a long history of anxiety and depression starting in childhood. She recalls as a child fleeing in a car to California from her home state to escape the law and CPS, only to be flown back and placed into foster care. She remembers her father pretending to kill himself on a couple of occasions, once putting ketchup on his shirt and shooting off a gun to scare her. Tricia describes herself hardening as an early teenager. She remembers getting into physical fights with her mother, as well as engaging in other forms of antisocial behavior (skipping school, running away, vandalism, and becoming sexually active at an early age). She started smoking regularly at age 8 years, had her first drink of alcohol at age 13 years, and began using other drugs at age 14 years. Alcohol and drug use problems were worse between the ages of 14 and 19 years, but they continued into her early 30s when we saw her last (alcohol and marijuana). Tricia is currently married and has two daughters. Her functioning improved during her 20s and early 30s, but she continues to be anxious, depressed, and has some substance use problems, along with frequent fighting in her marriage.

We first had the opportunity to work with Alex when he was 15 years old. He was residing in an inpatient program for teenagers with substance abuse problems. This was a year after his father's death from the drug overdose, which shook Alex up substantially even though he had minimal contact with his father for a number of years prior to his death. By age 15 years, Alex had used almost every substance imaginable other than opioids and PCP. Not surprisingly, he already had a history of antisocial behavior, along with depression, anxiety, and obsessive–compulsive behavior. He regularly smoked cigarettes; started to drink alcohol at age 12 years, with problem usage starting at age 13 years; and started to use and misuse drugs at approximately the same time alcohol use began. During the next 12 years, Alex continued to struggle. He was involved in various relationships with women, with the longest one being very conflictual. This relationship included physical fights resulting in Alex being arrested and jailed for domestic violence. He dropped out of school not too long after being released from his substance abuse treatment program, had a series of jobs (several from which he was fired), and continued to experience depression and substance abuse. When we last saw him at age 27 years, Alex had made some significant improvements in his life. He was again living with the woman with whom he had the historically conflictual relationship, but they were doing better and expecting a child. Alex had a steady job, and he had ceased all use of substances, including tobacco. He said that 2 years earlier he really saw himself being like his biological father and decided he did not want to be like that anymore. Especially now with the upcoming birth of his first child, he wanted something different for his children than what he had had in his own life.

Joe's Story

We first saw Joe when he was 3½ years old. He was a scrawny-looking young boy who was chewing gum throughout his first assessment. Although engaged early in the session, he quickly became oppositional with the examiner, and he also showed significant hyperactivity. Developmental milestones were all within the normal range. There was little positive affect noted by the examiner during the assessment other than a sense of glee when Joe had been able to escape the work a couple of times. Noteworthy was the last sentence of the case report during this first assessment, which stated, "It is the examiner's opinion that this child is well on his way to encountering major life difficulties." How true and how sad, and this was recognized when Joe was age 3!

We next saw Joe 7 years later, after his parents had divorced, when he was living with his two older siblings, his mother, and his stepfather in another state. His intellectual and academic functioning were in the normal range, with strong arithmetic skills noted. He appeared much more likeable at this time, although he was still quite hyperactive. He was experiencing symptoms of anxiety, especially excessive worrying about harm befalling himself and his parents and also about how others viewed him. At age 11 years, he was beginning to show some oppositional behavior more publically, and he had been in trouble with the law for vandalizing (egging) someone's home.

At age 13 years, Joe exhibited bright affect while working with the examiner. His intellectual functioning was still within the average range, and some of his academic skills were in the superior range. This assessment of Joe followed the death of his biological father, which impacted him even though he had not seen him for quite some time. There was excessive worry about death and dying noted. Anxiety in other areas continued as well, along with oppositional behavior. Joe had started smoking cigarettes regularly at this age, and he had also started to use alcohol and marijuana during the past year. At the end of his report, the examiner predicted that the next 3 years were important to this child's long-term trajectory and expected to hear about bad things happening during that time frame.

Unfortunately, the prediction rang true, and at age 16 years when seen next, Joe had experienced problems with the law during the past year for stealing (jewelry from someone's home) and having drug paraphernalia. Reportedly, Joe stole the merchandise in order to obtain money to buy marijuana. Joe had regularly been using tobacco, alcohol, and marijuana during the time frame prior to the legal problems. A family counselor became involved with the family as a result of the problems, with some immediate positive impact as Joe started playing on his school's football team and ceased his interactions with a negative peer group with whom he had previously been involved. Joe stopped using marijuana but continued his use of tobacco and alcohol.

We next saw Joe at age 19 years while he was visiting his parents on leave from the US Army. Joe had graduated high school and enlisted in the Army 4 months later. During high school, Joe had a girlfriend whose father was a police officer. This led to various problems for Joe and his girlfriend because the father did not like Joe. Also prior to joining the Army, Joe and his brother Alex had been in a serious physical fight, with Joe's nose broken as a result.

Prior to joining the Army, Joe continued to use and abuse tobacco, alcohol, and marijuana, ceasing only the use of marijuana when he entered the Army. Of note during basic training was an incident in which Joe observed the death of a fellow soldier while practicing jumps from an airplane.

At age 23 years when we saw Joe next, he was married (during the previous year) and out of the Army. Of importance was Joe's deployment in Iraq 2 years before our visit with him. While there, a truck in which he was riding was hit by an improvised explosive device, which resulted in him sustaining a traumatic brain injury and partial deafness, along with the experience of continuing significant pain. After the injury, Joe's mood was volatile, his ability to concentrate was impaired, and his overall cognitive functioning and response time were altered. Joe also witnessed people being killed and injured while in Iraq. He clearly met diagnostic criteria for PTSD. Antisocial behavior continued, as well as alcohol problems (but not drug use) during that 3-year period.

We last saw Joe at age 26 years when he was living with a new girlfriend who was expecting their child in another month. During the previous 3 years, Joe had been in counseling for his PTSD and was taking an antidepressant. He had made a suicide attempt by taking an entire bottle of pills, but he blamed it on the feelings produced by the antidepressant he was taking. Therefore, he discontinued using the medication. He had separated from his wife, who had also filed a personal protection order against him (he claimed there was never any violence between them before the split). Joe had been in a serious motorcycle accident a year previously, which obviously did not help both the physical and the mental problems he was already experiencing. After the breakup with his wife, he used marijuana daily for a while, as well as drank significant amounts of alcohol. However, for most of the 3-year period, Joe had stayed away from substances (other than chewing tobacco). Although laid off from a job, Joe completed an Associate of Arts degree from a local community college and had recently been admitted to a surgical technician program that he was about to start. It appeared that good things might be happening for him in his future.

We do not know what happened during the next 2 years that led to Joe's death from a drug overdose.

Was it truly accidental as reported by his mother? Or did the long history of a troubled life finally catch up with him? It seems ironic that Joe died the same way his father did 16 years before him. A tragic story—but one that is far too common.

SEEKING AN UNDERSTANDING OF THE DEVELOPMENT OF ALCOHOL USE DISORDERS

The topic of this book is the etiology of substance abuse disorders (SUDs), with the primary focus on alcohol. We hope the reader will learn a great deal about our field and the significant growth of knowledge gained throughout the years regarding our understanding of this complex disorder. Important to remember, however, is that the object of our discourse is real people, affected by serious and sometimes life-threatening problems. This is not just science for the sake of exploration. It is hoped that the case of Joe and his family is a reminder of that fact as one reads the research that is presented in the remainder of this book.

Joe's case information, collected during a 26-year interval as part of the Michigan Longitudinal Study (Zucker et al., 2000), is also an excellent example of what can be learned about the human element through the use of longitudinal studies. We recognize our major debt of gratitude to Joe and his family, along with all study participants, for being willing to open up their lives to us over such an extended period of time. The data we obtain are a gift of the intimate details of individual lives and of the settings in which they live them out. Sometimes the sharing is of experiences that have never before been told to another. This is truly an act of altruism.

From a scientific standpoint, longitudinal studies allow us the opportunity to study behavior and events prospectively while they are happening rather than relying on retrospective data with more error due to memory recollection issues and with much less richness of detail. They are a major reason why the understanding of etiology and course of adult disorders have progressed as far as they have. However, their importance as a methodology to describe the emergence and development of risk for disorder was not always so evident. There typically have been concerns about cost, as well as about the potential relevance of early child behavior to the ultimate endpoint of severe, chronic, and problematic substance use and the issue of whether, at the end of the road, there will be a scientific payoff valuable enough to justify the effort. We digress briefly about this issue as it reflects the history of this prospective research.

The Back Story and the Development of Substance Use Disorders

The project that provided the impetus for all the interviews and assessments of Joe's family during their 26-year interval was part of a now 30-year-long effort to prospectively characterize the etiology of substance use disorder, albeit with a primary focus on alcohol, the world's most common drug of abuse. This project was the Michigan Longitudinal Study (Zucker et al., 2000). The study was conceived by Robert Zucker in the late 1970s and was driven by information that later came to be understood as the core material of developmental psychopathology (Cicchetti, 1984). The specific impetus for this work originated from several sources. One was findings being reported from longitudinal studies of high-risk offspring of schizophrenic parents (Erlenmeyer-Kimling et al.,1997; Mednick & McNeil, 1968) and parallel reports of clinical encounters with the members of these families (Anthony & Chiland, 1974; Anthony, Koupernik, & Chiland, 1978). This work was beginning to document that the schizophrenic disorder of adulthood was preceded by harbingers detectable long before the full-blown clinical syndrome appeared.

Another stimulus was the observation that some of the retrospective family characteristics reported by alcoholics in their 40s resembled the concurrent reports of family behavior being provided in a community study of problem drinkers during adolescence. This raised the possibility that the patterning occurring during adolescence was actually an early indicator of a life course pattern leading to problematic alcohol use during adulthood. If this hypothesis was correct, then it indicated that there was a potential to carry out in-depth mapping of the etiologic course of alcoholism significantly prior to its onset, which would in turn open up possibilities for early identification and prevention of this chronic and recurring disorder long before it had become chronic.

At that point, it was not clear that such a project would be feasible because of its need for very long-term support. Equally important was the question of how early in developmental time should one begin. The answer to that question was posed as both an empirical and a practical issue. First, such a study should begin as early as it was possible to demonstrate that there were differences between putative high- and low-risk children. In other words, there needed to be some demonstrated etiologic variance indicating the potential that some process(es) was already operating. Second, a practical issue was that one needed to be able to demonstrate it was feasible to recruit a viable sample containing sufficient numbers of both higher and lower risk children. The third, and perhaps most daunting, issue was whether the scientific community was willing to acknowledge that such a long-term project was scientifically worthwhile in an era in which the scientific climate still conceived of alcoholism as a disorder of adulthood (Kissin & Begleiter, 1971–1983).

A detailed account of the manner in which those early challenges were answered is provided by Zucker, Baxter, Noll, Theado, and Weil (1982) and Zucker et al. (2000). The pilot work to establish that differences could be demonstrated between 3-year-olds who were and those who were not children of alcoholics was successfully carried out in 1981 and 1982, and local pilot funding was obtained to begin data collection on a subset of 70 families who would become the first enrollees of the long-term study. After two National Institutes of Health (NIH) reviews questioned the relevance of such early behavior to the adult disorder of alcoholism, reviews of the third submission indicated the committee's acknowledgment of the major importance of the study, and the project's first R01 was funded in 1987. NIH funding has continued thereafter through the present day.

Hiram Fitzgerald joined the study as co-principal investigator in 1987 to contribute his major expertise in child development, a content area that was much in need of representation (Fitzgerald et al., 1993). In 1998, Margit Burmeister began collaborating on molecular genetic analyses and became a collaborator on that activity in 2008 (Villafuerte et al., 2012). In 2000, Joel Nigg joined as a collaborator to lead the initiative on the role of neurocognitive functioning in the development of risk (Nigg et al., 2004). In 2003, the study began to probe the neural circuitry of risk via functional magnetic resonance imaging, with Mary Heitzeg as the major collaborator on that work (Martz et al., 2016). In 2012, Elisa Trucco joined the group as a collaborator, with major focus on gene × environment × development interactions (Trucco et al., 2016). Those domains of inquiry also continue to the present. As these collaborations have deepened, our multilevel, multidomain conceptualization of the risk development process has become more mechanistically detailed, in ways that were not conceivable in 1980. Some of this work is described in this volume in Chapters 6, 8, 9, 19, and 21. Other integrative accounts of this recent work may be found in Zucker (2014) and Zucker, Hicks, and Heitzeg (2016).

The Development of Alcohol Use Disorders

Our understanding of the development of alcohol use disorders (AUDs) has been greatly enhanced not just by our methodology. Conceptually, utilization of a developmental perspective has stimulated exploration of the pathways of risk for early antecedents and intervening mechanisms of AUDs (Hussong et al., 2007), including pathways that involve equifinal as well as multifinal outcomes. Equifinality refers to different pathways leading to the same endpoint (in this case, AUD), whereas multifinality refers to the same pathway resulting in different expressed outcomes (e.g., AUD, delinquency, antisocial behavior, or combinations of comorbid psychopathologies). Our current acquired knowledge of these pathways suggests that facing many individuals who go on to develop AUDs is a complex and dynamic system of genes, epigenetic processes, brain, family, peers, community, and culture. This system undergoes change as development proceeds and enhances the risk for future problems in these individuals if nothing is done to disrupt the risky pathways. Thus, both equifinal and multifinal pathways are operative.

The dynamic and systemic complexity of such pathways has been described in numerous articles and chapters (Fitzgerald, Davies, Zucker & Klinger, 1994; Fitzgerald, Zucker, & Yang, 1995; Zucker, 1987, 2006, 2014; Zucker et al., 2016) and is captured in part by the risk–resilience framework described in the overview of Part 1 of this volume. In addition, a formal heuristic model developed by Zucker et al. (2016) illustrates the multiple levels of influence across time, and it provides an empirically anchored guide to investigate the transactions involving genes, epigenetic processes, brain response/reactivity systems, intermediate alcohol nonspecific phenotypes (encompassing personality/temperament and behavior), and environmental influences leading first to the initiation of alcohol use and culminating in the occurrence of an AUD (depicted as SUD in

the model because AUD is but one of the SUDs). Current research is being done to test parts of the Zucker et al. model depicted in Figure 1.1.

Despite a categorical diagnostic system for AUD, it is clearly a heterogeneous disorder in terms of both developmental pathways that result in meeting diagnostic criteria and comorbidity in its expression. Early work in this area focused on type I proposed by Cloninger, or type A proposed by Babor (found in men and women and having adult onset, moderate symptomatology, a relatively short course, and little comorbidity) and type II, or type B (found primarily in males with early onset, strong heritability, and antisocial comorbidity) (Babor, 1996). Zucker (1987, 1994) extended this work by proposing four alcoholism subtypes: antisocial, developmentally cumulative, developmentally limited, and negative affect.

Figure 1.2, from earlier work (Zucker, 2006), shows six subtypes, three of which show associations with specific comorbidities and three that do not. Antisocial alcoholism is similar to type B alcoholism and involves a developmental pathway linked to a history of antisocial behavior starting during childhood and continuing into adult years. The antisocial behavior is a prime part of the emergence of alcohol problems. Probable underlying genetic factors are likely related to both antisociality and alcoholism.

Developmentally limited alcoholism also has antisocial behavior as a central component, but both the conduct problems/impulsivity and the subsequent alcohol problems are time-limited, appearing only during adolescence. The third subtype, negative affect alcoholism, emerges from internalizing symptomatology during childhood and adolescence, with sustained alcohol problems usually beginning as an adult. This subtype is more common in women than in men, and it may be linked to genetic factors common to depression and alcoholism.

The other three subtypes are perhaps closer examples of a true addiction. They appear more linked to diagnostic criteria and their drinking-related consequences than to any underlying etiology. Nevertheless, alcohol-specific vulnerabilities, such as sensitivity to ethanol's intoxicating effects, or environmental stressors occurring in a social context that supports alcohol use for tension reduction are likely contributors to these subtypes. Episodic alcoholism occurs when stress situations are recurrent, such as those associated with work, family conflict, and so on. Isolated abuse occurs when nonsustained stressors emerge, such as

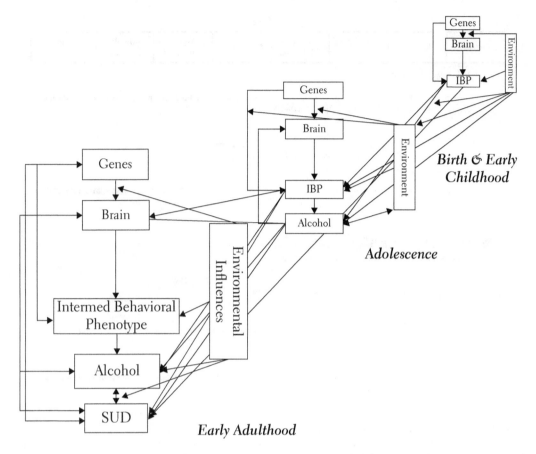

FIGURE 1.1 Developmental systems framework for the development of alcohol use disorder: A heuristic model of the flow over time. IBP, intermediate behavioral phenotype; SUD, substance use disorder.

Source: Zucker, R. A., Hicks, B. M., & Heitzeg, M. M. (2016). Alcohol use and the alcohol use disorders over the life course: A cross-level developmental review. In D. Cicchetti (Ed.), *Developmental psychopathology: Volume 3. Maladaptation and psychopathology* (3rd ed., pp. 793–832). New York, NY: Wiley. Reprinted with permission.

major life changes (e.g., divorce). However, for a certain segment of the population, drinking adaptation to stress is sustained, resulting in the developmentally cumulative subtype.

Many of these developmental pathways leading to psychopathology proposed 30 years ago (Zucker, 1987) are reinforced by the empirical research described throughout this volume. They are also reinforced by contemporary research on broader literatures investigating systems and stress regulation (Oken, Chamine, & Wakeland, 2015), lifetime influences of epigenetics on dynamic organizational processes affecting gene expression (Kanherkar, Bhatia-Dey, & Csoka, 2014), complex modeling of the hypothalamic–pituitary–adrenal axis (Hosseinichimeh, Rahmandad, & Wittenborn,

2015), and the association of toxic stress via adverse childhood experiences in infancy and early childhood with relationship difficulties (Humphreys & Zeanah, 2014).

The case study describing the life experiences of Steven, Sarah, and their children gives substance to quantitative studies and heuristic and empirical models of the dynamic, cascading effects of family psychopathology across three generations. Their childhood experiences clearly did not promote positive development, and they, in turn, created lifetime negative influences on their children that expressed across generations as early onset of substance use (smoking, alcohol, and other drugs), individual mental health difficulties (antisocial behavior, depression, anxiety, and conduct disorder), crime/delinquency, and serious relationship difficulties

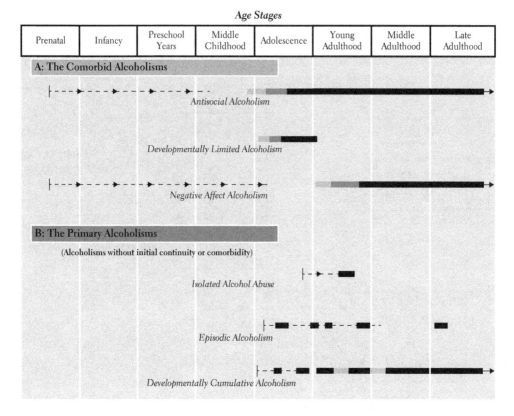

FIGURE 1.2 Course of the comorbid and primary alcoholisms.

Source: Figure 17.6, p. 639, in Zucker, R. A. (2006). Alcohol use and the alcohol use disorders: A developmental-biopsychosocial systems formulation covering the life course. In D. Cicchetti & D. J. Cohen (Eds.), *Developmental psychopathology: Volume 3. Risk, disorder and adaptation* (2nd ed., pp. 620–656). New York, NY: Wiley. Reprinted with permission.

(including emotional and physical aggression) evident as early as infancy (Edwards, Eiden, & Leonard, 2004; Eiden, Leonard, Hoyle, & Chavez, 2004; Eiden et al., 2016) and the preschool years (Fitzgerald et al., 1993; Fitzgerald, Wong, & Zucker, 2013; Puttler, Fitzgerald, Heitzeg, & Zucker, 2017).

The interdisciplinary field of infant mental health has provided strong empirical support spanning behavior to neurobiological and neuroendocrinological evidence. During infancy and toddlerhood, the very young child organizes perceptual, sensory, and internal working models (mental models, schemas, and expectancies) about self, others, and self–other relationships (Bretherton & Munholland, 2016; Fitzgerald et al., 2013; Puttler et al., 2017) that become embodied into neural networks (Ammaniti & Gallese, 2014; Bretherton & Munholland, 2016), stress regulatory systems (Oken et al., 2015), and relationship dysregulation (Schore, 2001), which serve as

modulators of child–other relationship transactions. Relationship dysregulation affects such factors as the degree of secure attachment between parent and child, the degree of certainty in the child's expectations in relation to another's behavior, the degree of self-efficacy and internal control, and the degree of emotional and behavioral self-regulation achieved. We posited a model of the early organization of the development of intersubjectivity (Ammaniti & Gallese, 2014; Trevarthen, 1980) that may serve to prime the very young child via cascading dysregulation in interpersonal relationship dynamics (Figure 1.3: Fitzgerald et al., 2013), including the very young child's sense of self. Thus, during the first 3 years of life, self-regulatory systems organize and develop within the context of self–other relationship contingencies, which synergistically generate procedural knowledge and conscious awareness of those relationships (Trevarthen, 1980).

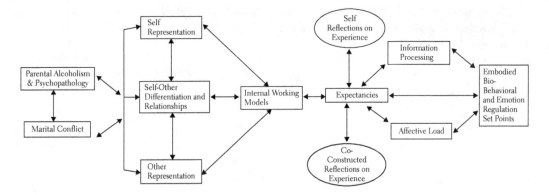

FIGURE 1.3 Development of internal working models of self and self–other relationships and the organization of set points for embodied biobehavioral and emotion regulation.

Source: Adapted from Fitzgerald, H. E., Wong, M. M., & Zucker, R. A. (2013). Early origins of alcohol use and abuse: Mental representations, relationships, and the risk–resilience continuum. In N. Suchman, M. Pajulo, & L. C. Mayes (Eds.), *Parenting and substance abuse: Developmental approaches to intervention* (pp. 126–155). New York, NY: Oxford University Press.

Ammaniti and Gallese's (2014) systematic review of evidence from neurobiology, developmental psychology, endocrinology, and psychodynamics suggests that relationship expectancies (child to other; child to experience and observed world) become embodied into neurobiological systems that integrate regulatory aspects of the child's developing world view. A major overriding theme of this volume is that when the child's birth to age 5 years life experience is dominated by psychopathological relationships and behavior of primary caregivers, the dynamics of psychopathology become part of (embodied) the child's emergent sense of self, self–other relationships, and overall world view. Longitudinal studies provide evidence of the continuities and discontinuities within pathways of risk through childhood to emergent adulthood (Eiden et al., 2016; Moffitt, Caspi, Rutter, & Silva, 2001; Shaw & Gilliam, 2016; Zucker et al., 2016). When life course experiences of psychopathology and disorganization persist, they strengthen continuity, not only behaviorally but also within all the biological systems that contribute to the individual's lack of social competence and increase in relationship disorders.

The formalization of developmental (Ford & Lerner, 1992; Gottlieb, 1991; Schneirla, 1957; Werner, 1957) and systems science theory (Abraham, Abraham, & Shaw; 1992; Miller, 1978; Sameroff, 1983; von Bertalanffy, 1968) during the last half of the 20th century, and its spread of effects across a broad range of disciplines, has produced a general consensus that development is modulated by dynamic systems, organism–environment transactions, and probabilistic–contextual influences on organization and change (Zucker, 1989). Modern scientific findings resulting from studies of epigenetics, and the neurobiology of the brain, demonstrate the work of these dynamic systems organizations and reorganizations over the lifespan.

The chapters in this volume summarize empirical findings related to the organization and development of SUD, AUD, and coactive psychopathology from the transdisciplinary developmental science of today. There is a heavy emphasis on studies that have been able to identify the precursive evidence of risk that is present long before the adult disorder appears. The methodology of choice for such work is the longitudinal study of emergent pathways of risk and resilience. Such studies contribute generative methods for assessing change and have led to the development of new approaches for integrative data analysis. Focusing on systemic influences of biobehavioral development over time has great potential for informing prevention science and practice for when and how to optimally intervene in order to support developmental pathways that sustain efforts to strengthen the individual's presence on the resilient side of the risk–resilience continuum. The evidence from developmental science clearly indicates that the dynamics forming etiologic pathways to SUD/AUD and coactive psychopathology begin to organize in infancy and early childhood—a very different view than what was in vogue just two or three decades ago. Much of this newer work has been developed by the contributors to this volume, and the work they describe here indicates that this process is still very much a live one. We hope the reader will be as edified and energized as we have been in reading these contributions.

ACKNOWLEDGMENTS

This research is currently being supported by grants from the National Institute on Alcohol Abuse and Alcoholism (R01 AA07065, R01 AA12217) and the National Institute on Drug Abuse (R01 DA039112), with previous support also from the National Institute on Drug Abuse (R01 DA027261).

NOTE

1. The names of the people, along with minor details, have been changed to protect the anonymity and confidentiality of the persons involved.

REFERENCES

Abraham, F. D., Abraham, R., & Shaw, C. (1992). Basic principles of dynamical systems. In R. L. Levine & H. E. Fitzgerald (Eds.), *Analysis of dynamic psychological systems: Basic approaches to general systems, dynamic systems, and cybernetics* (pp. 35–143). New York, NY: Plenum.

Ammaniti, M., & Gallese, V. (2014). *The birth of intersubjectivity: Psychodynamics, neurobiology and the self.* New York, NY: Norton.

Anthony, E. J., & Chiland, C. (Eds.). (1974). *The child in his family: Children at psychiatric risk.* New York, NY: Wiley.

Anthony, E. J., Koupernik, C., & Chiland, C. (Eds.). (1978). *The child in his family: Vulnerable children.* New York, NY: Wiley.

Babor, T. F. (1996). The classification of alcoholics. *Alcohol Health & Research World, 1,* 6–14.

Bretherton, I., & Munholland, K. A. (2016). The internal working model construct in light of contemporary neuroimaging research. In J. Cassidy & P. R. Shaver (Eds.), *Handbook of attachment: Theory, research, and clinical applications* (3rd ed., pp. 64–88). New York, NY: Guilford.

Cicchetti, D. (1984). The emergence of developmental psychopathology. *Child Development, 55,* 1–7.

Edwards, E. P., Eiden, R. D., & Leonard, K. E. (2004). Impact of fathers' alcoholism and associated risk factors on parent–infant attachment stability from 12 to 18 months. *Infant Mental Health Journal, 25*(6), 556–579.

Eiden, R. D., Leonard, K. E., Hoyle, R. H., & Chavez, F. (2004). A transactional model of parent–infant interactions in alcoholic families. *Psychology of Addictive Behaviors, 18*(4), 350–361.

Eiden, R. D., Lessard, J., Colder, C. R., Livingston, J., Casey, M., & Leonard, K. E. (2016). Developmental cascade model for adolescent substance use from infancy to late adolescence. *Developmental Psychology, 52*(10), 1619–1633. doi:10.1037/dev0000199

Erlenmeyer-Kimling, L., Hilldoff-Adamo, U., Rock, D., Roberts, S. A., Bassett, A. S., Squires-Wheeler, E., . . . Gottesman, I. I. (1997). The New York High-Risk Project: Prevalence and comorbidity of Axis I disorders in offspring of schizophrenic parents at 25-year follow-up. *Archives of General Psychiatry, 54*(12), 1096–1102.

Fitzgerald, H. E., Davies, W. H., Zucker, R. A., & Klinger, M. T. (1994). Developmental systems theory and substance abuse: A conceptual and methodological framework for analyzing patterns of variation in families. In L. L'Abate (Ed.), *Handbook of developmental family psychology and psychopathology* (pp. 350–372). New York, NY: Wiley.

Fitzgerald, H. E., Sullivan, L. A., Ham, H. P., Zucker, R. A., Bruckel, S., & Schneider, A. (1993). Predictors of behavior problems in three-year-old sons of alcoholics: Early evidence for the onset of risk. *Child Development, 64,* 110–123.

Fitzgerald, H. E., Wong, M. M., & Zucker, R. A. (2013). Early origins of alcohol use and abuse: Mental representations, relationships, and the risk–resilience continuum. In N. Suchman, M. Pajulo, & L. C. Mayes (Eds.), *Parenting and substance addiction: Developmental approaches to intervention* (pp. 126–155). New York, NY: Oxford University Press.

Fitzgerald, H. E., Zucker, R. A., & Yang, H.-Y. (1995). Developmental systems theory and alcoholism: Analyzing patterns of variation in high-risk families. *Psychology of Addictive Behavior, 9,* 8–22.

Ford, D. H., & Lerner, R. M. (1992). *Developmental system theory.* Newbury Park, CA: Sage.

Gottlieb, G. (1991). Experiential canalization of behavior development: Theory. *Developmental Psychology, 27,* 4–13.

Hosseinichimeh, N., Rahmandad, H., & Wittenborn, A. L. (2015). Modeling the hypothalamus–pituitary–adrenal axis: A review and extension. *Mathematical Biosciences, 268*, 52–65.

Humphreys, K., & Zeanah, C. H. (2014). Deviations from the expectable environment in early childhood and emerging psychopathology. *Neuropsychopharmacology Reviews, 165*, 1–17.

Hussong, A. M., Wirth, R. J., Edwards, M. C., Curran, P. J., Chassin, L. A., & Zucker, R. A. (2007). Externalizing symptoms among children of alcoholic parents: Entry points for an antisocial pathway to alcoholism. *Journal of Abnormal Psychology, 116*, 529–542.

Kanherkar, R. R., Bhatia-Dey, N., & Csoka, A. B. (2014). Epigenetics across the human lifespan. *Frontiers in Cell and Developmental Biology, 2*, 1–19.

Kissin, B., & Begleiter, H. (1971–1983). *The biology of alcoholism, Volumes 1–7*. New York, NY: Plenum.

Martz, M., Trucco, E. M., Cope, L., Hardee, J., Jennifer, J., Zucker, R. A., & Heitzeg, M. M. (2016). Association of marijuana use with blunted nucleus accumbens response to reward anticipation: Prospective effects over four years in early adulthood. *JAMA Psychiatry, 73*, 838–844.

Mednick, S., & McNeil, T. (1968). Current methodology in research on the etiology of schizophrenia: Serious difficulties which suggest the use of the high-risk-group method. *Psychological Bulletin, 70*, 681–693.

Miller, J. G. (1978). *Living systems*. New York, NY: McGraw-Hill.

Moffitt, T. E., Caspi, A., Rutter, M., & Silva, P. A. (2001). *Sex differences in antisocial behavior: Conduct disorder, delinquency, and violence in the Dunedin Longitudinal Study*. Cambridge, UK: Cambridge University Press.

Nigg, J. T., Glass, J. M., Poon, E., Wong, M. M., Fitzgerald, H. E., Puttler, L. I., . . . Zucker, R. A. (2004). Neuropsychological executive functioning in children at elevated risk for alcoholism: Findings in early adolescence. *Journal of Abnormal Psychology, 113*, 302–314.

Oken, B. S., Chamine, I., & Wakeland, W. (2015). A systems approach to stress, stressors and resilience in humans. *Behavioral Brain Research, 282*, 144–154.

Puttler, L. I., Fitzgerald, H. E., Heitzeg, M. M., & Zucker, R. A. (2017). Boys, early risk factors for alcohol problems, and the development of the self: An interconnected matrix. *Infant Mental Health Journal, 38*, 83–96.

Sameroff, A. J. (1983). Developmental systems: Contexts and evolution. In P. H. Mussen (Ed.), *Handbook of child psychology: Vol. 1. History, theory, and methods* (pp. 237–294). New York, NY: Wiley.

Schneirla, T. C. (1957). The concept of development in comparative psychology. In D. B. Harris (Ed.), *The concept of development* (pp. 78–108). Minneapolis, MN: University of Minnesota Press.

Schore, A. (2001). The effects of relational trauma on right brain development, affect regulation, and infant mental health. *Infant Mental Health Journal, 22*, 7–66.

Shaw, D. S., & Gilliam, M. (2016). Early childhood predictors of low-income boys' antisocial behavior. *Infant Mental Health Journal, 37*, 68–82.

Trevarthen, C. (1980). The foundations of intersubjectivity: Development of interpersonal and cooperative understanding in infants. In D. Olson (Ed.), *The social foundation of language and thought* (pp. 216–242). New York, NY: Norton.

Trucco, E. M., Hicks, B. M., Villafuerte, S., Nigg, J. T., Burmeister, M., & Zucker, R. A. (2016). Temperament and externalizing behavior as mediators of genetic risk on adolescent substance use. *Journal of Abnormal Child Psychology, 125*(4), 565–575.

Villafuerte, S., Heitzeg, M. M., Foley, S., Yau, W. W., Majczenko, K., Zubieta, J. K., . . . Burmeister, M. (2012). Impulsiveness and insula activation during reward anticipation are associated with genetic variants in *GABRA2* in a family sample enriched for alcoholism. *Molecular Psychiatry, 17*, 511–519.

von Bertalanffy, L. (1968). *General systems theory*. New York, NY: Braziller.

Werner, H. (1957). The concept of development from a comparative and organismic point of view. In D. B. Harris (Ed.), *The concept of development* (pp. 125–148). Minneapolis, MN: University of Minnesota Press.

Zucker, R. A. (1987). The four alcoholisms: A developmental account of the etiologic process. In P. C. Rivers (Ed.), *Alcohol and addictive behavior: Nebraska Symposium on Motivation, 1986* (pp. 27–83). Lincoln, NE: University of Nebraska Press.

Zucker, R. A. (1989). Is risk for alcoholism predictable? A probabilistic approach to a developmental problem. *Drugs and Society, 3*, 69–93.

Zucker, R. A. (1994). Pathways to alcohol problems and alcoholisms: A developmental account of the evidence for multiple alcoholisms and for contextual contributions to risk. In R. A. Zucker, J. Howard, & G. M. Boyd (Eds.), *The development of alcohol problems: Exploring the biopsychosocial matrix of risk* (Research Monograph No. 26, pp. 255–290). Rockville, MD: National Institute on Alcohol Abuse and Alcoholism.

Zucker, R. A. (2006). Alcohol use and the alcohol use disorders: A developmental–biopsychosocial systems formulation covering the life course. In D. Cicchetti & D. J. Cohen (Eds.), *Developmental psychopathology: Vol. 3. Risk, disorder and adaptation* (2nd ed., pp. 620–656). New York, NY: Wiley.

Zucker, R. A. (2014). Genes, brain, behavior and context: The developmental matrix of addictive behavior. In S. F. Stoltenberg (Ed.), *Genes and the motivation to use substances: Nebraska Symposium on Motivation* (pp. 51–69). New York, NY: Springer.

Zucker, R. A., Baxter, J. A., Noll, R. B., Theado, D. P., & Weil, C. M. (1982, August). *An alcoholic risk study: Design and early health related findings.* Paper presented at the American Psychological Association meeting, Washington, DC.

Zucker, R. A., Fitzgerald, H. E., Refior, S., Puttler, L. I., Pallas, D. M., & Ellis, D. A. (2000). The clinical and social ecology of childhood for children of alcoholics: Description of a study and implications for a differentiated social policy. In H. E. Fitzgerald, B. M. Lester, & B. S. Zuckerman (Eds.), *Children of addiction: Research, health, and policy issues* (pp. 109–141). New York: RoutledgeFalmer.

Zucker, R. A., Hicks, B. M., & Heitzeg, M. M. (2016). Alcohol use and the alcohol use disorders over the life course: A cross-level developmental review. In D. Cicchetti (Ed.), *Developmental psychopathology: Vol. 3. Maladaptation and psychopathology* (3rd ed., pp. 793–832). New York, NY: Wiley.

2

A Developmental Psychopathology Perspective on Substance Use

Illustrations from the Research on Child Maltreatment

Dante Cicchetti

Fred A. Rogosch

Substance use and alcohol disorders typically do not emerge until adolescence or later in adulthood. Despite onset in these life stages, Robert Zucker has been a pioneer in advocating for an appreciation of alcoholism as a developmental disorder, with a full lifespan understanding of developmental processes that unfold in the etiology of these serious outcomes. His work fully espouses a deeply integrative developmental psychopathology formulation that forms a solid foundation for advancing research and theory, as well as direction for prevention and treatment. We find substantial consistency in Zucker's work with our perspective on developmental psychopathology. Herein, we present a developmental psychopathology conceptualization of child maltreatment and provide examples from our research on how child maltreatment contributes to problem substance use during adolescence.

Child maltreatment represents one of the greatest failures of the caregiving environment to provide many of the expectable experiences necessary to facilitate normal developmental processes (Cicchetti & Lynch, 1993). Maltreatment ushers in a probabilistic epigenesis for children characterized by an increased likelihood of failure and disruption in the successful resolution of major developmental tasks that have great implications for functioning over the lifespan. These repeated disruptions create a profile of enduring vulnerability factors that increase the probability of the emergence of maladaptation, psychopathology,

and substance abuse as negative transactions between the child and the environment ensue (Cicchetti & Toth, 2015; Cicchetti & Valentino, 2006). Maltreated children exhibit elevated levels of disturbance across a wide range of areas. They are at higher risk for the emergence of both externalizing and internalizing behavior problems, both of which are risk factors for substance use and abuse (Cicchetti & Rogosch, 1999, 2002; Rogosch, Oshri, & Cicchetti, 2010; Zucker, Donovan, Masten, Mattson, & Moss, 2008). Although numerous studies have linked child maltreatment and substance use in adolescence and adulthood, the developmental mechanisms through which the experience of child maltreatment results in substance use/abuse have received only minimal attention (Masten, Faden, Zucker, & Spear, 2008; Zucker et al., 2008).

Biological, psychological, and social systems undergo marked developmental changes from childhood through adolescence to adulthood (Masten et al., 2008). From a developmental perspective, changes in contexts, processes, and developmental tasks all play critical roles in the evolution of substance abuse (Windle et al., 2009). This heightened vulnerability is a consequence of both the continuity of risk from earlier developmental stages and the unique neurobiological, cognitive, and social changes that occur (Cicchetti, 2000; Spear, 2000; Zucker, 2006, Zucker, Hicks, & Heitzeg, 2016).

Substance abuse unfolds over time in a developing individual. Thus, it is critical to adopt a developmental perspective in order to understand the processes, mechanisms, and moderators underlying individual pathways to adaptive and maladaptive outcomes. It is necessary to consider developmental variations in cognitive, socioemotional, representational, interpersonal, and social–cognitive capacities, in addition to biological domains of functioning, in order to ascertain how individual differences in these domains may impact the developing individual's use of drugs.

Because there is diversity in pathways (known as equifinality) and outcomes (known as multifinality) evident in development (Cicchetti & Rogosch, 1996), not surprisingly, a developmental psychopathology approach to substance abuse does not advocate a unitary etiologic explanation (Cicchetti & Luthar, 1999; Glantz & Leshner, 2000). Although commonalties in pathways among different relatively homogeneous clusters of individuals diagnosed with a substance use disorder may be delineated, it also is likely that drug abuse is not the only outcome associated with those pathways. Consideration of the various etiological models of substance abuse is important for understanding the phenomenon and suggesting prevention and intervention targets and pathways. Thus, there are likely to be generic pathways that contribute to a range of dysfunctions and disorders, of which drug abuse may be only one. Consequently, individuals interested in developing prevention and intervention strategies grounded in a developmental psychopathology perspective need to identify deviations from normative pathways, articulate the developmental courses, and discover the processes that may deflect an individual off a particular trajectory and onto a more or less adaptive course (Cicchetti, 2000).

Substance misuse leading to abuse, dependence, and addiction will involve changes in biological systems, including alterations to the hypothalamic–pituitary–adrenal (HPA) axis, brain processing, stress regulation, biological functions, and so on. This must be understood on a biological and behavioral level. Changes in these systems could be important in preventive intervention outcomes. Most of what is known about the correlates, causes, pathways, and sequelae of substance abuse has been gleaned from investigations that focused on relatively narrow domains of variables. To understand substance abuse in its full complexity, all levels of analysis must be examined and integrated (Cicchetti & Dawson, 2002; Cicchetti & Rogosch, 1999). Moreover, the influence of levels on

one another is almost always bidirectional. Therefore, no component subsystem or level of organization possesses causal privilege in the developmental system (Cicchetti & Cannon, 1999; Thelen & Smith, 1998). It is the reciprocally interactive relationship between at least two components of the developmental system that influences developmental organization or disorganization (Gottlieb, 1991).

A DEVELOPMENTAL PSYCHOPATHOLOGY PERSPECTIVE

A focus on the boundary between normal and abnormal development is central to the developmental psychopathology perspective (Cicchetti, 1993; Cicchetti & Toth, 1991, 2009). This viewpoint emphasizes not only how understanding of normal development provides a framework for conceptualizing atypical development but also how knowledge from the study of high-risk conditions, psychopathology, and substance use and abuse can contribute to an understanding of normal development.

"Experiments of nature" are "naturally arising conditions in which there is a possibility of separating otherwise confounding processes or opportunities to examine processes that for practical or ethical reasons would not have been possible" (O'Connor, 2003, p. 837). Because they enable us to isolate the components of the integrated system, investigation of these natural experiments sheds light on the normal structure of the system. If we choose to ignore or bypass the investigation of these experiments of nature, we are likely to construct theories that will eventually be contradicted by critical discoveries in research on psychopathology (Lenneberg, 1967). The utilization of a diversity of natural experiments is critical because when extrapolating from non-normal populations with the goal of informing developmental theory, it is important that a range of populations and conditions be considered. To make generalizations beyond the risk process or mental disorder investigated, it is necessary to examine an entire spectrum of disordered modifications.

The examination of individuals with high-risk conditions and mental disorders can provide a natural entrée into the study of system organization, disorganization, and reorganization that is otherwise not possible due to constraints associated with research involving human participants. Through investigating a variety of high-risk and mentally disordered conditions, it is possible to gain significant insight into processes of development not generally achieved through sole reliance on investigations of relatively homogeneous nondisordered populations. Research conducted with atypical populations also can elucidate the behavioral and biological consequences of alternative pathways of development, provide important information about the range and variability of individual response to challenge and adversity, and help specify the limits of behavioral and biological plasticity.

Developmental psychopathologists strive to engage in a comprehensive evaluation of biological, psychological, social, and cultural processes and to ascertain how the interaction among these multiple levels of analysis may influence individual differences, the continuity or discontinuity of adaptive or maladaptive behavioral patterns, and the pathways by which normal and pathological developmental outcomes may be achieved (Cicchetti & Blender, 2006; Cicchetti & Dawson, 2002). In practice, this entails comprehension of the appreciation for the developmental transformations and reorganizations that occur over time; an analysis of the risk and protective factors and mechanisms operating within and outside the individual and his or her environment over the course of development; the investigation of how emergent functions, competencies, and developmental tasks modify the expression of a disorder or lead to new symptoms and difficulties; and the recognition that a particular stressor or set of stressful circumstances may eventuate in different biological and psychological difficulties, depending on when in the developmental period the stress occurs. Moreover, various difficulties will constitute different meanings for an individual depending on cultural considerations (Causadias, 2013; Garcia-Coll, Akerman, & Cicchetti, 2000), as well as an individual's experiential history and current level of psychological and biological organization and functioning. The integration of the experience, in turn, will affect the adaptation or maladaptation that ensues.

The course of adaptation once drug abuse has remitted also warrants investigation from a developmental perspective. It would be very revealing, for example, to study the characteristics of individuals formerly diagnosed (or undiagnosable) as drug abusers who have successfully re-entered the mainstream.

In keeping with the concept of multifinality, it may be possible to identify core characteristics such as impulsivity, sensation seeking, or executive functioning deficits that remain stable but no longer culminate in drug abuse because of protective or buffering factors in the environmental context or within the person. Research such as this might reveal that certain circumstances that once were causally relevant to drug-abusing behavior in an earlier environment have become positively adaptive in a new environment. They may actually facilitate adaptive and successful functioning. For example, a person who has used manipulation to attain drugs may be able to channel this attribute into a career involving persuasive abilities, such as sales. Again, just as it is unwise to assume that drug-abusing behavior is always caused by an underlying dysfunction, it also may be misdirected to assume that normalized behavior necessarily reflects improvements in processes that were once causal to drug-abusing behavior. Thus, a developmental psychopathology perspective would encourage one to remain open to the possibility that many of the characteristics that are typically viewed as functioning deficits (e.g., impulsivity, sensation seeking, or insecurity) in fact may be neutral. That is, they may translate into deficits or assets depending on other characteristics of the individual and/or the environmental context.

DEVELOPMENTAL PATHWAYS

Since its inception as an emergent interdisciplinary science, diversity in process and outcome has been conceived as among the hallmarks of the developmental psychopathology perspective. As Sroufe (1990, p. 335) asserted, "One of the principal tasks of developmental psychopathology is to define families of developmental pathways, some of which are associated with psychopathology with high probability, others with low probability." Even before a mental disorder emerges, certain pathways signify adaptational failures that probabilistically forebode subsequent substance abuse or psychopathology (Sroufe, 1990).

Equifinality refers to the observation that in any open system, a diversity of pathways may lead to the same outcome. In contrast, in a closed system, the end state is inextricably linked to and determined by the initial conditions. Within the discipline of developmental psychopathology, equifinality has been invoked to explain why a variety of pathways may eventuate in the same outcome rather than expecting a singular primary pathway to adaptive or maladaptive outcome.

Multifinality suggests that any one component may function differently depending on the organization of the system in which it operates. In other words, a particular adverse event should not necessarily be viewed as leading to the same outcome in every individual. The meaning of any one attribute, process, or psychopathological condition needs to be considered in light of the complex matrix of individual characteristics, experiences, and social–contextual influences involved; the timing of events and experiences; and the developmental history of the individual.

The parameters of developmental psychopathology lend themselves to fostering translational research that has implications for society, policymakers, and individuals with drug abuse and mental disorders and their families. The very subject matter of the field, which encompasses risk and resilience, prevention and intervention, the elucidation of the precipitants of substance abuse and mental illness, the mediating and moderating processes that contribute to or mitigate against the emergence and maintenance of psychopathology and substance abuse, a multiple levels of analysis approach, and the incorporation of principles of normal development into the conduct of empirical investigations, necessitates thinking clearly about the implications of the work and devising strategies that will remedy the problems being studied.

ORGANIZATIONAL PERSPECTIVE ON DEVELOPMENT

Understanding the process of progressive vulnerability for drug use problems is advanced by conceptualizing development from an organizational perspective (Cicchetti, 2000; Cicchetti & Rogosch, 2002). Development is conceived as a series of qualitative reorganizations among and within biological, psychological, and social systems as growth of the individual proceeds (Cicchetti & Schneider-Rosen, 1986; Sroufe & Rutter, 1984: see also Werner & Kaplan, 1963). At each stage of development, the individual is confronted with a stage-salient task that constitutes the primary developmental issue

of the period. Across the early years into elementary school, these issues include the development of homeostatic regulation, early differentiation of affect states, the development of a secure attachment relationship with the primary caregiver, the emergence of an autonomous self, representational and symbolic development, the development of effective peer relations, and successful adaptation to school (Cicchetti & Schneider-Rosen, 1986; Sroufe & Rutter, 1984). Resolving the stage-salient issue of the period becomes the central organizing goal of the individual, generating preparedness for subsequent developmental challenges as growth proceeds. The quality of the manner in which individuals meet the principal stage-salient issue of the developmental period is crucial for the course of development. Competent resolution fosters more adaptive preparedness for dealing with subsequent developmental challenges. In contrast, incompetent resolution leaves the individual more vulnerable to having difficulty in successfully resolving later developmental tasks. Through differentiation and hierarchic integration, continuity of functioning may be perpetuated over time, as prior patterns of adaptation are incorporated into successive reorganizations as development proceeds. As a result of probabilistic epigenesis, early competence tends to promote later competence, whereas early incompetence portends greater difficulty in attaining positive adjustment (Cicchetti & Tucker, 1994).

The dynamic interplay of risk and protective processes operating at successive stages of development influences the quality of developmental organization that unfolds. Excessive adverse inputs to the system, accompanied by few compensatory or growth-promoting resources, will detract from the individual's success in competently resolving the stage-salient tasks of the developmental period. As a result, developmental lags, deficits, or deviations in component systems of the individual (i.e., biological, emotional, cognitive, representational, and interpersonal) will occur, and these aberrations will influence subsequent development. Moreover, given that development is characterized by differentiation and hierarchic integration within and across component biological and psychological systems at successive periods of developmental reorganization, prior aberrations acquired in one system begin to impact other systems detrimentally. As incompetence is engendered within the individual, negative reactions from levels of the social ecology may further perpetuate a maladaptive developmental trajectory.

Over the course of development, diverse prototypic organizations of biological and psychological systems emerge, and some of these prototypes will exhibit vulnerability for drug abuse. The quality of the organization among systems, rather than individual components in isolation, influences the potential for drug use outcomes. Adaptively functioning individuals exhibit a coherence in the organization among biological and psychological systems. In contrast, an individual who is vulnerable to drug abuse will evidence an incoherence in the organization across systems, with aberrations in one component system adversely impinging on other systems. Rather than a singular vulnerable prototype, different prototypes of incoherent organization that are vulnerable to drug use disorders are likely to exist. For example, one such prototype would involve an antisocial developmental organization with poor impulse control; impoverished, conflictual interpersonal relationships; difficulties in sustaining commitments to school or work; and a desire for thrill-seeking and excitement (Zucker, Fitzgerald, & Moses, 1995). Another prototype may consist of individuals with difficulty in negative affect regulation, difficulties in forming fulfilling interpersonal relationships, representations of others as abandoning and rejecting, and lack of confidence in one's self and one's abilities. Different prototypes may exhibit vulnerability to drug use problems at different stages of the life course. Different developmental demands faced at various stages of the life course may strain particular prototypes differentially, leading to different timing of onset for drug difficulties. Such variation in timing of vulnerability for drug problems is an important consideration in developmental research focused on a particular developmental period. For example, some prototypic organizations may not be vulnerable during the adolescent periods, whereas vulnerability for subsequent drug abuse problems in adulthood may emerge. Thus, a lifespan perspective is necessary for a full appreciation of the potential for vulnerability for drug abuse problems (Zucker et al., 2016).

Our research on the sequelae of child maltreatment is grounded in a developmental psychopathology perspective. Next, we examine developmental findings from childhood into the teenage years, with a focus on emerging substance use problems, specifically marijuana use during the adolescence period.

ILLUSTRATIONS OF DEVELOPMENTAL MODELS LINKING CHILD MALTREATMENT TO SUBSTANCE ABUSE

Research in our laboratory has been guided by the premise that substance abuse does not emerge in adolescence based on current contextual risk processes alone. Rather, we have sought to examine earlier patterns of developmental organization in childhood that contribute to substance abuse engagement later in adolescence. The work is based on research conducted with maltreated and nonmaltreated children in the school-age years in the context of a summer research camp. Half of the children had experienced previous abuse and/or neglect as documented in official Department of Human Services records, which were cumulative over each child's life. A demographically comparable group of low-income nonmaltreated children served as comparisons. The camp setting provided a rich context in which to observe children in a naturalistic peer context with extensive opportunity to assess broad aspects of interpersonal functioning with other children and adults; diverse aspects of psychological functioning, personality, and symptomatology; and multilevel indicators of biological regulation and reactivity. More than 600 youth were followed into adolescence and assessed at two time points with an extensive measurement battery assessing current organization of diverse developmental domains, with a particular interest in psychopathology and substance use involvement.

DEVELOPMENTAL CASCADES MODEL OF PROBLEM ADOLESCENT SUBSTANCE USE

In a first study (Rogosch, Oshri, & Cicchetti, 2010), our developmental model was based on a developmental cascades conceptualization. These models strive to demonstrate a developmental sequence of risk processes, whereby early risk factors generate subsequent vulnerabilities in development, which in turn transact to produce further risk for competent adaptation. Such cascade models are consistent with the transactional–ecological formulation of the sequelae of maltreatment (Cicchetti & Lynch, 1993; Cicchetti & Valentino, 2006). Consistent with Zucker et al.'s (2016) developmental–biopsychosocial systems formulation of alcoholism, an important empirical demonstration of a cascade model has been supported previously. This model charted a developmental sequence from family risk due to paternal alcoholism to early childhood difficult temperamental traits (i.e., negative emotionality, reactive control, and low ego resiliency), the emergence of childhood attention problems and subsequent disruptive behavior problems, and ensuing substance abuse in adolescence (Martell et al., 2009). The model illustrates the influence of compromises in one domain unfolding to difficulties in subsequent areas of behavioral control and regulation. Notably, early risk processes coalesced to promote conduct disturbance as an important link in the cascade to adolescent substance problems.

Similarly, Dodge et al. (2009) also have evaluated a developmental cascade model of adolescent substance use onset based on a social learning theory formulation. This model originates with problems in early parenting that are promoted by adverse sociocultural contexts and difficult child characteristics that present challenges to parenting. Through these difficulties in early parenting, early behavior problems emerge. As children develop relationships with peers, their behavior problems lead to peer rejection, which further escalates their conduct problems. In turn, parenting these children is progressively more challenging, and parents have difficulty monitoring their child's interactions with peers, who increasingly are more deviant, given the larger peer group social rejection they experience. Consequently, deviant peer models provide exposure to substances, and the vulnerable child is initiated into substance involvement.

Both the Martell et al. (2009) and the Dodge et al. (2009) cascade models provide poignant illustrations of the unfolding progression of risks that transact over development to promote substance use involvement. Both models focus on one risk process at a time at successive stages of development. A somewhat different model of developmental cascades (Burt, Obradovic, Long, & Masten, 2008; Burt & Roisman, 2010; Masten et al., 2005) stresses the importance of evaluating, whenever feasible, all of the developmental constructs successively at each time period in the developmental cascade model. There has been particular interest within these models in examining the transactions between different forms of psychopathology (internalizing and externalizing) and competence (social and academic) across different developmental periods. By addressing both the continuity across

development within domains and the within-time period covariance among domains, stronger conclusions can be made about cross-domain influences contributing to change as development proceeds. Through this approach (Burt et al., 2008; Burt & Roisman, 2010; Masten et al., 2005), the cascade models have been able to demonstrate how internalizing problems can suppress the later development of externalizing problems, how childhood externalizing problems contribute negatively to academic competence in adolescence, and how social and academic competence in emerging adulthood contribute to lower internalizing problems in young adulthood.

We evaluated a developmental cascades model of the emergence of cannabis abuse and dependence in adolescents who experienced child abuse and neglect earlier in development. We sought to determine how child maltreatment influences the development of externalizing and internalizing psychopathology, as well as social competence, from childhood to late adolescence. Because we were interested in the development of cannabis abuse and dependence, our model includes this emergent adolescent outcome only during adolescence, given the virtually nonexistent use of marijuana during childhood. A series of nested longitudinal models were tested, progressively evaluating within-domain stability across time, the influence of maltreatment status, and cross-lag effects whereby one domain contributes to subsequent change in another domain. Constructs were assessed by multiple informants and measures, and the methodology allowed for examination of long-term longitudinal cross-domain paths while controlling for both cross-domain within-time associations and rank-order stability of each domain over time (Cole & Maxwell, 2003).

Support was found for continuity of behavior problems, both internalizing and externalizing symptomatology, across the four developmental waves of assessment, from the earlier school-age years to later adolescence. These findings support the concept of rank-order stability in these two broadband forms of psychopathology across development and indicate that early occurring behavior problems are not transient concerns. Moreover, earlier social competence was related to late childhood social competence, and early adolescent cannabis use problems portended continuity of these problems later in adolescence. Child maltreatment prior to age 8 years significantly predicted the three early school-age domains, externalizing and internalizing problems, as well as low social competence. These findings are consistent with prior work that demonstrated the risk for heightened behavioral disturbance occurring among maltreated children, as well as compromises in the development of social competence, an important overarching stage-salient issue of childhood (Cicchetti & Valentino, 2006; Masten et al., 1999; Sroufe, 1989). Importantly, we also found evidence for a direct effect of early child maltreatment on higher levels of cannabis abuse and dependence symptoms in the early adolescent period. Moreover, early maltreatment continued to contribute independently to increases in problem cannabis use in late adolescence. Thus, our expectation of higher risk for substance use problems among youth with a history of maltreatment was confirmed.

Evaluation of cross-lagged relations occurring among domains from earlier to later childhood indicated that internalizing problems played an influential role. In particular, early internalizing problems served to curb the development of later increases in childhood externalizing difficulties, a finding consistent with the braking effect of internalizing symptoms on antisocial development (Burt et al., 2008; Masten et al., 2005). In addition, early internalizing difficulties contributed to decreases in social competence later in childhood: Children who socially withdraw and struggle with anxiety and depression increasingly are less successful in engaging with their peers, forming friendships, and developing prosocial behaviors. It also should be noted that maltreatment was directly related to social competence while also contributing to internalizing problems, leading to further decrements in competence among peers.

Cross-lagged influences across the transition from late childhood into the early adolescent years indicated a significant path linking late childhood externalizing problems to cannabis abuse and dependence symptoms in early adolescence. This finding is consistent with a substantial range of findings linking adolescent substance use to conduct disturbance. This relation was further instantiated by a significant path between early adolescent externalizing problems and late adolescent cannabis use problems. Thus, continuities in externalizing problems further contribute to increases in substance abuse difficulties later in adolescence. Of note, in addition to the direct influence of child maltreatment on cannabis abuse and dependence symptoms, indirect pathways to early substance problems and increases in these problems

in late adolescence via externalizing pathology were supported.

It is important to note that we obtained independent direct pathways between child maltreatment and early as well as late adolescent cannabis problem use, and the influence of late childhood antisocial behavior did not account for this association. These direct effects suggest that there are other processes associated with child maltreatment that are not accounted for by the development of behavioral problems or poor social competence. In determining what these processes are, it is important to note that the non-maltreated youth reside in the same impoverished neighborhood contexts as the maltreated youth, suggesting that other familial influences are likely involved. A potentially higher likelihood of parental substance use in the maltreating families, greater exposure to substance use in the home, and/or poor parental monitoring in maltreating families are possible processes that may account for this effect. Further investigation of mediators of the direct effect of maltreatment on adolescent problem use is needed.

There was limited evidence of linkages between child and adolescent internalizing difficulties and cannabis problem use in these analyses. Rather than contributing to substance use problems, early adolescent internalizing problems were found to reduce increases in late adolescent cannabis abuse and dependence symptoms, as well as externalizing problems. These relations are similar to the braking influence of internalizing symptomatology on externalizing difficulties observed in the current study during childhood. The more restricted contribution of internalizing difficulties to substance use is consistent with the more equivocal role for internalizing pathology in substance abuse during the adolescent period of development. Contrary to expectations, an association between late childhood social competence and cannabis use problems also was not supported. It may be that the influence of social difficulties and rejection by peers, and the development of relations with deviant peers in adolescence, on substance involvement, is accounted for more directly and fully by child externalizing problems. However, a very interesting significant path was found between late childhood social competence and increases in late adolescent externalizing problems. This effect is above and beyond the influence of stability in externalizing difficulties stemming from the childhood years. Moreover, it is noteworthy that this pathway also links early childhood internalizing problems to increases in late adolescent antisocial behaviors via diminished social competence in late childhood. Thus, cascading influences across development among the three domains are demonstrated, and these linkages again are sequelae of early maltreatment experiences. The externalizing stability pathway from child maltreatment to late adolescent externalizing problems is suggestive of Moffitt's (1993) life course persistent trajectory, whereas the cascading pathway from maltreatment to early internalizing difficulties to late childhood decrements in social competence to increases in late adolescent antisocial behavior may reflect youth following an adolescent-onset or adolescent-limited trajectory.

Finally, we did not find support for early adolescent cannabis abuse and dependence symptoms contributing to changes in late adolescent externalizing and internalizing pathology. It may be the case that the adverse consequences of substance use problems on functioning have not yet emerged during the adolescent period. However, if further assessment of this sample were available, then the influence of adolescent substance abuse problems on young adult functioning may become apparent.

CHILDHOOD PERSONALITY ORGANIZATION AS A DEVELOPMENTAL MEDIATOR

Two additional papers from our laboratory examined longitudinal models of adolescent marijuana abuse and dependence, with a particular emphasis on the role of childhood personality organization (Oshri, Rogosch, Burnette, & Cicchetti, 2011; Oshri, Rogosch, & Cicchetti, 2013). In these papers, broad domains of child personality, ego control (EC) and ego resiliency (ER), were assessed by camp counselors using the California Child Q-set (CCQ). EC refers to the degree to which individuals express their emotional impulses, varying between spontaneous and immediate to constrained and inhibited. ER involves the dynamic capacity to modify one's modal level of ego control in adapting flexibly to meet environmental contextual demands. In the first study (Oshri et al., 2011), a progressive longitudinal model was evaluated that included child maltreatment prior to age 7 years as the exogenous variable, ER and EC personality dimensions at age 7–9 years, externalizing and internalizing symptoms at age 10–12 years, and

early marijuana use symptoms at age 13–15 years. A more nuanced measure of early maltreatment was used involving a composite of the severity of each of four subtypes of maltreatment the child had experienced: emotional maltreatment, neglect, physical abuse, and sexual abuse.

The findings supported a developmental sequence in which early childhood maltreatment severity potentiates less adaptive childhood personality functioning, followed by externalizing problems in preadolescence and, ultimately, adolescent cannabis abuse and dependence symptoms. Notably, a corresponding internalizing pathway was not supported, although internalizing symptoms were related to maltreatment status, EC, and ER. The findings indicate that maltreatment acts as a major catalyst for many children to develop maladaptive childhood personality characteristics that contribute to preadolescent externalizing problems, which in turn influence adolescent cannabis abuse and dependence. The externalizing path observed in the current study among maltreated youth is consistent with prior studies of nonmaltreated youth, in which behaviorally undercontrolled personality functioning was associated with affective dysregulation and problem behaviors (Cornelius et al., 2010; Kirisci et al., 2009; Ridenour et al., 2009; Tarter, Kirisci, Habeych, Reynolds, & Vanyukov, 2004; Tarter, Kirisci, Ridenour, & Vanyukov, 2008; Zucker et al., 2008).

In the second paper focused on child personality functioning (Oshri et al., 2013), a more person-centered approach in characterizing child personality organization was used. In particular, using multireported CCQ assessments of children ages 10–12 years, latent profile analysis was used to identify three child personality types: undercontrolled, overcontrolled, and resilient (Hart, Hofmann, Edelstein, & Keller, 1997; Robins, John, Caspi, Moffitt, & Stouthamer-Loeber, 1996). Longitudinal models were evaluated linking child maltreatment density (i.e., the number of maltreatment subtypes experienced) to the differential likelihood of undercontrolled and overcontrolled child personality types and subsequent marijuana and alcohol abuse/dependence symptoms, as well as externalizing and internalizing symptoms at ages 15–18 years. Both the undercontrolled and the overcontrolled personality types showed elevated prevalence among maltreated children, relative to the resilient type. Separate longitudinal models were conducted contrasting the undercontrolled versus resilient personality profiles and the overcontrolled versus resilient profiles. Variations in the distribution of personality configurations were found to mediate the relation between the number of child maltreatment subtypes and the development of adolescent maladaptation. The findings revealed that children with a higher number of maltreatment subtypes were significantly more likely to be classified into the undercontrolled and overcontrolled profiles compared to the resilient profile. Members of the two less flexible profiles were at differential risk for problem behaviors and marijuana and alcohol use problems in adolescence, after controlling the variance related to the cumulative number of maltreatment subtypes. The undercontrolled profile significantly mediated the link between the number of child maltreatment subtypes and adolescent cannabis use problems and externalizing symptoms. In contrast, a greater number of maltreatment subtypes were related to greater likelihood of an overcontrolled versus a resilient personality profile, which in turn was related to fewer alcohol use problems and greater internalizing symptomatology. Thus, evaluating a pattern-based mediation model (Bergman, 2009; Schulenberg, Sameroff, & Cicchetti, 2004; Schulenberg, Wadsworth, O'Malley, Backman, & Johnston, 1996) improved our ability to methodologically and conceptually demonstrate diverse developmental pathways by showing the contribution of latent personality configurations as an underlying mechanism linking child maltreatment and the development of problem behaviors and substance abuse in adolescence.

GENETIC MODERATION OF DEVELOPMENTAL PATHWAYS TO SUBSTANCE USE

Our findings have provided clear support for an externalizing pathway leading from earlier childhood maltreatment experiences to subsequent problem adolescent marijuana use, whereas an internalizing pathway has not been supported. These models have been at the behavioral levels and have not considered concomitant biological contributions. Such extension is essential for a multilevel developmental perspective. Child maltreatment constitutes a profound source of chronic stress that disrupts stress regulatory systems, and considerable work has demonstrated adverse effects among maltreated children (Cicchetti, Rogosch, Gunnar, & Toth, 2010). Genetic variation has been shown to moderate the adverse sequelae of child maltreatment and provide insight into individual differences in susceptibility. In a recent paper (Handley, Rogosch, & Cicchetti, 2015), we evaluated the role of the FK506 binding protein 5 gene (FKBP5) in moderating the impact of maltreatment on the externalizing pathway to substance abuse. FKBP5 was chosen given its central role in influencing stress responsivity. Evidence for moderated mediation was found. As previously mentioned, child externalizing symptoms mediated the effect of child maltreatment on adolescent marijuana dependence symptoms. However, this pathway was found only for adolescents with one or two copies of the FKBP5 CATT haplotype. Although child maltreatment conferred risk for child externalizing symptoms regardless of FKBP5 polymorphism, whether externalizing symptoms in childhood progressed into marijuana dependence in adolescence depended on the presence of the FKBP5 CATT haplotype. These findings indicate that the snowballing of childhood externalizing symptoms into adolescent substance disorder may be dependent on gene variants that affect stress sensitivity. Preliminary support also was found for FKBP5 genetic variation as a moderator of the direct effect of child maltreatment on adolescent marijuana dependence. Our externalizing models demonstrated that adolescents with maltreatment experiences prior to age 8 years reported more marijuana dependence symptoms in adolescence only if they carried one or two copies of the FKBP5 CATT haplotype. For adolescents without copies of the FKBP5 CATT haplotype, child maltreatment was unrelated to marijuana dependence in adolescence. It is worth noting that moderation of this direct effect did not reach statistical significance in our internalizing models. Together, these results contribute to a growing literature demonstrating that FKBP5 moderates the effect of childhood adversity on the development of later psychopathology (for a review, see Zannas & Binder, 2014). Our test of gene–environment interaction within the externalizing pathway highlights the importance of examining individual differences within this risk pathway and, more broadly, the criticality of a multiple levels of analysis approach to understanding the etiology of substance use disorders.

CONCLUSIONS AND FUTURE DIRECTIONS

Robert Zucker's theoretical work and empirical research have greatly influenced the ways in which investigators have examined the processes underlying substance abuse. The knowledge base of the development and course of substance abuse and psychopathology will be significantly increased by advances in genomics, gene–environment interactions, and epigenetics, including microarrays and whole genome sequencing of DNA and RNA; an increase in the understanding of neurobiology, neural plasticity, and resilience; and progress in the development of methodological and technological tools. In addition, advances in neural circuitry, hormone assays, immunology, social and environmental influences on brain development, and statistical analysis of developmental change pave the way for interdisciplinary and multilevel research and prevention programs that will contribute greatly to the understanding of substance abuse in its full complexity.

Steps Forward

1. Most investigations of the causes and consequences of substance use and abuse have examined neurobiological and psychological systems separately. Longitudinal research that examines biological and psychological systems concurrently over developmental time is required.

2. Although some progress in this area has occurred, it is imperative that future research continues to examine mediators that contribute to our understanding of the mechanisms that underlie both the developmental consequences of substance use and abuse and intervention efficacy.

3. Despite rapid, promising advances, our understanding of the genetic moderation of intervention outcome remains in its infancy. Most interventions have attempted to change the environment with no consideration for genetic involvement. Thus, interventions targeting both gene and environment are in a nascent state, and such work must occur more frequently in the future.

4. Research on G×E and on epigenetics needs to incorporate, as well as emphasize, a developmental perspective (i.e., G×E×D). Genes may influence how environmental experience affects the developmental process, and this may operate differently at various developmental periods. Moreover, the effects of genes and experience during a particular period may be influenced by the effects of prior development. Environments may affect the timing of genetic effects and gene expression. In addition, there are experience effects on the epigenome, and these also may operate differently across the course of development.

5. Prevention and intervention strive to alter the environment in order to bring about positive outcomes. Research on epigenetics suggests that prevention and intervention may also change the epigenome and that this could result in improved outcomes. If researchers are to understand the processes through which early adverse experiences impart maladaptation, psychopathology, or resilience, then it is critical that genetic variation (functional polymorphisms) and epigenetic modifications be examined.

6. Genetic effects on intervention efficacy may occur in a number of ways (Belsky & van Ijzendoorn, 2015). Are some individuals, based on genetic variation, more susceptible to the positive effects of intervention? Are particular interventions more effective on particular individuals based on genetic differences (i.e., should interventions match genotype groups)? Does intervention affect DNA methylation, resulting in changes in gene expression? DNA methylation changes in response to experience could lead to the design of both prevention and intervention strategies that alter the expression of genes to promote healthy physical and mental outcomes. Given that the demethylated epigenome is transmitted to the next generation, it is important to determine if decreased substance use and abuse risk through efficacious intervention would alter the epigenome, which in turn would result in a less risky epigenome being transmitted to the next generation.

ACKNOWLEDGMENTS

The research reported in this chapter was supported by funding from the National Institute on Drug Abuse

(DA 12903 and DA 17741) to Dante Cicchetti and Fred A. Rogosch and the Spunk Fund, Inc., to Dante Cicchetti.

REFERENCES

Belsky, J., & van Ijzendoorn, M. H. (2015). What works for whom? Genetic moderation of intervention efficacy. *Development and Psychopathology*, 27(1), 617–627. doi:10.1017/S0954579414001254

Bergman, L. R. (2009). Mediation and causality at the individual level. *Integrative Psychological Behavioral Science*, 43, 248–252.

Burt, K. B., Obradovic, J., Long, J. D., & Masten, A. S. (2008). The interplay of social competence and psychopathology over 20 years: Testing transactional and cascade models. *Child Development*, 79, 359–374.

Burt, K. B., & Roisman, G. I. (2010). Competence and psychopathology: Cascade effects in the NICHD Study of Early Child Care and Youth Development. *Development and Psychopathology*, 22(3), 557–567.

Causadias, J. M. (2013). A roadmap for the integration of culture into developmental psychopathology. *Development and Psychopathology*, 25(4 Pt. 2), 1375–1398.

Cicchetti, D. (1993). Developmental psychopathology: Reactions, reflections, projections. *Developmental Review*, 13, 471–502. doi:10.1006/drev.1993.1021

Cicchetti, D. (2000). A developmental psychopathology perspective on drug abuse. In M. D. Glantz & C. R. Hartel (Eds.), *Drug abuse: Origins and interventions* (pp. 97–118). Washington, DC: American Psychological Association.

Cicchetti, D. (Ed.). (2003). Experiments of nature: Contributions to developmental theory [Special issue]. *Development and Psychopathology*, 15, 833–1106.

Cicchetti, D., & Blender, J. A. (2006). A multiple-levels-of-analysis perspective on resilience: Implications for the developing brain, neural plasticity, and preventive interventions. *Annals of the New York Academy of Sciences*, 1094, 248–258.

Cicchetti, D., & Cannon, T. D. (1999). Neurodevelopmental processes in the ontogenesis and epigenesis of psychopathology. *Development and Psychopathology*, 11, 375–393.

Cicchetti, D., & Dawson, G. (2002). Multiple levels of analysis. *Development and Psychopathology*, 14, 417–420.

Cicchetti, D., & Luthar, S. S. (Eds.). (1999). Developmental approaches to substance use and abuse [Special issue]. *Development and Psychopathology*, 11, 655–988.

Cicchetti, D., & Lynch, M. (1993). Toward an ecological/transactional model of community violence and child maltreatment: Consequences for children's development. *Psychiatry*, 56, 96–118.

Cicchetti, D., & Rogosch, F. A. (1996). Equifinality and multifinality in developmental psychopathology. *Development and Psychopathology*, 8, 597–600.

Cicchetti, D., & Rogosch, F. A. (1999). Psychopathology as risk for adolescent substance use disorders: A developmental psychopathology perspective. *Journal of Clinical Child Psychology*, 28, 355–365.

Cicchetti, D., & Rogosch, F. A. (2002). A developmental psychopathology perspective on adolescence. *Journal of Consulting and Clinical Psychology*, 70(1), 6–20.

Cicchetti, D., Rogosch, F. A., Gunnar, M. R., & Toth, S. L. (2010). The differential impacts of early physical and sexual abuse and internalizing problems on daytime cortisol rhythm in school-aged children. *Child Development*, 81(1), 252–269.

Cicchetti, D., & Schneider-Rosen, K. (1986). An organizational approach to childhood depression. In M. Rutter, C. E. Izard, & P. B. Read (Eds.), *Depression in young people: Clinical and developmental perspectives* (pp. 71–134). New York, NY: Guilford.

Cicchetti, D., & Toth, S. L. (2009). The past achievements and future promises of developmental psychopathology: The coming of age of a discipline. *Journal of Child Psychology and Psychiatry*, 50, 16–25.

Cicchetti, D., & Toth, S. L. (2015). Child maltreatment. In M. Lamb (Ed.), *Handbook of child psychology and developmental science: Volume 3. Socioemotional process* (7th ed., pp. 513–563). New York, NY: Wiley.

Cicchetti, D., & Tucker, D. (1994). Development and self-regulatory structures of the mind. *Development and Psychopathology*, 6, 533–549.

Cicchetti, D., & Valentino, K. (2006). An ecological transactional perspective on child maltreatment: Failure of the average expectable environment and its influence upon child development. In D. Cicchetti & D. J. Cohen (Eds.), *Developmental psychopathology: Volume 3. Risk, disorder, and adaptation* (2nd ed., pp. 129–201). New York, NY: Wiley.

Cole, D. A., & Maxwell, S. E. (2003). Testing mediational models with longitudinal data: Questions and tips in the use of structural equation modeling. *Journal of Abnormal Psychology*, 112, 558–577.

Cornelius, J. R., Kirisci, L., Reynolds, M., Clark, D. B., Hayes, J., & Tarter, R. (2010). PTSD contributes to teen and young adult cannabis use disorders. *Addictive Behaviors*, 35(2), 91–94.

Dodge, K. A., Malone, P. S., Landsford, J. E., Miller, S., Pettit, G. S., & Bates, J. E. (2009). A dynamic cascade model of the development of substance-use onset. *Monographs of the Society for Research in Child Development*, 74(3), 1–120.

Garcia-Coll, C., Akerman, A., & Cicchetti, D. (2000). Cultural influences on developmental processes and outcomes: Implications for the study of development and psychopathology. *Development and Psychopathology*, 12, 333–356.

Glantz, M. D., & Leshner, A. I. (2000). Drug abuse and developmental psychopathology. *Development & Psychopathology*, 12(4), 795–814.

Gottlieb, G. (1991). Experiential canalization of behavioral development: Theory. *Developmental Psychology*, 27, 4–13.

Handley, E. D., Rogosch, F. A., & Cicchetti, D. (2015). Developmental pathways from child maltreatment to adolescent marijuana dependence: Examining moderation by FKBP5. *Development and Psychopathology*, 27(4 Pt. 2), 1489–1502.

Hart, D., Hofmann, V., Edelstein, W., & Keller, M. (1997). The relation of childhood personality types to adolescent behavior and development: A longitudinal study of Icelandic children. *Developmental Psychology*, 33(2), 195–205.

Kirisci, L., Tarter, R., Mezzich, A., Ridenour, T., Reynolds, M., & Vanyukov, M. (2009). Prediction of cannabis use disorder between boyhood and young adulthood: Clarifying the phenotype and environtype. *American Journal on Addictions*, 18(1), 36–47.

Lenneberg, E. (1967). *Biological foundations of language*. New York, NY: Wiley.

Martell, M. M., Pierce, L., Nigg, J. T., Jester, J. M., Adams, K., Puttler, L. I., . . . Zucker, R. A. (2009). Temperamental pathways to childhood disruptive behavior and adolescent substance abuse: Testing a cascade model. *Journal of Abnormal Child Psychology*, 37, 363–373.

Masten, A. S., Faden, V. B., Zucker, R. A., & Spear, L. P. (2008). Underage drinking: A developmental framework. *Pediatrics*, 121(Suppl. 4), S235–S251.

Masten, A. S., Hubbard, J. J., Gest, S. D., Tellegen, A., Garmezy, N., & Ramirez, M. (1999). Competence in the context of adversity: Pathways to resilience and maladaptation from childhood to late adolescence. *Development and Psychopathology*, 11, 143–169.

Masten, A. S., Roisman, G. I., Long, J. D., Burt, K. B., Obradovic, J., Riley, J. R., . . . Tellegen, A. (2005).

Developmental cascades: Linking academic achievement and externalizing and internalizing symptoms over 20 years. *Developmental Psychology*, 41, 733–746.

Moffitt, T. E. (1993). "Life-course persistent" and "adolescence-limited" antisocial behavior: A developmental taxonomy. *Psychological Review*, 100, 674–701.

O'Connor, T. G. (2003). Natural experiments to study the effects of early experience: Progress and limitations. *Development and Psychopathology*, 15(4), 837–852.

Oshri, A., Rogosch, F. A., Burnette, M. L., & Cicchetti, D. (2011). Developmental pathways to adolescent cannabis abuse and dependence: Child maltreatment, emerging personality, and internalizing versus externalizing psychopathology. *Psychology of Addictive Behaviors*, 25(4), 634.

Oshri, A., Rogosch, F. A., & Cicchetti, D. (2013). Child maltreatment and mediating influences of childhood personality types on the development of adolescent psychopathology. *Journal of Clinical Child & Adolescent Psychology*, 42(3), 287–301.

Ridenour, T. A., Tarter, R. E., Reynolds, M., Mezzich, A., Kirisci, L., & Vanyukov, M. (2009). Neurobehavior disinhibition, parental substance use disorder, neighborhood quality and development of cannabis use disorder in boys. *Drug and Alcohol Dependence*, 102(1–3), 71–77.

Robins, R. W., John, O. P., Caspi, A., Moffitt, T. E., & Stouthamer-Loeber, M. (1996). Resilient, overcontrolled, and undercontrolled boys: Three personality types in early adolescence. *Journal of Personality and Social Psychology*, 70, 157–171.

Rogosch, F. A., Oshri, A., & Cicchetti, D. (2010). From child maltreatment to adolescent cannabis abuse and dependence: A developmental cascade model. *Development and Psychopathology*, 22(4), 883–897.

Schulenberg, J. E., Sameroff, A. J., & Cicchetti, D. (2004). The transition to adulthood as a critical juncture in the course of psychopathology and mental health. *Development and Psychopathology*, 16(4), 799–806.

Schulenberg, J. E., Wadsworth, K. N., O'Malley, P. M., Bachman, J. G., & Johnston, L. D. (1996). Adolescent risk factors for binge drinking during the transition to young adulthood: Variable- and pattern-centered approaches to change. *Developmental Psychology*, 32(4), 659–674.

Spear, L. P. (2000). The adolescent brain and age-related behavioral manifestations. *Neuroscience and Behavioral Reviews*, 24, 417–463.

Sroufe, L. A. (1989). Relationships, self, and individual adaptation. In A. J. Sameroff & R. N. Emde (Eds.),

Relationship disturbances in early childhood (pp. 70–94). New York, NY: Basic Books.

Sroufe, L. A. (1990). Considering normal and abnormal together: The essence of developmental psychopathology. *Development and Psychopathology, 2,* 335–347.

Sroufe, L. A., & Rutter, M. (1984). The domain of developmental psychopathology. *Child Development, 55,* 17–29.

Tarter, R. E., Kirisci, L., Habeych, M., Reynolds, M., & Vanyukov, M. (2004). Neurobehavior disinhibition in childhood predisposes boys to substance use disorder by young adulthood: Direct and mediated etiologic pathways. *Drug and Alcohol Dependence, 73*(2), 121–132.

Tarter, R. E., Kirisci, L., Ridenour, T., & Vanyukov, M. (2008). Prediction of cannabis use disorder between childhood and young adulthood using the Child Behavior Checklist. *Journal of Psychopathology and Behavioral Assessment, 30*(4), 272–278.

Thelen, E., & Smith, L. B. (1998). Dynamic systems theories. In W. Damon & R. Lerner (Eds.), *Handbook of child psychology: Volume 1. Theoretical models of human development* (pp. 563–634). New York, NY: Wiley.

Werner, H., & Kaplan, B. (1963). *Symbol formation.* New York, NY: Wiley.

Windle, M., Spear, L. P., Fuligni, A. J., Angold, A., Brown, J. D., Pine, D., . . . Dahl, R. E. (2009). Transitions into underage and problem drinking: Summary of developmental processes and mechanisms: Ages 10–15. *Alcohol Research & Health, 32*(1), 30–40.

Zannas, A. S., & Binder, E. B. (2014). Gene–environment interactions at the FKBP5 locus: Sensitive periods, mechanisms and pleiotropism. *Genes, Brain, and Behavior, 13,* 25–37.

Zucker, R. A. (2006). Alcohol use and the alcohol use disorders: A developmental–biopsychosocial systems formulation covering the life course. In D. Cicchetti & D. J. Cohen (Eds.), *Developmental psychopathology: Volume 3. Risk, disorder, and adaptation* (2nd ed., pp. 620–656). New York, NY: Wiley.

Zucker, R. A., Donovan, J. E., Masten, A. S., Mattson, M. E., & Moss, H. B. (2008). Early developmental processes and the continuity of risk for underage drinking and problem drinking. *Pediatrics, 121*(Suppl. 4), S252–S272.

Zucker, R. A., Fitzgerald, H. E., & Moses, H. D. (1995). Emergence of alcohol problems and the several alcoholisms: A developmental perspective on etiologic theory and life course trajectory. In D. Cicchetti & D. Cohen (Eds.), *Developmental psychopathology: Risk, disorder, and adaptation* (Vol. 2, pp. 677–711). New York, NY: Wiley.

Zucker, R. A., Hicks, B. M., & Heitzeg, M. M. (2016). Alcohol use and the alcohol use disorders over the life course: A cross-level developmental review. In D. Cicchetti (Ed.), *Developmental psychopathology: Volume 3. Maladaptation and psychopathology* (3rd ed., pp. 793–832). New York, NY: Wiley.

3

Implications of Heterogeneity in Alcohol Use Disorders for Understanding Developmental Pathways and Prevention Programming

Andrea M. Hussong

W. Andrew Rothenberg

Ruth K. Smith

Maleeha Haroon

Highly heterogeneous diagnostic classifications present long-acknowledged challenges for understanding etiology, mapping epidemiology, identifying effective treatments, and developing successful prevention programs for psychiatric disorders (Olbert, Gala, & Tupler, 2014). Alcoholism is one such highly heterogeneous disorder. Studies dating back to Jellinek's (1960) articulation of five alcoholism subtypes that vary both diachronically (or along the dimension of time) and synchronically (or across people) began a wave of research to identify the key dimensions that meaningfully distinguish among those who share this psychiatric diagnosis. However, not all dimensions of heterogeneity have meaningful implications for perhaps the most salient purpose of diagnostic classification: guiding treatment and prevention efforts.

Several research efforts have sought to determine whether targeted treatments for subgroups of individuals with an alcohol use disorder (AUD) (i.e., treatments that consider heterogeneity in AUDs as part of treatment planning) are more effective than universal treatments (i.e., treatments that do not consider such heterogeneity in treatment planning). The challenges associated with developing targeted treatments were reflected in reactions of

the scientific community to Project MATCH (which stands for Matching Alcoholism Treatment to Client Heterogeneity; Cooney, Babor, DiClemente, & Del Boca, 2003), the first large-scale treatment study to examine the efficacy of targeted psychosocial treatments for AUDs in alcohol-dependent adults. In this study, investigators examined whether three randomly assigned treatments (i.e., cognitive–behavioral, motivational enhancement, and Alcoholics Anonymous-based interventions) were more effective for some clients than for others by testing whether a variety of statistical interactions between treatment condition and client characteristics (e.g., comorbid disorders) predicted abstinence-based outcomes. Because few effects of matching were consistently supported and clients generally improved in all treatment conditions, Project MATCH investigators concluded that their body of work provided only limited support for the efficacy of targeting AUD treatments for specific individuals (for details, see Cooney et al., 2003). However, other researchers sharply criticized this conclusion on methodological as well as theoretical grounds, in part calling into question what it means to provide targeted treatment and on which individual and treatment characteristics matching should occur (e.g., see Marlatt, 1999). These questions remain relevant today and are reflected in the ongoing search for salient dimensions of heterogeneity to guide targeted treatments.

The implications of heterogeneity among those with an AUD diagnosis for prevention programming (vs. treatment development) are less often a focus in the literature. Few efforts currently tailor prevention programs with an eye specifically toward heterogeneity in the AUD outcomes for which subsets of youth are at risk. A clear step toward this goal is to articulate the developmental pathways that lead to different subtypes of AUDs along with risk factors to identify who may be on which pathway at what point in development. In this chapter, we first consider current conceptualizations of heterogeneity in AUDs and then focus on developmental pathways that are best articulated for two subtypes of AUDs. We then consider how developmental pathways may be related to diagnostic subgroups more generally before discussing implications for prevention programming.

CHARACTERIZING HETEROGENEITY IN ALCOHOL USE DISORDERS

Although several frameworks for conceptualizing subtypes of AUDs have been offered throughout the years (Babor, 1996; Cloninger, Sigvardsson, Gilligan, & von Knorring, 1988; Moss, Chen, & Yi, 2007), perhaps the most developmentally embedded of these is that proposed by Dr. Robert Zucker. In his seminal work, Zucker and colleagues (Zucker, 2006; Zucker, Fitzgerald, & Moses, 1995) utilized a developmental psychopathology framework (Cicchetti & Cohen, 1995) to identify several developmental factors that precede initial alcohol use and influence the development of AUDs across ontogeny. Invoking the concept of equifinality (i.e., that several distinct processes can operate to produce a common phenotypic endpoint across individuals; Cicchetti & Rogosch, 1996), Zucker (2006) articulated how experiencing different childhood precursors could lead individuals down distinct developmental pathways that each ultimately lead to the onset of an AUD. The form of AUD, however, may differ across pathways, and Zucker distinguished among six forms of AUD based on individual differences in developmental trajectories, adult functioning, comorbidity, course, and prognosis. These six

types of AUD included both "comorbid alcoholisms" that are characterized by their co-occurrence with other types of psychopathology and their demarcation by a set of childhood precursors and "primary alcoholisms" that have no clear childhood antecedents and are related to drinking consequences rather than developmental etiology.

Zucker identified three forms of AUD as primary alcoholisms, labeling them isolated alcohol abuse (i.e., characterized by infrequent, non-recurring instances of problematic drinking), episodic alcoholism (i.e., characterized by occasional recurrent, but not chronic, instances of problematic drinking), and developmentally cumulative alcoholism (i.e., characterized by chronic instances of problematic drinking). He offered two hypotheses for how primary alcoholisms develop. First, primary alcoholisms may be driven by an individual's low sensitivity to ethanol's intoxicating effects and an individual's positive subjective experiences with alcohol that reinforce consumption. According to this hypothesis, an individual moves from isolated abuse to episodic abuse and then to developmentally cumulative abuse over time as these addictive properties of alcohol become further reinforced. An alternative (although not necessarily competing) hypothesis is that primary alcoholisms are driven by the presence of environmental stressors that propel individuals toward alcohol use as a means of reducing stress. The nature of the stressors, in turn, distinguishes among the forms of primary alcoholism. For example, isolated abuse could be associated with the experience of one-time environmental stressors (e.g., the breakup of a marriage), whereas episodic abuse could be associated with recurring environmental stressors (e.g., continued long-term occupational stress). Developmentally cumulative abuse could in turn be associated with sustained environmental stressors; individuals with the greatest vulnerability to the addictive properties of alcohol may be particularly vulnerable to developmentally cumulative abuse and as a result evidence a chronic pattern of alcoholism. Importantly, Zucker posits that these three forms of AUD have no developmental antecedents in early or middle childhood, making empirically based early preventive programming for these types of AUD difficult to develop.

In the comorbid class of AUD, Zucker included antisocial alcoholism, developmentally limited alcoholism, and negative affect alcoholism. Both the antisocial and developmentally limited AUDs focus on comorbidities between antisocial behavior and problematic alcohol use, but they distinguish among those who experience AUDs as a chronic disorder (the antisocial subtype that is similar to Moffitt's [1993] life course persistent form of antisocial behavior) or as a time-limited disorder. Whereas the antisocial AUD subtype is characterized by temperamental and behavioral characteristics in early childhood that persist across ontogeny, the developmentally limited AUD subtype emerges as a consequence of the common delinquent behaviors in which many adolescents engage. Adolescent alcohol use is itself a common delinquent behavior, and problematic alcohol use may escalate into an AUD for some youth vulnerable to the reinforcing properties of alcohol (Zucker, 2006). However, many adolescents "mature out" of problematic drinking patterns in young adulthood (Donovan, Jessor, & Jessor, 1983), resulting in a developmentally limited pattern of AUD. Researchers posit that developmentally limited alcoholism dissipates as social goals in young adulthood (e.g., finding a long-term romantic partner and establishing a career) become incompatible with problematic substance use (Jackson, Sher, Gotham, & Wood, 2001).

Following a more chronic course, Zucker's antisocial subtype of AUD emerges from a history of persistent externalizing behavior evident in childhood and eventually concomitant problematic alcohol use in adolescence and adulthood. Forming an "externalizing pathway" to antisocial AUD, associated developmental risk is posited to begin in infancy with the emergence of a genetically mediated disinhibited temperament characterized by high activity level, low attention span, and behavioral dysregulation. This temperamental style is hypothesized to lead to the development of oppositional and conduct problems throughout childhood when coupled with deleterious environmental circumstances (e.g., living in a home with high levels of marital conflict, family stress, or parent psychopathology). These externalizing behaviors create risk for associations with deviant peers during the school years that in turn exacerbate externalizing behavior over time, leading to delinquent activity (including problematic alcohol use) and ultimately the emergence of an antisocial personality in adulthood. In this way, an externalizing pathway is predicted to lead to the antisocial behavior and comorbid alcoholism that define the antisocial AUD subtype.

The third form of comorbid AUD proposed by Zucker is the negative affect AUD subtype. Like the antisocial AUD subtype, this type of AUD is posited to be the culmination of a developmental trajectory that begins in early childhood. Zucker initially hypothesized that dispositional tendencies toward behavioral inhibition, shyness, and social fearfulness in childhood predicted the emergence of concomitant internalizing symptomatology (e.g., symptoms of negative affect, depression, and anxiety) and problematic alcohol use in adolescence, culminating in the development of comorbid negative affectivity and severe alcohol-related symptoms in adulthood. Since Zucker's identification of the negative affect AUD subtype and accompanying internalizing developmental pathway, other researchers have delineated how early temperamental characteristics, social skill deficits, deviant peer groups, alcohol expectancies, coping motives, and other vulnerability factors that emerge throughout development facilitate progression down this pathway (Hussong, Jones, Stein, Baucom, & Boeding, 2011).

The antisocial and negative affect AUDs described by Zucker are reflected in many other articulations of AUD subtypes (Babor, 1996; Cloninger et al., 1988; Moss et al., 2007). What is unique about Zucker's articulation of these subtypes is their connection to developmental pathways. These pathways reflect a core developmental tenant, namely that AUDs often do not emerge only in adulthood but, rather, emerge as part of a developmental process that includes childhood and adolescent precursors that precede drinking behavior (Masten, Faden, Zucker, & Spear, 2008). Other researchers have since identified early childhood internalizing and externalizing behaviors as promising targets for early interventions to prevent AUDs (Chung, 2013; Hussong et al., 2011; Masten et al., 2008), although programs to prevent AUDs early in development are still uncommon. Addressing this gap, the remainder of this chapter describes existing and recent work delineating the externalizing and internalizing pathways to the antisocial and negative affect AUD subtypes and considers prevention implications associated with each of these developmental pathways. Because more literature has reviewed the externalizing pathway than the internalizing pathway, we review the first briefly and more fully articulate predictions associated with the second.

ANTISOCIAL ALCOHOL USE DISORDERS AND THE EXTERNALIZING PATHWAY

Although the externalizing pathway to AUD—also termed the antisocial, behavioral undercontrol, or behavioral disinhibition pathway—is most often described with respect to co-occurring aggression and delinquent behavior, researchers posit that the primary operative deficit is in controlling behavior (Sher, Walitzer, Wood, & Brent, 1991; Zucker, Heitzeg, & Nigg, 2011). Behavioral control or disinhibition deficits operate at several levels and subsume both observable (e.g., aggression) and inferential (e.g., impulsivity) traits such as inattention, aggression, impulsivity, and low persistence (for a review, see Iacono, Malone, & McGue, 2008). Formulations of this pathway overlap with those for antisocial behavior more generally (Dishion, Capaldi, & Yoerger, 1999; Dodge et al., 2009; Sher, 1991) and often reflect a process of heterotypic continuity in which individuals show continuity in some "core deficit" over time (i.e., behavioral control) but different expressions of the deficit emerge across development (Caspi & Moffitt, 1995; Rutter, 1996). At a molar level, the externalizing pathway to AUD is often posited to first emerge as a difficult temperament style in infancy, followed by externalizing symptoms (e.g., attentional deficits and oppositional behavior) in childhood and then by an early onset and escalation of alcohol use and worsening antisocial behavior in adolescence (Tarter et al., 1999; Zucker, 2006). These externalizing symptoms are often considered to be part of a larger constellation of problem behavior that continues into adulthood (Jessor & Jessor, 1977) and escalates into an eventual AUD that is comorbid with antisocial behavior (Zucker, 2006).

Previous studies show that early emerging externalizing symptoms are a reliable predictor of later AUDs. As reviewed by Zucker (2006), several prospective studies support a direct association between early indicators of behavioral undercontrol (including aggression) in childhood and later alcohol-related problems and disorder in adolescence and adulthood. Notably, Caspi, Moffitt, Newman, and Silva (1996) found that behavioral undercontrol in children at age 3 years increased the likelihood of alcohol dependence at age 21 years in their population study of a New Zealand birth cohort, and Zucker, Chermack, and Curran (2000) found that externalizing symptoms in 3- to 5-year-olds elevated risk for drinking onset in

early adolescence in their high-risk sample of sons of alcoholic parents and matched controls. A strong evidence base also supports the prospective prediction of alcohol involvement and related problems into adulthood from aggression, conduct problems, and delinquency in adolescence (Chassin, Colder, Hussong, & Sher, 2016; Zucker, 2006).

Building on these findings, researchers have identified several mechanisms that each partially account for the association between externalizing symptoms and alcohol use (for a review, see Chassin et al., 2016). An important implication of these studies is that the strong and consistent association between externalizing symptoms and alcohol use may be so commonly supported because externalizing symptoms index multiple mechanisms working at multiple levels (e.g., genetic, neural, and behavioral) to incur risk for problematic alcohol use. In this review, we consider the externalizing (and internalizing) pathway as emerging through the intersection of genetic, neural, and behavioral elements that transact with an environmental context across ontogeny (according to developmental principles described by Gottlieb, 2007). The behavioral level of analysis here involves the heterotypic expression of behavioral undercontrol that extends to antisocial AUDs in adolescence and adulthood.

A substantial research focus now concerns the underlying genetic and neural correlates of behavioral undercontrol and associated AUDs. Two neural systems implicated in the development of behavioral undercontrol that are most consistently associated with alcohol involvement are those that regulate cognitive control over behavior (also termed cognitive constraint or effortful control) and sensitivity to reward (Chassin et al., 2016). Poor regulatory control and greater sensitivity to reward are each associated with both externalizing symptoms and adolescent alcohol use in prior research (Beauchaine, 2001; Colder & O'Connor, 2004; Khurana et al., 2013; Knyazev, 2004; Zucker et al., 2011). Moreover, tripartite models indicate that these two neural systems may operate jointly, with weak regulatory control failing to inhibit antisocial and alcohol use behaviors and greater sensitivity to reward simultaneously enhancing motivation for these behaviors (Ernst & Fudge, 2009). Although these systems have been associated with indices of alcohol use and behavioral undercontrol, we could find no studies that tested the unique effect of these neural systems on co-occurring externalizing and alcohol-related symptoms, over and above associations with these symptoms occurring individually.

Behavioral genetic studies, however, do indicate that co-occurring externalizing symptoms and alcohol-related problems may share a common genetic liability for behavioral undercontrol or disinhibition (for a review, see Tully & Iacono, 2014). Genome-wide association studies (GWAS) and candidate gene studies that seek to identify specific genetic risk mechanisms, however, more often focus on phenotypes for externalizing symptoms and alcohol-related problems separately (although see Hill, Stoltenberg, Bullard, Li, Zucker, & Burmeister, 2002). As reviewed by Chassin et al. (2016), several candidate genes have been associated with indices of behavioral undercontrol and alcohol involvement in adolescence, including the monoamine oxidase A (MAO-A; Nilsson, Wargelius, Sjöberg, Leppert, & Oreland, 2008) and dopamine genes (Derringer et al., 2010), as well as genes involving the serotonin transporter (Nilsson et al., 2005) and variants of the GABRA2 gene (Dick & Mustanski, 2006; Dick et al., 2013). The connection between these candidate genes and the neural circuitry contributing to behaviors associated with the heterotypic expression of the externalizing pathway to AUDs over the early life course is not yet understood (Agrawal et al., 2012).

However, increasing evidence indicates the importance of complex gene–environment interactions in the expression of risk behaviors associated with this pathway. Previous studies implicate many different protective and risk factors within the environmental context that may change the course and rate of acceleration of youth along the externalizing pathway to AUDs as well as change the likelihood that neurogenetic factors may impact risk for AUDs. Several important contextual factors that are related to both externalizing symptoms and alcohol use include the caregiving environment, peers, schools, and neighborhoods/communities (Chassin et al., 2016; Zucker, 2006), and recent studies demonstrate the potential complexities in gene–environmental interactions related to this pathway. For example, twin studies show that genetic influences on adolescent substance use as well as externalizing symptoms are stronger when parent monitoring is lower and substance-using peers are present (for a review, see Dick, 2011), and specific candidate genes, such as GABRA2, show stronger associations with externalizing symptoms across adolescence for those experiencing lower parental

monitoring (Dick et al., 2009; Trucco, Villafuerte, Heitzeg, Burmeister, & Zucker, 2016).

In summary, the externalizing pathway involves a deficit in behavioral control (Chassin et al., 2016) that may be expressed through a variety of risky, oppositional, and antisocial behaviors that escalate over the early life course. Neurobiological factors posited to underlie behavioral undercontrol and risk for an antisocial AUD associated with the externalizing pathway include the intersection of two neural regulatory systems involved in behavioral control and sensitivity to reward as well as an emerging array of genetic factors associated with both antisocial behavior and AUDs. Complex interactions among these neurobiological factors and salient environmental contexts appear to influence the likelihood that risk associated with behavioral undercontrol will manifest in AUDs in adolescence and adulthood. High-risk environments such as those often surrounding children with alcohol or drug-involved parents are likely to expose neurobiologically vulnerable children to compounded environmental risks and hasten the onset of antisocial AUDs (Zucker et al., 2011).

NEGATIVE AFFECT ALCOHOL USE DISORDER AND THE INTERNALIZING PATHWAY

Like the externalizing pathway, the internalizing pathway to AUDs may be described by an underlying core deficit that emerges across development in a process characterized by heterotypic continuity. In this case, the pathway is characterized by co-occurring internalizing symptoms (including depression and anxiety) and problematic alcohol use that develop in tandem across ontogeny as a result of a core deficit in regulating emotion (Chassin et al., 2016; Hussong et al., 2011; Zucker, 2006). Although multiple definitions of emotion regulation exist in the literature, Thompson's (1994) is perhaps most widely cited and defines emotion regulation as the "extrinsic and intrinsic processes responsible for monitoring, evaluating, and modifying emotional reactions, especially their intensive and temporal features, to accomplish one's goal" (pp. 27–28). Core deficits in emotion regulation are hypothesized to first manifest as a behaviorally inhibited temperament in infancy characterized by cautious or avoidant reactions to unfamiliar persons, objects, events, or places (Kagan, 2008). Underlying deficits in emotion regulation are posited to subsequently lead to the development of internalizing behavior in early childhood and accompanying social skills deficits upon school entry that may persist into adolescence and beyond (Lillehoj, Trudeau, Spoth, & Wickrama, 2004).

As with the externalizing pathway, empirical support is slowly amassing for the role of internalizing symptoms in childhood as a risk factor for problematic alcohol involvement in adolescence and young adulthood (Hussong et al., 2011; Zucker, 2006). For example, Ensminger, Juon, and Fothergill (2002) found that first-grade boys (although not girls) who were both shy and aggressive had higher risk for drug use in adulthood. Similarly, Caspi et al. (1996) found that inhibited (fearful, shy, and easily upset) 3-year olds, compared to their peers, had higher rates of depression and, for boys, alcohol-related problems at age 21 years. Other studies also provide some support that indices of internalizing behavior between ages 3 and 10 years are predictive of more alcohol-related problems and disorder in mid-adolescence to early adulthood (for a review, see Zucker, 2006). When gender differences are found in these studies, they generally demonstrate a stronger effect for boys than for girls.

However, studies that examine the association between internalizing symptoms and alcohol use during adolescence are less conclusive, perhaps in part due to differences in the relation between depression versus anxiety symptoms and alcohol use (Colder, Chassin, Lee, & Villalta, 2010; Kassel et al., 2010). For example, Pardini, White, and Stouthamer-Loeber (2007) found that adolescent boys had a greater risk for later alcohol-related consequences if they reported higher rates of depression symptoms; however, these boys had a lower risk for later alcohol-related consequences if they reported higher rates of anxiety symptoms. Other studies also report a protective effect of anxious symptoms on risk for substance use in adolescence (Kaplow, Curran, Angold, & Costello, 2001; Masse & Tremblay, 1997). In addition, unique effects of an overall index of internalizing symptoms (that combines symptoms of depression and anxiety) on substance use are more frequently nonsignificant or weak (Brook, Zhang, & Brook, 2011; Fite, Colder, & O'Connor, 2006). In contrast, effects associated with depression tend to be risk-promoting across studies (as reviewed later).

One explanation for this distinction is that anxious youth are more harm avoidant, and they may be less likely to engage in illegal or delinquent activities as well as the peer contexts in which such behaviors are often encouraged. On the other hand, depression symptoms are less likely to be associated with harm avoidance and may reflect feelings of distress that underlie coping motives related to substance use (vis-à-vis a self-medicating mechanism; Kassel et al., 2010; Khantzian, 1997). Depression symptoms are also often associated with interpersonal difficulties (Kochel, Ladd, & Rudolph, 2012), which may decrease adolescents' acceptance by mainstream peers and thereby increase the likelihood of affiliating with deviant peer groups that provide access to, encouragement of, and reinforcement for substance use (vis-à-vis the self-derogation hypothesis; Kaplan, 1980).

Nonetheless, given the consistently strong association between externalizing symptoms and alcohol use and the high co-occurrence of depression and externalizing symptoms in children and adolescents (Angold, Costello, & Erkanli, 1999), some researchers have questioned whether the effect of depression symptoms on alcohol use is indirect (as defined by Copeland, Shanahan, Erkanli, Costello, & Angold, 2013) and primarily due to the confounding effect of externalizing symptoms. Recent longitudinal studies testing the prospective prediction of alcohol use outcomes from depression symptoms while controlling for externalizing symptoms address this question. Most of these studies show that depression symptoms are unique prospective predictors of alcohol outcomes in adolescents, even after controlling for indicators of such externalizing disorders as conduct disorder, oppositional defiant disorder, and attention deficit hyperactivity disorder (Huurre et al., 2010; King, Iacono, & McGue, 2004; Kumpulainen, 2000; Mackie, Castellanos-Ryan, & Conrod, 2011; Meier et al., 2013; Pardini et al., 2007; Sung, Erkanli, Angold, & Costello, 2004; but see Bardone et al., 1998; Fergusson & Woodward, 2002; Tartter, Hammen, & Brennan, 2014). Moreover, available studies that test gender differences in this association often find a stronger association for boys than for girls (Huurre et al., 2010; Kumpulainen, 2000; Sung et al., 2004; but see McCarty et al., 2012). Together, these studies indicate that internalizing symptoms early in childhood predict later alcohol and substance involvement and that depression symptoms are uniquely related to alcohol use after controlling for co-occurring externalizing symptoms. However, associations between internalizing symptoms and alcohol use are consistently weaker than those between externalizing symptoms and alcohol use.

The self-medication hypothesis is the primary mechanism invoked by researchers to explain why deficits in emotion regulation and depression symptoms lead to alcohol-related behaviors (Khantzian, 1997). The self-medication hypothesis is a negative reinforcement model in which drinking behavior is motivated by a desire to reduce stress and negative affect that is reinforced by the pharmacological properties of alcohol (McCarthy, Curtin, Piper, & Baker, 2010). Individuals progressing along the internalizing pathway are expected to engage in problematic drinking beginning in adolescence to reduce the aversive distress they experience as a result of their internalizing symptoms. These drinking behaviors may in turn be exacerbated by continued adolescent experiences of social withdrawal or associations with deviant peers and by the development of positive expectancies and motivations for using alcohol as a coping response (Hussong et al., 2011).

Studies regarding the mechanisms underlying risk for the internalizing pathway have received much less attention than those for the externalizing pathway. Nonetheless, recent genetic and neural studies are beginning to identify potential associations of interest (Tully & Iacono, 2014). Family linkage and twin studies demonstrate modest cotransmission for internalizing disorders (primarily depression) and alcoholism in adult samples (Kendler, Neale, Heath, Kessler, & Eaves, 1994; Merikangas, Weissman, Prusoff, Pauls, & Leckman, 1985; Zucker, 2006). Moreover, in their multivariate behavioral genetic analysis, Silberg, Rutter, D'Onofrio, and Eaves (2003) reported that genetic influences played a greater role in the comorbidity of depression and drug use in girls versus boys, although substantial environmental variance was found for both sexes. Relatively recent candidate gene and GWAS studies are beginning to identify potential markers of genetic risk for co-occurring internalizing symptoms and alcohol-related problems in adolescents and young adults. In a review of these studies, Saraceno, Munafó, Heron, Craddock, and Van Den Bree (2009) reported that four genetic markers of risk include the dopamine receptor D2 (DRD2) Taq A1 genetic polymorphism, variants within the 5'-untranslated region (UTR) of the cholinergic

muscarinic receptor 2 (CHRM2 SNPs 5'-UTR), the short variant of the serotonin transporter gene (5-HTT S-allele), and the MAO-A variable number tandem repeat low-activity allele (MAOA promoter VNTR); however, effects for only two of these markers (CHRM2 SNPs 5'-UTR and the 5-HTT S-allele) have been replicated for studies that examine co-occurring AUD and internalizing disorders specifically. In addition to challenges with replication, these genetic analyses do not control for risk associated with externalizing symptoms, and some of the emerging genetic risk markers overlap with current candidates associated with the externalizing pathway.

Despite these challenges, some researchers are trying to bridge the gap between genetic risk for negative affect AUDs and behavior by investigating neural systems. For example, Glaser et al. (2014) found indirect effects of polymorphisms in the corticotropin-releasing hormone receptor (CRHR1) on alcohol use via greater activation in the right ventrolateral prefrontal cortex (rVLPFC) during an emotion-arousal task. Greater rVLPFC response to negative emotional words was associated with lower levels of trait negative emotionality and fewer alcohol-related problems, suggesting that the rVLPFC may be involved in reappraisal of negative emotion. This, in turn, may modulate negative affect-related alcohol use. Although this line of work is nascent, investigations of links from genetic markers to behavior via neural activation are potentially novel ways to better understand how risk associated with AUD subtypes manifests.

Although studies of environmental moderators of neurobiological risk for co-occurring internalizing and alcohol-related symptoms or negative affect AUD in particular, rather than AUDs in general, are clearly still needed, researchers have posited several environmental factors that may play a particular role in risk for AUDs associated with the internalizing pathway (Hussong et al., 2011, 2016). Two leading environmental risk factors are stress exposure and failures in the caregiving environment. These general risk factors are implicated in a broad array of developmental outcomes, likely including risk associated with both internalizing and externalizing pathways to AUDs. However, maltreatment and violence exposure may also bear specific risk for internalizing AUDs when occurring alongside additional risk factors that fuel self-medication processes as a particular coping response, especially for at-risk children (Hussong et al., 2016).

Notably, child maltreatment and neglect are more likely to occur in children with alcohol- or drug-involved parents (Besinger, Garland, Litrownik, & Landsverk, 1999; Harrington, Dubowitz, Black, & Binder, 1995; Thomas, Leicht, Hughes, Madigan, & Dowell, 2003; Turner, Finkelhor, Hamby, & Shattuck, 2013; Walsh, MacMillan, & Jamieson, 2003). Studies estimate that between 10% and 20% of child maltreatment cases involve children of substance abusing parents, with some estimates as high as 80% (US Department of Health and Human Services, 2012; also see Young, Boles, & Otero, 2007). A growing literature documents the long-term deleterious effects of early maltreatment (and other forms of stress exposure) on the development of the neurobiological stress response (Gunnar & Quevedo, 2007). The nature of these changes is complex but may be profound, leading to prolonged dysregulation of the hypothalamic–pituitary–adrenal axis that can be a risk factor for later psychiatric symptoms (McCrory, De Brito, & Viding, 2010). Research on the negative cascading effects of early stress exposure indicates that negative life stressors in young children can heighten subsequent stress reactivity to future life stressors, with this negative escalating cycle between neurobiological responsivity and environmental insult continuing into the adolescent years (Gunnar & Quevedo, 2007). Despite the notable consensus regarding the dysregulating impact of trauma and chronic stress exposure on the neurobiological stress response, there is clearly less consensus regarding the mechanisms mediating the relation between stress and later adjustment problems (McCrory et al., 2010). Studies directly linking early childhood stress and trauma with emotion dysregulation and later substance use are needed to test this model.

Nonetheless, the likelihood that early stress exposure may result in subsequent deficits in emotion regulation and inadequate coping responses is exacerbated in poor caregiving or parenting contexts (Calkins & Hill, 2007). Although multiple aspects of parenting are associated with risk for alcohol involvement (Donovan, 2016), parent emotion socialization may be particularly relevant in understanding children's emotion regulation. Parent emotion socialization broadly includes the ways in which parents explicitly and implicitly teach their children about if, when, and how it is appropriate to feel and express emotions and also how to manage or cope with emotions (Eisenberg, Cumberland, & Spinrad, 1998).

Parents socialize their children around emotion in several key ways, including reactions to their children's emotions, modeling of emotion and regulation, awareness and acceptance of emotions, and direct teaching about children's emotional expression (Eisenberg et al., 1998; Gottman, Katz, & Hooven, 1997). Emotion-coaching parents are aware of and accepting of children's emotions and respond supportively to children's expression of emotion through validation, teaching, and problem-solving, whereas emotion-dismissing parents may minimize children's emotions and avoid teaching or problem-solving around children's emotional experiences (Gottman et al., 1997). Parents' use of emotion-dismissing styles is associated with externalizing and internalizing symptoms (Lunkenheimer, Shields, & Cortina, 2007), whereas emotion-coaching styles are associated with more positive outcomes physically, socially, and academically (Gottman et al., 1997).

There is little empirical work that characterizes parent emotion socialization behaviors in relation to alcohol-related behaviors and risk contexts. Efforts to address these questions have been a focus of our work, in which we found that the context of maternal drug use negatively impacted emotion socialization behaviors among mothers in addiction treatment (Shadur & Hussong, 2013). Specifically, mothers reported less supportive and less consistent emotion socialization practices during periods of problematic drug use compared to periods of sobriety. Moreover, we found support for cross-sectional mediation such that more severe maternal drug use predicted higher levels of nonsupportive reactions to children's emotions that, in turn, predicted poorer emotion regulation in children. Parent emotion socialization is an important predictor of children's emotion regulation in other at-risk samples as well, including low-income families (Brophy-Herb, Stansbury, Bocknek, & Horodynski, 2012), maltreated children (Shipman et al., 2007), and families impacted by maternal depression (Silk et al., 2011). Critical to the internalizing pathway, parent emotion socialization practices have also been shown to predict adolescent substance use as a means of coping with negative affect. In contrast to findings regarding symptomatology in younger children, Hersh and Hussong (2009) found that families characterized by high levels of both emotion-coaching and emotion-dismissing styles of parent emotion socialization, perhaps reflecting an overinvolved and critical interaction style, had adolescents who were more likely to use substances in a self-medicating manner. Together, these results suggest that parent emotion socialization practices may be an important aspect of the caregiving context that influences risk for progressing along the internalizing pathway.

In summary, whereas several studies examine the relationship between negative affect and substance use, particularly via the self-mediation hypothesis, in adolescent and adult samples, the mechanisms that perpetuate this association across ontogeny are not well understood. The internalizing pathway is characterized by a core deficit in emotion regulation that leads to internalizing symptoms, social skills deficits and interpersonal difficulties, cognitions supportive of drinking as a coping mechanism, an eventual drinking onset, and escalation to the point of a negative affect AUD. Analogous to the externalizing pathway, the core deficit of this pathway is said to be detectable in infancy. Empirical support examining the relationship between internalizing symptoms and alcohol use has varied, with studies indicating potential symptom-specific relations (reflecting stronger relationships between depression and alcohol use when controlling for externalizing symptoms) and frequent support for gender differences with worse outcomes for males than for females. Although empirical support is accumulating, much work is needed to better explicate the transacting neurobiological and environmental risk factors associated with the development of drinking-related problems and the internalizing pathway.

USING PATHWAYS TO DEVELOP PREVENTION PROGRAMS

The study of pathways is a core component of a developmental psychopathology approach (Cicchetti & Rogosch, 1996), in part because of its clear link to informing prevention and intervention programming. Pathways can elucidate which risk and protective factors impact whom for what outcome at what period in development. A point of frequent confusion is whether such pathways define mechanisms (sometimes discussed as variable-oriented approaches in a parallel methodological literature) or groups of homogeneous individuals (similarly, person-oriented approaches; Magnusson & Cairns, 1996). Moreover, theoretical pathways focused on underlying mechanisms vary in whether they posit associations among constructs

(or elements) in the pathway that reflect etiological processes, heterotypic continuity in the expression of an underlying deficit over ontogeny, or epidemiological patterns of related behaviors. We expect that, in practice, pathways that reflect mechanisms versus homogeneous groups of individuals are somewhat less distinct. For example, at one level the externalizing and internalizing pathways may be defined by the heterotypic expression of different core deficits in each pathway over maturation. To the extent that any one deficit is the sole or dominant contributor to alcohol use for a group of individuals, then the development pathway associated with that mechanism defines both the risk mechanism (i.e., the underlying deficit) and the risk group (i.e., those with the deficit as expressed at any given point in development). However, for some individuals, multiple mechanisms may underlie their alcohol involvement at a given time; these individuals may reflect a more heterogeneous pattern of risk that straddles multiple pathways depending on the other contributing core deficits that fuel alcohol involvement. In this chapter, we describe these pathways heuristically, with a focus on the simplest case in which each pathway defines a risk mechanism that is the single core deficit contributing to AUDs over maturation, thereby defining both a single risk pathway and a homogeneous group of individuals. We expect that for many youth there are multiple mechanisms that underlie their risk for AUDs and that some youth may even change pathways across development such that the dominant risk mechanism associated with their alcohol involvement shifts over time.

A number of researchers, for example, have examined whether the intersection of internalizing and externalizing symptoms created greater risk for alcohol involvement in youth than either set of symptoms alone. One theoretical rationale for this model is derived from an extension of the dual failure model. Patterson and Capaldi (1990) offered this model to explain their findings that the accumulation of failure experiences (i.e., in academic and social experiences) predicted greater depressed mood in boys. Capaldi (1991) extended this model, recognizing that similar risk factors also predicted conduct disorder, and showed that young boys with greater depression and conduct problems reported higher rates of substance use than did their peers. Because youth with co-occurring depression and externalizing symptoms experience greater peer rejection and have a history of conduct problems, they may have eased entry into deviant peer groups, a context associated with substance-using behaviors. Early studies using a group comparison approach showed that groups with co-occurring symptoms reported higher substance use at later time points compared to those reporting depression only and asymptomatic groups (and sometimes conduct problems only; Capaldi, 1991; Miller-Johnson, Lochman, Coie, Terry, & Hyman, 1998).

However, this method is limited due to the reliance on median splits that reduce statistical power (MacCallum, Zhang, Preacher, & Rucker, 2002) and, more important, to the confounding of co-occurring symptomatology and symptom severity. Recognizing this limitation, researchers have also used statistical interactions to test the co-occurring symptom prediction of the dual failure hypothesis. Results of these studies generally support the accumulated risk model (Marmorstein, 2010; Miller-Johnson et al., 1998; Sung, Erkanli, Angold, & Costello, 2004). For example, Pardini et al. (2007) found the expected pattern of risk such that among boys in the Pittsburgh youth study, greater levels of depression symptoms in eighth grade were only related to increased risk for AUDs and symptom counts in early adulthood (ages 20–25 years) in the presence of conduct problems. However, a few studies show a different pattern. For example, Mason, Hitchings, and Spoth (2008) found that higher rates of depression symptoms at age 11 years served to dampen risk for substance use and related problems at age 18 years related to conduct problems at age 11 years. To reconcile these inconsistent findings, examinations of how core deficits in the internalizing and externalizing pathways (i.e., emotion regulation and behavioral undercontrol respectively) intersect to create or dampen risk for alcohol use outcomes across development are needed to move beyond symptom indices to more clearly test questions about intersecting mechanisms at the level of endophenotypes.

CONCLUSIONS AND FUTURE DIRECTIONS

Consistent with a prevention science perspective (Ialongo et al., 2006), we believe the study of early emerging developmental pathways is critical in identifying when in child development prevention programming would be most effective, who would benefit most from such programming, and what deleterious behaviors should be targeted for remediation.

The early emerging nature of both internalizing and externalizing pathways to AUDs suggests early childhood may be an ideal developmental period in which to introduce preventive interventions (Hussong et al., 2011; Zucker, 2006). Prevention science emphasizes the critical importance of intervention during early childhood to reduce the need for later treatment of more entrenched deleterious behaviors in adolescence and adulthood. In this vein, knowledge about early emerging pathways to alcohol use can inform the development of early prevention programming for AUDs in children as young as preschool age, when risk is more malleable and intervention perhaps more successful. To encourage research that fills the translational gap, we offer five critical directions for future research.

First, few interventions have been developed or evaluated to treat precursors to AUDs in the early childhood period (although Haggerty, Skinner, Fleming, Gainey, and Catalano [2008] focused on 3- to 14-year-old children of parents in methadone treatment). However, interventions to treat markers of early childhood progression along externalizing and internalizing pathways, including childhood disruptive behaviors (e.g., behavioral parent training programs) and anxiety (e.g., cognitive–behavioral therapy and exposure) have been empirically supported in children as young as 3 years (Chorpita et al., 2011). These interventions represent promising foundations for the development of AUD-specific preventive therapies. A first step forward is to provide existing interventions to children at risk for AUDs and to track substance use outcomes in these children as they mature into adolescence. Furthermore, future intervention studies could compare the efficacy of established treatments for early childhood internalizing and externalizing problems with the efficacy of such treatments modified to include modules specifically targeting prevention of problematic substance use. In this way, prevention scientists may be able to better identify whether already efficacious treatments for early childhood internalizing and externalizing problems should be modified or supplemented to specifically target prevention of AUDs or if these existing programs' emphasis on remediating non-alcohol-related AUD developmental precursors is sufficient to prevent progression toward AUD.

Second, because early emerging AUDs occur in a vulnerable minority of the population, better methods for identifying these at-risk individuals are clearly needed. These methods inform both more focused study of how risk mechanisms unfold over development and the development of targeted prevention and intervention programming. Risk factors integral to the etiology of both internalizing and externalizing pathways to AUDs serve as important markers for vulnerable populations. Specifically, individuals with a family history of AUD, exposure to elevated and chronic stress (particularly associated with maltreatment and family conflict), or exposure to impoverished childcare environments (characterized by insensitive parenting, insecure attachment, and poor parent emotion socialization practices) may be especially at risk for progression along early emerging pathways to AUD (Chassin et al., 2016; Hussong et al., 2016). These risk mechanisms launch and sustain individuals along pathways that demonstrate both multifinality (e.g., development of emotion dysregulation and internalizing symptoms or development of behavioral undercontrol and externalizing symptoms in childhood) and equifinality (e.g., culmination of both externalizing and internalizing pathways to AUD in adulthood) across development. The study of heterogeneity in pathways to AUD brings into focus the breadth and magnitude of effects from such risk mechanisms. Consequently, study of these early emerging pathways can inform the development of preventive interventions that identify and treat individuals at highest risk for AUD and thus in most need of early intervention.

Third, early emerging risk pathways identify core deficits to target in AUD prevention programming, but we have to yet to fully understand how these core deficits operate at different points in development. The neurobiological and environmental contexts in which these core deficits manifest risk associated with AUDs are often viewed as dynamic and transacting across development. Attention to developmental context is critically needed; studies that examine early emerging risk for AUDs beginning in early childhood as well as longitudinal studies that track risk expression into adolescence and young adulthood are important designs to address this need. Particular attention should be paid to the varying time frames across which different mechanisms that affect developmental risk manifest themselves. For instance, an adolescent's experience of negative affect throughout *a single week* could influence his or her decision to engage in problematic alcohol consumption to self-medicate. However, it could take repeated experiences

of negative affect as a result of environmental stress exposure and subsequent problematic alcohol use over *a matter of months* to chronically alter one's neurophysiological stress-regulatory systems. Moreover, it could take repeated pairings of environmental insult and neurophysiological stress-regulatory system dysregulation over *a matter of years* to alter the expression of high-risk genes. Investigations establishing the time frames over which different risk mechanisms operate, and establishing how these disparate timings interact, are sorely needed. Although novel primary data collection efforts are necessary to address these questions, research efforts that take advantage of secondary designs that use existing data to examine extended developmental contexts through the pooling of longitudinal studies (e.g., via integrative data analysis; Hussong, Curran, & Bauer, 2013) are another option for addressing this need.

Fourth, as attention to the underlying neurobiology of developing AUDs increases, similar attention to the rich and intersecting environmental factors that likely modify and shape the expression of neurobiological factors is essential. Environmental risk and protective factors have been a mainstay of research on the development of addictions for several decades, and new research avenues regarding neurobiology should consider the ways in which established risk factors moderate neurobiological risk (creating gene–environmental interactions) as well as how they are selected on the basis of neurobiological risk (through gene–environmental correlations). Given widely cited challenges in identifying replicable effects of specific genetic mechanisms that predict heterogeneous phenotypes such as AUDs, attention to environmental context and to more homogeneous subtypes of AUDs is likely to be beneficial. Future investigations in this vein could start by examining interactions between candidate genes repeatedly implicated in progression along both internalizing and externalizing pathways (e.g., the serotonin transporter genes) and risk factors specific to each pathway (e.g., behaviorally disinhibited temperament vs. behaviorally inhibited temperament in infancy). Such research would be able to isolate the effects of specific gene–environment configurations in launching individuals down specific developmental pathways toward AUD.

Fifth, research regarding the development of AUDs is largely focused on risk mechanisms associated with the externalizing pathway. Recognizing the heterogeneity of risk pathways to AUDs and increasing attention to alternate pathways, such as the internalizing pathway, is likely to provide a richer and more complete heuristic for understanding the development of AUDs. Given the complexity of influences on AUDs and potential for individuals to "jump" risk pathways over time, a focus on those most at risk for given pathways and related AUD subtypes may provide a more clear picture of the underlying mechanisms associated with the development of a particular AUD subtype in a more homogeneous group of individuals.

Ultimately, continued investigation of heterogeneity in AUDs has enormous potential to inform prevention programming because such investigations clarify the developmental periods, populations, and deleterious core deficits most in need of redress. Identification of early emerging pathways to AUD has the potential to guide interventions in early childhood, in which swift developmental changes offer families multiple opportunities to adapt to children's needs and redefine family interaction patterns (Hussong et al., 2011).

REFERENCES

Agrawal, A., Verweij, K. J. H., Gillespie, N. A., Heath, A. C., Lessov-Schlaggar, C. N., Martin, N. G., . . . Lynskey, M. T. (2012). The genetics of addiction—A translational perspective. *Translational Psychiatry*, 2(7), e140. doi:10.1038/tp.2012.54

Angold, A., Costello, E. J., & Erkanli, A. (1999). Comorbidity. *Journal of Child Psychology and Psychiatry*, 40(1), 57–87. doi:10.1111/1469-7610.00424

Babor, T. F. (1996). The classification of alcoholics: Typology theories from the 19th century to the present. *Alcohol Health & Research World*, 20(1), 6–17.

Bardone, A. M., Moffitt, T. E., Caspi, A., Dickson, N., Stanton, W. R., & Silva, P. A. (1998). Adult physical health outcomes of adolescent girls with conduct disorder, depression, and anxiety. *Journal of the American Academy of Child & Adolescent Psychiatry*, 37(6), 594–601. doi:10.1097/00004583-199806000-00009

Beauchaine, T. (2001). Vagal tone, development, and Gray's motivational theory: Toward an integrated model of autonomic nervous system functioning in psychopathology. *Development and Psychopathology*, 13(2), 183–214. doi:10.1017/S0954579401002012

Besinger, B. A., Garland, A. F., Litrownik, A. J., & Landsverk, J. A. (1999). Caregiver substance abuse among maltreated children placed in out-of-home care. *Child Welfare*, 78(2), 221.

Brook, J. S., Zhang, C., & Brook, D. W. (2011). Developmental trajectories of marijuana use from adolescence to adulthood: Personal predictors. *Archives of Pediatrics & Adolescent Medicine*, 165(1), 55–60. doi:10.1001/archpediatrics.2010.248

Brophy-Herb, H. E., Stansbury, K., Bocknek, E., & Horodynski, M. A. (2012). Modeling maternal emotion-related socialization behaviors in a low-income sample: Relations with toddlers' self-regulation. *Early Childhood Research Quarterly*, 27(3), 352–364. doi:10.1016/j.ecresq.2011.11.005

Calkins, S., & Hill, A. (2007). Caregiver influences on emerging emotion regulation. In J. J. Gross (Ed.), *Handbook of emotion regulation* (pp. 229–248). New York, NY: Guilford.

Capaldi, D. M. (1991). Co-occurrence of conduct problems and depressive symptoms in early adolescent boys: I. Familial factors and general adjustment at grade 6. *Development and Psychopathology*, 3(3), 277–300. doi:10.1017/S0954579409000169

Caspi, A., & Moffitt, T. E. (1995). The continuity of maladaptive behavior: From description to understanding in the study of antisocial behavior. In D. Cicchetti & D. J. Cohen (Eds.), *Developmental psychopathology: Volume 2. Risk, disorder, and adaptation* (pp. 472–511). Oxford, UK: Wiley.

Caspi, A., Moffitt, T. E., Newman, D. L., & Silva, P. A. (1996). Behavioral observations at age 3 years predict adult psychiatric disorders: Longitudinal evidence from a birth cohort. *Archives of General Psychiatry*, 53(11), 1033–1039. doi:10.1001/archpsyc.1996.01830110071009

Chassin, L., Colder, C. R., Hussong, A., & Sher, K. J. (2016). Substance use and substance use disorders. In D. Cicchetti & D. J. Cohen (Eds.), *Developmental Psychopathology: Volume 3. Maladaptation and Psychopathology*(3rd ed., 833–897). New York, NY: Wiley.

Chorpita, B. F., Daleiden, E. L., Ebesutani, C., Young, J., Becker, K. D., Nakamura, B. J., . . . Starace, N. (2011). Evidence-based treatments for children and adolescents: An updated review of indicators of efficacy and effectiveness. *Clinical Psychology: Science and Practice*, 18(2), 154–172. doi:10.1111/j.1468-2850.2011.01247.x

Chung, T. (2013). Adolescent substance use: Course and symptoms. In P. Miller (Ed.), *Principles of addiction: Comprehensive addictive behaviors and disorders* (Vol. 1, pp. 97–106). San Diego, CA: Academic Press.

Cicchetti, D., & Cohen, D. J. (1995). Perspectives on developmental psychopathology. In D. Cicchetti & D. J. Cohen (Eds.), *Developmental psychopathology: Volume 1. Theory and methods* (pp. 3–20). Oxford, UK: Wiley.

Cicchetti, D., & Rogosch, F. A. (1996). Equifinality and multifinality in developmental psychopathology. *Development and Psychopathology*, 8(4), 597–600. doi:10.1017/S0954579400007318

Cloninger, C. R., Sigvardsson, S., Gilligan, S. B., & von Knorring, A. (1988). Genetic heterogeneity and the classification of alcoholism. *Advances in Alcohol & Substance Abuse*, 7, 3–16. doi:10.1300/J251v07n03_02

Colder, C. R., Chassin, L., Lee, M. R., & Villalta, I. K. (2010). Developmental perspectives: Affect and adolescent substance use. In J. D. Kassel (Ed.), *Substance abuse and emotion* (pp. 109–135). Washington, DC: American Psychological Association.

Colder, C. R., & O'Connor, R. M. (2004). Gray's reinforcement sensitivity model and child psychopathology: Laboratory and questionnaire assessment of the BAS and BIS. *Journal of Abnormal Child Psychology*, 32(4), 435–451. doi:10.1023/B:JACP.0000030296.54122.b6

Cooney, N. L., Babor, T. F., DiClemete, C. C., & Del Boca, F. K. (2003). Clinical and scientific implications of Project MATCH. In T. F. Babor & F. K. Del Boca (Eds.), *Treatment matching in alcoholism* (pp. 222–237). Cambridge, UK: Cambridge University Press.

Copeland, W. E., Shanahan, L., Erkanli, A., Costello, E. J., & Angold, A. (2013). Indirect comorbidity in childhood and adolescence. *Frontiers in Psychiatry*, 4, 144. doi:10.3389/fpsyt.2013.00144

Derringer, J., Krueger, R. F., Dick, D. M., Saccone, S., Grucza, R. A., Agrawal, A., . . . Bierut, L. J.; Gene Environment Association Studies (GENEVA) Consortium (2010). Predicting sensation seeking from dopamine genes: A candidate-system approach. *Psychological Science*, 21(9), 1282–1290. doi:10.1177/0956797610380699

Dick, D. M. (2011). Gene–environment interaction in psychological traits and disorders. *Annual Review of Clinical Psychology*, 7, 383. doi:10.1146/annurev-clinpsy-032210-104518

Dick, D. M., Aliev, F., Latendresse, S., Porjesz, B., Schuckit, M., Rangaswamy, M., . . . Kramer, J. (2013). How phenotype and developmental stage affect the genes we find: GABRA2 and impulsivity. *Twin Research and Human Genetics*, 16(3), 661–669. doi:10.1017/thg.2013.20

Dick, D. M., Latendresse, S. J., Lansford, J. E., Budde, J. P., Goate, A., Dodge, K. A., . . . Bates, J. E.

(2009). Role of GABRA2 in trajectories of externalizing behavior across development and evidence of moderation by parental monitoring. *Archives of General Psychiatry*, 66(6), 649–657. doi:10.1001/archgenpsychiatry.2009.48

Dick, D. M., & Mustanski, B. S. (2006). Pubertal development and health-related behavior. In L. Pulkkinen, J. Kaprio, & R. J. Rose (Eds.), *Socioemotional development and health from adolescence to adulthood* (pp. 108–125). Cambridge, UK: Cambridge University Press.

Dishion, T. J., Capaldi, D. M., & Yoerger, K. (1999). Middle childhood antecedents to progressions in male adolescent substance use: An ecological analysis of risk and protection. *Journal of Adolescent Research*, 14(2), 175–205. doi:10.1177/0743558499142003

Dodge, K. A., Malone, P. S., Lansford, J. E., Miller, S., Pettit, G. S., & Bates, J. E. (2009). A dynamic cascade model of the development of substance-use onset. *Monographs of the Society for Research in Child Development*, 74, 1–130. doi:10.1111/j.1540-5834.2009.00528.x

Donovan, J. E. (2016). Child and adolescent socialization into substance use. In S. Brown & R. A. Zucker (Eds.), *The Oxford handbook of adolescent substance abuse* (pp. 1–57). New York, NY: Oxford University Press.

Donovan, J. E., Jessor, R., & Jessor, L. (1983). Problem drinking in adolescence and young adulthood: A follow-up study. *Journal of Studies on Alcohol*, 44(1), 109–137. doi:10.15288/jsa.1983.44.109

Eisenberg, N., Cumberland, A., & Spinrad, T. L. (1998). Parental socialization of emotion. *Psychological Inquiry*, 9(4), 241–273. doi:10.1207/s15327965pli0904_1

Ensminger, M. E., Juon, H. S., & Fothergill, K. E. (2002). Childhood and adolescent antecedents of substance use in adulthood. *Addiction*, 97(7), 833–844. doi:10.1046/j.1360-0443.2002.00138.x

Ernst, M., & Fudge, J. L. (2009). A developmental neurobiological model of motivated behavior: Anatomy, connectivity and ontogeny of the triadic nodes. *Neuroscience & Biobehavioral Reviews*, 33(3), 367–382. doi:10.1016/j.neubiorev.2008.10.009

Fergusson, D. M., & Woodward, L. J. (2002). Mental health, educational, and social role outcomes of adolescents with depression. *Archives of General Psychiatry*, 59(3), 225–231. doi:10.1001/archpsyc.59.3.225

Fite, P. J., Colder, C. R., & O'Connor, R. M. (2006). Childhood behavior problems and peer selection and socialization: Risk for adolescent alcohol use.

Addictive Behaviors, 31(8), 1454–1459. doi:10.1016/j.addbeh.2005.09.015

Glaser, Y. G., Zubieta, J. K., Hsu, D. T., Villafuerte, S., Mickey, B. J., Trucco, E. M., . . . Heitzeg, M. M. (2014). Indirect effect of corticotropin-releasing hormone receptor 1 gene variation on negative emotionality and alcohol use via right ventrolateral prefrontal cortex. *Journal of Neuroscience*, 34(11), 4099–4107. doi:10.1523/JNEUROSCI.3672-13.2014

Gottlieb, G. (2007). Probabilistic epigenesis. *Developmental Science*, 10(1), 1–11. doi:10.1111/j.1467-7687.2007.00556.x

Gottman, J. M., Katz, L. F., & Hooven, C. (1997). *Meta-emotion: How families communicate emotionally*. Mahwah, NJ: Erlbaum.

Gunnar, M., & Quevedo, K. (2007). The neurobiology of stress and development. *Annual Review of Psychology*, 58, 145–173. doi:10.1146/annurev.psych.58.110405.085605

Haggerty, K. P., Skinner, M., Fleming, C. B., Gainey, R. R., & Catalano, R. F. (2008). Long-term effects of the Focus on Families project on substance use disorders among children of parents in metha-done treatment. *Addiction*, 103(12), 2008–2016. doi:10.1111/j.1360-0443.2008.02360.x

Harrington, D., Dubowitz, H., Black, M. M., & Binder, A. (1995). Maternal substance use and neglectful par-enting: Relationships with children's development. *Journal of Child Clinical Psychology*, 24, 258–263.

Hersh, M. A., & Hussong, A. M. (2009). The associa-tion between observed parental emotion social-ization and adolescent self-medication. *Journal of Abnormal Child Psychology*, 37(4), 493–506. doi:10.1007/s10802-008-9291-z

Hill, E. M., Stoltenberg, S. F., Bullard, K. H., Li, S., Zucker, R. A., & Burmeister, M. (2002). Antisocial alcoholism and serotonin-related polymor-phisms: Association tests. *Psychiatric Genetics*, 12(3), 143–153. doi:10.1097/00041444-200209000-00005

Hussong, A. M., Curran, P. J., & Bauer, D. J. (2013). Integrative data analysis in clinical psychology research. *Annual Review of Clinical Psychology*, 9, 61. doi:10.1146/annurev-clinpsy-050212-185522

Hussong, A. M., Jones, D. J., Stein, G. L., Baucom, D. H., & Boeding, S. (2011). An internalizing pathway to alcohol use and disorder. *Psychology of Addictive Behaviors*, 25(3), 390–404. doi:10.1037/a0024519

Hussong, A. M., Shadur, J. M., Burns, A. R., Stein, G. L., Jones, D. J., Solis, J. M., & McKee, L. (2016). An early emerging internalizing pathway to substance use and disorder. In S. Brown & R. A. Zucker (Eds.), *The Oxford handbook of adolescent substance abuse* (pp. 1–48). New York, NY: Oxford University Press.

Huurre, T., Lintonen, T., Kaprio, J., Pelkonen, M., Marttunen, M., & Aro, H. (2010). Adolescent risk factors for excessive alcohol use at age 32 years: A 16-year prospective follow-up study. *Social Psychiatry and Psychiatric Epidemiology*, 45(1), 125–134. doi:10.1007/s00127-009-0048-y

Iacono, W. G., Malone, S. M., & McGue, M. (2008). Behavioral disinhibition and the development of early-onset addiction: Common and spe-cific influences. *Annual Review of Clinical Psychology*, 4, 325–348. doi:10.1146/annurev.clinpsy.4.022007.141157

Ialongo, N. S., Rogosch, F. A., Cicchetti, D., Toth, S. L., Buckley, J., Petras, H., & Neiderhiser, J. (2006). A developmental psychopathology approach to the prevention of mental health disorders. In D. Cicchetti & D. Cohen (Eds.), *Developmental psy-chopathology: Volume 1. Theory and method* (2nd ed., pp. 968–1018). Hoboken, NJ: Wiley.

Jackson, K. M., Sher, K. J., Gotham, H. J., & Wood, P. K. (2001). Transitioning into and out of large-effect drinking in young adulthood. *Journal of Abnormal Psychology*, 110(3), 378–391. doi:10.1037/0021-843X.110.3.378

Jellinek, E. M. (1960). *The disease concept of alcoholism*. Oxford, UK: Hillhouse.

Jessor, R., & Jessor, S. L. (1977). *Problem behavior and psychosocial development: A longitudinal study of youth*. New York, NY: Academic Press.

Kagan, J. (2008). Behavioral inhibition as a risk fac-tor for psychopathology. In T. P. Beauchaine, S. P. Hinshaw, T. P. Beauchaine, & S. P. Hinshaw (Eds.), *Child and adolescent psychopathology* (pp. 157–179). Hoboken, NJ: Wiley.

Kaplan, H. B. (1980). *Deviant behavior in defense of self*. New York, NY: Academic Press.

Kaplow, J. B., Curran, P. J., Angold, A., & Costello, E. J. (2001). The prospective relation between dimen-sions of anxiety and the initiation of adolescent alco-hol use. *Journal of Clinical Child Psychology*, 30(3), 316–326. doi:10.1207/S15374424JCCP3003_4

Kassel, J. D., Hussong, A. M., Wardle, M. C., Veilleux, J. C., Heinz, A., Greenstein, J. E., & Evatt, D. P. (2010). Affective influences in drug use etiol-ogy. In L. Scheier (Ed.), *Handbook of drug use etiology: Theory, methods, and empirical find-ings* (pp. 183–205). Washington, DC: American Psychological Association.

Kendler, K. S., Neale, M. C., Heath, A. C., Kessler, R. C., & Eaves, D. L. J. (1994). A twin-family study of alco-holism in women. *American Journal of Psychiatry*, 151(5), 707–715. doi:10.1176/ajp.151.5.707

Khantzian, E. J. (1997). The self-medication hypothesis of substance use disorders: A reconsideration and recent applications. *Harvard Review of Psychiatry*, 4(5), 231–244. doi:10.3109/10673229709030550

Khurana, A., Romer, D., Betancourt, L. M., Brodsky, N. L., Giannetta, J. M., & Hurt, H. (2013). Working memory ability predicts trajectories of early alcohol use in adolescents: The mediational role of impulsivity. *Addiction*, 108(3), 506–515. doi:10.1111/add.12001

King, S. M., Iacono, W. G., & McGue, M. (2004). Childhood externalizing and internalizing psychopathology in the prediction of early substance use. *Addiction*, 99(12), 1548–1559. doi:10.1111/j.1360-0443.2004.00893.x

Knyazev, G. G. (2004). Behavioural activation as predictor of substance use: Mediating and moderating role of attitudes and social relationships. *Drug and Alcohol Dependence*, 75(3), 309–321. doi:10.1016/j.drugalcdep.2004.03.007

Kochel, K. P., Ladd, G. W., & Rudolph, K. D. (2012). Longitudinal associations among youth depressive symptoms, peer victimization, and low peer acceptance: An interpersonal process perspective. *Child Development*, 83(2), 637–650. doi:10.1111/j.1467-8624.2011.01722.x

Kumpulainen, K. (2000). Psychiatric symptoms and deviance in early adolescence predict heavy alcohol use 3 years later. *Addiction*, 95(12), 1847–1857. doi:10.1080/09652140020011144

Lillehoj, C. J., Trudeau, L., Spoth, R., & Wickrama, K. A. S. (2004). Internalizing, social competence, and substance initiation: Influence of gender moderation and a preventive intervention. *Substance Use & Misuse*, 39, 963–991. doi:10.1081/JA-120030895

Lunkenheimer, E. S., Shields, A. M., & Cortina, K. S. (2007). Parental emotion coaching and dismissing in family interaction. *Social Development*, 16(2), 232–248. doi:10.1111/j.1467-9507.2007.00382.x

MacCallum, R. C., Zhang, S., Preacher, K. J., & Rucker, D. D. (2002). On the practice of dichotomization of quantitative variables. *Psychological Methods*, 7(1), 19. doi:10.1037/1082-989X.7.1.19

Mackie, C. J., Castellanos-Ryan, N., & Conrod, P. J. (2011). Developmental trajectories of psychotic-like experiences across adolescence: Impact of victimization and substance use. *Psychological Medicine*, 41(1), 47–58. doi:10.1017/S0033291710000449

Magnusson, D., & Cairns, R. B. (1996). *Developmental science: Toward a unified framework*. Cambridge, UK: Cambridge University Press.

Marlatt, G. A. (1999). From hindsight to foresight: A commentary on Project MATCH. In J. A. Tucker, D. M. Donovoan, & G. A. Marlatt (Eds.), *Changing addictive behavior: Bridging clinical and public health strategies* (pp. 45–66). New York, NY: Guilford.

Marmorstein, N. R. (2010). Longitudinal associations between depressive symptoms and alcohol problems: The influence of comorbid delinquent behavior. *Addictive Behavior*, 35, 564–571.

Mason, W. A., Hitchings, J. E., & Spoth, R. L. (2008). The interaction of conduct problems and depressed mood in relation to adolescent substance involvement and peer substance use. *Drug and Alcohol Dependence*, 96(3), 233–248. doi:10.1016/j.drugalcdep.2008.03.012

Masse, L. C., & Tremblay, R. E. (1997). Behavior of boys in kindergarten and the onset of substance use during adolescence. *Archives of General Psychiatry*, 54(1), 62–68. doi:10.1001/archpsyc.1997.01830130068014

Masten, A. S., Faden, V. B., Zucker, R. A., & Spear, L. P. (2008). Underage drinking: A developmental framework. *Pediatrics*, 121(Suppl. 4), S235–S251. doi:10.1542/peds.2007-2243A

McCarthy, D. E., Curtin, J. J., Piper, M. E., & Baker, T. B. (2010). Negative reinforcement: Possible clinical implications of an integrative model. In J. Kassel (Ed.), *Substance abuse and emotion* (pp. 15–42). Washington, DC: American Psychological Association.

McCarty, C. A., Wymbs, B. T., King, K. M., Mason, W. A., Stoep, A. V., McCauley, E., & Baer, J. (2012). Developmental consistency in associations between depressive symptoms and alcohol use in early adolescence. *Journal of Studies on Alcohol and Drugs*, 73(3), 444–453. doi:10.15288/jsad.2012.73.444

McCrory, E., De Brito, S. A., & Viding, E. (2010). Research review: The neurobiology and genetics of maltreatment and adversity. *Journal of Child Psychology and Psychiatry*, 51(10), 1079–1095. doi:10.1111/j.1469-7610.2010.02271.x

Meier, M. H., Caspi, A., Houts, R., Slutske, W. S., Harrington, H., Jackson, K. M., . . . Moffitt, T. E. (2013). Prospective developmental subtypes of alcohol dependence from age 18 to 32 years: Implications for nosology, etiology, and intervention. *Development and Psychopathology*, 25(3), 785–800. doi:10.1017/S0954579413000175

Merikangas, K. R., Weissman, M. M., Prusoff, B. A., Pauls, D. L., & Leckman, J. F. (1985). Depressives with secondary alcoholism: Psychiatric disorders in offspring. *Journal of Studies on Alcohol*, 46(3), 199–204. doi:10.15288/jsa.1985.46.199

Miller-Johnson, S., Lochman, J. E., Coie, J. D., Terry, R., & Hyman, C. (1998). Comorbidity of conduct and depressive problems at sixth grade: Substance use outcomes across adolescence. *Journal of Abnormal*

Child Psychology, 26(3), 221–232. doi:10.1023/A:1022676302865

Moffitt, T. E. (1993). Adolescence-limited and life-course-persistent antisocial behavior: A developmental taxonomy. *Psychological Review*, 100(4), 674–701. doi:10.1037/0033-295X.100.4.674

Moss, H. B., Chen, C. M., & Yi, H. Y. (2007). Subtypes of alcohol dependence in a nationally representative sample. *Drug and Alcohol Dependence*, 91(2), 149–158. doi:10.1016/j.drugalcdep.2007.05.016

Nilsson, K. W., Sjöberg, R. L., Damberg, M., Leppert, J., Öhrvik, J., Alm, P. O., . . . Oreland, L. (2005). Role of the serotonin transporter gene and family function in adolescent alcohol consumption. *Alcoholism: Clinical and Experimental Research*, 29(4), 564–570. doi:10.1097/01.ALC.0000159112.98941.B0

Nilsson, K. W., Wargelius, H. L., Sjöberg, R. L., Leppert, J., & Oreland, L. (2008). The MAO-A gene, platelet MAO-B activity and psychosocial environment in adolescent female alcohol-related problem behaviour. *Drug and Alcohol Dependence*, 93(1), 51–62. doi:10.1016/j.drugalcdep.2007.08.022

Olbert, C. M., Gala, G. J., & Tupler, L. A. (2014). Quantifying heterogeneity attributable to polythetic diagnostic criteria: Theoretical framework and empirical application. *Journal of Abnormal Psychology*, 123(2), 452. doi:10.1037/a0036068

Pardini, D., White, H. R., & Stouthamer-Loeber, M. (2007). Early adolescent psychopathology as a predictor of alcohol use disorders by young adulthood. *Drug and Alcohol Dependence*, 88, S38–S49. doi:10.1016/j.drugalcdep.2006.12.014

Patterson, G. R., & Capaldi, D. M. (1990). A mediational model for boys' depressed mood. In J. Rolf, A. S. Masten, D. Cicchetti, K. H. Nuechterlein, & S. Weintraub (Eds.), *Risk and protective factors in the development of psychopathology* (pp. 141–163). Cambridge, UK: Cambridge University Press.

Rutter, M. (1996). Developmental psychopathology: Concepts and prospects. In M. F. Lenzenweger & J. J. Haugaard (Eds.), *Frontiers of developmental psychopathology* (pp. 209–237). New York, NY: Oxford University Press.

Saraceno, L., Munafó, M., Heron, J., Craddock, N., & Van Den Bree, M. (2009). Genetic and non-genetic influences on the development of co-occurring alcohol problem use and internalizing symptomatology in adolescence: A review. *Addiction*, 104(7), 1100–1121. doi:10.1111/j.1360-0443.2009.02571.x

Shadur, J. M., & Hussong, A. M. (2013). *Parent emotion socialization and emotion regulation in substance abusing families*. Symposium presentation at the 36th Annual Research Society on Alcoholism Scientific Meeting, Orlando, FL.

Sher, K. J. (1991). *Children of alcoholics: A critical appraisal of theory and research*. Chicago, IL: University of Chicago Press.

Sher, K. J., Walitzer, K. S., Wood, P. K., & Brent, E. E. (1991). Characteristics of children of alcoholics: Putative risk factors, substance use and abuse, and psychopathology. *Journal of Abnormal Psychology*, 100, 427–448. doi:10.1037/0021-843X.100.4.427

Shipman, K. L., Schneider, R., Fitzgerald, M. M., Sims, C., Swisher, L., & Edwards, A. (2007). Maternal emotion socialization in maltreating and non-maltreating families: Implications for children's emotion regulation. *Social Development*, 16(2), 268–285. doi:10.1111/j.1467-9507.2007.00384.x

Silberg, J., Rutter, M., D'Onofrio, B., & Eaves, L. (2003). Genetic and environmental risk factors in adolescent substance use. *Journal of Child Psychology and Psychiatry*, 44(5), 664–676. doi:10.1111/1469-7610.00153

Silk, J. S., Shaw, D. S., Prout, J. T., O'Rourke, F., Lane, T. J., & Kovacs, M. (2011). Socialization of emotion and offspring internalizing symptoms in mothers with childhood-onset depression. *Journal of Applied Developmental Psychology*, 32(3), 127–136. doi:10.1016/j.appdev.2011.02.001

Sung, M., Erkanli, A., Angold, A., & Costello, E. J. (2004). Effects of age at first substance use and psychiatric comorbidity on the development of substance use disorders. *Drug and Alcohol Dependence*, 75(3), 287–299. doi:10.1016/j.drugalcdep.2004.03.013

Tarter, R. E., Vanyukov, M., Giancola, P., Dawes, M., Blackson, T., Mezzich, A., & Clark, D. B. (1999). Etiology of early age onset substance use disorder: A maturational perspective. *Development and Psychopathology*, 11, 657–683. doi:10.1017/S0954579499002266

Tartter, M., Hammen, C., & Brennan, P. (2014). Externalizing disorders in adolescence mediate the effects of maternal depression on substance use disorders. *Journal of Abnormal Child Psychology*, 42(2), 185–194. doi:10.1007/s10802-013-9786-0

Thomas, D., Leicht, C., Hughes, C., Madigan, A., & Dowell, K. (2003). *Emerging practices in the prevention of child abuse and neglect*. Washington, DC: US Department of Health and Human Services.

Thompson, R. A. (1994). Emotion regulation: A theme in search of definition. *Monographs of the Society for Research in Child Development*, 59(2–3), 25–52, 250–283. doi:10.2307/1166137

Trucco, E. M., Villafuerte, S., Heitzeg, M. M., Burmeister, M., & Zucker, R. A. (2016).

Susceptibility effects of GABA receptor subunit alpha-2 (GABRA2) variants and parental monitoring on externalizing behavior trajectories: Risk and protection conveyed by the minor allele. *Development and Psychopathology, 28*, 15–26. doi:10.1017/S0954579415000255

Tully, E. C., & Iacono, W. G. (2014). An integrative common liabilities model for the comorbidity of substance use disorders with externalizing and internalizing disorders. In K. Sher (Ed.), *The Oxford handbook of substance use disorders* (Vol. 2, pp. 187–212). New York, NY: Oxford University Press.

Turner, H. A., Finkelhor, D., Hamby, S. L., & Shattuck, A. (2013). Family structure, victimization, and child mental health in a nationally representative sample. *Social Science & Medicine, 87*, 39–51. doi:10.1016/j.socscimed.2013.02.034

United States Department of Health and Human Services (2012). *Child Maltreatment 2011*. Washington, DC: United States Department of Health and Human Services.

Walsh, C., MacMillan, H. L., & Jamieson, E. (2003). The relationship between parental substance abuse and child maltreatment: Findings from the Ontario Health Supplement. *Child Abuse & Neglect, 27*(12), 1409–1425.

Young, N. K., Boles, S. M., & Otero, C. (2007). Parental substance use disorders and child maltreatment: Overlap, gaps, and opportunities. *Child Maltreatment, 12*(2), 137–149. doi:10.1177/1077559507300322

Zucker, R. A. (2006). Alcohol use and the alcohol use disorders: A developmental–biopsychosocial systems formulation covering the life course. In D. Cicchetti & D. J. Cohen (Eds.), *Developmental psychopathology: Volume 3. Risk, disorder, and adaptation* (2nd ed., pp. 620–656). Hoboken, NJ: Wiley.

Zucker, R. A., Chermack, S. T., & Curran, G. M. (2000). Alcoholism. In A. J. Sameroff, M. Lewis, & S. M. Miller (Eds.), *Handbook of developmental psychopathology* (pp. 569–587). New York, NY: Springer.

Zucker, R. A., Fitzgerald, H. E., & Moses, H. D. (1995). Emergence of alcohol problems and the several alcoholisms: A developmental perspective on etiologic theory and life course trajectory. In D. Cicchetti & D. J. Cohen (Eds.), *Developmental psychopathology: Volume 2. Risk, disorder, and adaptation* (pp. 677–711). Oxford, UK: Wiley.

Zucker, R. A., Heitzeg, M. M., & Nigg, J. T. (2011). Parsing the undercontrol–disinhibition pathway to substance use disorders: A multilevel developmental problem. *Child Development Perspectives, 5*(4), 248–255. doi:10.1111/j.1750-8606.2011.00172.x

PART II

ALCOHOL USE DISORDERS

Developmental Neurobiology and Early Organization of Risk

OVERVIEW

Addictive behaviors, as well as all behaviors, are the expressed or observable outcomes of the synergy between the individual organism and its environment (experience). They are also the expression of the complex relationship dynamics among genetic, epigenetic, and experience. Many human characteristics are a reflection of species membership (e.g., upright locomotion and language), and for the vast majority of the species, these species-specific characteristics are expressed if one is reared in a just adequate environment. Goodenough, Black, and Wallace (1987) referred to species-specific characteristics as experience expectant, and they contrasted these with experience-dependent characteristics—those that are expressed as a result of the individual's interplay with experience. Experience-expectant and experience-dependent aspects of plasticity, the organization of the brain and central nervous system, and cellular structure and function are fundamental concerns to researchers focusing on the genetics, epigenetics, and neurobiological aspects of alcohol use disorder (AUD) and other forms of psychopathology.

In Chapter 4, Trucco, Schlomer, and Hicks observe that heritable variation in AUD ranges from 48% to 66% across studies. They provide an overview of the genetic influences that contribute to AUD within a developmental perspective. They assert that the risk for AUD is a function of age-related changes in the relative contribution of genetic and environmental factors. Designs used to identify genetic factors relevant to problematic alcohol use are reviewed,

as are studies examining developmental pathways to AUD, with a focus on endophenotypes and intermediate phenotypes. Endophenotypes refer to those hereditary characteristic that are normally associated with some condition but are not direct symptoms for that condition. An intermediate phenotype describes an expressed phenotypic characteristic that cannot be traced to a specific dominant or recessive trait. All of these phenomenon are most likely influenced by epigenetic processes.

In Chapter 5, Ponomarev draws attention to epigenetics and its role in moderating gene expression. Epigenetics refers to gene–experience interplay, a process that affects the epigenome throughout the lifespan. The epigenome is characterized by "a dynamic and flexible response to intra- and extracellular stimuli, through cell–cell contact, by neighboring cells, by physiology, or entirely by the environment that the organism is exposed to" (Kanherkar, Bhatia-Dey, & Csoka, 2014, p. 1). Epigenetic influences act to regulate the epigenome without changing the genetic sequence. Experiential factors that affect the epigenome can influence how cells recode, a process that affects the expression of the phenotype. In short, epigenetics plays a major role in ensuring diversity within the species. Prenatal epigenetics influences have been linked to poor nutrition, maternal depression, endemic stress, post-traumatic stress disorder, prematurity, and neurodevelopmental disorders. Postnatal epigenetic factors include exposure to adverse children experiences, child maltreatment, psychopathology, behavioral disorders, and other factors. Many of these factors have also been investigated as predictors of psychopathology, including substance use disorder (SUD). Ponomarev discusses the role of epigenetic mechanisms and processes within the context of AUD etiology. He explores the potential for epigenetic research to improve diagnosis, to examine risks specific to diverse pathways for expression of AUD, and to lead to greater diversity in preventive interventions and treatments of AUD.

Epigenetics, therefore, plays a critical role in neurobiological and behavioral plasticity of the species and individual. In Chapter 6, Heitzeg reviews studies of behavioral undercontrol and negative affectivity, two pathways consistently linked to risk for SUD. She focuses on studies that probe the neural systems underlying these behavioral phenotypes in high-risk youth who are participants in a 30-year population-based prospective longitudinal study of families with high levels of parental SUDs (Zucker et al., 2000). Her work integrates behavioral trait, developmental, neurobiological, and, in some cases, genetic and epigenetic frameworks to develop a better understanding of the risk factors leading to SUDs.

REFERENCES

Goodenough, W., Black, J. E., & Wallace, C. S. (1987). Experience and brain development. *Child Development, 58,* 539–559.

Kanherkar, R. R., Bhatia-Dey, N., & Csoka, A. B. (2014). Epigenetics across the human lifespan. *Frontiers in Cell and Developmental Biology, 2,* 1–19.

Zucker, R. A., Fitzgerald, H. E., Refior, S. K., Puttler, L. I., Pallas, D. M., & Ellis, D. A. (2000). The clinical and social ecology of childhood for children of alcoholics: Description of a study and implications for a differentiated social policy. In H. E. Fitzgerald, B. M. Lester, & B. Zuckerman (Eds.), *Children of addiction: Research, health, and policy issues* (pp. 109–140). New York, NY: Garland.

4

A Developmental Perspective on the Genetic Basis of Alcohol Use Disorder

Elisa M. Trucco

Gabriel L. Schlomer

Brian M. Hicks

Like with other mental health disorders, substantial evidence indicates that alcohol use disorder (AUD) is affected by genetic influences. However, being a carrier of these genetic vulnerabilities is not deterministic in terms of developing AUD. Instead, the impact of genetic risk varies as a function of age and across different environmental exposures. This chapter starts with a discussion on how a developmental framework is useful for understanding the role of genetic and environmental influences on pathways to AUD. Next, an overview of research designs used to identify variants of genetic markers that influence risk for AUD is provided. Emerging work examining mechanistic pathways from genetic risk to the development of AUD, how genetic and environmental contributions to AUD risk may vary across age, and candidate gene–environment (cG×E) and candidate gene–intervention (cG×I) interactions on AUD outcomes are reviewed. We conclude with a discussion of future research directions. Some definitions are provided in Box 4.1 to assist the reader with certain more technical terms throughout the chapter.

ALCOHOL USE DISORDER WITHIN A DEVELOPMENTAL FRAMEWORK

The role of genetics in psychological disorders, including AUD, is not straightforward. Several factors contribute to its complexity. One factor is that

AUD is characterized by a progression of different stages of use (i.e., initiation, regular use, and problematic use), with each stage characterized by unique risk factors and etiological influences. Another factor is evidence for heterogeneous pathways to AUD. Substantial evidence supports an externalizing pathway to AUD characterized by a difficult temperament (e.g., impulsivity) in infancy, externalizing symptoms in childhood, and escalation in antisocial behavior leading to AUD (Iacono, Malone, & McGue, 2008). An internalizing pathway to AUD has also been posited, which is characterized by behaviorally inhibited temperament in infancy, internalizing symptoms and social skill deficits in childhood, and the eventual onset of substance use to cope with internalizing symptoms to the point of addiction (Hussong, Jones, Stein, Baucom, & Boeding, 2011). Risk for AUD is also influenced by genetic differences in alcohol metabolism such that persons who are unable to efficiently break down alcohol into its metabolites are less likely to develop AUD (Takeshita & Morimoto, 1999). As such, an investigation of the genetic etiology of AUD must be (1) informed by a developmental perspective, (2) modeled using a longitudinal study design, and (3) understood within a framework whereby AUD represents the endpoint of developmental processes that begin early in life. Unfortunately, the importance of longitudinal study designs and developmental theory on the genetics of AUD has received little attention.

BOX 4.1 **Glossary of Terms**

Candidate gene: This is an approach to conducting genetic association studies that focuses on the relation between a prespecified gene of interest and a phenotype.

Genome-wide association studies (GWAS): This is an approach to conducting genetic association studies that scans the entire genome for common genetic variation in a phenotype of interest.

Genotype: The genetic makeup of an organism.

Linkage disequilibrium (LD): Linkage disequilibrium occurs when genotypes at two or more loci are not independent of each other (i.e., they are highly correlated).

Phenotype: A set of observable traits of an organism, such as appearance and behavior.

Polygenic risk scores (PRSs): A score capturing the aggregation of genetic variation in multiple loci.

Reference single nucleotide polymorphism (rs): rs numbers are used to identify single nucleotide polymorphisms.

Single nucleotide polymorphism (SNP): Genetic variation in a single nucleotide that occurs at a specific position in a DNA sequence.

Variable number tandem repeats (VNTR): A location in a genome where a short nucleotide sequence is organized as a tandem repeat, which often show variations in length between individuals.

Variant: This is a general term used to describe variation in the DNA sequence in the genome. A single-nucleotide polymorphism is an example of a common genetic variant. Variable number tandem repeats is another type of genetic variant.

A critical time frame for understanding the role of genetics on AUD spans adolescence to young adulthood. Adolescence is when most individuals initiate alcohol use (Johnston, O'Malley, Miech, Bachman, & Schulenberg, 2016). For some, this experimentation is followed by more established patterns of use and rapid escalation of heavy and problematic use in early adulthood (Tucker, Ellickson, Orlando, Martino, & Klein, 2005). Late adolescence to early adulthood is often the period when early signs of problematic use are apparent, rates of use reach their peak, and levels of AUD symptomatology are at their highest (Vrieze, Hicks, Iacono, & McGue, 2012). Thus, developmental frameworks are necessary to capture multiple stages of use.

Environmental contexts, although not a focus of this chapter, are critical in understanding the development of alcohol use during adolescence and young adulthood. A host of parental factors have been examined in relation to adolescent substance use. The following are supported as robust predictors of adolescent alcohol use: parental monitoring/knowledge (i.e., tracking of a child's whereabouts and activities; Kerr, Stattin, & Burk, 2010), parental attitudes toward substance use (e.g., anti-alcohol parenting strategies; Handley & Chassin, 2013), and parental control (e.g., discipline; Barnes, Reifman, Farrell, & Dintcheff, 2000).

The shift from a more parent-dominated social experience during childhood to more time being spent with peers during adolescence marks a period when peers are highly influential due, in part, to a heightened concern for gaining autonomy from parents and avoiding social exclusion (Trucco, Wright, & Colder, 2014). Research demonstrates that adolescents who affiliate with peers who engage in externalizing behavior, or use substances, are more likely to initiate alcohol use (Trucco, Colder, & Wieczorek, 2011). Aspects of the neighborhood, including poverty and social connections among neighbors, also have an influence on adolescent substance use. However, this influence is more distal and may be mediated by more proximal contexts such as parenting and peer influences (Trucco, Colder, Wieczorek, Lengua, & Hawk, 2014). As described later, not only does the relative influence of genetic and environmental factors on adolescent substance use tend to vary with age (Rose, Dick, Viken, Pulkkinen, & Kaprio, 2001) but also certain genetic factors may impact the degree to which individuals are susceptible to these social contexts (Trucco, Villafuerte, Heitzeg, Burmeister, & Zucker, 2016). Thus, it is important to also understand the role of the environment in the field of addiction genetics.

COMMON VULNERABILITY
TO EXTERNALIZING PSYCHOPATHOLOGY

When conceptualizing the role of genetics on AUD, it is important to keep in mind that it is best viewed as an emerging phenotype preceded by a sequential progression of risk behaviors across development. Developmental cascade models help organize the multiple processes underlying complex developmental phenomena such as AUD. According to these models, there is a progression from early childhood risk to sequentially higher risk and more problematic behaviors across development. Namely, there is a sequential progression from childhood temperament (e.g., behavioral disinhibition) to adolescent behavior problems (e.g., externalizing) and to problematic substance use in early adulthood (Dodge et al., 2009). One study demonstrated that family risk of alcohol use was associated with low reactive control in early childhood. Low reactive control predicted inattention/hyperactivity, which in turn predicted conduct problems in middle childhood. Conduct problems predicted substance use in middle adolescence (Martel et al., 2009).

The associations between AUD and childhood disruptive disorders led researchers to posit that some individuals may inherit a common genetic liability that accounts for comorbidities among phenotypes across the broad spectrum of externalizing behaviors (Iacono et al., 2008). This common genetic liability is often described as a propensity toward behavioral disinhibition. During childhood, this common liability is relatively nonspecific, expressed behaviorally as temperament traits reflecting dispositional characteristics that either precede or co-occur with disruptive behavior disorders. In adulthood, this genetic liability is more differentiated given the effect of other genetic factors and exposure to different environmental contexts. Thus, the risk for AUD is best understood as joint genetic and environmental influences that operate at a general nonspecific level contributing to all forms of externalizing psychopathology as well as at the specific level by influencing the risk of abuse for a specific substance. This explains high rates of polysubstance abuse and why some people are more at risk for developing certain disorders (Iacono et al., 2008).

Several studies support the common genetic liability model. For example, one twin study demonstrated that genetic influences contributing to variation in behavioral disinhibition accounted for almost half of the genetic variation in conduct disorder and alcohol dependence and approximately 90% of the common genetic risk for conduct disorder and alcohol dependence (Slutske et al., 2002). Another study found that what is passed down from parents to the next generation is a vulnerability to a spectrum of externalizing disorders rather than increased risk for a particular disorder (Hicks, Krueger, Iacono, McGue, & Patrick, 2004). Namely, the general vulnerability to externalizing disorders was demonstrated as being highly heritable ($h^2 = 0.80$) compared to that of individual disorders in the spectrum ($h^2 = 0.35$–0.60; Slutske et al., 1998), suggesting that the residual genetic variance in AUD is relatively small. These results suggest that genetic factors contributing to variation in behavioral disinhibition and conduct disorder likely account for a significant portion of the genetic liability for AUD.

OVERVIEW OF GENETIC METHODOLOGY

Research designs used to evaluate genetic and environmental contributions to phenotypes are classified into two broad categories: *quantitative genetic* and *molecular genetic*. Quantitative genetic methods utilize information about genetic asymmetries between family members and family types along with principles of genetic inheritance to estimate the relative genetic and environmental contributions to phenotypes. Genetic and environmental sources of phenotypic variance are inferred without identifying specific genes or environments. Molecular genetic designs involve DNA and measured genetic variance (i.e., polymorphisms). These designs are used to evaluate the relation between DNA polymorphisms and phenotypic differences, such as AUD. Next, we outline the more common quantitative and molecular genetic research designs and introduce some of the commonly studied DNA polymorphisms.

Quantitative Genetic Designs

Twin Studies

Twin studies are a type of sibling design (Schlomer & Ellis, in press) in which concordance between pairs of monozygotic (MZ) and dizygotic (DZ) twins are compared. Because MZ twins are genetically identical and DZ twins share, on average, 50% of their genes, differences in within-pair correlations between MZ and

DZ twins can be used to infer genetic and environmental contributions to phenotype variance. Using robust statistical assumptions (Barnes et al., 2014), the phenotypic variance is partitioned into additive genetic, shared, and non-shared environmental components through latent variable modeling. Stemming from these are more complex methods such as twins reared apart (Bouchard, Lykken, McGue, Segal, & Tellegen, 1990), children of twins (Silberg & Eaves, 2004), and extended children of twins (Narusyte et al., 2008) designs that can be used to investigate gene–environment interplay.

Adoption Studies

As a natural experiment, adoption studies are designs for evaluating environment- and gene–phenotype associations (Rutter et al., 1990). The strength of adoption designs is in separating biological and social parentage, which is done by comparing an adoptee to his or her biological and adoptive parents. Phenotypic similarity, such as for AUD, between the adoptee and his or her biological parent suggests genetic transmission (Cloninger, Bohman, & Sigvardsson, 1981). Inferences can also be made regarding shared environmental influences by comparing adopted and non-adopted siblings within the same family (Hicks, Foster, Iacono, & McGue, 2013). Like twin studies, however, the validity of findings from adoption studies rests on a set of (largely testable) assumptions (Plomin, DeFries, Knopik, & Neiderhiser, 2013).

Molecular Genetic Designs

Candidate Genes

Candidate gene studies usually include one or a few measured genes or genetic markers. A gene is considered a good candidate if prior research and theory suggest the variant(s) is relevant to the phenotype and/or environment of interest. At the forefront of candidate gene research are candidate gene–environment (cG×E) studies that test how measured environments and genes co-act on the development of phenotypes. Recently, cG×E has been a productive but somewhat controversial area of study due to replication difficulties. This has led to greater attention and critical evaluation of the methods employed in this research area (Dick et al., 2015).

Because cG×E studies use a confirmational, hypothesis-driven approach to testing gene–environment interplay, researchers often rely on genetic markers that have been well studied. For example, genes involved in dopamine regulation have been studied widely due to associations with reward-seeking behaviors (Gan, Walton, & Phillips, 2010), substance use, and addiction risk (Volkow, Fowler, & Wang, 2002). Namely, the catechol-O-methyltransferase (COMT) gene encodes the enzyme COMT, which is involved in degrading neurotransmitters, including dopamine. COMT is often identified by rs4680, an A/G single nucleotide polymorphism (SNP) that results in an amino acid change from valine (A) to methionine (G) at the 158 codon (i.e., COMT Val^{158}Met). COMT variation has been linked to alcoholism (Kreek, Nielsen, & LaForge, 2004), heroin addiction (Horowitz et al., 2000), and methamphetamine abuse (Li et al., 2004).

The dopamine transporter gene DAT1 contains a variable number of tandem repeats (VNTR) in the polymorphic region related to dopamine transporter expression, a protein involved in the reuptake of synaptic dopamine. Given its role in dopamine regulation, it has also been the focus of research on substance use/abuse. DAT1 variation may be particularly relevant for cocaine abuse because cocaine binds to the DAT protein, which then prevents dopamine reuptake (Han & Gu, 2006), and has been linked to differences in subjective feelings of being "high" during acute cocaine exposure (Brewer et al., 2015). DAT1 is also linked to alcohol use among adolescent girls who report high stressful life events (Stogner, 2015).

Another commonly studied gene involved in dopamine regulation is the dopamine receptor D2 gene (DRD2). Two polymorphisms are often studied in relation to DRD2. First is the –141 insertion/deletion identified by the C allele (insertion) or no allele (deletion) in rs1799732. The second is the Taq1A polymorphism (rs1800497), which is located within another gene (ANKK1) but the polymorphism, or a variant in high linkage disequilibrium (LD) with it, affects D2 receptor binding and subsequent extracellular chemical communication associated with the D2 receptor protein. Both polymorphisms have been linked to addiction (Chen et al., 2011), but stronger evidence exists for Taq1A (Wang, Simen, Arias, Lu, & Zhang, 2013).

The dopamine receptor D4 gene (DRD4) codes for the D4 receptor protein. DRD4 contains a VNTR that ranges from 2 to 11 repeats, the most common of which are 2, 4, and 7 (Asghari et al., 1995). The 7-repeat allele has been associated with less effective receptor signaling and *DRD4* gene expression (Schoots & Van Tol, 2003), which is linked to greater physiological reactivity and exploratory behavior in mice (Falzone et al., 2002). Relations between *DRD4* and novelty seeking in humans have been extensively studied (Kluger, Siegfried, & Ebstein, 2002; Munafò, Yalcin, Willis-Owen, & Flint, 2008), and the link between *DRD4* and drinking behaviors is hypothesized to be mediated by novelty seeking (Ray et al., 2009).

Genes related to regulation of the serotonin system have also been examined in conjunction with AUD and other substance use/abuse. A large body of research has centered on the *5-HTTLPR* VNTR in the promoter region of *SLC6A4*, which produces a protein involved in the reuptake of serotonin from the synaptic cleft. *5-HTTLPR* is typically identified by long versus short repeat lengths (16 and 14 repeats; Lesch et al., 1996), and the short allele has been related to the lower expression of the serotonin transporter (Bradley, Dodelzon, Sandhu, & Philibert, 2005). Variability in expression due to *5-HTTLPR* has ambiguous functional effects; however, imaging research suggests that short allele carriers may be more neurologically reactive and susceptible to the negative effects of stressors (Hariri et al., 2002). In turn, greater stress sensitivity due to *5-HTTLPR* variants can result in greater substance use problems (Covault et al., 2007), and these effects may be age dependent (Merenäkk et al., 2011).

The *GABRA2* gene has been widely studied due to its involvement in alcohol use phenotypes and its role in how ethanol affects the central nervous system (Covault, Gelernter, Hesselbrock, Nellissery, & Kranzler, 2004; Edenberg et al., 2004). The γ-aminobutyric acid (GABA) neurotransmitter binds to the GABA α_2 receptor, which is encoded by *GABRA2* and inhibits neural potentials. Variation in *GABRA2* is linked to a neural endophenotype common to alcoholics (Edenberg et al., 2004). However, the role of *GABRA2* in substance use phenotypes, including alcohol use, is limited to adults (Corley et al., 2008). Among adolescents, SNPs in *GABRA2* are associated with more general conduct disorder symptoms and not alcohol dependence symptoms (Dick, Bierut, et al., 2006). Similarly, *GABRA2* has been linked to only subclinical-level externalizing behavior problems and

not to disorders/syndromes (Dick et al., 2013; Trucco, Villafuerte, Heitzeg, Burmeister, & Zucker, 2014).

Genome-wide Association Studies

Genome-wide association studies (GWAS) represent a powerful genomic design for discovering genotype–phenotype associations. This method entails genotyping hundreds of thousands to millions of SNPs and estimating correlations with a phenotype, often measured as a binary case–control (disease or no disease) such as AUD diagnosis. Correlations—characterized by frequency of the less common (minor) allele—are calculated for each SNP with the phenotype, and a stringent significance threshold is applied—typically $p < .05 \times 10^{-8}$ (i.e., $p < .00000005$). There are two primary reasons for adopting this p value. First is multiple testing; given the number of SNPs evaluated, a family-wise error correction is necessary. The second reason stems from replication failures in small sample size genomic studies prior to GWAS (McCarthy et al., 2008), which placed Type I error aversion at the forefront of GWAS research. The stringent p value necessitates large samples, on the order of tens of thousands, to achieve sufficient power to meet this criterion. GWAS are an exploratory, hypothesis-free approach designed to discover gene–phenotype associations that can inform hypotheses-driven analyses. As such, GWAS are not a direct result of a priori theories regarding the function of SNPs and the causal relation between SNPs and the phenotype studied (Pearson & Manolio, 2008).

Notably, most GWAS include only adults, and systematic research on adolescents is limited (Corley et al., 2008; Hart & Kranzler, 2015). However, genetic variants identified using gene discovery methods among adults can be examined in adolescents for associations with similar phenotypes. For example, *GABRA2* was initially identified in an association study of GABA$_A$ receptor genes in chromosome 4 using an adult sample at risk for AUD (Edenberg et al., 2004) and has since been examined in adolescent populations. *GABRA2* variability has been linked to adolescent externalizing behavior problems, which suggests that genetic variation in *GABRA2* may show developmentally contingent phenotypic associations. In this case, *GABRA2* may be related to AUD among adults but more general externalizing among adolescents (Dick, Bierut, et al., 2006; Dick, Prescott, & McGue, 2009; Trucco et al., 2014).

Polygenic Risk Scores

Polygenic risk scores (PRSs) "describe metrics comprising a large number of SNPs pooled together to represent a measured set of variants underlying a particular trait or disease" (Maher, 2015, p. 240). In effect, PRSs are SNP aggregates, such as a mean or sum of a set of alleles that are related to a phenotype. In this approach, an initial GWAS is conducted using a discovery sample to determine which SNPs meet or exceed a predetermined significance threshold. SNPs that meet threshold are then aggregated into a PRS, and phenotypic associations are evaluated in a separate prediction sample. Clarke et al. (2015) showed a significant, although modest, association between two PRSs and alcohol consumption, which is consistent with other research that examined PRS associations with alcohol use-onset phenotypes (Kapoor et al., 2016). Related to this approach, Belsky et al. (2013) used findings from existing GWAS to construct a PRS related to adult heavy cigarette smoking. This PRS included SNPs from the *CHRNA5–CHRNA3–CHRNB4* genetic cluster, which has been consistently related to smoking in several GWAS (Vandenbergh & Schlomer, 2014). The PRS was related to progression to dependence but not smoking initiation. This research further underscores the importance of considering development issues when evaluating gene–phenotype associations.

Another approach to creating PRSs is based on biological relevance and mechanism, such as aggregating genetic markers with the same neurotransmitter system. Using a set of dopamine-related genes (*DRD2*, *DAT1*, *DRD4*, and *COMT*), Nikolova, Ferrell, Manuck, and Hariri (2011) found a relation between a dopamine PRS and ventral striatum reactivity. Chhangur et al. (2017) found that a behavioral intervention was most effective in reducing problem behavior in boys higher on a similar dopamine PRS. PRS research using this approach in the AUD context is still needed.

GENETIC PATHWAYS TO ALCOHOL USE DISORDERS

Diagnostic classification systems often create heterogeneous groups within each clinical syndrome. For example, to meet a diagnosis of AUD using current practices, an individual must endorse at least 2 of 11 possible symptoms (American Psychiatric Association, 2013). In this way, individuals can meet criteria for AUD based on a multitude of symptom presentation combinations. This heterogeneity has made it challenging to identify susceptibility genes that replicate across samples due to nonspecific phenotypic measurement (Dick, 2013). Effect sizes of a single genetic marker on AUD are often small and difficult to detect (Ioannidis, Trikalinos, & Khoury, 2006). That is, one specific gene alone does not determine AUD onset; rather, various genes impact the neurobiological and biochemical processes that lead to increased susceptibility to AUD over time. Moreover, AUD represents an endpoint of a long history of developmental processes, including neurobiology and heritable temperament traits of nonspecific risk factors (Dodge et al., 2009). This realization has led to increased interest in identifying quantitative traits, physiology, and behavior that may be closer to the underlying genetic composition than a diagnostic classification. Approaches focused on capturing factors that represent pathways characterizing the effect of genetic architecture on downstream risk for psychopathology have made a significant contribution to the field of addiction by moving beyond binary diagnostic classifications of outcomes. Both endophenotype and intermediate phenotype approaches allow researchers to identify pathways that are key in the development of AUD before onset and at younger ages. Next, several key terms that are important for understanding the work on genetic pathways to AUD are defined. Then findings highlighting factors that are critical for genetic transmission of risk on AUD are reviewed.

Endophenotype Versus Intermediate Phenotype

The terms *endophenotype* and *intermediate phenotype* are often used interchangeably, despite important distinctions. Traditionally, an endophenotype is defined as a heritable biologically based phenotype that underlies and predicts a certain disorder but is not part of the disorder itself. Gottesman and Gould (2003) believe endophenotypes should be (1) associated with the disorder, (2) heritable, (3) state independent (i.e., not dependent on symptom presentation or expression), (4) co-segregated with the disorder within families, and (5) more prevalent in family members not meeting criteria for the disorder than in the general population. Endophenotypes can be grouped into several categories: anatomical (e.g., abnormalities in gray matter), electrophysiological (e.g., event-related potential and P300 amplitude), metabolic (e.g., cortisol secretion), sensory (e.g., olfactory sensitivity), or psychological/cognitive (e.g., response inhibition). An emerging area is the identification of key endophenotypes of complex disorders through imaging genetics (Fauth-Bühler & Kiefer, 2016). This approach combines genetics and imaging techniques (e.g., functional magnetic resonance imaging) to identify endophenotypes specific to differences in brain structure and function related to genetic variants and disorders.

Intermediate phenotypes tend to have less rigid criteria for classification. Some researchers state that intermediate phenotypes related to disorders should be heritable traits (Rasetti & Weinberger, 2011), whereas others believe that this is not necessary (Meyer-Lindenberg & Weinberger, 2006). Overall, the term intermediate phenotype is reserved for traits or behaviors that do not reflect an endogenous attribute or biological process. Intermediate phenotypes tend to represent traits that are observable, such as overt behaviors, and tend to bear some resemblance to the outcome. Also, it is often assumed that intermediate phenotypes act as intermediaries between the underlying genetic architecture and clinical disorders. Intermediate phenotypes receiving recent attention in the addiction literature include temperament (e.g., impulsivity) as well as child externalizing (e.g., aggression) and internalizing (e.g., depression) problems.

Mediational Versus Liability Index Models

Researchers have noted that even the term intermediate phenotype may not be used correctly. Namely, Kendler and Neale (2010) state that researchers adopting the term often assume a mediational model but tend not to state this specifically. These authors make a distinction between mediational and liability-index models. A liability-index model is consistent with pleiotropy, which presumes that a common set of genetic factors underlie susceptibility to both the intermediate phenotype and risk for disease. In this way, intermediate phenotypes are associated with risk for disease but are not necessarily causal factors. That is, in liability-index models, genetic factors are directly linked to clinical outcomes and do not need to operate via intermediate phenotypes. In contrast, mediational models make a causal assumption that the pathway from genetic vulnerability to risk for disease operates primarily via the intermediate phenotypes. Given the complexity of AUD, each intermediate phenotype tends to only represent a portion of relevant risk mechanisms. Mediational models imply that if it were possible to alter a key intermediate phenotype, doing so would result in a reduction of disease risk. However, this is not necessarily the case in liability-index models (Kendler & Neale, 2010).

Brief Review of Relevant Endophenotypes and Intermediate Phenotypes in Alcohol Use Disorder Risk

Electroencephalogram and Event-Related Potentials

There is a growing body of literature to support the role of electrophysiological factors as relevant endophenotypes for risk of AUD. For example, the amplitude of the P300 area of the visual event-related potential (ERP) has proven useful in identifying potential genes relevant to AUD (Dick, Jones, et al., 2006; Iacono & Malone, 2011). P300 reflects a voltage change elicited in response to stimuli that stand out (i.e., a rare target) when embedded with other like stimuli (i.e., frequent nontarget) because they are rare and require a response such as a button press (Iacono & Malone, 2011). A meta-analysis demonstrated that sons of paternal alcoholics who had never been exposed to alcohol had smaller P300 amplitudes compared to those of sons of non-alcoholics, and this effect is stronger with younger participants (Polich, Pollock, & Bloom, 1994). This suggests that P300 amplitude may represent a heritable precursor of AUD risk that is apparent at a young age. Some suggest that P300 amplitude may be due in part to differences in central nervous system hyperexcitability (Polich, 2007), whereas others state that it reflects attention allocation, information processing, and working memory (Enoch, Schuckit, Johnston, & Goldman, 2003). Dick, Jones, and colleagues (2006) observed two linkage peaks on chromosome 4 for alcohol-related phenotypes and with the beta 2 electroencephalogram (EEG) trait: one near the ADH gene cluster and one near the $GABA_A$ cluster. In addition, on chromosome 7, peaks in the CHRM2 gene were observed for alcohol-related phenotypes and the event-related theta band of the P300 ERP. In neither gene clusters in chromosome 4 or 7 were the peaks observed with AUD (Dick, Jones, et al., 2006). Other work indicates that reduced P300 is not associated with alcohol problems but, rather, an externalizing factor that underlies substance dependence, conduct disorder, and antisocial behavior (Patrick et al., 2006). As such, reduced P300 may be an endophenotypic indicator of overall externalizing risk rather than a specific syndrome. Future work should examine whether P300 and externalizing behavior are phenotypic expressions of genetic variants and also whether they mediate the association between genetic risk and later AUD.

Another potential electrophysiological endophenotype reflecting genetic risk for alcoholism is the low-voltage alpha (LVA) resting EEG trait. Alpha power has been demonstrated as highly heritable (Van Beijsterveldt, Molenaar, de Geus, & Boomsma, 1996). When experiencing states of high arousal, alpha oscillations tend to diminish greatly. Individuals with LVA resting EEG tend to have very few alpha oscillations. Accordingly, the LVA resting EEG trait is believed to resemble increased arousal. Individuals with LVA are at risk for AUD (Enoch et al., 2003). As noted previously, the low-activity Met158 allele (i.e., Met/Met) has been associated with problematic alcohol use. When examining LVA as an endophenotype, there was evidence for the association between the Met/Met genotype and LVA across two independent populations (Enoch et al., 2003). This suggests that the low-activity Met158 allele may be associated with AUD due in part to abnormalities in arousal.

Other work supports the association between increased power in the beta frequency band (13–28 Hz) of the EEG in individuals with AUD compared to controls (Rangaswamy et al., 2002), as well as a significant degree of heritability of EEG power in the beta frequency band in children of male alcoholics (Rangaswamy et al., 2004). Variations in the GABRA2 gene were also associated with both brain oscillations in the beta frequency range and AUD (Edenberg et al., 2004). Findings indicate that neural excitation may act as a pathway through which certain genes impact vulnerability for AUD. However, this work has focused primarily on adults.

Alcohol Sensitivity

The way a person experiences the pharmacological effects of alcohol impacts patterns of alcohol use

(Iacono et al., 2008). Alcohol sensitivity is heritable and can be either protective against or increase the risk for AUD. Work on genetic variants in alcohol dehydrogenase (ADH1B) and aldehyde dehydrogenase (ALDH2) that code for the enzymes that metabolize alcohol and acetaldehyde provide good examples. Approximately 50% of people of East Asian ancestry inherit these variants (Luczak, Glatt, & Wall, 2006). Individuals with ADH1B or ALDH2 variants experience flushing, headaches, and nausea when consuming alcohol due to the accumulation of acetaldehyde and reduced enzyme activity. Thus, people who inherit ALDH deficiency have reduced AUD risk due to the unpleasant feelings they experience while drinking alcohol. One study involving college students indicated that those with the ALDH2 variant reported more alcohol-associated symptoms but lower drinking frequency as well as binge drinking rates, reflecting a protective effect (Takeshita & Morimoto, 1999).

Another study tested the subjective effects of alcohol and the A118G polymorphism of the OPRM1 gene given research indicating that the opiodergic system plays an important role in the rewarding properties of substances (Ray & Hutchison, 2004). After an alcohol-administration paradigm, individuals with the G allele reported greater subjective feelings of intoxication, self-reported stimulation and sedation after alcohol consumption, and increases in positive mood compared to participants with the A allele. This might explain not only why these individuals are at increased risk for AUD but also why they have higher success rates with naltrexone. Naltrexone may have a stronger impact in blocking the positive effects produced by alcohol that place individuals carrying this polymorphism at increased risk (Volpicelli, Watson, King, Sherman, & O'Brien, 1995). There is also preliminary work suggesting that adolescents who carry the 5-HTTLPR short allele may be at increased risk for problematic alcohol use based on lower levels of alcohol response (Cope et al., 2017). This finding suggests that targeting adolescents with low responsivity to alcohol early on may help prevent AUD onset.

Cue Processing

Identification of functional polymorphisms on alcohol cue-induced brain activation has dominated the field of imaging genetics. Environmental stimuli are continuously paired with the effects of alcohol.

In this way, secondary conditioned reinforcers are established, which can trigger cue-elicited reactions (Fauth-Bühler & Kiefer, 2016). These alcohol-specific cues are thought to be related to the maintenance of compulsive drug-taking behavior that characterizes AUD (Grüsser et al., 2004). Imaging genetic studies of AUD support associations between genetic polymorphisms and variability in processing of alcohol cues within specific brain regions. For example, one study examined OPRM1 A118G during a gustatory alcohol cue reactivity paradigm before and after alcohol priming (Courtney, Ghahremani, & Ray, 2015). Results indicated that G allele carriers exhibited greater decreases in activation during alcohol priming in the left caudate, thalamus, putamen, and parietal cortex compared to A allele homozygotes (Courtney et al., 2015). Similarly, polymorphisms in glutamatergic neurotransmission genes (GRIK1 and GRIN2C) that have previously been associated with AUD were associated with altered cue-induced brain activation. GRIK1 risk allele carriers showed increased cue-induced activation in the medial prefrontal and orbitofrontal cortex and in the lateral prefrontal and orbitofrontal cortex, whereas GRIN2C risk allele carriers showed increased activation in the anterior cingulate cortex and dorsolateral prefrontal cortex (Bach et al., 2015).

Reward Processing

Individual differences in reinforcement processes, including sensitivity to rewards, are also supported as potential endophenotypes to later AUD. Namely, it has been demonstrated that individuals who are more prone to using alcohol may do so because of a genetic predisposition that may lead to defective reward pathway functioning. That is, some people have a genetic predisposition to be less satisfied with natural rewards and seek out substances for enhanced reward stimulation. One study tested the role of GABRA2 variants on brain activation during anticipation of monetary reward (Heitzeg et al., 2014). G allele carriers had greater nucleus accumbens activation during anticipation of monetary reward, and this effect was greatest in adolescence compared to childhood and adulthood. There was also support for an indirect effect of GABRA2 SNPs on later alcohol problems via nucleus accumbens activation during reward anticipation, supporting a possible endophenotype (Heitzeg et al., 2014).

Another group examined the role of the DAT1 9-repeat VNTR and the Val[158]Met COMT polymorphism on reward responsivity (Dreher, Kohn, Kolachana, Weinberger, & Berman, 2009). Findings indicated that COMT Met/Met carriers exhibited increased brain activity during anticipation of uncertain rewards in the ventral striatum, the left superior prefrontal gyrus, and the dorsolateral prefrontal cortex. In addition, 9-repeat allele carriers exhibited more bilateral ventral striatal and caudate nuclei activities compared to 10-repeat DAT1 allele carriers. Although AUD was not directly assessed, findings suggest that genetic risk associated with reward responsivity may lead to increased vulnerability to riskier reward-seeking behavior, including compulsive alcohol and drug use (Dreher et al., 2009).

Limitations of Endophenotype and Intermediate Phenotype Approaches

With the recent emphasis on endophenotype and intermediate phenotypes, key contributions have been made to the field of addiction genetics. These approaches may be useful for identifying factors early in life to inform prevention programs that may alter risk processes. For example, work by Trucco, Hicks, and colleagues (2016) indicates that intermediate phenotypes may offer glimpses into the utility of offering individualized treatments based on genetic makeup. In this study, some individuals carried genetic risk that was expressed as early difficulties modulating distress, whereas for other youth, genetic risk was expressed as difficulties controlling impulses. Accordingly, some youth may benefit from increased self-control, whereas others may benefit from interventions targeting emotion regulation to prevent AUD risk (Trucco, Hicks, et al., 2016).

Nevertheless, these approaches also have several limitations. Perhaps the most notable limitation is that these models often exclude environmental exposures, despite strong evidence of the importance of these factors in understanding AUD (MacKillop & Munafò, 2013). The development of more comprehensive models that assess how genetic pathways to AUD may differ across environmental exposures is critical. However, modeling the natural complexity inherent in these processes necessitates large prospective data sets, data across extensive domains, and data across various methodologies (genotyping, imaging, observation, and survey). There is also disagreement regarding the degree to which endophenotypes are useful for identifying genetic variants that contribute to disease susceptibility. Some researchers suggest that endophenotypes may offer an efficient approach to gene identification (Dick & Foroud, 2003), whereas others state that despite being conceptually simpler than syndromes, endophenotypes are not sufficiently less complex to aid in gene discovery (Iacono, Vaidyanathan, Vrieze, & Malone, 2014). Thus, endophenotypic approaches may not be as useful as previously reported and not likely to address current challenges (Iacono et al., 2014).

DYNAMIC DEVELOPMENTAL CHANGES IN THE ROLE OF GENETICS ON ALCOHOL USE DISORDER

The importance of genetic factors on AUD is likely to vary across development. This is largely due to the joint contribution of genetic influences and social contexts as etiological factors involved in the onset and pattern of drinking behavior. Overall, studies demonstrate that the relative impact of genetic factors on drinking behavior increases with time, whereas the influence of environmental contexts decreases (Rose et al., 2001). This has been demonstrated using cross-sectional designs with twins, as well as longitudinal studies focused on specific candidate genes.

Twin Studies

One study examined the relative impact of additive genetic, shared environmental, and unique environmental influences on AUD across twins between the ages of 15 and 32 years (van Beek et al., 2012). Findings indicated that shared environmental factors accounted for a majority of the variance in alcohol abuse and dependence in adolescence but significantly declined thereafter. Namely, 57% of the variance in alcohol abuse and dependence was attributed to environmental factors at ages 15–17 years, 18% at ages 18–20 years, 2% at ages 21–23 years, and none thereafter. In contrast, genetic influences increased from adolescence to early adulthood and then leveled off (28% at ages 15–17 years, 36% at ages 18–20 years, and 58% at ages 21–23 years; van Beek et al., 2012). Another study demonstrated that the total percentage

of variance accounted for by genetic factors increased from age 16 years to age 18½ years (33% compared to 50%, respectively), in contrast to the variance accounted for by common environmental factors that decreased with age (37% compared to 14%, respectively; Rose et al., 2001). It is important to note that one meta-analysis demonstrated that although a general pattern of increased heritability from early adolescence to early adulthood in overall externalizing behavior emerged, there was weak support for increasing heritability in alcohol consumption (Bergen, Gardner, & Kendler, 2007). This indicates that the relative impact of genes on problematic alcohol use from adolescence to adulthood is not consistent across studies.

Candidate Gene Studies

Although only a small number of candidate gene studies have examined developmental questions regarding the relative contribution of genetic and environmental influences on alcohol-related phenotypes over time, a similar pattern emerges. For example, one study examined the effect of five monoamine genes (i.e., 5HTT, DAT1, DRD4, DRD2, and MAOA) on the frequency of alcohol consumption in adolescence compared to young adulthood (Guo, Wilhelmsen, & Hamilton, 2007). Although none of the genetic factors were related to alcohol consumption in adolescence, all five genes predicted alcohol use in young adulthood. Another study employed piecewise linear growth models to examine the unique impact of GABRA2 variants on increases in drunkenness from early adolescence to early adulthood (14–18 years old), during the transition to adulthood (18 to 19 years old), and in early adulthood (19 years of age or older; Dick et al., 2013). Findings indicated that GABRA2 variants were associated with the increase in drunkenness from age 18 to age 19 years but not in early adolescence or early adulthood. Trucco and colleagues (2014) used structural equation modeling to determine age-specific effects of GABRA2 on rule-breaking behavior and substance use outcomes. GABRA2 variants had a significant effect on rule-breaking behavior from mid- to late adolescence (ages 13 to 18 years) but not during pre-adolescence (ages 11 and 12 years). In contrast, GABRA2 did not predict problematic alcohol use or substance use disorder symptoms. These studies indicate that genetic effects have a stronger association on AUD starting in early adulthood compared to adolescence. However, this may also be a function of greater variability in alcohol use during later developmental periods.

Explanations Posed for Dynamic Effects of Genes on Alcohol Use Disorder

Currently, there is no clear explanation regarding what accounts for the developmentally modulated contribution of genetic versus environmental influences. One study found that age-related increases in genetic influences and age-related decreases in family-level environmental influences in externalizing behaviors were better accounted for by pubertal status than by age (Harden et al., 2015). Other studies have demonstrated that developmental differences may be confounded by stage of alcohol use. That is, what might appear to be differences in the relative contribution of genetic and environmental effects across age may be a result of whether the individual is initiating alcohol use or engaging in problematic use. Because stages of alcohol use are highly correlated with developmental period (e.g., initiation is more typical during adolescence, and problematic use is more typical during adulthood), it is important that studies tease apart these effects. For example, one study examined the environmental and genetic contributions on initiation of alcohol use compared to progression to more severe use of alcohol (e.g., binge drinking and getting drunk) among twins aged 11–19 years (Fowler et al., 2007). Results demonstrated that shared environmental influences accounted for a majority (~65%) of the variance in alcohol use initiation compared to genetic factors (~26%) when controlling for age of the individual. This is in contrast to findings on alcohol use progression: Almost half (47%) of the variance was due to shared environmental influences, and approximately one-third (35%) was due to genetic factors (Fowler et al., 2007). Moreover, regarding the variance of alcohol progression explained by factors influencing initiation, 26% was due to genetic factors, 65% was due to shared environmental factors, and 9% was due to non-shared environmental factors. This suggests that the relative significance of genetic and environmental factors changes across stages of use, and it supports the role of separate but related genetic liabilities for initiation versus escalation of alcohol use (Fowler et al., 2007).

Another explanation that has been posed involves differences in the social world of an adolescent compared to that of an adult. Parents tend to monitor and regulate the social world of an adolescent. When individuals gain autonomy and have more freedom to shape their social worlds during the transition from adolescence to adulthood, genetic vulnerabilities may be more likely to be expressed (Dick & Foroud, 2003). Moreover, research demonstrates that substance use initiation is largely driven by socialization contexts (high rates of peer substance use and low parental monitoring), but as alcohol use becomes more established and regular, genetic factors become increasingly important and may reflect individual differences in response to alcohol.

CG×E AND CG×I INTERACTION STUDIES

cG×E are the primary designs used to study alcohol use phenotypes in the developmental literature, largely in conjunction with known contextual influences on adolescent alcohol use, such as parents and peers. For example, Pieters et al. (2012) tested whether DRD2 Taq1A variation moderates the association between parent rule setting and alcohol use risk. Results showed main effects of DRD2 and parent rule setting on adolescent alcohol use, as well as an interaction. Adolescents who were at DRD2 genetic risk had higher alcohol use if they had parents who had permissive alcohol use attitudes compared to adolescents who had parents with stricter attitudes and whose alcohol use was similar to that of adolescents not at genetic risk. This finding replicated those from a prior study of Dutch adolescents (van der Zwaluw et al., 2010). Other research suggests the DRD2–alcohol use link may be specific to nonsocial motivations for drinking, such as coping (van der Zwaluw, Kuntsche, & Engels, 2011). In a series of studies, Cleveland et al. (2015) found that a substance use preventive intervention was most effective at reducing alcohol use among early adolescents who had at least one copy of the DRD4 7-repeat and had higher maternal involvement. In a follow-up study, Cleveland et al. (2017) found that the intervention mitigated ADH1C genetic risk for alcohol use progression in early but not late adolescence. Using a novel statistical approach, Russell et al. (2017) found that an intervention moderated the effect of GABRA2 (rs279845) variation on alcohol use across adolescence, particularly between ages 13 and 16 years. Similar results have been found in other studies regarding dopaminergic and GABAergic gene effects on substance use moderated by substance use interventions (Brody, Chen, & Beach, 2013). Nonintervention research using experimental designs has revealed that young adults with at least one copy of the DRD4 7-repeat allele are more likely to drink when exposed to peer drinking (Larsen et al., 2010). A potential mechanism for increased sensitivity to peer alcohol consumption may be greater experiences of social bonding among 7-repeat carriers when consuming alcohol, as evidenced in a second experimental study of DRD4, peers, and alcohol consumption (Creswell et al., 2012).

Genetic studies that implement experimental designs such as cG×I are a burgeoning area of research that holds promise for elucidating molecular genetic associations with substance use phenotypes (Belsky & van Ijzendoorn, 2015; Musci & Schlomer, in press). Randomization in experimental cG×E designs is an important methodological advancement over nonrandomized, correlational designs. Importantly, randomization breaks possible gene–environment correlation (rGE) confounds that might occur in the absence of randomization because genotype is unrelated to intervention and control assignment. Adjusting for rGE is key for cG×E effects because interactions could reflect rGE processes and not genetic or environmental moderation. In addition, because interventions are designed to change phenotypes, intervention effects can create between-group differences that may be larger than those observed in non-intervention studies. Statistical power is enhanced when larger group differences result in larger effect sizes. Last, measurement error terms for intervention status (control vs. intervention) can be relatively small compared to those of typical psychometric assessments of environments and can also be more directly evaluated through intervention fidelity assessments. Intervention designs are a powerful method for evaluating cG×E when these factors are maximized (Belsky & van Ijzendoorn, 2015).

Developmental Plasticity

A unique aspect of cG×E relative to other genomic designs is that these studies are often heavily theoretically guided. Much of this work is underlain by evolution-based theories of developmental plasticity, or the ability of a phenotype associated with a single genotype to take on different forms, depending on specific external (e.g., environmental) or internal (e.g., psychological) conditions (West-Eberhard, 2003). The most general of these is differential susceptibility theory (DST; Ellis, Boyce, Belsky, Bakermans-Kranenburg, & van Ijzendoorn, 2011), which posits that evolutionary processes favor phenotypes that vary in their sensitivity to parenting and socialization. Because the future is inherently uncertain, it would be beneficial for parents to produce some offspring who are relatively phenotypically fixed and who would thrive in particular contexts (Belsky, 1997), as well as those who are more phenotypically responsive to environmental variation. A more contextually responsive phenotype could reap more gains when conditions are favorable, but it risks greater losses during adversity. The hallmark of DST is the proposition that those who are more sensitive to their environment are at higher risk for negative outcomes in adverse conditions but can gain exceptional benefits in more positive contexts. For example, one study demonstrated that adolescents homozygous for the GABRA2 minor allele (G) are especially sensitive to parental monitoring/knowledge compared to A carriers (Trucco, Villafuerte, et al., 2016). That is, at high parental monitoring, GG homozygous adolescents were more likely to belong to lower risk externalizing trajectory classes across adolescence compared to A carriers. However, at low parental monitoring, these same individuals were less likely to belong to a lower risk externalizing trajectory class compared to A carriers (Trucco, Villafuerte, et al., 2016). This indicates that GABRA2 variants may act as plasticity factors. More work regarding differences in environmental sensitivity may be worth undertaking with developmental models of genetic associations because this sensitivity to environmental context may change over time.

CONCLUSION AND FUTURE DIRECTIONS

Research examining the role of genetic factors in the development of AUD has proliferated during the past decade. Not only have technological advances, such as GWAS, increased confidence in our ability to detect novel and reliable genetic variants involved in AUD but also research has started to refine the mechanistic pathways through which genes impact AUD risk over time. Research has identified several genetic factors that show replicated associations with AUD, including COMT Val[158]Met, ANKK1/DRD2 TaqlA, 5-HTTLPR VNTR, and GABRA2 (rs279858). An increase in multidisciplinary collaborations has also contributed to the identification of replicated endophenotypes and intermediate phenotypes that act as intermediaries in the pathway to later AUD pathology. As these etiological models become increasingly refined, early risk factors associated with genetic vulnerabilities can be identified and targeted through personalized preventive interventions before the onset of alcohol use. The field of addiction genetics has also seen a dramatic shift from candidate approaches heavily grounded in a priori hypotheses to GWAS, a data-driven atheoretical approach. It is likely that in the near future, more researchers will attempt to maximize the relative strengths of each approach through more integrative methods, such as calculating PRSs across GWAS-identified SNPs. These risk scores are then included in theoretically informed models to track the relation of particular variants on the development of substance use over time. Despite these notable advances, we propose four future directions within the field of AUD genetics.

Gene–Environment–Development Models

Few studies have been successfully integrated the complexity of interactions between genetic factors and environmental contexts with the nuances that unfold across development. An important future direction is to test gene–environment–development (G×E×D) models. One obstacle has been the lack of statistical methods to test these models adequately. Conventional methods, such as structural equation modeling, are not ideal for this type of analysis given that time-varying effects are typically implicitly tested using interactions with limited options for modeling functions of time (e.g., linear and quadratic; Buu, Dabrowska, Heinze, Hsieh, & Zimmerman, 2015). Accounting for changes over time in this manner is too simplistic for the inherent complexity of

synergistic effects of genes and the environment on alcohol use behavior.

Time-varying effect modeling is a novel approach to address this limitation because time-varying effects can be modeled more flexibly through nonparametric regression functions. The utility of this approach has been demonstrated using long-term longitudinal data of substance use patterns (Buu et al., 2015). This new methodology also holds great promise for testing G×E×D effects on AUD. Namely, this methodology could pinpoint the developmental stage in which genes have the strongest impact on susceptibility to environmental contexts and also whether specific genetic influences change from being protective during one phase of life to increasing AUD risk in another. For example, Russell et al. (2017) found that the effect of a substance use intervention on adolescent (ages 11–20 years) alcohol misuse differed by GABRA2 genotype. Differences were strongest between ages 13 and 16 years, a critical period for the development of AUD.

Genome-wide Complex Trait Analysis

Heritability of most quantitative traits averages approximately 50% (Polderman et al., 2015), which suggests that 50% of the variation in many traits can be explained by additive genetics. Molecular genetic studies, however, have fallen short of explaining this magnitude of phenotypic variance. Most individual genetic markers explain only a small fraction of the phenotypic variance, and PRSs have shown only modest improvement over single-gene/marker approaches (Manolio et al., 2009). This disjunction between the phenotypic variance explained in quantitative genetics and what has been found using molecular approaches is known as the missing heritability problem. Genome-wide complex trait analysis (GCTA) uses information about the genetic relationships between individuals using SNP data to estimate trait heritability with molecular data (Yang, Lee, Goddard, & Visscher, 2011). This approach has shown promise for addressing the missing heritability problem, although there is currently some debate about the accuracy of GCTA heritability estimates (Kumar, Feldman, Rehkopf, & Tuljapurkar, 2016). In addition, this method is potentially ideal for addressing the missing heritability problem but provides limited insight into specific genetic liabilities beyond what has already been inferred by quantitative genetic studies. Nonetheless, it does appear that this approach could be used to address interesting questions about genes and development. For example, does SNP-based heritability for AUD differ between adult and adolescent populations?

Capturing Complex Environmental Contexts

cG×E studies have received significant criticism for their high false-positive rates and low rates of replication due to measurement error, low effect and sample sizes, and limited distribution of genotypes and exposure. The National Institute on Alcohol Abuse and Alcoholism (NIAAA) and the National Institute on Drug Abuse (NIDA) are in agreement that a roadblock in advancing the field of addiction genetics has been that the operationalization of environments has lagged behind genetic innovations (Conway, Compton, & Miller, 2006; Gunzerath & Goldman, 2003). One effort to improve the reliability of environmental and phenotypic measures is the PhenX Toolkit, a web-based catalog of widely used and reliable measures related to the study of complex disease, environments, and phenotypic traits. Including measures from the PhenX Toolkit in protocols will improve reliability and allow for direct comparisons of findings across studies.

Another limitation is that current studies tend to focus on one specific environmental context at a time. Although these findings have been useful for understanding the specific synergistic effects of a particular environmental context and genetic factor, environmental exposures seldom occur in isolation. That is, adolescents who use alcohol tend to affiliate more with deviant peers, have a poor relationship with their parents, and are more disconnected from their school. Future work should also consider generality in the effects of environmental variables by considering methods to aggregate contextual risk across key domains. One strategy for characterizing complex environments is to create a broad omnibus construct through latent variable modeling. For example, one group created a family environment latent variable by including key factors demonstrated to impact substance use, including family management, conflict, bonding, and positive involvement (Bailey, Hill, Meacham, Young, & Hawkins, 2011). These models could be extended to include various environmental contexts.

Data Sharing and Consortia

The Achilles heel of genetics of addiction research has primarily centered around small sample and effects sizes for individual candidate genes. There is a strong need for large consortia to first identify key genetic factors in GWAS and then pool resources across longitudinal studies to examine G×E, G×D, and G×E×D effects using larger sample sizes.

This has led to a recent push to create open-access data repositories and data sharing across sites. This includes NIDA's Center for Genetic Studies' Gene, Environment, and Development Initiative (GEDI), which solicits applications for the integration of data sets that assess rich developmental, environmental, and genetic factors related to substance abuse. Another effort has been initiated by multiple centers in Europe through the IMAGEN study, in which 2000 14-year-old children and their families are assessed at multiple time points. This initiative includes the collection of neuroimaging and genetic information. The Psychiatric Genomics Consortium (PGC) is another initiative that includes more than 800 investigators from 38 countries who conduct meta-analyses of genome-wide genomic data for various psychiatric disorders. In 2014, the PGC received funding from NIDA and NIAAA to create the Substance Use Disorder Workgroup, which focuses on the use and misuse of alcohol, tobacco, marijuana, cocaine, and opioids. These data-pooling efforts hold great promise to increase our understanding of the neural basis of AUD.

ACKNOWLEDGMENTS

Preparation of this chapter was supported by grant K08 AA023290 from the National Institution on Alcohol Abuse and Alcoholism awarded to Dr. Trucco. The contents are solely the responsibility of the authors and do not necessarily represent the official views of the National Institutes of Health.

REFERENCES

American Psychiatric Association. (2013). *Diagnostic and statistical manual of mental disorders* (5th ed.). Arlington, VA: American Psychiatric Publishing.

Asghari, V., Sanyal, S., Buchwaldt, S., Paterson, A., Jovanovic, V., & Van Tol, H. H. (1995). Modulation of intracellular cyclic AMP levels by different human dopamine D4 receptor variants. *Journal of Neurochemistry*, 65, 1157–1165.

Bach, P., Kirsch, M., Hoffmann, S., Jorde, A., Mann, K., Frank, J., . . . Rietschel, M. (2015). The effects of single nucleotide polymorphisms in glutamatergic neurotransmission genes on neural response to alcohol cues and craving. *Addiction Biology*, 20(6), 1022–1032.

Bailey, J. A., Hill, K. G., Meacham, M. C., Young, S. E., & Hawkins, J. D. (2011). Strategies for characterizing complex phenotypes and environments: General and specific family environmental predictors of young adult tobacco dependence, alcohol use disorder, and co-occurring problems. *Drug and Alcohol Dependence*, 118, 444–451.

Barnes, G. M., Reifman, A. S., Farrell, M. P., & Dintcheff, B. A. (2000). The effects of parenting on the development of adolescent alcohol misuse: A six-wave latent growth model. *Journal of Marriage and the Family*, 62(1), 175–186.

Barnes, J. C., Wright, J. P., Boutwell, B. B., Schwartz, J. A., Connolly, E. J., Nedelec, J. L., & Beaver, K. M. (2014). Demonstrating the validity of twin research in criminology. *Criminology*, 52(4), 588–626.

Belsky, J. (1997). Theory testing, effect-size evaluation, and differential susceptibility to rearing influence: The case of mothering and attachment. *Child Development*, 68(4), 598–600.

Belsky, J., & van Ijzendoorn, M. H. (2015). What works for whom? Genetic moderation of intervention efficacy. *Development and Psychopathology*, 27(1), 1–6.

Belsky, D. W., Moffitt, T. E., Baker, T. B., Biddle, A. K., Evans, J. P., Harrington, H., . . . Poulton, R. (2013). Polygenic risk and the developmental progression to heavy, persistent smoking and nicotine dependence: evidence from a 4-decade longitudinal study. *JAMA Psychiatry*, 70(5), 534–542.

Bergen, S. E., Gardner, C. O., & Kendler, K. S. (2007). Age-related changes in heritability of behavioral phenotypes over adolescence and young adulthood: A meta-analysis. *Twin Research and Human Genetics*, 10(3), 423–433.

Bouchard, T. J., Jr., Lykken, D. T., McGue, M., Segal, N., & Tellegen, A. (1990). Sources of human psychological differences: The Minnesota Study of Twins Reared Apart. *Science*, 250, 223–228.

Brewer, A. J., Nielsen, D. A., Spellicy, C. J., Hamon, S. C., Gingrich, J., Thompson-Lake, D. G. Y., . . . De La Garza, R. (2015). Genetic variation of the dopamine transporter (DAT1) influences the acute subjective responses to cocaine in volunteers with cocaine use disorders. *Pharmacogenetic Genomics*, 25, 296–304.

Bradley, S. L., Dodelzon, K., Sandhu, H. K., & Philibert, R. A. (2005). Relationship of serotonin transporter gene polymorphisms and haplotypes to mRNA transcription. *American Journal of Medical Genetics Part B: Neuropsychiatric Genetics*, 136B, 58–61.

Brody, G. H., Chen, Y. F., & Beach, S. R. (2013). Differential susceptibility to prevention: GABAergic, dopaminergic, and multilocus effects. *Journal of Child Psychology and Psychiatry*, 54(8), 863–871.

Buu, A., Dabrowska, A., Heinze, J. E., Hsieh, H.-F., & Zimmerman, M. A. (2015). Gender differences in the developmental trajectories of multiple substance use and the effect of nicotine and marijuana use on heavy drinking in a high-risk sample. *Addictive Behaviors*, 50, 6–12.

Chen, D., Liu, F., Shang, Q., Song, X., Miao, X., & Wang, Z. (2011). Association between polymorphisms of DRD2 and DRD4 and opioid dependence: Evidence from the current studies. *American Journal of Medical Genetics Part B: Neuropsychiatric Genetics*, 156(6), 661–670.

Chhangur, R. R., Weeland, J., Overbeek, G., Matthys, W., Orobio de Castro, B., van der Giessen, D., & Belsky, J. (2017). Genetic moderation of intervention efficacy: Dopaminergic genes, The Incredible Years, and externalizing behavior in children. *Child Development*, 88(3), 796–811.

Clarke, T.-K., Smith, A. H., Gelernter, J., Kranzler, H. R., Farrer, L. A., Hall, L. S., . . . McIntosh, A. M. (2015). Polygenic risk for alcohol dependence associates with alcohol consumption, cognitive function and social deprivation in a population-based cohort. *Addiction Biology*, 21, 469–480.

Cleveland, H. H., Schlomer, G. L., Vandenbergh, D. J., Feinberg, M., Greenberg, M., Spoth, R., . . . Hair, K. L. (2015). The conditioning of intervention effects on early adolescent alcohol use by maternal involvement and dopamine receptor D4 (DRD4) and serotonin transporter linked polymorphic region (5-HTTLPR) genetic variants. *Development and Psychopathology*, 27(1), 51–67.

Cleveland, H. H., Schlomer, G. L., Vandenbergh, D. J., Wolf, P. S. A., Feinberg, M. E., Greenberg, M. T., . . . Redmond, C. (2017). Associations between alcohol dehydrogenase genes and alcohol use across early and late adolescence: Moderation by preventive intervention. *Development and Psychopathology*.

Cloninger, C. R., Bohman, M., & Sigvardsson, S. (1981). Inheritance of alcohol abuse: Cross-fostering analysis of adopted men. *Archives of General Psychiatry*, 38(8), 861–868.

Conway, K. P., Compton, W. M., & Miller, P. M. (2006). Novel approaches to phenotyping drug abuse. *Addictive Behaviors*, 31, 923–928.

Cope, L. M., Munier, E. C., Trucco, E. M., Hardee, J. E., Burmeister, M., Zucker, R. A., & Heitzeg, M. M. (2017). Effects of the serotonin transporter gene, sensitivity of response to alcohol, and parental monitoring on risk for problem alcohol use. *Alcohol*, 59, 7–16.

Corley, R. P., Zeiger, J. S., Crowley, T., Ehringer, M. A., Hewitt, J. K., Hopfer, C. J., . . . Krauter, K. (2008). Association of candidate genes with antisocial drug dependence in adolescents. *Drug and Alcohol Dependence*, 96(1), 90–98.

Courtney, K. E., Ghahremani, D. G., & Ray, L. A. (2015). The effect of alcohol priming on neural markers of alcohol cue-reactivity. *American Journal of Drug and Alcohol Abuse*, 41(4), 300–308.

Covault, J., Tennen, H., Armeli, S., Conner, T. S., Herman, A. I., Cillessen, A. H. N., & Kranzler, H. R. (2007). Interactive effects of the serotonin transporter 5-HTTLPR polymorphism and stressful life events on college student drinking and drug use. *Biological Psychiatry*, 61, 609–616.

Covault, J., Gelernter, J., Hesselbrock, V., Nellissery, M., & Kranzler, H. R. (2004). Allelic and haplotypic association of GABRA2 with alcohol dependence. *American Journal of Medical Genetics Part B: Neuropsychiatric Genetics*, 129(1), 104–109.

Creswell, K. G., Sayette, M. A., Manuck, S. B., Ferrell, R. E., Hill, S. Y., & Dimoff, J. D. (2012). DRD4 polymorphism moderates the effect of alcohol consumption on social bonding. *PLoS One*, 7(2), e28914.

Dick, D. M. (2013). Developmental considerations in gene identification efforts. In J. MacKillop & M. R. Munafò (Eds.), *Genetic influences on addiction: An intermediate phenotype approach* (pp.141–156). Cambridge, MA: MIT Press.

Dick, D. M., Agrawal, A., Keller, M. C., Adkins, A., Aliev, F., Monroe, S., . . . Sher, K. J. (2015). Candidate gene-environment interaction research: reflections and recommendations. *Perspectives on Psychological Science*, 10, 37–59.

Dick, D. M., Bierut, L., Hinrichs, A., Fox, L., Bucholz, K. K., Kramer, J., . . . Foroud, T. (2006). The role of GABRA2 in risk for conduct disorder and alcohol and drug dependence across developmental stages. *Behavior Genetics*, 36(4), 577–590.

Dick, D. M., Cho, S. B., Latendresse, S. J., Aliev, F., Nurnberger, J. I., Edenberg, H. J., . . . Kuperman, S. (2013). Genetic influences on alcohol use

across stages of development: GABRA2 and longitudinal trajectories of drunkenness from adolescence to young adulthood. *Addiction Biology*, 19, 1055–1064.

Dick, D. M., & Foroud, T. (2003). Candidate genes for alcohol dependence: A review of genetic evidence from human studies. *Alcoholism: Clinical and Experimental Research*, 27(5), 868–879.

Dick, D. M., Jones, K., Saccone, N., Hinrichs, A., Wang, J. C., Goate, A., . . . Tischfield, J. (2006). Endophenotypes successfully lead to gene identification: Results from the collaborative study on the genetics of alcoholism. *Behavior Genetics*, 36, 112–126.

Dick, D. M., Prescott, C., & McGue, M. (2009). The genetics of substance use and substance use disorders. In Y.-K. Kim (Ed.), *Handbook of behavior genetics* (pp. 433–453). New York, NY: Springer.

Dodge, K. A., Malone, P. S., Lansford, J. E., Miller, S., Pettit, G. S., & Bates, J. E. (2009). A dynamic cascade model of the development of substance-use onset. *Monographs of the Society for Research in Child Development*, 74(3), vii–119.

Dreher, J. C., Kohn, P., Kolachana, B., Weinberger, D. R., & Berman, K. F. (2009). Variation in dopamine genes influences responsivity of the human reward system. *Proceedings of the National Academy of Sciences of the USA*, 106(2), 617–622.

Edenberg, H. J., Dick, D. M., Xuei, X., Tian, H., Almasy, L., Bauer, L. O., . . . Begleiter, H. (2004). Variations in GABRA2, encoding the α_2 subunit of the GABA$_A$ receptor, are associated with alcohol dependence and with brain oscillations. *American Journal of Human Genetics*, 74(4), 705–714.

Ellis, B. J., Boyce, W. T., Belsky, J., Bakermans-Kranenburg, M. J., & van Ijzendoorn, M. H. (2011). Differential susceptibility to the environment: An evolutionary–neurodevelopmental theory. *Development and Psychopathology*, 23, 7–28.

Enoch, M., Schuckit, M. A., Johnston, B. A., & Goldman, D. (2003). Genetics of alcoholism using intermediate phenotypes. *Alcoholism: Clinical and Experimental Research*, 27(2), 169–176.

Falzone, T. L., Gelman, D. M., Young, J. I., Grandy, D. K., Low, M. J., & Rubinstein, M. (2002). Absence of dopamine D4 receptors results in enhanced reactivity to unconditioned, but not conditioned, fear. *European Journal of Neuroscience*, 15(1), 158–164.

Fauth-Bühler, M., & Kiefer, F. (2016). Alcohol and the human brain: A systematic review of recent functional neuroimaging and imaging genetics findings. *Current Addiction Reports*, 3, 109–124.

Fowler, T., Lifford, K., Shelton, K., Rice, F., Thapar, A., Neale, M. C., . . . van den Bree, M. B. M. (2007).

Exploring the relationship between genetic and environmental influences on initiation and progression of substance use. *Addiction, 101*, 413–422.

Gan, J. O., Walton, M. E., & Phillips, P. E. M. (2010). Dissociable cost and benefit encoding of future rewards by mesolimbic dopamine. *Nature Neuroscience, 13*, 25–27.

Gottesman, I. I., & Gould, T. D. (2003). The endophenotype concept in psychiatry: Etymology and strategic intentions. *American Journal of Psychiatry, 160*, 636–645.

Grüsser, S. M., Wrase, J., Klein, S., Hermann, D., Smolka, M. N., Ruf, M., . . . Heinz, A. (2004). Cue-induced activation of the striatum and medial prefrontal cortex is associated with subsequent relapse in abstinent alcoholics. *Psychopharmacology, 175*(3), 296–302.

Gunzerath, L., & Goldman, D. (2003). G×E: A NIAAA workshop on gene–environment interactions. *Alcoholism: Clinical and Experimental Research, 27*, 540–562.

Guo, G., Wilhelmsen, K., & Hamilton, N. (2007). Gene–lifecourse interaction for alcohol consumption in adolescence and young adulthood: Five monoamine genes. *American Journal of Medical Genetics Part B: Neuropsychiatric Genetics, 144B*, 417–423.

Han, D. D., & Gu, H. H. (2006). Comparison of the monoamine transporters from human and mouse in their sensitivities to psychostimulant drugs. *BMC Pharmacology, 6*, 6.

Handley, E. D., & Chassin, L. (2013). Alcohol-specific parenting as a mechanism of parental drinking and alcohol use disorder risk on adolescent alcohol use onset. *Journal of Studies on Alcohol and Drugs, 74*(5), 684–693.

Harden, K. P., Patterson, M. W., Briley, D. A., Engelhardt, L. E., Kretsch, N., Mann, F. D., . . . Tucker-Drob, E. M. (2015). Developmental changes in genetic and environmental influences on rule-breaking and aggression: Age and pubertal development. *Journal of Child Psychology and Psychiatry, 56*(12), 1370–1379.

Hariri, A. R., Mattay, V. S., Tessitore, A., Bhaskar, K., Fera, F., Goldman, D., . . . Weinberger, D. R. (2002). Serotonin transporter genetic variation and the response of the human amygdala. *Science, 297*, 400–403.

Hart, A. B., & Kranzler, H. R. (2015). Alcohol dependence genetics: Lessons learned from genome-wide association studies (GWAS) and post-GWAS analyses. *Alcoholism: Clinical and Experimental Research, 39*(8), 1312–1327.

Heitzeg, M. M., Villafuerte, S., Weiland, B. J., Enoch, M. A., Burmeister, M., Zubieta, J. K., & Zucker,

R. A. (2014). Effect of GABRA2 genotype on development of incentive–motivation circuitry in a sample enriched for alcoholism risk. *Neuropsychopharmacology, 39*(13), 3077–3086.

Hicks, B. M., Foster, K. T., Iacono, W. G., & McGue, M. (2013). Genetic and environmental influences on the familial transmission of externalizing disorders in adoptive and twin offspring. *JAMA, 70*(10), 1076–1083.

Hicks, B. M., Krueger, R. F., Iacono, W. G., McGue, M., & Patrick, C. J. (2004). Family transmission and heritability of externalizing disorders. *Archives of General Psychiatry, 61*, 922–928.

Horowitz, R., Kotler, M., Shufman, E., Aharoni, S., Kremer, I., Cohen, H., & Ebstein, R. P. (2000). Confirmation of an excess of the high enzyme activity COMT val allele in heroin addicts in a family-based haplotype relative risk study. *American Journal of Medical Genetics, 96*(5), 599–603.

Hussong, A. M., Jones, D. J., Stein, G. L., Baucom, D. H., & Boeding, S. (2011). An internalizing pathway to alcohol use and disorder. *Psychology of Addictive Behaviors, 25*(3), 390–404.

Iacono, W. G., & Malone, S. M. (2011). Developmental endophenotypes: Indexing genetic risk for substance abuse with the P300 brain event-related potential. *Child Development Perspectives, 5*(4), 239–247.

Iacono, W. G., Malone, S. M., & McGue, M. (2008). Behavioral disinhibition and the development of early-onset addiction: Common and specific influences. *Annual Review of Clinical Psychology, 4*, 325–348.

Iacono, W. G., Vaidyanathan, U., Vrieze, S. I., & Malone, S. M. (2014). Knowns and unknowns for psychophysiological endophenotypes: Integration and response to commentaries. *Psychophysiology, 51*, 1339–1347.

Ioannidis, J. P. A., Trikalinos, T. A., & Khoury, M. J. (2006). Implications of small effect sizes of individual genetic variants on the design and interpretation of genetic association studies of complex diseases. *American Journal of Epidemiology, 164*, 609–614.

Johnston, L. D., O'Malley, P. M., Miech, R. A., Bachman, J. G., & Schulenberg, J. E. (2016). *Monitoring the Future national survey results on drug use, 1975–2015: Overview, key findings on adolescent drug use.* Ann Arbor, MI: Institute for Social Research, University of Michigan.

Kapoor, M., Chou, Y.-L., Edenberg, H. J., Foroud, T., Martin, N. G., Madden, P. A. F., . . . Agrawal, A. (2016). Genome-wide polygenic scores for age at onset of alcohol dependence and association with alcohol-related measures. *Translational Psychiatry*, 6, e761.

Kendler, K. S., & Neale, M. C. (2010). Endophenotype: A conceptual analysis. *Molecular Psychiatry*, 15, 789–797.

Kerr, M., Stattin, H., & Burk, W. J. (2010). A reinterpretation of parental monitoring in longitudinal perspective. *Journal of Research on Adolescence*, 20(1), 39–64.

Kluger, A. N., Siegfried, Z., & Ebstein, R. P. (2002). A meta-analysis of the association between DRD4 and novelty seeking. *Molecular Psychiatry*, 7, 712–717.

Kreek, M. J., Nielsen, D. A., & LaForge, K. S. (2004). Genes associated with addiction. *Neuromolecular Medicine*, 5(1), 85–108.

Kumar, S. K., Feldman, M. W., Rehkopf, D. H., & Tuljapurkar, S. (2016). Reply to Yang et al.: GCTA produces unreliable heritability estimates. *Proceedings of the National Academy of Sciences of the USA*, 113(2), E4581.

Larsen, H., van der Zwaluw, C. S., Overbeek, G., Granic, I., Franke, B., & Engels, R. C. (2010). A variable-number-of-tandem-repeats polymorphism in the dopamine D4 receptor gene affects social adaptation of alcohol use investigation of a gene–environment interaction. *Psychological Science*, 21(8), 1064–1068.

Lesch, K. P., Bengel, D., Heils, A., Sabol, S. Z., Greenberg, B. D., Petri, S., . . . Murphy, D. L. (1996). Association of anxiety-related traits with a polymorphism in the serotonin transporter gene regulatory region. *Science*, 274, 1527–1531.

Li, T., Chen, C. K., Hu, X., Ball, D., Lin, S. K., Chen, W., . . . Collier, D. A. (2004). Association analysis of the DRD4 and COMT genes in methamphetamine abuse. *American Journal of Medical Genetics Part B: Neuropsychiatric Genetics*, 129(1), 120–124.

Luczak, S. E., Glatt, S. J., & Wall, T. L. (2006). Meta-analyses of ALDH2 and ADH1B with alcohol dependence in Asians. *Psychological Bulletin*, 132, 607–621.

MacKillop, J., & Munafò, M. R. (2013). *Genetic influences on addiction: An intermediate phenotype approach*. Cambridge, MA: MIT Press.

Maher, B. S. (2015). Polygenic scores in epidemiology: Risk prediction, etiology, and clinical utility. *Current Epidemiology Reports*, 2(4), 239–244.

Manolio, T. A., Collins, F. S., Cox, N. J., Goldstein, D. B., Hindorff, L. A., Hunter, D. J., . . . Visscher, P. M. (2009). Finding the missing heritability of complex diseases. *Nature*, 461, 747–753.

Martel, M. M., Pierce, L., Nigg, J. T., Jester, J. M., Adams, K., Puttler, L. I., . . . Zucker, R. A. (2009). Temperament pathways to childhood disruptive

behavior and adolescent substance abuse: Testing a cascade model. *Journal of Abnormal Child Psychology*, 37, 363–373.

McCarthy, M. I., Abecasis, G. R., Cardon, L. R., Goldstein, D. B., Little, J., Ioannidis, J. P., & Hirschhom, J. N. (2008). Genome-wide association studies for complex traits: Consensus, uncertainty and challenges. *Nature Reviews Genetics*, 9(5), 356–369.

Merenäkk, L., Maestu, J., Nordquist, N., Parik, J., Oreland, L., Loit, H., & Harro, J. (2011). Effects of the serotonin transporter (5-HTTLPR) and α2A-adrenoceptor (C-1291G) genotypes on substance use in children and adolescents: A longitudinal study. *Psychopharmacology*, 215, 13–22.

Meyer-Lindenberg, A., & Weinberger, D. R. (2006). Intermediate phenotypes and genetic mechanisms of psychiatric disorders. *Nature Reviews Neuroscience*, 7(10), 818–827.

Munafò, M. R., Yalcin, B., Willis-Owen, S. A., & Flint, J. (2008). Association of the dopamine D4 receptor (DRD4) gene and approach-related personality traits: Meta-analysis and new data. *Biological Psychiatry*, 63(1), 197–206.

Musci, R., & Schlomer, G. L. (in press). The implications of genetics for prevention and intervention programming. *Prevention Science*.

Narusyte, J., Neiderhiser, J. M., D'Onofrio, B. M., Reiss, D., Spotts, E. L., Ganiban, J., & Lichtenstein, P. (2008). Testing different types of genotype–environment correlation: An extended children-of-twins model. *Developmental Psychology*, 44(6), 1591–1603.

Nikolova, Y. S., Ferrell, R. E., Manuck, S. B., & Hariri, A. R. (2011). Multilocus genetic profile for dopamine signaling predicts ventral striatum reactivity. *Neuropsychopharmacology*, 36(9), 1940–1947.

Patrick, C. J., Bernat, E. M., Malone, S. M., Iacono, W. G., Krueger, R. F., & McGue, M. (2006). P300 amplitude as an indicator of externalizing in adolescent males. *Psychophysiology*, 43(1), 84–92.

Pearson, T. A., & Manolio, T. A. (2008). How to interpret a genome-wide association study. *JAMA*, 299, 1335–1344.

Pieters, S., van der Zwaluw, C. S., van der Vorst, H., Wiers, R. W., Smeets, H., Lambrichs, E., . . . Engels, R. C. M. E. (2012). The moderating effect of alcohol-specific parental rule-setting on the relation between the dopamine D2 receptor gene (DRD2), the mu-opioid receptor gene (OPRM1) and alcohol use in young adolescents. *Alcohol and Alcoholism*, 47(6), 663–670.

Plomin, R., DeFries, J., Knopik, V. S., & Neiderhiser, J. M. (2013). *Behavioral genetics* (6th ed.). London, UK: Worth.

Polderman, T. J., Benyamin, B., De Leeuw, C. A., Sullivan, P. F., Van Bochoven, A., Visscher, P. M., & Posthuma, D. (2015). Meta-analysis of the heritability of human traits based on fifty years of twin studies. *Nature Genetics, 47*(7), 702–709.

Polich, J. (2007). Updating P300: An integrative theory of P3a and P3b. *Clinical Neurophysiology, 118,* 2128–2148.

Polich, J., Pollock, V. E., & Bloom, F. E. (1994). Meta-analysis of P300 amplitude from males at risk for alcoholism. *Psychological Bulletin, 115,* 55–73.

Rangaswamy, M., Porjesz, B., Chorlian, D. B., Wang, K., Jones, K. A., Bauer, L. O., . . . Begleiter, H. (2002). Beta power in the EEG of alcoholics. *Biological Psychiatry, 52*(8), 831–842.

Rangaswamy, M., Porjesz, B., Chorlian, D. B., Wang, K., Jones, K. A., Kuperman, S., . . . Begleiter, H. (2004). Resting EEG in offspring of male alcoholics: Beta frequencies. *International Journal of Psychophysiology, 51*(3), 239–251.

Rasetti, R., & Weinberger, D. R. (2011). Intermediate phenotypes in psychiatric disorders. *Current Opinion in Genetics and Development, 21*(3), 340–348.

Ray, L. A., Bryan, A., MacKillop, J., McGeary, J., Hesterberg, K., & Hutchinson, K. E. (2009). The dopamine D4 Receptor (DRD4) gene exon III polymorphism, problematic alcohol use and novelty seeking: Direct and mediated genetic effects. *Addiction Biology, 4*(2), 238–244.

Ray, L. A., & Hutchison, K. E. (2004). A polymorphism of the μ-opioid receptor gene (OPRM1) and sensitivity to the effect of alcohol in humans. *Alcoholism: Clinical and Experimental Research, 28,* 1789–1795.

Rose, R. J., Dick, D. M., Viken, R. J., Pulkkinen, L., & Kaprio, J. (2001). Drinking or abstaining at age 14? A genetic epidemiological study. *Alcoholism: Clinical and Experimental Research, 25*(11), 1594–1604.

Russell, M. A., Schlomer, G. L., Cleveland, H. H., Feinberg, M. E., Greenberg, M. T., Spoth, R. L., . . . Vandenbergh, D. J. (2017). PROSPER intervention effects on adolescents' alcohol misuse by GABRA2 genotype and age. *Prevention Science.*

Rutter, M., Bolton, P., Harrington, R., Couteur, A., Macdonald, H., & Simonoff, E. (1990). Genetic factors in child psychiatric disorders—I. A review of research strategies. *Journal of Child Psychology and Psychiatry, 31*(1), 3–37.

Schlomer, G. L., Cleveland, H. H., Feinberg, M. E., Wolf, P. S. A., Greenberg, M. T., Spoth, R. L., . . . Vandenbergh, D. J. (2017). Extending previous cG×I findings on 5-HTTLPR's moderation of intervention effects on adolescent substance misuse initiation. *Child Development.*

Schlomer, G. L., & Ellis, B. J. (in press). Sibling studies. In T. K. Shackelford & V. A. Weekes-Shackelford (Eds.), *Encyclopedia of evolutionary psychological science.* New York, NY: Springer.

Schoots, O., & Van Tol, H. H. (2003). The human dopamine D4 receptor repeat sequences modulate expression. *Pharmacogenomics Journal, 3,* 343–348.

Silberg, J. L., & Eaves, L. J. (2004). Analysing the contributions of genes and parent–child interaction to childhood behavioural and emotional problems: A model for the children of twins. *Psychological Medicine, 34*(2), 347–356.

Slutske, W. S., Heath, A. C., Dinwiddie, S. H., Madden, P. A., Bucholz, K. K., Dunne, M. P., . . . Martin, N. G. (1998). Common genetic risk factors for conduct disorder and alcohol dependence. *Journal of Abnormal Psychology, 107*(3), 363–374.

Slutske, W. S., Heath, A. C., Madden, P. A., Bucholz, K. K., Statham, D. J., & Martin, N. G. (2002). Personality and the genetic risk for alcohol dependence. *Journal of Abnormal Psychology, 111*(1), 124–133.

Stogner, J. M. (2015). DAT1 and alcohol use: Differential responses to life stress during adolescence. *Criminal Justice Studies, 28*(1), 18–38.

Takeshita, T., & Morimoto, K. (1999). Self-reported alcohol-associated symptoms and drinking behavior in three *ALDH2* genotypes among Japanese university students. *Alcoholism: Clinical and Experimental Research, 23*(6), 1065–1069.

Trucco, E. M., Colder, C. R., & Wieczorek, W. F. (2011). Vulnerability to peer influence: A moderated mediation study of early adolescent alcohol use initiation. *Addictive Behaviors, 36,* 729–736.

Trucco, E. M., Colder, C. R., Wieczorek, W. F., Lengua, L. J., & Hawk, L. W. J. (2014). Early adolescent alcohol use in context: How neighborhoods, parents, and peers impact youth. *Development and Psychopathology, 26,* 425–436.

Trucco, E. M., Hicks, B. M., Villafuerte, S., Nigg, J. T., Burmeister, M., & Zucker, R. A. (2016). Temperament and externalizing behavior as mediators of genetic risk on adolescent substance use. *Journal of Abnormal Child Psychology, 125*(4), 565–575.

Trucco, E. M., Villafuerte, S., Heitzeg, M. M., Burmeister, M., & Zucker, R. A. (2014). Rule breaking mediates the developmental association between GABRA2 and adolescent substance abuse. *Journal of Child Psychology and Psychiatry, 55*(12), 1372–1379.

Trucco, E. M., Villafuerte, S., Heitzeg, M. M., Burmeister, M., & Zucker, R. A. (2016). Susceptibility effects of GABA receptor subunit alpha-2 (GABRA2) variants and parental monitoring on externalizing behavior trajectories: Risk and protection conveyed by the minor allele. *Development and Psychopathology*, 28(1), 15–26.

Trucco, E. M., Wright, A. G. C., & Colder, C. R. (2014). Stability and change of social goals in adolescence. *Journal of Personality*, 82(5), 379–389.

Tucker, J. S., Ellickson, P. L., Orlando, M., Martino, S. C., & Klein, D. J. (2005). Substance use trajectories from early adolescence to emerging adulthood: A comparison of smoking, binge drinking, and marijuana use. *Journal of Drug Issues*, 35(2), 307–332.

van Beek, J. H. D. A., Kendler, K. S., de Moor, M. H. M., Geels, L. M., Bartels, M., Vink, J. M., . . . Boomsma, D. I. (2012). Stable genetic effects on symptoms of alcohol abuse and dependence from adolescence into early adulthood. *Behavior Genetics*, 42, 40–56.

Van Beijsterveldt, C. E., Molenaar, P. C., de Geus, E. J., & Boomsma, D. (1996). Heritability of human brain functioning as assessed by electroencephalography. *American Journal of Human Genetics*, 58, 562–573.

Vandenbergh, D. J., & Schlomer, G. L. (2014). Finding genomic function for genetic associations in nicotine addiction research: The ENCODE project's role in future pharmacogenomic analysis. *Pharmacology Biochemistry and Behavior*, 123, 34–44.

van der Zwaluw, C. S., Engels, R. C. M. E., Vermulst, A. A., Franke, B., Buitelaar, J., Verkes, R. J., & Scholte, R. H. J. (2010). Interaction between dopamine D2 receptor genotype and parental rule-setting in adolescent alcohol use: Evidence for a gene–parenting interaction. *Molecular Psychiatry*, 15(7), 727–735.

van der Zwaluw, C. S., Kuntsche, E., & Engels, R. C. M. E. (2011). Risky alcohol use in adolescence: The role of genetics (DRD2, SLC6A4) and coping motives. *Alcoholism: Clinical and Experimental Research*, 35(4), 756–764.

Volkow, N. D., Fowler, J. S., & Wang, G. J. (2002). Role of dopamine in drug reinforcement and addiction in humans: Results from imaging studies. *Behavioral Pharmacology*, 13, 355–366.

Volpicelli, J. R., Watson, N. T., King, A. C., Sherman, C. E., & O'Brien, C. P. (1995). Effect of naltrexone on alcohol "high" in alcoholics. *American Journal of Psychiatry*, 152(4), 613–615.

Vrieze, S. I., Hicks, B. M., Iacono, W. G., & McGue, M. (2012). Decline in genetic influence on the co-occurrence of alcohol, marijuana, and nicotine dependence symptoms from age 14 to 29. *American Journal of Psychiatry*, 169(10), 1073–1081.

Wang, F., Simen, A., Arias, A., Lu, Q. W., & Zhang, H. (2013). A large-scale meta-analysis of the association between the ANKK1/DRD2 Taq1A polymorphism and alcohol dependence. *Human Genetics*, 132, 347–358.

West-Eberhard, M. J. (2003). *Developmental plasticity and evolution*. New York, NY: Oxford University Press.

Yang, J., Lee, S. H., Goddard, M. E., & Visscher, P. M. (2011). GCTA: A tool for genome-wide complex trait analysis. *American Journal of Human Genetics*, 88(1), 76–82.

5

Alcohol Use Disorder

Role of Epigenetics

Igor Ponomarev

Although most people consume alcohol (ethanol) in moderation, nearly 40% of US adults drink in excess of the low-risk guidelines established by the National Institute on Alcohol Abuse and Alcoholism (NIAAA, 2016). Alcohol misuse can lead to clinically significant impairments in health and social function. The fifth edition of the *Diagnostic and Statistical Manual of Mental Disorders* (DSM-5; American Psychiatric Association, 2013) integrates alcohol abuse and alcohol dependence into a single disorder called alcohol use disorder (AUD). Twin, adoption, and family studies have established that genetic factors account for approximately half a person's risk for developing AUD. The other half is influenced by environmental factors, the most critical of which is the repeated exposure to alcohol. Despite decades of research, the exact mechanisms underlying genetic contributions to AUD etiology, as well as the role of gene–environment interactions, are not well understood. The search for genetic variants affecting the development of AUD in humans has been somewhat challenging because findings from genome-wide association studies could account for only a small portion of the epidemiologically estimated heritability. A growing resolve to discover the mechanisms underlying this "missing heritability" contributed to a recent influx of studies focusing on the epigenetics of alcohol-related conditions.

The term *epigenetics*, first coined by Conrad Waddington in the 1940s as a "whole complex of developmental processes" connecting genotype to phenotype (Waddington, 1942/2012), has evolved into the current generally accepted definition of "'the study of changes in gene function that are mitotically and/or

meiotically heritable and that do not entail a change in DNA sequence'" (Wu & Morris, 2001, p. 1104). To become "functional," genes must first be transcribed. The transcriptional status (activation or repression) of a gene is determined by the conformational state of chromatin (the complex of chromosomal DNA and proteins) and by the recruitment of transcription factors to DNA regulatory sites (Copeland, Olhava, & Scott, 2010). The fundamental unit of chromatin is the nucleosome, which consists of approximately 147 base pairs of DNA wrapped around a core of eight histone proteins, with each octamer containing two copies of the histones H2A, H2B, H3, and H4. Both DNA and amino acid residues on the N-terminal tails of histones can be modified by covalent addition of several chemical groups, including methyl (DNA and histones), acetyl, and phosphate (histones), which can result in altered chromatin states and downstream gene expression (Bernstein, Meissner, & Lander, 2007; Borrelli, Nestler, Allis, & Sassone-Corsi, 2008). In addition to DNA and histone modifications (epigenetic marks), the incorporation of histone variants, nucleosome repositioning, and regulation of gene expression by small noncoding RNAs, such as microRNAs (miRNAs), are also considered epigenetic phenomena that play important roles in regulating gene expression.

A central biological question is to understand how a single genome can give rise to an organism comprising hundreds of distinct cell types. Epigenetic systems play a critical role in embryonic development and cellular differentiation. By activating some genes while inhibiting the expression of others during development, epigenetic programs define cell identity. Embryonic development progresses from a single fertilized egg cell to a zygote that continues to divide, ultimately resulting in different cell types in an organism, including neurons, glia, and immune cells. Epigenetic modifications can occur as early as fertilization with the removal of methyl groups in paternal DNA, followed by similar changes in the zygote and embryo, and also during germ cell lineage specification and organ-specific cell differentiation (Cortessis et al., 2012).

Three important features of epigenetic changes are heritability, stability, and reversibility. Mitotic heritability refers to transmission of epigenetic states from progenitor to daughter cells through cell division within a single organism, whereas transmission of epigenetic information between generations via germ line cells represents meiotic heritability (Wu & Morris, 2001). It has been suggested that the latter may, at least in part, explain cases of "missing heritability" in complex disorders (Miranda, Salem, Fincher, Mahnke, & Burrowes, 2016). Many chromatin marks, especially DNA methylation, are stable modifications that can remain unchanged during a lifespan, whereas others, such as histone acetylation, are transient in nature (Barth & Imhof, 2010). Importantly, unlike genetic mutations, epigenetic modifications are reversible and, therefore, can change in response to environmental challenges and have the potential to be manipulated therapeutically. For example, the notion of irreversibility of epigenetic states in terminally differentiated cells has been critically challenged by Takahashi and Yamanaka (2006), who demonstrated that the introduction of only four transcription factors epigenetically reprogrammed differentiated fibroblasts into induced pluripotent stem cells capable of differentiation to endodermal, ectodermal, and mesodermal lineages. Chromatin modifications in terminally differentiated post-mitotic cells, such as most neurons, are not heritable but can nevertheless be stable, leading to long-term changes in patterns of gene expression. Such changes can also be considered epigenetic. However, there is some debate in the field concerning whether to promote a more narrow definition that only includes heritable modifications (Isles, 2015; Ptashne, 2007).

Early epigenetic research of neuropsychiatric conditions, including drug addiction, targeted different chromatin marks at promoters of individual genes, revealing disease-associated molecular changes (Nestler, Pena, Kundakovic, Mitchell, & Akbarian, 2016; Renthal & Nestler, 2009). The development of genome-wide DNA methylation and chromatin immunoprecipitation followed by next-generation sequencing (ChIP-Seq) approaches allowed parallel measurements of chromatin marks at multiple genomic locations on a massive scale. More important, combined with global gene expression (transcriptome) profiling by microarrays or RNA-Seq, this approach revealed fundamental mechanisms of epigenetic control of gene expression. In a seminal paper, Ernst and colleagues (2011) used a combination of the ChIP-Seq approach and transcriptome profiling by microarrays to study genomic distributions of several chromatin marks and DNA-binding proteins in nine cell types. By studying correlations between chromatin marks and gene expression, the authors distinguished 15 distinct chromatin states classified into six broad categories, which they referred to as promoter, enhancer, insulator, transcribed, repressed, and inactive states. Importantly, they identified chromatin marks that could describe these states in a non-redundant manner. These findings also indicate that in simplified terms, chromatin exists in two states: a relaxed, open state (euchromatin), which allows individual genes to be regulated and transcribed, and a condensed, closed state (heterochromatin), which represses gene transcription.

Various chromatin marks contribute differently to chromatin states and regulation of gene expression. For example, DNA methylation of gene promoters is generally associated with transcriptional repression, whereas histone acetylation is generally associated with transcriptional activation (Bernstein et al., 2007). Detailed discussion of basic mechanisms of chromatin modifications and current literature on epigenetics of alcohol-related conditions is beyond the scope of this chapter but can be found in several recent reviews (Andersen, Dogan, Beach, & Philibert, 2015; Finegersh, Rompala, Martin, & Homanics, 2015; Krishnan, Sakharkar, Teppen, Berkel, & Pandey, 2014; Marballi, Ponomarev, Mayfield, & Harris, 2014; Miranda et al., 2016; Ponomarev, 2013; Schuebel, Gitik, Domschke, & Goldman, 2016; Tulisiak, Harris, & Ponomarev, 2017). The goal of the current review is to provide critical discussion of the role of epigenetic systems in the etiology of AUD and the potential of epigenetic research to improve diagnosis, prevention, and treatment of alcohol-related problems. Challenges of the current epigenetic approaches and future directions are also discussed.

EPIGENETICS OF ALCOHOL: A PRIMER

With the invention of new genomic and transcriptomic approaches to study global gene expression, there has been considerable progress in our understanding of the molecular mechanisms of alcohol and other drugs of abuse. Microarray and RNA-Seq studies have successfully identified multiple candidate genes associated with either genetic predisposition to alcohol consumption (Mulligan et al., 2006) or the effects of alcohol self-administration in humans and animal models (Farris, Arasappan, Hunicke-Smith, Harris, & Mayfield, 2015; Flatscher-Bader et al., 2006; Liu et al., 2006; Ponomarev, Wang, Zhang, Harris, & Mayfield, 2012; Z. Zhou, Yuan, Mash, & Goldman, 2011). Increasing evidence indicates that alcohol-induced changes in gene expression are mediated, at least in part, by epigenetic mechanisms that alter chromatin structure.

As with many other complex traits, AUD can be viewed in the framework of systems biology, a cross-disciplinary field frequently defined as "the study of all of the elements in a biological system and their relationship to one another in response to perturbation" (Stephens & Rung, 2006, p. 240). In the context of AUD, systems biology seeks to understand the mechanistic transitions between variations in DNA

sequence (the genome) and variations in cellular and behavioral phenotypes, as well as how neurobiological systems as a whole respond to environmental challenges, such as alcohol, stress, diet, and toxins (Figure 5.1).

The epigenome plays a critical role in "translating" the genomic information into cell type-specific transcriptional programs and also in mediating environmental effects. Thus, epigenetic mechanisms may be key regulators of gene–environment interactions and may explain why some people are more likely than others to develop alcohol-related diseases, which could not be explained by genetic factors alone. A hypothetical diagram of the role of DNA methylation in gene–environment interactions is shown in Figure 5.2. Genomic DNA is modified by methylation of cytosines within 5′—cytosine (C)—phosphate (p)—guanine (G)—3′ dinucleotide sites (CpGs) of genes by the DNA methyltransferase (DNMT) class of enzymes. A cytosine (C) to thymine (T) single nucleotide polymorphism introduces a possibility of cytosine methylation in genotype 1, but not genotype 2, which represents a *cis*-regulated methylation quantitative trait locus (mQTL)—that is, a genetic variant leading to differential methylation. Alcohol can produce DNA demethylation by a variety of mechanisms (Hamid, Wani, & Kaur, 2009), and environmental exposure to alcohol during a critical stage can result in the removal of the methyl group in genotype 1 and downstream changes in gene expression, as well as altered cellular and behavioral

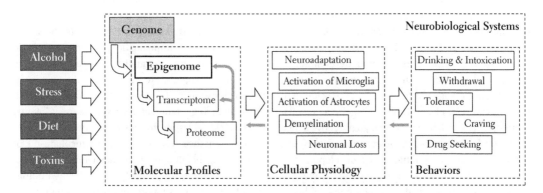

FIGURE 5.1 A systems biology view of AUD in the context of neurobiological mechanisms. AUD, characterized by behavioral changes such as alcohol tolerance and drug seeking, is a result of the complex interplay between genetic and environmental factors. Chemical modifications of chromatin (epigenome) may serve as an intermediary mechanism in the gene–environment interaction effects, resulting in downstream molecular and cellular changes associated with the disease.

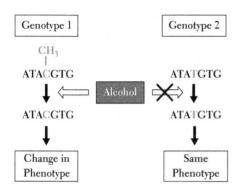

FIGURE 5.2 A simplified example of how epigenetics (DNA methylation) can play a mechanistic role in gene–environment interactions. Alcohol exposure can cause a loss in DNA methylation (epimutation) in genotype 1 but not genotype 2. This epimutation can be meiotically and/or mitotically heritable and cause downstream changes in gene expression and functional abnormalities associated with AUD. CH_3, methylation of cytosine (C) in genotype 1.

phenotypes. If occurring early in life, this epimutation can be transmitted to other cells in the body via mitotic inheritance, resulting in an abnormal phenotype. At the same time, alcohol exposure will not affect genotype 2.

Because of the critical role of epigenetic mechanisms in prenatal and early postnatal development, environmental exposures during early development may have broader impact on epigenetic states and brain circuits than similar exposures later in life. It is therefore important to evaluate the effects of alcohol across the life cycle. The NIAAA-adopted "lifespan approach" to alcohol research considers how the emergence and progression of drinking behavior and related outcomes interact with developmental changes and environmental inputs across the lifespan, from the embryonic and fetal stages of development to adolescence and adulthood. Epigenetic mechanisms of gene regulation may offer an attractive explanation for how early life exposures to alcohol, stress, and other stimuli contribute to the development of AUD and induce long-lasting changes in the brain.

Alcohol is particularly damaging to the fetal brain. Alcohol consumption during pregnancy can result in a complex of physiological and anatomical abnormalities including neurocognitive deficits, which are collectively termed "fetal alcohol spectrum disorders" (FASD) (Miranda et al., 2016). There is abundant

evidence from FASD research that prenatal ethanol exposure causes chromatin modifications, particularly in terms of altered DNA methylation. For example, fetuses from ethanol-treated mice exhibit global DNA hypomethylation in addition to inhibited DNMT activity (Garro, McBeth, Lima, & Lieber, 1991). Alcohol exposure can cause widespread perturbations in methylation programming and cellular differentiation, which can contribute to developmental disorders and neurobehavioral deficits that can persist into adulthood (Lunde et al., 2016; F. C. Zhou, Balaraman, et al., 2011; F. C. Zhou, Chen, & Love, 2011).

Although prenatal alcohol models have typically focused on maternal exposure, there is accumulating evidence that paternal ethanol exposure may modify the sperm epigenome, which may be meiotically inherited, leading to functional changes in the offspring. Paternal drinking may lead to altered DNMT activity and methylation profiles in gametes, which can potentially cause alterations in methylation reprogramming and epigenetic inheritance (Finegersh et al., 2015). For example, paternal ethanol exposure in rats produced decreased cytosine methyltransferase mRNA levels in sperm and significantly decreased the mean fetal weight, suggesting that decreased DNA methylation in the germ line could produce anatomical abnormalities in the offspring (Bielawski, Zaher, Svinarich, & Abel, 2002). Another example of transgenerational effects is heritable hypermethylation of the gene encoding pro-opiomelanocortin (POMC), which further demonstrates the diverse effects of alcohol on DNA methylation (Govorko, Bekdash, Zhang, & Sarkar, 2012). Govorko and colleagues showed that fetal alcohol-induced hypermethylation of the *Pomc* promoter transferred across generations in the sperm and hypothalamus, implying both meiotic and mitotic inheritance of this epimutation. Importantly, these molecular changes were associated with deficits in gene expression and POMC-related neuronal functions, including an increased stress response (Govorko et al., 2012). Despite the growing interest in epigenetic inheritance research, the exact mechanisms of these transgenerational phenomena remain unclear (Heard & Martienssen, 2014). Collectively, findings from FASD studies support epigenetic mechanisms as potential contributors to the deficits observed following prenatal alcohol exposure. They also illustrate that alcohol-induced effects depend on particular time points during development, which further highlights the dynamic nature of epigenetic modifications.

The recent focus on epigenetic mechanisms of AUD produced an inpouring of studies encompassing different species, animal models, experimental designs, and developmental time points (reviewed in Schuebel et al., 2016; Tulisiak et al., 2017). Current evidence supports the hypothesis that alcohol exposure is associated with global epigenetic changes, which may mechanistically contribute to alcohol-induced changes in cellular functions and behaviors. Overall, there is a relationship between alcohol and epigenetic modifications in a wide variety of contexts. In humans, multiple studies have reported alcohol-associated changes in global DNA methylation in both brain and blood, with a general tendency of hypomethylation effects in brain and the opposite trend in blood (Ponomarev, 2013). Differences between the two tissues may reflect the cell type specificity of DNA modification profiles. Compared to human studies, animal models offer the advantage of discovering causative factors related to alcohol exposure. This includes identifying critical epigenetic factors controlling alcohol-induced gene expression, specific roles of epigenetic enzymes in different cell types, and the effects of epigenetic drugs on brain and behavior. Multiple CpG sites have been discovered that may mediate alcohol-induced gene expression in neurons and other brain cells. Time-course studies suggest that epigenetic modifications are involved in neuroadaptive responses to alcohol. Taken together, these studies indicate that the relationships between epigenetic modifications and alcohol traits are complex and depend on many factors, such as species, gender, tissue and cell type, method and duration of alcohol exposure, and the developmental stage of the animal model. Most important, the collective knowledge obtained from these studies can potentially be used to identify reliable biomarkers to improve diagnosis and/or evaluate risks for alcohol-induced pathologies and to promote development of novel therapies for the treatment of AUD.

EPIGENETIC BIOMARKERS AND DIAGNOSTICS

Epigenetic modifications have been recognized as valuable biomarkers for cancer and other disease states. A general purpose of a clinical biomarker is to inform clinicians about the presence or absence of a disease (diagnostic value), the patient prognosis (prognostic value), the response to a specific treatment (predictive value), or future risks of disease development or recurrence (García-Giménez et al., 2012). Critical properties of clinical biomarkers are specificity, sensitivity, and stability. Some epigenetic factors (e.g., DNA methylation and miRNAs) are highly stable and represent excellent targets for biomarker development. One of the most promising features of epigenetic biomarkers is that they may be useful for the development of improved personalized/precision medicine tools. Some epigenetic biomarkers may undergo dynamic changes based on environmental exposures, disease progression, or responses to treatment, which can be used to adjust existing or develop new treatment strategies. For many central disorders, brain tissue is not routinely accessible in clinical practice, but peripheral tissues, such as blood and saliva, have been used instead in biomarker research.

Developing molecular diagnostic tools and identifying risk biomarkers may complement the existing methods used to detect alcohol-induced pathologies and advance therapeutics for AUD (Portales-Casamar et al., 2016). The number of human studies using genome-wide measurements of DNA methylation and miRNAs in peripheral tissues as potential biomarkers of AUD has increased in recent years (Andersen et al., 2015; Portales-Casamar et al., 2016; Soares do Amaral, Cruz E Melo, de Melo Maia, & Malagoli Rocha, 2016; Szabo & Satishchandran, 2015). The vast majority of these studies have examined samples pre-exposed to alcohol, which provided some valuable information on epigenetic changes associated with alcohol-induced pathologies. However, this approach is limited because it is usually impossible to establish whether altered epigenetic patterns are a risk factor *for* or a consequence *of* alcohol use, which limits their predictive value as a biomarker. In addition, most studies have focused on a single time point, which given the dynamic nature of epigenetic changes may not capture the full spectrum of responses that occur over time. To identify reliable risk biomarkers for various alcohol-associated conditions, longitudinal studies with measurements taken over different time periods—spanning alcohol pre-exposure, exposure, and abstinence—may be required.

Early identification of problematic drinking patterns and relapse drinking during and after treatment is needed to advance the treatment outlook for AUD. A recent longitudinal study of 244 subjects from the

Avon Longitudinal Study of Parents and Children examined whether DNA methylation patterns in early life were prospectively associated with substance use in adolescence (Cecil et al., 2016). DNA methylation was measured at birth and at age 7 years, and substance use (tobacco, alcohol, and cannabis) was evaluated at ages 14–18 years. When measured at birth, 65 methylation loci were associated with greater levels of substance use during adolescence, as well as an earlier age of onset among users. Despite a relatively weak association between epigenetic marks and behavior and lack of consistency between measurements taken at different time points, this study nevertheless presents a valuable approach to discovering risk biomarkers for substance use disorders. Another study examined DNA methylation in peripheral mononuclear cells in subjects with heavy alcohol use at two time points—before and 4 weeks after alcohol treatment (Philibert et al., 2014). Compared with abstinent controls, subjects with heavy alcohol use showed widespread changes in DNA methylation that had a tendency to reverse following a period of abstinence. This approach could help identify biomarkers for monitoring treatment response and assessing the risk of relapse. If validated, the methylation panels from these studies may potentially be used as epigenetic biomarkers of alcohol-associated conditions.

Additional factors must be taken into consideration when developing biomarker panels based on peripheral tissue samples. Because DNA methylation is cell type specific, individual variability in blood cell counts is an important factor. Blood is a renewable resource: The circulating half-life for most nuclear blood cells is days to weeks (Hasegawa et al., 2009). If alcohol-associated methylation changes occur in differentiated circulating cells, and not in the progenitor cells, these changes may disappear when the cells are replaced. Despite these limitations, using peripheral blood to identify biomarkers for central disorders remains a promising area of study.

EPIGENETIC ADVANCES IN THE PREVENTION AND TREATMENT OF ALCOHOL USE DISORDER

Prevention of alcohol-related problems relies heavily on recognizing the risk of developing AUD. This task not only involves reliable diagnostics and risk biomarkers but also requires mechanistic knowledge. For central conditions, such as AUD, this knowledge can be obtained from a wealth of epigenetic data collected from postmortem human brains (Tulisiak et al., 2017; Z. Zhou et al., 2011) and animal models (Krishnan et al., 2014; Marballi et al., 2014; Miranda et al., 2016) by comparing alcohol and control groups. Some biomarker studies have suggested that epigenetic changes occurring in peripheral tissues, such as blood, parallel those in the brain. This has led to the generation of hypotheses about central mechanisms based on findings from peripheral tissues. However, given the cell type specificity of epigenetic profiles, results obtained from peripheral tissues cannot be easily extrapolated to central mechanisms. One way to better predict brain-related changes based on peripheral findings is to identify a subset of epigenetic marks that are consistently correlated across tissues. One example of such an analysis is the identification of the "epigenetic clock," a panel of 353 CpG sites that can reliably predict biological aging based on their methylation profiles across various human tissues (Horvath, 2013). Identifying such a panel in response to alcohol exposure in humans will be challenging, but different animal models are readily available and can help identify the common molecular networks across tissues. Interestingly, another biological marker of aging, chromosome telomere length in peripheral blood leucocytes, was shown to be altered by alcohol; for example, heavy alcohol users had significantly shorter telomeres, which correlated with early onset of cancer and other aging-related diseases (Pavanello et al., 2011). Telomere length is regulated epigenetically (Blasco, 2007), and if this marker is proven to be consistent across tissues, alcohol-induced telomere shortening in peripheral blood could be used as a predictor for brain abnormalities associated with AUD.

As with other disease states, the effect of diet is an important area of research in the context of prevention and treatment of alcohol-related problems. Chronic alcohol causes vitamin B and folate deficiencies that negatively affect one-carbon metabolism and can result in homocysteinemia and decreased production of S-adenosylmethionine (SAM), the methyl group donor in most transmethylation reactions (Hamid et al., 2009). Alcohol-induced decreases in SAM, as well as other alcohol-mediated effects, such as acetaldehyde-induced inhibition of DNMT1 (Garro et al., 1991) and 5-methylcytosine demethylation induced by DNA damage and repair (Chen,

Pan, Chen, & Huang, 2011), can cause global DNA hypomethylation. DNA hypomethylation was reported in several peripheral tissues from alcohol-related models, and it has been proposed to play a role in alcoholic liver disease, fetal alcohol syndrome, and colon cancer (Choi et al., 1999; Garro et al., 1991; Lu et al., 2000; Shukla et al., 2008).

One of the first indications that dietary changes regulate alcohol consumption can be traced back to the 1940s and 1950s to the work of Roger J. Williams, a biochemistry professor at The University of Texas at Austin. He showed that diets deficient in B vitamins, folic acid, and choline increased, whereas vitamin-enriched diets decreased, consumption of 10% ethanol in some rats (Williams, Berry, & Beerstecher, 1949). It is now well established that folates and several other vitamins from the B group are critical for one-carbon metabolism and the synthesis of SAM (Hamid et al., 2009). It is possible that these dietary changes affect alcohol consumption via changes in DNA methylation and methylation-regulated gene expression. Human studies have tested SAM, folates, choline, and other "methyl-enriched" components to prevent/treat alcohol-related problems with mixed success. Nevertheless, the potential to decrease excessive drinking through dietary changes remains high.

There are only three US Food and Drug Administration (FDA)-approved drugs (disulfiram, naltrexone, and acamprosate) for the treatment of alcohol dependence, and none of these have shown consistent effects in clinical trials. Therefore, research aimed at developing prevention and treatment strategies for AUD is certainly warranted. Small molecule inhibitors of enzymes that modify DNA and histones, such as DNA methyltransferase inhibitors (DNMTi) and histone deacetylase inhibitors (HDACi), have the potential to change gene expression and downstream behaviors via regulation of chromatin structure (Abel & Zukin, 2008; Spanagel, 2009). These epigenetic drugs have been extensively studied in the treatment of somatic diseases such as cancer, leading to their approval for use in patients (Copeland et al., 2010), and have recently emerged as potential therapeutics for neurodegenerative disorders and drug addiction (Coppedè, 2014; Ponomarev, 2013; Walker, Cates, Heller, & Nestler, 2015).

The effects of HDACi and DNMTi on different alcohol behaviors were demonstrated by several research groups (Barbier et al., 2015; Pandey, Ugale, Zhang, Tang, & Prakash, 2008; Sanchis-Segura, Lopez-Atalaya, & Barco, 2009; Warnault, Darcq, Levine, Barak, & Ron, 2013; Wolstenholme et al., 2011). High alcohol consumption is a prerequisite for developing AUD, and compounds that can reduce drinking are of particular importance for drug development. For example, the FDA-approved drugs azacitidine (a DNMTi) and vorinostat, also known as SAHA (an HDACi), both reduced ethanol consumption in mice (Warnault et al., 2013). It has been hypothesized that these drugs act by altering brain gene expression; however, the specific mechanisms underlying these drug-induced changes in alcohol behaviors have not been determined. Examining the central mechanisms of action of FDA-approved drugs that are known to target peripheral diseases may assist in repurposing these compounds for drug addiction and other brain disorders.

FUTURE DIRECTIONS

The most important contribution of animal research is to ultimately offer implications for the human condition. The translation of results from animal models to clinical settings remains one of the major challenges in alcohol research because it is not clear how well some animal models represent different aspects of alcohol use and abuse in humans. Given the discrepancies between some animal and human studies, it is important to identify mechanistic similarities and differences between human conditions and their animal models. This can be done via carefully designed meta-analytical studies across experiments and species, with results of such analyses building a foundation for future clinical studies. Such comparisons can provide insights into the epigenetic mechanisms of AUD, distinguishing pre-existing epigenetically driven susceptibility to alcohol abuse and alcohol-induced epigenetic states that mediate downstream changes in cellular function and behavior.

There have been increasing efforts to repurpose (reposition) FDA-approved drugs for the treatment of various conditions, including drug addiction. The primary advantage of such strategies is that the time to clinical trial can be greatly reduced. As discussed previously, some FDA-approved epigenetic drugs have shown promising effects in animal models of alcohol consumption. AUD is a multigenic disease, and one advantage of identifying epigenetic compounds that act as "master regulators" is that their effects on gene networks, rather than single genes, could offer greater potential to correct abnormal gene expression patterns associated with the disease.

A promising approach to drug repurposing is based on the reanalysis of large amounts of genomic data collected during the past two decades. A fundamental challenge in biomedicine is to understand the association among diseases, their cellular and molecular processes (e.g., epigenetic modifications and gene expression), and the action of small molecule therapeutics. Developing reference databases and integrating resources across biological modalities offer a solution to this problem. The goal of the National Institutes of Health-funded Connectivity Map (CMAP) database and its extension, the Library of Integrated Network-based Cellular Signatures (LINCS) database, is to create a reference data set of gene expression profiles from cultured human cells treated with bioactive small molecules, including FDA-approved drugs (Lamb et al., 2006). These resources allow researchers studying a particular disease state in human or animal models to compare gene expression profiles associated with the disease to those associated with the treatment compound in cell cultures and to discover compounds with matching profiles. This analysis provides a rationale for testing FDA-approved drugs in animal models and may even point to repurposing these drugs for the treatment of other diseases. The relevance of computational drug repurposing is highlighted in a recent review (Li et al., 2016).

Current strategies for data-driven drug repurposing are based on transcriptome profiling, whereas future studies may use epigenomes to predict drug-related responses. Epigenetic modifications are more stable than mRNA levels and may provide a better platform for reliably predicting FDA-approved compounds that can be repurposed for the prevention/treatment of AUD. In addition to recent efforts to repurpose known drugs, continued efforts to discover new therapeutics are fueled by rapid advances in statistical genomics and in public data repositories, which provide a foundation for systematic data integration. Figure 5.3 shows a general approach for data-driven drug discovery. To achieve a systems-level understanding of brain function in health and disease, integration of data within and across biological domains is required. On the one hand, novel computational approaches allow researchers to shift focus from individual genes to gene networks by elucidating the relationships among all genes expressed in large-scale experiments. On the other hand, a wealth of biological data stored in public databases are used for gene annotations—that is, to classify individual genes into groups with similar function, regulation, or localization—which in turn can be used to determine biological properties of the gene networks, leading to a better understanding of the mechanisms of disease and to the development of more effective therapeutics. This approach also highlights the importance of integrating epigenomic and transcriptomic data to understand the full scope of molecular changes associated with disease (Farris, Harris, & Ponomarev, 2015).

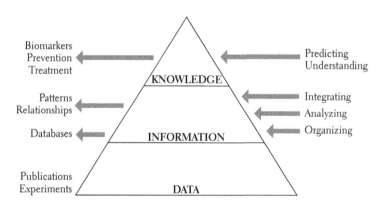

FIGURE 5.3 A data-to-knowledge approach presenting a series of steps required for the organization, analysis, and integration of large amounts of biological data to advance our understanding of human health and disease and to develop molecular biomarkers and novel therapeutics for the prevention and/or treatment of AUD.

Determination of cell type-specific epigenetic profiles is critical to our understanding of alcohol-induced changes in gene expression, cellular functions, and behavior. Future efforts should be directed toward cell type-specific mechanisms of AUD. Although this will be challenging in human research, animal models offer the advantage of being amenable to molecular genetics approaches. INTACT (Isolation of Nuclei TAgged in specific Cell Types) uses genetically modified mice for rapid and efficient extraction of nuclei from specific cell types for downstream molecular analysis and is a relatively new technique that could be useful for study of cell type-specific epigenetic states (Deal & Henikoff, 2010). Combined with transcriptome profiling, this method may reveal the molecular mechanisms contributing to alcohol-induced changes in cellular functions. Compared to gene expression profiling, which usually provides a snapshot of molecular activity at a single time point, epigenomic states may represent long-lasting attributes of cellular identity, including patterns of past gene expression, current gene expression, and/or potential future experience-related responses (Mo et al., 2015). These findings may, at least in part, explain how drugs of abuse establish long-lasting changes in brain plasticity that underlie compulsive drug use, craving, and relapse, even following years of abstinence.

ACKNOWLEDGMENTS

This work was supported by the National Institutes of Health (grants AA021462, AA020683, and AA024568). I thank Dr. Adron Harris and Dr. Jody Mayfield for critical reading of the manuscript.

REFERENCES

Abel, T., & Zukin, R. S. (2008). Epigenetic targets of HDAC inhibition in neurodegenerative and psychiatric disorders. *Current Opinion in Pharmacology*, 8(1), 57–64. http://doi.org/10.1016/j.coph.2007.12.002

American Psychiatric Association. (2013). *Diagnostic and statistical manual of mental disorders* (5th ed.). Arlington, VA: American Psychiatric Publishing.

Andersen, A. M., Dogan, M. V., Beach, S. R. H., & Philibert, R. A. (2015). Current and future prospects for epigenetic biomarkers of substance use disorders. *Genes*, 6(4), 991–1022. http://doi.org/10.3390/genes6040991

Barbier, E., Tapocik, J. D., Juergens, N., Pitcairn, C., Borich, A., Schank, J. R., . . . Hellig, M. (2015). DNA methylation in the medial prefrontal cortex regulates alcohol-induced behavior and plasticity. *Journal of Neuroscience*, 35(15), 6153–6164. http://doi.org/10.1523/JNEUROSCI.4571-14.2015

Barth, T. K., & Imhof, A. (2010). Fast signals and slow marks: The dynamics of histone modifications. *Trends in Biochemical Sciences*, 35(11), 618–626. http://doi.org/10.1016/j.tibs.2010.05.006

Bernstein, B. E., Meissner, A., & Lander, E. S. (2007). The mammalian epigenome. *Cell*, 128(4), 669–681. http://doi.org/10.1016/j.cell.2007.01.033

Bielawski, D. M., Zaher, F. M., Svinarich, D. M., & Abel, E. L. (2002). Methyltransferase messenger RNA levels. *Alcoholism: Clinical and Experimental Research*, 26(3), 347–351.

Blasco, M. A. (2007). The epigenetic regulation of mammalian telomeres. *Nature Reviews Genetics*, 8(4), 299–309. http://doi.org/10.1038/nrg2047

Borrelli, E., Nestler, E. J., Allis, C. D., & Sassone-Corsi, P. (2008). Decoding the epigenetic language of neuronal plasticity. *Neuron*, 60(6), 961–974. http://doi.org/10.1016/j.neuron.2008.10.012

Cecil, C. A. M., Walton, E., Smith, R. G., Viding, E., McCrory, E. J., Relton, C. L., . . . Barker, E. D. (2016). DNA methylation and substance-use risk: A prospective, genome-wide study spanning gestation to adolescence. *Translational Psychiatry*, 6(12), e976. http://doi.org/10.1038/tp.2016.247

Chen, C. H., Pan, C. H., Chen, C. C., & Huang, M. C. (2011). Increased oxidative DNA damage in patients with alcohol dependence and its correlation with alcohol withdrawal severity. *Alcoholism: Clinical and Experimental Research*, 35(2), 338–344. http://doi.org/10.1111/j.1530-0277.2010.01349.x

Choi, S. W., Stickel, F., Baik, H. W., Kim, Y. I., Seitz, H. K., & Mason, J. B. (1999). Chronic alcohol consumption induces genomic but not p53-specific DNA hypomethylation in rat colon. *Journal of Nutrition*, 129(11), 1945–1950.

Copeland, R. A., Olhava, E. J., & Scott, M. P. (2010). Targeting epigenetic enzymes for drug discovery. *Current Opinion in Chemical Biology*, 14(4), 505–510. http://doi.org/10.1016/j.cbpa.2010.06.174

Coppedè, F. (2014). The potential of epigenetic therapies in neurodegenerative diseases. *Frontiers in Genetics*, 5(243), 220. http://doi.org/10.3389/fgene.2014.00220

Cortessis, V. K., Thomas, D. C., Levine, A. J., Breton, C. V., Mack, T. M., Siegmund, K. D., . . . Laird, P. W.

(2012). Environmental epigenetics: Prospects for studying epigenetic mediation of exposure–response relationships. *Human Genetics, 131*(10), 1565–1589. http://doi.org/10.1007/s00439-012-1189-8

Deal, R. B., & Henikoff, S. (2010). A simple method for gene expression and chromatin profiling of individual cell types within a tissue. *Developmental Cell, 18*(6), 1030–1040. http://doi.org/10.1016/j.devcel.2010.05.013

Ernst, J., Kheradpour, P., Mikkelsen, T. S., Shoresh, N., Ward, L. D., Epstein, C. B., . . . Bernstein, B. E. (2011). Mapping and analysis of chromatin state dynamics in nine human cell types. *Nature, 473*(7345), 43–49. http://doi.org/10.1038/nature09906

Farris, S. P., Arasappan, D., Hunicke-Smith, S., Harris, R. A., & Mayfield, R. D. (2015). Transcriptome organization for chronic alcohol abuse in human brain. *Molecular Psychiatry, 20*(11), 1438–1447. http://doi.org/10.1038/mp.2014.159

Farris, S. P., Harris, R. A., & Ponomarev, I. (2015). Epigenetic modulation of brain gene networks for cocaine and alcohol abuse. *Frontiers in Neuroscience, 9*, 176. http://doi.org/10.3389/fnins.2015.00176

Finegersh, A., Rompala, G. R., Martin, D. I. K., & Homanics, G. E. (2015). Drinking beyond a lifetime: New and emerging insights into paternal alcohol exposure on subsequent generations. *Alcohol, 49*(5), 461–470. http://doi.org/10.1016/j.alcohol.2015.02.008

Flatscher-Bader, T., van der Brug, M. P., Landis, N., Hwang, J. W., Harrison, E., & Wilce, P. A. (2006). Comparative gene expression in brain regions of human alcoholics. *Genes, Brain, and Behavior, 5*(Suppl. 1), 78–84. http://doi.org/10.1111/j.1601-183X.2006.00197.x

García-Giménez, J. L., Sanchis-Gomar, F., Lippi, G., Mena, S., Ivars, D., Gomez-Cabrera, M. C., . . . Pallardo, F. V. (2012). Epigenetic biomarkers: A new perspective in laboratory diagnostics. *Clinica Chimica Acta, 413*(19–20), 1576–1582. http://doi.org/10.1016/j.cca.2012.05.021

Garro, A. J., McBeth, D. L., Lima, V., & Lieber, C. S. (1991). Ethanol consumption inhibits fetal DNA methylation in mice: Implications for the fetal alcohol syndrome. *Alcoholism: Clinical and Experimental Research, 15*(3), 395–398.

Govorko, D., Bekdash, R. A., Zhang, C., & Sarkar, D. K. (2012). Male germline transmits fetal alcohol adverse effect on hypothalamic proopiomelanocortin gene across generations. *Biological Psychiatry, 72*(5), 378–388. http://doi.org/10.1016/j.biopsych.2012.04.006

Hamid, A., Wani, N. A., & Kaur, J. (2009). New perspectives on folate transport in relation to alcoholism-induced folate malabsorption: Association with epigenome stability and cancer development. *FEBS Journal, 276*(8), 2175–2191. http://doi.org/10.1111/j.1742-4658.2009.06959.x

Hasegawa, A., Liu, H., Ling, B., Borda, J. T., Alvarez, X., Sugimoto, C., . . . Kuroda, M. J. (2009). The level of monocyte turnover predicts disease progression in the macaque model of AIDS. *Blood, 114*(14), 2917–2925. http://doi.org/10.1182/blood-2009-02-204263

Heard, E., & Martienssen, R. A. (2014). Transgenerational epigenetic inheritance: Myths and mechanisms. *Cell, 157*(1), 95–109. http://doi.org/10.1016/j.cell.2014.02.045

Horvath, S. (2013). DNA methylation age of human tissues and cell types. *Genome Biology, 14*(10), R115. http://doi.org/10.1186/gb-2013-14-10-r115

Isles, A. R. (2015). Neural and behavioral epigenetics: What it is, and what is hype. *Genes, Brain, and Behavior, 14*(1), 64–72. http://doi.org/10.1111/gbb.12184

Krishnan, H. R., Sakharkar, A. J., Teppen, T. L., Berkel, T. D. M., & Pandey, S. C. (2014). The epigenetic landscape of alcoholism. *International Review of Neurobiology, 115*, 75–116. http://doi.org/10.1016/B978-0-12-801311-3.00003-2

Lamb, J., Crawford, E. D., Peck, D., Modell, J. W., Blat, I. C., Wrobel, M. J., . . . Golub, T. R. (2006). The Connectivity Map: Using gene-expression signatures to connect small molecules, genes, and disease. *Science, 313*(5795), 1929–1935. http://doi.org/10.1126/science.1132939

Li, J., Zheng, S., Chen, B., Butte, A. J., Swamidass, S. J., & Lu, Z. (2016). A survey of current trends in computational drug repositioning. *Briefings in Bioinformatics, 17*(1), 2–12. http://doi.org/10.1093/bib/bbv020

Liu, J., Lewohl, J. M., Harris, R. A., Iyer, V. R., Dodd, P. R., Randall, P. K., & Mayfield, R. D. (2006). Patterns of gene expression in the frontal cortex discriminate alcoholic from nonalcoholic individuals. *Neuropsychopharmacology, 31*(7), 1574–1582. http://doi.org/10.1038/sj.npp.1300947

Lu, S. C., Huang, Z. Z., Yang, H., Mato, J. M., Avila, M. A., & Tsukamoto, H. (2000). Changes in methionine adenosyltransferase and S-adenosylmethionine homeostasis in alcoholic rat liver. *American Journal of Physiology: Gastrointestinal and Liver Physiology, 279*(1), G178–85.

Lunde, E. R., Washburn, S. E., Golding, M. C., Bake, S., Miranda, R. C., & Ramadoss, J. (2016). Alcohol-induced developmental origins of adult-onset diseases. *Alcoholism: Clinical and Experimental*

Research, 40(7), 1403–1414. http://doi.org/10.1111/acer.13114

Marballi, K., Ponomarev, I., Mayfield, R. D., & Harris, R. A. (2014). Alcohol and the brain. In A. Noronha, C. Cui, R. A. Harris, J. C. Crabbe (Eds.), *Neurobiology of alcohol dependence* (pp. 349–358). New York, NY: Elsevier. http://doi.org/10.1016/B978-0-12-405941-2.00017-1

Miranda, R. C., Salem, N. A., Fincher, A. S., Mahnke, A. H., & Burrowes, S. G. (2016). Epigenetic mechanisms and inheritance of acquired susceptibility to disease. In T. Tollefsbol (Ed.), *Medical epigenetics* (pp. 531–552). New York, NY: Elsevier. http://doi.org/10.1016/B978-0-12-803239-8.00030-2

Mo, A., Mukamel, E. A., Davis, F. P., Luo, C., Henry, G. L., Picard, S., . . . Nathans, J. (2015). Epigenomic signatures of neuronal diversity in the mammalian brain. *Neuron, 86*(6), 1369–1384. http://doi.org/10.1016/j.neuron.2015.05.018

Mulligan, M. K., Ponomarev, I., Hitzemann, R. J., Belknap, J. K., Tabakoff, B., Harris, R. A., . . . Bergeson, S. E. (2006). Toward understanding the genetics of alcohol drinking through transcriptome meta-analysis. *Proceedings of the National Academy of Sciences of the USA, 103*(16), 6368–6373. http://doi.org/10.1073/pnas.0510188103

National Institute on Alcohol Abuse and Alcoholism. (2016). *Draft strategic plan for research.* Retrieved from https://www.niaaa.nih.gov/sites/default/files/publications/DraftSP/NIAAA_Draft_Strategic_Plan_11_04_16_final.pdf

Nestler, E. J., Pena, C. J., Kundakovic, M., Mitchell, A., & Akbarian, S. (2016). Epigenetic basis of mental illness. *The Neuroscientist, 22*(5), 447–463. http://doi.org/10.1177/1073858415608147

Pandey, S. C., Ugale, R., Zhang, H., Tang, L., & Prakash, A. (2008). Brain chromatin remodeling: A novel mechanism of alcoholism. *Journal of Neuroscience, 28*(14), 3729–3737. http://doi.org/10.1523/JNEUROSCI.5731-07.2008

Pavanello, S., Hoxha, M., Dioni, L., Bertazzi, P. A., Snenghi, R., Nalesso, A., . . . Baccarelli, A. (2011). Shortened telomeres in individuals with abuse in alcohol consumption. *International Journal of Cancer, 129*(4), 983–992. http://doi.org/10.1002/ijc.25999

Philibert, R. A., Penaluna, B., White, T., Shires, S., Gunter, T., Liesveld, J., . . . Osborn, T. (2014). A pilot examination of the genome-wide DNA methylation signatures of subjects entering and exiting short-term alcohol dependence treatment programs. *Epigenetics, 9*(9), 1212–1219. http://doi.org/10.4161/epi.32252

Ponomarev, I. (2013). Epigenetic control of gene expression in the alcoholic brain. *Alcohol Research : Current Reviews, 35*(1), 69–76.

Ponomarev, I., Wang, S., Zhang, L., Harris, R. A., & Mayfield, R. D. (2012). Gene coexpression networks in human brain identify epigenetic modifications in alcohol dependence. *Journal of Neuroscience, 32*(5), 1884–1897.

Portales-Casamar, E., Lussier, A. A., Jones, M. J., MacIsaac, J. L., Edgar, R. D., Mah, S. M., . . . Kobor, M. S. (2016). DNA methylation signature of human fetal alcohol spectrum disorder. *Epigenetics & Chromatin, 9*(1), 25. http://doi.org/10.1186/s13072-016-0074-4

Ptashne, M. (2007). On the use of the word "epigenetic." *Current Biology, 17*(7), R233–R236. http://doi.org/10.1016/j.cub.2007.02.030

Renthal, W., & Nestler, E. J. (2009). Histone acetylation in drug addiction. *Seminars in Cell & Developmental Biology, 20*(4), 387–394. http://doi.org/10.1016/j.semcdb.2009.01.005

Sanchis-Segura, C., Lopez-Atalaya, J. P., & Barco, A. (2009). Selective boosting of transcriptional and behavioral responses to drugs of abuse by histone deacetylase inhibition. *Neuropsychopharmacology, 34*(13), 2642–2654. http://doi.org/10.1038/npp.2009.125

Schuebel, K., Gitik, M., Domschke, K., & Goldman, D. (2016). Making sense of epigenetics. *International Journal of Neuropsychopharmacology, 19*(11), pyw058. http://doi.org/10.1093/ijnp/pyw058

Shukla, S. D., Velazquez, J., French, S. W., Lu, S. C., Ticku, M. K., & Zakhari, S. (2008). Emerging role of epigenetics in the actions of alcohol. *Alcoholism: Clinical and Experimental Research, 32*(9), 1525–1534. http://doi.org/10.1111/j.1530-0277.2008.00729.x

Soares do Amaral, N., Cruz E Melo, N., de Melo Maia, B., & Malagoli Rocha, R. (2016). Noncoding RNA profiles in tobacco- and alcohol-associated diseases. *Genes, 8*(1), 6. http://doi.org/10.3390/genes8010006

Spanagel, R. (2009). Alcoholism: A systems approach from molecular physiology to addictive behavior. *Physiological Reviews, 89*(2), 649–705. http://doi.org/10.1152/physrev.00013.2008

Stephens, S. M., & Rung, J. (2006). Advances in systems biology: Measurement, modeling and representation. *Current Opinion in Drug Discovery & Development, 9*(2), 240–250.

Szabo, G., & Satishchandran, A. (2015). MicroRNAs in alcoholic liver disease. *Seminars in Liver Disease, 35*(1), 36–42. http://doi.org/10.1055/s-0034-1397347

Takahashi, K., & Yamanaka, S. (2006). Induction of pluripotent stem cells from mouse embryonic and adult fibroblast cultures by defined factors. *Cell*, *126*(4), 663–676. http://doi.org/10.1016/j.cell.2006.07.024

Tulisiak, C. T., Harris, R. A., & Ponomarev, I. (2017). DNA modifications in models of alcohol use disorders. *Alcohol*, *60*, 19–30. http://doi.org/10.1016/j.alcohol.2016.11.004

Waddington, C. H. (2012). The epigenotype. *International Journal of Epidemiology*, *41*, 10–13. (Original work published 1942) http://doi.org/10.1093/ije/dyr184

Walker, D. M., Cates, H. M., Heller, E. A., & Nestler, E. J. (2015). Regulation of chromatin states by drugs of abuse. *Current Opinion in Neurobiology*, *30*, 112–121. http://doi.org/10.1016/j.conb.2014.11.002

Warnault, V., Darcq, E., Levine, A., Barak, S., & Ron, D. (2013). Chromatin remodeling—A novel strategy to control excessive alcohol drinking. *Translational Psychiatry*, *3*(2), e231. http://doi.org/10.1038/tp.2013.4

Williams, R. J., Berry, L. J., & Beerstecher, E. (1949). Individual metabolic patterns, alcoholism, genetotrophic diseases. *Proceedings of the National Academy of Sciences of the USA*, *35*(6), 265–271.

Wolstenholme, J. T., Warner, J. A., Capparuccini, M. I., Archer, K. J., Shelton, K. L., & Miles, M. F. (2011). Genomic analysis of individual differences in ethanol drinking: Evidence for non-genetic factors in C57BL/6 mice. *PLoS One*, *6*(6), e21100. http://doi.org/10.1371/journal.pone.0021100

Wu, C.-t., & Morris, J. R. (2001). Genes, genetics, and epigenetics: a correspondence. *Science*, *293*(5532), 1103–1105. http://doi.org/10.1126/science.293.5532.1103

Zhou, F. C., Balaraman, Y., Teng, M., Liu, Y., Singh, R. P., & Nephew, K. P. (2011). Alcohol alters DNA methylation patterns and inhibits neural stem cell differentiation. *Alcoholism: Clinical and Experimental Research*, *35*(4), 735–746. http://doi.org/10.1111/j.1530-0277.2010.01391.x

Zhou, F. C., Chen, Y., & Love, A. (2011). Cellular DNA methylation program during neurulation and its alteration by alcohol exposure. *Birth Defects Research Part A: Clinical and Molecular Teratology*, *91*(8), 703–715. http://doi.org/10.1002/bdra.20820

Zhou, Z., Yuan, Q., Mash, D. C., & Goldman, D. (2011). Substance-specific and shared transcription and epigenetic changes in the human hippocampus chronically exposed to cocaine and alcohol. *Proceedings of the National Academies of Science of the USA*, *108*(16), 6626–6631. http://doi.org/10.1073/pnas.1018514108

6

Brain Functional Contributors to Vulnerability for Substance Abuse

Neuroimaging Findings from the Michigan Longitudinal Study

Mary M. Heitzeg

Substance use disorder (SUD) is associated with a host of negative outcomes and is one of the most significant health concerns worldwide (Gmel & Rehm, 2003; Rehm, Gmel, Sempos, & Trevisan, 2003; Rehm, Room, et al., 2003). Early substance use is linked to greater risk of developing SUD, with use by age 13 years associated with significantly increased rates of alcohol dependence (Grant & Dawson, 1997) and drug dependence (Grant & Dawson, 1998). Even at very low levels of use, age of first use impacts speed of transition from use to SUD (Behrendt, Wittchen, Hofler, Lieb, & Beesdo, 2009), and a growing literature suggests the possibility that early use may cause lasting changes on brain maturation (Batalla et al., 2013; Jacobus & Tapert, 2013) , which may further impact transition to SUD. Understanding the mechanisms that precede the onset and contribute to the escalation of substance use from childhood to adulthood is vital for understanding this cascading process.

Multiple factors influence the risk for SUDs. It is well known that parental SUD raises risk for offspring SUD (Caspi, Moffitt, Newman, & Silva, 1996), and numerous studies conducted in diverse populations have demonstrated that an individual's risk for SUDs is partially influenced by heredity (Bierut et al., 1998; Kendler, Jacobson, Prescott, & Neale, 2003). Genetic influences have been estimated to account for 40–60% of the variance in SUD risk, with the remaining variance attributed to environmental factors (Agrawal et al., 2012). Furthermore, there is significant overlap

in genetic influences on alcohol, nicotine, marijuana, and other drug dependence, which suggests a role of common pathways underlying the problem use of multiple drugs (Agrawal et al., 2012). There is considerable evidence that behavioral undercontrol and negative affectivity are two such pathways (Hussong, Hicks, Levy, & Curran, 2001; Zucker, Heitzeg, & Nigg, 2011).

During approximately the past decade, there has been an emergence of studies investigating the neural basis of the behavioral phenotypes associated with risk for SUD using functional magnetic resonance imaging (fMRI). Indices of brain function not only provide an objective measure of individual differences, circumventing limitations of self-report measures, but also are more proximal to the genetic sources of variance (Sweitzer, Donny, & Hariri, 2012). Here, I review fMRI studies conducted in offspring from the Michigan Longitudinal Study (MLS), an ongoing, prospective, high-risk family study of the development of SUD and related conditions that began in 1988 (Zucker, Ellis, Fitzgerald, Bingham, & Sanford, 1996; Zucker et al., 2000). Risk level of the offspring in the MLS was varied through recruitment of a population-based sample that differed in level of alcohol use disorder (AUD) among the fathers. Forty-one percent were drunk drivers with at least 0.15% blood alcohol levels who also met other ascertainment criteria; they were recruited from all district courts in the four counties. Twenty-nine percent were community alcoholics, uncovered during the canvass for controls. All had an AUD diagnosis, were coupled with a partner, and had a 3- to 5-year-old male offspring living in the home. Thirty percent were an ecologically comparable set of control families (no parental SUD at recruitment) accessed via door-to-door canvassing in neighborhoods in which the court alcoholics lived. The MLS involves repeated measurement of behavioral and psychological functioning, environment, substance use and problems, and psychiatric symptoms on the entire family. The current review focuses on work conducted within the MLS that integrates behavioral trait, developmental, neurobiological, and, in some cases, genetic frameworks. This integration across multiple levels of analysis is necessary for a better understanding of the risk factors leading to SUDs.

BEHAVIORAL UNDERCONTROL

The neural underpinnings of behavioral control involve a "top-down" inhibitory control system and a "bottom-up" incentive reactivity system (Eisenberg et al., 1997; Nigg, 2000). Work in the MLS has probed these systems with two tasks during fMRI. The go/no-go task is a well-validated measure of inhibition (Durston, Thomas, Worden, Yang, & Casey, 2002). Correct inhibition during the task is dependent on frontoparietal and frontostriatal-thalamic networks (Garavan, Ross, & Stein, 1999 ; Stevens, Kiehl, Pearlson, & Calhoun, 2007). The monetary incentive delay (MID) task is used to study neural circuitry involved in anticipation of reward (Knutson, Fong, Adams, Varner, & Hommer, 2001). This task is associated with robust ventral striatal activation, including the nucleus accumbens (NAcc) (Knutson, Adams, Fong, & Hommer, 2001).

Inhibitory Control

A weakness in response inhibition has been found to be a general liability factor for psychopathology related to behavioral undercontrol, including SUD. Poor inhibitory control has been associated with earlier substance use (Miller & Plant, 2002; Wills, Vaccaro, McNamara, & Hirky, 1996) and SUD diagnosis in adolescents (Rohde, Lewinsohn, & Seeley, 1996). Furthermore, adolescents and adults with SUD have alterations in the frontostriatal system

involved in regulating impulsive responses (Li, Luo, Yan, Bergquist, & Sinha, 2009; Tapert et al., 2007). However, studies of patient populations are not able to disentangle neurofunctional differences related to pre-existing traits that predispose to problem substance use from those that are secondary to chronic substance use. This was the goal of our early work investigating inhibitory control in MLS offspring (Heitzeg, Nigg, Yau, Zucker, & Zubieta, 2010). Sixty-one 16- to 22-year-olds were tested using the go/no-go task during fMRI. Forty-one participants were at high risk for SUD based on having at least one parent with an AUD diagnosis (FH+). The remaining 20 participants had no parent with AUD (FH−). Two FH+ subgroups were created to disentangle alcohol involvement from pre-existing risk: a FH+ control group ($n = 20$) with low levels of alcohol use and problems, which differed from the FH− group only by family history, and a FH+ problem group ($n = 21$) with high alcohol problems. We found a difference in caudate functioning during successful inhibition in both FH+ groups, regardless of problem alcohol involvement, compared with the FH− group. Specifically, FH+ youth had greater activation in the caudate, which was related to more externalizing problems, suggesting a neural risk marker for SUD. In contrast, orbital and left medial prefrontal regions were deactivated in both the FH− and the FH+ control groups but not the FH+ problem group. Activation in these regions was associated with levels of alcohol and other drug use, suggesting an effect related to chronic substance use. Taken together, the findings suggest a pre-existing abnormality in striatal functioning in youth at risk for SUD, which may lead to inappropriate motivational responding, and they also suggest an effect of substance use on a prefrontal "control" mechanism, resulting in a loss of efficiency and further dysregulation of the frontostriatal circuitry involved in control of motivational responding.

Other cross-sectional fMRI studies have shown altered inhibitory control processing in FH+ adolescents as well, supporting a pre-existing risk factor related to frontostriatal functioning (Schweinsburg et al., 2004; Silveri, Rogowska, McCaffrey, & Yurgelun-Todd, 2011). However, no consistent picture has emerged across these studies regarding the specific neural structures involved or whether they are overactive or underactive in youth at risk. We have suggested that this might be due to variation in the developmental periods that have been investigated, which have ranged from studies of 12- to 14-year-olds (Schweinsburg et al., 2004) to studies of 8- to 19-year-olds (Silveri et al., 2011). Given that inhibitory control improves from childhood into early adulthood, concomitant with the maturation of the underlying neural circuitry, the identification of specific neural abnormalities in this circuitry may represent a moving target when viewed across development. Therefore, we investigated developmental trajectories related to familial risk in MLS offspring across the ages of 7–17 years (Hardee et al., 2014). Longitudinal fMRI was conducted in 43 FH+ youth and 30 FH– youth beginning at ages 7–12 years. Participants performed a go/no-go task during fMRI at 1- to 2-year intervals. We found that although performance improved with age in both groups, there were significant group differences in age-related activation changes in the caudate, middle cingulate, and middle frontal gyrus during successful inhibition. Specifically, caudate and middle frontal gyrus activation decreased with age in FH– subjects. These changes reflect normative maturational improvements in efficiency—an effect that was not observed in FH+ youth. Importantly, these differences were evident as early as ages 7–12 years, even in alcohol- and drug-naive participants, with the FH+ group showing significantly blunted activation compared to FH– subjects at baseline. Thus, risk-related differences in response inhibition circuitry are present in childhood and continue into adolescence. Youth at risk for SUD have maturational trajectories that are inconsistent with normal response inhibition development, which may be a contributing factor for subsequent problem substance use.

The work discussed thus far has been focused on correct inhibition of responses during the go/no-go task. However, errors are frequently made during no-go trials, representing a failure of inhibition. Error processing is an important aspect of inhibitory control, critical to adaptive adjustment of performance (Ridderinkhof, Ullsperger, Crone, & Nieuwenhuis, 2004), but few studies have investigated error processing in relation to risk for SUD. The medial prefrontal cortex (PFC), including the anterior cingulate, has been consistently associated with error detection (Garavan, Ross, Murphy, Roche, & Stein, 2002; Kiehl, Liddle, & Hopfinger, 2000) and interacts with lateral PFC to support performance adjustment (Ridderinkhof et al., 2004;

Stevens, Kiehl, Pearlson, & Calhoun, 2009). Using a prospective design, we investigated brain activation during successful and failed no-go trials as predictors of early problem substance use (Heitzeg, Nigg, et al., 2014). A total of 45 MLS offspring completed the go/no-go task during fMRI when they were 9–12 years old. They were then followed for approximately 4 years, completing assessments of substance use through regular MLS assessments. Participants with marijuana or other drug use or significant alcohol use (drunk, binged, and/or have reported a problem due to use of alcohol) by ages 13–16 years were considered problem users. The problem users were individually matched by gender, age, and family history of AUD with non-substance-using children (non-user group). No differences were observed between these groups in brain activation during successful inhibition. However, the problem user group showed a significant blunting of activation in the left dorsolateral PFC (dlPFC) during failed inhibition. Furthermore, dlPFC activation was inversely correlated with externalizing problems at ages 11–13 years—that is, those with less activation had more externalizing problems approximately 2 years later. Using logistic regression, we found that activation of dlPFC significantly predicted group membership (problem user vs. non-user) over and above externalizing problems. The dlPFC is part of a network that is engaged during errors and involved in subsequent performance adjustment (Ridderinkhof et al., 2004; Stevens et al., 2009). Therefore, blunted dlPFC activation during errors may underlie problems adapting behavior appropriately, leading to undercontrolled behavior and early problem substance use, thereby heightening risk for SUD. This is the earliest beginning neuroimaging study to prospectively investigate neural risk factors for SUD and the first to specifically differentiate between response suppression and error responding aspects of inhibitory control during the go/no-go task. Work in older participants (ages 12–14 years) has uncovered differences related to SUD risk specifically in circuitry supporting successful inhibition (Norman et al., 2011; Whelan et al., 2012)—a network that is dissociable from the error detection and performance adjustment network (Garavan et al., 2002; Stevens et al., 2007, 2009). Therefore, a weakness in error detection and performance adjustment may be a critical risk factor for SUD at earlier ages (9–12 years), whereas at later ages (12–14 years), the critical liability may begin to shift toward circuitry supporting response inhibition.

Reward/Incentive Responding

Substances of abuse exert their reinforcing effects by activating the mesolimbic reward circuitry in the brain (Robinson & Berridge, 2000; Schultz, 1998). Thus, reward system functioning has emerged as an important target in the study of neurofunctional risk markers for SUD (McBride & Li, 1998; Volkow et al., 2002). Most studies of the involvement of the reward system in risk for SUD have focused on the opposing hypotheses of overreactive (Hariri et al., 2006; McClure et al., 2004) and underreactive (Blum et al., 2000) reward systems with respect to risky personality, risky behaviors, or familial risk (Bjork, Knutson, & Hommer, 2008; Schneider et al., 2012), with support emerging for each hypothesis. However, little attention has been given to factors that may moderate the relationship between risky phenotype and reward responding. Our work in MLS offspring (Yau et al., 2012) found that activation of the NAcc to reward anticipation during the MID task was blunted in FH+ young adults (aged 18–22 years) compared with an FH– group, who were matched for age, alcohol consumption, drug use, and externalizing problems to the FH+ group. On the surface, this suggests that an underreactive reward system is related to risk for SUD. However, additional analyses revealed that NAcc activation increased as a function of externalizing problems, and both variables correlated with drinking volumes in the FH+ group. In contrast, this relationship was not observed in the FH– group. This suggests a multilevel developmental process whereby lower behavioral risk may be protective of later problem substance use in FH+ youth, an effect further associated with a blunted NAcc response to incentive anticipation, potentially reflecting a resilience mechanism. Moreover, the results suggest that a close association between motivational responses, alcohol consumption, and behavioral risk may underlie SUD vulnerability uniquely in FH+ youth.

As a follow-up to this study, Weiland and colleagues (2013) investigated whether functional connectivity of the NAcc during reward anticipation differed based on familial risk in MLS offspring. The NAcc receives inputs from cortical and limbic regions involved in cognitive control (Camara,

Rodriguez-Fornells, & Munte, 2009). Differences in frontostriatal connectivity in problem substance users have suggested reduced influence of cognitive regions on reward functioning (Ma et al., 2010). Seventy 18- to 22-year-old offspring from the MLS (49 FH+/21 FH–) performed the MID task during fMRI. Group differences in NAcc connectivity during incentive (reward or loss) compared with neutral conditions were investigated with psychophysiological interaction analysis. NAcc connectivity with a region centered in the paracentral lobule and extending into the precuneus and sensorimotor areas was decreased in FH– youth but increased in FH+ youth during incentive anticipation. This brain region maps onto the supplementary sensorimotor area (SSMA), which is involved in the initiation and integration of motor function with emotional guidance (Lim et al., 1994). In FH+ youth, functional connectivity between the NAcc and the SSMA correlated positively with sensation seeking and drinking volume, and the strength of connectivity significantly mediated a positive relationship between sensation seeking and amount of drinking. In contrast, NAcc–SSMA connectivity correlated negatively with sensation seeking and was not related to drinking in FH– youth. These findings suggest pre-existing differences in reward-related functional connectivity between NAcc and regions involved in motivational responding. This difference in connectivity may act to mediate the effect of sensation-seeking phenotypes on drinking in individuals at risk for SUD. Furthermore, both this finding and that by Yau et al. (2012) illustrate heterogeneity in the relationship between reward system functioning and a measure of risky phenotype. They highlight the importance of potential moderating effects, such as those associated with familial risk, which may involve both genetic influences and influences related to the rearing environment.

In more recent work, we sought to directly investigate genetic influences on reward responding. The GABRA2 gene encodes the α_2 subunit of the γ-aminobutyric acid A receptor, which is a predominant receptor subtype in the NAcc, contributing to inhibitory regulation of dopaminergic functioning (Steffensen, Svingos, Pickel, & Henriksen, 1998). Variants in GABRA2 have been associated with adult alcohol dependence (Edenberg et al., 2004) as well as phenotypic precursors, including impulsiveness and externalizing behaviors (Dick et al., 2009; Villafuerte et al., 2012). We demonstrated an association between GABRA2 and insula activation during reward anticipation, linked to impulsive behavior, with the putative risk allele conferring heightened activation (Villafuerte et al., 2012). Follow-up work demonstrated that impulsiveness mediates the association between GABRA2 and lifetime alcohol problems in adults (Villafuerte, Strumba, Stoltenberg, Zucker, & Burmeister, 2013). Heitzeg, Villafuerte, et al. (2014) investigated the impact of GABRA2 on the developmental trajectory of NAcc activation during the MID from childhood to young adulthood in MLS youth. Participants (N = 175) completed the MID during fMRI, with the majority (n = 151) undergoing repeated scanning at 1- or 2-year intervals. One group entered the study at ages 8–13 years (n = 76) and another at ages 18–23 years (n = 99); with repeated measurement, this study covered ages 8–27 years. GABRA2 genotype was associated with individual differences in NAcc activation specifically during adolescence, with the putative risk allele associated with greater activation. Furthermore, NAcc activation mediated an effect of genotype on later alcohol problems, an effect that was significant even when accounting for amount of substance use. This work demonstrates an impact of GABRA2 genotype on the functional neurocircuitry involved in reward responding during adolescence, and it represents an important step toward understanding the genetic and neural basis of individual differences in how risk for SUD unfolds across development.

NEGATIVE AFFECTIVITY

Various measures of negative affectivity (e.g., neuroticism and depressive and anxiety symptoms) have been correlated with substance use in adults (Degenhardt & Hall, 2001; White, Xie, Thompson, Loeber, & Stouthamer-Loeber, 2001) and adolescents (Griesler, Kandel, & Davies, 2002; Miller & Plant, 2002). Associations between negative affectivity and SUDs have also been described (Conway, Swendsen, Rounsaville, & Merikangas, 2002; Jackson, Sher, & Wood, 2000). However, there have been very few studies designed to investigate the underlying neural correlates of this risk phenotype in relation to SUDs. The majority of this work has been conducted in MLS offspring, as described later. Work in the MLS has probed the neural basis of negative emotionality

using an emotion-arousal word task. In this task, positive, negative, and neutral words are selected from the Affective Norms for English Words list, which provides words normed on valence and arousal (Bradley & Lang, 1999). To investigate the neural correlates of negative emotion, brain activation to the reading of negative words is compared with brain activation to the reading of neutral words.

Heitzeg, Nigg, Yau, Zubieta, and Zucker (2008) described a small preliminary study of emotion arousal in MLS offspring designed to identify neurofunctional markers of SUD risk, as well as resilience to SUDs in high-risk youth. Twenty-two FH+ participants (ages 16–20 years) were categorized as either vulnerable (n = 11) or resilient (n = 11) based on level of problem drinking during the course of adolescence. Six FH– participants from the MLS with no evidence of their own problem drinking were labeled as low-risk controls. We found heightened activation in the orbital frontal gyrus and left insula to emotional stimuli in the resilient FH+ group compared with both the FH+ vulnerable group and FH– control group. This pattern of heightened activation is consistent with active emotional monitoring, which may be a protective factor in this group. In contrast, the vulnerable FH+ group had greater activation in the dorsomedial PFC and less activation in the ventral striatum and extended amygdala compared to the other groups, and activation in these regions was correlated with externalizing behavior. This pattern of activation is consistent with active suppression of affective responses, which may confer heightened vulnerability by impairing the ability to engage adaptively with emotional stimuli. This was the first report of dissociable patterns of neural activation underlying vulnerability and resiliency in youth at risk for SUDs based on their family history.

In a follow-up to the study by Heitzeg et al. (2008), we sought to directly investigate genetic influences on emotional responding. Variation in corticotropin-releasing hormone receptor 1 (CRHR1) genotype has been found to be associated with both problem alcohol use (Ray et al., 2013) and negative emotionality traits, including trait anxiety (Mahon, Zandi, Potash, Nestadt, & Wand, 2013) and depression (R. G. Bradley et al., 2008). We examined the influence of an intronic CRHR1 gene variant, rs110402, on neural responses during the emotion-arousal word task and associations with negative emotional traits and substance use in MLS offspring aged 16–21 years (Glaser et al., 2014). Furthermore, evidence suggests that *CRHR1* may interact with stress in modulating alcohol consumption (Bradley et al., 2008; Ray et al., 2013); therefore, childhood stress was also included as a potential moderating factor. We found that a region in the right ventrolateral prefrontal cortex (VLPFC) was more engaged during negative emotional word processing in homozygotes for the risk allele compared with other genotypes. In addition, genotype indirectly influenced problem alcohol use via VLPFC activation to negative words and negative emotionality, such that the risk allele was associated with decreased negative emotionality through heightened VLPFC activation and decreased negative emotionality was associated with fewer binge drinking days and fewer alcohol problems. This was a somewhat surprising finding given that we would expect the risk allele to confer increased negative emotionality and problem alcohol use. However, the effect was further moderated by childhood stress—the indirect effect was present only at low levels of childhood stress. The VLPFC is involved in re-evaluating an emotional situation to decrease its emotional impact (Gross & John, 2003). Thus, we propose that the development of enhanced reappraisal functioning is a compensatory mechanism for at-risk youth that allows them to neutralize their sensitivity to negative emotional stimuli. However, this compensatory mechanism may only develop in low-stress rearing environments. These findings highlight the importance of integration across multiple levels of analysis in seeking to understand developmental pathways of risk for SUDs.

An additional critical consideration when investigating neurofunctional risk for SUDs across development is the potential for substance use to impact brain maturation and have long-lasting consequences on adaptive functioning. Heitzeg, Cope, Martz, Hardee, and Zucker (2015) investigated the impact of heavy marijuana use during adolescence on emotional functioning, as well as the brain functional mediators of this effect in MLS offspring. Data on frequency of marijuana use were collected prospectively beginning in childhood as part of the MLS, and participants were classified as heavy marijuana users ($n = 20$) or controls with minimal marijuana use ($n = 20$). We investigated two facets of emotional functioning, negative emotionality and resiliency (a self-regulatory mechanism), assessed as part of the MLS at three time points from early adolescence to early adulthood: mean age, 13.4 years; mean age, 19.6 years; and mean age, 23.1 years. Heavy users began marijuana use at age 13 years, on average. We found that negative emotionality and resiliency did not differ between the heavy users and controls in early adolescence when marijuana use was initiated, whereas in early adulthood, heavy marijuana users had more negative emotionality and less resiliency than controls. Furthermore, across time, negative emotionality decreased and resiliency increased from early adolescence to adulthood in controls but not in heavy marijuana users. These findings add to the growing evidence of a causal relationship between early marijuana use and later difficulties in emotional functioning (Chadwick, Miller, & Hurd, 2013; Lev-Ran et al., 2014).

To investigate the impact of adolescent marijuana use on emotion-related brain functioning, participants also completed the emotion-arousal word task during fMRI at a mean age of 20.2 years. Compared with controls, heavy marijuana users had less activation to negative words in emotion processing and integration regions, including the amygdala, insula, PFC, and occipital cortex. Activation of the caudal dlPFC to negative words mediated an association between marijuana use and later negative emotionality. This brain region is involved in emotion processing and empathy (Lamm, Decety, & Singer, 2011) and has previously been found to be blunted in individuals with difficulties experiencing and processing emotions (van der Velde et al., 2013). Thus, the finding suggests that heavy marijuana use during adolescence may impair neural processing and integration of emotional stimuli, leading to increased negative emotionality. In addition, we found that less activation of the cuneus/lingual gyrus in the occipital cortex mediated an association between marijuana use and later low levels of resiliency. This brain region has been linked to numerous aspects of emotional functioning, including the evaluation of one's own emotional state (Terasawa, Fukushima, & Umeda, 2013). This suggests that heavy marijuana use during adolescence may impair the neural underpinning of emotional self-regulation. This longitudinal work demonstrates a neural pathway through which the use of substances during adolescence, concomitant with continuing brain maturation, may impact behavioral phenotypes associated with risk for SUDs.

CONCLUSIONS AND FUTURE DIRECTIONS

The development of SUD is a multistage process, beginning with the initiation of substance use, followed by escalation of use and, finally, compulsive use for a subset of users. Individual differences in the functioning of neural circuitry critical to behavioral control and emotionality may uniquely impact the risk for SUD depending on stage of use (Hommer, Bjork, & Gilman, 2011) as well as age (Hardee et al., 2014; Heitzeg, Villafuerte, et al., 2014). Furthermore, of major concern is that substance use during adolescence has the potential to affect the functioning and development of behavioral control and emotion systems and, as a result, increase the likelihood of transitioning into problem use.

Using fMRI in MLS offspring, we have made significant progress in describing developmental trajectories of brain function related to risk for SUD (Hardee et al., 2014; Heitzeg, Villafuerte, et al., 2014), as well as genetic contributions to intermediate neural phenotypes (Glaser et al., 2014; Heitzeg, Villafuerte, et al., 2014; Villafuerte et al., 2012). This work uncovers different genetic and neural mechanisms underlying behavioral undercontrol compared with negative emotionality, highlighting the heterogeneity that exists in risk pathways. We also demonstrate that biological mechanisms underlying risk are changing throughout development. This not only highlights the necessity of a longitudinal, developmental framework for understanding the emergence of problem substance use and SUD but also suggests that targets for prevention and intervention may be changing across development as well. Finally, we show that substance use itself impacts neural mechanisms of risk (Heitzeg et al., 2010, 2015). Thus, characterization of neural systems, behavioral and emotional functioning, stages of substance use, and genetic and environmental influences in parallel is critical to understand the biopsychosocial cascade of risk across development.

ACKNOWLEDGMENT

This work was supported by National Institutes of Health grants R01 AA07065, R01 AA012217, and R01 DA027261.

REFERENCES

Agrawal, A., Verweij, K. J., Gillespie, N. A., Heath, A. C., Lessov-Schlaggar, C. N., Martin, N. G., . . . Lynskey, M. T. (2012). The genetics of addiction—A translational perspective. *Translational Psychiatry*, 2, e140. doi:10.1038/tp.2012.54

Andrews, M. M., Meda, S. A., Thomas, A. D., Potenza, M. N., Krystal, J. H., Worhunsky, P., . . . Pearlson, G. D. (2011). Individuals family history positive for alcoholism show functional magnetic resonance imaging differences in reward sensitivity that are related to impulsivity factors. *Biological Psychiatry*, 69(7), 675–683. doi:10.1016/j.biopsych.2010.09.049

Batalla, A., Bhattacharyya, S., Yucel, M., Fusar-Poli, P., Crippa, J. A., Nogue, S., . . . Martin-Santos, R. (2013). Structural and functional imaging studies in chronic cannabis users: A systematic review of adolescent and adult findings. *PLoS One*, 8(2), e55821. doi:10.1371/journal.pone.0055821

Behrendt, S., Wittchen, H. U., Hofler, M., Lieb, R., & Beesdo, K. (2009). Transitions from first substance use to substance use disorders in adolescence: Is early onset associated with a rapid escalation? *Drug and Alcohol Dependence*, 99(1–3), 68–78. doi:10.1016/j.drugalcdep.2008.06.014

Bierut, L. J., Dinwiddie, S. H., Begleiter, H., Crowe, R. R., Hesselbrock, V., Nurnberger, J. I., Jr., . . . Reich, T. (1998). Familial transmission of substance dependence—Alcohol, marijuana, cocaine, and habitual smoking: A report from the Collaborative Study on the Genetics of Alcoholism. *Archives of General Psychiatry*, 55(11), 982–988.

Bjork, J. M., Chen, G., Smith, A. R., & Hommer, D. W. (2010). Incentive-elicited mesolimbic activation and externalizing symptomatology in adolescents. *Journal of Child Psychology and Psychiatry*, 51(7), 827–837. doi:10.1111/j.1469-7610.2009.02201.x

Bjork, J. M., Knutson, B., & Hommer, D. W. (2008). Incentive-elicited striatal activation in adolescent children of alcoholics. *Addiction*, 103(8), 1308–1319. doi:10.1111/j.1360-0443.2008.02250.x

Bjork, J. M., Smith, A. R., Chen, G., & Hommer, D. W. (2011). Psychosocial problems and recruitment of incentive neurocircuitry: Exploring individual differences in healthy adolescents. *Developmental Cognitive Neuroscience*, 1(4), 570–577. doi:10.1016/j.dcn.2011.07.005

Blum, K., Braverman, E. R., Holder, J. M., Lubar, J. F., Monastra, V. J., Miller, D., . . . Comings, D. E. (2000). Reward deficiency syndrome: A biogenetic model for the diagnosis and treatment of impulsive, addictive, and compulsive behaviors. *Journal of Psychoactive Drugs*, 32(Suppl.), i–iv, 1–112.

Bradley, M. M., & Lang, P. J. (1999). *Affective norms for English words (ANEW)*. Gainesville, FL: NIMH Center for the Study of Emotion and Attention, University of Florida.

Bradley, R. G., Binder, E. B., Epstein, M. P., Tang, Y., Nair, H. P., Liu, W., . . . Ressler, K. J. (2008). Influence of child abuse on adult depression: Moderation by the corticotropin-releasing hormone receptor gene. *Archives of General Psychiatry*, 65(2), 190–200. doi:10.1001/archgenpsychiatry.2007.26

Camara, E., Rodriguez-Fornells, A., & Munte, T. F. (2009). Functional connectivity of reward processing in the brain. *Frontiers of Human Neuroscience*, 2(19), 1–14. doi:10.3389/neuro.09.019.2008

Caspi, A., Moffitt, T. E., Newman, D. L., & Silva, P. A. (1996). Behavioral observations at age 3 years predict adult psychiatric disorders: Longitudinal evidence from a birth cohort. *Archives of General Psychiatry*, 53(11), 1033–1039.

Chadwick, B., Miller, M. L., & Hurd, Y. L. (2013). Cannabis use during adolescent development: Susceptibility to psychiatric illness. *Frontiers of Psychiatry*, 4, 129. doi:10.3389/fpsyt.2013.00129

Conway, K. P., Swendsen, J. D., Rounsaville, B. J., & Merikangas, K. R. (2002). Personality, drug of choice, and comorbid psychopathology among substance abusers. *Drug and Alcohol Dependence*, 65(3), 225–234.

Degenhardt, L., & Hall, W. (2001). The relationship between tobacco use, substance-use disorders and mental health: Results from the National Survey of Mental Health and Well-being. *Nicotine and Tobaco Research*, 3(3), 225–234.

Dick, D. M., Latendresse, S. J., Lansford, J. E., Budde, J. P., Goate, A., Dodge, K. A., . . . Bates, J. E. (2009). Role of GABRA2 in trajectories of externalizing behavior across development and evidence of moderation by parental monitoring. *Archives of General Psychiatry*, 66(6), 649–657. doi:66/6/649 [pii] 10.1001/archgenpsychiatry.2009.48

Durston, S., Thomas, K. M., Worden, M. S., Yang, Y., & Casey, B. J. (2002). The effect of preceding context on inhibition: An event-related fMRI study. *Neuroimage*, 16(2), 449–453. doi:10.1006/nimg.2002.1074

Edenberg, H. J., Dick, D. M., Xuei, X., Tian, H., Almasy, L., Bauer, L. O., . . . Begleiter, H. (2004). Variations in GABRA2, encoding the alpha 2 subunit of the GABA(A) receptor, are associated with alcohol dependence and with brain oscillations. *American Journal of Human Genetics*, 74(4), 705–714.

Eisenberg, N., Guthrie, I. K., Fabes, R. A., Reiser, M., Murphy, B. C., Holgren, R., . . . Losoya, S. (1997). The relations of regulation and emotionality to

resiliency and competent social functioning in elementary school children. *Child Development*, 68(2), 295–311.

Garavan, H., Ross, T. J., Murphy, K., Roche, R. A., & Stein, E. A. (2002). Dissociable executive functions in the dynamic control of behavior: Inhibition, error detection, and correction. *Neuroimage*, 17(4), 1820–1829.

Garavan, H., Ross, T. J., & Stein, E. A. (1999). Right hemispheric dominance of inhibitory control: An event-related functional MRI study. *Proceedings of the National Academy of Science of the USA*, 96(14), 8301–8306.

Glaser, Y. G., Zubieta, J. K., Hsu, D. T., Villafuerte, S., Mickey, B. J., Trucco, E. M., . . . Heitzeg, M. M. (2014). Indirect effect of corticotropin-releasing hormone receptor 1 gene variation on negative emotionality and alcohol use via right ventrolateral prefrontal cortex. *Journal of Neuroscience*, 34(11), 4099–4107. doi:10.1523/JNEUROSCI.3672-13.2014

Gmel, G., & Rehm, J. (2003). Harmful alcohol use. *Alcohol and Research Health*, 27(1), 52–62.

Grant, B. F., & Dawson, D. A. (1997). Age at onset of alcohol use and its association with DSM-IV alcohol abuse and dependence: Results from the National Longitudinal Alcohol Epidemiologic Survey. *Journal of Substance Abuse*, 9, 103–110.

Grant, B. F., & Dawson, D. A. (1998). Age of onset of drug use and its association with DSM-IV drug abuse and dependence: Results from the National Longitudinal Alcohol Epidemiologic Survey. *Journal of Substance Abuse*, 10(2), 163–173.

Griesler, P. C., Kandel, D. B., & Davies, M. (2002). Ethnic differences in predictors of initiation and persistence of adolescent cigarette smoking in the National Longitudinal Survey of Youth. *Nicotine and Tobacco Research*, 4(1), 79–93.

Gross, J. J., & John, O. P. (2003). Individual differences in two emotion regulation processes: Implications for affect, relationships, and well-being. *Journal of Personality and Social Psychology*, 85(2), 348–362.

Hardee, J. E., Weiland, B. J., Nichols, T. E., Welsh, R. C., Soules, M. E., Steinberg, D. B., . . . Heitzeg, M. M. (2014). Development of impulse control circuitry in children of alcoholics. *Biological Psychiatry*, 76(9), 708–716. doi:10.1016/j.biopsych.2014.03.005

Hariri, A. R., Brown, S. M., Williamson, D. E., Flory, J. D., de Wit, H., & Manuck, S. B. (2006). Preference for immediate over delayed rewards is associated with magnitude of ventral striatal activity. *Journal of Neuroscience*, 26(51), 13213–13217.

Heitzeg, M. M., Cope, L. M., Martz, M. E., Hardee, J. E., & Zucker, R. A. (2015). Brain activation to negative stimuli mediates a relationship between adolescent marijuana use and later emotional functioning. *Developmental Cognitive Neuroscience, 16,* 71–83. doi:10.1016/j.dcn.2015.09.003

Heitzeg, M. M., Nigg, J. T., Hardee, J. E., Soules, M., Steinberg, D., Zubieta, J. K., & Zucker, R. A. (2014). Left middle frontal gyrus response to inhibitory errors in children prospectively predicts early problem substance use. *Drug and Alcohol Dependence, 141,* 51–57. doi:10.1016/j.drugalcdep.2014.05.002

Heitzeg, M. M., Nigg, J. T., Yau, W. Y., Zubieta, J. K., & Zucker, R. A. (2008). Affective circuitry and risk for alcoholism in late adolescence: Differences in frontostriatal responses between vulnerable and resilient children of alcoholic parents. *Alcoholism: Clinical and Experimental Research,* 32(3), 414–426. doi:ACER605 [pii] 10.1111/j.1530-0277.2007.00605.x

Heitzeg, M. M., Nigg, J. T., Yau, W. Y., Zucker, R. A., & Zubieta, J. K. (2010). Striatal dysfunction marks preexisting risk and medial prefrontal dysfunction is related to problem drinking in children of alcoholics. *Biological Psychiatry,* 68(3), 287–295. doi:10.1016/j.biopsych.2010.02.020

Heitzeg, M. M., Villafuerte, S., Weiland, B. J., Enoch, M. A., Burmeister, M., Zubieta, J. K., & Zucker, R. A. (2014). Effect of GABRA2 genotype on development of incentive–motivation circuitry in a sample enriched for alcoholism risk. *Neuropsychopharmacology,* 39(13), 3077–3086. doi:10.1038/npp.2014.161

Hommer, D. W., Bjork, J. M., & Gilman, J. M. (2011). Imaging brain response to reward in addictive disorders. *Annals of the New York Academy of Science,* 1216, 50–61. doi:10.1111/j.1749-6632.2010.05898.x

Hussong, A. M., Hicks, R. E., Levy, S. A., & Curran, P. J. (2001). Specifying the relations between affect and heavy alcohol use among young adults. *Journal of Abnormal Psychology,* 110(3), 449–461.

Jackson, K. M., Sher, K. J., & Wood, P. K. (2000). Trajectories of concurrent substance use disorders: A developmental, typological approach to comorbidity. *Alcoholism: Clinical and Experimental Research,* 24(6), 902–913.

Jacobus, J., & Tapert, S. F. (2013). Neurotoxic effects of alcohol in adolescence. *Annual Review of Clinical Psychology,* 9, 703–721. doi:10.1146/annurev-clinpsy-050212-185610

Kendler, K. S., Jacobson, K. C., Prescott, C. A., & Neale, M. C. (2003). Specificity of genetic and environmental risk factors for use and abuse/dependence of cannabis, cocaine, hallucinogens, sedatives, stimulants, and opiates in male twins. *American Journal of Psychiatry,* 160(4), 687–695.

Kiehl, K. A., Liddle, P. F., & Hopfinger, J. B. (2000). Error processing and the rostral anterior cingulate: An event-related fMRI study. *Psychophysiology,* 37(2), 216–223.

Knutson, B., Adams, C. M., Fong, G. W., & Hommer, D. (2001). Anticipation of increasing monetary reward selectively recruits nucleus accumbens. *Journal of Neuroscience,* 21(16), RC159. doi:20015472 [pii]

Knutson, B., Fong, G. W., Adams, C. M., Varner, J. L., & Hommer, D. (2001). Dissociation of reward anticipation and outcome with event-related fMRI. *Neuroreport,* 12(17), 3683–3687.

Lamm, C., Decety, J., & Singer, T. (2011). Meta-analytic evidence for common and distinct neural networks associated with directly experienced pain and empathy for pain. *Neuroimage,* 54(3), 2492–2502. doi:10.1016/j.neuroimage.2010.10.014

Lev-Ran, S., Roerecke, M., Le Foll, B., George, T. P., McKenzie, K., & Rehm, J. (2014). The association between cannabis use and depression: A systematic review and meta-analysis of longitudinal studies. *Psychological Medicine,* 44(4), 797–810. doi:10.1017/s0033291713001438

Li, C. S., Luo, X., Yan, P., Bergquist, K., & Sinha, R. (2009). Altered impulse control in alcohol dependence: Neural measures of stop signal performance. *Alcoholism: Clinical and Experimental Research,* 33(4), 740–750. doi:10.1111/j.1530-0277.2008.00891.x

Lim, S. H., Dinner, D. S., Pillay, P. K., Luders, H., Morris, H. H., Klem, G., . . . Awad, I. A. (1994). Functional anatomy of the human supplementary sensorimotor area: Results of extraoperative electrical stimulation. *Electroencephalography and Clinical Neurophysiology,* 91(3), 179–193.

Ma, N., Liu, Y., Li, N., Wang, C. X., Zhang, H., Jiang, X. F., . . . Zhang, D. R. (2010). Addiction related alteration in resting-state brain connectivity. *Neuroimage,* 49(1), 738–744. doi:10.1016/j.neuroimage.2009.08.037

Mahon, P. B., Zandi, P. P., Potash, J. B., Nestadt, G., & Wand, G. S. (2013). Genetic association of FKBP5 and CRHR1 with cortisol response to acute psychosocial stress in healthy adults. *Psychopharmacology (Berlin),* 227(2), 231–241. doi:10.1007/s00213-012-2956-x

McBride, W. J., & Li, T. K. (1998). Animal models of alcoholism: Neurobiology of high alcohol-drinking behavior in rodents. *Critical Reviews in Neurobiology,* 12(4), 339–369.

McClure, E. B., Monk, C. S., Nelson, E. E., Zarahn, E., Leibenluft, E., Bilder, R. M., . . . Pine, D. S. (2004). A developmental examination of gender differences in brain engagement during evaluation of threat. *Biological Psychiatry,* 55(11), 1047–1055.

Miller, P., & Plant, M. (2002). Heavy cannabis use among UK teenagers: An exploration. *Drug and Alcohol Dependence*, 65(3), 235–242.

Nigg, J. T. (2000). On inhibition/disinhibition in developmental psychopathology: Views from cognitive and personality psychology and a working inhibition taxonomy. *Psychological Bulletin*, 126(2), 220–246.

Norman, A. L., Pulido, C., Squeglia, L. M., Spadoni, A. D., Paulus, M. P., & Tapert, S. F. (2011). Neural activation during inhibition predicts initiation of substance use in adolescence. *Drug and Alcohol Dependence*, 119(3), 216–223. doi:10.1016/j.drugalcdep.2011.06.019

Ray, L. A., Sehl, M., Bujarski, S., Hutchison, K., Blaine, S., & Enoch, M. A. (2013). The CRHR1 gene, trauma exposure, and alcoholism risk: A test of G × E effects. *Genes, Brain and Behavior*, 12(4), 361–369. doi:10.1111/gbb.12032

Rehm, J., Gmel, G., Sempos, C. T., & Trevisan, M. (2003). Alcohol-related morbidity and mortality. *Alcohol Research & Health*, 27(1), 39–51.

Rehm, J., Room, R., Monteiro, M., Gmel, G., Graham, K., Rehn, N., . . . Jernigan, D. (2003). Alcohol as a risk factor for global burden of disease. *European Addiction Research*, 9(4), 157–164. doi:72222

Ridderinkhof, K. R., Ullsperger, M., Crone, E. A., & Nieuwenhuis, S. (2004). The role of the medial frontal cortex in cognitive control. *Science*, 306(5695), 443–447. doi:306/5695/443 [pii]10.1126/science.1100301

Robinson, T. E., & Berridge, K. C. (2000). The psychology and neurobiology of addiction: An incentive-sensitization view. *Addiction*, 95(Suppl. 2), S91–S117.

Rohde, P., Lewinsohn, P. M., & Seeley, J. R. (1996). Psychiatric comorbidity with problematic alcohol use in high school students. *Journal of the American Academy of Child and Adolescent Psychiatry*, 35(1), 101–109.

Schneider, S., Peters, J., Bromberg, U., Brassen, S., Miedl, S. F., Banaschewski, T., . . . Buchel, C. (2012). Risk taking and the adolescent reward system: A potential common link to substance abuse. *American Journal of Psychiatry*, 169(1), 39–46. doi:appi.ajp.2011.11030489 [pii] 10.1176/appi.ajp.2011.11030489

Schultz, W. (1998). Predictive reward signal of dopamine neurons. *Journal of Neurophysiology*, 80(1), 1–27.

Schweinsburg, A. D., Paulus, M. P., Barlett, V. C., Killeen, L. A., Caldwell, L. C., Pulido, C., . . . Tapert, S. F. (2004). An FMRI study of response inhibition in youths with a family history of alcoholism. *Annals of the New York Academy of Sciences*, 1021, 391–394. doi:10.1196/annals.1308.050

Silveri, M. M., Rogowska, J., McCaffrey, A., & Yurgelun-Todd, D. A. (2011). Adolescents at risk for alcohol abuse demonstrate altered frontal lobe activation during Stroop performance. *Alcoholism: Clinical and Experimental Research*, 35(2), 218–228. doi:10.1111/j.1530-0277.2010.01337.x

Steffensen, S. C., Svingos, A. L., Pickel, V. M., & Henriksen, S. J. (1998). Electrophysiological characterization of GABAergic neurons in the ventral tegmental area. *Journal of Neuroscience*, 18(19), 8003–8015.

Stevens, M. C., Kiehl, K. A., Pearlson, G. D., & Calhoun, V. D. (2007). Functional neural networks underlying response inhibition in adolescents and adults. *Behavior and Brain Research*, 181(1), 12–22. doi:S0166-4328(07)00165-9 [pii] 10.1016/j.bbr.2007.03.023

Stevens, M. C., Kiehl, K. A., Pearlson, G. D., & Calhoun, V. D. (2009). Brain network dynamics during error commission. *Human Brain Mapping*, 30(1), 24–37. doi:10.1002/hbm.20478

Sweitzer, M. M., Donny, E. C., & Hariri, A. R. (2012). Imaging genetics and the neurobiological basis of individual differences in vulnerability to addiction. *Drug and Alcohol Dependence*, 123(Suppl. 1), S59–S71. doi:10.1016/j.drugalcdep.2012.01.017

Tapert, S. F., Schweinsburg, A. D., Drummond, S. P., Paulus, M. P., Brown, S. A., Yang, T. T., & Frank, L. R. (2007). Functional MRI of inhibitory processing in abstinent adolescent marijuana users. *Psychopharmacology (Berlin)*, 194(2), 173–183. doi:10.1007/s00213-007-0823-y

Terasawa, Y., Fukushima, H., & Umeda, S. (2013). How does interoceptive awareness interact with the subjective experience of emotion? An fMRI study. *Human Brain Mapping*, 34(3), 598–612. doi:10.1002/hbm.21458

van der Velde, J., Servaas, M. N., Goerlich, K. S., Bruggeman, R., Horton, P., Costafreda, S. G., & Aleman, A. (2013). Neural correlates of alexithymia: A meta-analysis of emotion processing studies. *Neuroscience Biobehavior Review*, 37(8), 1774–1785. doi:10.1016/j.neubiorev.2013.07.008

Villafuerte, S., Heitzeg, M. M., Foley, S., Yau, W. Y., Majczenko, K., Zubieta, J. K., . . . Burmeister, M. (2012). Impulsiveness and insula activation during reward anticipation are associated with genetic variants in GABRA2 in a family sample enriched for alcoholism. *Molecular Psychiatry*, 17(5), 511–519. doi:10.1038/mp.2011.33

Villafuerte, S., Strumba, V., Stoltenberg, S. F., Zucker, R. A., & Burmeister, M. (2013). Impulsiveness mediates the association between GABRA2 SNPs and lifetime alcohol problems. *Genes, Brain and Behavior*, 12(5), 525–531. doi:10.1111/gbb.12039

Volkow, N. D., Wang, G. J., Maynard, L., Fowler, J. S., Jayne, B., Telang, F., . . . Pappas, N. (2002). Effects of alcohol detoxification on dopamine D2 receptors in alcoholics: A preliminary study. *Psychiatry Research*, 116(3), 163–172.

Weiland, B. J., Welsh, R. C., Yau, W. Y., Zucker, R. A., Zubieta, J. K., & Heitzeg, M. M. (2013). Accumbens functional connectivity during reward mediates sensation-seeking and alcohol use in high-risk youth. *Drug and Alcohol Dependence*, 128(1–2), 130–139. doi:10.1016/j.drugalcdep.2012.08.019

Whelan, R., Conrod, P. J., Poline, J. B., Lourdusamy, A., Banaschewski, T., Barker, G. J., . . . Consortium, I. (2012). Adolescent impulsivity phenotypes characterized by distinct brain networks. *Nature Neuroscience*, 15(6), 920–925. doi:10.1038/nn.3092

White, H. R., Xie, M., Thompson, W., Loeber, R., & Stouthamer-Loeber, M. (2001). Psychopathology as a predictor of adolescent drug use trajectories. *Psychology of Addictive Behavior*, 15(3), 210–218.

Wills, T. A., Vaccaro, D., McNamara, G., & Hirky, A. E. (1996). Escalated substance use: A longitudinal grouping analysis from early to middle adolescence. *Journal of Abnormal Psychology*, 105(2), 166–180.

Yau, W. Y., Zubieta, J. K., Weiland, B. J., Samudra, P. G., Zucker, R. A., & Heitzeg, M. M. (2012). Nucleus accumbens response to incentive stimuli anticipation in children of alcoholics: Relationships with precursive behavioral risk and lifetime alcohol use. *Journal of Neuroscience*, 32(7), 2544–2551. doi:10.1523/JNEUROSCI.1390-11.2012

Zucker, R. A., Ellis, D. A., Fitzgerald, H. E., Bingham, C. R., & Sanford, K. (1996). Other evidence for at least two alcoholisms: II. Life course variation in antisociality and heterogeneity of alcoholic outcome. *Development and Psychopathology*, 8(4), 831–846. doi:http://dx.doi.org/10.1017/S0954579400007458

Zucker, R. A., Fitzgerald, H. E., Refior, S. K., Puttler, L. I., Pallas, D. M., & Ellis, D. A. (2000). The clinical and social ecology of childhood for children of alcoholics: Description of a study and implications for a differentiated social policy. In H. E. Fitzgerald, B. M. Lester, & R. A. Zucker (Eds.), *Children of addiction: Research, health and policy issues* (pp. 221–254). New York, NY: RoutledgeFalmer.

Zucker, R. A., Heitzeg, M. M., & Nigg, J. T. (2011). Parsing the undercontrol/disinhibition pathway to substance use disorders: A multilevel developmental problem. *Child Development Perspectives*, 5(4), 248–255. doi:10.1111/j.1750-8606.2011.00172.x

PART III

ALCOHOL USE DISORDERS

Developmental Transitions from Infancy to Early Adolescence

OVERVIEW

The human newborn is completely dependent on caregivers to provide the essential nutrition and safety needed to sustain his or her survival. Beyond survival, the newborn is also dependent on caregivers to provide the essentials necessary for him or her to construct a developmental pathway that prepares him or her to successfully negotiate toddlerhood. Packing away a successful life course through the first 2 years of postnatal life, the next step is to handle the preschool years, and on it goes throughout the life course. These dynamic and systemic postnatal reorganizations occur in a fairly orderly sequence (experience expectant) but can be seriously disrupted when children are exposed to adverse childhood experiences (experience dependent):

- 1–3 months: Shift from external regulation to internal regulation; differentiation of self, other, and self–other relationships
- 7–9 months: Emotional and cognitive reorganizations along with significant changes in memory processes and retention
- 12–14 months: Transition to upright locomotion
- 18–24 months: Transition to language as the major form of communication
- 24–48 months: Emergence and consolidation of autobiographical self
- 5–7 years: Transition from preschool to formal schooling; significant changes in peer network
- 9–14 years: Biological, emotional, social, and cognitive changes of puberty; influence of peers; shift to "if–then" thinking

18–25 years: Identity, independence, and the transition to adulthood

Within each of these segments of the early life course, the individual resides somewhere on the risk to resilience continuum, with that positioning dependent on the quality of the life course pathway being constructed by the individual and the others who provide care and a care environment (Fitzgerald & Zucker, 2006). It is during the critical period from birth to age 5 years that children are exposed to parents who have realistic or unrealistic expectations about child development; who do or do not have mental health problems or high degrees of marital conflict; and who may or may not have other issues, such as low frustration tolerance and poor social skills. Regardless of the quality of the rearing environment, epigenetic processes are at work, as well as the child's sense of self and intersubjectivity, which results in internalized views of how the world works (Ammaniti & Gallese, 2014), particularly with respect to interpersonal dynamics.

In Chapter 7, Eiden draws upon evidence from the Buffalo Longitudinal Study, whose participants at the onset were parents and their infants. Working from a developmental cascade model investigating stage-salient outcomes, Eiden focuses on factors that increased risk or resilience for developmental outcomes. Discussed is the co-occurrence of parental alcohol use disorder (AUD) with depression and antisocial behavior, along with its impact on the quality of parent–child relationships, especially the parent–infant attachment relationship. A critical aspect of the quality of this parent–child relationship is the extent to which it contributes positively to the child's emerging ability to self-regulate emotions and behavior. Eiden posits that the quality of the parent–child relationship and child self-regulation may be important influences affecting continuity of externalizing problems from childhood to adolescence within a developmental pathway leading to AUDs. Finally, based on the results from the Buffalo Longitudinal Study, as well as other longitudinal outcomes, Eiden discusses implications for development of preventive interventions for adolescent substance use disorders.

In Chapter 8, Wong delves into an aspect of regulation that provides developmental difficulties for children as well as the child–parent relationships. It is well established that sleep disturbance is part of the symptomatology of problem drinking, but sleep disturbance during the preschool years has rarely been connected with etiologic issues related to AUD. Wong reviews the functional significance of sleep for human development as a prelude to considering its relationship to alcohol use and related problems. She notes that sleep problems as early as the preschool years (e.g., difficulties falling or staying asleep) increase the risk of early onset of alcohol use and related problems. By the third or fourth postnatal month, human growth hormone production synchronizes with the sleep–wake cycle such that significant release of human growth hormone occurs from 2 to 4 hours after sleep onset. Although it is the case that the growth hormone has not been linked to risk for AUD, the cycle pattern is interrupted in children with sleep disturbance. Sleep research has fully documented the negative psychological effects of sleep absence and sleep disruption, so sufficient corollary evidence suggests that sleep problems during the preschool years may be symptomatic of ongoing problems in self-regulation. Wong proposes a theoretical model of sleep and alcohol use, highlighting the role of self-regulatory processes as mediators of this relationship, and reviews evidence in support of the model.

The intraindividual aspects of addiction liability are described in Chapter 9. Nigg posits that self-regulation is best conceived as having top-down and bottom-up components. He provides evidence that this dual-process model is helpful for understanding the organization of emotional and behavioral self-regulation. From this perspective, addictive behavior emerges early, and expression of risk is first driven by bottom-up appetitive systems (brain systems) and subsequently involves organization of top-down control and executive processes (higher brain functions). This results in either an adaptive functioning system of self-regulation or a disruptive system that is highly likely to be linked to psychopathology such as attention deficit hyperactivity disorder, conduct problems, and substance use disorder. Finally, Nigg suggests that continued research on executive functioning, effortful control, and self-control is important to our understanding of early protective factors to reduce the propensity toward addiction and other problematic outcomes.

As key agents in the socialization of children, parents play a critical role in helping children gain control of their emotions and behavior. In Chapter 10, Donovan provides a thorough overview of parental socialization, with particular attention to parental modeling of substance use, parental approval, parental monitoring and control practices, parent–child relationship quality, emergent child expectancies, peer substance use, and child use of substances. It should not be surprising that parental substance use (alcohol, tobacco, and other drugs) is predictive of substance use by their children. What is less known is that such parental behaviors are also correlated with poorer parent–child relationship quality, which in turn is related to stronger influences of substance-using peers on child/adolescent use. Resilience is provided by parental non-use, effective parenting practices, and good-quality parent–child relationships. Donovan offers a model of parent–child relationships and socialization that will generate new research on the socialization of adolescent substance use.

In Chapter 11, Bacio and colleagues focus on adolescence as a time of transition and change that augers growing independence from family and transformational changes associated with puberty. The authors draw attention to the synergistic changes in biological, cognitive, affective, and social systems that accompany puberty at the same time that many adolescents begin to experiment with alcohol consumption (average age of onset of drinking in the United States is 14 years). They draw upon data from a longitudinal study of alcohol and other drug use on adolescents' neuroanatomy, neurocognition, and behavior (National Consortium on Alcohol and NeuroDevelopment in Adolescence), as well as data from a high school-based intervention study (Project Options), to examine how diverse developmental process and emergent transformations related to puberty affect alcohol and other drug use.

REFERENCES

Ammaniti, M., & Gallese, V. (2014). *The birth of inter-subjectivity: Psychodynamics, neurobiology, and the self.* New York, NY: Norton.

Fitzgerald, H. E., & Zucker, R. A. (2006). Pathways of risk aggregation for alcohol use disorders. In K. Freeark & W. S. Davidson, III (Eds.), *The crisis in youth mental health: Issues for families, schools, and communities* (pp. 249–272). Westport, CT: Praeger.

7

Etiological Processes for Substance Use Disorders Beginning in Infancy

Rina D. Eiden

Understanding and documenting etiological pathways to substance abuse disorders necessitates a lifespan developmental framework beginning in infancy (Zucker & Fitzgerald, 1991). The importance of early experience has also been underscored in recent reviews (Chassin, Presson, Il-Cho, Lee, & Macy, 2013) as well as studies of differences in brain morphology across a number of different high-risk samples, including adults with post-traumatic stress disorder who were maltreated as children (McCrory, De Brito, & Viding, 2010), orphanage-reared children (Mehta et al., 2009; Tottenham et al., 2010), children of mothers with chronic depression (Lupien et al., 2011), and those who experienced insecure attachment with mothers as infants (Moutsiana et al., 2015). Beginning in early childhood is also important given recent literature on the enduring effects of maternal sensitivity in early childhood for child outcomes from early childhood through adolescence (Haltigan, Roisman, & Fraley, 2013) and adulthood (Raby, Roisman, Fraley, & Simpson, 2015).

CHILDREN OF ALCOHOLIC FATHERS

There are robust and consistent associations between parents' alcohol and drug dependence and children's substance use disorders, including alcohol abuse and dependence, earlier onset of use, and a more rapid progression from use to disorder (Chassin, Curran, Hussong, & Colder, 1997; Donovan, 2004; Duncan et al., 2006; Grant et al., 2015). However, not all children of alcoholic parents (COAs) develop substance use disorders, and there is considerable heterogeneity

in outcomes (Hussong, Flora, Curran, Chassin, & Zucker, 2008; Hussong et al., 2007; Puttler, Zucker, Fitzgerald, & Bingham, 1998). In order to understand developmental pathways to risk and resilience, it is important to begin at the earliest developmental time points, as noted by Zucker in 1976. Although there have been many developmental studies of COAs since then (Chassin, Rogosch, & Barrera, 1991; Hussong & Chassin, 1997; Noll, Zucker, & Greenberg, 1990; Sher, 1991), none (except studies of fetal alcohol syndrome) have spanned infancy through late adolescence, with the exception of the Buffalo Longitudinal Study (BLS; Eiden et al., 2016).

THE BUFFALO LONGITUDINAL STUDY

The BLS began in 1995 with a community-recruited sample of intact (both biological parents in the household) families, identified through New York state birth records (Eiden et al., 2016). The sample consisted of 227 families (116 girls and 111 boys) with 12-month-old infants at the time of recruitment. Families were classified as being in one of two groups: the non-alcoholic or control group consisting of parents with no or few alcohol problems since the child's birth ($n = 102$) and the alcoholic group with families in which the father met criteria for alcohol abuse or dependence ($n = 125$). Within the father alcoholic group, 95 mothers were light drinkers or abstainers, and 30 mothers were heavy drinkers or had current alcohol problems. The study used a developmental psychopathology framework, the constructs of equifinality (that there may be multiple pathways to the same outcome) and multifinality (there is heterogeneity in outcomes among children exposed to the same risk condition; Cicchetti & Rogosch, 1996), and discussions regarding the importance of examining family interactions as significant etiological processes (Jacob, Seilhamer, & Rushe, 1989) to guide hypotheses. Multimethod family assessments were conducted at 10 different child ages with fathers, mothers, and children in early childhood (12, 18, 24, 36, and 48 months), at kindergarten age (5–6 years of age), in middle childhood (when they were in 4th and 6th grades; 9–10 and 11–12 years of age, respectively), in early adolescence (when they were in 8th grade; 13–14 years of age), and in later adolescence (when they were in 11th and 12th grades; 15–19 years of age). The long-term goal was to understand etiological processes for substance use and associated disorders beginning in infancy, with a focus on stage-salient developmental outcomes. In other words, how children negotiate the salient developmental issues at each stage of development may set the stage for adaptive or maladaptive outcomes in the next stage. Although the study used a case–control design in order to control for potential demographic differences between alcoholic and control families, the results may be applicable for understanding etiological processes for substance use disorders beginning in infancy for non-alcoholic families as well. Given the focus of this chapter on etiological processes beginning in infancy, most of the results discussed concern early childhood predictors (12, 18, 24, and 36 months) of adolescent substance use or associated risks.

EXTERNALIZING PROBLEMS AS A PATHWAY TO ADOLESCENT SUBSTANCE USE

One of the most consistent risk pathways to adolescent substance use is via continuity of externalizing problem behaviors from childhood to adolescence (Jester et al., 2008). Both theoretical discussions (Costello, Erkanli, Federman, & Angold, 1999; Ellickson & Hays, 1991; Jessor, 1991; Kellam & Anthony, 1998) and empirical evidence (Colder et al., 2013; Hussong, Huang, Curran, Chassin, & Zucker, 2010; Sartor, Lynskey, Heath, Jacob, & True, 2007; Timmermans, van Lier, & Koot, 2008) highlight the importance of externalizing problems as a significant risk pathway for adolescent substance use in prospective studies. Children with continuing externalizing

problems are also more likely to affiliate with deviant peers (Dodge et al., 2009), a significant proximal risk factor for adolescent substance use (Van Ryzin & Dishion, 2014).

PARENT PSYCHOPATHOLOGY IN EARLY CHILDHOOD

As in other studies of COAs beginning later in childhood (Buu et al., 2012; Chassin et al., 1997; Jacob et al., 2003; Sher, Walitzer, Wood, & Brent, 1991; Windle, 1990), results from the BLS indicated significant associations between parent alcohol problems in infancy and adolescent substance use (Table 7.1; Eiden et al., 2016). COAs reported higher levels of alcohol, marijuana, cigarette, and other drug use compared to children of non-alcoholic parents. Within COAs, children who had two parents with alcohol problems reported significantly higher frequency of marijuana and cigarette use compared to those with alcoholic fathers (see Table 7.1). Although these results are not unique in the literature, it is worth noting that there are no other studies of COAs reporting associations between fathers' current alcohol diagnosis in infancy and higher rates of adolescent substance use. These results cannot be attributed to genetic link alone, as noted in studies using genetically informative designs (Jacob et al., 2003; McAdams et al., 2014). Although there may be some degree of genetic association, this association was also mediated via a cascade of processes supportive of developmental cascade models (Dodge et al., 2009) of substance use etiology (Eiden et al., 2016).

Parent alcohol problems often co-occur with other comorbid disorders, particularly antisocial personality disorder (Cloninger, Sigvardsson, & Bohman, 1988; Hussong et al., 2007, 2008) and depression among both parents (for a review, see Fitzgerald & Eiden, 2007). The role of comorbid antisocial behavior has been well studied in the COA literature as an important explanatory variable for heterogeneity in risk processes, although it has not been studied as much in the general developmental literature. Results from papers examining risk trajectories of children from 2 to 17 years of age and pooling data across multiple studies indicate significant increases in risk for internalizing and externalizing symptoms when parent alcohol problems were comorbid with antisocial behavior or depression or children had two

TABLE 7.1 Group Differences in Adolescent Substance Use as a Function of Early Parental Alcohol Use

Variable	Control Group (n = 102)	Father Alcoholic Group (n = 95)	Both Parents Alcoholic Group (n = 30)	F Value	η_p^2
Alcohol use	6.03 (7.38)[a]	8.21 (8.42)	11.04 (10.22)[b]	3.83[*]	.04
Cigarette use	0.38 (1.51)[a]	1.02 (2.85)[a]	3.28 (6.93)[b]	7.38[**]	.08
Marijuana use	0.80 (1.47)[a]	1.44 (2.12)[a]	2.68 (2.91)[b]	8.63[**]	.09
Other drugs	0.39 (1.51)[a]	1.48 (3.42)[b]	2.68 (2.91)[b]	3.92[*]	.04

Note: The frequency of cigarette and other drug use was low.

[*]$p < .05$; [**]$p < .01$.

a, b: The means with superscripts a and b were significantly different from each other.

alcoholic parents (Hussong et al., 2007, 2008). Only a few studies have examined the predictive role of maternal or paternal depression for adolescent substance use beginning in infancy or early childhood. However, the literature linking maternal depression to different aspects of adverse child behaviors, including externalizing problem behaviors, is much larger, and meta-analytic reviews report small but significant associations (Goodman et al., 2011). One important aspect of the meta-analytic review by Goodman et al. (2011) was the examination of moderators. Of note, the association between maternal depression and child psychopathology was significantly stronger among younger samples, suggesting the possibility that early experience of maternal depression may have long-lasting effects on children's development.

In addition to associations with developmental risks such as externalizing problems, a small number of studies have examined the role of maternal depression in predicting adolescent substance use in older cohorts. Clinically depressed mothers of children recruited in middle childhood were five times more likely to report alcohol dependence compared to non-depressed mothers (Weissman, Warner, Wickramaratne, Moreau, & Olfson, 1997). In a community-recruited sample of low-income boys, maternal depressive symptoms from 18 months to 3½ years of child age were indirectly associated with adolescent substance use by increasing risk for externalizing problems in early adolescence, which in turn predicted lower parental knowledge of child activities in mid-adolescence, leading to higher substance use in late adolescence (Sitnick, Shaw, & Hyde, 2014). In a sample of Chilean adolescents, maternal depression at 10 years of age predicted higher adolescent cigarette use via lower parental monitoring (Bares, Delva, & Andrade, 2015), even in the context of maternal

cigarette use. In contrast, in a sample of students recruited from schools, maternal depression in middle childhood (grades 3–7) was not associated with changes in adolescent substance use from grades 7 to 11 (Cortes, Fleming, Mason, & Catalano, 2009). Thus, although the literature linking maternal depression to adolescent substance use using longitudinal design is small, three out of four studies reported significant associations, with two studies reporting indirect associations via lower maternal monitoring.

In one of the few prospective studies examining the role of maternal antisocial behavior in the context of recurrent maternal depressive disorder among 9- to 17-year-old children (Sellers et al., 2014), the authors noted complex associations between maternal and child psychopathology via maternal warmth and hostility. This study highlighted the comorbidity of maternal depression and antisocial behavior. Results also indicated that the association of depression and disruptive behaviors was no longer significant when comorbid antisocial behavior was included in the model. The association between antisocial behavior and child disruptive behaviors was mediated by maternal hostility. These results are remarkably similar to those obtained by Harold, Elam, Lewis, Rice, and Thapar (2012) using a genetically informed design. Studies using genetically informative designs indicate that the association between parent and child antisocial behavior is influenced by both genes and environment (for a review, see McAdams et al., 2014).

For a number of reasons, paternal depression has received much less attention in the general developmental literature compared to maternal depression (O'Hara & Fisher, 2010). However, it is increasingly recognized that depression is common among both mothers and fathers with young children (Keller, Cummings, Peterson, & Davies, 2009),

TABLE 7.2 Group Differences in Parent Psychopathology and Family Processes in Infancy

Variable	Control Group (n = 102)	Father Alcoholic (n = 95)	Both Parents Alcoholic (n = 30)	F Value	η_p^2
M antisocial behavior	34.27 (4.42)[a]	36.70 (5.39)[b]	39.27 (6.88)[b]	12.41**	.10
M depression	7.09 (6.16)[a]	9.71 (8.02)[b]	9.73 (8.13)[b]	3.67*	.03
M marital satisfaction	108.26 (22.99)[a]	92.94 (27.69)[b]	100 (29.20)	8.63**	.07
F antisocial behavior	36.16 (6.33)[a]	42.33 (8.41)[b]	43.80 (12.66)[b]	17.84**	.14
F depression	6.35 (6.25)[a]	8.97 (7.27)[b]	7.44 (7.00)	3.53*	.03
F marital satisfaction	107.04 (23.68)[a]	97.28 (23.61)[b]	103 (24.07)	4.17*	.04
Marital aggression	1.35 (2.62)[a]	3.19 (5.61)	3.28 (5.58)	4.76**	.04

F, father; M, mother.

*$p < .05$; **$p < .01$.

a, b: The means with superscripts a and b were significantly different from each other.

although the rates are much higher among mothers (Goodman, 2007). Recent studies have noted the importance of both maternal and paternal depression for increased child psychopathology, including externalizing behavior problems (Fisher, Brock, O'Hara, Kopelman, & Stuart, 2015), although the results for paternal depression have been more mixed compared to those for maternal depression (Goodman, 2007; Gutierrez-Galve, Stein, Hanington, Heron, & Ramchandani, 2015; O'Hara & McCabe, 2013).

As with other cohorts of COAs beginning beyond the first 3 years of life, results from BLS indicate higher symptoms of depression and antisocial behavior among alcoholic compared to control group families (Table 7.2). Fathers' antisocial behavior in infancy (12 months) was associated with higher frequency of adolescent marijuana ($r = .20$, $p = .01$) and cigarette use ($r = .27$, $p = .00$) during the past 30 days. Mothers' antisocial behavior in infancy was associated with higher frequency of marijuana use in later adolescence ($r = .17$, $p = .02$). In the context of mediated pathways including parenting and externalizing behaviors from childhood to adolescence, these associations were no longer significant (Eiden et al., 2016), implicating these processes as explanatory developmental mechanisms. These results are similar to those reported previously in COA samples at older ages (Loukas, Fitzgerald, Zucker, & Von Eye, 2001). Although there were no direct associations between parents' depressive symptoms in infancy and substance use in adolescence in the BLS data, higher parental depressive symptoms in infancy were significantly associated with a strong risk factor for substance use liability, externalizing behavior problems at kindergarten age ($r = .26$ and .21 for fathers

and mothers, respectively; $p < .01$). Thus, in the BLS, the association between parental depression and adolescent substance use was mediated by continuity of externalizing behavior problems from childhood through adolescence (Eiden et al., 2016).

INFANT–PARENT ATTACHMENT

In addition to potential direct effects of parental psychopathology on child behaviors that increase risk for substance abuse, parents' alcohol problems and comorbid psychopathology are significant risk factors for one of the most salient developmental issues of infancy: the quality of the parent–child relationship (Bowlby, 1969, 1973). The development of a secure attachment relationship with a caring adult is one crucial aspect of social–emotional development during infancy. Insecure attachment with a mother or father or both may set the stage for difficulties in negotiating the salient developmental issues at toddler age and beyond (Bowlby, 1969, 1973).

Results from the BLS indicate significant associations between fathers' alcohol problems and attachment insecurity (Edwards, Eiden, & Leonard, 2004; Eiden, Edwards, & Leonard, 2002) and also between attachment insecurity with mothers at 12 months and adolescent substance use (Table 7.3). Results from multivariate analysis of variance (MANOVA) with the adolescent substance use variables and dependent measures, and three group attachment classifications (secure, avoidant, and resistant), yielded a significant multivariate effect of attachment security with mother [$F (8, 346) = 2.05$, $p = .04$, $\eta_p^2 = .04$]. Univariate analyses indicated significant effects of attachment security

TABLE 7.3 Infant–Mother Attachment Classifications and Substance Use in Adolescence

Variable	Secure	Avoidant	Resistant	F Value	η_p^2
Alcohol use	7.49 (8.83)	9.47 (7.72)	6.41 (7.48)	1.17	.01
Cigarette use	0.66 (2.71)[a]	2.33 (5.46)[b]	1.10 (2.37)	3.33*	.04
Marijuana use	1.18 (1.89)[a]	2.03 (2.81)[b]	1.03 (1.52)	2.69+	.03
Other drug use	0.69 (1.87)[a]	2.33 (4.62)[b]	0.59 (1.59)[b]	5.78**	.06

Note: The means and standard deviations for the disorganized classification were as follows: 10 (8.88), 1.65 (4.37), 1.71 (2.44), and 2.12 (4.88) for alcohol, cigarette, marijuana, and other drug use, respectively. There were no significant differences between the disorganized and other classifications.

+$p < .10$; *$p < .05$; **$p < .01$.

a, b: The means with superscripts a and b were significantly different from each other.

on cigarette and other drug use and a marginal effect on marijuana use. Children who were avoidant with their mothers in infancy reported higher levels of cigarette, marijuana, and other drug use compared to those who were secure with their mothers in infancy. A similar pattern emerged when the four group classifications were used, although the multivariate results were nonsignificant (see Table 7.3). There were no significant associations with attachment security with father at 12 months and adolescent substance use.

Although these results suggest that children who had an avoidant attachment relationship with mothers in infancy were at higher risk for substance use in adolescence for the sample as a whole, the next question was whether infant–mother attachment served as a protective factor in the context of fathers' alcohol problems. Earlier results from the BLS had indicated that among children with alcoholic fathers, those who were secure with their mothers at 12 months had lower externalizing problems at 24 and 36 months (Edwards, Eiden, & Leonard, 2006). When an ANOVA was conducted to examine if infant attachment security with mothers moderated the association between fathers' alcohol problems and adolescent substance use, there was a significant interaction effect of attachment security with mothers (secure vs. insecure) and parent alcohol problems [F (1, 175) = 5.25, $p = .02$, $\eta_p^2 = .03$]. COAs who were insecure with their mothers in infancy had significantly higher levels of other drug use (mean [M] = 2.50, standard deviation [SD] = 4.58) compared to those who were secure ($M = .88$, $SD = 1.92$) or those in the control group ($M = .47$ and .22 and $SD = 1.81$ and .57 for the secure and insecure groups, respectively). Results with the four group attachment classifications indicated a significant interaction effect of infant–mother attachment classifications and alcohol group

status on frequency of marijuana use in adolescence [F (3, 171) = 2.98, $p = .03$, $\eta_p^2 = .05$] and frequency of other drug use in adolescence [F (3, 171) = 2.79, $p = .04$, $\eta_p^2 = .05$]. Results indicated that there were no associations between fathers' alcohol problems and adolescent marijuana or other drug use for those who had a secure attachment relationship with their mother in infancy or those who had a resistant attachment classification (Figure 7.1). However, there was a significant association between fathers' alcohol problems in infancy and adolescent marijuana and other drug use among those who had an avoidant or disorganized with their mother in infancy. These results with the four level classifications need to be viewed with caution and replicated given the small cell sizes ($n = 7$ for avoidant infants in the control group) for some groups, but they are suggestive of the long-term protective effects of attachment security with mothers in the context of fathers' psychopathology. The results with regard to avoidant and disorganized classifications are partially supportive of previous work (Fearon et al., 2010), indicating that disorganized boys from risky social contexts had increases in behavior problems over time.

BEYOND ATTACHMENT: PARENT–INFANT INTERACTIONS

Attachment theory argues that infants form attachment relationships on the basis of repeated interactions with caregivers. Although the exact nature of parent–infant interactions predictive of attachment security has been under debate for some time (Belsky, 1997; De Wolff & van Ijzendoorn, 1997), the theoretical link between parent–infant interactions and attachment security has been well validated (De Wolff

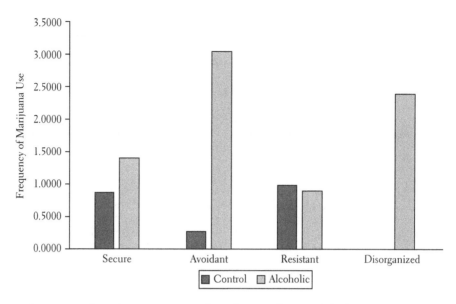

FIGURE 7.1 Interaction of attachment security with mother in infancy and alcohol group status on frequency of marijuana use in adolescence. Note that the pattern of interaction was very similar for frequency of other drug use.

& van Ijzendoorn, 1997). Few studies have examined if parent–child interactions in early childhood beginning in infancy have enduring effects on adolescent substance use in the general developmental literature, with some exceptions noted later. Results from the Minnesota Longitudinal Study of firstborn children of mothers below the poverty level (Siebenbruner, Englund, Egeland, & Hudson, 2006) indicated that maternal hostility experienced by the child from 24 to 42 months during mother–child interactions and externalizing problems in first grade predicted adolescent substance use patterns (experimenters vs. abusers). Similarly, results from the Pitt Mother and Child Project indicated that in a sample of low-income boys, maternal nurturance at 24 months was protective against adolescent substance use at 17 years of age, mainly by associations with higher parental monitoring/knowledge in earlier adolescence (Sitnick et al., 2014). In addition, others have noted the importance of parenting quality in the toddler–preschool period as a significant prospective predictor of early onset antisocial behavior (Moffitt & Caspi, 2001) and teacher reports of externalizing symptoms in childhood (Haltigan et al., 2013). Examining a dynamic, cascade model of adolescent substance use, Dodge et al. (2009) reported that nonsupportive parenting in early childhood was associated with higher externalizing

problems upon school entry, which predicted higher peer problems at school age. Peer problems at school age were then predictive of greater affiliation with deviant peers. Finally, deviant peer affiliation and nonsupportive parenting were predictive of higher adolescent substance use.

Results from the BLS indicated that alcoholic fathers displayed lower warmth and sensitivity and higher negative affect during play interactions with their infants (Eiden, Chavez, & Leonard, 1999). Fathers' alcohol problems and comorbid depression were also prospective predictors of more negative parenting behaviors at toddler age (24 months; Eiden, Leonard, Hoyle, & Chavez, 2004). Similarly, mothers with alcoholic partners displayed lower warmth and sensitivity and higher negative affect toward their infants (Eiden et al., 1999) and toddlers (Eiden et al., 2004). Maternal negative affect, low warmth, and low sensitivity in infancy, but not toddler age, were associated with higher frequency of marijuana use in adolescence ($r = .23$, $-.17$, and $-.15$ respectively; $p < .05$), and higher dyadic negative affect (negative affect expressed by both parent and child toward each other) during mother–infant interactions was significantly associated with higher frequency of marijuana, cigarette, and alcohol use in adolescence ($r = -.18$, .22, and .16, respectively; $p < .01$). Including data at later time points presented a different picture of continuity of maternal warmth and sensitivity predicting low maternal monitoring and higher adolescent substance use (Eiden et al., 2016). Among fathers, high negative affect and low sensitivity at toddler age were associated with higher frequency of marijuana use, cigarette use, and other drug use in adolescence (correlations ranged from –.18 for other drugs to –.23 for marijuana use; $p < .01$). However, when mothers and fathers were included in the same model predicting adolescent substance use, most of the variance was accounted for by continuity in maternal behaviors (Eiden et al., 2016). Taken together, both the general developmental literature and results from the BLS indicate that the quality of parent–child interactions in early childhood may have both enduring effects on adolescent substance use and associated risk processes, and it may be explained by a continuity of risk processes from infancy to adolescence.

TEMPERAMENT

The importance of child temperamental characteristics in etiological pathways to adolescent substance use has been discussed in several theoretical papers (Tarter et al., 1999; Vanyukov et al., 2003; Wills & Ainette, 2010). However, empirical evidence regarding the importance of particular temperamental characteristics as posing risk or being protective against substance use has mostly come from studies beginning in the preschool period (Block, Block, & Keyes, 1988; Caspi et al., 1997; Lerner & Vicary, 1984). For instance, results from a community-recruited longitudinal study in New Zealand indicated that two profiles of temperament—undercontrolled (high activity level, irritability, and low persistence) and inhibited (fearful, uncommunicative, and easily upset)—assessed by examiner ratings at age 3 years were associated with higher substance use disorders at age 21 years. However, the comorbid risks for the two profiles were different, with the undercontrolled profile associated with antisocial personality disorder and the inhibited profile associated with depressive disorders in adulthood. Similarly, children's difficult temperament at ages 3–5 years assessed via maternal reports was associated with higher frequency of substance use in late adolescence (16–18 years; Lerner & Vicary, 1984). Finally, in a study of children recruited from a university-run preschool, adolescents who were using

substances by age 14 years were more likely to have been rated by examiners as having higher activity level, reactivity to frustration, negative emotionality, and low delay of gratification at 3 and 4 years of age (Block et al., 1988).

In addition to the previously discussed studies that examined direct associations between temperamental risk in early childhood and adolescent substance use, a larger literature and theoretical models have focused on mediated processes via childhood variables or interactions of temperament with contextual risk and protective processes in both COA and non-COA samples (Kirisci, Tarter, Ridenour, Reynolds, & Vanyukov, 2013; Martel et al., 2009; Scalco & Colder, 2016; Wills & Ainette, 2010). For instance, in a study examining a developmental cascade model (Martel et al., 2009), temperamental traits of reactive control, negative emotionality, and resiliency measured at child age between 3 and 5 years were associated with disruptive behaviors in adolescence via higher inattention/hyperactivity at ages 6–11 years. Composite disruptive behavior across development (ages 3–17 years) was associated with higher adolescent substance use (ages 11–17 years).

The lack of empirical evidence linking early childhood temperament (first 3 years of life) to substance use risk is surprising. Theoretical models of temperament suggest that individual differences in temperament are evident in the first 3 years of life, reflect biological influences in early childhood and are modified based on environmental experiences, and include closely associated affective and cognitive processing systems (Shiner et al., 2012). One important aspect of temperament that develops during the second year of life is effortful control, often defined as the ability to suppress inappropriate approach responses given environmental demands and to be planful (Kochanska, Murray, Jacques, Koenig, & Vandegeest, 1996; Rothbart & Ahadi, 1994). This is similar to the concept of self-control thought to be critical in etiological models of adolescent substance use (Wills & Ainette, 2010). Results from the BLS indicated that boys with alcoholic fathers had lower effortful control compared to controls assessed in laboratory paradigms at 2 and 3 years of age, but there were no differences among girls (Eiden, Edwards, & Leonard, 2004). These differences in effortful control were evident in middle childhood as well, for the sample as a whole (Adkison et al., 2013). Fathers' warmth during father–toddler interactions during the second year of life mediated the association between fathers' alcohol problems and child effortful control for both boys and girls, when father–child and mother–child interactions were examined separately. Higher effortful control at toddler age was associated with lower marijuana and other illicit drug use in late adolescence ($r = -.21$, $p = .00$).

FAMILY/CONTEXTUAL PROCESSES

In addition to parent characteristics, child characteristics, and parent–child interactional processes, the family context may have a significant impact on adolescent substance use. Theories such as the ecological theory (Bronfenbrenner, 1977), relational developmental systems theory (Belsky, Lerner, & Spanier, 1984), and family systems theories (Cox & Paley, 2003; Cummings, Davies, & Campbell, 2000) highlight the importance of the relationship between parents as having a significant influence on the parent–child relationship and child health and development. The quality of intimate partner relationships may impact children's development either directly by providing social learning contexts (Bandura, Ross, & Ross, 1961) or increasing child distress (Cummings, Pellegrini, Notarius, & Cummings, 1989) or indirectly by spilling over into parent–child interactions (Cox & Paley, 2003; Repetti, Taylor, & Seeman, 2002). Results from reviews of the literature provide support for both alternatives and indicate moderate associations between intimate partner relationships and quality of parenting (Erel & Burman, 1995; Krishnakumar & Buehler, 2000). Parental separation and divorce are also predictive of earlier onset of alcohol use (Doherty & Needle, 1991; Grant et al., 2015; Needle, Su, & Doherty, 1990). Thus, the intimate partner context may be a significant source of influence in developmental processes leading to adolescent substance use.

In one of the few studies examining the association between marital quality and adolescent substance use, Hair, Moore, and Hadley (2009) classified adolescents into groups based on marital adolescent–parent relationship quality. Results indicated that adolescents who were exposed to positive marital relationships and had positive relationships with both parents had lower levels of substance use compared to other groups. Similarly, in a diverse sample of South African 14- and 17-year-old adolescents,

higher marital hostility was associated with adolescent substance use via lower parental knowledge and limit setting (Amoateng, Barber, & Erickson, 2006). In contrast to the limited literature on interparental relationships and adolescent substance use, there is a large literature on the role of marital relationships in the development of children's externalizing problems, including children of twin studies that examine potential genetic influences. Results indicate that the association between marital conflict and children's internalizing and externalizing symptoms largely reflects environmental influences (McAdams et al., 2014). In addition to marital conflict, parental divorce or separation is also associated with higher risk for externalizing disorders and young adult alcohol problems (McAdams et al., 2014) and earlier onset of alcohol use even after accounting for parental alcohol and other drug dependence (Waldron et al., 2015). Thus, the intimate partner context is an important consideration in developmental pathways to adolescent substance use etiology, but it has received little attention in studies beginning in early childhood.

Results from the BLS indicate prospective associations between fathers' psychopathology in the infant/toddler years and increases in harsh parenting from early childhood to kindergarten age via higher marital aggression at preschool age (Finger, Kachadourian, et al., 2010). Marital aggression also mediated the association between parental psychopathology in early childhood and social competence in kindergarten (Finger, Eiden, Edwards, Leonard, & Kachadourian, 2010), as well as increases in child depression and anxiety from early to middle childhood (Eiden, Molnar, Colder, Edwards, & Leonard, 2009). With regard to associations with adolescent substance use, higher maternal experience of verbal aggression from partners in the infant/toddler years was associated with higher frequency of adolescent alcohol (correlations ranging from .22 to .26, $p < .01$) and marijuana use (correlations ranging from .15 to .17, $p < .05$). Higher levels of total aggression between parents in early childhood were associated with significantly higher frequency of adolescent cigarette and marijuana use (correlations ranging from .26 to .30, $p < .001$). To what extent these reflect continuity of family aggression, higher levels of separation and divorce, spillover effects on parenting, and associations with externalizing problems as a mediational pathway remains to be investigated. This is clearly an important area of investigation because the results may speak to the potential for positive effects of marital or couples therapy on adolescent health behaviors.

GENDER DIFFERENCES

Gender differences in adolescent substance use have been changing over time, although there are robust and more consistent patterns of gender differences in rates of substance use during adulthood, with men more likely to use substances compared to women (Substance Abuse and Mental Health Services Administration [SAMHSA], 2014). Men also have higher rates of dependence on alcohol and other drugs compared to women. However, the pattern of gender differences in adolescence is more complex (Hammerslag & Gulley, 2016). For instance, among 12- to 17-year-olds, girls are more likely to use some substances and more likely to enter treatment for prescription drug use, cocaine use, and methamphetamine use compared to boys; in addition, girls are as likely to be in treatment for heroin use as boys (SAMHSA, 2014). Results also differ by race/ethnicity, and there are differences in results within ethnic subgroups (Epstein, Botvin, & Diaz, 2001). For instance, some studies report higher rates of alcohol use and problems among Hispanic girls compared to boys (Vaughan, Gassman, Jun, & de Martinez, 2015), and others report the opposite (Epstein et al., 2001).

Results from the COA literature are similarly mixed, with theoretical and empirical evidence providing support for higher adolescent substance use among both boys (Sartor et al., 2007) and girls (Hammerslag & Gulley, 2016). There is evidence that girls may be more sensitive to stressful family interactions, resulting in higher rates of substance use among girls in alcoholic families (Hammerslag & Gulley, 2016), although the rates of alcohol problems have been higher among boys in alcoholic families (Buu et al., 2014), and sons of alcoholic parents are more likely to progress from alcohol initiation to alcohol dependence (Buu et al., 2012). Twin studies also provide support for the importance of examining gender differences in pathways to adolescent substance use. For instance, the association between parent antisocial behavior and child conduct disorder was largely genetic for girls, but there was a significant environmental effect for boys, after accounting for genetic transmission (for a review, see McAdams

et al., 2014). This is clearly an area for further investigation. However, examination of gender differences in etiological pathways is especially challenging because it requires large number of participants who are followed over time beginning before initiation and across periods of initiation, use, and desistance or problems.

Results from the BLS indicated significant gender differences in marijuana use [F (1, 180) = 4.35, p = .04], with boys reporting higher levels of use compared to girls (M = 1.66 and 1.02 and SD = 2.46 and 1.60 for boys and girls, respectively). More important, MANOVA indicated there were significant multivariate group (both parents alcoholic, father alcoholic, vs. control) by gender interaction effects when frequencies of use of alcohol, marijuana, cigarettes, and other drugs were used as the dependent measures [F (8, 346) = 2.63, p = .008, η_p^2 = .06]. Univariate analyses indicated a significant group by gender interaction on frequency of cigarette use in the past 30 days [F (2, 176) = 9.62, p = .00, η_p^2 = .10]. Boys with two alcoholic parents reported significantly higher frequency of cigarette use in the past 30 days compared to girls (M = 6.55 and 0.71 and SD = 9.47 and 1.86, respectively). The results regarding these group by gender interactions need to be viewed with caution given the small number of families who had two parents with alcohol problems, but they are suggestive of greater risk for boys.

FETAL ORIGINS

All of the studies discussed previously, including the BLS, begin in the postnatal period. This is a significant drawback given empirical evidence and theoretical discussions regarding fetal origins of health and disease (Wadhwa, Buss, Entringer, & Swanson, 2009). The prenatal period is a critical time for neurological development and, consequently, is a time of enhanced vulnerability during which a variety of exposures have been shown to have a long-term impact on both physical and behavioral development. The importance of the fetal period was noted years ago with the recognition of fetal alcohol syndrome (Jones & Smith, 1973) and in a series of papers by Barker and colleagues on infant mortality and morbidity (Barker, Martyn, Osmond, Hales, & Fall, 1993; Barker & Osmond, 1986; Barker, Winter, Osmond, Margetts, & Simmonds, 1989). Subsequently, there has been a growing body of literature examining fetal origins of child health and development (Schlotz & Phillips, 2009), theories of fetal programming (Coe & Lubach, 2008), and developmental origins of health and disease (Wadhwa et al., 2009). Relatively recently, a few of these studies have focused on adolescent substance use, primarily in the context of maternal substance use during pregnancy (Conradt et al., 2014; Frank et al., 2011, 2014; Minnes et al., 2014; Rando, Chaplin, Potenza, Mayes, & Sinha, 2013; Yip, Lacadie, Sinha, Mayes, & Potenza, 2015). However, consideration of fetal origins of adolescent substance use other than prenatal substance exposure samples has been largely lacking. Given discoveries regarding the long-lasting effects of prenatal stressors on a range of developmental outcomes that include physical and mental health, this is an important area for further research.

DEVELOPMENTAL CASCADE

We have recently published results from a developmental cascade model predicting adolescent substance use that included data from later time points (Eiden et al., 2016). This model had three hypothesized pathways from infancy to adolescent substance use (Figure 7.2). The first was a parenting pathway with parent depression, antisocial behavior, and alcohol problems in infancy predicting low parental warmth/sensitivity at toddler age to kindergarten age, predicting low parental monitoring in middle childhood to early adolescence and parents who viewed underage drinking as normative, predicting higher engagement with delinquent and substance-using peers and underage drinking, and predicting substance use in late adolescence. The second was an externalizing pathway with parent psychopathology in infancy predicting low warmth/sensitivity at toddler age, predicting low self-regulation at preschool age, and predicting high externalizing problems from kindergarten age to early adolescence, leading to higher engagement with delinquent and substance-using peers in early adolescence and higher substance use in late adolescence. The third was a social competence pathway beginning in early school age that may be protective against engagement with delinquent and substance-using peers in adolescence. Results were supportive of the first two pathways, the parenting pathway and the externalizing pathway, but not the social competence pathway.

FUTURE DIRECTIONS AND IMPLICATIONS FOR PREVENTION

Examining developmental processes beginning in the fetal period and testing theory-driven developmental pathways would add to the literature on adolescent substance use disorders and be of practical public health significance as well. One such heuristic is the dynamic cascade model (Dodge et al., 2009) that points to developmental processes that may increase risk or protect against adolescent substance use disorders. Examining whether etiological processes may be different for boys and girls may also be informative, but this requires large samples. This may be accomplished by combining data sets that include measures of individual, family, and contextual risk and protective processes. Examining long-term developmental processes and the role of early experiences for adolescent substance use is not an easy endeavor, but it may be critical given many recent advances in our knowledge about the importance of these experiences for developmental outcomes.

Results from the BLS have important implications with regard to timing and content of preventive interventions for children of alcoholic fathers and prevention of adolescent substance use in general. One of the most significant findings is the continuity of protective parenting processes from toddler to early adolescence as being a critical pathway for lowering substance use risk. Maternal warmth/sensitivity in toddler to kindergarten age and parental monitoring or knowledge of where and with whom their children are interacting in middle childhood resulted in lower engagement with substance-using and delinquent peers and less underage drinking. Thus, targeting preventive interventions in early childhood with content focused on increasing maternal warmth and sensitivity during mother–child interactions even in the context of fathers' psychopathology may result in a cascade of protective processes. Second, children's self-regulation, defined as internalization of rules of conduct or conscience, and effortful control at preschool age were a critical mediator of parental psychopathology in infancy and continuity of externalizing problems from kindergarten age to early adolescence. Children with higher externalizing problems were more likely to engage with delinquent and substance-using peers and engage in higher frequency of marijuana use in late adolescence. Thus, focusing interventions that are designed to promote self-regulation in the preschool years may not only

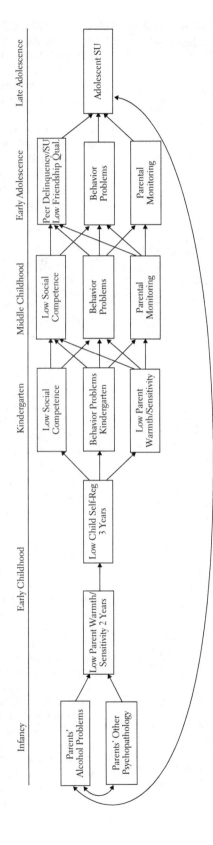

FIGURE 7.2 Hypothesized dynamic cascade model. SU, substance use.

prevent continuity of externalizing problems but also lower risk for adolescent substance use. Interventions targeted in middle childhood, before transition to high school, may also be beneficial, with a focus on preventing underage drinking and engagement with delinquent peers. Content focused on teaching parents how to increase child self-disclosure and their own knowledge of children's activities and peer groups may be important in preventing risk escalation from middle childhood to adolescence.

ACKNOWLEDGMENTS

The Buffalo Longitudinal Study was supported by grants R01 AA10042 and R21 AA021617 from the National Institute on Alcohol Abuse and Alcoholism of the National Institutes of Health and by grant 2012-W9-BX-0001 from the National Institute of Justice, Office of Justice Programs, US Department of Justice.

REFERENCES

Adkison, S. E., Grohman, K., Colder, C. R., Leonard, K., Orrange-Torchia, T., Peterson, E., & Eiden, R. D. (2013). Impact of fathers' alcohol problems on the development of effortful control in early adolescence. *Journal of Studies on Alcohol and Drugs*, 74(5), 674–683.

Amoateng, A. Y., Barber, B. K., & Erickson, L. D. (2006). Family predictors of adolescent substance use: The case of high school students in the Cape Metropolitan Area, Cape Town, South Africa. *Journal of Child and Adolescent Mental Health*, 18(1), 7–15. doi:10.2989/17280580609486612

Bandura, A., Ross, D., & Ross, S. A. (1961). Transmission of aggression through imitation of aggressive models. *Journal of Abnormal and Social Psychology*, 63(3), 575–582.

Bares, C. B., Delva, J., & Andrade, F. H. (2015). Pathways to adolescent depression and cigarette smoking: A longitudinal investigation of Chilean mothers and their children. *Social Work Research*, 39(1), 23–35. doi:10.1093/swr/svu029

Barker, D. J., Martyn, C. N., Osmond, C., Hales, C. N., & Fall, C. H. (1993). Growth in utero and serum cholesterol concentrations in adult life. *BMJ*, 307(6918), 1524–1527.

Barker, D. J., & Osmond, C. (1986). Infant mortality, childhood nutrition, and ischaemic heart disease in England and Wales. *Lancet*, 1(8489), 1077–1081.

Barker, D. J., Winter, P. D., Osmond, C., Margetts, B., & Simmonds, S. J. (1989). Weight in infancy and death from ischaemic heart disease. *Lancet*, 2(8663), 577–580.

Belsky, J. (1997). Attachment, mating, and parenting: An evolutionary interpretation. *Human Nature*, 8(4), 361–381.

Belsky, J., Lerner, R. M., & Spanier, G. B. (1984). *The child in the family*. Reading, MA: Addison-Wesley.

Block, J., Block, J. H., & Keyes, S. (1988). Longitudinally foretelling drug usage in adolescence: Early childhood personality and environmental precursors. *Child Development*, 59(2), 336–355. doi:10.2307/1130314

Bowlby, J. (1969). *Attachment and Loss: Vol. 1. Attachment*. New York, NY: Basic Books.

Bowlby, J. (1973). *Attachment and Loss: Vol. 2. Separation*. New York, NY: Basic Books.

Bronfenbrenner, U. (1977). Toward an experimental ecology of human development. *American Psychologist*, 32, 513–531.

Buu, A., Dabrowska, A., Mygrants, M., Puttler, L. I., Jester, J. M., & Zucker, R. A. (2014). Gender differences in the developmental risk of onset of alcohol, nicotine, and marijuana use and the effects of nicotine and marijuana use on alcohol outcomes. *Journal of Studies on Alcohol and Drugs*, 75(5), 850–858. doi:10.15288/jsad.2014.75.850

Buu, A., Wang, W., Schroder, S. A., Kalaida, N. L., Puttler, L. I., & Zucker, R. A. (2012). Developmental emergence of alcohol use disorder symptoms and their potential as early indicators for progression to alcohol dependence in a high risk sample: A longitudinal study from childhood to early adulthood. *Journal of Abnormal Psychology*, 121(4), 897–908. doi:10.1037/a0024926

Caspi, A., Begg, D., Dickson, N., Harrington, H., Langley, J., Moffitt, T. E., & Silva, P. A. (1997). Personality differences predict health-risk behaviors in young adulthood: Evidence from a longitudinal study. *Journal of Personality and Social Psychology*, 73(5), 1052–1063. doi:10.1037/0022-3514.73.5.1052

Chassin, L., Curran, P. J., Hussong, A. M., & Colder, C. R. (1997). The relation of parent alcoholism to adolescent substance use: A longitudinal follow-up study. In G. A. Marlatt & G. R. VandenBos (Eds.), *Addictive behaviors: Readings on etiology, prevention, and treatment* (pp. 509–533). Washington, DC: American Psychological Association.

Chassin, L., Presson, C., Il-Cho, Y., Lee, M., & Macy, J. (2013). Developmental factors in addiction: Methodological considerations. In J. MacKillop & H. de Wit (Eds.), *The Wiley-Blackwell handbook of addiction psychopharmacology* (pp. 7–26). Malden, MA: Wiley-Blackwell.

Chassin, L., Rogosch, F., & Barrera, M. (1991). Substance use and symptomatology among adolescent children of alcoholics. *Journal of Abnormal Psychology, 100*(4), 449–463.

Cicchetti, D., & Rogosch, F. A. (1996). Equifinality and multifinality in developmental psychopathology. *Development and Psychopathology, 8*(4), 597–600. doi:10.1017/S0954579400007318

Cloninger, C. R., Sigvardsson, S., & Bohman, M. (1988). Childhood personality predicts alcohol abuse in young adults. *Alcoholism: Clinical & Experimental Research, 12*(4), 494–505.

Coe, C. L., & Lubach, G. R. (2008). Fetal programming: Prenatal origins of health and illness. *Current Directions in Psychological Science, 17*(1), 36–41. doi:10.1111/j.1467-8721.2008.00544.x

Colder, C. R., Scalco, M., Trucco, E. M., Read, J. P., Lengua, L. J., Wieczorek, W. F., & Hawk, L. W., Jr. (2013). Prospective associations of internalizing and externalizing problems and their co-occurrence with early adolescent substance use. *Journal of Abnormal Child Psychology, 41*(4), 667–677. doi:10.1007/s10802-012-9701-0

Conradt, E., Lagasse, L. L., Shankaran, S., Bada, H., Bauer, C. R., Whitaker, T. M., . . . Lester, B. M. (2014). Physiological correlates of neurobehavioral disinhibition that relate to drug use and risky sexual behavior in adolescents with prenatal substance exposure. *Developmental Neuroscience, 36*(3–4), 306–315. doi:10.1159/000365004

Cortes, R. C., Fleming, C. B., Mason, W. A., & Catalano, R. F. (2009). Risk factors linking maternal depressed mood to growth in adolescent substance use. *Journal of Emotional and Behavioral Disorders, 17*(1), 49–64. doi:10.1177/1063426608321690

Costello, E. J., Erkanli, A., Federman, E., & Angold, A. (1999). Development of psychiatric comorbidity with substance abuse in adolescents: Effects of timing and sex. *Journal of Clinical Child Psychology, 28*(3), 298–311.

Cox, M. J., & Paley, B. (2003). Understanding families as systems. *Current Directions in Psychological Science, 12*(5), 193–196. doi:10.1111/1467-8721.01259

Cummings, E. M., Davies, P. T., & Campbell, S. B. (2000). *Developmental psychopathology and family process: Theory, research, and clinical implications.* New York, NY: Guilford.

Cummings, J. S., Pellegrini, D. S., Notarius, C. I., & Cummings, E. M. (1989). Children's responses to angry adult behavior as a function of marital distress and history of interparent hostility. *Child Development, 60*, 1035–1043.

De Wolff, M., & van Ijzendoorn, M. H. (1997). Sensitivity and attachment: A meta-analysis on parental antecedents of infant attachment. *Child Development, 68*(4), 571–591.

Dodge, K. A., Malone, P. S., Lansford, J. E., Miller, S., Pettit, G. S., & Bates, J. E. (2009). A dynamic cascade model of the development of substance-abuse onset. *Monographs of the Society for Research in Child Development, 73*(3), 1–31.

Doherty, W. J., & Needle, R. H. (1991). Psychological adjustment and substance use among adolescents before and after a parental divorce. *Child Development, 62*(2), 328–337. doi:10.2307/1131006

Donovan, J. E. (2004). Adolescent alcohol initiation: A review of psychosocial risk factors. *Journal of Adolescent Health, 35*(6), 529.

Duncan, A. E., Scherrer, J., Fu, Q., Bucholz, K. K., Heath, A. C., True, W. R., . . . Jacob, T. (2006). Exposure to paternal alcoholism does not predict development of alcohol-use disorders in offspring: Evidence from an offspring-of-twins study. *Journal of Studies on Alcohol, 67*(5), 649–656. doi:10.15288/jsa.2006.67.649

Edwards, E. P., Eiden, R. D., & Leonard, K. E. (2004). Impact of fathers' alcoholism and associated risk factors on parent–infant attachment stability from 12 to 18 months. *Infant Mental Health Journal, 25*(6), 556–579.

Edwards, E. P., Eiden, R. D., & Leonard, K. E. (2006). Behavior problems in 18- to 36-month-old children of alcoholic fathers: Secure mother–infant attachment as a protective factor. *Development and Psychopathology, 18*(2), 395–407. doi:10.1017/S0954579406060214

Eiden, R. D., Chavez, F., & Leonard, K. E. (1999). Parent–infant interactions among families with alcoholic fathers. *Development and Psychopathology, 11,* 745–762.

Eiden, R. D., Edwards, E. P., & Leonard, K. E. (2002). Mother–infant and father–infant attachment among alcoholic families. *Development and Psychopathology, 14*(2), 253–278.

Eiden, R. D., Edwards, E. P., & Leonard, K. E. (2004). Predictors of effortful control among children of alcoholic and nonalcoholic fathers. *Journal of Studies on Alcohol, 65*(3), 309–319.

Eiden, R. D., Leonard, K. E., Hoyle, R. H., & Chavez, F. (2004). A transactional model of parent–infant interactions in alcoholic families. *Psychology of Addictive Behaviors, 18*(4), 350–361.

Eiden, R. D., Lessard, J., Colder, C. R., Livingston, J., Casey, M., & Leonard, K. E. (2016). Developmental cascade model for adolescent substance use from infancy to late adolescence. *Developmental*

Psychology, 52(10), 1619–1633. doi:10.1037/dev0000199

Eiden, R. D., Molnar, D. S., Colder, C., Edwards, E. P., & Leonard, K. E. (2009). A conceptual model predicting internalizing problems in middle childhood among children of alcoholic and nonalcoholic fathers: The role of marital aggression. *Journal of Studies on Alcohol and Drugs, 70*(5), 741–750.

Ellickson, P. L., & Hays, R. D. (1991). Antecedents of drinking among young adolescents with different alcohol use histories. *Journal of Studies on Alcohol, 52*, 398–408.

Epstein, J. A., Botvin, G. J., & Diaz, T. (2001). Alcohol use among Dominican and Puerto Rican adolescents residing in New York City: Role of Hispanic group and gender. *Journal of Developmental and Behavioral Pediatrics, 22*(2), 113–118. doi:10.1097/00004703-200104000-00005

Erel, O., & Burman, B. (1995). Interrelatedness of marital relations and parent–child relations: A meta-analytic review. *Psychological Bulletin, 118*(1), 108–132.

Fearon, R. P., Bakermans-Kranenburg, M. J., van Ijzendoorn, M. H., Lapsley, A. M., & Roisman, G. I. (2010). The significance of insecure attachment and disorganization in the development of children's externalizing behavior: A meta-analytic study. *Child Development, 81*(2), 435–456.

Finger, B., Eiden, R. D., Edwards, E. P., Leonard, K. E., & Kachadourian, L. (2010). Marital aggression and child peer competence: A comparison of three conceptual models. *Personal Relationships, 17*(3), 357–376.

Finger, B., Kachadourian, L. K., Molnar, D. S., Eiden, R. D., Edwards, E. P., & Leonard, K. E. (2010). Alcoholism, associated risk factors, and harsh parenting among fathers: Examining the role of marital aggression. *Addictive Behaviors, 35*(6), 541–548.

Fisher, S. D., Brock, R. L., O'Hara, M. W., Kopelman, R., & Stuart, S. (2015). Longitudinal contribution of maternal and paternal depression to toddler behaviors: Interparental conflict and later depression as mediators. *Couple and Family Psychology: Research and Practice, 4*(2), 61–73. doi:10.1037/cfp0000037

Fitzgerald, H. E., & Eiden, R. D. (2007). Paternal alcoholism, family functioning, and infant mental health. *Zero to Three, 27*, 11–18.

Frank, D. A., Kuranz, S., Appugliese, D., Cabral, H., Chen, C., Crooks, D., . . . Rose-Jacobs, R. (2014). Problematic substance use in urban adolescents: Role of intrauterine exposures to cocaine and marijuana and post-natal environment. *Drug and Alcohol Dependence, 142*, 181–190. doi:10.1016/j.drugalcdep.2014.06.014

Frank, D. A., Rose-Jacobs, R., Crooks, D., Cabral, H. J., Gerteis, J., Hacker, K. A., . . . Heeren, T. (2011). Adolescent initiation of licit and illicit substance use: Impact of intrauterine exposures and post-natal exposure to violence. *Neurotoxicology and Teratology, 33*(1), 100–109. doi:10.1016/j.ntt.2010.06.002

Goodman, S. H. (2007). Depression in mothers. *Annual Review of Clinical Psychology, 3*, 107–135. doi:10.1146/annurev.clinpsy.3.022806.091401

Goodman, S. H., Rouse, M. H., Connell, A. M., Broth, M. R., Hall, C. M., & Heyward, D. (2011). Maternal depression and child psychopathology: A meta-analytic review. *Clinical Child and Family Psychology Review, 14*(1), 1–27. doi:10.1007/s10567-010-0080-1

Grant, J. D., Waldron, M., Sartor, C. E., Scherrer, J. F., Duncan, A. E., McCutcheon, V. V., . . . Bucholz, K. K. (2015). Parental separation and offspring alcohol involvement: Findings from offspring of alcoholic and drug dependent twin fathers. *Alcoholism: Clinical and Experimental Research, 39*(7), 1166–1173. doi:10.1111/acer.12766

Gutierrez-Galve, L., Stein, A., Hanington, L., Heron, J., & Ramchandani, P. (2015). Paternal depression in the postnatal period and child development: Mediators and moderators. *Pediatrics, 135*(2), e339–e347. doi:10.1542/peds.2014-2411

Hair, E. C., Moore, K. A., & Hadley, A. M. (2009). Parent marital quality and the parent–adolescent relationship: Effects on adolescent and young adult health outcomes. *Marriage & Family Review, 45*, 218–248.

Haltigan, J. D., Roisman, G. I., & Fraley, R. C. (2013). The predictive significance of early caregiving experiences for symptoms of psychopathology through midadolescence: Enduring or transient effects? *Development and Psychopathology, 25*(1), 209–221. doi:10.1017/S0954579412000260

Hammerslag, L. R., & Gulley, J. M. (2016). Sex differences in behavior and neural development and their role in adolescent vulnerability to substance use. *Behavioural Brain Research, 298*(Part A), 15–26. doi:10.1016/j.bbr.2015.04.008

Harold, G. T., Elam, K. K., Lewis, G., Rice, F., & Thapar, A. (2012). Interparental conflict, parent psychopathology, hostile parenting, and child antisocial behavior: Examining the role of maternal versus paternal influences using a novel genetically sensitive research design. *Development and Psychopathology, 24*(4), 1283–1295. doi:10.1017/S0954579412000703

Hussong, A. M., & Chassin, L. (1997). Substance use initiation among adolescent children of alcoholics: Testing protective factors. *Journal of Studies on Alcohol, 58*(3), 272–279.

Hussong, A. M., Flora, D. B., Curran, P. J., Chassin, L. A., & Zucker, R. A. (2008). Defining risk heterogeneity for internalizing symptoms among children of alcoholic parents. *Development and Psychopathology, 20*(1), 165–193. doi:10.1017/S0954579408000084

Hussong, A. M., Huang, W., Curran, P., Chassin, L., & Zucker, R. (2010). Parent alcoholism impacts the severity and timing of children's externalizing symptoms. *Journal of Abnormal Child Psychology, 38*(3), 367–380.

Hussong, A. M., Wirth, R. J., Edwards, M. C., Curran, P. J., Chassin, L. A., & Zucker, R. A. (2007). Externalizing symptoms among children of alcoholic parents: Entry points for an antisocial pathway to alcoholism. *Journal of Abnormal Psychology, 116*(3), 529–542. doi:10.1037/0021-843X.116.3.529

Jacob, T., Seilhamer, R. A., & Rushe, R. H. (1989). Alcoholism and family interaction: An experimental paradigm. *American Journal of Drug and Alcohol Abuse, 15*(1), 73–91. doi:10.3109/00952998908993401

Jacob, T., Waterman, B., Heath, A., True, W., Bucholz, K. K., Haber, R., . . . Fu, Q. (2003). Genetic and environmental effects on offspring alcoholism: New insights using an offspring-of-twins design. *Archives of General Psychiatry, 60*(12), 1265–1272. doi:10.1001/archpsyc.60.12.1265

Jessor, R. (1991). Risk behavior in adolescence: A psychosocial framework for understanding and action. *Journal of Adolescent Health, 12*(8), 597–605.

Jester, J. M., Nigg, J. T., Buu, A., Puttler, L. I., Glass, J. M., Heitzeg, M. M., . . . Zucker, R. A. (2008). Trajectories of childhood aggression and inattention/hyperactivity: Differential effects on substance abuse in adolescence. *Journal of the American Academy of Child and Adolescent Psychiatry, 47*(10), 1158–1165. doi:10.1097/CHI.0b013e3181825a4e

Jones, K. L., & Smith, D. W. (1973). Recognition of the fetal alcohol syndrome in early infancy. *Lancet, 2,* 999–1001.

Kellam, S. G., & Anthony, J. C. (1998). Targeting early antecedents to prevent tobacco smoking: Findings from an epidemiologically based randomized field trial. *American Journal of Public Health, 88*(10), 1490–1495.

Keller, P. S., Cummings, E. M., Peterson, K. M., & Davies, P. T. (2009). Marital conflict in the context of parental depressive symptoms: Implications for the development of children's adjustment problems. *Social Development, 18*(3), 536–555. doi:10.1111/j.1467-9507.2008.00509.x

Kirisci, L., Tarter, R. E., Ridenour, T., Reynolds, M., & Vanyukov, M. (2013). Longitudinal modeling of transmissible risk in boys who subsequently develop cannabis use disorder. *American Journal of Drug and Alcohol Abuse, 39*(3), 180–185. doi:10.3109/00952990.2013.774009

Kochanska, G., Murray, K., Jacques, T. Y., Koenig, A. L., & Vandegeest, K. A. (1996). Inhibitory control in young children and its role in emerging internalization. *Child Development, 67,* 490–507.

Krishnakumar, A., & Buehler, C. (2000). Interparental conflict and parenting behaviors: A meta-analytic review. *Family Relations, 49*(1), 25–44.

Lerner, J. V., & Vicary, J. R. (1984). Difficult temperament and drug use: Analyses from the New York longitudinal study. *Journal of Drug Education, 14*(1), 1–8.

Loukas, A., Fitzgerald, H. E., Zucker, R. A., & Von Eye, A. (2001). Parental alcoholism and co-occurring antisocial behavior: Prospective relationships to externalizing behavior problems in their young sons. *Journal of Abnormal Child Psychology, 29*(2), 91–106.

Lupien, S. J., Parent, S., Evans, A. C., Tremblay, R. E., Zelazo, P. D., Corbo, V., . . . Séguin, J. R. (2011). Larger amygdala but no change in hippocampal volume in 10-year-old children exposed to maternal depressive symptomatology since birth. *Proceedings of the National Academy of Sciences of the USA, 108*(34), 14324–14329. doi:10.1073/pnas.1105371108

Martel, M. M., Pierce, L., Nigg, J. T., Jester, J. M., Adams, K., Puttler, L. I., . . . Zucker, R. A. (2009). Temperament pathways to childhood disruptive behavior and adolescent substance abuse: Testing a cascade model. *Journal of Abnormal Child Psychology, 37*(3), 363–373. doi:10.1007/s10802-008-9269-x

McAdams, T. A., Neiderhiser, J. M., Rijsdijk, F. V., Narusyte, J., Lichtenstein, P., & Eley, T. C. (2014). Accounting for genetic and environmental confounds in associations between parent and child characteristics: A systematic review of children-of-twins studies. *Psychological Bulletin, 140*(4), 1138–1173. doi:10.1037/a0036416

McCrory, E., De Brito, S. A., & Viding, E. (2010). Research review: The neurobiology and genetics of maltreatment and adversity. *Journal of Child Psychology and Psychiatry, 51*(10), 1079–1095. doi:10.1111/j.1469-7610.2010.02271.x

Mehta, M. A., Golembo, N. I., Nosarti, C., Colvert, E., Mota, A., Williams, S. C. R., . . . Sonuga-Barke, E. J. S. (2009). Amygdala, hippocampal and corpus callosum size following severe early institutional deprivation: The English and Romanian Adoptees study pilot. *Journal of Child Psychology and Psychiatry, 50*(8), 943–951. doi:10.1111/j.1469-7610.2009.02084.x

Minnes, S., Singer, L., Min, M. O., Wu, M., Lang, A., & Yoon, S. (2014). Effects of prenatal cocaine/polydrug exposure on substance use by age 15. *Drug and Alcohol Dependence, 134*, 201–210. doi:10.1016/j.drugalcdep.2013.09.031

Moffitt, T. E., & Caspi, A. (2001). Childhood predictors differentiate life-course persistent and adolescence-limited antisocial pathways among males and females. *Development and Psychopathology, 13*(2), 355–375.

Moutsiana, C., Johnstone, T., Murray, L., Fearon, P., Cooper, P. J., Pliatsikas, C., . . . Halligan, S. L. (2015). Insecure attachment during infancy predicts greater amygdala volumes in early adulthood. *Journal of Child Psychology and Psychiatry, 56*(5), 540–548. doi:10.1111/jcpp.12317

Needle, R. H., Su, S. S., & Doherty, W. J. (1990). Divorce, remarriage, and adolescent substance use: A prospective longitudinal study. *Journal of Marriage and the Family, 52*(1), 157–169. doi:10.2307/352847

Noll, R. B., Zucker, R. A., & Greenberg, G. S. (1990). Identification of alcohol by smell among preschoolers: Evidence for early socialization about drugs occurring in the home. *Child Development, 51*, 1520–1527.

O'Hara, M. W., & Fisher, S. D. (2010). Psychopathological states in the father and their impact on parenting. In S. Tyano, M. Keren, H. Herrman, & J. Cox (Eds.), *Parenthood and mental health: A bridge between infant and adult psychiatry* (pp. 231–240). Hoboken, NJ: Wiley-Blackwell.

O'Hara, M. W., & McCabe, J. E. (2013). Postpartum depression: Current status and future directions. *Annual Review of Clinical Psychology, 9*, 379–407. doi:10.1146/annurev-clinpsy-050212-185612

Puttler, L. I., Zucker, R. A., Fitzgerald, H. E., & Bingham, C. R. (1998). Behavioral outcomes among children of alcoholics during the early and middle childhood years: Familial subtype variations. *Alcoholism: Clinical & Experimental Research, 22*(9), 1962–1972.

Raby, K. L., Roisman, G. I., Fraley, R. C., & Simpson, J. A. (2015). The enduring predictive significance of early maternal sensitivity: Social and academic competence through age 32 years. *Child Development, 86*(3), 695–708. doi:10.1111/cdev.12325

Rando, K., Chaplin, T. M., Potenza, M. N., Mayes, L., & Sinha, R. (2013). Prenatal cocaine exposure and gray matter volume in adolescent boys

and girls: Relationship to substance use initiation. *Biological Psychiatry, 74*(7), 482–489. doi:10.1016/j.biopsych.2013.04.030

Repetti, R. L., Taylor, S. E., & Seeman, T. E. (2002). Risky families: Family social environments and the mental and physical health of offspring. *Psychological Bulletin, 128*(2), 330–366.

Rothbart, M. K., & Ahadi, S. A. (1994). Temperament and the development of personality. *Journal of Abnormal Psychology, 103*(1), 55–66.

Sartor, C. E., Lynskey, M. T., Heath, A. C., Jacob, T., & True, W. (2007). The role of childhood risk factors in initiation of alcohol use and progression to alcohol dependence. *Addiction, 102*(2), 216–225. doi:10.1111/j.1360-0443.2006.01661.x

Scalco, M. D., & Colder, C. R. (2017). Trajectories of marijuana use from late childhood to late adolescence: Can temperament × experience interactions discriminate different trajectories of marijuana use? *Development and Psychopathology, 29*, 775–790. doi:10.1017/S0954579416000468

Schlotz, W., & Phillips, D. I. W. (2009). Fetal origins of mental health: Evidence and mechanisms. *Brain, Behavior, and Immunity, 23*(7), 905–916. doi:10.1016/j.bbi.2009.02.001

Sellers, R., Harold, G. T., Elam, K., Rhoades, K. A., Potter, R., Mars, B., . . . Collishaw, S. (2014). Maternal depression and co-occurring antisocial behaviour: Testing maternal hostility and warmth as mediators of risk for offspring psychopathology. *Journal of Child Psychology and Psychiatry, 55*(2), 112–120. doi:10.1111/jcpp.12111

Sher, K. J. (1991). *Children of alcoholics: A critical appraisal of theory and research.* Chicago, IL: University of Chicago Press.

Sher, K. J., Walitzer, K. S., Wood, P. K., & Brent, E. E. (1991). Characteristics of children of alcoholics: Putative risk factors, substance use and abuse, and psychopathology. *Journal of Abnormal Psychology, 100*(4), 427–448.

Shiner, R. L., Buss, K. A., McClowry, S. G., Putnam, S. P., Saudino, K. J., & Zentner, M. (2012). What is temperament now? Assessing progress in temperament research on the twenty-fifth anniversary of Goldsmith et al. (1987). *Child Development Perspectives, 6*(4), 436–444. doi:DOI 10.1111/j.1750-8606.2012.00254.x

Siebenbruner, J., Englund, M. M., Egeland, B., & Hudson, K. (2006). Developmental antecedents of late adolescence substance use patterns. *Development and Psychopathology, 18*(2), 551–571. doi:10.1017/S0954579406060287

Sitnick, S. L., Shaw, D. S., & Hyde, L. W. (2014). Precursors of adolescent substance use from early childhood and early adolescence: Testing a developmental cascade model. *Development and Psychopathology*, *26*(1), 125–140. doi:10.1017/S0954579413000539

Substance Abuse and Mental Health Services Administration, Center for Behavioral Health Statistics and Quality. (2014). *The TEDS report: Gender differences in primary substance of abuse across age groups*. Rockville, MD: Author.

Tarter, R. E., Vanyukov, M., Giancola, P. R., Dawes, M. A., Blackson, T. C., Mezzich, A. D., & Clark, D. B. (1999). Etiology of early age onset substance use disorder: A maturational perspective. *Development and Psychopathology*, *11*, 657–683.

Timmermans, M., van Lier, P. A., & Koot, H. M. (2008). Which forms of child/adolescent externalizing behaviors account for late adolescent risky sexual behavior and substance use? *Journal of Child Psychology and Psychiatry and Allied Disciplines*, *49*(4), 386–394. doi:10.1111/j.1469-7610.2007.01842.x

Tottenham, N., Hare, T. A., Quinn, B. T., McCarry, T. W., Nurse, M., Gilhooly, T., . . . Casey, B. J. (2010). Prolonged institutional rearing is associated with atypically large amygdala volume and difficulties in emotion regulation. *Developmental Science*, *13*(1), 46–61. doi:10.1111/j.1467-7687.2009.00852.x

Van Ryzin, M. J., & Dishion, T. J. (2014). Adolescent deviant peer clustering as an amplifying mechanism underlying the progression from early substance use to late adolescent dependence. *Journal of Child Psychology and Psychiatry*, *55*(10), 1153–1161. doi:10.1111/jcpp.12211

Vanyukov, M. M., Tarter, R. E., Kirisci, L., Kirillova, G. P., Maher, B. S., & Clark, D. B. (2003). Liability to substance use disorders: 1. Common mechanisms and manifestations. *Neuroscience and Biobehavioral Reviews*, *27*(6), 507–515. doi:10.1016/j.neubiorev.2003.08.002

Vaughan, E. L., Gassman, R. A., Jun, M. C., & de Martinez, B. J. S. (2015). Gender differences in risk and protective factors for alcohol use and substance use problems among Hispanic adolescents. *Journal of Child & Adolescent Substance Abuse*, *24*(5), 243–254. doi:10.1080/1067828X.2013.826609

Wadhwa, P. D., Buss, C., Entringer, S., & Swanson, J. M. (2009). Developmental origins of health and disease: brief history of the approach and current focus on epigenetic mechanisms. *Seminars in Reproductive Medicine*, *27*(5), 358–368. doi:10.1055/s-0029-1237424

Weissman, M. M., Warner, V., Wickramaratne, P., Moreau, D., & Olfson, M. (1997). Offspring of depressed parents: 10 years later. *Archives of General Psychiatry*, *54*(10), 932–940. doi:10.1001/archpsyc.1997.01830220054009

Wills, T. A., & Ainette, M. G. (2010). Temperament, self-control, and adolescent substance use: A two-factor model of etiological processes. In L. Scheier (Ed.), *Handbook of drug use etiology: Theory, methods, and empirical findings* (pp. 127–146). Washington, DC: American Psychological Association.

Windle, M. (1990). Temperament and personality attributes of children of alcoholics. In M. Windle & J. S. Searles (Eds.), *Children of alcoholics: Critical perspectives* (pp. 129–167). New York, NY: Guilford.

Yip, S. W., Lacadie, C. M., Sinha, R., Mayes, L. C., & Potenza, M. N. (2016). Prenatal cocaine exposure, illicit-substance use and stress and craving processes during adolescence. *Drug and Alcohol Dependence*, *158*, 76–85. doi:10.1016/j.drugalcdep.2015.11.012

Zucker, R. A. (1976). Parental influences upon drinking patterns of their children. In M. Greenblatt & M. A. Schuckit (Eds.), *Alcoholism problems in women and children*. New York, NY: Grune & Stratton.

Zucker, R. A., & Fitzgerald, H. E. (1991). Early developmental factors and risk for alcohol problems. *Alcohol Health and Research World*, *15*, 18–24.

8

Sleep Problems During the Preschool Years and Beyond as a Marker of Risk and Resilience in Substance Use

Maria M. Wong

Individuals with alcohol problems have well-described disturbances of sleep, but the development of these disturbances both before and after the onset of problem drinking is poorly understood (Brower, 2001; National Institute on Alcohol Abuse and Alcoholism, 2007). Approximately a decade ago, our group published the first longitudinal study documenting that early childhood sleep problems were a risk factor for early onset of alcohol and other drug use (Wong, Brower, Fitzgerald, & Zucker, 2004). Since then, several lines of evidence across the human lifespan now suggest that sleep disturbances may precede and represent a marker of risk for the development of alcohol use disorders (Brower, 2001; Weissman, Greenwald, Nino-Murcia, & Dement, 1997; Wong, Brower, & Zucker, 2009; Wong, Robertson, & Dyson, 2015).

This chapter examines sleep as a marker of risk and resilience to the development of alcohol use and related problems. It first discusses the physiology and measurement of sleep. Then, it examines the functions of sleep and its role in development. Finally, the chapter reviews recent research on the relationship between sleep and alcohol use and related problems. Most of the current work focuses on sleep problems as a risk factor of alcohol use. However, recent work also underscores the role of sleep as a marker of resilience to alcohol problems.

SLEEP PHYSIOLOGY AND MEASUREMENT IN HUMANS

Most animals sleep. Human beings are no exception. We spend approximately one-third of our life sleeping. Yet researchers do not fully understand the functions of this important behavior.

Sleep States

Extensive research has identified two different sleep states: rapid eye movement (REM) and non-rapid eye movement (NREM) sleep (Rechtschaffen & Kales, 1968; Roehrs & Roth, 2001). NREM sleep is now classified into three stages (it was previously classified into four stages; (Berry et al., 2015; Iber, Ancoli-Israel, & Quan, 2007). Stage 1 or drowsy sleep has the lowest arousal threshold, followed by stage 2 or light sleep. It is easy to awaken someone in these two stages. Stage 3 is referred to as deep sleep or slow wave sleep (SWS). It has the highest arousal threshold; thus, it is typically difficult to awaken someone in this stage. NREM and REM sleep alternate throughout the night; each cycle of NREM and REM sleep lasts approximately 90 minutes (Figure 8.1) (Roehrs & Roth, 2001; Walker, 2009). Thus, if someone sleeps for 8 hours, there are four or five cycles of NREM and REM sleep.

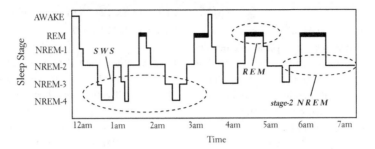

FIGURE 8.1 The human sleep cycle. Across the night, NREM and REM sleep cycle every 90 minutes in an ultradian manner, while the ratio of NREM to REM sleep shifts. During the first half of the night, NREM stages 3 and 4 NREM (SWS) dominate, while stage 2 NREM and REM sleep prevail in the latter half of the night. EEG patterns also differ significantly between sleep stages, with electrical oscillations such as slow delta waves developing in SWS, K-complexes and sleep spindles occurring during stage 2 NREM, and theta waves seen during REM.

Source: Walker, M. P. (2009). The role of sleep in cognition and emotion. *Annals of the New York Academy of Sciences, 1156,* 168–197. © 2009 New York Academy of Sciences. Reprinted with permission from John Wiley and Sons.

REM sleep is divided into tonic and phasic periods (Roehrs & Roth, 2001). During tonic periods, brain activity is similar to that of stage 1 of NREM sleep while muscle tone is decreased. The majority of REM sleep is classified as tonic periods. Phasic periods are characterized by events such as bursts of eye movement, muscle twitches, and irregular heart rate and breathing. These events occur intermittently in REM sleep.

Sleep Regulation

Human sleep–wake behavior is regulated by the complex interaction of biological, psychological, and social circumstances and cultural norms (Carskadon & Tarokh, 2013). Although it is beyond the scope of this chapter to examine all these factors and the many ways that they interact, it is still useful to briefly discuss the biological factors regulating human sleep and wake states. There are two biological processes that regulate sleep: sleep–wake homeostasis (also known as *Process* S) (Borbély, 1982) and circadian rhythms (also known as *Process* C) (Dunlap, Loros, & DeCoursey, 2004). The sleep homeostatic process affects sleep amount and intensity after a period of wakefulness. The longer one stays awake, the higher the pressure to sleep and the longer the sleep duration. Circadian (Latin: *circa* means "around," and *diem* means "day") rhythms are biological processes that

display endogenous (built in, self-sustained), entrainable (synchronized, adjusted to the environment) oscillations (Dunlap et al., 2004; Hasler, Soehner, & Clark, 2015; Wikipedia, 2016). These oscillations occur in approximately 24 hours. Circadian rhythms affect numerous physiological processes, including the sleep–wake cycle. In mammals and humans, circadian rhythms are controlled by a central clock located in the suprachiasmatic nucleus of the hypothalamus. This clock is entrained by many environmental cues, of which light is the most powerful. The presence of circadian rhythms means that the body favors resting or sleeping and waking at different times of the day (Carskadon & Tarokh, 2013).

Measurement of Sleep

Sleep states and stages are defined using scoring criteria established initially by the American Academy of Sleep Medicine (Berry et al., 2015). The gold standard of sleep measurement is polysomnography (PSG), which consists of three electrophysiological measurements: electroencephalogram (EEG), electrooculogram (EOG), and electromyogram (EMG). EEG measures electrical activity of the brain by placing electrodes on the scalp. EOG measures eye movement by electrodes placed on the skin around the eye. EMG measures electrical activity of muscles by electrodes placed on skin in different regions of the body. PSG provides information about sleep stages and states, as well as important parameters such as onset latency (amount of time it takes to fall asleep), sleep efficiency (percentage of time sleeping while in bed), wake time after sleep onset, sleep duration, and REM latency. PSG data are typically collected in research and clinical laboratories. These measurements require sophisticated machines, a highly controlled environment, and research staff with appropriate training.

Quality and quantity of sleep can also be measured by actigraphy (Ancoli-Israel et al., 2003; Sadeh & Acebo, 2002). Actigraphs are waterproof instruments that can be worn on the wrist like a watch. They electronically measure the number of movements that exceed 0.01 g (gravitational force per minute of recording). In addition, a photoconductive cell records light level exposure, measured in lux. Actigraphy allows researchers to verify bedtimes and rise times via body movement and light exposure, thus gathering information about sleep quantity. Moreover, actigraphy helps quantify the amplitude and phase of circadian rest–activity cycles, thus gathering information about sleep quality. Actigraphy data are typically collected for several consecutive nights (e.g., 1 week). Subjects are asked to keep a sleep diary, which provides important information for data scoring. Actigraphy obtains data on sleep duration, efficiency, onset latency, and wake time after onset. It has been shown that this method is consistent with PSG measurement. However, no information about brain activity, eye movement, and muscle movement of specific body regions is obtained through this method.

In addition to PSG and actigraphy, sleep is frequently measured by parent ratings (Chervin, Hedger, Dillon, & Pituch, 2000; Owens, Spirito, & McGuinn, 2000) and self-report (Buysse, Reynolds, Monk, Berman, & Kupfer, 1989; Owens, Spirito, McGuinn, & Nobile, 2000). Parent ratings and self-report provide subjective ratings of onset latency, sleep quality, and sleep duration. Obviously, no information about brain activity and body movement is available through this type of measurement. Due to the high costs associated with PSG and actigraphy, researchers have relied on parent ratings and self-report to measure both quantity and quality of sleep. In fact, the majority of the research reviewed in this chapter is based on subjective ratings. Although these ratings offer valuable information on sleep, they may not be consistent with sleep data collected by objective measurements.

FUNCTIONS OF SLEEP AND ITS ROLE IN DEVELOPMENT

Despite more than 100 years of sleep research, the functions of sleep are still not entirely known. Numerous theories have been proposed to explain why animals (including humans) sleep (Harvard Medical School Division of Sleep Medicine, 2007; Sheldon, 2005). Evolutionary and adaptive theories suggest that inactivity at night is adaptive for animals because it keeps them away from predators or other dangers in the dark. Sleep presumably evolves through natural selection because inactivity is adaptive to animals. However, critics of these theories are quick to point out that it seems safer for animals to be alert rather than becoming unconscious during sleep (Sheldon, 2005).

Energy conservation theory states that the primary function of sleep is to conserve energy resources for the animal, especially during times when the search for food is least efficient for the animal (e.g., at night). In humans, energy metabolism decreases during sleep compared to wakefulness. Both caloric demand and body temperature decrease. Thus, the body requires fewer resources while asleep than while awake. However, this theory has also been disputed. Compared to relaxed wakefulness, there is only an approximately 8–10% reduction in metabolic rate in sleep (Carpenter & Timiras, 1982; Sheldon, 2005). Moreover, an increase in sleep time does not correlate with an increase in metabolic rate.

Restorative theories argue that the function of sleep is to restore to the body what is lost during wakefulness. According to these theories, somatic and cerebral deficits occur during wakefulness. Sleep allows or promotes certain physiologic processes to repair and restore these deficits. In a classical study, rats were placed on a fiberglass disk above a tray that contained water (Rechtschaffen, Gilliland, Bergmann, & Winter, 1983). When the disk periodically rotated, rats had to walk in the opposite direction to avoid being forced into water. Whenever sleep onset was detected in the experimental rats, the disk would be activated until rats were awake for at least 6 seconds. Sleep-deprived rats suffered severe pathology compared to controls. Some of the sleep-deprived rats died as a result. Thus, sleep appears to serve a vital physiologic function.

Restorative theories suggest that both NREM sleep and REM sleep serve different restorative functions (Sheldon, 2005). NREM sleep is believed to repair body tissue. In prepubertal children, growth hormone occurs at sleep onset and reaches peak level during SWS. The release of endogenous anabolic steroids (e.g., testosterone and luteinizing hormone) is dependent on the sleep cycle. Moreover, the rate of bone growth increases during sleep. REM sleep is believed to restore the function of the central nervous system (CNS). A high level of CNS activation and an increase in the synthesis of CNS proteins occur during REM sleep. Increased protein synthesis may be critical for CNS development. However, critics of restorative theories note that sleep does not directly affect the physiologic process. For example, even though cell division reaches its peak during sleep, the process is likely not due to sleep.

Last, brain plasticity theory states that sleep affects changes in the structure and organization of the brain. Sleep appears to play a critical role in the development of the brain. Each 24-hour period, human fetuses and newborns sleep approximately 13 or 14 hours, and approximately 50% of that time is REM sleep, during which dream occurs (Roffwarg, Muzio, & Dement, 1966). This percentage gradually decreases in the first few years of life. The large amount of REM sleep in newborns is thought to serve as endogenous stimulation and provide excitation to different regions of the brain (Roffwarg et al., 1966). Sleep deprivation resulted in lower executive functions, especially lower ability of inhibition, in both children and adults. There is also evidence that sleep deprivation adversely affects inhibition or processes related to inhibition among adults, including the ability to suppress a prepotent response (Chuah, Venkatraman, Dinges, & Chee, 2006) and the ability to detect error and engage in error remedial action (Tsai, Young, Hsieh, & Lee, 2005). Critics of this theory note that it is unclear whether the brain changes as a result of sleep (Sheldon, 2005). Although sleep deprivation studies show that brain functions and connectivity of different brain regions change as a result, much more work needs to be done to identify the exact brain mechanisms that are causally linked to sleep loss and extension.

Thus, no single theory fully explains all functions of sleep. Nevertheless, sleep clearly plays an important role in development, particularly the development of the brain (e.g., learning, memory) and physical growth. The brain undergoes a great deal of neural maturation in childhood and adolescence (Casey, Getz, & Galvan, 2008; Steinberg, 2008), and evidence suggests that adequate sleep is essential to optimal brain development and functioning (Campbell & Feinberg, 2009; Feinberg & Campbell, 2010). The prefrontal cortex (PFC), one of the last brain regions to mature (Benes, 2001; Giedd et al., 1999; Gogtay et al., 2004), is particularly sensitive to insufficient sleep (Gujar, Yoo, Hu, & Walker, 2011; Mullin et al., 2013; Venkatraman, Chuah, Huettel, & Chee, 2007; Venkatraman, Huettel, Chuah, Payne, & Chee, 2011). The PFC is critically involved in inhibitory control, and it is functionally connected with limbic regions involved in emotion regulation (amygdala, hippocampus, and ventral striatum) (Blasi et al., 2006; Hariri, Mattay, Tessitore, Fera, & Weinberger, 2003). Dysregulation of this brain circuitry is associated with a number of risky behaviors, including problem alcohol use (Casey et al., 2008; Steinberg, 2008; Zucker, Heitzeg, & Nigg, 2011).

SLEEP PROBLEMS AND RISK OF ALCOHOL USE AND RELATED PROBLEMS

In this chapter, sleep problems broadly include insomnia (difficulty falling or staying asleep), circadian misalignment, and insufficient sleep duration. Both cross-sectional and longitudinal studies address these different sleep problems and their relationships with alcohol use and related problems.

Cross-Sectional Studies

Cross-sectional studies indicate that sleep patterns and problems are associated with substance use across different age groups. Here, these studies are divided based on the types of sleep problems investigated. Studies of sleep characteristics in individuals who are at risk for alcoholism (i.e., individuals with an alcoholic parent) are also reviewed.

Difficulties Falling or Staying Asleep and Other Sleep Problems

In a World Health Organization survey of schoolchildren's health behavior, irregular sleep schedules and perceived daytime tiredness were associated with increased use of cigarettes and alcohol in 1,057 15-year-old Finnish adolescents (Tynjala, Kannas,

& Levalahti, 1997). Among a group of French secondary school students ($N = 763$), poor sleepers (self-reports of insomnia and the use of sleeping pills) were more likely than others to use alcohol, cigarettes, and illicit drugs (Vignau et al., 1997). Similarly, in a group of 703 9th and 11th graders in South Africa, sleep problems (trouble falling or staying asleep, morning tiredness, and daytime sleepiness) were associated with an increased likelihood of use of alcohol, tobacco, cannabis, methamphetamine, and other illegal drugs. This relationship was significant even after learning difficulties were taken into account (Fakier & Wild, 2011). Data from the US National Household Survey on Drug Abuse ($N = 13,381$) also indicated a similar trend. Adolescents aged 12–17 years who reported having trouble sleeping were more likely than others to use alcohol, cigarettes, and other illicit drugs (Johnson & Breslau, 2001). In a study of adolescents with alcohol use disorder (AUD) and controls in the United States ($N = 259$), self-reports of sleep problems were associated with AUD, even after controlling for tobacco involvement and negative emotionality (Clark, Lynch, Donovan, & Block, 2001).

Insufficient Sleep and Irregular Sleep–Wake Times

In the 2007 Youth and Health Risk Behavior Survey ($N = 12,154$), a nationally representative sample of US high school students, insufficient sleep was associated with higher odds of current (during 30 days before the survey) alcohol, cigarette, and marijuana use (McKnight-Eily et al., 2011). Another study of 318 high school students aged 14–19 years also found a relationship between insufficient sleep and increased risk-taking behaviors (i.e., use of alcohol, tobacco, marijuana, and illicit drugs and sexual activity). Students who slept the least on school nights reported greater alcohol use compared to students who obtained more sleep. Moreover, students with the largest difference between school-night and weekend-night bedtimes reported more risk-taking behaviors and lower academic performance (O'Brien & Mindell, 2005). Another study corroborated the associations between weekday–weekend difference in bedtimes and substance use. In a sample of 242 9th to 11th graders (mean age = 16.4 years), larger difference between weekend and weekday bedtimes and wake times was associated with increased

substance use and truancy (Pasch, Laska, Lytle, & Moe, 2010). Moreover, longer weekday sleep duration was inversely associated with past-month alcohol use and drunkenness, as well as depressive symptoms in the past year.

Global Sleep Measures

The relationships among global sleep quality (self-report of items from seven subscales including sleep duration, onset latency, sleep disturbance, use of sleep medication, and daytime dysfunction due to sleepiness), sleep efficiency (actual hours of sleep vs. hours in bed), and perception of one's sleep quality and alcohol-related consequences were examined in 261 college students (Kenney, LaBrie, Hummer, & Pham, 2012). Poor sleep quality moderated the relationship between alcohol consumption and alcohol-related consequences. Compared to students with better sleep quality, quantity of drinking had a stronger relationship with negative alcohol-related consequences among students with poorer sleep quality. In another study with a larger sample of college students ($N = 1,044$), self-report of global sleep quality mediated the relationship between poor mental health (depression, anxiety, and stress) and quantity of drinking during a typical week in the past month. Poor sleep quality also directly predicted alcohol consequences (Kenney, Lac, LaBrie, Hummer, & Pham, 2013).

Patterns of Sleep Among Individuals with a Positive Parental History of Alcoholism

In studies using parental ratings of sleep, children and adolescents of alcoholic parents (COAs) did not differ from controls on prevalence rates of sleep problems (Wong et al., 2004, 2009; Wong, Brower, Nigg, & Zucker, 2010). However, studies using actigraphy and polysomnography reveal that there are differences in the sleep patterns and physiology of COAs compared to controls. An actigraph study found that among children of aged 7–13 years ($N = 92$; 68 COAs), COAs had fewer hours of sleep and more nighttime motor activity during sleep compared to non-COAs (Conroy, Hairston, Zucker, & Heitzeg, 2015). An EEG study compared children aged 9 and 10 years with (PH+) or without (PH–) a parental history of alcohol abuse or dependence ($N = 30$; 13 COAs) (Tarokh & Carskadon, 2010).

There were no signs of sleep disruption in sleep stages in PH+ and PH– children. However, PH+ children had lower NREM delta power and spindle range compared to PH– children. Reduced delta power among PH+ children may reflect a failure of the structures responsible for protecting sleep. EEG spectral differences suggest that certain circuits responsible for protecting sleep may be impaired among PH+ children.

Summary

The previously discussed cross-sectional studies indicate that sleep problems and alcohol use likely have a complex reciprocal relationship. Although sleep problems are likely a risk factor for alcohol use and related problems, the effects of alcohol on sleep have also been demonstrated (Roehrs & Roth, 2001). However, cross-sectional studies do not allow the testing of temporal order between sleep problems and substance use. Moreover, many of these studies did not separately analyze the relationship between sleep problems and substance use before and after onset of use. Once alcohol onset begins, excessive use of alcohol may lead to sleep disturbances, which can start a vicious cycle of drinking to aid sleep, more sleep disturbances, and more drinking (Brower, 2001). Thus, prospective, longitudinal studies are needed to establish the temporal relationship between sleep problems and substance use.

Longitudinal Studies

Prospective research on the relationship between sleep problems and alcohol use is less common than cross-sectional studies.

Sleep Difficulties and Alcohol Use and Related Problems

Our group was among the first to document the prospective relationship between childhood sleep problems and subsequent onset of alcohol and other drug use in adolescence and young adulthood (Wong et al., 2004). In one study, we examined the relationship between childhood sleep problems and onset of substance use in boys (N = 258) (Wong et al., 2004). Childhood sleep problems were measured by two items on the Child Behavior Checklist (Achenbach & Edelbrock, 1983): having trouble sleeping and

overtiredness. Controlling for parental alcoholism, sleep problems from ages 3 to 5 years significantly predicted onset of any use of alcohol, marijuana, and illicit drugs and also onset of occasional or regular use of cigarettes by ages 12–14 years. Sleep problems also predicted internalizing and externalizing problems. However, these problems did not mediate the relationship between sleep problems and onset of substance use. Parental alcoholism was not associated with children's sleep problems.

In another study of a larger mixed-gender sample (N = 386; 94 girls), we found that sleep problems at ages 3–8 years increased the probability of alcohol consumption onset among boys between 8 and 14 years old. Among girls, sleep problems did not significantly increase the hazard probability of drinking onset until they were 15 years old or older (Wong et al., 2009). Sleep problems also predicted onset of cigarette use and marijuana use for boys but not for girls. Adjusting for the effects of behavioral problems did not weaken the relationship between sleep problems and onset of substance use.

One study examined the longitudinal relationships among pubertal status, behavioral problems, sleep problems, and substance use in 555 adolescents (290 girls) (Pieters et al., 2015). Sleep problems were measured by items on the Adolescent Sleep–Wake Scale and Adolescent Sleep Hygiene Scale (LeBourgeois, Giannotti, Cortesi, Wolfson, & Harsh, 2005). After accounting for stability of sleep and alcohol use and controlling for pubertal status, sleep problems at Time 1 positively predicted alcohol use, cigarette smoking, marijuana smoking, as well internalizing and externalizing problems at Time 2. These results are consistent with those of the previous two studies reviewed here.

The relationship between childhood sleep difficulties and substance-related problems in emerging adulthood was examined in another study (N = 386) (Wong et al., 2010). Having trouble sleeping in childhood (3–8 years old) predicted a higher probability of "having trouble sleeping" in adolescence (11–17 years old), which in turn predicted the presence of drug-related problems in emerging adulthood (18–20 years old). Overtiredness in childhood predicted a lower response inhibition in adolescence, which in turn predicted number of illicit drugs used in emerging adulthood. Overtiredness in childhood also directly predicted the presence of binge drinking, blackouts, driving after drinking alcohol, and number of lifetime alcohol problems in young adulthood. Gender and parental alcoholism did not moderate the relationship between sleep and substance-related problems. To my knowledge, this is the first study showing a long-term relationship between childhood sleep measures and subsequent substance-related problems. The longitudinal relationship between sleep difficulties and lower response inhibition in this study was consistent with previous research showing that experimental manipulated sleep deprivation was associated with lower inhibition in children and adults (Drummond & Brown, 2001; Durmer & Dinges, 2005; Pilcher & Huffcutt, 1996).

The relationship between poor sleep and substance use has been demonstrated in nationally representative samples of adolescents. Concurrent associations between insomnia symptoms (defined as having trouble falling asleep or staying asleep almost every day or every day in the past 12 months) and substance use were reported in the National Longitudinal Study of Adolescent Health (ADD HEALTH; $N = 4,494$) (Roane & Taylor, 2008), the largest national study of adolescents in the United States (Harris et al., 2014). Adolescents in the Insomnia group were more likely than those in the No Insomnia group to report using alcohol, cannabis, and other illicit drugs at Time 1 (T1) (Roane & Taylor, 2008). However, longitudinal analyses using T1 insomnia to predict a new incidence of substance use at Time 2 (T2) did not find any significant relationship. The stringent definition of insomnia (insomnia symptoms almost every day or every day in the past 12 months) and the exclusion of adolescents who used any substances at T1 might have accounted for these findings.

Our group examined whether the frequency of trouble falling or staying asleep in the past 12 months increased the likelihood of alcohol-related problems in ADD HEALTH ($N = 6,504$) at a later time (Wong & Brower, 2012). Controlling for alcohol-related problems at a previous wave, a higher frequency of trouble falling or staying asleep predicted a higher likelihood of reporting any alcohol-related problems at a subsequent wave, including having problems at school, having problems with friends, having problems with someone they were dating, and getting into a physical fight during the past 12 months due to their drinking. Because the focus of this study was not alcohol use, we did not analyze the relationship between sleep difficulties and serious alcohol-related

problems—problems that are clearly detrimental to health.

This relationship was the focus of another study (Wong, Robertson, et al., 2015). The primary goal of the study was to examine whether difficulties falling or staying asleep and hours of sleep predicted alcohol-related problems in the ADD HEALTH study ($N = 6,504$). Holding T1 alcohol-related problems constant, T1 sleep difficulties significantly predicted binge drinking, gotten drunk or very high on alcohol, driving under the influence of alcohol, getting into a sexual situation one later regretted due to drinking, or ever using any illicit drugs and drugs-related problems at T2 (1 year later). In addition, T1 sleep duration negatively predicted T2 alcohol-related interpersonal problems and binge drinking. The relationship between T2 sleep variables and T3 substance-related problems was consistent with previous waves, although the effect was weaker, possibly due to a longer time lag between T2 and T3 (5 years).

The longitudinal relationship between poor sleep and substance use has been reported in both normal and clinical adult samples. Data from the Epidemiological Catchment Survey ($N = 18,571$) showed that healthy adults (no lifetime psychiatric disorder) with insomnia in the past year were more likely to experience the first onset of alcohol use during the following year (Weissman et al., 1997). An epidemiological study of a random sample of young adults in Michigan ($N = 979$) reported that insomnia increased the risk of any illicit drug use disorder and nicotine dependence 3½ years later (Breslau, Roth, Rosenthal, & Andreski, 1996).

Sleep Problems as a Risk Factor of Relapse to Drinking

Sleep problems are more common among alcoholics than non-alcoholics (Brower, 2001). Adults with alcohol dependence commonly experience sleep disturbances during periods of drinking and withdrawal, as indicated by polysomnographic data and self-report (Brower, 2003). Among patients who received treatment for alcohol dependence ($N = 172$), those with insomnia were more likely to use alcohol as a sleep aid, had longer sleep onset latency (time between going to bed and sleep onset), and had lower sleep efficiency (percentage of time in bed sleeping) compared to those without insomnia (Brower, Aldrich, Robinson, Zucker, & Greden, 2001). A subset of these patients ($n = 74$) had a follow-up 5 months after treatment. Alcoholics with baseline insomnia were more likely to relapse to alcohol use (Brower, 2001).

Patterns of Sleep Among Individuals with a Positive Parental History of Alcoholism

A relatively recent study gathered longitudinal sleep EEG data from children and teenagers with (PH+) or without (PH–) a parental history of alcoholism ($N = 48$; 20 COAs) (Tarokh et al., 2012). There were no differences in any sleep stage variables between PH+ and PH– participants. PH+ participants did not show any sign of sleep disruption. Modest differences in spectral EEG power among PH+ and PH– participants were found. Compared to PH– teens, NREM sleep EEG power was lower in the delta band for the central derivations among PH+ teens at both initial and follow-up assessments. Moreover, power in the sigma band for the right occipital derivation was lower among PH+ children only in both NREM and REM sleep.

Summary

Sleep difficulties and insomnia symptoms predicted earlier onset of alcohol use, alcohol- and drug-related problems, as well as substance use disorders among individuals across different developmental periods. Sleep problems are an important risk factor for relapse in drinking among alcoholics who received treatment for alcoholism. Modest differences in spectral EEG power among PH+ and PH– children and teens were found.

SLEEP PROBLEMS AND RESILIENCE TO ALCOHOL USE AND RELATED PROBLEMS

Resilience is positive adaption despite adversity (Luthar, Cicchetti, & Becker, 2000; Masten, 2001, 2007). Do sleep problems predict protective factors that are known to be related to alcohol use and related problems? Is good sleep a protective factor for those who are at high risk of developing alcohol-related problems? Is good sleep a facilitative factor for positive alcohol use outcome, regardless of risk background? Is the lack of sleep problems or good sleep a marker of resilience? The relationship between sleep problems and resilience among COAs has been largely unexplored. Given the association between sleep problems and alcohol use in previous studies, it is reasonable to ask whether sleep problems may be a risk factor or whether adequate sleep/the absence of sleep problems is a protective factor in COAs.

In one study, we examined whether maternal ratings of childhood sleep rhythmicity (defined as regular sleep and wake time and an absence of sleep difficulties) predicted behavioral control in early adolescence and whether behavioral control in turn predicted resilience in COAs in emerging adulthood (Wong, Puttler, Nigg, & Zucker, 2014, 2015). Behavioral control was defined as the tendency to express or contain one's impulses, motor responses, and behaviors and measured by interviewers' ratings on the child Q-setsort (Block & Block, 1980). COAs were considered resilient if they met one or more of the following criteria: (1) an absence of alcohol use disorder, (2) an absence of substance-related problems, (3) high work satisfaction, and (4) high relationship satisfaction. Similar analyses were conducted among age-matched controls. Participants were 517 boys and 210 girls who participated in the Michigan Longitudinal Study (Zucker et al., 2000). Sleep rhythmicity predicted higher behavioral control, which negatively predicted two resilience indicators—that is, an absence of AUD and substance-related problems (SRP). Higher behavioral control was a significant mediator of this relationship. Sleep also directly predicted one resilience outcome—that is, an absence of AUD and SRP and high relationship satisfaction. No group differences between COAs and controls were found. Thus, the absence of sleep problems and higher behavioral control were protective factors for both COAs and controls.

One major weakness of the study was that sleep data were gathered solely from maternal ratings. Moreover, no information regarding good sleep was available (e.g., sleep efficiency and percentage of SWS). However, this study provided preliminary evidence that self-regulatory processes may be an important mediator between sleep problems and resilience among COAs. The next section provides a more in-depth analysis of the relationships among sleep, self-regulatory processes, and alcohol involvement.

SLEEP AND ALCOHOL USE AND RELATED PROBLEMS: A HYPOTHESIZED MODEL

The research reviewed previously shows support for the relationship between sleep and alcohol

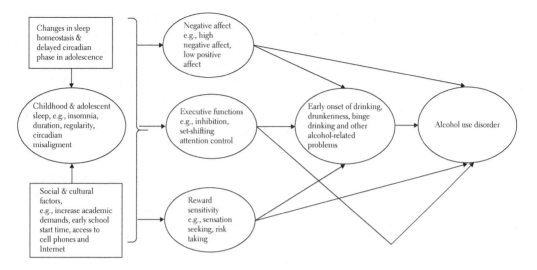

FIGURE 8.2 A hypothesized model of sleep, self-regulatory processes, and alcohol use.

involvement. However, relatively little is still known about mediators and moderators of this relationship. The conceptual model is illustrated in Figure 8.2 using three possible mediators.

Children have different sleep patterns and habits that are influenced by both biological factors, such as genes, sleep homeostasis drive, circadian rhythm, and temperament, and sociocultural factors, such as parenting and home environment. These patterns and habits predispose some children to develop certain sleep problems—for example, difficulty falling or staying asleep, low sleep efficiency, and circadian misalignment. These problems in turn predict adolescent sleep.

In adolescence, both sleep homeostasis and circadian timing undergo marked changes (Becker, Langberg, & Byars, 2015; Carskadon, Mindell, & Drake, 2006; Hasler et al., 2015). Compared to young children, the pressure to sleep builds up slowly during the day, making adolescents less likely to feel tired until late in the evening. The circadian rhythm also moves to a delayed position, resulting in a preference of eveningness, (i.e., a preference to engage in events in the evening). These factors lead to a tendency to have later bedtimes. However, the need to sleep does not change. Increased academic demands and earlier school start times for high school mean that many adolescents do not get enough sleep.

The National Sleep Foundation (2006) reported that approximately 60% of 6th to 8th graders did not sleep the recommended 9 hours per night on school

nights. The issue of insufficient sleep was more serious for older adolescents. Less than 10% of 9th to 12th graders reported getting the recommended amount of sleep in the same study. A total of 43% of 6th graders thought that they got the sleep they needed to feel their best, compared to 72% of 12th graders.

In addition to insufficient sleep, the issue of "social jet lag" (differences between weekday and weeknight sleep time) appears to be serious among adolescents (Hasler et al., 2015). Most adolescents (88%) went to bed later on non-school nights than on school nights (National Sleep Foundation, 2006). In the same study, 51% reported going to bed on non-school nights within 2 hours of their school-night sleep time, and 37% reported going to bed more than 2 hours later than their school-night sleep time. Social jet lag is even more common among older adolescents; 44% of 9th to 12th graders reported going to bed 2 hours or more later on non-school nights, compared to 26% of 6th to 8th graders (National Sleep Foundation, 2006). Due to recent changes in technology, many adolescents have access to the Internet 24 hours a day, 7 days a week via mobile phones and computers, providing an infinite supply of information and entertainment opportunities to keep them awake in the evenings. Later sleep and wake times lead to a later circadian timing, which reinforces the physical changes of circadian rhythm described previously (Carskadon & Tarokh, 2013; Hasler et al., 2015). The differences between weekday and weekend sleep times for some adolescents are the equivalent of traveling multiple time zones between Sunday and Monday (Hasler et al., 2015), resulting in sleepiness on school days and possibly insomnia symptoms on school nights.

A combination of biological (e.g., individual predisposition) and sociocultural factors (e.g., social jet lag and increased academic demands in school) may lead to sleep problems. The National Sleep Foundation (2006) reported that more than half of adolescents (51%) had trouble falling asleep and 31% had trouble staying asleep at least once a week within the past 2 weeks. In the National Longitudinal Study of Adolescent Health (Harris et al., 2014), one of the largest studies on adolescents in the United States, approximately one-fourth of adolescents had trouble falling or staying asleep approximately once a week, almost every day, or every day in the past 12 months (Wave 1: 23%; mean age = 15.99 years, SD = 1.75; Wave 2: 24%; mean age = 16.02 years, SD = 1.62) (Wong, Robertson, et al., 2015).

As discussed previously, the association between sleep problems and substance use may be due to three possible mediators: regulation of negative affect, regulation of cognitive/neurocognitive processes, and reward sensitivity. Next, supporting research that links these three variables to both sleep and alcohol involvement is discussed.

Regulation of Negative Affect

The relationship between sleep and negative affect regulation has been shown in both experimental and correlational studies with children/adolescent and adult samples. In a meta-analysis of 19 empirical studies, sleep deprivation had the greatest negative effect on mood, followed by negative effects on cognitive and motor tasks (Pilcher & Huffcutt, 1996). A comprehensive review of sleep deprivation studies also found that sleep deprivation negatively affects mood (Durmer & Dinges, 2005). In an experimental study, adolescent and adult participants (N = 64) experienced more anxiety in a catastrophizing task and believed that potential catastrophes were more likely to occur when sleep deprived compared to when rested (Talbot, McGlinchey, Kaplan, Dahl, & Harvey, 2010). The exaggerated response of participants when sleep deprived is an indication of an inability to regulate negative affect (e.g., anxiety). Persistent sleep problems in childhood longitudinally predicted anxiety disorder in adulthood (N = 980), providing yet another piece of evidence supporting

the link between sleep difficulties and negative affect regulation (Gregory et al., 2005).

Insufficient sleep and sleep difficulties were associated with less positive affect and more negative affect in adults (Durmer & Dinges, 2005; Goldstein & Walker, 2014; Pilcher & Huffcutt, 1996). Moreover, the relationship between the two appears to be causal. Acute sleep deprivation results in more subjective reports of emotional disturbance, as well as stress, anxiety, and anger in response to low-stress situations (Walker & van der Helm, 2009). In one functional magnetic resonance imaging study, participants were asked to view emotionally aversive pictures after one night of sleep deprivation (Yoo, Gujar, Hu, Jolesz, & Walker, 2007). Relative to controls, sleep-deprived subjects exhibited a 60% greater reactivity of magnitude of amygdala activation. There was also less functional connectivity between medial prefrontal cortex (mPFC) and amygdala in the sleep-deprived group compared to the control group. mPFC is believed to exert a top-down inhibitory control over the amygdala with adequate sleep. However, this functional connectivity is decreased in sleep deprivation—that is, the mPFC is less able to regulate emotional reactivity, resulting in an overly reactive amygdala.

The relationship between negative affect on alcohol involvement is controversial because the findings are mixed (Hussong, Jones, Stein, Baucom, & Boeding, 2011). This is likely due to the different definitions used to define negative affect and the failure to include other potential mediators or moderators, such as externalizing problems and gender (Hussong, Flora, Curran, Chassin, & Zucker, 2008). However, a consistent relationship between negative affect and alcohol consumption in both adolescents and adults has been found (Hussong et al., 2011; Shadur, Hussong, & Haroon, 2015), possibly due to the self-medication mechanism, in which individuals drink alcohol to alleviate negative affect (Cooper, Russell, & George, 1988; Khantzian, 1997).

Regulation of Cognitive/Neurocognitive Processes

The effects of sleep problems on the regulation of cognitive and neurocognitive processes have been demonstrated in previous research (Durmer & Dinges, 2005; Sadeh, Gruber, & Raviv, 2002, 2003). Children with fragmented sleep scored lower on a continuous performance test and a symbol–digit substitution test (N = 135), which required sustained attention and behavioral inhibition (Sadeh et al., 2002). Children who were asked to extend their sleep for 1 hour for three consecutive nights performed significantly better than baseline on a digit forward memory task and a continuous performance task that measured sustained visual attention, response inhibition, and motor speed ($N = 77$) (Sadeh et al., 2003). Childhood sleep problems appear to have long-term effects on behavioral inhibition. One of our studies found that childhood sleep problems predicted poor response inhibition in adolescence 14 years later (Wong et al., 2010). Sleep loss and difficulties were associated with lower executive functions and lower performance on divergent cognitive tasks such as multitasking and flexible thinking in adults (Durmer & Dinges, 2005; Pilcher & Huffcutt, 1996).

The relationship between sleep and cognitive/neurocognitive processes may be partially explained by the functions of the PFC, which regulates inhibitory processes, attention, and affect (Davidson, Jackson, & Kalin, 2000; Posner & Petersen, 1990; Yang & Raine, 2009). Sustained attention and inhibition are required to perform executive functions and other complex cognitive tasks such as decision-making. The PFC is particularly sensitive to prolonged periods of wakefulness (Horne, 1993, 2012). Thus, insufficient sleep or sleep difficulties may adversely affect functions of the PFC, which in turn have a negative effect on cognitive and neurocognitive processes.

Sleep also affects cognitive/neurocognitive processes via its effect on long-term memory. Previous research has demonstrated a robust relationship between sleep and the consolidation of procedural memory (i.e., memory about how to do something, such as how to ride a bicycle) (Walker & Stickgold, 2006). Specifically, sleep after learning is essential for the consolidation and enhancement of procedural memories. Research indicates that sleep plays an important role in the encoding of declarative memory (i.e., memory about facts and things). For instance, after 36 hours of sleep deprivation, adult subjects scored significantly lower on a retention task (Harrison & Horne, 2000). Another study examined the effects of 35 hours of sleep deprivation on verbal learning ($N = 13$) (Drummond et al., 2000). Sleep deprivation was associated with lower recall performance. Compared to controls, the medial temporal lobe was less activated, whereas the PFC and the parietal lobe showed a greater activation. Thus, sleep loss prior to learning appears to lead to an inability of the medial temporal lobe to function normally, leading to compensatory activation of the PFC and parietal lobe. Sleep also appears to play a critical role in the consolidation of declarative memory (Ellenbogen, Payne, & Stickgold, 2006). In a classic interference paradigm, subjects who slept performed significantly better than those who did not on recall in the interference conditions ($n = 60$) (Ellenbogen, Hulbert, Stickgold, Dinges, & Thompson-Schill, 2006). In the non-interference condition, sleep had a modest but still positive effect. After a night of sleep, memories appear to be more resistant to interference.

The cognitive and neurocognitive processes discussed previously are either components of or indirectly related to executive functions—a set of mechanisms that modulate the operation of other cognitive subprocesses (Miyake, Friedman, Emerson, Witzki, & Howerter, 2000). Poor executive functions are both a risk factor for and a consequence of problem alcohol use (Nixon, 2013). Longitudinal data showed that lower executive functions predicted increases in alcohol consumption (Deckel & Hesselbrock, 1996), as well as a higher number of alcohol- and drug-related problems (Nigg et al., 2006; Wong et al., 2010). In addition, individuals with a positive family history of alcoholism show lower executive functions (Nigg et al., 2004; Peterson, Finn, & Pihl, 1992).

Regulation of Reward-Related Perception and Behaviors

In addition to regulation of negative affect and cognitive/neurocognitive processes, another possible mediator is sensitivity to reward. Sleep and circadian rhythm appear to affect regulation of reward-related perception and behaviors (Hasler, Smith, Cousins, & Bootzin, 2012; Hasler et al., 2015). Research on adolescents indicates that sleep duration and misaligned circadian timing are associated with altered response to rewards. One study on adolescents aged 11–13 years ($N = 58$) showed that shorter sleep duration, later sleep onset time, and lower sleep quality were associated with less activation in the caudate (part of the ventral striatum) during reward anticipation (Holm et al., 2009). Moreover, later sleep onset time, earlier sleep offset time, and lower sleep quality were also associated with less caudate activation (Holm et al., 2009). Lower reactivity in reward-related areas may drive adolescents to increase reward-driven behavior, including increased risk-taking and alcohol use. Another study on adolescents aged 14–16 years ($N = 46$) showed that poorer sleep quality was associated with more decision-making complacency, lower decision-making self-esteem, a higher likelihood of engaging in risk-taking behavior, and greater perception of the positive consequences associated with such behavior (Telzer, Fuligni, Lieberman, & Galván, 2013). In the same study, lower sleep quality was associated with reduced recruitment of the dorsolateral prefrontal cortex (DLPFC) during the go/no-go task, as well as greater insula activation and the functional decoupling between DLPFC and affective regions including the insula and ventral striatum during a risk-taking task (Telzer, Fuligni, Lieberman, & Galván, 2013).

In experimentally induced sleep deprivation studies among adults, acute sleep deprivation is associated with an elevated response to gains and an attenuated response to losses (Gujar et al., 2011; Mullin et al., 2013; Venkatraman et al., 2007, 2011). Moreover, adults with AUD, substance use disorder, and affective disorders seem to show both sleep disturbances and altered reward sensitivity, providing further evidence that sleep problems are linked to changes in reward-related perception and behavior (Koob & Le Moal, 2001; Nestler et al., 2002; Nestler & Carlezon, 2006).

The research reviewed previously indicates that regulation of negative affect, cognitive/neurocognitive processes, and reward-related perception may mediate the relationship between sleep problems and problem alcohol use. Heavy alcohol use has also been documented to affect these regulatory processes (Hasler et al., 2015; Nixon, 2013), as well as sleep (Roehrs & Roth, 2001). Disentangling the effects of sleep, self-regulatory processes, and alcohol use have on one another is essential to understanding the contributions of sleep in alcohol use and related problems.

FUTURE DIRECTIONS

The studies reviewed in this chapter show that sleep problems have a robust relationship with alcohol use and related problems across different developmental periods. The relationship between sleep and resilience is less clear. Our work indicates that sleep may have a positive effect on developmental outcomes via various self-regulatory processes. During the past

decade, we have made much progress in understanding the effects of sleep difficulties on alcohol outcomes. However, less is known about the mediators and moderators of this relationship. We proposed a conceptual model of mediators and moderators to explain and further specify the relationships between sleep and alcohol involvement. Although there is some empirical support for these variables, more work remains to be done to clarify the relationships between these mediators/moderators and sleep, on the one hand, and alcohol use, on the other hand. It is unclear whether good sleep (e.g., longer sleep duration, less wake time after sleep onset, and better sleep hygiene) is protective of alcohol-related problems. All of the studies focus on the presence or absence of sleep problems as measured by parental ratings or self-report. Measuring the quality of sleep using actigraphy and polysomnography will allow us to understand the relationship between different sleep parameters and negative developmental outcomes, including alcohol use disorders. The results reviewed in the chapter have implications for intervention and prevention programs on youth alcohol use. Given the important role of sleep in alcohol use, it is necessary for these programs to incorporate a sleep hygiene component, including greater attention to sleep disorders during very early childhood. The effects of poor sleep on self-control and motivation could also be discussed in these programs.

ACKNOWLEDGMENT

The work presented here was supported in part by grant R01 AA020364 from the National Institute on Alcohol Abuse and Alcoholism and the National Institute of General Medical Sciences.

REFERENCES

Achenbach, T., & Edelbrock, C. (1983). *Manual for the Child Behavior Checklist and revised Child Behavior Profile*. Burlington, VT: University Associates in Psychiatry.

Ancoli-Israel, S., Cole, R., Alessi, C., Chambers, M., Moorcroft, W., & Pollak, C. P. (2003). The role of actigraphy in the study of sleep and circadian rhythms. *Sleep, 26*(3), 342–392.

Becker, S. P., Langberg, J. M., & Byars, K. C. (2015). Advancing a biopsychosocial and contextual model of sleep in adolescence: A review and introduction to the special issue. *Journal of Youth and Adolescence, 44*(2), 239–270. doi:10.1007/s10964-014-0248-y

Benes, F. M. (2001). The development of prefrontal cortex: The maturation of neurotransmitter systems and their interactions. In C. A. Nelson & M. Luciana (Eds.), *Handbook of developmental cognitive neuroscience* (pp. 79–92). Cambridge, MA: MIT Press.

Berry, R. B., Brooks, R., Gamaldo, C. E., Harding, S. M., Lloyd, R. M., Marcus, C. L., & Vaughn, B. V. (2015). *The AASM manual for the scoring of sleep and associated events: Rules, terminology and technical specifications, Version 2.2.* Darien, IL: American Academy of Sleep Medicine.

Blasi, G., Goldberg, T. E., Weickert, T., Das, S., Kohn, P., Zoltick, B., . . . Mattay, V. S. (2006). Brain regions underlying response inhibition and interference monitoring and suppression. *European Journal of Neuroscience, 23*(6), 1658–1664. doi:10.1111/j.1460-9568.2006.04680.x

Block, J., & Block, J. H. (1980). *The California Q-set: Orientation and introduction.* Berkeley, CA: University of California Press.

Borbély, A. A. (1982). A two process model of sleep regulation. *Human Neurobiology, 1*(3), 195–204.

Breslau, N., Roth, T., Rosenthal, L., & Andreski, P. (1996). Sleep disturbance and psychiatric disorders: A longitudinal epidemiological study of young adults. *Biological Psychiatry, 39*, 411–418.

Brower, K. J. (2001). Alcohol's effects on sleep in alcoholics. *Alcohol Research & Health, 25*(2), 110–125.

Brower, K. J. (2003). Insomnia, alcoholism and relapse. *Sleep Medicine Reviews, 7*(6), 523–539.

Brower, K. J., Aldrich, M. S., Robinson, E. A. R., Zucker, R. A., & Greden, J. F. (2001). Insomnia, self-medication, and relapse to alcoholism. *American Journal of Psychiatry, 158*(3), 399–404. doi:10.1176/appi.ajp.158.3.399

Buysse, D. J., Reynolds, C. F., 3rd, Monk, T. H., Berman, S. R., & Kupfer, D. J. (1989). The Pittsburgh Sleep Quality Index: A new instrument for psychiatric practice and research. *Psychiatry Research, 28*(2), 193–213.

Campbell, I. G., & Feinberg, I. (2009). Longitudinal trajectories of non-rapid eye movement delta and theta EEG as indicators of adolescent brain maturation. *Proceedings of the National Academy of Sciences of the USA, 106*(13), 5177–5180. doi:10.1073/pnas.0812947106

Carpenter, A. C., & Timiras, P. S. (1982). Sleep organization in hypo- and hyperthyroid rats. *Neuroendocrinology, 34*, 438.

Carskadon, M. A., Mindell, J. A., & Drake, C. (2006). *Sleep in America poll: Summary of findings.*

Washington, DC: National Sleep Foundation. Retrieved from https://www.sleepfoundation.org/sites/default/files/2006_summary_of_findings.pdf

Carskadon, M. A., & Tarokh, L. (2013). Developmental changes in circadian timing and sleep: Adolescence and emerging adulthood. In A. R. Wolfson & H. E. Montgomery-Downs (Eds.), *The Oxford handbook of infant, child, and adolescent sleep and behavior* (pp. 70–77). New York, NY: Oxford University Press.

Casey, B. J., Getz, S., & Galvan, A. (2008). The adolescent brain. *Developmental Review, 28*(1), 62–77. doi:10.1016/j.dr.2007.08.003

Chervin, R. D., Hedger, K. M., Dillon, J. E., & Pituch, K. J. (2000). Pediatric Sleep Questionnaire (PSQ): Validity and reliability of scales for sleep-disordered breathing, snoring, sleepiness, and behavioral problems. *Sleep Medicine, 1*, 21–32.

Chuah, Y. M. L., Venkatraman, V., Dinges, D. F., & Chee, M. W. L. (2006). The neural basis of inter-individual variability in inhibitory efficiency after sleep deprivation. *Journal of Neuroscience, 26*(27), 7156–7162.

Clark, D. B., Lynch, K. G., Donovan, J. E., & Block, G. D. (2001). Health problems in adolescents with alcohol use disorders: Self-report, liver injury, and physical examination findings and correlates. *Alcoholism: Clinical and Experimental Research, 25*(9), 1350–1359.

Conroy, D., Hairston, I., Zucker, R., & Heitzeg, M. (2015). Sleep patterns in children of alcoholics and the relationship with parental reports. *Austin Journal of Sleep Disorders, 2*(1), 1009.

Cooper, M. L., Russell, M., & George, W. H. (1988). Coping, expectancies, and alcohol abuse: A test of social learning formulations. *Journal of Abnormal Psychology, 97*(2), 218–230. doi:10.1037/0021-843X.97.2.218

Davidson, R. J., Jackson, D. C., & Kalin, N. H. (2000). Emotion, plasticity, context, and regulation: Perspectives from affective neuroscience. *Psychological Bulletin, 126*(6), 890–909. doi:10.1037/0033-2909.126.6.890

Deckel, A. W., & Hesselbrock, V. (1996). Behavioral and cognitive measurements predict scores on the MAST: A 3-year prospective study. *Alcoholism, Clinical & Experimental Research, 20*(7), 1173–1178.

Drummond, S. P. A., & Brown, G. G. (2001). The effects of total sleep deprivation on cerebral responses to cognitive performance. *Neuropsychopharmacology, 25*(Suppl. 5), S68–S73. doi:10.1016/s0893-133x(01)00325-6

Drummond, S. P. A., Brown, G. G., Gillin, J. C., Stricker, J. L., Wong, E. C., & Buxton, R. B. (2000).

Altered brain response to verbal learning following sleep deprivation. *Nature, 403*(6770), 655–657. doi:10.1038/35001068

Dunlap, J. C., Loros, J. J., & DeCoursey, P. J. (2004). *Chronobiology: Biological timekeeping.* Sunderland, MA: Sinauer.

Durmer, J. S., & Dinges, D. F. (2005). Neurocognitive consequences of sleep deprivation. *Seminars in Neurology, 25*(1), 117–129.

Ellenbogen, J. M., Hulbert, J. C., Stickgold, R., Dinges, D. F., & Thompson-Schill, S. L. (2006). Interfering with theories of sleep and memory: Sleep, declarative memory, and associative interference. *Current Biology, 16*(13), 1290–1294.

Ellenbogen, J. M., Payne, J. D., & Stickgold, R. (2006). The role of sleep in declarative memory consolidation: Passive, permissive, active or none? *Current Opinion in Neurobiology, 16*(6), 716–722.

Fakier, N., & Wild, L. G. (2011). Associations among sleep problems, learning difficulties and substance use in adolescence. *Journal of Adolescence, 34*(4), 717–726. doi:10.1016/j.adolescence.2010.09.010

Feinberg, I., & Campbell, I. G. (2010). Sleep EEG changes during adolescence: An index of a fundamental brain reorganization. *Brain and Cognition, 72*(1), 56–65. doi:10.1016/j.bandc.2009.09.008

Giedd, J. N., Blumenthal, J., Jeffries, N. O., Castellanos, F. X., Liu, H., Zijdenbos, A., . . . Rapoport, J. L. (1999). Brain development during childhood and adolescence: A longitudinal MRI study. *Nature Neuroscience, 2*(10), 861–863. doi:10.1038/13158

Gogtay, N., Giedd, J. N., Lusk, L., Hayashi, K. M., Greenstein, D., Vaituzis, A. C., . . . Thompson, P. M. (2004). Dynamic mapping of human cortical development during childhood through early adulthood. *Proceedings of the National Academy of Sciences of the USA, 101*(21), 8174–8179. doi:10.1073/pnas.0402680101

Goldstein, A. N., & Walker, M. P. (2014). The role of sleep in emotional brain function. *Annual Review of Clinical Psychology, 10,* 679–708. doi:10.1146/annurev-clinpsy-032813-153716

Gregory, A. M., Caspi, A., Eley, T. C., Moffitt, T. E., O'Connor, T. G., & Poulton, R. (2005). Prospective longitudinal associations between persistent sleep problems in childhood and anxiety and depression disorders in adulthood. *Journal of Abnormal Child Psychology, 33*(2), 157–163. doi:10.1007/s10802-005-1824-0

Gujar, N., Yoo, S.-S., Hu, P., & Walker, M. P. (2011). Sleep deprivation amplifies reactivity of brain reward networks, biasing the appraisal of positive emotional experiences. *Journal of Neuroscience, 31*(12), 4466–4474. doi:10.1523/JNEUROSCI.3220-10.2011

Hariri, A. R., Mattay, V. S., Tessitore, A., Fera, F., & Weinberger, D. R. (2003). Neocortical modulation of the amygdala response to fearful stimuli. *Biological Psychiatry, 53*(6), 494–501.

Harris, K. M., Halpern, C. T., Whitsel, E., Hussey, J., Tabor, J., Entzel, P., & Udry, J. R. (2014). *The National Longitudinal Study of Adolescent Health: Research design* [WWW Document]. Retrieved from http://www.cpc.unc.edu/projects/addhealth/design

Harrison, Y., & Horne, J. A. (2000). Sleep loss and temporal memory. *Quarterly Journal of Experimental Psychology A: Human Experimental Psychology, 53A*(1), 271–279. doi:10.1080/027249800390772

Harvard Medical School Division of Sleep Medicine. (2007). *Why do we sleep, anyway?* Retrieved from http://healthysleep.med.harvard.edu/healthy/matters/benefits-of-sleep/why-do-we-sleep

Hasler, B. P., Smith, L. J., Cousins, J. C., & Bootzin, R. R. (2012). Circadian rhythms, sleep, and substance abuse. *Sleep Medicine Reviews, 16*(1), 67–81. doi:10.1016/j.smrv.2011.03.004

Hasler, B. P., Soehner, A. M., & Clark, D. B. (2015). Sleep and circadian contributions to adolescent alcohol use disorder. *Alcohol, 49*(4), 377–387. doi:10.1016/j.alcohol.2014.06.010

Holm, S. M., Forbes, E. E., Ryan, N. D., Phillips, M. L., Tarr, J. A., & Dahl, R. E. (2009). Reward-related brain function and sleep in pre/early pubertal and mid/late pubertal adolescents. *Journal of Adolescent Health, 45*(4), 326–334. doi:10.1016/j.jadohealth.2009.04.001

Horne, J. A. (1993). Human sleep, sleep loss and behaviour: Implications for the prefrontal cortex and psychiatric disorder. *British Journal of Psychiatry, 162,* 413–419. doi:10.1192/bjp.162.3.413

Horne, J. A. (2012). Working throughout the night: Beyond "sleepiness" — Impairments to critical decision making. *Neuroscience and Biobehavioral Reviews, 36*(10), 2226–2231. doi:10.1016/j.neubiorev.2012.08.005

Hussong, A. M., Flora, D. B., Curran, P. J., Chassin, L. A., & Zucker, R. A. (2008). Defining risk heterogeneity for internalizing symptoms among children of alcoholic parents. *Development and Psychopathology, 20*(1), 165–193. doi:10.1017/S0954579408000084

Hussong, A. M., Jones, D. J., Stein, G. L., Baucom, D. H., & Boeding, S. (2011). An internalizing pathway to alcohol use and disorder. *Psychology of Addictive Behaviors, 25*(3), 390–404. doi:10.1037/a0024519

Iber, C., Ancoli-Israel, S., & Quan, S. F. (2007). *The AASM manual for the scoring of sleep and associated events: Rules, terminology and technical specifications, Version 1.* Westchester, IL: American Academy of Sleep Medicine.

Johnson, E. O., & Breslau, N. (2001). Sleep problems and substance use in adolescence. *Drug and Alcohol Dependence, 64*, 1–7.

Kenney, S. R., LaBrie, J. W., Hummer, J. F., & Pham, A. T. (2012). Global sleep quality as a moderator of alcohol consumption and consequences in college students. *Addictive Behaviors, 37*(4), 507–512. doi:http://dx.doi.org/10.1016/j.addbeh.2012.01.006

Kenney, S. R., Lac, A., LaBrie, J. W., Hummer, J. F., & Pham, A. (2013). Mental health, sleep quality, drinking motives, and alcohol-related consequences: A path-analytic model. *Journal of Studies on Alcohol and Drugs, 74*(6), 841–851.

Khantzian, E. J. (1997). The self-medication hypothesis of substance use disorders: A reconsideration and recent applications. *Harvard Review of Psychiatry, 4*(5), 231–244. doi:10.3109/10673229709030550

Koob, G. F., & Le Moal, M. (2001). Drug addiction, dysregulation of reward, and allostasis. *Neuropsychopharmacology, 24*(2), 97–129. doi:10.1016/S0893-133X(00)00195-0

LeBourgeois, M. K., Giannotti, F., Cortesi, F., Wolfson, A. R., & Harsh, J. (2005). The relationship between reported sleep quality and sleep hygiene in Italian and American adolescents. *Pediatrics, 115*(1), 257–265.

Luthar, S. S., Cicchetti, D., & Becker, B. (2000). The construct of resilience: A critical evaluation and guidelines for future work. *Child Development, 71*(3), 543–562. doi:10.1111/1467-8624.00164

Masten, A. S. (2001). Ordinary magic: Resilience processes in development. *American Psychologist, 56*(3), 227–238. doi:10.1037/0003-066x.56.3.227

Masten, A. S. (2007). Resilience in developing systems: Progress and promise as the fourth wave rises. *Development and Psychopathology, 19*(3), 921–930. doi:10.1017/S0954579407000442

McKnight-Eily, L. R., Eaton, D. K., Lowry, R., Croft, J. B., Presley-Cantrell, L., & Perry, G. S. (2011). Relationships between hours of sleep and health-risk behaviors in US adolescent students. *Preventive Medicine, 53*(4–5), 271–273. doi:http://dx.doi.org/10.1016/j.ypmed.2011.06.020

Miyake, A., Friedman, N. P., Emerson, M. J., Witzki, A. H., & Howerter, A. (2000). The unity and diversity of executive functions and their contributions to complex "frontal lobe" tasks: A latent variable analysis. *Cognitive Psychology, 41*(1), 49–100.

Mullin, B. C., Phillips, M. L., Siegle, G. J., Buysse, D. J., Forbes, E. E., & Franzen, P. L. (2013). Sleep deprivation amplifies striatal activation to monetary reward. *Psychological Medicine, 43*(10), 2215–2225. doi:10.1017/S0033291712002875

National Institute on Alcohol Abuse and Alcoholism. (2007). *Epidemiology and prevention in alcohol research* (R01 PA-07-448). Retrieved from http://grants.nih.gov/grants/guide/pa-files/PA-07-448.html

National Sleep Foundation. (2006). *Sleep in America poll: Teens and sleep*. Washington, DC: National Sleep Foundation.

Nestler, E. J., Barrot, M., DiLeone, R. J., Eisch, A. J., Gold, S. J., & Monteggia, L. M. (2002). Neurobiology of depression. *Neuron, 34*(1), 13–25.

Nestler, E. J., & Carlezon, W. A., Jr. (2006). The mesolimbic dopamine reward circuit in depression. *Biological Psychiatry, 59*(12), 1151–1159. doi:10.1016/j.biopsych.2005.09.018

Nigg, J. T., Glass, J. M., Wong, M. M., Poon, E., Jester, J. M., Fitzgerald, H. E., . . . Zucker, R. A. (2004). Neuropsychological executive functioning in children at elevated risk for alcoholism: Findings in early adolescence. *Journal of Abnormal Psychology, 113*(2), 302–314. doi:10.1037/0021-843x.113.2.302

Nigg, J. T., Wong, M. M., Martel, M. M., Jester, J. M., Puttler, L. I., Glass, J. M., . . . Zucker, R. A. (2006). Poor response inhibition as a predictor of problem drinking and illicit drug use in adolescents at risk for alcoholism and other substance use disorders. *Journal of the American Academy of Child and Adolescent Psychiatry, 45*(4), 468–475.

Nixon, S. J. (2013). Executive functioning among young people in relation to alcohol use. *Current Opinion in Psychiatry, 26*(4), 305–309. doi:10.1097/YCO.0b013e328361ea3c

O'Brien, E. M., & Mindell, J. A. (2005). Sleep and risk-taking behavior in adolescents. *Behavioral Sleep Medicine, 3*(3), 113–133.

Owens, J. A., Spirito, A., & McGuinn, M. (2000). The Children's Sleep Habits Questionnaire (CSHQ): Psychometric properties of a survey instrument for school-aged children. *Sleep, 23*(8), 1043–1051.

Owens, J. A., Spirito, A., McGuinn, M., & Nobile, C. (2000). Sleep habits and sleep disturbance in elementary school-aged children. *Journal of Developmental and Behavioral Pediatrics, 21*(1), 27–36.

Pasch, K. E., Laska, M. N., Lytle, L. A., & Moe, S. G. (2010). Adolescent sleep, risk behaviors, and depressive symptoms: Are they linked? *American Journal of Health Behavior, 34*(2), 237–248. doi:10.5993/AJHB.34.2.11

Peterson, J., Finn, P., & Pihl, R. O. (1992). Cognitive dysfunction and the inherited predisposition to alcoholism. *Journal of Studies on Alcohol, 53*(2), 154–160.

Pieters, S., Burk, W. J., Van der Vorst, H., Dahl, R. E., Wiers, R. W., & Engels, R. C. M. E. (2015). Prospective relationships between sleep problems and substance use, internalizing and externalizing problems. *Journal of Youth and Adolescence, 44*(2), 379–388. doi:10.1007/s10964-014-0213-9

Pilcher, J. J., & Huffcutt, A. I. (1996). Effects of sleep deprivation on performance: A meta-analysis. *Sleep, 19*(4), 318–326.

Posner, M. I., & Petersen, S. E. (1990). The attention system of the human brain. *Annual Review of Neuroscience, 13*, 25–42. doi:10.1146/annurev. ne.13.030190.000325

Rechtschaffen, A., Gilliland, M. A., Bergmann, B. M., & Winter, J. B. (1983). Physiological correlates of prolonged sleep deprivation in rats. *Science, 221*(4606), 182–184.

Rechtschaffen, A., & Kales, A. (1968). *A manual of standardized terminology, techniques and scoring system for sleep stages of human subjects.* Washington, DC: US Department of Health, Education, and Welfare, National Institutes of Health.

Roane, B. M., & Taylor, D. J. (2008). Adolescent insomnia as a risk factor for early adult depression and substance abuse. *Sleep, 31*(10), 1351–1356.

Roehrs, T., & Roth, T. (2001). Sleep, sleepiness, and alcohol use. *Alcohol Research & Health, 25*(2), 101–109.

Roffwarg, H. P., Muzio, J. N., & Dement, W. C. (1966). Ontogenetic development of the human sleep–dream cycle. *Science, 152*(3722), 604–619. doi:10.1126/science.152.3722.604

Sadeh, A., & Acebo, C. (2002). The role of actigraphy in sleep medicine. *Sleep Medicine Reviews, 6*(2), 113–124.

Sadeh, A., Gruber, R., & Raviv, A. (2002). Sleep, neurobehavioral functioning, and behavior problems in school-age children. *Child Development, 73*(2), 405–417.

Sadeh, A., Gruber, R., & Raviv, A. (2003). The effects of sleep restriction and extension on school-age children: What a difference an hour makes. *Child Development, 74*(2), 444–455.

Shadur, J. M., Hussong, A. M., & Haroon, M. (2015). Negative affect variability and adolescent self-medication: The role of the peer context. *Drug and Alcohol Review, 34*(6), 571–580. doi:10.1111/dar.12260

Sheldon, S. H. (2005). Introduction to pediatric sleep medicine. In S. H. Sheldon, R. Ferber, & M. H. Kryger (Eds.), *Principles and practice of pediatric sleep medicine* (pp. 1–6). Philadelphia, PA: Elsevier Saunders.

Steinberg, L. (2008). A social neuroscience perspective on adolescent risk-taking. *Developmental Review, 28*(1), 78–106. doi:10.1016/j.dr.2007.08.002

Talbot, L. S., McGlinchey, E. L., Kaplan, K. A., Dahl, R. E., & Harvey, A. G. (2010). Sleep deprivation in adolescents and adults: Changes in affect. *Emotion, 10*(6), 831–841. doi:10.1037/a0020138

Tarokh, L., & Carskadon, M. A. (2010). Sleep electroencephalogram in children with a parental history of alcohol abuse dependence. *Journal of Sleep Research, 19*(1, Pt. 2), 165–174. doi:10.1111/j.1365-2869.2009.00763.x

Tarokh, L., Van Reen, E., Acebo, C., LeBourgeois, M., Seifer, R., Fallone, G., & Carskadon, M. A. (2012). Adolescence and parental history of alcoholism: Insights from the sleep EEG. *Alcoholism: Clinical and Experimental Research, 36*(9), 1530–1541. doi:10.1111/j.1530-0277.2012.01756.x

Telzer, E. H., Fuligni, A. J., Lieberman, M. D., & Galván, A. (2013). The effects of poor quality sleep on brain function and risk taking in adolescence. *Neuroimage, 71*, 275–283. doi:10.1016/j.neuroimage.2013.01.025

Tsai, L. L., Young, H. Y., Hsieh, S., & Lee, C. S. (2005). Impairment of error monitoring following sleep deprivation. *Sleep, 28*(6), 707–713.

Tynjala, J., Kannas, L., & Levalahti, E. (1997). Perceived tiredness among adolescents and its association with sleep habits and use of pyschoactive substances. *Journal of Sleep Research, 6*, 189–198.

Venkatraman, V., Chuah, Y. M. L., Huettel, S. A., & Chee, M. W. L. (2007). Sleep deprivation elevates expectation of gains and attenuates response to losses following risky decisions. *Sleep, 30*(5), 603–609.

Venkatraman, V., Huettel, S. A., Chuah, L. Y. M., Payne, J. W., & Chee, M. W. L. (2011). Sleep deprivation biases the neural mechanisms underlying economic preferences. *Journal of Neuroscience, 31*(10), 3712–3718. doi:10.1523/JNEUROSCI.4407-10.2011

Vignau, J., Bailly, D., Duhamel, A., Vervaecke, P., Beuscart, R., & Collinet, C. (1997). Epidemiologic study of sleep quality and troubles in French secondary school adolescents. *Journal of Adolescent Health, 21*, 343–350.

Walker, M. P. (2009). The role of sleep in cognition and emotion. *Annals of the New York Academy of Sciences, 1156*, 168–197. doi:http://dx.doi.org/10.1111/j.1749-6632.2009.04416.x

Walker, M. P., & Stickgold, R. (2006). Sleep, memory, and plasticity. *Annual Review of Psychology, 57*, 139–166. doi:10.1146/annurev.psych.56.091103.070307

Walker, M. P., & van der Helm, E. (2009). Overnight therapy? The role of sleep in emotional brain processing. *Psychological Bulletin, 135*(5), 731–748. doi:10.1037/a0016570

Weissman, M. M., Greenwald, S., Nino-Murcia, G., & Dement, W. C. (1997). The morbidity of insomnia uncomplicated by psychiatric disorders. *General Hospital Psychiatry, 19*, 245–250.

Wikipedia. (2016). *Circadian rhythm.* Retrieved from https://en.wikipedia.org/wiki/Circadian_rhythm

Wong, M. M., & Brower, K. J. (2012). The prospective relationship between sleep problems and suicidal behavior in the National Longitudinal Study of Adolescent Health. *Journal of Psychiatric Research, 46*(7), 953–959. doi:10.1016/j.jpsychires.2012.04.008

Wong, M. M., Brower, K. J., Fitzgerald, H. E., & Zucker, R. A. (2004). Sleep problems in early childhood and early onset of alcohol and other drug use in adolescence. *Alcoholism: Clinical and Experimental Research, 28*(4), 578–587. doi:10.1097/01.alc.0000121651.75952.39

Wong, M. M., Brower, K. J., Nigg, J. T., & Zucker, R. A. (2010). Childhood sleep problems, response inhibition, and alcohol and drug outcomes in adolescence and young adulthood. *Alcoholism: Clinical and Experimental Research, 34*(6), 1033–1044. doi:10.1111/j.1530-0277.2010.01178.x

Wong, M. M., Brower, K. J., & Zucker, R. A. (2009). Childhood sleep problems, early onset of substance use and behavioral problems in adolescence. *Sleep, 10*(7), 787–796. doi:10.1016/j.sleep.2008.06.015

Wong, M. M., Puttler, L. I., Nigg, J. T., & Zucker, R. A. (2014). Sleep problems, self-regulation and resilience to problem alcohol use: A prospective study. *Alcoholism: Clinical and Experimental Research, 38*(Suppl. S1), 314A, 388.

Wong, M. M., Puttler, L. I., Nigg, J. T., & Zucker, R. A. (2015). *Sleep and self-regulatory processes in earlier life predicted resilience in young adulthood: A prospective study of children of alcoholics and controls.* Submitted for publication.

Wong, M. M., Robertson, G. C., & Dyson, R. B. (2015). Prospective relationship between poor sleep and substance-related problems in a national sample of adolescents. *Alcoholism: Clinical and Experimental Research, 39*(2), 355–362. doi:10.1111/acer.12618

Yang, Y., & Raine, A. (2009). Prefrontal structural and functional brain imaging findings in antisocial, violent, and psychopathic individuals: A meta-analysis. *Psychiatry Research: Neuroimaging, 174*(2), 81–88. doi:10.1016/j.pscychresns.2009.03.012

Yoo, S.-S., Gujar, N., Hu, P., Jolesz, F. A., & Walker, M. P. (2007). The human emotional brain without sleep—A prefrontal amygdala disconnect. *Current Biology, 17*(20), R877–878.

Zucker, R. A., Fitzgerald, H. E., Refior, S. K., Puttler, L. I., Pallas, D. M., & Ellis, D. A. (2000). The clinical and social ecology of childhood for children of alcoholics: Description of a study and implications for a differentiated social policy. In H. E. Fitzgerald, B. M. Lester, & B. S. Zuckerman (Eds.), *Children of addiction: Research, health, and policy issues* (pp. 109–141). New York, NY: RoutledgeFalmer.

Zucker, R. A., Heitzeg, M. M., & Nigg, J. T. (2011). Parsing the undercontrol–disinhibition pathway to substance use disorders: A multilevel developmental problem. *Child Development Perspectives, 5*(4), 248–255. doi:10.1111/j.1750-8606.2011.00172.x

9

Self-Regulation, Behavioral Inhibition, and Risk for Alcoholism and Substance Use Disorders

Joel T. Nigg

Substance addiction emerges in at least two stages of risk (Audrain-McGovern, Nigg, & Perkins, 2009). The first stage involves increased liability for experimenting or exploring drugs and alcohol. The second stage follows and entails risk factors for recurrent usage and addiction following exposure. Distinct risk factors are involved for each stage. This chapter focuses on liability for the first stage: atypical or early exposure and use or risk for "first-stage behaviors" in the form of early use onset, early drunkenness, early use of illicit drugs, or early emergence of problems related to use.

What causes some children to enter the first risk stage of early potentially problematic usage? Addiction emerges from a multifactorial interplay of genetic, familial, personal, and contextual risk and protective factors (Zucker, 2014). One major source of liability is thought to be personality or temperament. However, personality and temperament are also related to measures of cognition and emotion regulation, enabling cross-talk of measures at different levels of analysis (e.g., global rating scales and laboratory measures of reaction time) (Nigg, 2000; 2017). Here, I offer framing considerations, followed by a discussion of the conceptual model and some key empirical findings and conclusions.

First, personality and temperament can be conceptualized in different ways. As used here, they refer to behavioral tendencies that are typical for an individual in a given context and that can be measured by global ratings of behavior. Temperament refers to these traits in children, and personality refers to them in adults. Despite substantial literature arguing

that temperament is more biological and personality more socially determined, empirical studies indicate that measures of temperament in children and of personality in adults have quite similar factorial, biological, and other correlates and features, suggesting they are developmentally closely related (Nigg, 2006). Temperament in this perspective is hierarchically organized, with three or four higher order traits defined as (1) extraversion/surgency/positive affect, (2) negative affect/neuroticism, (3) effortful control, and (4) in some views, agreeableness/hostility. For adults, three-, four-, and five-factor models are popular. In the five-factor version, the factors are (1) extraversion/surgency, (2) neuroticism/negative emotions, (3) conscientiousness, (4) agreeableness versus hostility, and (5) openness to experience. A glossary concerning these and other terms is provided in Box 9.1.

Second, the cognitive terms involved in risk have included *executive function* and *reward discounting* as well as *impulsivity*, but these are in need of better definition as outlined in Nigg (2017). Although I address this issue in more detail in the section on the conceptual model developed by me and my colleagues (Nigg, 2000, 2006, 2017; Zucker, Heitzeg, & Nigg, 2011), an initial remark is in order here. Executive function is a centrally important domain, but there is only limited agreement on its components and boundaries. The critical domain of reward-related decision-making is sometimes referred to as "hot" executive function, in contrast to planning and focused attention under less salient reward conditions, which are "cool" executive function(Zelazo et al., 2012). While

---

BOX 9.1 **Glossary of Term and Definitions Related to Temperamental and Cognitive Liability for Alcoholism and Substance Use Disorders**

Behavioral inhibition: A term, associated most often with the work of Jerome Kagan, that refers to the tendency to interrupt ongoing behavior in the presence of a novel or ambiguous stimulus, particularly a novel social encounter. It is associated with anxiety and anxiety disorders.

Effortful control: A term originating in the work of Mary Rothbart that connotes top-down suppression of behavior or affect in the service of a goal held in working memory. It is necessary but not sufficient for the emergence of executive functioning.

Emotion regulation: Adjustment of emotional response via both automatic and deliberate (attentional and cognitive) strategies to maintain homeostasis and adaptation.

Executive functioning: Ability to ignore interfering information and/or suppress automatic responses in the service of long-terms goals, to carry out multistep plans projected forward in time, and to maintain two task sets in mind at the same time and switch between them to achieve superordinate goals represented in memory. It is also a multicomponent construct that includes sub-abilities such as set shifting, working memory, and response inhibition.

Impulsivity: Ill-considered action that yields a result opposite to one's goals. It may be influenced by poor response inhibition or by steep reward delay discounting. It is a multicomponent construct that subsumes several types of impulsive behavior based on affective tone, urgency, and other influences.

Liability: Propensity to engage in illness-enhancing behavior or develop an illness.

Personality: Characteristic behavioral response style of adolescents and adults. It is interpreted by some as the compilation of values, goals, motives, and decision-making styles accumulated through both temperament and learning history; it is viewed by others as the structure of trait responses. When viewed in this second way, it is indistinguishable from trait models of temperament.

Reactive inhibition: Bottom-up interruption of a planned behavior due to anxiety or novelty; largely synonymous with behavioral inhibition.

Response inhibition: The top-down ability to interrupt a behavior one is about to perform, in order to achieve a task-related goal. The "check swing" in baseball is the paradigm. It is a component of effortful control.

Self-control: The compilation of deliberate and effortful abilities, including cognitive control, effortful control, and emotional regulation, to direct behavior and affect toward social and instrumental goals. It is part of self-regulation.

Self-regulation: The overarching assembling of top-down and bottom-up functions that combine to provide for both autonomic and psychological, as well as automatic and effortful, adjustment to maintain an optimal emotional and arousal state for adaptation to context. It subsumes self-control.

Temperament: Characteristic emotional and behavioral response style of children; interpreted by some as the characteristic situation-specific nervous system response (e.g., autonomic response) and by others as the characteristic situation-specific behavioral response style. When viewed as behavioral response style, it has psychometric characteristics largely indistinguishable from psychobiological and trait models of personality.

---

that approach has been generative, and although we acknowledge these two types of functions are related, our model does not fully accept this approach. Our caution to the hot/cool idea is that so-called "hot" decision-making involves substantial bottom-up neural processes (i.e., originating in affective systems and relatively automatic subcortical responses including feed-forward neural transmission), whereas "cool" processes favor top-down neural processes (and relatively deliberate response and feed-backward or downward neural transmission). Although these neural "hot" and "cool" circuits are both closely linked anatomically and quite heuristic (Petrovic), this cru-cial distinction can be muddied by calling both of them "executive." Furthermore, executive function still has multiple inter-related components, such as working memory, interference control, and response inhibition, that have to be considered.

Third, attempting to clarify the temperamental component of alcoholism or substance use liabil-ity in itself is not new: It has been a perennial goal in the field for at least two decades (Caspi, Moffitt, Newman, & Silva, 1996; Young Mun, Fitzgerald, Von Eye, Puttler, & Zucker, 2001). The question has been how to organize or unify this broad liabil-ity domain given the heavy overlap of substance use with other psychopathologies that often precede and accompany it both developmentally and across life. These other psychopathologies include attention-deficit/hyperactivity disorder (ADHD: in older lit-erature, hyperactivity or hyperkinesis), conduct problems, antisocial behavior, oppositional defiant disorder (ODD), and antisocial personality disor-der. In a seminal paper, Gorenstein and Newman (1980) suggested that *disinhibitory psychopathology* as a framework might unify disparate conditions such as antisocial behavior, alcoholism, hyperactivity, and some personality disorders. Basing their thinking on foundational work by Gray (e.g., Gray, 1982) on impulsivity and the brain's septal–hippocampal sys-tem, they argued that these were all part of a larger "septal syndrome." Although work in cognitive and neural sciences suggests that the neuropsychological portion of that theory is too simplistic, subsequent work indeed has borne out this fundamental struc-tural and behavioral integration.

For example, large-scale factor analytic studies of multiple data sets have suggested that psychopathology can be organized in a hierarchical taxonomy (Lahey et al., 2017). In this taxonomy, most of the common psychopathologies cluster into two broad domains labeled for convenience "externalizing" (aggression, antisocial behavior, oppositional defiant behavior, and ADHD as well as substance use disorders) and "internalizing" (anxiety, depression, and mood dis-orders). This picture was well known in children for decades (Achenbach, Howell, Quay, & Conners, 1991; Hudziak, Achenbach, Althoff, & Pine, 2007), but more recently it has also been supported in major studies on adults (Achenbach, Krukowski, Dumenci, & Ivanova, 2005; Carragher, Krueger, Eaton, & Slade, 2015; Eaton, Rodriguez-Seijas, Carragher, &

Krueger, 2015). We can ask what behavioral or per-sonality trait underlies the externalizing factor, for example. A superfactor of psychopathology liability, or a psychopathology "g" factor, may account for the positive correlation of externalizing and internalizing problems as well (Lahey et al., 2017; Tackett et al., 2013). Presumably, the liability for substance addic-tion is narrower than that the psychopathology super-factor but broader than any one personality trait—but this is unclear.

Fourth, risk factors and predictors are not identi-cal for alcohol, marijuana, and other drugs. However, there are sufficient overlaps in terms of the risk fac-tors discussed and sufficient evidence that the tem-perament or personality aspect of liability is partially shared that, for simplicity, they are discussed inter-changeably here unless otherwise specified. It has long been thought that alcoholism, as well as some other drug addictions, is correlated with problems in executive functioning, reward discounting, con-trolled attention, and other measures related to *self-control* or *self-regulation* (De Wilde, Verdejo-Garcia, Sabbe, Hulstijn, & Dom, 2013; Giancola, Mezzich, & Tarter, 1998; Giancola & Moss, 1998). Less was initially known about personality or temperament, but similar correlations have been reported. However, because drugs or alcohol over time damage the brain, it has often been unclear what occurred first: the addiction or the executive function problem.

For that reason, investigators some time ago began prospective high-risk studies of offspring of alcoholic parents. The studies discussed in the current review emerged from the Michigan Longitudinal Study (MLS) (Zucker et al., 2000). This study recruited boys at ages 3–5 years from alcoholic fathers identi-fied by survey of court records, with a control group from the same neighborhood recruited by door-to door canvassing. Later, girls were included, as were other supplemental groups. The sample was followed annually for some measures and every 3 years for a detailed, all-day evaluation that included measures of behavioral adjustment, and after approximately age 11 years, laboratory assessment of neuropsychological functioning began as well as annual brief assessments to capture onset of alcohol use. Beginning in mid-adolescence, a subset began to undergo MRI brain imaging. The cohort, now mostly in their twenties, has yielded a wealth of data (discussed in this vol-ume; see also Zucker, 2010). With these preliminary notes in mind, this chapter outlines progress on this problem during the past two decades in our work involving the MLS.

CONCEPTUALIZATION AND GUIDING MODEL

Presumably, addiction liability is related to a propensity for problems in self-regulation or self-control. However, this simple statement begs the following questions: What is the basic structure of self-control and how does it relate to the welter of related terms and constructs from the fields of personality, temperament, and cognition(Nigg, 2017)? How does self-control, or what is sometimes called behavioral inhibition, occur psychologically? How is it mediated in the mind, the brain, and the human psychological process?

Several lines of work have highlighted the importance of self-control and self-regulation to life outcomes. This was initially hinted at in a book by Block (1971). It became central and widespread with Mischel's classic work on delay of gratification (Mischel, Shoda, & Rodriguez, 1989). That work, showing that preschool children who could delay gratification (wait for two marshmallows rather than impulsively take one that is available) had better academic outcomes. Early work from the MLS also showed that this "discounting" or "impulsive response pattern" was seen more often in offspring of alcoholic parents (Fitzgerald et al., 1993). Mischel's work set the stage for subsequent work on impulsivity related to delay discounting ("hot" decision-making). Perhaps the most conclusive documentation came from Clausen (1993), who examined the Berkeley longitudinal data from childhood to old age. He showed that across the lifespan from childhood to old age, the best predictor of long-term life success as well as satisfaction was a characteristic he labeled *planfulness*— doubtless closely related to self-control. Relatively recently, several reviews and empirical papers have documented the importance to multiple life outcomes of measures associated with self control or self regulation (Moffitt et al., 2011; Tagney et al., 2004).

However, although all the previously mentioned studies show that self-control is critically important, and although their authors are extraordinarily thoughtful about their definitions of self-control and/ or self-regulation, the constructs remain rather undifferentiated and, indeed, are at times seen unhelpfully as unitary(Nigg, 2017). Our contention has been that a more differentiated analysis of the self-regulation domain is crucial to unpack developmental dynamics and, in particular, to be able to relate it to theories of neural instantiation of liability.

To approach this problem, we and others have begun with the fundamental dual-process model that guides much of contemporary understanding of cognition and emotion. This general model, while not a complete account, is valuable and is supported in numerous experiments, suggests that human cognition (and, for our purposes, self-regulation) relies on two kinds of psychological functions. These are first explained and then related to the numerous interrelated concepts that make this domain complex, including effortful control, behavioral undercontrol, behavioral inhibition, response inhibition, self-regulation, emotion regulation, attention, controlled attention, cognitive control, and executive functioning. See Box 9.1 for a glossary of these terms and see Nigg (2017) for a more detailed discussion.

The two basic types of processes are, in brief, *reactive* and *effortful*. The first., the reactive domain, refers to responses or processes that are relatively automatic and governed by immediate incentives. A child stops whispering because the teacher suddenly looms overhead (a signal of impending punishment). An adult, driving a car, sees red and blue lights flashing in the rearview mirror. There is a burst of cortisol, attention is captured, and perhaps even without realizing it, the driver has released the gas pedal and applied the brakes. With regard to children, when a larger, unknown child enters a playroom, the child in the room will immediately stop what she is doing and appraise the stranger. That interruption is not deliberate but, rather, automatic. It is a response to cues for uncertainty, or potential threat or loss of reward. This response varies in intensity: Some children are very reactive to the novel or uncertain event, whereas others are less concerned with it. This trait is called behavioral inhibition (Kagan & Snidman, 2004), and a closely related construct is called reactive inhibition (Eisenberg et al., 2004). In either formulation, it is a bottom-up process in that it emanates from subcortical neural activation (probably via thalamic–amygdala connections) projecting forward to prefrontal cortex to interrupt motor and mental routines that are represented there in attention and working memory. Eisenberg and colleagues (Eisenberg, Spinrad, & Eggum, 2010; Eisenberg et al., 2004) conducted a series of studies suggesting that this form of reactive control is a powerful predictor (inversely) of childhood behavioral problems in conjunction with parenting behaviors and effortful control. Kagan and colleagues (see Kagan & Snidman, 2004) have provided a large program of work demonstrating that early markers of this behavioral trait in children are correlated with amygdala activation, autonomic response, and subsequent emergence of anxiety disorders.

The second type of regulatory control is relatively effortful or deliberate in terms of subjective experience, and behaves as if it is resource-limited in terms of objective measurement. These "top down" processes respond to distal goals held in working memory rather than incentives for which immediate cues are seen or heard. The child stops whispering because she remembers the day's rule and hopes to earn points at the end of the hour. Imagine your child telling you a long story and you remaining patient because you are determined to pay attention to your child even though you really need to get to work, taking only one bite of dessert because you are determined to remain on a diet, or setting aside your anxiety in order to present a confident report to the company board of directors. These are examples of inhibiting behavior or suppressing emotion in order to achieve a goal that is represented in working memory. This process, unlike bottom-up inhibition, requires mental effort, it occupies apparent mental resources(experiments demonstrate that people cannot do as much mental work when trying to inhibit a behavior or an emotion), and it is a limited capacity resource (only so much inhibition and attention can occur, and the process fatigues with time). This process is top-down because it emanates from goals represented in working memory (principally in the dorsolateral prefrontal cortex) and projections from the prefrontal cortex to posterior and subcortical systems (notably, the thalamus) suppress motor and emotional responses in the service of the goal.

Impulsivity is a related concept to both processes. While considerable nuance is needed for a full account (Nigg, 2017), in general, impulsivity refers to a hasty ill-considered action, which results in consequences contrary to an individual's goals. Theory and data suggest it may be related to either top-down or bottom-up mechanisms. One key theory is that it is related to faulty response inhibition—that is, failure to inhibit rapidly triggered responses. Although this may seem self-evident, it is not. Rapid response patterns

(moment-to-moment behavior), of the sort to which the formal definition of response inhibition refers, are also susceptible to executive function. It biases these responses and interacts with them. A second theory is that impulsivity is related to reward delay discounting. The principal here is that we all value sooner more than later rewards; however, we discount later rewards at varying rates. An impulsive or addicted person greatly discounts later rewards, so much so that their ultimate goals are defeated. From this emerges the paradigmatic predicament of the alcoholic who wants to be sober in the long term but also wants a drink now. The immediate reward wins out over the later reward, and he takes the drink only to regret it.

CONCEPTUAL SUMMARY AND APPLICATION TO SUBSTANCE ABUSE

Drawing on the previous discussion, we have proposed that a higher order trait of behavioral inhibition, here defined broadly to subsume bottom-up and top-down abilities, involves the interplay of the bottom-up classic "behavioral inhibition" or, more precisely, reactive control or reactive inhibition and top-down or effortful control or effortful inhibition (Zucker et al., 2011). These processes can be partially distinguished in psychological measurement, but they are mutually influencing during behavior, such that bottom-up processes can interfere with controlled processes, and controlled processes can bias or suppress bottom-up processes. They are also dynamically related during development, such that they anticipate and depend on one another for their respective development. However, they do not develop in parallel. With some exceptions, the brain develops in a general rostral-to-caudal and posterior-to-anterior sequence (Brain Development Cooperative Group, 2012; Huttenlocher & Dabholkar, 1997; Sowell, Trauner, Gamst, & Jernigan, 2002). As a result, bottom-up or reactive control mechanisms emerge and mature earlier than top-down or control mechanisms. This affects attention, self-control, and response inhibition differentially during development, with particular implications during adolescence.

These developmental sequences are nonlinear. Substantial disagreement exists as to the extent to which the process of cognitive and neural development is fundamentally staged (a series of plateaus and relative stability and consolidation interspersed with periods of reorganization and rapid change) or continuous (gradual growth and change). We know, nonetheless, that different regions and networks of the brain do not all develop in parallel but, rather, organize and develop at different times and rates, and we also know that dramatic nonlinearity occurs at least in the first year of life and again in adolescence for some brain networks. The first period reflects the period of risk for neurodevelopmental disorders (e.g., ADHD and autism), whereas the latter is during the period of maximum risk for substance use and substance use disorder onset. During the adolescent transition, the development and growth of the limbic system and particularly responsivity to social cues and rewards is more rapid than that of prefrontal systems (Casey, Jones, & Hare, 2008). As a result, adolescents, while gaining considerable capacity for planning and self-control, are also uniquely prone to impulsive and risk-taking behavior, particularly when potential social rewards (e.g., status within the peer group or attention from the opposite sex) are involved. The evolutionary basis of this developmental tendency is not difficult to speculate on because it helps adolescents establish their status, their independence, and find sexual partners.

Both bottom-up and top-down inhibitory processes are considered to be part of a comprehensive temperament model (Eisenberg et al., 2004, 2010; Nigg et al., 2006; Rothbart, 1981; 2011); in adulthood, the terminology changes to personality traits, but the constructs are similar. These two domains (temperament and personality) also share similar heritability, neural correlates, and factor structures (see Box 9.1).

Thus, we can clarify some of the overlapping yet distinct functions that are in play here. First, reactive control is a bottom-up or automatic (often fear- or anxiety-based) response to a stimulus, that in turn interrupts behavior. It is closely related to the idea of behavioral undercontrol, which is a broad, superordinate impulsivity construct correlated with both reactive and effortful control. It is also related closely to behavioral inhibition as identified by Kagan and colleagues (Kagan & Snidman, 2004)—that is, the automatic interruption of behavior in response to novelty.

Effortful control is top-down suppression of habitual response or distracting information to achieve a goal. Emotion regulation can occur in response to both bottom-up and top-down mechanisms when they serve to adjust emotional response or experience

to assist with either coping and homeostatic regulation or goal achievement, respectively. Executive function depends on effortful control but entails additional capabilities such as task switching and particularly projecting activity forward in time by representing future steps of behavior in mind and protecting those from interference (Diamond, 2013; Shipstead & Engle, 2013). Because of the close relationship between effortful control and executive functioning, our work examines both constructs, viewing them as different levels of measurement of a related ability. Self-regulation is an umbrella term that subsume all of the bottom-up and top-down capacities for adjusting behavior to context.

EMPIRICAL FINDINGS AND STEPS FORWARD

How do both bottom-up and top-down aspects behavioral regulation relate to substance abuse risk and alcoholism onset? Our work has outlined several principles that clarify the empirical basis for this association.

The first is that a characteristic developmental sequence or cascade seems to exist for many individuals. In the thinking that has guided our work on the MLS, this cascade is proposed to occur as follows for an important subgroup of children. In early life, these children exhibit extremes of disinhibition, irritability, and hyperactivity. By school age, they are inattentive, hyperactive, and impulsive, and they often meet diagnostic criteria for ADHD. Many also meet criteria for ODD, a syndrome characterized by a combination of defiance for authority and resentment and irritability toward others. By late childhood and adolescence, a further subset of children have begun to engage in antisocial and rule-breaking behavior and may meet criteria for conduct disorder (CD), defined by covert or overt rule-breaking behavior, or meet the statutory definition of delinquency, or both.

Although this is not the only route to addiction (Zucker et al., 1996), this group is at perhaps the highest risk for both experimentation and addiction to alcohol and other substances, accounting for the high comorbidity of alcoholism and antisocial personality disorder in adults that is a key focus of the MLS. This framework is illustrated in Figure 9.1. It is supported by longitudinal studies showing elevated

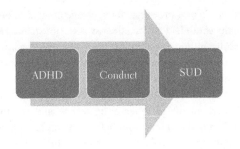

FIGURE 9.1 Basic conceptual schematic model of the developmental cascade for disinhibitory psychopathology.

CD in children with ADHD and ODD and substance use in these children (Sibley et al., 2014) and also by meta-analyses indicating that ADHD confers markedly elevated risk of subsequent alcoholism and other drug use and abuse (Charach, Yeung, Climans, & Lillie, 2011; Lee, Humphreys, Flory, Liu, & Glass, 2011), including the finding that this risk for most drugs seems to be "carried" by a subgroup who develop conduct disorder (Serra-Pinheiro et al., 2013). Because ADHD can be viewed as carrying or conveying a kind of temperamental liability (Nigg et al., 2006) from early in life, ADHD can be considered a liability factor, and the related temperamental trait is of keen interest. ADHD in turn is thought to be related to altered development of both top-down control and reactive mechanisms.

Our work supported this model in novel ways using longitudinal data. A key paper (Martel et al., 2009) examined parent-rated reactive control in preschool, hyperactivity and aggression during school age, and initiation of problem use by age 15 years. We found that, indeed, the model in Figure 9.1 fit the data well. We then took the next step of linking family history of alcoholism (a presumed proxy for a blend of genetic, epigenetic, and psychosocial risk transmitted through the parents to the child). Family history of alcoholism is known to predict offspring alcoholism, but how is this mediated developmentally? We showed that the process described in Figure 9.1 mediated the association of family history with offspring alcohol use in adolescence.

We then asked about temperament as a mediator. That is, we asked whether the path from family risk to substance use is perhaps explained by intermediate emergence of a certain temperament style and, in turn, ADHD. Here, we consider a basic model of self-control that includes two components. Because we were starting with preschoolers, we focused on reactive control, which is a domain of temperament. We fit a more complex model involving early measures of reactive control, as schematically portrayed in Figure 9.2. This model also fit the data well, with a reliable indirect path to teen alcohol use via the intervening developmental markers of reduced reactive control, increased childhood inattention and hyperactivity, and increased later childhood antisocial and aggressive behaviors. This type of finding has converged in prospective work by other investigators using other methods. For example, Herting, Schwartz, Mitchell, and Nagel (2010) found steeper delay discounting in children with a family history of alcoholism prior to onset of drug or alcohol use. This supports the idea of reactive mechanisms related to impulsivity as a key marker of familial liability.

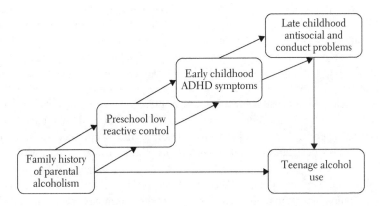

FIGURE 9.2 A cascade model of the emergence of psychopathology from early temperament as a mediator of adolescent onset of alcohol and drug use.

The second component is that, at least at some ages, this risk can also be indicated via laboratory measures of top-down inhibitory control. In these studies (Nigg et al., 2004, 2006), we used the stop signal task as a laboratory measure of the integrity of top-down control. This task measures how much warning time a child needs to interrupt a computer response that he or she was making. (The typical child needs approximately 0.25 seconds of warning in this fast-paced task.) It is mediated by a well-understood neural circuit involving the thalamus, striatum, and inferior frontal gyrus (Congdon et al., 2010), with some lateralization occurring with development.

We found that reduced response inhibition in childhood indeed predicted increased risk of alcohol and illicit drug use in adolescence. This effect held over and above childhood ADHD, conduct problems, IQ, or family history, suggesting it is an additional effect not explained fully by the cascade just described. Instead, it is likely that in some form, both reactive and controlled response inhibitory processes are involved in liability for substance use and alcoholism onset behaviors in the teen years.

The third major point that we considered was the question of distinct behavioral trajectories, using this model, that might relate problematic behavior to drug and alcohol use onset in adolescence. We were particularly interested in determining whether in fact ADHD effects were fully accounted for by conduct disorder effects or were an additional risk. In these studies (Jester et al., 2005, 2008), we conducted analyses designed to identify distinct developmental groups of children. We identified four basic, similarly sized groups in a sample of more than 300 children comprising youth from high- and low-risk families: (1) a "normative" group with low levels of inattention and aggression (33% of the sample), (2) an inattentive group (high in inattention/hyperactivity but low in aggression) (39% of the sample), (3) a rare "aggressive-but-not-inattentive" group (only 4% of the sample), and (4) a group that was both inattentive and aggressive (24% of the sample). Note that this breakdown illustrates how rare it is for children to develop sustained and substantial aggressive/antisocial behaviors in the absence of a history of significant inattention/hyperactivity.

We examined several very important markers of risk that are of continuing interest in our society: first marijuana use, first alcohol use, ever drunk, and using any hard drugs. A survival analysis was used, meaning

we could plot the curves for each age point as to how many youth had entered the risk behavior status. The results, although rather differentiated with regard to specific outcome measures, provided a fundamental finding: The risk for substance use disorders is amplified by the presence of high inattention/hyperactivity even in the presence of aggression and conduct problems. The group with both problems had significantly more risk behavior compared to the group with aggression alone. This underscores the importance of the temperamental liability aspect of risk pathways.

It is crucial to recognize that these effects are not determinative. Some children with problems in reactive control do not develop substance abuse problems. Why is this? Our principal hypothesis is that these outcomes are moderated by other cognitive skills, as well as by early family environment. To evaluate this second hypothesis, we examined the same trajectories as described previously, but this time in relation to specific associations to preschool home environment (Jester et al., 2005). We found that variation in symptoms of ADHD and variation in symptoms of aggression had distinct family correlates. Thus, it is likely that some children are more sensitive than others to variation in family environment, which can either enhance or protect against risk. Interestingly, Belsky and colleagues (Ellis, Boyce, Belsky, Bakermans-Kranenburg, & van Ijzendoorn, 2011) have subsequently argued that early temperamental liability may confer not risk but, rather, responsivity or *plasticity*, making children more responsive *for good or for ill* to characteristics of their early environment. They suggest several methods for testing this idea statistically that we anticipate will be part of future work in relation to alcoholism.

We have amplified this work in a series of studies of brain imaging that considered emotional response, reward discounting, and executive function (for details, see Heitzeg, 2016). One question was whether in fact alterations in neural response to a response inhibition task actually corresponded to alterations in the hypothesized neural circuitry mentioned previously. We have indeed found that prior to the occurrence of substance use problems, children from parents with alcoholism show alterations in subcortical functioning in response to an inhibition task (a go/no-go task). Alterations in cortical response were also noted in the group that went on to substance use (Heitzeg, Nigg, Yau, Zucker, & Zubieta, 2010). In a subsequent study, we specifically examined brain activation from 9 to 12 years of age on an inhibition task, prior to substance use onset. It was inferior frontal gyrus activation changes during errors, but not during correct responses, that predicted problematic drug use 4 years later. This again suggests that alterations in neural development related to cognitive supports for top-down response inhibition confer a preexisting liability for substance use onset (Heitzeg et al., 2014).

CONCLUSIONS AND FUTURE DIRECTIONS

The snapshot of selected studies presented in this chapter falls in the context of a larger literature asking about the behavioral, temperamental, and personality liability that sets individuals at risk for addiction in the wrong environment or context. In the past two decades, there has been significant progress in the characterization of this liability. We are proud to have contributed in some small way to that progress.

In view of the extant literature that preceded our work, it is not surprising that this broad ability would be so closely related to addiction. What is more striking is the increased precision and differentiation with which we can characterize components or aspects of self-regulation, measure them, and relate them to neural systems as well as to early life and genetic determinants. The hope is that eventually this work can help us understand who is at risk and how to help those at risk be more resilient.

Finally, there has been substantially increased recognition that a particular subdomain known as executive functioning has important ramifications for early life success and virtuous cycle of positive outcome. For example, behaviors of inattention (related to executive function) predict school success over and above externalizing behavior problems in longitudinal data (Breslau et al., 2010). Likewise, executive functioning is viewed as critical to academic success (Nesbitt, Farran, & Fuhs, 2015), which in turn influences peer selection, risk-taking, and other components of the complex pathway to experimentation and problem use. Executive functioning, effortful control, and top down aspects of self-regulation are closely related to development of the prefrontal cortex and its extensive connections to posterior and subcortical neural structures and regions. These networks and regions are among the last to develop and the most vulnerable to

insult in early development. Thus, their role in addiction will speak to the importance of not only understanding early brain development but also protecting early development generally in our society to reduce the propensity toward addiction and other problem outcomes.

Of course, development of addiction is a specific outcome that depends on societal and local context: If no drugs are available, or if immediate treatment and help are at hand, a child is unlikely to become addicted to them. Appropriate social policy related to drugs, availability of treatment, and other contextual supports are of paramount importance. However, the course of development that places children on the path of risk to alcoholism and other addictions is very closely related to the course of development for other negative life outcomes. Therefore, it will remain important to understand these developmental cascades in relation to a range of health and life outcomes in addition to addiction.

REFERENCES

Achenbach, T. M., Howell, C. T., Quay, H. C., & Conners, C. K. (1991). National survey of problems and competencies among four- to sixteen-year-olds: Parents' reports for normative and clinical samples. *Monographs of the Society for Research in Child Development, 56*(3), 1–131.

Achenbach, T. M., Krukowski, R. A., Dumenci, L., & Ivanova, M. Y. (2005). Assessment of adult psychopathology: Meta-analyses and implications of cross-informant correlations. *Psychology Bulletin, 131*(3), 361–382. doi:10.1037/0033-2909.131.3.361

Audrain-McGovern, J., Nigg, J. T., & Perkins, K. (2009). Endophenotypes for nicotine dependence risk at or before initial nicotine exposure. In G. E. Swan, T. B. Baker, L. Chassin, D. V. Conti, C. Lerman, & K. A. Perkins (Eds.), *Phenotypes and endophenotypes: Foundations for genetic studies of nicotine use and dependence* (Vol. 20, pp. 339–402). Washington, DC: US Department of Health & Human Services, National Institutes of Health.

Brain Development Cooperative Group. (2012). Total and regional brain volumes in a population-based normative sample from 4 to 18 years: The NIH MRI Study of Normal Brain Development. *Cerebral Cortex, 22*(1), 1–12. doi:10.1093/cercor/bhr018

Breslau, N., Breslau, J., Peterson, E., Miller, E., Lucia, V. C., Bohnert, K., & Nigg, J. T. (2010). Change in teachers' ratings of attention problems and subsequent change in academic achievement: A prospective analysis. *Psychological Medicine*, 40(1), 159–166. doi:10.1017/s0033291709005960

Carragher, N., Krueger, R. F., Eaton, N. R., & Slade, T. (2015). Disorders without borders: Current and future directions in the meta-structure of mental disorders. *Social Psychiatry and Psychiatric Epidemiology*, 50(3), 339–350. doi:10.1007/s00127-014-1004-z

Casey, B. J., Jones, R. M., & Hare, T. A. (2008). The adolescent brain. *Annals of the New York Academy of Sciences*, 1124, 111–126. doi:10.1196/annals.1440.010

Caspi, A., Moffitt, T. E., Newman, D. L., & Silva, P. A. (1996). Behavioral observations at age 3 years predict adult psychiatric disorders: Longitudinal evidence from a birth cohort. *Archives of General Psychiatry*, 53(11), 1033–1039.

Charach, A., Yeung, E., Climans, T., & Lillie, E. (2011). Childhood attention-deficit/hyperactivity disorder and future substance use disorders: Comparative meta-analyses. *Journal of the American Academy of Child & Adolescent Psychiatry*, 50(1), 9–21. doi:10.1016/j.jaac.2010.09.019

Congdon, E., Mumford, J. A., Cohen, J. R., Galvan, A., Aron, A. R., Xue, G., . . . Poldrack, R. A. (2010). Engagement of large-scale networks is related to individual differences in inhibitory control. *Neuroimage*, 53(2), 653–663. doi:10.1016/j.neuroimage.2010.06.062

Diamond, A. (2013). Executive functions. *Annual Review of Clinical Psychology*, 64, 135–168. doi:10.1146/annurev-psych-113011-143750

De Wilde, B., Verdejo-Garcia, A., Sabbe, B., Hulstijn, W., & Dom, G. (2013). Affective decision-making is predictive of three-month relapse in polysubstance-dependent alcoholics. *European Addiction Research Journal*, 19(1), 21–28. doi:10.1159/000339290

Eaton, N. R., Rodriguez-Seijas, C., Carragher, N., & Krueger, R. F. (2015). Transdiagnostic factors of psychopathology and substance use disorders: A review. *Social Psychiatry and Psychiatric Epidemiology*, 50(2), 171–182. doi:10.1007/s00127-014-1001-2

Eisenberg, N., Spinrad, T. L., & Eggum, N. D. (2010). Emotion-related self-regulation and its relation to children's maladjustment. *Annual Review of Clinical Psychology*, 6, 495–525. doi:10.1146/annurev.clinpsy.121208.131208

Eisenberg, N., Spinrad, T. L., Fabes, R. A., Reiser, M., Cumberland, A., Shepard, S. A., . . . Thompson, M. (2004). The relations of effortful control and

impulsivity to children's resiliency and adjustment. *Child Development*, 75(1), 25–46.

Ellis, B. J., Boyce, W. T., Belsky, J., Bakermans-Kranenburg, M. J., & van Ijzendoorn, M. H. (2011). Differential susceptibility to the environment: An evolutionary–neurodevelopmental theory. *Development and Psychopathology*, 23(1), 7–28. doi:10.1017/s0954579410000611

Fitzgerald, H. E., Sullivan, L. A., Ham, H. P., Zucker, R. A., Bruckel, S., Schneider, A. M., & Noll, R. B. (1993). Predictors of behavior problems in three-year-old sons of alcoholics: early evidence for the onset of risk. *Child Development*, 64(1), 110–123.

Giancola, P. R., Mezzich, A. C., & Tarter, R. E. (1998). Disruptive, delinquent and aggressive behavior in female adolescents with a psychoactive substance use disorder: Relation to executive cognitive functioning. *Journal of Studies on Alcohol*, 59(5), 560–567.

Giancola, P. R., & Moss, H. B. (1998). Executive cognitive functioning in alcohol use disorders. *Recent Developments in Alcoholism*, 14, 227–251.

Gorenstein, E. E., & Newman, J. P. (1980). Disinhibitory psychopathology: A new perspective and a model for research. *Psychological Review*, 87(3), 301–315. doi:10.1037/0033-295X.87.3.301

Gray, J. A. (1982). *The neuropsychology of anxiety: An enquiry into the functions of the septo-hippocampal system*. New york: ClarendonPress/Oxford University Press.

Heitzeg, M. M., Nigg, J. T., Hardee, J. E., Soules, M., Steinberg, D., Zubieta, J. K., & Zucker, R. A. (2014). Left middle frontal gyrus response to inhibitory errors in children prospectively predicts early problem substance use. *Drug and Alcohol Dependence*, 141, 51–57. doi:10.1016/j.drugalcdep.2014.05.002

Heitzeg, M. M., Nigg, J. T., Yau, W. Y., Zucker, R. A., & Zubieta, J. K. (2010). Striatal dysfunction marks preexisting risk and medial prefrontal dysfunction is related to problem drinking in children of alcoholics. *Biological Psychiatry*, 68(3), 287–295. doi:10.1016/j.biopsych.2010.02.020

Hudziak, J. J., Achenbach, T. M., Althoff, R. R., & Pine, D. S. (2007). A dimensional approach to developmental psychopathology. *International Journal of Methods in Psychiatric Research*, 16(Suppl. 1), S16–S23. doi:10.1002/mpr.217

Huttenlocher, P. R., & Dabholkar, A. S. (1997). Regional differences in synaptogenesis in human cerebral cortex. *Journal of Comparative Neurology*, 387(2), 167–178.

Iaboni, F., Douglas, V. I., & Ditto, B. (1997). Psychophysiological response of ADHD children to reward and extinction. *Psychophysiology*, 34(1), 116–123.

Jester, J. M., Nigg, J. T., Adams, K., Fitzgerald, H. E., Puttler, L. I., Wong, M. M., & Zucker, R. A. (2005). Inattention/hyperactivity and aggression from early childhood to adolescence: Heterogeneity of trajectories and differential influence of family environment characteristics. *Development and Psychopathology*, 17(1), 99–125.

Jester, J. M., Nigg, J. T., Buu, A., Puttler, L. I., Glass, J. M., Heitzeg, M. M., . . . Zucker, R. A. (2008). Trajectories of childhood aggression and inattention/hyperactivity: Differential effects on substance abuse in adolescence. *Journal of the American Academy of Child & Adolescent Psychiatry*, 47(10), 1158–1165. doi:10.1097/CHI.0b013e3181825a4e

Kagan, J., & Snidman, N. C. (2004). *The long shadow of temperament*. Cambridge, MA: Belknap.

Lahey, B. B., Krueger, R. F., Rathouz, P. J., Waldman, I. D., & Zald, D. H. (2017). A hierarchical causal taxonomy of psychopathology across the life span. *Psychological Bulletin*, 143(2), 142–186.

Lee, S. S., Humphreys, K. L., Flory, K., Liu, R., & Glass, K. (2011). Prospective association of childhood attention-deficit/hyperactivity disorder (ADHD) and substance use and abuse/dependence: A meta-analytic review. *Clinical Psychology Review*, 31(3), 328–341. doi:10.1016/j.cpr.2011.01.006

Martel, M. M., Pierce, L., Nigg, J. T., Jester, J. M., Adams, K., Puttler, L. I., . . . Zucker, R. A. (2009). Temperament pathways to childhood disruptive behavior and adolescent substance abuse: Testing a cascade model. *Journal of Abnormal Child Psychology*, 37(3), 363–373. doi:10.1007/s10802-008-9269-x

Mischel, W., Shoda, Y., & Rodriguez, M. I. (1989). Delay of gratification in children. *Science*, 244(4907), 933–938.

Moffitt, T. E., Arseneault, L., Belsky, D., Dickson, N., Hancox, R. J., Harrington, H., . . . Caspi, A. (2011). A gradient of childhood self-control predicts health, wealth, and public safety. *Proceedings of the National Academy of Sciences of the USA*, 108(7), 2693–2698. doi:10.1073/pnas.1010076108

Nesbitt, K. T., Farran, D. C., & Fuhs, M. W. (2015). Executive function skills and academic achievement gains in prekindergarten: Contributions of learning-related behaviors. *Developmental Psychology*, 51(7), 865–878. doi:10.1037/dev0000021

Nigg, J. T. (2000). On inhibition/disinhibition in developmental psychopathology: Views from cognitive and personality psychology and a working inhibition taxonomy. *Psychology Bulletin*, 126(2), 220–246.

Nigg, J. T. (2006). Temperament and developmental psychopathology. *Journal of Child Psychology and Psychiatry*, 47(3–4), 395–422. doi:10.1111/j.1469-7610.2006.01612.x

Nigg, J. T. (2017). On the relations between self-regulation, executive function, effortful control, cognitive control, impulsivity, inhibition, and risk taking for developmental psychopathology. *Journal of Child Psychology and Psychiatry*, 58, 361–383.

Nigg, J. T., Glass, J. M., Wong, M. M., Poon, E., Jester, J. M., Fitzgerald, H. E., . . . Zucker, R. A. (2004). Neuropsychological executive functioning in children at elevated risk for alcoholism: Findings in early adolescence. *Journal of Abnormal Psychology*, 113(2), 302–314. doi:10.1037/0021-843x.113.2.302

Nigg, J. T., Wong, M. M., Martel, M. M., Jester, J. M., Puttler, L. I., Glass, J. M., . . . Zucker, R. A. (2006). Poor response inhibition as a predictor of problem drinking and illicit drug use in adolescents at risk for alcoholism and other substance use disorders. *Journal of the American Academy of Child & Adolescent Psychiatry*, 45(4), 468–475. doi:10.1097/01.chi.0000199028.76452.a9

Rothbart, M. K. (1981). Measurement of temperament in infancy. *Child Development*, 52(2), 569–578. doi:10.2307/1129176

Rothbart, M. K. (2011). *Becoming who we are: Temperament and personality in development*. New York: Guilford Press.

Serra-Pinheiro, M. A., Coutinho, E. S., Souza, I. S., Pinna, C., Fortes, D., Araujo, C., . . . Mattos, P. (2013). Is ADHD a risk factor independent of conduct disorder for illicit substance use? A meta-analysis and meta-regression investigation. *Journal of Attention Disorders*, 17(6), 459–469. doi:10.1177/1087054711435362

Shipstead, Z., & Engle, R. W. (2013). Interference within the focus of attention: Working memory tasks reflect more than temporary maintenance. *Journal of Experimental Psychology: Learning, Memory, and Cognition*, 39(1), 277–289. doi:10.1037/a0028467

Sibley, M. H., Pelham, W. E., Molina, B. S., Coxe, S., Kipp, H., Gnagy, E. M., . . . Lahey, B. B. (2014). The role of early childhood ADHD and subsequent CD in the initiation and escalation of adolescent cigarette, alcohol, and marijuana use. *Journal of Abnormal Psychology*, 123(2), 362–374. doi:10.1037/a0036585

Sowell, E. R., Trauner, D. A., Gamst, A., & Jernigan, T. L. (2002). Development of cortical and subcortical brain structures in childhood and adolescence: A structural MRI study. *Developmental Medicine & Child Neurology*, *44*(1), 4–16.

Tackett, J. L., Lahey, B. B., van Hulle, C., Waldman, I., Krueger, R. F., & Rathouz, P. J. (2013). Common genetic influences on negative emotionality and a general psychopathology factor in childhood and adolescence. *Journal of Abnormal Psychology*, *122*(4), 1142–1153. doi:10.1037/a0034151

Tangney, J. P., Baumeister, R. F., & Boone, A. L. (2004). High self-control predicts good adjustment, less pathology, better grades, and interpersonal success. *Journal of Personality*, *72*(2), 271–324.

Young Mun, E., Fitzgerald, H. E., Von Eye, A., Puttler, L. I., & Zucker, R. A. (2001). Temperamental characteristics as predictors of externalizing and internalizing child behavior problems in the contexts of high and low parental psychopathology. *Infant Mental Health Journal*, *22*(3), 393–415. doi:10.1002/imhj.1008

Zelazo, P. D., & Carlson, S. M. (2012). Hot and cool executive function in childhood and adolescence: Development and plasticity. *Child Development Perspectives*, *6*(4), 354–360. doi:10.1111/j.1750-8606.2012.00246.x

Zucker, R. A. (2010). Addiction research centres and the nurturing of creativity. University of Michigan Addiction Research Center (UMARC): Development, evolution, and direction. *Addiction*, *105*(6), 966–973. doi:10.1111/j.1360-0443.2010.02904.x

Zucker, R. A. (2014). Genes, brain, behavior, and context: The developmental matrix of addictive behavior. *Nebraska Symposium on Motivation*, *61*, 51–69.

Zucker, R. A., Ellis, D. A., Fitzgerald, H. E. (1994). Developmental evidence for at least two alcoholisms. I. Biopsychosocial variation among pathways into symptomatic difficulty. *Abdominal Aortic Aneurysm: Genetics, Pathophysiology, and Molecular Biology*, *708*, 134–146.

Zucker, R. A., Fitzgerald, H. E., Refior, S. K., Puttler, L. I., Pallas, D. M., & Ellis, D. A. (2000). The clinical and social ecology of childhood for children of alcoholics: Description of a study and implications for a differentiated social policy. In H. E. Fitzgerald, B. M. Lester, & B. Zuckerman (Eds.), *Children of addiction: Research, health, and policy issues*. New York, NY: Garland.

Zucker, R. A., Heitzeg, M. M., & Nigg, J. T. (2011). Parsing the undercontrol/disinhibition pathway to substance use disorders: A multilevel developmental problem. *Child Development Perspectives*, *5*(4), 248–255. doi:10.1111/j.1750-8606.2011.00172.x

10

A Framework for Studying Parental Socialization of Child and Adolescent Substance Use

John E. Donovan

Since the early 1970s, the major focus of social–psychological research on the development of substance use in adolescence has been on peer influence, without much attention to the interaction of the peer environment and the family environment (even when both are assessed in the same theoretical framework). It is hoped that this chapter provides some grist for the millwheel of progress toward a fuller understanding of the influence of the family environment on child and adolescent substance use and of the interrelations between the family environment and the peer environment in the socialization of youth into substance use. An influential review of parenting research by Collins, Maccoby, Steinberg, Hetherington, and Bornstein (2000) importantly stated,

> Any psychological snapshot taken during adolescence, when peers are undeniably an important force in children's lives, rightly should be viewed as the end of a long process of socialization that began early in childhood and most likely has its origins in the family. (p. 227)

Socialization is defined here as a lifelong process through which an individual's personality, attitudes, and behaviors are shaped by agents in their evolving social environments of origin and selection. The social environment is conceptualized as a field of forces impacting the individual through a variety of different mechanisms and processes (Lewin, 1939). Social agents include the members of the adolescent's immediate family (parents, guardians, and siblings) and extended family (grandparents, aunts, uncles, and cousins; close friends, classmates, and schoolmates; social-media peers, online video game competitors, and the denizens of multiple intersecting subcultures and cultures inhabiting the Internet/blogosphere; and the mass media of literature, magazines, art, advertising, television, movies, radio, and music. This chapter focuses on the impact of two of these sets of social agents—parents and peers—on the socialization of children and adolescents into substance use (for the other social agents, see Donovan, 2015). A number of theories are relevant to understanding the socialization processes influencing adolescent involvement in substance use. Some of the most relevant are listed and briefly reviewed in Box 10.1.

FAMILY ENVIRONMENT INFLUENCES

As can be seen in Box 10.1, the socialization theories include a variety of family environment variables, including parent substance use (alcohol consumption, smoking, marijuana use, and other drug use) reflecting their modeling of these behaviors, parents' substance-specific approval for child/adolescent use, parenting practices (e.g., monitoring, positive parenting, and discipline), the quality of the parent–child relationship (warmth, bonding, support, closeness, and low conflict), and parents' beliefs (e.g., outcome expectancies) regarding child and adolescent substance use.

BOX 10.1 Important Socialization Theories

BANDURA'S SOCIAL LEARNING THEORY

Briefly, social learning theory (SLT) states that children learn about drinking, smoking, and drug use through observation of the behaviors of others in their social environment (including models observed on television and in the movies) and through their vicarious learning of the positive and negative consequences for these individuals of their substance use (thereby developing outcome expectancies for these behaviors). According to the theory (Bandura, 1977, p. 88), responsiveness to modeling cues is determined by the characteristics of the models, the attributes of the observers, and the outcome expectancies associated with matching the modeled behavior. Important characteristics of the models include their high status, competence, and power. Based on these criteria, parents and close friends are considered highly salient models for child and adolescent involvement in substance use behavior.

AKER'S SOCIAL LEARNING THEORY

Aker's social learning theory (Akers, 1985) focuses on the influence of behavioral models on the social learning of children and adolescents and also on the influence of perceived parent and peer approval (norms), their expected reactions to substance use (positive and negative reinforcement), and their involvement with substance-using or non-using peers (differential association) on the development of the adolescents' own attitudes (definitions) toward substance use and their consequent use. Imitation of others' use is expected to have a stronger effect on the initiation of use than on the maintenance of use.

HIRSCHI'S SOCIAL BONDING THEORY

Social control theories (also called bonding theories) generally derive from the sociological literature focused on delinquency (e.g., Hirschi, 1969). The underlying premise is that people will engage in such behavior (including substance use) unless they have a reason not to do so—specifically, strong bonds to conventional social agents and to the conventional institutions of society such as the family, religion, and school systems.

KANDEL'S ADOLESCENT SOCIALIZATION THEORY

Kandel's adolescent socialization theory (Kandel, 1980) encompasses aspects of both social learning and social control theories. Adolescent drug use behavior is considered to depend on intergenerational influences from parents and peers. Consistent with SLT, imitation of others' behavior as well as social reinforcement lead to the internalization of definitions and values held by significant others and to the adoption of substance use behaviors. Closeness to parents is viewed as a control against involvement in deviant behavior, regardless of the parents' own behavior. It posits that parents are the primary source of socialization for the initiation of licit substance use (alcohol and tobacco) in childhood and early adolescence and that peer influence becomes more important in adolescence.

OETTING'S PRIMARY SOCIALIZATION THEORY

Oetting's primary socialization theory (Oetting & Donnermeyer, 1998) states that adolescent drug use is socialized by three primary contexts of interaction—the family, schools, and peers—and focuses on the role of each context in transmitting norms concerning substance use. When child bonding to the family or to the schools is low, children or adolescents are considered more likely to bond with deviant peers and to engage in substance use.

INTERACTIONAL THEORY

Interactional theory (Thornberry, 1987) also combines elements of both social control and social learning theories. The theory proposes that deviant behavior (e.g., drug use) results both from a weakening of the individual's bonds to conventional society and its agents and from the individual's exposure to a social environment in which deviant behavior (including substance use) can be learned and reinforced.

PATTERSON'S COERCION THEORY

Patterson's coercion theory (Patterson, 1982) suggests that conflict within the family and poor family management skills lead early adolescents to affiliate with deviant peers, resulting in involvement in delinquent behavior and substance use. Parental influence is thus hypothesized to influence adolescent substance use through the mediation of deviant peer affiliation.

PROBLEM BEHAVIOR THEORY

Problem behavior theory (Jessor & Jessor, 1977) proposes that involvement in drinking, drug use, and risky sex is more likely when risk for problem behavior in the personality system (low self-esteem, low expectations of success, and hopelessness), social environment system (family and peer models and approval for problem behavior), and behavior system (involvement in other problem behaviors) is high and protective factors in these systems (e.g., attitudinal intolerance of deviance, positive attitudes toward school, positive relations with adults, family rules, friend models for conventional behavior, and involvement in church and school activities) are low. Overall, it is the balance between risk and protection across the three systems that determines the likelihood of involvement in problem behavior, including substance use.

Generally unacknowledged in most studies of adolescent substance use are the relationships of these family environment constructs to each other, to important constructs in the peer environment (e.g., peer modeling and peer approval for substance use), and to the personality system, including child and adolescent cognitions (attitudes, outcome expectancies, and perceptions of parent and peer approval and models or norms) with respect to drinking, smoking, and other drug use.

In the following sections, I review empirical support for the linkages among the family environment, peer environment, and child/adolescent personality constructs. Many of the linkages described were determined through examination of correlation matrices included in articles focused on other variables. Each of the relationships of the family environment, peer environment, and personality constructs to child/adolescent substance use was considered with respect to alcohol use, smoking, marijuana use, and other drug use, but it is important to remember that these substance use behaviors are significantly correlated in adolescence (Catalano, White, Fleming, & Haggerty, 2011; Donovan & Jessor, 1985; Jessor & Jessor, 1977; Palmer et al., 2009). On the other hand, they can alternatively be seen as constituting stages in a developmental sequence of progression in substance involvement in adolescence (Kandel, 2002), generally starting with either alcohol or tobacco use, then marijuana use, followed by other illicit drug use and the nonmedical use of prescription drugs. Importantly, these interrelations suggest that one can generalize findings across substance use behaviors to a certain extent. Due to space limitations, the literature reviewed includes only a sample of those studies that have been done in each area.

The Linkage Between Parental Modeling and Child/Adolescent Substance Use

The first linkage between the family environment and child/adolescent substance use involves parental modeling of drinking, smoking, marijuana use, and other drug use. There is substantial evidence in the literature for the influence of exposure to parental substance use on offspring use of the same substance within childhood and adolescence, as well as evidence that parental alcohol use also has an impact on adolescents' use of other substances (Dishion, Capaldi, & Yoerger, 1999; Johnson, Shontz, & Locke, 1984). There is also evidence supporting exposure to older sibling substance use as an important family environment factor contributing to the adolescent's own substance use, but this linkage is less relevant to this chapter's focus on parental socialization, and it has been reviewed elsewhere (Donovan, 2015).

In regard to parental alcoholism, early adolescent children of alcoholics are more likely to have ever used alcohol, to have used it in the past 3 months, and to have ever had an alcohol- or drug-related social consequence or dependence symptom than are children of non-alcoholic parents (Chassin, Rogosch, & Barrera, 1991). They also drank more alcohol in the past 6 months than adolescents without an alcoholic parent (Ohannessian, 2009). Parental alcoholism has also been shown to predict onset of alcohol use and onset of drunkenness by ages 12–14 years (Wong, Brower, Fitzgerald, & Zucker, 2004), as well as adolescent symptoms of alcohol use disorder (Buu et al., 2009).

Although there is not a large literature on alcohol use among children in relation to actual parent drinking behavior rather than alcoholism, research shows that child exposure to parental drinking is associated with both sipping or tasting of alcohol (Donovan & Molina, 2008, 2014; Jackson, Ennett, Dickinson, & Bowling, 2012, 2013) and drinking among elementary schoolchildren (Chen et al., 2011; Macleod et al., 2008). Parental drinking is also significantly associated with drinking in adolescence. This has been shown in numerous studies that relied on adolescent perceptions of parent drinking (Bjorkqvist, Batman, & Aman-Back, 2004; Brook et al., 2010; Epstein, Griffin, & Botvin, 2008; Müller & Kuntsche, 2011; Pieters, Burk, van der Vorst, Wiers, & Engels, 2012; Smith et al., 2014), as well as studies that relied on parent reports of their own drinking (Ali & Dwyer, 2010; Armstrong et al., 2013; Duncan, Duncan, & Strycker, 2006; Fagan & Najman, 2005; Handley & Chassin, 2013; Kendler et al., 2013; Latendresse et al., 2008; Windle, 2000).

Parental drinking has also been shown to be a significant antecedent risk factor for the *initiation* of drinking among adolescent abstainers (Donovan, 2004; Handley & Chassin, 2013). In addition, research shows that parental drinking is a significant

antecedent predictor of younger ages of onset of drinking (Stoolmiller et al., 2012) or early onset drinking (Donovan & Molina, 2011; Hayatbakhsh et al., 2008), as well as of adolescent alcohol misuse (Seljamo et al., 2006) and smoking and marijuana use (Dishion et al., 1999). Regarding the question of which parent's drinking is more influential for modeling, more than 30 studies found that both mother's and father's drinking relate to adolescent drinking (Aas, Jacobsen, & Anderssen, 1996; Brook et al., 2010; Epstein et al., 2008), with far fewer studies finding a relation for only one or the other parent when both were examined.

As was true for alcohol use, research found that children and adolescents who have parents who smoke are more likely to start smoking themselves. A systematic review and meta-analysis of 58 studies published since 2000 (Leonardi-Bee, Jere, & Britton, 2011) concluded that the relative odds of initiation of smoking in children and adolescents increased significantly if at least one parent smoked. There was also significant support for a dose–response relationship between the number of parents who smoked and child/adolescent smoking.

Longitudinal research has shown that exposure to parental smoking in elementary school not only predicted initiation of smoking 1 or 2 years later (Jackson & Henriksen, 1997; O'Loughlin et al., 2014) but also increased the children's likelihood of smoking as adolescents (Bricker et al., 2006). In longitudinal research within adolescence, parental smoking has repeatedly been shown to predict initiation of smoking 1–3 years later (Gritz et al., 2003; Skinner, Haggerty, & Catalano, 2009; Wang et al., 1999). Perceived parental smoking was as strong a predictor of smoking initiation over 1 year as best friends' perceived smoking (de Vries, Engels, Kremers, Wetzels, & Mudde, 2003). Parents' smoking at child grade 7 was also found to predict escalation of the child's smoking involvement by grade 12 (Kim, Fleming, & Catalano, 2009).

The age of smoking initiation was predicted by parental smoking and by the duration of the adolescent's exposure to smoking parents (Gilman et al., 2009). This effect was equally strong for mother and father smoking, and it was stronger if exposure was before age 13 years, if both parents smoked, and if smoking fathers resided with the adolescent. On the other hand, Leonardi-Bee et al. (2011) concluded from their meta-analysis that although *both* mother smoking and father smoking increased the relative odds of child/adolescent smoking initiation, the effect was stronger for mother smoking than for father smoking. The analysis also found some support for a stronger effect for same-sex than for opposite-sex socialization. Finally, child and adolescent exposure to parental smoking may be confounded by their exposure to second-hand smoke in the home and in the family automobile. These secondary exposures have been shown to be risk factors for children's initiation of smoking (Wang, Ho, & Lam, 2011).

There is much less research on the influence of parental use of marijuana or other illicit drugs on adolescents' frequency of use or initiation of use of such drugs. Nevertheless, similar to alcohol and tobacco, when children were introduced to marijuana use during early elementary school, it was generally by a parent or close family friend, whereas in later elementary school and junior high school, it was generally by peers (Baumrind, 1985). Parental modeling of marijuana use has been found to be a significant correlate of child and adolescent use in cross-sectional studies (Ellickson, Tucker, Klein, & Saner, 2004; Vermeulen-Smit, Verdurmen, Engels, & Vollebergh, 2015). Parents' use of other drugs (cocaine, opiates, amphetamines, barbiturates, inhalants, and PCP) correlated with their children's use of these same drugs (Johnson et al., 1984; Smart & Fejer, 1972), and father (but not mother) use of prescription drugs was associated with adolescent marijuana use (Prendergast, 1974). Longitudinal studies have demonstrated a linkage between parent-reported marijuana use and later child use, both between childhood and adolescence (Brook, Brook, Arencibia-Mireles, Richter, & Whiteman, 2001) and within adolescence for marijuana use (Ellickson et al., 2004; Miller, Siegel, Hohman, & Crano, 2013) and for substance use more generally (Gibbons et al., 2004).

The Linkage of Parental Approval/Disapproval to Child/Adolescent Substance Use

A second category of relevant family environment variables includes parental approval/disapproval of child/adolescent substance use and parents' anticipated reactions to learning of their child's substance use. Parent approval can refer to either acceptance of one's own child's substance use or acceptance of substance use by children the same age as their child or by adolescents in general. Parental offers of alcohol and cigarettes may also signal parental approval of child substance use.

Regarding alcohol use, a greater expectation of getting into trouble with parents for using alcohol was found among child abstainers than drinkers (Jackson, 1997). Greater mother and father disapproval of adolescent alcohol use was associated with a lower likelihood of an adolescent being a drinker (Barnes & Welte, 1986; Osaki, Suzuki, Wada, & Hitsumoto, 2011), and parent approval (or lack of disapproval) of their own child's/adolescent's drinking correlated with an adolescent's frequency of alcohol use (Abar & Turrisi, 2008; Ary, Tildesley, Hops, & Andrews, 1993; Hummer, LaBrie, & Ehret, 2013; Kelly, O'Flaherty, Toumbourou, et al., 2011; Li et al., 2014; Smith et al., 2014), heavy drinking (Lipperman-Kreda, Grube, & Paschall, 2010), and variation in daily intake of alcohol (Barnes & Welte, 1986). Parent disapproval of substance use in general also related to less alcohol use (Beal, Ausiello, & Perrin, 2001; Clark, Belgrave, & Abell, 2012). Greater parental acceptance of drinking by adolescents in general (not just their own child) is also associated with greater adolescent drinking (Aas et al., 1996; Koning, Engels, Verdurmen, & Vollebergh, 2010; Thompson & Wilsnack, 1987).

Longitudinal studies also demonstrate associations between the expectation of parental negative reaction and the decreased likelihood of starting to drink among sixth graders (Simons-Morton, 2004) and among 11- to 15-year-olds (Andrews, Hops, Ary, Tildesley, & Harris, 1993). Similarly, parent disapproval was associated with abstaining from heavy drinking across adolescence (Martino, Collins, Ellickson, Schell, & McCaffrey, 2009) and with decreased binge drinking among college freshmen (Walls, Fairlie, & Wood, 2009, 2012). Abar and Turrisi (2008) found that parental disapproval during the summer before college significantly predicted second-semester alcohol intake. Finally, Ryan, Jorm, and Lubman's (2010) review of longitudinal adolescent alcohol research concluded that greater parental disapproval of drinking related consistently to later levels of alcohol use, but it did not relate consistently to younger ages of onset of drinking.

Parental disapproval of smoking is associated with a lower likelihood of adolescent smoking (Osaki et al., 2011); less frequent adolescent smoking (Bahr, Hoffmann, & Yang, 2005); and middle school students' frequency of use of cigars, cigarillos, and little cigars (Trapl, Yoder, Frank, Borawski, & Sattar, 2016).

A relaxed parental attitude toward youth smoking was also found to be related to a greater likelihood of students initiating weekly smoking 2 years later (Forrester, Biglan, Severson, & Smolkowski, 2007). Perceived parent approval also predicted the transition from experimental to regular smoking (Tucker, Ellickson, & Klein, 2003) and from never smoker to established smoker less than 2 years later (Sargent & Dalton, 2001). Finally, there is evidence of a reciprocal effect from adolescent smoking to perceptions of parent approval of smoking (Tucker, Martinez, Ellickson, & Edelen, 2008).

Regarding marijuana and other drug use, greater parental tolerance (or less disapproval) of adolescent drug use is related to greater involvement with marijuana use among adolescents (Bahr et al., 2005; Ellickson et al., 2004; Hemphill et al., 2011; Napper, Hummer, Chithambo, & LaBrie, 2015) and young adults (LaBrie, Hummer, & Lac, 2011; LaBrie, Hummer, Lac, & Lee, 2010; Napper, Kenney, Hummer, & Fiorot, 2016). Perceived parental injunctive anti-ATOD (alcohol, tobacco, other drugs) norms correlate negatively with adolescents' ATOD use (Kam, Matsunaga, Hecht, & Ndiaye, 2009; Parsai, Voisine, Marsiglia, Kulis, & Nieri, 2008). Strong parent disapproval of marijuana use was also associated with a lower likelihood of opioid misuse in the past year (Sung, Richter, Vaughn, Johnson, & Thom, 2005). In a national sample of adolescents, greater parental disapproval of substance use related to a lower likelihood of prescription opiate drug misuse (Ford & Rigg, 2015) and prescription drug misuse in general (Conn & Marks, 2014).

The Linkage of Parenting Practices to Child/Adolescent Substance Use

The third linkage between the family environment and child/adolescent substance use involves parenting or family management practices. Included in this category are variables such as parental monitoring or knowledge (Stattin & Kerr, 2000) of child behavior, consistent discipline practices, positive parenting (involving positive reinforcement of desired behavior and consistent negative reinforcement of problematic behavior), and parenting styles (e.g., authoritative parenting, which involves both parental responsiveness and demandingness) (Steinberg, Lamborn, Darling, Mounts, & Dornbusch, 1994). In this review, we distinguish between general parenting (e.g., parental monitoring)

and substance-specific parenting (e.g., household rules regarding child/adolescent use of alcohol, tobacco, marijuana, or other drugs). There is a sizable literature showing that parenting practices are significantly related to child and adolescent involvement with alcohol, tobacco, marijuana, and other drugs.

Among third- through fifth-grade children, greater parental monitoring was found to be associated 1 year later with a lower likelihood of starting to drink without parental permission (Chilcoat, Dishion, & Anthony, 1995) and with delayed initiation of smoking (Chilcoat & Anthony, 1996). Greater parental monitoring also related to less change in drinking involvement among fifth graders across a school year (Yabiku et al., 2010) and with less child risk for drinking (susceptibility) among 9- to 12-year-olds (Dalton et al., 2006). In a short-term longitudinal study of sixth graders, greater parent monitoring in the fall predicted a lower likelihood of starting to drink by spring (Simons-Morton, 2004).

Among elementary school children, more effective parenting was associated with less likelihood of drinking (Jackson, Henriksen, Dickinson, & Levine, 1997). Authoritative parenting was also associated with a lower likelihood of having initiated drinking (Jackson, Henriksen, & Foshee, 1998), whereas low parental demandingness (one aspect of authoritative parenting style) was associated with a higher likelihood of current alcohol use 2 years later (Jackson, Henriksen, & Dickinson, 1999).

Similarly, numerous studies of adolescents report a significant negative relationship between parental monitoring and offspring drinking (Abar, Jackson, Colby, & Barnett, 2014; Doumas, Hausheer, & Esp, 2015; Rioux et al., 2015; Urberg, Luo, Pilgrim, & Değirmencioğlu, 2003). Inept parent discipline practices are also associated with more frequent drinking in adolescent boys (Dishion & Loeber, 1985).

Middle adolescents who drank alcohol perceived their parents as less authoritative and more permissive compared to adolescents who did not drink (Cohen & Rice, 1997). Among middle adolescents, both mother's and father's lax control and the use of psychological control were associated with more frequent adolescent drinking (Prendergast & Schaefer, 1974). Adolescents exposed to good family functioning were less likely to start drinking in early adolescence (Geels, Vink, van Beijsterveldt, Bartels, & Boomsma, 2013).

Longitudinal research also supports the association of parenting to adolescent drinking. A review concluded that less parental monitoring and poorer general communication generally relate to both earlier initiation of drinking and higher levels of later adolescent alcohol use (Ryan et al., 2010). In a study of Australian early adolescents, poor family management practices and parental permissiveness related to more alcohol use 1 year later (Shortt, Hutchinson, Chapman, & Toumbourou, 2007), whereas in a Finnish study of early adolescents, less parental monitoring predicted initiation of drinking 2 years later (Rose, Dick, Viken, Pulkkinen, & Kaprio, 2001). In US early and middle adolescents, harsh and inconsistent parenting related to their later frequency of drinking (Conger & Rueter, 1996; Pears, Capaldi, & Owen, 2007), whereas authoritative parenting was associated with a lower likelihood of initiating alcohol use in a US national sample of 10- to 14-year-olds (Stoolmiller et al., 2012). Parental monitoring and knowledge assessed prior to college matriculation were also predictive of first-semester college drinking (Abar & Turrisi, 2008) and binge drinking (Fairlie, Wood, & Laird, 2012).

Parenting factors relate as well to *growth* (change over time) in adolescent alcohol involvement. There is slower growth in adolescent drinking when there is greater parental monitoring (Barnes, Reifman, Farrell, & Dintcheff, 2000). Increases (or maintenance) in parental monitoring were also associated with less growth in adolescent alcohol use (Simons-Morton & Chen, 2005). In panel analyses of a national sample, parental monitoring related negatively and linearly to alcohol involvement during middle school (Jackson & Schulenberg, 2013).

With respect to alcohol-specific parenting, fourth- through sixth-grade children who had started to drink perceived their parents as being less likely to know if they were drinking with friends (i.e., low alcohol-specific monitoring), as communicating with them less often about not drinking, and as less likely to react if they knew the children were drinking than did children who had not yet started drinking (Jackson, 1997). In a longitudinal follow-up study of fifth-grade children, Jackson et al. (1999) found that children's report of having had a drink of alcohol in the past 30 days in seventh grade was predicted by lower levels of parental alcohol use monitoring, greater permission to drink at home, and greater parental permissiveness at baseline.

In cross-sectional analyses of early adolescent girls, family rules against alcohol use were associated with less adolescent drinking (Fang, Schinke, & Cole, 2009), whereas greater enforcement of family rules against drinking, or stricter rules, was associated with less frequent drinking in Dutch adolescents (Pieters et al., 2012; van den Eijnden, van de Mheen, Vet, & Vermulst, 2011). In addition, child alcohol problems can lead to the imposition of stricter parental rules against drinking (van den Eijnden et al., 2011).

General parenting styles and practices have also been found to relate to both child and adolescent smoking. In cross-sectional research among children, child smoking was associated with less effective parenting (Jackson et al., 1997) and indulgent, authoritarian, or neglectful parenting (vs. authoritative parenting) (Jackson et al., 1998); child risk for smoking (susceptibility) was also associated with less parental monitoring (Dalton et al., 2006). In a longitudinal study of third- through fifth-grade children, greater parental monitoring was associated 1 year later with a lower likelihood of starting to smoke (Chilcoat et al., 1995) and with older age of initiation of smoking (Chilcoat & Anthony, 1996). In fifth graders, greater parental monitoring related to less change in smoking involvement across a school year (Yabiku et al., 2010). Among sixth graders, greater parental monitoring in the fall semester predicted a lower likelihood of starting to smoke by spring (Simons-Morton, 2002).

Smoking among adolescents is similarly related to less parental monitoring (Bahr et al., 2005; Clark et al., 2012; Harakeh, Scholte, Vermulst, de Vries, & Engels, 2004), harsh and inconsistent parenting (Melby, Conger, Conger, & Lorenz, 1993), and less parental supervision (Kim & Chun, 2016). Less parental monitoring related to middle school students' current frequency of smoking cigars, cigarillos, and little cigars (Trapl et al., 2016). Authoritative parenting, on the other hand, related to lower levels of adolescent smoking (Adamczyk-Robinette, Fletcher, & Wright, 2002; Mewse, Eiser, Slater, & Lea, 2004). Middle adolescents who smoked perceived their parents as less authoritative and more permissive compared to adolescents who did not smoke (Cohen & Rice, 1997). In one study, less supervision related to greater smoking among boys but not girls (Wu & Kandel, 1995).

In short-term longitudinal studies within adolescence, lower levels of parental monitoring predicted later cigarette use (Abar et al., 2014; Urberg et al., 2003), and low levels of mother responsiveness and mother demandingness (aspects of authoritative parenting) among adolescent nonsmokers aged 10–14 years predicted initiation of smoking 8 months later (Wills, Sargent, Stoolmiller, Gibbons, & Gerrard, 2008). A decrease in parental monitoring over 2 or 3 years significantly increased the likelihood of starting to smoke in a national sample of adolescents (Mahabee-Gittens, Xiao, Gordon, & Khoury, 2012). Decreases in parental monitoring were associated with greater growth in adolescent smoking (Simons-Morton, Chen, Abroms, & Haynie, 2004).

Several tobacco-specific parenting practices predict a lower likelihood of child or adolescent smoking, including more monitoring of the child's smoking (Jackson, 1997), more anti-smoking communication (Jackson, 1997; Jackson & Henriksen, 1997), having household rules against smoking (Andersen, Leroux, Bricker, Rajan, & Peterson, 2004; Wu & Kandel, 1995), and greater restrictions on adolescent smoking (Ditre, Coraggio, & Herzog, 2008). However, the likelihood of starting to smoke among children was higher when there was a smoking parent than when no parent smoked, regardless of whether there was a household smoking ban (and was highest when both parents smoked *and* there was a home smoking ban) (O'Loughlin et al., 2014).

Generally, the same parenting practices and styles that relate to adolescent drinking and smoking also relate to adolescent marijuana use. In a longitudinal study of third- through fifth-grade children, greater parental monitoring was associated 1 year later with a lower likelihood of starting to use marijuana or other drugs (Chilcoat et al., 1995) and with later initiation of drug use (Chilcoat & Anthony, 1996).

Among adolescents, marijuana use is associated with lower levels of parental behavioral control and monitoring (Bahr et al., 2005; Clark et al., 2012), fewer parental rules (Brook et al., 1998), poorer family management (Hemphill et al., 2011), and less authoritative parenting (Baumrind, 1991; Lambourn, Mounts, Steinberg, & Dornbusch, 1991). Lax control by the mother and the use of psychological control by the father were associated with more frequent marijuana use (Prendergast, 1974). Less parental control was associated with more illicit drug use among high school seniors (Stice, Myers, & Brown, 1998).

In longitudinal studies, less parental knowledge of the adolescent's activities was associated with more frequent marijuana use 1 year later (Lac, Alvaro, Crano, & Siegel, 2009). Lower levels of parental monitoring are also associated with greater nonmedical use of prescription opioid and stimulant drugs (Donaldson, Nakawaki, & Crano, 2015; Nargiso, Ballard, & Skeer, 2015). Less parental supervision was associated with substance use 2 years later (Erickson, Crosnoe, & Dornbusch, 2000). Greater parental monitoring related both cross-sectionally and longitudinally to less adolescent drug use (Li, Stanton, & Feigelman, 2000; Mounts, 2002). Finally, less monitoring predicted initiation of drug use 1 year later among high school students (Steinberg, Fletcher, & Darling, 1994).

The Linkage of Parent–Child Relationship to Child/Adolescent Substance Use

The fourth linkage between the family environment and child/adolescent substance use involves variables reflecting the quality of the relationship between the child/adolescent and his or her parents. Conceptually similar relevant variables include warmth, closeness, bonding, support, parental involvement, intimacy of communication, and lack of conflict.

In a sample of fourth graders, Dielman, Leech, and Loveland-Cherry (1995) found that greater perceived warmth and parental involvement was associated with less alcohol use. Similarly, greater parental support was associated with less likelihood of child alcohol use among third- and fifth-grade children (Jackson et al., 1997). Among Taiwanese fifth-grade students, greater parental support and less family conflict predicted a lower likelihood of initiating drinking by sixth grade (Hung, Yen, & Wu, 2009). In a longitudinal study of sixth graders over the course of a school year, greater parental involvement predicted a lower likelihood of starting to drink (Simons-Morton, 2004).

Both cross-sectional and longitudinal studies among adolescents have demonstrated that less adolescent drinking (or a lower likelihood of drinking) is associated with greater parental involvement with the adolescent and greater trust and concern (Hundleby & Mercer, 1987), a better relationship with the mother (Urberg et al., 2003), a better relationship with parents (Clark, Nguyen, Belgrave, & Tademy, 2011; Clark et al., 2012), greater closeness or bonding to parents (Bahr et al., 2005; Kelly, O'Flaherty, Toumbourou, et al., 2011), greater parental support (Abar et al., 2014; Windle, 2000), greater parental emotional support (van Zundert, van der Vorst, Vermulst, & Engels, 2006), greater family harmony (less conflict and more cohesion) (Webb & Baer,

1995), less conflict (Kelly, O'Flaherty, Toumbourou, et al., 2011), fewer negative interchanges with parents (Abar et al., 2014), and greater parental acceptance (Prendergast & Schaefer, 1974). Less parental involvement and less mother–daughter communication relate to more frequent drinking among female adolescents (Fang et al., 2009). Greater identification with parents is associated with less frequent drinking in both pre-adolescence and adolescence (Brook & Brook, 1987).

A more positive parent–adolescent relationship (Gerrard, Gibbons, Zhao, Russell, & Reis-Bergan, 1999) and less parent–child conflict (Thompson & Wilsnack, 1987) were associated both cross-sectionally and longitudinally (over 4 years) with less adolescent drinking in a national sample study. In a short-term follow-up study of Australian seventh graders, both high family attachment and low family conflict related to less frequent alcohol use 1 year later (Shortt et al., 2007). A review of the longitudinal literature on adolescent drinking (Ryan et al., 2010) concluded that lower parent–child relationship quality and poorer general communication related to both earlier initiation of drinking and higher levels of later adolescent alcohol use. This review also concluded that greater parental involvement related to delayed initiation of drinking but not to later levels of alcohol use and that parent–child conflict did not show a consistent relationship. A second review of longitudinal studies (Visser, de Winter, & Reijneveld, 2012) concluded that a negative parent–child relationship was only weakly related to later adolescent alcohol use.

The parent–adolescent relationship also relates to *growth* in adolescent alcohol involvement. There is slower growth in adolescent drinking when there is greater positive identification with parents (Gutman, Eccles, Peck, & Malanchuk, 2011), greater parental support (King, Molina, & Chassin, 2009), and greater family cohesion and less family conflict (Bray, Adams, Getz, & Baer, 2001). In one study (Simons-Morton & Chen, 2005), growth in parental involvement was associated with slower growth in adolescent alcohol involvement (i.e., negatively correlated slopes).

Again, similar results can be seen in the literature on smoking. In a study of third- through fifth-grade children, greater parental support was associated with less likelihood of child smoking (Jackson et al., 1997). Among sixth- and seventh-grade children, greater attachment to parents related to less likelihood of smoking (Fleming, Kim, Harachi, & Catalano, 2002).

Among sixth graders, greater parental involvement in the fall predicted a lower likelihood of starting to smoke by spring (Simons-Morton, 2002).

Family relationship variables also relate to smoking among adolescents. Adolescent smoking was associated with a lower quality relationship between parents and youth (Clark et al., 2012; Nowlin & Colder, 2007), lower parental support (Brown & Rinelli, 2010; Simons-Morton, Haynie, Crump, Eitel, & Saylor, 2001; Walter, Vaughan, & Cohall, 1993), less closeness to parents (Foster et al., 2007), lower cohesion among family members (Baer, McLaughlin, Burnside, Pokorny, & Garmezy, 1987), less trust and concern and lower parental involvement (Hundleby & Mercer, 1987), and more parent–child conflict (Simons-Morton et al., 2001). Lower quality relationships with their mothers predicted more smoking 6 months later (Urberg et al., 2003). Initiation of smoking was predicted 1 year later among early adolescents who reported less parental support and more negative interchanges with parents (Abar et al., 2014). The transition to regular smoking was predicted by poor parental support in both early and middle adolescence (Tucker et al., 2003). In a national sample of adolescents, smoking initiation was predicted by less parent–child connectedness (Kandel, Kiros, Schaffran, & Hu, 2004).

In longer term longitudinal studies, parent–child attachment and parental involvement with the child's school in first or second grade predicted a lower likelihood of the child smoking in sixth grade (Fleming et al., 2002), and lower family cohesion at ages 11–13 years predicted smoking 6 years later (Doherty & Allen, 1994). Latent growth modeling showed that greater parental involvement at baseline was associated with less involvement in adolescent smoking and that growth in parental involvement was associated with less growth in adolescent smoking (Simons-Morton et al., 2004).

Generally, the same relationship variables associated with adolescent drinking and smoking also relate to marijuana use. Lower levels of parent involvement with their child in fourth grade were associated with younger ages (reported 10 years later) at which children were first offered the chance to use marijuana (Chen, Storr, & Anthony, 2005). Frequency of marijuana use in adolescence is associated with a lower quality parent–child relationship (Brook et al., 1998; Clark et al., 2012), less parental support (Potvin & Lee, 1980), less closeness (Bahr et al., 2005; Kandel

& Andrews, 1987), less maternal affection and less identification with mother and father (Brook et al., 1998, 2001), less family cohesion (Baer et al., 1987), greater parent–child conflict (Brook et al., 1998), less trust and concern and lower parental involvement (Hundleby & Mercer, 1987), and less likelihood of talking to parents if they have a problem (Ellickson et al., 2004). Greater parental support related to less use of illicit drugs (Stice et al., 1998). Less parental warmth was associated with more frequent marijuana use 1 year later (Lac et al., 2009). Greater parent–child conflict was associated with greater adolescent substance use (alcohol, tobacco, and marijuana use) and with greater growth in adolescent substance use during a 3-year period (Wills, Sandy, Yaeger, & Shinar, 2001). Greater problems in the parent–adolescent relationship were associated with adolescents' use of more substances (Walden, McGue, Iacono, Burt, & Elkins, 2004). Parental attachment related negatively to adolescent substance use (alcohol, tobacco, marijuana, and other drug use) 1 year later (Erickson et al., 2000). Greater parental bonding reduced the likelihood of prescription opiate drug misuse in a national sample of adolescents (Ford & Rigg, 2015).

Bonding to Heavy Users

Consistent with Social Control Theory, studies examining bonding to parents who smoke or are heavy drinkers found that greater bonding is generally associated with *less* likelihood of adolescent imitation of parent behavior (Ennett et al., 2010; Foster et al., 2007). Interestingly, bonding to a parent in methadone treatment for opiate abuse was negatively related to child drug use if the parent had stopped using drugs, but it was positively related if the parent continued to use drugs (Fleming, Brewer, Gainey, Haggerty, & Catalano, 1997).

The Linkage of Parental Modeling to Child/Adolescent Cognitions

According to Bandura's (1977) Social Learning Theory, children develop attitudes and expectancies about substance use through their observation of the outcomes and reinforcements that occur when social agents in their environment engage in these behaviors. This vicarious learning can occur long before they themselves ever engage in substance use. The research literature tends to support this linkage

between parent modeling of substance use and child/adolescent cognitions.

Among third graders, more frequent parent drinking related to greater child susceptibility to drinking, as measured by child alcohol expectancies, intentions, attitudes toward drinking, and perceptions of peer norms (Ennett, Jackson, Bowling, & Dickinson, 2013). The greater the child's (Casswell, Brasch, Gilmore, & Silva, 1985) or adolescent's (Bank et al., 1985) exposure to parent drinking, the more positive was their attitude toward drinking. Children or adolescents with parents who drank also had greater intentions of drinking in the future (Epstein et al., 2008; Glanton & Wulfert, 2013), and they showed faster growth in their intentions through eighth grade. Perceived parental drinking (Dal Cin et al., 2009), parent-reported drinking (Gerrard et al., 1999; Ouellette, Gerrard, Gibbons, & Reis-Bergan, 1999), and perceived parental approval of drinking (Spijkerman, van den Eijnden, Overbeek, & Engels, 2007) are also associated with more positive adolescent prototypes of the typical teen drinker.

Alcohol outcome expectancies (beliefs about the effects of alcohol) are also more positive or less negative among children of parents who drink (Chen et al., 2011; Dal Cin et al., 2009; Glanton & Wulfert, 2013; Martino et al.2006, ; Ouellette et al., 1999). However, the relation between alcohol expectancies and parental alcoholism is less clear (Brown, Tate, Vik, Haas, & Aarons, 1999; Campbell & Oei, 2010b; Cranford, Zucker, Jester, Putler, & Fitzgerald, 2010).

Parent alcohol consumption also predicts adolescents' drinking motives (Müller & Kuntsche, 2011), including social, enhancement, coping, and conformity motives, which have been shown to partially mediate the relation between parent and adolescent drinking. Parent drinking related to late adolescent drinking motives less consistently, with paternal drinking related to enhancement motives whereas maternal drinking related to social motives (Van Damme et al., 2015).

Parental smoking is also positively associated with greater intentions to smoke in both children (Jackson & Henriksen, 1997; Quine & Stephenson, 1990) and adolescents (Grube, Morgan, & McGree, 1986; Harakeh et al., 2004; Leatherdale, McDonald, Cameron, Jolin, & Brown, 2006; Mak, Ho, & Day, 2012), more positive attitudes toward smoking (Harakeh et al., 2004), more positive prototypes of adolescent smokers (Blanton, Gibbons, Gerrard, Conger, & Smith, 1997), more positive smoking expectancies (Chung, White, Hipwell, Stepp, & Loeber, 2010; Wills et al., 2008), fewer negative smoking outcome expectancies (Flay et al., 1994), and overestimation of the number of peers who smoke (i.e., exaggerated descriptive norms) (Reid, Manske, & Leatherdale, 2008).

There has been little research on the relation of parent drug use to offspring drug-specific cognitions. One study found that recent parental marijuana use was related to more positive attitudes toward marijuana use in their adolescent children (Miller et al., 2013). A longitudinal study found that parental substance use significantly predicted adolescent intentions and behavioral willingness to try drugs approximately 2 years later (Gibbons et al., 2004).

The Linkage of Parenting to Child/Adolescent Substance-Specific Cognitions

There is relatively little research on the relation of parenting practices to child and adolescent substance-related cognitions. In Hispanic fifth graders, greater parental monitoring related to less child approval of substance use, lower intentions to use, and less positive substance use expectancies across a school year (Yabiku et al., 2010). Among early adolescents, effective parenting practices were negatively associated with adolescent pro-drug attitudes (Macaulay, Griffin, Gronewold, Williams, & Botvin, 2005). In Mexican American middle school students, parental monitoring was associated with higher personal norms against drugs and with lower intentions to use (Parsai et al., 2008; Parsai, Marsiglia, & Kulis, 2010). Among Dutch early adolescents, parental knowledge was associated with less positive adolescent attitudes toward smoking and lower intentions to smoke (Harakeh et al., 2004). Finally, in samples of college students, greater parental monitoring (or perceived knowledge) was associated with less student approval for drinking (Hummer et al., 2013) and for marijuana use (Napper et al., 2015).

The Linkage of Parent to Child Substance-Specific Cognitions

Despite the importance of substance-specific cognitions (e.g., attitudes, outcome expectancies, and prototypes) for the explanation of adolescent substances, little explicit attention has been paid to the socialization of these cognitions.

Direct examinations of the transmission of parent alcohol-specific cognitions to their children are rare (Campbell & Oei, 2010a), but studies of other substance-specific cognitions are even less common. Mother and father norms concerning the acceptability of child drinking predicted the norms held by their 10- to 12-year-old children, even after controlling for child temperament (Brody, Flor, Hollett-Wright, & McCoy, 1998), and mother and father norms when children were aged 10–12 years significantly predicted the children's norms 1 year later (Brody, Ge, Katz, & Arias, 2000). Koning et al. (2010) found that parent and child norms correlated 0.18 ($p < .001$) in Dutch early adolescents. Prins, Donovan, and Molina (2011) found that although both child and parent personal norms were strongly disapproving of child sipping, drinking, and drunkenness at child ages 8–10 years, there was significant divergence in their norms as the children moved into early and middle adolescence, with child (but not parent) norms becoming more accepting of alcohol involvement.

Parent and adolescent attitudes toward alcohol use are also positively correlated (Hummer et al., 2013; Kline, Canter, & Robin, 1987). Adolescent perceptions of parent disapproval if they were to drink are predictive of their personal norms for adolescent drinking (Voisine, Parsai, Marsiglia, Kulis, & Nieri, 2008). Perceived parent approval and students' own approval of drinking correlate significantly in college students (Hummer et al., 2013; LaBrie, Hummer, Neighbors, & Larimer, 2010).

Beyond norms and approval, there has been little research attention on the influence of other parent alcohol-specific cognitions on offspring cognitions. With respect to expectancies, Handley and Chassin (2009) found no relation between mother or father alcohol outcome expectancies and those of their adolescent child. With respect to prototypes, parental prototypes of the typical adolescent frequent drinker longitudinally predicted their adolescents' prototypes (Gerrard et al., 1999).

Only a few studies of the transmission of positive attitudes toward smoking, marijuana, or other drug use have been performed. Adolescents' personal approval of smoking correlated significantly with their parents' perceived approval (Krohn, Skinner, Massey, & Akers, 1985). Similarly, adolescent perceptions of their parents' disapproval if they smoked were found to correlate with their personal norms for adolescent smoking (Voisine et al., 2008).

Parent and adolescent attitudes toward marijuana use were positively correlated (Akers, Krohn, Lanza-Kaduce, & Radosevich, 1979; Kandel & Andrews, 1987). Perceived parental injunctive anti-ATOD norms correlate significantly with early adolescents' personal anti-ATOD norms (Kam et al., 2009; Parsai et al., 2008, 2010). Adolescent perceptions of their parents' disapproval if they used marijuana are predictive of their personal norms for marijuana use (Akers et al., 1979; Krohn et al., 1982). Adolescent perceptions of their parents' disapproval if they used marijuana correlate significantly with the favorability of adolescents' own attitudes (Teichman & Kefir, 2000) as well as with their personal norms for adolescent marijuana use (Voisine et al., 2008). Among college students, personal approval of marijuana use correlated significantly with their perceptions of their parents' approval of marijuana use (LaBrie, Hummer, Lac, & Lee, 2010; Napper et al., 2015).

The Linkage of Parent Approval to Other Child/Adolescent Substance-Specific Cognitions

Mother's attitude toward the child's drinking was associated with both positive and negative alcohol expectancies among Taiwanese adolescents (Hung, Chiang, Chang, & Yen, 2011). Among middle school students in South Dakota, parental approval of drinking related to adolescents' positive alcohol expectancies (Martino et al., 2009). Perceived parent approval of smoking related to greater intentions to smoke among non0smokers (Flay et al., 1994). Perceived parental injunctive anti-ATOD norms were associated with lower intentions to use drugs among middle school students (Parsai et al., 2008, 2010). Teichman and Kefir (2000) found no significant relation in Israeli adolescents between perceived parent approval of marijuana use and adolescents' intentions to experiment with marijuana. Greater perceived parental approval of student marijuana use was found to be associated with greater coping, enhancement, and expansion motives for use among college students (Buckner, 2013).

Parental Influence on Peer Susceptibility

In addition to research linking peer substance use to adolescent use (discussed later), studies have examined adolescents' beliefs regarding their own vulnerability to peer influence. Relevant conceptually related variables include susceptibility to peer pressure, behavioral willingness, and refusal self-efficacy. Peer susceptibility and behavioral willingness refer to children's and adolescents' evaluations of the likelihood that they would try a substance if peers offered it, whereas refusal efficacy refers to their self-rated confidence in their ability to turn down offers of substances. Although there is not yet a sizable literature in this area, research supports the influence of parents on these variables.

Parent Modeling

Quine and Stephenson (1990) found that children whose parents drank at least weekly were more likely to accept a drink from a close friend. Teenagers whose parents drank frequently were more willing to accept peer offers of a drink (Blanton et al., 1997; Dal Cin et al., 2009; Gerrard et al., 1999). Parental smoking significantly correlated with teens' willingness to smoke if offered a cigarette (Blanton et al., 1997). Having parents who smoked was associated with lower smoking refusal self-efficacy (Harakeh et al., 2004). Parent substance use was significantly associated with teen susceptibility to offers of alcohol and marijuana (Cleveland, Gibbons, Gerrard, Pomery, & Brody, 2005).

Parent Approval

Parent approval of adolescent drinking related significantly to adolescents' susceptibility to peer pressure (Dielman, Butchart, & Shope, 1993). Perceived parental approval of smoking related negatively to adolescent refusal self-efficacy (Flay et al., 1994). Greater parental disapproval of drug use related to greater alcohol and drug refusal efficacy among 5th-, 8th-, and 12th-grade African Americans (Clark et al., 2011, 2012).

Parenting

Parenting practices relate to both adolescent reports of susceptibility to peer influence and adolescent alcohol refusal self-efficacy. Parental monitoring was associated with greater alcohol refusal self-efficacy in 4th-grade students (Loveland-Cherry, Leech, Laetz, & Dielman, 1996) and with less vulnerability to peer offers of drugs in Hispanic 5th graders (Yabiku et al., 2010); authoritative parenting was associated with greater resistance to peer influence among 4th- and 6th-grade children (Jackson et al., 1998). Among African American 5th graders, effective parenting (greater communication, monitoring, and warmth) predicted less susceptibility to friends' offers of substances 2 years later (Cleveland et al., 2005). Parental monitoring related to greater drug refusal efficacy among 5th-, 8th-, and 12th-grade African American students (Clark et al., 2012). Among high school students, lower levels of parental supervision were associated with greater susceptibility to peer influence (Erickson et al., 2000). One study found that adolescents' refusal self-efficacy completely mediated the relation of parental monitoring to adolescent alcohol use (Watkins, Howard-Barr, Moore, & Werch, 2006).

Parenting Relationships

Among middle and high school students, higher parental nurturance was associated with less susceptibility to peer influence (Dielman et al., 1993). A better parent–child relationship in middle adolescence was associated with less willingness to accept a drink from a peer 1 year later (Gerrard et al., 1999). Adolescents with higher parental attachment had fewer friends 1 year later who used substances and were less susceptible to peer influence (Erickson et al., 2000). Better mother–adolescent, but not father–adolescent, relationship correlated with less willingness to smoke, and better mother and father relationships correlated with less willingness to accept a drink from peers (Blanton et al., 1997).

LINKAGES AMONG FAMILY ENVIRONMENT CONSTRUCTS

There has been little explicit attention in the literature to the interrelations *among* the measures of the family environment that are relevant to the explanation of adolescent substance use.

The Linkage of Parent Substance Use to Parent Approval

In studies of children, more frequent parent drinking is associated with parent beliefs that child sipping has fewer negative consequences and possibly protective

outcomes (pro-sipping beliefs) and with less disapproval of their own child's sipping alcohol (Ennett et al., 2013; Jackson et al., 2012). In studies of adolescents as well, the more parents drink, the higher their approval (or lack of disapproval) for adolescent drinking (Hummer et al., 2013; Spijkerman et al., 2007). Parent drinking was also associated with their beliefs that children should be allowed to drink before age 21 years (Kerr, Capaldi, Pears, & Owens, 2012). Heavier drinking parents also reported more positive prototypes of the typical adolescent frequent drinker (Gerrard et al., 1999).

Parental smoking and parental approval for adolescent smoking also correlate positively (den Exter Blokland, Hale, Meeus, & Engels, 2006; Otten, Engels, van de Ven, & Bricker, 2007). In a sample of 4th through 11th graders, if both parents smoked, they were both perceived as less likely to react negatively to finding out the student smoked (Sargent & Dalton, 2001). Last, more frequent marijuana use by parents during their adolescence was associated with offspring perceptions of less parent disapproval of marijuana use (Kerr, Tiberio, & Capaldi, 2015).

The Linkage of Parents' Substance Use to Their Parenting

The second linkage within the family environment is between parental substance use and parents' parenting practices. Although understudied, there is evidence for this linkage with respect to parental alcohol and tobacco, but the evidence is equivocal for parental marijuana use.

The literature supports a linkage between parental drinking and parents' use of less optimal family management practices. For example, there is greater alcohol-impaired parenting, child abuse, and neglect in the households of alcoholic parents (Dube et al., 2001). Sher (1991) proposed several models for the influence of parental alcoholism on offspring behavior. The *deviance-proneness submodel* specifies that parental alcoholism impacts offspring behavior through deficits in parenting (e.g., failure to monitor child behavior) that impact child temperament and that also moderate the relations between temperament and peer influence as well as between school failure and peer influence. In partial support of this model, Chassin, Pillow, Curran, Molina, and Barrera (1993) found that alcoholic fathers tend to monitor their children less than do non-alcoholic fathers (also

Clark, Kirisci, Mezzich, & Chung, 2008). Alcoholic parents were also rated by their children as being less consistent in their discipline and rule setting (King & Chassin, 2004). In the general population, greater parental drinking is associated with parents' greater use of discipline (or inconsistent discipline) and less parental monitoring (Conger & Rueter, 1996; Kerr et al., 2012; Latendresse et al., 2008; Wills, Sargent, Gibbons, Gerrard, & Stoolmiller, 2009), less emotional and instrumental support (fathers only; van Zundert et al., 2006), and less supervision (Dal Cin et al., 2009).

Parental drinking is also associated with more permissive alcohol-specific parenting, including having fewer household rules against teen drinking (Pieters et al., 2012; van der Vorst, Engels, Meeus, & Deković, 2006; van der Vorst, Engels, Meeus, Deković, & Vermulst, 2006) and providing more frequent sips of alcohol (Ennett et al., 2013). Reimuller, Hussong, and Ennett (2011) found that the more parents drank, the more permissive were their communications about alcohol with their children.

Parental smoking has been found to relate to less positive parenting and more inconsistent discipline (Kandel & Wu, 1995), less consistent discipline (Chassin, Presson, Todd, Rose, & Sherman, 1998), less knowledge of children's activities (den Exter Blokland et al., 2006; Harakeh et al., 2004), lower levels of perceived authoritativeness (Mewse et al., 2004), and less maternal demandingness (Wills et al., 2008). Compared to non-smoking parents, parents who smoke are likely to have fewer household rules about child smoking (den Exter Blokland et al., 2006), more likely not to have a household smoking ban (Hilliard et al., 2015), more likely to have fewer restrictions on child smoking (Ditre et al., 2008), less likely to punish child smoking (Pennanen, Vartainen, & Haukkala, 2012), and more likely to have a lower quality of communication about smoking issues (Harakeh, Scholte, Vermulst, de Vries, & Engels, 2010) and weaker anti-smoking beliefs (Kodl & Mermelstein, 2004). Parental smoking was also associated with a lower quality of communication about smoking (Otten et al., 2007).

Parental substance use was associated in earlier US studies with less optimal parenting practices, including poorer monitoring (Dishion, Patterson, & Reid, 1988; Dishion et al., 1999) and poorer discipline (Dishion et al., 1999). A study of Dutch families, however, found no differences in parental support, monitoring, or knowledge between parents differing in their ever-use of cannabis, but it found that ever-using parents had less strict rules about adolescent cannabis use (Vermeulen-Smit et al., 2015). Kerr et al. (2015), however, found that US parents who had used marijuana as adolescents monitored their children's behavior less than did parents who had not used marijuana as adolescents.

The Linkage of Parent Substance Use to Relationship Quality

Within the family environment, the third linkage of interest is between parental substance use and the quality of relationship with the child or adolescent, as assessed by measures of bonding, warmth, or closeness. This linkage has been relatively unexplored thus far. Latendresse et al. (2008) found that greater parental drinking at child age 12 years was associated with greater tension in the relationship between parent and child and with fewer shared family activities. Other research has shown a significant correlation between parent drinking and less relationship warmth, closeness, bonding, or support (Barnes et al., 2000; Dal Cin et al., 2009; Gerrard et al., 1999). Not only does greater parental alcohol use relate to greater conflict and less cohesion in the family (Webb & Baer, 1995), but also the greater the number of parents in the family who drink or smoke (0–2), the greater the level of parent–child conflict (Wills et al., 2001). There has been little research examining the link between parental smoking and the quality of the relationship between parents and their children. However, maternal smoking has been found to relate to less maternal support (Chassin et al., 1998) and to less maternal responsiveness (Wills et al., 2008). Finally, parental drug use is associated with less involvement in the child's life (Dishion et al., 1988) and with less mutual attachment between the parent and the son or daughter (Brook, Whiteman, Balka, & Cohen, 1995). Similarly, parental marijuana use is associated with less affection in the parent–child relationship (Brook, Balka, Fei, & Whiteman, 2006).

The Linkage of Parental Approval to Parenting and Relationships

There is evidence that parental disapproval of substance use is associated with greater parental monitoring and with higher quality parent–adolescent relationships. Stronger parental injunctive anti-ATOD norms were associated with greater parental monitoring among 5th-grade students (Yabiku et al., 2010) and with greater parental behavioral control among 5th- to 7th-grade students (Kam et al., 2009). Among early adolescents, parent disapproval of drinking correlated positively with mother and father closeness and negatively with family conflict (Kelly, O'Flaherty, Toumbourou, et al., 2011). Among 9th graders, monitoring and approval correlated negatively for both mothers and fathers (Doumas et al., 2015). Also among middle school students, parental monitoring, consistent discipline, and parental anti-drug messages all loaded strongly on an effective parenting latent variable (Macaulay et al., 2005). Among 5th-, 8th-, and 12th-grade African American students, parent disapproval of substance use related to greater parental control and better parent–child relationships (Clark et al., 2011, 2012). Greater parent disapproval of child marijuana use correlated with greater parental monitoring (Kerr et al., 2015). Similarly, lower perceived parental approval for risky drinking was associated with greater perceived parental monitoring in the summer before college (Abar & Turrisi, 2008). For freshman college students, perceived parental disapproval for heavy drinking was associated with greater parental support, parental monitoring, and parental permissiveness (Wood, Read, Mitchell, & Brand, 2004).

The Linkage of Parenting and Parent–Child Relationships

There is consistent evidence of a moderate positive correlation between parental monitoring and the quality of parent–child relationships across a variety of adolescent samples in the substance use literature. Monitoring and warmth correlated 0.42 among pre-adolescent African American students (Cleveland et al., 2005). Mother and father consistent discipline correlated significantly and positively with mother and father social support among early adolescents (Marshal & Chassin, 2000). Among Dutch early adolescents, strict control (monitoring and supervision) and parental attachment correlated cross-sectionally and showed reciprocal cross-lagged correlations longitudinally (van der Vorst, Engels, Meeus, Dekovic, & Vermulst, 2006). Wills et al. (2009) reported a correlation of 0.38 between warmth/responsiveness and monitoring in a US national sample of adolescents. In

another US national sample, parent monitoring and warmth correlated 0.43 (Hemovich, Lac, & Crano, 2011). Chuang, Ennett, Bauman, and Foshee (2005) report a correlation of 0.61 between latent-variable measures of parental monitoring and parental closeness in a third US national sample of early adolescents, and parental monitoring and family closeness correlated 0.53 in a sample of Welsh adolescents (Moore, Rothwell, & Segrott, 2010). In a national sample of US adolescents, Lac et al. (2009) found that latent-variable measures of warmth and parent knowledge correlated 0.54. Finally, parental support and control correlated 0.38 among high school seniors (Stice et al., 1998), and parental support and parental monitoring correlated 0.42 in incoming college students (Wood et al., 2004).

FAMILY ENVIRONMENT INFLUENCES ON THE PEER ENVIRONMENT

Although research has generally shown that peer models for substance use are generally stronger influences on adolescent use compared to parental models, there has been relatively little theoretical recognition of the significant relationships between the parent and peer environments and also little recognition that family factors in childhood may influence the adolescent's selection among available peer environments varying in their support for substance use. To set up consideration of the influence of the family environment on the peer environment, I first briefly review the impact of peer substance use on the child's or adolescent's own substance use.

Linkages of Peer Substance Use and Approval to Adolescent Substance Use

Peer Models

Peer involvement in substance use is commonly cited as the strongest risk factor for adolescent use of alcohol, tobacco, marijuana, and other drugs. The influence of peer use is apparent even in studies of children's drinking and smoking (Jackson, 1997; Kelly et al., 2016; Quine & Stephenson, 1990). In general, the more friends an adolescent has who have used a substance (or the greater the proportion of friends), the more likely the adolescent is to also have used it. This has been shown with respect to alcohol use

(Blanton et al., 1997; Dal Cin et al., 2009; Windle, 2000), tobacco use (Blanton et al., 1997; Kelly, O'Flaherty, Connor, et al., 2011; Liao, Huang, Huh, Pentz, & Chou, 2013), and marijuana or other drug use (Ellickson et al., 2004; Windle, 2000). These relations are not limited to US adolescents. Cross-national studies replicate these associations between friend and target adolescent substance use (Farhat et al., 2012; Kokkevi, Richardson, Florescu, Kuzman, & Stergar, 2007).

Child or adolescent perceptions of their friends' substance use relate more strongly to their own substance use than do friends' self-reported substance use (Bauman & Fisher, 1986; Iannotti & Bush, 1992). Kandel (1996) estimated that cross-sectional research relying on adolescent perceptions of friends' behavior overestimates the predictive power of peer influence by a factor of five (see also Aseltine, 1995; Bauman & Ennett, 1996).

Although adolescent perceptions of friends' substance use may exaggerate the influence of peers, there is nonetheless evidence of peer modeling in studies using friends' self-reported substance use. There are significant correlations in both cross-sectional and longitudinal research (over 1 or 2 years) between adolescent and friends' reported alcohol use (Aikins, Simon, & Prinstein, 2010; Ali & Dwyer, 2010; Ennett et al., 2006), smoking (Adamczyk-Robinette et al., 2002; Aikins et al., 2010), marijuana use (Ennett et al., 2006), illicit drug use (Crosnoe, Erickson, & Dornbusch, 2002), and substance use in general (Allen, Chango, Szwedo, Schad, & Marston, 2012; Mounts, 2002). Evidence from social network analyses, which involve friend self-reports of substance use, generally supports both peer influence and peer selection as processes responsible for this similarity in use (Donovan, 2015).

In short-term longitudinal studies with two waves of data collection, the number of friends who drank, smoked, used marijuana, or used illicit drugs in the fall predicted, respectively, initiation of drinking (Stice et al., 1998; Urberg, Değirmencioğlu, & Pilgrim, 1997), smoking (Urberg et al., 1997), marijuana use (Kandel, Kessler, & Margulies, 1978), and illicit drug use (Stice et al., 1998) in the spring of the same school year. Among seventh-grade non-smokers, friends' smoking predicted initiation of smoking 15 months later (Flay et al., 1994). Friends' reported drug use predicted initiation of drug use 1 year later

among high school students (Steinberg, Lamborn, et al., 1994). In other longitudinal research, adolescents were more likely to increase their smoking or drinking if their chosen friends drank or smoked more than they did *and* if they had a higher quality relationship with them (Urberg et al., 2003). A prospective study of three samples found that perceived peer marijuana use predicted initiation of use at follow-up (Brook et al., 2001).

Peer Approval

In addition to the influence of peer models for substance use, there is also evidence for substantial influence from peer approval or disapproval of substance use (more recently called injunctive peer norms). Greater perceived peer approval (particularly friends' approval) is associated with more frequent adolescent drinking (Beal et al., 2001; Callas, Flynn, & Worden, 2004; Donovan, Jessor, & Costa, 1999; K. Jackson et al., 2014; LaBrie, Hummer, Neighbors, et al., 2010), smoking (Beal et al., 2001; Krohn et al., 1985), marijuana use (LaBrie, Hummer, Lac, & Lee, 2010; Napper et al., 2016), and substance use in general (Parsai et al., 2010).

Among abstainers, peer approval of alcohol use was a significant predictor of frequency of early adolescent drinking 1 year later (Ellickson & Hays, 1991). In a two-wave panel study within a school year, perceived peer approval of drug use in the fall predicted initiation of marijuana use in the spring (Kandel et al., 1978).

The Linkage of Parent Substance Use to Peer Substance Use

An important, but generally underrecognized, relationship between the family and peer environments is the association between the substance use of parents and that of the child's or adolescent's friends. Cross-sectional studies have shown that adolescents with drinking parents are more likely to have friends who drink than are adolescents with parents who abstain or who drink less (Ary et al., 1993; Dal Cin et al., 2009; Epstein et al., 2008).

There is also longitudinal evidence suggesting that parental drinking influences the adolescent's choice of friends who drink or use drugs. Children age 11 years who had heavy drinking parents were more likely at age 15 years to affiliate with peers who used substances (Fergusson, Horwood, & Lynskey, 1995) or who drank (Conger & Rueter, 1996). Adolescents whose parents drank or smoked were more likely to associate with peers who drank, smoked, or used marijuana (Wills et al., 2001), and teens whose parents drank or smoked were more likely to have friends 1 year later who drank or smoked, respectively (Blanton et al., 1997).

Parent and peer smoking also correlate positively. Adolescents with parents who smoke are more likely to have friends who smoke (Chuang et al., 2005; Krohn et al., 1985; Liao et al., 2013; Wills et al., 2007). In a longitudinal study of six European countries, parental weekly smoking at time 1 correlated with friends' weekly smoking 1 year later (de Vries, Candel, Engels, & Mercken, 2006). In addition, adolescents who had parents who both smoked tended to choose a smoker when choosing a new friend (Engels, Vitaro, den Exter Blokland, de Kemp, & Scholte, 2004). Parental smoking also correlates positively with perceived friends' approval for smoking (Harakeh et al., 2004).

Both family and friend marijuana use correlate as well. Children and adolescents who perceived that their parents had used marijuana were more likely to have friends who had used marijuana (Bush, Weinfurt, & Iannotti, 1994). In a sample of early adolescents, greater parental substance use (alcohol, tobacco, and marijuana) correlated with friends' drug use (Hansen et al., 1987).

The Linkage of Parental Approval to Peer Approval and Modeling

Just as parent and friends' involvement with alcohol are significantly associated, so are parent and friends' approval of adolescent drinking. Within a large metropolitan US sample of 6th to 12th graders, parent and peer disapproval of drinking correlated 0.46 (Mrug & McCay, 2013). Parental approval of adolescent drinking correlated 0.48 with peer alcohol approval (Kline et al., 1987). Perceptions of parent and peer approval for alcohol use correlated significantly in other adolescent samples (Akers et al., 1979; Ary et al., 1993) and correlated 0.49–0.52 in late adolescent college students (Hummer et al., 2013; LaBrie, Hummer, Neighbors, et al., 2010). Among college freshmen, perceived parent approval of risky drinking behaviors correlated 0.37 with perceived friends' approval (Neighbors et al., 2008).

In addition, adolescents whose parents drank more also perceived their friends as more approving of people their age drinking (Webb, Baer, Caid, McLaughlin, & McKelvey, 1991). Analogously, perceived parental disapproval of drinking is associated with having fewer friends who drink (Dielman et al., 1993; Lipperman-Kreda et al., 2010; Smith et al., 2014). Adolescents' perceived parental alcohol permissiveness correlated significantly ($r = 0.40$) with friends' approval for and modeling of drinking among incoming college students (Fairlie et al., 2012).

With respect to smoking, 4th- to 11th-grade students were less likely to have any smoking friends if both parents were perceived as likely to react negatively to finding out the student smoked (Sargent & Dalton, 2001). Parent and friends' approval for smoking were moderately correlated (0.34–0.49) both cross-sectionally and longitudinally in a study of Dutch families (Otten et al., 2007). Parents' and friends' approval for smoking correlated 0.30–0.34 in adolescent non-smokers and smokers (Krohn et al., 1985). Parent approval of smoking is associated longitudinally with best friend's smoking and hanging out with peers who smoke (Tucker et al., 2008). Decreases in expected parental negative reactions to problem behavior in early adolescence were associated with greater growth in the number of friends who smoked (Simons-Morton et al., 2004).

With respect to other drug use, perceived parental and peer injunctive anti-ATOD norms correlated significantly among fifth- and sixth graders (Kam et al., 2009). Greater expectations of a negative parental reaction to offspring marijuana use were associated with having fewer friends who had used marijuana (Kerr et al., 2015). Perceived parents' and friends' approval of marijuana use correlated significantly ($r = 0.35$–0.43) in samples of college students (Buckner, 2013; LaBrie, Hummer, Lac, & Lee, 2010; Napper et al., 2016).

The Linkage of Parenting Practices to Peer Substance Use

In addition to parent modeling and approval of substance use, family management variables also predict affiliation with substance-using peers. Less parent monitoring in fourth grade was associated with younger ages (reported 10 years later) at which children were first offered marijuana (Chen et al., 2005). In a national sample of 9- to 18-year-olds, greater parental knowledge was associated with receiving fewer offers of marijuana in the past 30 days (and offers mediated the relation between monitoring and marijuana use) (Siegel, Tan, Navarro, Alvaro, & Crano, 2015). Among African American fifth graders, effective parenting (greater monitoring, communication, and warmth) was associated with less substance use among friends 2 years later (Cleveland et al., 2005).

Among adolescents, greater parental monitoring (or knowledge) is associated with having fewer friends who drink (Chuang et al., 2005; Wills et al., 2009), smoke (Chuang et al., 2005), use drugs (Erickson, Crosnoe, & Dornbusch, 2000), engage in drug use and other risky behaviors (Clark et al., 2012), or who are involved in delinquent behavior (Dishion & Loeber, 1985). Parental monitoring and knowledge prior to college matriculation also predicted having fewer friends who drank and got drunk during the first semester of college (Abar & Turrisi, 2008). In a parallel process model, Simons-Morton (2007) found that declines between grades 6 and 9 in parent monitoring were associated with greater growth in the number of friends who drank (Simons-Morton & Chen, 2005) and the number of friends who smoked (Simons-Morton et al., 2004).

Other parenting practices also relate to affiliation with substance-using friends. Among fourth-grade children, greater monitoring and nurturance were associated with having fewer friends who drank (Loveland-Cherry et al., 1996), and greater monitoring and better discipline related to having fewer deviant friends (Dishion et al., 1999). Authoritative parenting among eighth-grade students was associated with less frequent smoking self-reported by nominated friends (Adamczyk-Robinette et al., 2002). Greater parental supervision (Dal Cin et al., 2009), good family functioning (Geels et al., 2013), and proactive parenting (Hawkins et al., 1997) in adolescence related to having fewer friends who drank. In high school students, authoritative parenting related to less friends' reported drug use (Mounts & Steinberg, 1995). In early adolescents, parent hostility and inconsistent discipline related cross-sectionally to friends' smoking in a sample of boys (Melby et al., 1993) and longitudinally to later friends' drinking for both sexes (Conger & Rueter, 1996). Greater father (but not mother) discipline was associated with less affiliation with drug-promoting friends (Marshal & Chassin, 2000). Among high school seniors, greater parental control

was associated with having fewer friends who drank or who used illicit drugs (Stice et al., 1998). With respect to substance-specific parenting, when smoking parents banned smoking indoors, adolescents had fewer friends who smoked (Rodriguez, Tscherne, & Audrain-McGovern, 2007).

The Linkage of Parent–Child Relationship Quality to Peer Substance Use

There is somewhat less research exploring the relation of parent–child relationship quality to child or adolescent affiliation with substance-using friends. A good relationship with parents is associated with both less perceived peer approval and fewer peer models for drinking (Webb et al., 1991) and also with fewer friends using substances and engaging in other risky behaviors (Clark et al., 2011). Parent–child relationship problems are associated with having more friends who use substances (Walden et al., 2004). Greater parental support was associated with having fewer friends who used illicit drugs (Stice et al., 1998) or substances in general (Marshal & Chassin, 2000). Adolescents with higher parental attachment had fewer friends 1 year later who used substances (Erickson et al., 2000). In a national sample of US adolescents, Wills et al. (2009) found that greater maternal warmth and responsiveness were associated with having fewer drinking friends. Dal Cin et al. (2009) reported that greater parental warmth related to having fewer drinking friends. Blanton et al. (1997) found that a warm parent–child relationship was associated 1 year later with having fewer friends who drank and fewer friends who smoked. Greater parent–child conflict was associated with having more friends who drank, smoke, or used marijuana and also with greater growth in friends' substance use during a 3-year period (Wills et al., 2001). Decreases in parent involvement in early adolescence were associated with greater growth in the number of friends who drank (Simons-Morton & Chen, 2005) and the number of friends who smoked (Simons-Morton et al., 2004).

THE PARENTAL SOCIALIZATION FRAMEWORK

The parental socialization framework presented in Figure 10.1 represents one way of depicting the linkages among the higher order constructs. The figure should be interpreted as a series of hypothesized relations among these constructs that need to be examined in greater detail (and using more sophisticated statistical procedures) in longitudinal studies of children and adolescents because many of the relations derive from cross-sectional research. A similar method was utilized by Sher (1991) in his important critical review summarizing the literature on children of alcoholics.

Whereas the preceding sections focused on the direct linkages among the classes of explanatory variables, the current section incorporates findings from path analyses and structural equation modeling analyses in the literature. Due to the varying designs of the published path analysis studies and their inclusion of diverse sets of exogenous and endogenous variables, the indirect paths and moderating effects in shown in Figure 10.1 should best be interpreted as hypotheses subject to empirical examination.

In Figure 10.1 (and succeeding figures), the following conventions are employed. Solid lines represent paths for which there is some empirical support in the literature. Dotted lines represent paths for which support is equivocal or that have yet to be examined. Arrows between boxes denote hypothesized directions of influence, and double-headed arrows denote correlations among constructs. Arrows intersecting other paths denote moderating effects (i.e., the magnitude

of the relation differs for different levels of the intersecting variable).

On the basis of the previous review, and following from the results of published multivariate analyses, I have identified three major pathways of parental influence within this larger parental socialization framework: a social control pathway, an internalization pathway, and a bonding pathway. Each is described here. The basic premise of these pathways is that the parental constructs structure the child's/adolescent's downstream personal and social risk and protection with respect to substance use.

The Social Control Pathway

The social control pathway (Figure 10.2) represents a series of hypotheses about the mechanisms through which parent modeling, parent approval, and parent–child relationships influence child/adolescent substance use directly and also indirectly through their effects on both parental monitoring (social control) and friends' substance use. The major questions for further longitudinal research are (1) whether parent modeling, parent approval, and parent–child relationships influence friends' substance use modeling only (or primarily) through their influences on parental monitoring and (2) whether the influence of parental monitoring on adolescent substance use is fully

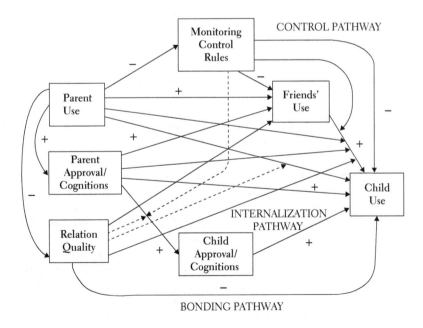

FIGURE 10.1 The parental socialization framework.

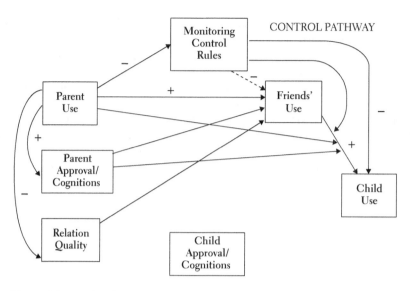

FIGURE 10.2 The social control pathway.

mediated by its effects on adolescents' choice of (or exposure to) substance-using or non-substance-using friends.

Relations Among Parent Use, Approval, and Relationship Quality

As presented previously, cross-sectional research shows that parental substance use correlates positively with approval of child substance use and that both constructs correlate negatively with the quality of parent–child relationships. Although longitudinal research has not yet established the directionality of these linkages, it is most likely that parental substance use predates and influences the other parental constructs. All three of these constructs have direct linkages to child/adolescent substance use. The major question for further research is whether these direct paths remain significant once the additional mediating and moderating variables in Figure 10.2 are examined. The following sections present evidence from previous studies supporting the indirect paths in the figure.

Parent Monitoring Mediates Parent Modeling's Effect on Substance Use

Latendresse et al. (2008) found in a longitudinal study of Finnish adolescents that both perceived parental discipline and parental monitoring were significant partial mediators of the relation of parent drinking to

adolescent drinking at ages 14 and 17 years. Kerr et al. (2012), however, reported that parent monitoring did not mediate the effect of mother and father drinking on child early onset drinking. A number of other studies, although not explicitly testing for the significance of potentially mediating variables, found in hierarchical regression analyses that parent drinking became nonsignificant as a predictor (complete mediation) or was reduced in magnitude but still significant (partial mediation) when parenting variables were added to the equation in a later step. In children, for example, effective parenting partially mediated the influence of parental modeling on child drinking and smoking (Jackson et al., 1997), whereas substance-specific parenting completely mediated the effect of parental drinking on child drinking (Jackson et al., 1999). Dishion et al. (1999) also found that parent monitoring and discipline completely mediated the influence of parent substance use on the initiation of boys' drinking. For tobacco use, Kandel and Wu (1995) found that in early adolescents the influence of parental smoking was partially mediated by parental closeness, discipline, and rules against smoking. In contrast, family management practices did not mediate the effect of parental drinking on the initiation of current drinking by grade 8 or 9 (Peterson, Hawkins, Abbott, & Catalano, 1994). Overall, these studies suggest that the influence of parent modeling of substance use is at least partially mediated by parental monitoring and control (i.e., greater parental modeling is associated with less monitoring, which is associated with greater child/adolescent substance use).

Monitoring Mediates Effect of Parent Modeling on Friends' Use

Currently, there is little support for this mediational path (see Figure 10.2, dotted line). Conger and Rueter (1996) found that parent history of substance use problems related to friends' alcohol use through its relation to harsh and inconsistent parenting.

Friends' Use Mediates Parent Modeling

There is relatively little elaboration of this relationship in the literature. Kandel and Andrews (1987) found that parent modeling of drinking had an indirect effect on adolescent drinking through its relation to best friend's drinking, suggesting that this effect was determined by parental influence on the adolescent's choice of friends. Kerr et al. (2015) found that peer use of marijuana mediated the relation between parents' use as adolescents and the onset of marijuana use among adolescent offspring.

Friends' Use Mediates Parent Disapproval

Only a single study of Australian adolescents (Kelly, O'Flaherty, Toumbourou, et al., 2011) found that the influence of parent disapproval on adolescent drinking was not mediated by friends' drinking. Other research has found support for at least partial mediation. The relations of parent disapproval of drug use to adolescent alcohol, tobacco, and marijuana use were found to be partially mediated by peer risky behavior and parent monitoring in a study of African American students (Clark et al., 2012). Similarly, in a study of 7th- to 12th-grade students, Bahr et al. (2005) found that the introduction of peer modeling reduced the relation of parental approval only slightly (supporting partial mediation) when predicting students' alcohol use, tobacco use, and marijuana use. Given the evidence, friends' use is hypothesized to mediate the influence of parental approval on adolescent substance use (see Figure 10.2, dotted line).

Friends' Use Mediates Parent Monitoring

The evidence suggests that the relation of parent monitoring to adolescent substance use is mediated by its negative relation to affiliation with substance-using peers. Dishion et al. (1999) found that deviant peer affiliation mediated the influence of parent discipline and monitoring on the initiation of boys' drinking and marijuana use between grades 4 and 10. Among African American 5th-, 8th-, and 12th graders, peer risky behavior completely mediated the influence of parent monitoring on adolescent tobacco and marijuana use and partially mediated its influence on adolescent alcohol use (Clark et al., 2012). Among 7th-grade students, peer pressure for drug use partially mediated the relation of poor parenting (less monitoring and inconsistent discipline) on adolescent drug use (Kung & Farrell, 2000). In early adolescents, the effect of parental monitoring and discipline on adolescent use of alcohol, tobacco, and marijuana use was partially mediated by peer substance use (Macaulay et al., 2005). Among high school students, the relation of parental supervision to adolescent substance use 1 year later was mediated by both susceptibility to peer influence and the number of substance-using friends (Erickson et al., 2000). The negative relation of authoritative parenting to early adolescent tobacco use was partially mediated by the influence of peers' self-reported frequency of smoking (Adamczyk-Robinette et al., 2002). Harsh and inconsistent parenting in early adolescence related to later drinking through its relation to friends' alcohol use (Conger & Rueter, 1996). In a longitudinal study of a national sample of adolescents, the relation of parent monitoring to adolescent marijuana use 2 years later was mediated by the number of peer offers of marijuana (Siegel et al., 2015). In longitudinal research, the number of friends who drank and got drunk during the first semester of college mediated the relation of parental monitoring and knowledge prior to college matriculation to the students' college drinking (Abar & Turrisi, 2008).

Mediation is also found in studies using parallel process modeling. The same studies that show that growth in parent monitoring in early adolescence significantly predicts slower growth in adolescent drinking (Simons-Morton & Chen, 2005) and smoking (Simons-Morton et al., 2004) also demonstrated that this relation is mediated by growth in the number of friends who drink or smoke. That is, parent monitoring decreases growth in friends' substance use, which in turn decreases growth in the adolescent's own substance use (the direct path, although significant, is only half as strong).

Friends' Use Mediates Parent Relationships

There is also evidence that peer modeling mediates the influence of parent–adolescent relationship quality on adolescent substance use. Kandel and Andrews (1987) found that closeness to parents had a direct effect on frequency of alcohol use and marijuana use, as well as an indirect effect through its relation to best friend's drinking, suggesting that this effect was determined by parental influence on the adolescent's choice of non-using friends. Walden et al. (2004) reported that the influence of parent–adolescent relationship problems on adolescent substance use was completely mediated by peer deviance/substance use. Erickson et al. (2000), however, found that parental attachment's relation to substance use was only partially reduced when friends' substance use and peer susceptibility were added to the regression. Similarly, in their study of 5th-, 8th-, and 12th-grade African American students, Clark et al. (2012) found that risky peer behavior did not mediate the relation of mother–adolescent relationship on adolescent alcohol, tobacco, or marijuana use. In addition, Bahr et al. (2005) found in a study of 7th- to 12th-grade students that the introduction of peer modeling reduced the relation of attachment to parents only slightly (finding only partial mediation) when predicting their alcohol use, tobacco use, and marijuana use. Support for this mediating link is therefore equivocal (meriting a dotted line in Figure 10.2).

Mediation has been found in studies using parallel process modeling. In studies of adolescent drinking (Simons-Morton & Chen, 2005) and smoking (Simons-Morton et al., 2004), growth in parent involvement decreases growth in friends' substance use, which in turn decreases growth in the adolescent's own substance use (the direct path, although significant, is only half as strong).

There is also evidence in the literature that the parental constructs of parent modeling, parent disapproval, and parent monitoring moderate the influence of peer modeling on adolescent substance use (for parent–child relationships, see The Bonding Pathway).

Parent Modeling Moderates Peer Modeling

One path through which parents can reduce their children's substance use is their modeling of abstinence from substance use. Research has shown that parental abstinence weakens the influence of peer modeling on adolescent substance use (Brook, 1993; Kandel, 1973, 1974; Li, Pentz, & Chou, 2002).

Parent Disapproval Moderates Peer Modeling

Parental acceptance of adolescent substance use also has an effect on this relationship. Sargent and Dalton (2001) found that the effect of peer smoking was reduced when both parents were perceived as being strongly against smoking. The relation between peer marijuana use and adolescent current marijuana use was also reduced when adolescents rated their parents as more likely to catch them if they broke family rules about drinking, skipping school, and carrying a handgun (Dorius, Bahr, Hoffmann, & Harmon, 2004). Perceived parental alcohol permissiveness (pre-matriculation) buffered the positive relation between peer influences (approval and modeling) and first-semester college binge-drinking frequency (Fairlie et al., 2012). Greater perceived parental disapproval of teen drinking also accentuated (strengthened) the relations of positive parenting practices to greater self-efficacy to resist peer offers and to less peer approval and models for drinking (Nash, McQueen, & Bray, 2005).

Parent Monitoring Moderates Peer Modeling

A variety of parenting variables have also been shown to moderate the influence of peer substance use. The expectation is that adolescents with at least moderate levels of parental monitoring will be less influenced by the substance use of their friends. The relation between peer substance use and the adolescent's own substance use has been shown to be reduced in the presence of greater parent monitoring or supervision (Clark et al., 2012; Ennett et al., 2008), more consistent discipline (Marshal & Chassin, 2000), more monitoring and consistent discipline (Kung & Farrell, 2000), and greater parental authoritativeness (Mounts & Steinberg, 1995). It is possible that this moderational pathway will be stronger than the previous mediational pathway (less monitoring → friends' use → child/adolescent use) as teens move into middle adolescence. Adamczyk-Robinette and colleagues (2002) also reported an amplification effect, wherein adolescents were especially unlikely to smoke if their friends reported using little tobacco use *and* their parents employed an authoritative style of parenting.

The Internalization Pathway

This second pathway represents an alternative set of hypothesized mechanisms for the influence of the parental constructs on child/adolescent substance use. The internalization pathway (Figure 10.3) is concerned with the effects of parent modeling, parent approval (and other substance-specific cognitions), and relationship quality on the development of adolescent substance-specific cognitions, and thereby on child/adolescent substance use.

As noted previously, there is evidence in the literature supporting the relation of parent substance use to their approval for child/adolescent substance use and also for the relation of both these parent variables to child/adolescent approval and beliefs concerning substance use. There is substantially less evidence concerning the relation of parents' other substance-specific beliefs (e.g., expectancies and prototypes) to the same beliefs in their children. What has been missing thus far is examination of the mechanisms by which parent substance-specific modeling, attitudes, and beliefs influence the development of the child's own attitudes and beliefs and their subsequent use.

This intergenerational transmission of parental attitudes and beliefs has historically been considered to result from child identification with the parent, but it can also be considered to fit within the compass of Social Cognitive Theory (Bandura, 1969, 1986). The developmental literature suggests that child/ adolescent internalization of parental values and beliefs is accentuated by higher quality parent–child relationships and by moderate levels of parental discipline/control (Brody et al., 2000) (see dotted moderating paths in Figure 10.3).

This pathway generally posits that the effects of parental modeling, approval, and beliefs on adolescent substance use are mediated by their influence on the child's internalization of their parents' approval/ disapproval, prototypes, and expectancies regarding substance use. Due to the nascent quality of this literature, there are few path analyses or structural equation models to draw upon to support the paths depicted in Figure 10.1. Thus far, the literature supports only a few of the hypothesized mediating paths.

Parent Approval Mediates Parent Modeling

Although parent modeling of substance use correlates with parental approval of child/adolescent use, few studies have examined which variable is more influential in explaining child and adolescent substance use. After classifying parents on both their drinking behavior and their attitudes, Hung, Chang, Luh, Wu, and Yen (2015) concluded that parental attitudes toward adolescent drinking were more important than parent models for drinking. McDermott (1984) found that parent permissive attitudes related to adolescent drug use whether the parents used drugs or not. In hierarchical analyses predicting initiation of current

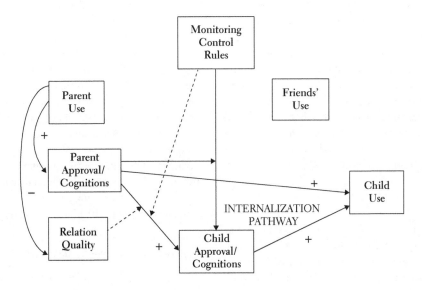

FIGURE 10.3 The internalization pathway.

drinking by grade 8 or 9, parental attitudes and norms mediated the effect of parental drinking (Peterson et al., 1994). In the longitudinal prediction of adolescent smoking, perceived parent approval mediated the effect of parental smoking models on intentions, which predicted both onset and escalation of smoking (Flay et al., 1994). Only a single study (Hummer et al., 2013) found the opposite effect—that parent drinking mediated the effect of parental approval on college student approval of risky drinking.

Own Approval Mediates Parent Approval's Effect on Substance Use

Napper et al. (2016) found that college students' own approval of marijuana use mediated the effect of parental (and friends') approval on the students' use of marijuana. This is probably the best example of the more general relationship put forward by this internalization pathway.

Own Approval Mediates Parent Monitoring Effect on Substance Use

Hummer et al. (2013) found that college student approval of risky drinking mediated the relation between perceived parental knowledge and student drinking.

Parent Approval Moderates Effect of Knowledge on Own Approval

Hummer et al. (2013) also found that at low levels (but not high levels) of parental approval, greater perceived parental knowledge of their student's activities was associated with less student approval of risky drinking.

Future research is needed to examine the influence of parental beliefs and attitudes other than just approval/disapproval of adolescent substance use (i.e., expectancies and prototypes). Further research could also profitably focus on the relative contributions of, and overlap between, the social control pathway and the internalization pathway.

The Bonding Pathway

The third pathway by which parental variables influence child/adolescent substance use is the bonding pathway (Figure 10.4). In this pathway, there is a direct relation between parent–child relationship quality and child/adolescent substance use; this relation has been found in a large number of the studies reviewed previously. Although the effect of parent–child relationships on adolescent substance use is mediated by friends' use (see The Social Control Pathway), its effect does not appear to be mediated by other parental influences.

No Mediation by Parent Use or Approval

Prendergast and Schaefer (1974) found that neither parent drinking nor parent attitudes toward adolescent drinking mediated the relation between measures of parental relationship and adolescent involvement with alcohol. This finding is in line with Social Control Theory, which states that positive parent–child bonding should result in low levels of child substance use, regardless of parent substance use.

Parent–Child Relationship Moderates Parent Modeling

A hypothesis often attributed to Social Learning Theory is that children will model parent substance use *only* if they have a good relationship (usually tested as an interaction effect). Support for this hypothesized interaction effect has been mixed. Yu (2003) found that the more time adolescents spent with alcohol-using parents, the more likely they were to use alcohol and to start drinking at an earlier age. Foshee and Bauman (1992) found that attachment to a parent resulted in smoking initiation if the parent was a smoker but no initiation if the parent was not a smoker. Similarly, connectedness to non-smoking parents predicted a lower likelihood of current adolescent smoking (Tilson, McBride, Lipkus, & Catalano, 2004). Two studies (Brook, Whiteman, Gordon, & Brook, 1984, 1986) found that greater identification with a drug-using father was associated with greater marijuana use among late adolescents. Andrews et al. (1997) provided partial support, finding that parent–child relationship moderated the association of parent use to adolescent use for cigarettes and marijuana use for mothers and for alcohol and marijuana use for fathers. Given this mixed support, a dotted line is included in Figure 10.4 for this moderating path.

Relationship Does Not Moderate Monitoring

Van der Vorst, Engels, Meeus, Dekovic, and Vermulst (2006) found that parental attachment does not

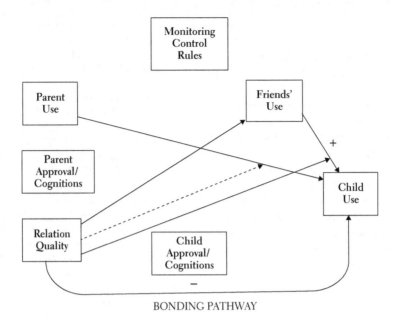

BONDING PATHWAY

FIGURE 10.4 The bonding pathway.

moderate the effect of parent strict control (moni-toring) on early adolescents' alcohol consumption. Additional examination of this relation is warranted.

Relationship Moderates Friends' Use

The quality of the parent–child relationship has been shown to moderate the magnitude of relation between peer and adolescent substance use. Greater family support (Frauenglass, Routh, Pantin, & Mason, 1997), greater maternal support (Allen et al., 2012), a stronger mother–adolescent relationship (Farrell & White, 1998), and greater closeness to their father (but not mother) (Dorius et al., 2004) reduce the relationship between friends' substance use and the adolescent's own substance use. Marshal and Chassin (2000) found a moderating relationship for parental support for girls but not for boys. Mother–adolescent relationship did not, however, moderate the relation of peer risky behavior to current adolescent substance use in a cross-sectional study of African American students (Clark et al., 2012). Greater maternal support did moderate the relation between peer substance use and change in teen drug use during a 1-year period (Allen et al., 2012).

Future longitudinal research is needed to deter-mine the level of support for the components of this pathway and to determine the relative contribution of this pathway to the explanation of adolescent sub-stance use in contrast to those of the social control and internalization pathways.

FUTURE DIRECTIONS

Many of the hypothesized paths comprising the parental socialization framework can be addressed through secondary analyses of data sets already in hand. Optimally, this would involve integrative data analyses (Hussong, Curran, & Bauer, 2013). The major thrust of this chapter is to encourage more targeted research on the relation of childhood fam-ily environment factors to the development of per-sonal and social vulnerability for, and protection against, adolescent involvement in substance use and its escalation into substance abuse and dependence. The findings reviewed in this chapter argue for more systematic attention to the interaction of the parent and peer environments in the socialization of ado-lescent substance use. Of particular consequence is longitudinal modeling of the mechanisms by which greater parental monitoring (or knowledge) and bet-ter relationships between parents and their children diminish affiliation with substance-using peers and reduce adolescent vulnerability to peer influence for use (Mounts, 2002).

It is hoped that more researchers will come to appreciate the importance of understanding the explanatory role of mediational relations in the longitudinal development of adolescent substance use. Given the present overreliance on cross-sectional data for the examination of mediation, it is understandable that the primary emphasis has been on the statistical importance of the mediator (e.g., friends' use) and not on the theoretical importance of the factors contributing to the development (or influence) of the mediator. Through a better understanding of these contributing factors, including parental influences, it should be possible to design more effective early interventions to short-circuit children's movement onto the slippery slope leading to substance abuse.

ACKNOWLEDGMENT

Work on this chapter was supported by grant AA-012342 from the National Institute on Alcohol Abuse and Alcoholism.

REFERENCES

Aas, H., Jakobsen, R., & Anderssen, N. (1996). Predicting 13-year-olds' drinking using parents' self-reported alcohol use and restrictiveness compared with offspring's perception. *Scandinavian Journal of Psychology, 37*, 113–120.

Abar, C. C., Jackson, K. M., Colby, S. M., & Barnett, N. P. (2014). Common and unique parenting predictors of adolescent tobacco and alcohol use. *Addictive Behaviors, 39*, 1528–1532.

Abar, C. C., & Turrisi, R. (2008). How important are parents during the college years? A longitudinal perspective of indirect influences parents yield on their college teens' alcohol use. *Addictive Behaviors, 33*, 1360–1368.

Adamczyk-Robinette, S. L., Fletcher, A. C., & Wright, K. (2002). Understanding the authoritative parenting-early adolescent tobacco use link: The mediating role of peer tobacco use. *Journal of Youth and Adolescence, 31*, 311–318.

Aikins, J. W., Simon, V. A., & Prinstein, M. J. (2010). Romantic partner selection and socialization of young adolescents' substance use and behavior problems. *Journal of Adolescence, 33*, 813–826.

Akers, R. L. (1985). *Deviant behavior: A social learning approach* (3rd ed.). Belmont, CA: Wadsworth.

Akers, R. L., Krohn, M. D., Lanza-Kaduce, L., & Radosevich, M. (1979). Social learning and deviant behavior: A specific test of a general theory. *American Sociological Review, 44*, 636–655.

Ali, M. M., & Dwyer, D. S. (2010). Social network effects in alcohol consumption among adolescents. *Addictive Behaviors, 35*, 337–342.

Allen, J. P., Chango, J., Szwedo, D., Schad, M., & Marston, E. (2012). Predictors of susceptibility to peer influence regarding substance use in adolescence. *Child Development, 83*, 337–350.

Andersen, M. R., Leroux, B. G., Bricker, J. B., Rajan, K. B., & Peterson, A. V., Jr. (2004). Antismoking parenting practices are associated with reduced rates of adolescent smoking. *Archives of Pediatrics and Adolescent Medicine, 158*, 348–352.

Andrews, J. A., Hops, H., Ary, D., Tildesley, E., & Harris, J. (1993). Parental influence on early adolescent substance use: Specific and nonspecific effects. *Journal of Early Adolescence, 13*, 285–310.

Armstrong, J. M., Ruttle, P. A., Burk, L. R., Costanzo, P. R., Strauman, T. J., & Essex, M. J. (2013). Early risk factors for alcohol use across high school and its covariation with deviant friends. *Journal of Studies on Alcohol and Drugs, 74*, 746–756.

Ary, D. V., Tildesley, E., Hops, H., & Andrews, J. (1993). The influence of parent, sibling, and peer modeling and attitudes on adolescent use of alcohol. *International Journal of the Addictions, 28*, 853–880.

Aseltine, R. H., Jr. (1995). A reconsideration of parental and peer influences on adolescent deviance. *Journal of Health and Social Behavior, 36*, 103–121.

Baer, P. E., McLaughlin, R. J., Burnside, M. A., Pokorny, A. D., & Garmezy, L. B. (1987). Stress, family environment, and multiple substance use among seventh graders. *Psychology of Addictive Behaviors, 1*, 92–103.

Bahr, S. J., Hoffmann, J. P., & Yang, X. (2005). Parental and peer influences on the risk of adolescent drug use. *Journal of Primary Prevention, 2005*, 529–551.

Bandura, A. (1969). Social-learning theory of identificatory processes. In D. R. Goslin (Ed.), *Handbook of socialization theory and research* (pp. 213–262). Skokie, IL: Rand McNally.

Bandura, A. (1977). *Social learning theory*. Englewood Cliffs, NJ: Prentice-Hall.

Bandura, A. (1986). *Social foundations of thought and action: A social cognitive theory*. Englewood Cliffs, NJ: Prentice-Hall.

Bank, B. J., Biddle, B. J., Anderson, D. S., Hauge, R., Keats, D. M., Keat, J. A., . . . Valentin, S. (1985). Comparative research on the social determinants of adolescent drinking. *Social Psychology Quarterly*, 48, 164–177.

Barnes, G. M., Reifman, A. S., Farrell, M. P., & Dintcheff, B. A. (2000). The effects of parenting on the development of adolescent alcohol misuse: A six-wave latent growth model. *Journal of Marriage and Family*, 62, 175–186.

Barnes, G. M., & Welte, J. W. (1986). Patterns and predictors of alcohol use among 7–12th grade students in New York state. *Journal of Studies on Alcohol*, 47, 53–62.

Bauman, K. A., & Ennett, S. T. (1996). On the importance of peer influence for adolescent drug use: Commonly neglected considerations. *Addiction*, 91, 185–198.

Bauman, K. A., & Fisher, L. A. (1986). On the measurement of friend behavior in research on friend influence and selection: Findings from longitudinal studies of adolescent smoking and drinking. *Journal of Youth and Adolescence*, 15, 345–353.

Baumrind, D. (1985). Familial antecedents of adolescent drug use: A developmental perspective. In C. L. Jones & R. J. Battjes (Eds.), *Etiology of drug abuse: Implications for prevention* (NIDA Research Monograph No. 56, pp. 13–44). Rockville, MD: National Institute on Drug Abuse.

Baumrind, D. (1991). The influence of parenting style on adolescent competence and substance use. *Journal of Early Adolescence*, 11, 56–95.

Beal, A. C., Ausiello, J., & Perrin, J. M. (2001). Social influences on health-risk behaviors among minority middle school students. *Journal of Adolescent Health*, 28, 474–480.

Bjorkqvist, K., Batman, A., & Aman-Back, S. (2004). Adolescents' use of tobacco and alcohol: Correlations with habits of parents and friends. *Psychological Reports*, 95, 418–420.

Blanton, H., Gibbons, F. X., Gerrard, M., Conger, K. J., & Smith, G. E. (1997). Role of family and peers in the development of prototypes associated with substance use. *Journal of Family Psychology*, 11, 271–288.

Bray, J. H., Adams, G. J., Getz, J. G., & Baer, P. E. (2001). Developmental, family, and ethnic influences on adolescent alcohol usage: A growth curve approach. *Journal of Family Psychology*, 25, 301–314.

Bricker, J. B., Peterson, A. V., Jr., Leroux, B. G., Andersen, M. R., Rajan, K. B., & Sarason, I. G. (2006). Prospective prediction of children's smoking transitions: Role of parents' and older siblings' smoking. *Addiction*, 101, 128–138.

Brody, G. H., Flor, D. L., Hollett-Wright, N., & McCoy, J. K. (1998). Children's development of alcohol use norms: Contributions of parent and sibling norms, children's temperaments, and parent–child discussions. *Journal of Family Psychology*, 12, 209–219.

Brody, G. H., Ge, X., Katz, J., & Arias, I. (2000). A longitudinal analysis of internalization of parental alcohol-use norms and adolescent alcohol use. *Applied Developmental Science*, 4, 71–79.

Brook, J. (1993). Interactional theory: Its utility in explaining drug use behavior among African-American and Puerto Rican youth. In M. de la Rosa & J. R. Adrados (Eds.), *Drug abuse among minority youth: Methodological issues and reent research advances* (NIDA Research Monograph No. 130, pp. 79–101). Rockville, MD: National Institute on Drug Abuse.

Brook, J. E., & Brook, J. S. (1987). A developmental approach examining social and personal correlates in relation to alcohol use over time. *Journal of Genetic Psychology*, 149, 93–110.

Brook, J. S., Balka, E. B., Crossman, A. M., Dermatis, H., Galanter, M., & Brook, D. W. (2010). The relationship between parental alcohol use, early and late adolescent alcohol use, and young adult psychological symptoms: A longitudinal study. *American Journal on Addictions*, 19, 534–542.

Brook, J. S., Balka, E. B., Fei, K., & Whiteman, M. (2006). The effects of parental tobacco and marijuana use and personality attributes on child rearing in African-American and Puerto Rican young adults. *Journal of Child and Family Studies*, 15, 157–168.

Brook, J. S., Brook, D. W., Arencibia-Mireles, O., Richter, L., & Whiteman, M. (2001). Risk factors for adolescent marijuana use across cultures and across time. *Journal of Genetic Psychology*, 162, 357–374.

Brook, J. S., Brook, D. W., de la Rosa, M., Duque, L. F., Rodriguez, E., Montoya, I. D., & Whiteman, M. (1998). Pathways to marijuana use among adolescents: Cultural/ecological, family, peer, and personality influences. *Journal of the American Academy of Child and Adolescent Psychiatry*, 37, 759–766.

Brook, J. S., Whiteman, M., Balka, E. B., & Cohen, P. (1995). Parent drug use, parent personality, and parenting. *Journal of Genetic Psychology*, 156, 137–151.

Brook, J. S., Whiteman, M., Gordon, A. S., & Brook, D. W. (1984). Identification with paternal attributes and its relationship to the son's personality and drug use. *Developmental Psychology*, 20, 1111–1119.

Brook, J. S., Whiteman, M., Gordon, A. S., & Brook, D. W. (1986). Father–daughter identification and its impact on her personality and drug use. *Developmental Psychology*, 22, 743–748.

Brown, S. A., Tate, S. R., Vik, P. W., Haas, A. L., & Aarons, G. A. (1999). Modeling of alcohol use mediates the effect of family history of alcoholism on adolescent alcohol expectancies. *Experimental and Clinical Psychopharmacology, 7,* 20–27.

Brown, S. L., & Rinelli, L. N. (2010). Family structure, family processes, and adolescent smoking and drinking. *Journal of Research on Adolescence, 20,* 259–273.

Buckner, J. D. (2013). College cannabis use: The unique roles of social norms, motives, and expectancies. *Journal of Studies on Alcohol and Drugs, 74,* 720–726.

Bush, P. J., Weinfurt, K. P., & Iannotti, R. J. (1994). Families versus peers: Developmental influences on drug use from grade 4–5 to grade 7–8. *Journal of Applied Developmental Psychology, 15,* 437–456.

Buu, A., DiPiazza, C., Wang, J., Puttler, L. I., Fitzgerald, H. E., & Zucker, R. A. (2009). Parent, family, and neighborhood effects on the development of child substance use and other psychopathology from preschool to the start of adulthood. *Journal of Studies on Alcohol and Drugs, 70,* 489–498.

Callas, P. W., Flynn, B. S., & Worden, J. K. (2004). Potentially modifiable psychosocial factors associated with alcohol use during early adolescence. *Addictive Behaviors, 29,* 1503–1515.

Campbell, J. M., & Oei, T. P. (2010a). A cognitive model for the intergenerational transference of alcohol use behavior. *Addictive Behaviors, 35,* 73–83.

Campbell, J. M., & Oei, T. P. (2010b). The intergenerational transference of alcohol use behavior from parents to offspring: A test of the cognitive model. *Addictive Behaviors, 35,* 714–716.

Casswell, S., Brasch, P., Gilmore, L., & Silva, P. (1985). Children's attitudes to alcohol and awareness of alcohol-related problems. *British Journal of Addiction, 80,* 191–194.

Catalano, R. F., White, H. R., Fleming, C. B., & Haggerty, K. P. (2011). Is nonmedical prescription opiate use a unique form of illicit drug use? *Addictive Behaviors, 36,* 79–86.

Chassin, L., Pillow, D. R., Curran, P. J., Molina, B. S. G., & Barrera, M., Jr. (1993). Relation of parental alcoholism to early adolescent substance use: A test of three mediating mechanisms. *Journal of Abnormal Psychology, 102,* 3–19.

Chassin, L., Presson, C. C., Todd, M., Rose, J. S., & Sherman, S. J. (1998). Maternal socialization of adolescent smoking: The intergenerational transmission of parenting and smoking. *Developmental Psychology, 34,* 1189–2101.

Chassin, L., Rogosch, F., & Barrera, M. (1991). Substance use and symptomatology among adolescent children of alcoholics. *Journal of Abnormal Psychology, 100,* 449–463.

Chen, C., Storr, C. L., & Anthony, J. C. (2005). Influences of parenting practices on the risk of having a chance to try cannabis. *Pediatrics, 115,* 1631–1639.

Chen, C., Storr, C. L., Liu, C., Chen, K., Chen, W. J., & Lin, K. (2011). Differential relationships of family drinking with alcohol expectancy among urban school children. *BMC Public Health, 11,* 87.

Chilcoat, H. D., & Anthony, J. C. (1996). Impact of parental monitoring on initiation of drug use through late childhood. *Journal of the American Academy of Child and Adolescent Psychiatry, 35,* 91–100.

Chilcoat, H. D., Dishion, T. J., & Anthony, J. C. (1995). Parent monitoring and the incidence of drug sampling in urban elementary school children. *American Journal of Epidemiology, 141,* 25–31.

Chuang, Y., Ennett, S. T., Bauman, K. E., & Foshee, V. A. (2005). Neighborhood influences on adolescent cigarette and alcohol use: Mediating effects through parent and peer behaviors. *Journal of Health and Human Behavior, 46,* 187–204.

Chung, T., White, H. R., Hipwell, A. E., Stepp, S. D., & Loeber, R. (2010). A parallel process model of the development of positive smoking expectancies and smoking behavior during early adolescence in Caucasian and African American girls. *Addictive Behaviors, 35,* 647–650.

Clark, D. B., Kirisci, L., Mezzich, A., & Chung, T. (2008). Parental supervision and alcohol use in adolescence: Developmentally specific interactions. *Journal of Developmental and Behavioral Pediatrics, 29,* 285–292.

Clark, T. T., Belgrave, F. Z., & Abell, M. (2012). The mediating and moderating effects of parent and peer influences upon drug use among African American adolescents. *Journal of Black Psychology, 38,* 52–80.

Clark, T. T., Nguyen, A. B., Belgrave, F. Z., & Tademy, R. (2011). Understanding the dimensions of parental influence on alcohol use and alcohol refusal efficacy among African American adolescents. *Social Work Research, 35,* 147–157.

Cleveland, M. J., Gibbons, F. X., Gerrard, M., Pomery, E. A., & Brody, G. H. (2005). The impact of parenting on risk cognition and risk behavior: A study of mediation and moderation in a panel of African American adolescents. *Child Development, 76,* 900–916.

Cohen, D. A., & Rice, J. (1997). Parenting styles, adolescent substance use, and academic achievement. *Journal of Drug Education, 27,* 199–211.

Collins, W. A., Maccoby, E. E., Steinberg, L., Hetherington, E. M., & Bornstein, M. H. (2000).

Contemporary research on parenting: The case for nature versus nurture. *American Psychologist, 55,* 218–232.

Conger, R. D., & Rueter, M. A. (1996). Siblings, parents, and peers: A longitudinal study of social influences in adolescent risk for alcohol use and abuse. In G. H. Brody (Ed.), *Sibling relationships: Their causes and consequences* (pp. 1–30). Norwood, NJ: Ablex.

Conn, B. M., & Marks, A. K. (2014). Ethnic/racial differences in peer and parent influence on adolescent prescription drug misuse. *Journal of Developmental and Behavioral Pediatrics, 35,* 257–265.

Cranford, J. A., Zucker, R. A., Jester, J. M., Putler, L. I., & Fitzgerald, H. E. (2010). Parental alcohol involvement and adolescent alcohol expectancies predict alcohol involvement in male adolescents. *Psychology of Addictive Behaviors, 24,* 386–396.

Crosnoe, R., Erickson, K. G., & Dornbusch, S. M. (2002). Protective functions of family relationships and school factors on the deviant behavior of adolescent boys and girls: Reducing the impact of risky friendships. *Youth and Society, 33,* 515–544.

Dal Cin, S., Worth, K. A., Gerrard, M., Gibbons, F. X., Stoolmiller, M., . . . Sargent, J. D. (2009). Watching and drinking: Expectancies, prototypes, and friends' alcohol use mediate the effect of exposure to alcohol use in movies on adolescent drinking. *Health Psychology, 28,* 473–483.

Dalton, M. A., Adachi-Mejia, A. M., Longacre, M. R., Titus-Ernstoff, L. T., Gibson, J. J., . . . Beach, M. L. (2006). Parental rules and monitoring of children's movie viewing associated with children's risk for smoking and drinking. *Pediatrics, 118,* 1932–1942.

de Vries, H., Candel, M., Engels, R., & Mercken, L. (2006). Challenges to the peer influence paradigm: Results for 12–13 year olds from six European countries from the European Smoking Prevention Framework Approach study. *Tobacco Control, 15,* 83–89.

de Vries, H., Engels, R., Kremers, S. Wetzels, J., & Mudde, A. (2003). Parents' and friends' smoking status as predictors of smoking onset: Findings from six European countries. *Health Education Research, 18,* 627–636.

den Exter Blokland, E., Hale, W. W., Meeus, W., & Engels, R. (2006). Parental anti-smoking socialization: Associations between parental anti-smoking socialization practices and early adolescent smoking initiation. *European Addiction Research, 12,* 25–32.

Dielman, T. E., Butchart, A. T., & Shope, J. T. (1993). Structural equation model tests of patterns of family interaction, peer alcohol use, and intrapersonal predictors of adolescent alcohol use and misuse. *Journal of Drug Education, 23,* 273–316.

Dielman, T. E., Leech, S. L., & Loveland-Cherry, C. (1995). Parents' and children's reports of parenting practices and parent and child alcohol use. *Drugs & Society, 8*(3–4), 83–101.

Dishion, T. J., Capaldi, D. M., & Yoerger, K. (1999). Middle childhood antecedents to progressions in male adolescent substance use: An ecological analysis of risk and protection. *Journal of Adolescent Research, 14,* 175–205.

Dishion, T. J., & Loeber, R. (1985). Adolescent marijuana and alcohol use: The role of parents and peers revisited. *American Journal of Drug and Alcohol Abuse, 11,* 11–25.

Dishion, T. J., Patterson, G. R., & Reid, J. R. (1988). Parent and peer factors associated with drug sampling in early adolescence: Implications for treatment. In E. R. Rahdert & J. Grabowski (Eds.), *Adolescent drug abuse: Analyses of treatment research* (NIDA Research Monograph No. 77, pp. 69–93). Rockville, MD: National Institute on Drug Abuse.

Ditre, J. W., Coraggio, J. T., & Herzog, T. A. (2008). Associations between parental smoking restrictions and adolescent smoking. *Nicotine & Tobacco Research, 10,* 975–983.

Doherty, W. J., & Allen, W. (1994). Family functioning and parental smoking as predictors of adolescent cigarette use: A six-year prospective study. *Journal of Family Psychology, 8,* 347–353.

Donaldson, C. D., Nakawaki, B., & Crano, W. D. (2015). Variations in parental monitoring and predictions of adolescent prescription opioid and stimulant misuse. *Addictive Behaviors, 45,* 14–21.

Donovan, J. E. (2004). Adolescent alcohol initiation: A review of psychosocial risk factors. *Journal of Adolescent Health, 35,* 529.e7–529.e18.

Donovan, J. E. (2015). Child and adolescent socialization into substance use. In S. A. Brown & R. A. Zucker (Eds.), *The Oxford handbook on adolescent substance abuse.* New York, NY: Oxford University Press.

Donovan, J. E., & Jessor, R. (1985). Structure of problem behavior in adolescence and young adulthood. *Journal of Consulting and Clinical Psychology, 53,* 890–904.

Donovan, J. E., Jessor, R., & Costa, F. M. (1999). Adolescent problem drinking: Stability of psychosocial and behavioral correlates across a generation. *Journal of Studies on Alcohol, 60,* 352–361.

Donovan, J. E., & Molina, B. S. G. (2008). Children's introduction to alcohol use: Sips and tastes. *Alcoholism: Clinical and Experimental Research, 32,* 108–119.

Donovan, J. E., & Molina, B. S. G. (2011). Childhood risk factors for early-onset drinking. *Journal of Studies on Alcohol and Drugs, 72,* 741–751.

Donovan, J. E., & Molina, B. S. G. (2014). Antecedent predictors of children's initiation of sipping/tasting alcohol. *Alcoholism: Clinical and Experimental Research*, 38(9), 2488–2495.

Dorius, C. J., Bahr, S. J., Hoffmann, J. P., & Harmon, E. L. (2004). Parenting practices as moderators of the relationship between peers and adolescent marijuana use. *Journal of Marriage and the Family*, 66, 163–178.

Doumas, D. M., Hausheer, R., & Esp, S. (2015). Sex-specific parental behaviors and attitudes as predictors of alcohol use and alcohol-related consequences among ninth grade students. *Journal of Child and Adolescent Counseling*, 1, 100–118.

Dube, S. R., Anda, R. F., Felitti, V. J., Croft, J. B., Edwards, V. J., & Giles, W. H. (2001). Growing up with parental alcohol abuse: Exposure to childhood abuse, neglect, and household dysfunction. *Child Abuse & Neglect*, 25, 1627–1640.

Duncan, S. C., Duncan, T. E., & Strycker, L. A. (2006). Alcohol use from ages 9 to 16: A cohort-sequential latent growth model. *Drug and Alcohol Dependence*, 81, 71–81.

Ellickson, P. L., & Hays, R. D. (1991). Antecedents of drinking among young adolescents with different alcohol use histories. *Journal of Studies on Alcohol*, 52, 398–408.

Ellickson, P. L., Tucker, J. S., Klein, D. J., & Saner, H. (2004). Antecedents and outcomes of marijuana use initiation during adolescence. *Preventive Medicine*, 39, 976–984.

Engels, R. C. M. E., Vitaro, F., den Exter Blokland, E., de Kemp, R., & Scholte, R. H. J. (2004). Influence and selection processes in friendships and adolescent smoking behavior: The role of parental smoking. *Journal of Adolescence*, 27, 531–544.

Ennett, S. T., Bauman, K. E., Hussong, A., Faris, R., Foshee, V. A., & Cai, L. (2006). The peer context of adolescent substance use: Findings from social network analysis. *Journal of Research on Adolescence*, 16, 159–186.

Ennett, S. T., Foshee, V. A., Bauman, K. E., Hussong, A., Cai, L., . . . DuRant, R. (2008). The social ecology of adolescent alcohol misuse. *Child Development*, 79, 1777–1791.

Ennett, S. T., Foshee, V. A., Bauman, K. E., Hussong, A., Faris, R., Hipp, J. R., & Cai, L. (2010). A social contextual analysis of youth cigarette smoking development. *Nicotine & Tobacco Research*, 12, 950–962.

Ennett, S. T., Jackson, C., Bowling, J. M., & Dickinson, D. M. (2013). Parental socialization and children's susceptibility to alcohol use initiation. *Journal of Studies on Alcohol and Drugs*, 74, 694–702.

Epstein, J. A., Griffith, K. W., & Botvin, G. J. (2008). A social influence model of alcohol use for inner-city adolescents: Family drinking, perceived drinking norms, and perceived social benefits of drinking. *Journal of Studies on Alcohol and Drugs*, 69, 397–405.

Erickson, K. G., Crosnoe, R., & Dornbusch, S. M. (2000). A social process model of adolescent deviance: Combining social control and differential association perspectives. *Journal of Youth and Adolescence*, 29, 395–425.

Fagan, A. A., & Najman, J. M. (2005). The relative contributions of parental and sibling substance use to adolescent tobacco, alcohol, and other drug use. *Journal of Drug Issues*, 34, 869–883.

Fairlie, A. M., Wood, M. D., & Laird, R. D. (2012). Prospective protective effect of parents on peer influences and college alcohol involvement. *Psychology of Addictive Behaviors*, 26, 30–41.

Fang, L., Schinke, S. P., & Cole, K. C. (2009). Underage drinking among young adolescent girls: The role of family processes. *Psychology of Addictive Behaviors*, 23, 708–714.

Farhat, T., Simons-Morton, B. G., Kokkevi, A., van der Sluijs, W., Fotiou, A., & Kuntsche, E. (2012). Early adolescent and peer drinking homogeneity: Similarities and differences among European and North American countries. *Journal of Early Adolescence*, 32, 81–103.

Farrell, A. D., & White, K. S. (1998). Peer influences and drug use among urban adolescents: Family structure and parent-adolescent relationship as protective factors. *Journal of Consulting and Clinical Psychology*, 66, 248–258.

Fergusson, D. M., Horwood, L. J., & Lynskey, M. T. (1995). The prevalence and risk factors associated with abusive or hazardous alcohol consumption in 16-year-olds. *Addiction*, 90, 935–946.

Flay, B. R., Hu, F. B., Siddiqui, O., Day, L. E., Hedeker, D., Petraitis, J., . . . Sussman, S. (1994). Differential influence of parental smoking and friends' smoking on adolescent initiation and escalation of smoking. *Journal of Health and Social Behavior*, 35, 248–264.

Fleming, C. B., Brewer, D. D., Gainey, R. R., Haggerty, K. P., & Catalano, R. F. (1997). Parent drug use and bonding to parents as predictors of substance use in children of substance abusers. *Journal of Child and Adolescent Substance Abuse*, 6(4), 75–87.

Fleming, C. B., Kim, H., Harachi, T. W., & Catalano, R. F. (2002). Family processes for children in early elementary school as predictors of smoking initiation. *Journal of Adolescent Health*, 30, 184–189.

Ford, J. A., & Rigg, K. K. (2015). Racial/ethnic differences in factors that place adolescents at risk for prescription opioid misuse. *Prevention Science, 16,* 633–641.

Forrester, K., Biglan, A., Severson, H. H., & Smolkowski, K. (2007). Predictors of smoking onset over two years. *Nicotine & Tobacco Research, 12,* 1259–1267.

Foshee, V., & Bauman, K. E. (1992). Parental and peer characteristics as modifiers of the bond–behavior relationship: An elaboration of control theory. *Journal of Health and Social Behavior, 33,* 66–76.

Foster, S. E., Jones, D. J., Olson, A. L., Forehand, R., Gaffney, C. A., . . . Bau, J. J. (2007). Family socialization of adolescent's self-reported cigarette use: The role of parents' history of regular smoking and parenting style. *Journal of Pediatric Psychology, 32,* 481–493.

Frauenglass, S., Routh, D. K., Pantin, H. M., & Mason, C. A. (1997). Family support decreases influence of deviant peers on Hispanic adolescents' substance use. *Journal of Clinical Child Psychology, 26,* 15–23.

Geels, L. M., Vink, J. M., van Beijsterveldt, C. E. M., Bartels, M., & Boomsma, D. I. (2013). Developmental prediction model for early alcohol initiation in Dutch adolescents. *Journal of Studies on Alcohol and Drugs, 74,* 59–70.

Gerrard, M., Gibbons, F. X., Zhao, L., Russell, D. W., & Reis-Bergan, M. (1999). The effect of peers' alcohol consumption on parental influence: A cognitive mediational model. *Journal of Studies on Alcohol, Supplement 13,* 32–44.

Gibbons, F. X., Gerrard, M., Lune, L. S. V., Wills, T. A., Brody, G., & Conger, R. D. (2004). Context and cognitions: Environmental risk, social influence, and adolescent substance use. *Personality and Social Psychology Bulletin, 30,* 1048–1061.

Gilman, S. E., Rende, R., Boergers, J., Abrams, D. B., Buka, S. L., . . . Niaura, R. S. (2009). Parental smoking and adolescent smoking initiation: An intergenerational perspective on tobacco control. *Pediatrics, 123,* e274–e281.

Glanton, C. F., & Wulfert, E. (2013). The relationship between parental alcohol use and college students' alcohol-related cognitions. *Addictive Behaviors, 38,* 2761–2767.

Gritz, E. R., Prokhorov, A. V., Hudmon, K. S., Jones, M. M., Rosenblum, C., . . . de Moor, C. (2003). Predictors of susceptibility to smoking and ever smoking: A longitudinal study in a triethnic sample of adolescents. *Nicotine & Tobacco Research, 5,* 493–506.

Grube, J. W., Morgan, M., & McGree, S. T. (1986). Attitudes and normative beliefs as predictors of smoking intentions and behaviours: A test of three models. *British Journal of Social Psychology, 25,* 81–93.

Gutman, L. M., Eccles, J. S., Peck, S., & Malanchuk, O. (2011). The influence of family relations on trajectories of cigarette and alcohol use from early to late adolescence. *Journal of Adolescence, 34,* 119–128.

Handley, E. D., & Chassin, L. (2009). Intergenerational transmission of alcohol expectancies in a high-risk sample. *Journal of Studies on Alcohol and Drugs, 70,* 675–682.

Handley, E. D., & Chassin, L. (2013). Alcohol-specific parenting as a mechanism of parental drinking and alcohol use disorder risk on adolescent alcohol use onset. *Journal of Studies on Alcohol and Drugs, 74,* 684–693.

Hansen, W. B., Graham, J. W., Sobel, J. L., Shelton, D. R., Flay, B. R., & Anderson, C. A. (1987). The consistency of peer and parent influences on tobacco, alcohol, and marijuana use among young adolescents. *Journal of Behavioral Medicine, 10,* 559–579.

Harakeh, Z., Scholte, R. H. J., Vermulst, A. A., de Vries, H., & Engels, R. C. M. E. (2004). Parental factors and adolescents' smoking behavior: An extension of the theory of planned behavior. *Preventive Medicine, 39,* 951–961.

Harakeh, Z., Scholte, R. H. J., Vermulst, A. A., de Vries, H., & Engels, R. C. M. E. (2010). The relations between parents' smoking, general parenting, parental smoking communication, and adolescents' smoking. *Journal of Research on Adolescence, 20,* 140–165.

Hawkins, J. D., Graham, J. W., Maguin, E., Abbott, R., Hill, K. G., & Catalano, R. F. (1997). Exploring the effects of age of alcohol use initiation and psychosocial risk factors on subsequent alcohol misuse. *Journal of Studies on Alcohol, 58,* 280–290.

Hayatbakhsh, M. R., Mamun, A. A., Najman, J. M., O'Callaghan, M. J., Bor, W., & Alati, R. (2008). Early childhood predictors of early substance use and substance use disorders: Prospective study. *Australian and New Zealand Journal of Psychiatry, 42,* 720–731.

Hemovich, V., Lac, A., & Crano, W. D. (2011). Understanding early-onset drug and alcohol outcomes among youth: The role of family structure, social factors, and interpersonal perceptions of use. *Psychology, Heath & Medicine, 16,* 249–267.

Hemphill, S. A., Heerde, J. A., Herrenkohl, T. I., Patton, G. C., Toumbourou, J. W., & Catalano, R. F. (2011). Risk and protective factors for adolescent substance use in Washington State, the United States and Victoria, Australia: A longitudinal study. *Journal of Adolescent Health, 49,* 312–320.

Hilliard, M. E., Riekert, K. A., Hovell, M. F., Rand, C. S., Welkom, J. S., & Eakin, M. N. (2015). Family beliefs and behaviors about smoking and young children's secondhand smoke exposure. *Nicotine & Tobacco Research*, 17, 1067–1075.

Hirschi, T. (1969). *Causes of delinquency*. Berkeley, CA: University of California Press.

Hummer, J. F., LaBrie, J. W., & Ehret, P. J. (2013). Do as I say, not as you perceive: Examining the roles of perceived parental knowledge and perceived parental approval in college students' alcohol-related approval and behavior. *Parenting: Science and Practice*, 13, 196–212.

Hundleby, J. D., & Mercer, G. W. (1987). Family and friends as social environments and their relationship to young adolescents' use of alcohol, tobacco, and marijuana. *Journal of Marriage and the Family*, 49, 151–164.

Hung, C., Chang, H., Luh, D., Wu, C., & Yen, L. (2015). Do parents play different roles in drinking behaviors of male and female adolescents? A longitudinal follow-up study. *BMJ Open*, 5, e007179.

Hung, C., Chiang, Y., Chang, H., & Yen, L. (2011). Path of socialization and cognitive factors effects on adolescent alcohol use in Taiwan. *Addictive Behaviors*, 36, 807–813.

Hung, C., Yen, L., & Wu, W. (2009). Association of parents' alcohol use and family interaction with the initiation of alcohol use by sixth graders: A preliminary study in Taiwan. *BMC Public Health*, 9, 172.

Hussong, A. M., Curran, P. J., & Bauer, D. J. (2013). Integrative data analysis in clinical psychology research. *Annual Review of Clinical Psychology*, 9, 61–89.

Iannotti, R. J., & Bush, P. J. (1992). Perceived vs. actual friends' use of alcohol, cigarettes, marijuana, and cocaine: Which has the most influence? *Journal of Youth and Adolescence*, 21, 375–389.

Jackson, C. (1997). Initial and experimental stages of tobacco and alcohol use during late childhood: Relation to peer, parent, and personal risk factors. *Addictive Behaviors*, 22, 685–698.

Jackson, C., Ennett, S. T., Dickinson, D. M., & Bowling, J.M. (2012). Letting children sip: Understanding why parents allow alcohol use by elementary school children. *Archives of Pediatrics and Adolescent Medicine*, 166, 1053–1057.

Jackson, C., Ennett, S. T., Dickinson, D. M., & Bowling, J.M. (2013) Attributes that differentiate children who sip alcohol from abstinent peers. *Journal of Youth and Adolescence*, 42, 1687–1692.

Jackson, C., & Henriksen, L. (1997). Do as I say: Parent smoking, antismoking socialization, and smoking onset among children. *Addictive Behaviors*, 22, 107–114.

Jackson, C., Henriksen, L., & Dickinson, D. (1999). Alcohol-specific socialization, parenting behaviors and alcohol use by children. *Journal of Studies on Alcohol*, 60, 362–367.

Jackson, C., Henriksen, L., Dickinson, D., & Levine, D. W. (1997). The early use of alcohol and tobacco: Its relation to children's competence and parents' behavior. *American Journal of Public Health*, 87, 359–364.

Jackson, C., Henriksen, L., & Foshee, V. A. (1998). The authoritative parenting index: Predicting health risk behaviors among children and adolescents. *Heath Education & Behavior*, 25, 319–337.

Jackson, K. M., Roberts, M. E., Colby, S. M., Barnett, N. P., Abar, C. C., & Merrill, J. E. (2014). Willingness to drink as a function of peer offers and peer norms in early adolescence. *Journal of Studies on Alcohol and Drugs*, 75, 404–414.

Jackson, K. M., & Schulenberg, J. E. (2013). Alcohol use during the transition from middle school to high school: National panel data on prevalence and moderators. *Developmental Psychology*, 49, 2147–2158.

Jessor, R., & Jessor, S. L. (1977). *Problem behavior and psychosocial development: A longitudinal study of youth*. New York, NY: Academic Press.

Johnson, G. M., Shontz, F. C., & Locke, T. P. (1984). Relationships between adolescent drug use and parental drug behaviors. *Adolescence*, 19(74), 295–298.

Kam, J. A., Matsunaga, M., Hecht, M. L., & Ndiaye, K. (2009). Extending the theory of planned behavior to predict alcohol, tobacco, and marijuana use among youth of Mexican heritage. *Prevention Science*, 10, 41–53.

Kandel, D. B. (1973). Adolescent marijuana use: Role of parents and peers. *Science*, 181, 1067–1070.

Kandel, D. B. (1974). Inter- and intragenerational influences on adolescent marijuana use. *Journal of Social Issues*, 30, 107–135.

Kandel, D. B. (1980). Drug and drinking behavior among youth. *Annual Review of Sociology*, 6, 235–285.

Kandel, D. B. (1996). The parental and peer contexts of adolescent deviance: An algebra of interpersonal influences. *Journal of Drug Issues*, 26, 289–315.

Kandel, D. B. (Ed.). (2002). *Stages and pathways of drug involvement*. New York, NY: Cambridge University Press.

Kandel, D. B., & Andrews, K. (1987). Processes of adolescent socialization by parents and peers. *International Journal of the Addictions*, 22, 319–342.

Kandel, D. B., Kessler, R. C., & Margulies, R. Z. (1978). Antecedents of adolescent initiation into stages of drug use: A developmental analysis. *Journal of Youth and Adolescence*, 7, 13–40.

Kandel, D. B., Kiros, G., Schaffran, C., & Hu, M. (2004). Racial/ethnic differences in cigarette smoking initiation and progression to daily smoking: A multilevel analysis. *American Journal of Public Health*, *94*, 128–135.

Kandel, D. B., & Wu, P. (1995). The contributions of mothers and fathers to the intergenerational transmission of cigarette smoking in adolescence. *Journal of Research on Adolescence, 5*, 225–252.

Kelly, A. B., O'Flaherty, M., Connor, J. P., Homel, R., Toumbourou, J. W., Patton, G. C., & Williams, J. (2011). The influence of parents, siblings and peers on pre- and early-teen smoking: A multilevel model. *Drug and Alcohol Review, 30*, 381–387.

Kelly, A. B., O'Flaherty, M., Toumbourou, J. W., Connor, J. P., Hemphill, S. A., & Catalano, R. F. (2011). Gender differences in the impact of families on alcohol use: A lagged longitudinal study of early adolescents. *Addiction, 106*, 1427–1436.

Kelly, Y., Goisis, A., Sacker, A., Cable, N., Watt, R. G., & Britton, A. (2016). What influences 11-year-olds to drink? Findings from the Millennium Cohort Study. *BMC Public Health, 16*, 169.

Kendler, K. S., Gardner, C. O., Edwards, A., Hickman, M., Heron, J., Macleod, J., . . . Dick, D. M. (2013). Dimensions of parental alcohol use/problems and offspring temperament, externalizing behaviors, and alcohol use/problems. *Alcoholism: Clinical and Experimental Research, 37*, 2118–2127.

Kerr, D. C. R., Capaldi, D. M., Pears, K. C., & Owens, L. D. (2012). Intergenerational influences on early alcohol use: Independence from the problem behavior pathway. *Development and Psychopathology, 24*, 889–906.

Kerr, D. C. R., Tiberio, S. S., & Capaldi, D. M. (2015). Contextual risks linking parents' adolescent marijuana use to offspring onset. *Drug and Alcohol Dependence, 154*, 222–228.

Kim, H. H., & Chun, J. (2016). Examining the effects of parental influence on adolescent smoking behaviors: A multilevel analysis of the Global School-based Student Health Survey (2003–2011). *Nicotine & Tobacco Research, 18*, 934–942.

Kim, M. J., Fleming, C. B., & Catalano, R. F. (2009). Individual and social influences on progression to daily smoking during adolescence. *Pediatrics, 124*, 895–902.

King, K. M., & Chassin, L. (2004). Mediating and moderating effects of adolescent behavioral undercontrol and parenting in the prediction of drug use disorders in emerging adulthood. *Psychology of Addictive Behaviors, 18*, 239–249.

King, K. M., Molina, B. S. G., & Chassin, L. (2009). Prospective relations between growth in drinking and familial stressors across adolescence. *Journal of Abnormal Psychology, 118*, 610–622.

Kline, R. B., Canter, W. A., & Robin, A. (1987). Parameters of teenage alcohol use: A path analytic conceptual model. *Journal of Consulting and Clinical Psychology, 55*, 521–528.

Kodl, M. M., & Mermelstein, R. (2004). Beyond modeling: Parenting practices, parental smoking history, and adolescent cigarette smoking. *Addictive Behaviors, 29*, 17–32.

Kokkevi, A., Richardson, C., Florescu, S., Kuzman, M., & Stergar, E. (2007). Psychosocial correlates of substance use in adolescence: A cross-national study in six European countries. *Drug and Alcohol Dependence, 86*, 67–74.

Koning, I. M., Engels, R. C. M. E., Verdurmen, J. E. E., & Vollebergh, W. A. M. (2010). Alcohol-specific socialization practices and alcohol use in Dutch early adolescents. *Journal of Adolescence, 33*, 93–100.

Krohn, M. D., Akers, R. L., Radosevich, M. J., & Lanza-Kaduce, L. (1982). Norm qualities and adolescent drinking and drug behavior: The effects of norm quality and reference group on using and abusing alcohol and marijuana. *Journal of Drug Issues, 12*, 343–359.

Krohn, M. D., Skinner, W. F., Massey, J. L., & Akers, R. L. (1985). Social learning theory and adolescent cigarette smoking: A longitudinal study. *Social Problems, 32*, 455–473.

Kung, E. M., & Farrell, A. D. (2000). The role of parents and peers in early adolescent substance use: An examination of mediating and moderating effects. *Journal of Child and Family Studies, 9*, 509–528.

LaBrie, J. W., Hummer, J. F., & Lac, A. (2011). Comparing injunctive marijuana use norms of salient reference groups among college student marijuana users and nonusers. *Addictive Behaviors, 36*, 717–720.

LaBrie, J. W., Hummer, J. F., Lac, A., & Lee, C. M. (2010). Direct and indirect effects of injunctive norms on marijuana use: The role of reference groups. *Journal of Studies on Alcohol and Drugs, 71*, 904–908.

LaBrie, J. W., Hummer, J. F., Neighbors, C., & Larimer, M. E. (2010). Whose opinion matters? The relationship between injunctive norms and alcohol consequences in college students. *Addictive Behaviors, 35*, 343–349.

Lac, A., Alvaro, E. M., Crano, W. D., & Siegel, J. T. (2009). Pathways from parental knowledge and warmth to adolescent marijuana use: An extension to the theory of planned behavior. *Prevention Science, 10*, 22–32.

Lambourn, S. D., Mounts, N. S., Steinberg, L., & Dornbusch, S. M. (1991). Patterns of competence and adjustment among adolescents from authoritative, authoritarian, indulgent, and neglectful families. *Child Development, 62,* 1049–1065.

Latendresse, S. J., Rose, R. J., Viken, R. J., Pulkkinen, L., Kaprio, J., & Dick, D. M. (2008). Parenting mechanisms in links between parents' and adolescents' alcohol use behaviors. *Alcoholism: Clinical and Experimental Research, 32,* 322–330.

Leatherdale, S. T., McDonald, P. W., Cameron, R., Jolin, M. A., & Brown, K. S. (2006). A multi-level analysis examining how smoking friends, parents, and older students in the school environment are risk factors for susceptibility to smoking among non-smoking elementary school youth. *Prevention Science, 7,* 397–402.

Leonardi-Bee, J., Jere, M. L., & Britton, J. (2011). Exposure to parental and sibling smoking and the risk of smoking uptake in childhood and adolescence: A systematic review and meta-analysis. *Thorax, 66,* 847–855.

Lewin, K. (1939). Field theory and experiment in social psychology: Concepts and methods. *American Journal of Social Psychology, 44,* 873–884.

Li, C., Pentz, M. A., & Chou, C. (2002). Parental substance use as a modifier of adolescent substance use risk. *Addiction, 97,* 1537–1550.

Li, H. K., Kelly, A. B., Chan, G. C. K., Toumbourou, J. W., Patton, G. C., & Williams, J. W. (2014). The association of puberty and young adolescent alcohol use: Do parents have a moderating role? *Addictive Behaviors, 39,* 1389–1393.

Li, X., Stanton, B., & Feigelman, S. (2000). Impact of perceived parental monitoring on adolescent risk behavior over 4 years. *Journal of Adolescent Health, 27,* 49–56.

Liao, Y., Huang, Z., Huh, J., Pentz, M. A., & Chou, C. (2013). Changes in friends' and parental influences on cigarette smoking from early through late adolescence. *Journal of Adolescent Health, 53,* 132–138.

Lipperman-Kreda, S., Grube, J. W., & Paschall, M. J. (2010). Community norms, enforcement of minimum legal drinking age laws, personal beliefs and underage drinking: An explanatory model. *Journal of Community Health, 35,* 249–257.

Loveland-Cherry, C. J., Leech, S., Laetz, V. B., & Dielman, T. E. (1996). Correlates of alcohol use and misuse in fourth-grade children: Psychosocial, peer, parental, and family factors. *Health Education & Behavior, 23,* 497–511.

Macaulay, A. P., Griffin, K. W., Gronewold, E., Williams, C., & Botvin, G. J. (2005). Parenting practices and adolescent drug-related knowledge, attitudes, norms and behavior. *Journal of Alcohol and Drug Education, 49,* 67–83.

Macleod, J., Hickman, M., Bowen, E., Alati, R., Tilling, K., & Smith, G. D. (2008). Parental drug use, early adversities, later childhood problems and children's use of tobacco and alcohol at age 10: Birth cohort study. *Addiction, 103,* 1731–1743.

Mahabee-Gittens, E. M., Xiao, Y., Gordon, J. S., & Khoury, J. C. (2012). Continued importance of family factors in youth smoking behavior. *Nicotine & Tobacco Research, 14,* 1458–1466.

Mak, K., Ho, S., & Day, J. R. (2012). Smoking of parents and best friend—Independent and combined effects on adolescent smoking and intention to initiate and quit smoking. *Nicotine & Tobacco Research, 9,* 1057–1064.

Marshal, M. P., & Chassin, L. (2000). Peer influence on adolescent alcohol use: The moderating role of parental support and discipline. *Applied Developmental Science, 4,* 80–88.

Martino, S. C., Collins, R. L., Ellickson, P. L., Schell, T. L., & McCaffrey, D. (2006). Socio-environmental influences on adolescents' alcohol outcome expectancies: A prospective analysis. *Addiction, 101,* 971–983.

McDermott, D. (1984). The relationship of parental drug use and parents' attitude concerning adolescent drug use to adolescent drug use. *Adolescence, 19*(73), 89–97.

Melby, J. N., Conger, R. D., Conger, K. J., & Lorenz, F. O. (1993). Effects of parental behavior on tobacco use by young male adolescents. *Journal of Marriage and the Family, 55,* 439–454.

Mewse, A. J., Eiser, J. R., Slater, A. M., & Lea, S. E. G. (2004). The smoking behaviors of adolescents and their friends: Do parents matter? *Parenting Science and Practice, 4,* 51–72.

Miller, S. M., Siegel, J. T., Hohman, Z., & Crano, W. D. (2013). Factors mediating the association of the recency of parent's marijuana use and their adolescent children's subsequent initiation. *Psychology of Addictive Behaviors, 27,* 848–853.

Moore, G. F., Rothwell, H., Segrott, J. (2010). An exploratory study of the relationship between parental attitudes and behavior and young people's consumption of alcohol. *Substance Abuse Treatment, 5,* 1–14.

Mounts, N. S. (2002). Parental management of adolescent peer relationships in context: The role of parenting style. *Journal of Family Psychology, 16,* 58–69.

Mounts, N. S., & Steinberg, L. (1995). An ecological analysis of peer influence on adolescent grade point average and drug use. *Developmental Psychology, 31,* 915–922.

Mrug, S., & McCay, R. (2013). Parental and peer disapproval of alcohol use and its relationship to adolescent drinking: Age, gender, and racial differences. *Psychology of Addictive Behaviors, 27,* 604–614.

Müller, S., & Kuntsche, E. (2011). Do the drinking motives of adolescents mediate the link between their parents' drinking habits and their own alcohol use? *Journal of Studies on Alcohol and Drugs, 72,* 429–437.

Napper, L. E., Hummer, J. F., Chithambo, T. P., & LaBrie, J. W. (2015). Perceived parent and peer marijuana norms: The moderating effect of parental monitoring during college. *Prevention Science, 16,* 364–373.

Napper, L. E., Kenney, S. R., Hummer, J. F., & Fiorot, S. (2016). Longitudinal relationships among perceived injunctive and descriptive norms and marijuana use. *Journal of Studies on Alcohol and Drugs, 77,* 457–463.

Nargiso, J. E., Ballard, E. L., & Skeer, M. R. (2015). A systematic review of risk and protective factors associated with nonmedical use of prescription drugs among youth in the United States: A social ecological perspective. *Journal of Studies on Alcohol and Drugs, 76,* 5–20.

Nash, S. G., McQueen, A., & Bray, J. H. (2005). Pathways to adolescent alcohol use: Family environment, peer influence, and parental expectations. *Journal of Adolescent Health, 37,* 19–28.

Neighbors, C., O'Connor, R. M., Lewis, M. A., Chawla, N., Lee, C. M., & Fossos, N. (2008). The relative impact of injunctive norms on college student drinking: The role of the reference group. *Psychology of Addictive Behaviors, 22,* 576–581.

Nowlin, P. R., & Colder, C. R. (2007). The role of ethnicity and neighborhood poverty on the relationship between parenting and adolescent cigarette use. *Nicotine & Tobacco Research, 9,* 545–556.

Oetting, E. R., & Donnermeyer, J. F. (1998). Primary socialization theory: The etiology of drug use and deviance: I. *Substance Use & Misuse, 33,* 995–1026.

Ohannessian, C. M. (2009). Does technology use moderate the relationship between parental alcoholism and adolescent alcohol and cigarette use? *Addictive Behaviors, 34,* 606–609.

O'Loughlin, J. L., Barry, A., O'Loughlin, E. K., Tremblay, M.; on behalf of the AdoQuest Team. (2014). Home smoking bans may increase the risk of smoking onset in children when both parents smoke. *Nicotine & Tobacco Research, 16,* 1009–1013.

Osaki, Y., Suzuki, K., Wada, K., & Hitsumoto, S. (2011). Association of parental factors with student smoking and alcohol use in Japan. *Japanese Journal of Alcohol and Drug Dependence, 46,* 270–278.

Otten, R., Engels, R., van de Ven, M., & Bricker, J. (2007). Parental smoking and adolescent smoking

stages: The role of parents' current and former smoking, and family structure. *Journal of Behavioral Medicine, 30,* 143–154

Ouellette, J. A., Gerrard, M., Gibbons, F. X., & Reis-Bergan, M. (1999). Parents, peers, and prototypes: Antecedents of adolescent alcohol expectancies, alcohol consumption, and alcohol-related life problems in rural youth. *Psychology of Addictive Behaviors, 13,* 185–197.

Palmer, R. H. C., Young, S. E., Hopfer, C. J., Corley, R. P., Stallings, M. C., . . . Hewitt, J. K. (2009). Developmental epidemiology of drug use and abuse in adolescence and young adulthood: Evidence of generalized risk. *Drug and Alcohol Dependence, 102,* 78–87.

Parsai, M., Marsiglia, F. F., & Kulis, S. (2010). Parental monitoring, religious involvement and drug use among Latino and non-Latino youth in the southwestern United States. *British Journal of Social Work, 40,* 100–114.

Parsai, M., Voisine, S., Marsiglia, F. F., Kulis, S., & Nieri, T. (2008). The protective and risk effects of parents and peers on substance use, attitudes, and behaviors of Mexican and Mexican-American female and male adolescents. *Youth & Society, 40,* 353–376.

Patterson, G. R. (1982). *A social learning approach to family intervention: Vol. 3. Coercive family processes.* Eugene, OR: Castalia.

Pears, K., Capaldi, D. M., & Owen, L. D. (2007). Substance use risk across three generations: The roles of parent discipline practices and inhibitory control. *Psychology of Addictive Behaviors, 21,* 373–386.

Pennanen, M., Vartiainen, E., & Haukkala, A. (2012). The role of family factors and school achievement in the progression of adolescents to regular smoking. *Health Education Research, 27,* 57–68.

Peterson, P. L., Hawkins, J. D., Abbott, R. D., & Catalano, R. F. (1994). Disentangling the effects of parental drinking, family management, and parental alcohol norms on current drinking by Black and White adolescents. *Journal of Research on Adolescence, 4,* 203–227.

Pieters, S., Burk, W. J., van der Vorst, H., Wiers, R. W., & Engels, R. C. M. E. (2012). The moderating role of working memory capacity and alcohol-specific rule-setting on the relation between approach tendencies and alcohol use in young adolescents. *Alcoholism: Clinical and Experimental Research, 36,* 915–922.

Potvin, R. H., & Lee, C. (1980). Multistage path models of adolescent alcohol and drug use. *Journal of Studies on Alcohol, 41,* 531–542.

Prendergast, T. J. (1974). Family characteristics associated with marijuana use among adolescents. *International Journal of the Addictions, 9,* 827–839.

Prendergast, T. J., & Schaefer, E. S. (1974). Correlates of drinking and drunkenness among high-school students. *Quarterly Journal of Studies on Alcohol, 35*, 232–242.

Prins, J. C., Donovan, J. E., & Molina, B. S. G. (2011). Parent–child divergence in the development of alcohol use norms from middle childhood into middle adolescence. *Journal of Studies on Alcohol and Drugs, 72*, 438–443.

Quine, S., & Stephenson, J. A. (1990). Predicting smoking and drinking intentions and behavior of pre-adolescents: The influence of parents, siblings, and peers. *Family Systems Medicine, 8*, 191–200.

Reid, J. L., Manske, S. R., & Leatherdale, S. T. (2008). Factors related to adolescents' estimation of peer smoking prevalence. *Health Education Research, 23*, 81–93.

Reimuller, A., Hussong, A., & Ennett, S. T. (2011). The influence of alcohol-specific communication on adolescent alcohol use and alcohol-related consequences. *Prevention Science, 12*, 389–400.

Rioux, C., Castellanos-Ryan, N., Parent, S., Vitaro, F., Tremblay, R. E., & Seguin, J. R. (2015). Differential susceptibility to environmental influences: Interactions between child temperament and parenting in adolescent alcohol use. *Development and Psychopathology, 28*, 265–275.

Rodriguez, D., Tscherne, J., & Audrain-McGovern, J. (2007). Contextual consistency and adolescent smoking: Testing the indirect effect of home indoor smoking restrictions on adolescent smoking through peer smoking. *Nicotine & Tobacco Research, 9*, 1155–1161.

Rose, R. J., Dick, D. M., Viken, R. J., Pulkkinen, L., & Kaprio, J. (2001). Drinking or abstaining at age 14? A genetic epidemiological study. *Alcoholism: Clinical and Experimental Research, 25*, 1594–1604.

Ryan, S. M., Jorm, A. F., & Lubman, D. I. (2010). Parenting factors associated with reduced adolescent alcohol use: A systematic review of longitudinal studies. *Australian and New Zealand Journal of Psychiatry, 44*, 774–783.

Sargent, J. D., & Dalton, M. (2001). Does parental disapproval of smoking prevent adolescents from becoming established smokers? *Pediatrics, 108*, 1256–1262.

Seljamo, S., Aromaa, M., Koivusilta, L., Rautava, P., Sourander, A., . . . Silanpää, M. (2006). Alcohol use in families: A 15-year prospective follow-up study. *Addiction, 101*, 984–992.

Sher, K. J. (1991). *Children of alcoholics: A critical appraisal of theory and research*. Chicago, IL: University of Chicago Press.

Shortt, A. L., Hutchinson, D. M., Chapman, R., & Toumbourou, J. W. (2007). Family, school, peer, and individual influences on early adolescent alcohol use: First-year impact of the Resilient Families programme. *Drug and Alcohol Review, 26*, 625–634.

Siegel, J. T., Tan, C. N., Navarro, M. A., Alvaro, E. M., & Crano, W. D. (2015). The power of the proposition: Frequency of marijuana offers, parental knowledge, and adolescent marijuana use. *Drug and Alcohol Dependence, 148*, 34–39.

Simons-Morton, B. (2002). Prospective analysis of peer and parent influences on smoking initiation among early adolescents. *Prevention Science, 3*, 275–283.

Simons-Morton, B. (2004). Prospective association of peer influence, school engagement, drinking expectancies, and parent expectations with drinking initiation among sixth graders. *Addictive Behaviors, 29*, 299–309.

Simons-Morton, B. (2007). Social influences on adolescent substance use. *American Journal of Health Behavior, 31*, 672–684.

Simons-Morton, B., & Chen, R. (2005). Latent growth curve analyses of parent influences on drinking progression among early adolescents. *Journal of Studies on Alcohol, 66*, 5–13.

Simons-Morton, B., Chen, R., Abroms, L., & Haynie, D. L. (2004). Latent growth curve analysis of peer and parent influences on smoking progression among early adolescents. *Health Psychology, 23*, 612–621.

Simons-Morton, B., Haynie, D. L., Crump, A. D., Eitel, P., & Saylor, K. E. (2001). Peer and parent influences on smoking and drinking among early adolescents. *Health Education and Behavior, 28*, 95–107.

Skinner, M. L., Haggerty, K. P., & Catalano, R. F. (2009). Parental and peer influences on teen smoking: Are White and Black families different? *Nicotine & Tobacco Research, 11*, 558–563.

Smart, R. G., & Fejer, D. (1972). Drug use among adolescents and their parents: Closing the generation gap in mood modification. *Journal of Abnormal Psychology, 79*, 153–160.

Smith, D. T., Kelly, A. B., Chan, G. C. K., Toumbourou, K. W., Patton, G. C., & Williams, J. W. (2014). Beyond the primary influences of parents and peers on very young adolescent alcohol use: Evidence of independent community associations. *Journal of Early Adolescence, 34*, 569–584.

Spijkerman, R., van den Eijnden, R. J. J. M., Overbeek, G., & Engels, R. C. M. E. (2007). The impact of peer and parental norms and behavior on adolescent drinking: The role of drinker prototypes. *Psychology and Health, 22*, 7–29.

Stattin, H., & Kerr, M. (2000). Parental monitoring: A reinterpretation. *Child Development*, 71, 1072–1085.

Steinberg, L., Fletcher, A., & Darling, N. (1994). Parental monitoring and peer influences on adolescent substance use. *Pediatrics*, 93, 1060–1064.

Steinberg, L., Lamborn, S., Darling, N., Mounts, N., & Dornbusch, S. (1994). Over-time changes in adjustment and competence among adolescents from authoritative, authoritarian, indulgent, and neglectful families. *Child Development*, 65, 754–770.

Stice, E., Myers, M. G., & Brown, S. A. (1998). A longitudinal grouping analysis of adolescent substance use escalation and de-escalation. *Psychology of Addictive Behaviors*, 12, 14–27.

Stoolmiller, M., Wills, T. A., McClure, A. C., Tanski, S. E., Worth, K. A., Gerrard, M., & Sargent, J. D. (2012). Comparing media and family predictors of alcohol use: A cohort study of US adolescents. *BMJ Open*, 2, e000543.

Sung, H., Richter, L., Vaughan, R., Johnson, P. B., & Thom, B. (2005). Nonmedical use of prescription opioids among teenagers in the United States: Trends and correlates. *Journal of Adolescent Health*, 37, 44–51.

Teichman, M., & Kefir, E. (2000). The effects of perceived parental behaviors, attitudes, and substance-use on adolescent attitudes toward and intent to use psychoactive substances. *Journal of Drug Education*, 30, 193–204.

Thompson, K. M., & Wilsnack, R. W. (1987). Parental influence on adolescent drinking: Modeling, attitudes, or conflict? *Youth & Society*, 19, 22–43.

Thornberry, T. P. (1987). Toward an interactional theory of delinquency. *Criminology*, 25, 863–891.

Tilson, E. C., McBride, C. M., Lipkus, I. M., & Catalano, R. F. (2004). Testing the interaction between parent–child relationship factors and parent smoking to predict youth smoking. *Journal of Adolescent Health*, 35, 182–189.

Trapl, E. S., Yoder, L. D., Frank, J. L., Borawski, E. A., & Sattar, A. (2016). Individual, parental, and environmental correlates of cigar, cigarillo, and little cigar use among middle school students. *Nicotine & Tobacco Research*, 18, 834–841.

Tucker, J. S., Ellickson, P. L., & Klein, D. J. (2003). Predictors of the transition to regular smoking during adolescence and young adulthood. *Journal of Adolescent Health*, 32, 314-324.

Tucker, J. S., Martinez, J. F., Ellickson, P. L., & Edelen, M. O. (2008). Temporal associations of cigarette smoking with social influences, academic performance, and delinquency: A four-wave longitudinal study from ages 13 to 23. *Psychology of Addictive Behaviors*, 22, 1–11.

Urberg, K. A., Değirmencioğlu, S. M., & Pilgrim, C. (1997). Close friend and group influence on adolescent cigarette smoking and alcohol use. *Developmental Psychology*, 33, 834–844.

Urberg, K. A., Luo, Q., Pilgrim, C., & Değirmencioğlu, S. M. (2003). A two-stage model of peer influence in adolescent substance use: Individual and relationship-specific differences in susceptibility to influence. *Addictive Behaviors*, 28, 1243–1256.

Van Damme, J., Maes, L., Kuntsche, E., Crutzen, R., De Clercq, B., Van Lippevelde, W., & Hublet, A. (2015). The influence of parental drinking on offspring' drinking motives and drinking: A mediation analysis on 9 year follow-up data. *Drug and Alcohol Dependence*, 149, 63–70.

van den Eijnden, R., van de Mheen, D., Vet, R., & Vermulst, A. (2011). Alcohol-specific parenting and adolescents' alcohol-related problems: The interacting role of alcohol availability at home and parental rules. *Journal of Studies on Alcohol and Drugs*, 72, 408–417.

van der Vorst, H., Engels, R. C. M. E., Meeus, W., & Deković, M. (2006). The impact of alcohol-specific rules, parental norms about early drinking and parental alcohol use on adolescents' drinking behavior. *Journal of Child Psychology and Psychiatry*, 47, 1299–1306.

van der Vorst, H., Engels, R. C. M. E., Meeus, W., Deković, M., & Vermulst, A. (2006). Parental attachment, parental control, and early development of alcohol use: A longitudinal study. *Psychology of Addictive Behaviors*, 20, 107–116.

Van Zundert, R. M. P., van der Vorst, H., Vermulst, A. A., & Engels, R. C. M. E. (2006). Pathways to alcohol use among Dutch students in regular education and education for adolescents with behavioral problems: The role of parental alcohol use, general parenting practices, and alcohol-specific parenting practices. *Journal of Family Psychology*, 20, 456–467.

Vermeulen-Smit, E., Verdurmen, J. E. E., Engels, R. C. M. E., & Vollebergh, W. A. M. (2015). The role of general parenting and cannabis-specific parenting practices in adolescent cannabis and other illicit drug use. *Drug and Alcohol Dependence*, 147, 222–228.

Visser, L., de Winter, A. F., & Reijneveld, S. A. (2012). The parent–child relationship and adolescent alcohol use: A systematic review of longitudinal studies. *BMC Public Health*, 12, 886.

Voisine, S., Parsai, M., Marsiglia, F. F., Kulis, S., & Nieri, T. (2008). Effects of parental monitoring, permissiveness, and injunctive norms on substance use among Mexican American adolescents. *Families in Society*, 89, 264–273.

Walden, B., McGue, M., Iacono, W. G., Burt, A., & Elkin, I. (2004). Identifying shared environmental contributions to early substance use: The respective roles of peers and parents. *Journal of Abnormal Psychology, 113*, 440–450.

Walls, T. A., Fairlie, A. M., & Wood, M. D. (2009). Parents do matter: A longitudinal two-part mixed model of early college alcohol participation and intensity. *Journal of Studies on Alcohol and Drugs, 70*, 908–918.

Walter, H. J., Vaughn, R. D., & Cohall, A. T. (1993). Comparison of three theoretical models of substance use among urban minority high school students. *Journal of the American Academy of Child and Adolescent Psychiatry, 32*, 975–981.

Wang, M. Q., Fitzhugh, E. C., Green, B. L., Turner, L. W., Eddy, J. M., & Westerfield, R. C. (1999). Prospective social–psychological factors of adolescent smoking progression. *Journal of Adolescent Health, 24*, 2–9.

Wang, M. P., Ho, S. Y., & Lam, T. H. (2011). Parental smoking, exposure to secondhand smoke at home, and smoking initiation among young children. *Nicotine & Tobacco Research, 13*, 827–832.

Watkins, J. A., Howard-Barr, E. M., Moore, M. J., & Werch, C. C. (2006). The mediating role of adolescent self-efficacy in the relationship between parental practices and adolescent alcohol use. *Journal of Adolescent Health, 38*, 448–450.

Webb, J. A., & Baer, P. R. (1995). Influence of family disharmony and parental alcohol-use on adolescent social skills, self-efficacy, and alcohol use. *Addictive Behaviors, 20*, 127–135.

Webb, J. A., Baer, P. E., Caid, C. D., McLaughlin, R. J., & McKelvey, R. S. (1991). Concurrent and longitudinal assessment of risk for alcohol use among seventh graders. *Journal of Early Adolescence, 11*, 450–465.

Wills, T. A., Sandy, J. M., Yaeger, A., & Shinar, O. (2001). Family risk factors and adolescent substance use: Moderation effects for temperament dimensions. *Developmental Psychology, 37*, 283–297.

Wills, T. A., Sargent, J. D., Gibbons, F. X., Gerrard, M., & Stoolmiller, M. (2009). Movie exposure to alcohol cues and adolescent alcohol problems: A longitudinal analysis in a national sample. *Psychology of Addictive Behaviors, 23*, 23–35.

Wills, T. A., Sargent, J. D., Stoolmiller, M., Gibbons, F. X., & Gerrard, M. (2008). Movie smoking exposure and smoking onset: A longitudinal study of mediation processes in a representative sample of U.S. adolescents. *Psychology of Addictive Behaviors, 22*, 269–277.

Wills, T. A., Sargent, J. D., Stoolmiller, M., Gibbons, F. X., Worth, K. A., & Dal Cin, S. (2007). Movie exposure to smoking cues and adolescent smoking onset: A test for mediation through peer affiliations. *Health Psychology, 26*, 769–776.

Windle, M. (2000). Parental, sibling, and peer influences on adolescent substance use and alcohol problems. *Applied Developmental Science, 4*, 98–110.

Wong, M. M., Brower, K. J., Fitzgerald, H. E., & Zucker, R. A. (2004). Sleep problems in early childhood and early onset of alcohol and other drug use in adolescence. *Alcoholism: Clinical and Experimental Research, 28*, 578–587.

Wood, M. D., Read, J. P., Mitchell, R. E., & Brand, N. H. (2004). Do parents still matter? Parent and peer influences on alcohol involvement among recent high school graduates. *Psychology of Addictive Behaviors, 18*, 19–30.

Wu, P., & Kandel, D. B. (1995). The roles of mothers and fathers in intergenerational behavioral transmission: The case of smoking and delinquency. In H. B. Kaplan (Ed.), *Drugs, crime and other deviant adaptations: Longitudinal studies* (pp. 49–81). New York, NY: Plenum.

Yabiku, S. T., Marsiglia, F. F., Kulis, S., Parsai, M. B., Becerrra, D., & Del-Colle, M. (2010). Parental monitoring and changes in substance use among Latino/a and non-Latino/a preadolescents in the Southwest. *Substance Use & Misuse, 45*, 2524–2550.

Yu, J. (2003). The association between parental alcohol-related behaviors and children's drinking. *Drug and Alcohol Dependence, 69*, 253–262.

11

Alcohol and Youth

Evaluations of Developmental Impact

Guadalupe A. Bacio

Ty Brumback

Sandra A. Brown

ADOLESCENT DEVELOPMENT: PROGRESSION TO INDEPENDENCE

Adolescence is a period of intense change and transition across nearly every life domain, from physical changes associated with the onset of puberty to corresponding social and emotional changes that coincide with increased independence from family of origin. Throughout this period of development, individuals are exposed to and must learn to function in new environments with increasing demands. The functional transition from dependent child to independent adult overarches this developmental epoch, and desynchronous maturation in underlying functional and physical domains exemplifies this progression. Simultaneous with the interrelated biological, cognitive, affective, and social changes are behavioral changes including the onset of alcohol and drug involvement. In mid- to late adolescence, hazardous drinking behaviors begin to emerge, culminating in the peak incidence rate of alcohol use disorders from 18 to 25 years old (Substance Abuse and Mental Health [SAMHSA], 2015). In an effort to understand the interrelationships of the various developmental processes occurring throughout adolescence and their effects on adolescent alcohol consumption and risk for problematic drinking, all aspects of functioning must be considered.

Biologically, adolescence is marked by the onset of and progression through puberty (Dorn, Dahl, Woodward, & Biro, 2006). Hormonal changes initiate a cascade of physical and neurobiological changes that alter the way adolescents behave and interact with others (Schulz, Molenda-Figueira, & Sisk, 2009; Spear, 2000). Specifically, the biological changes associated with puberty tend to orient motivational goals more toward social interaction highlighted by sensation seeking and intensification of peer influences (Forbes & Dahl, 2010). Thus, underlying biological changes serve as the basis for the dramatic shifts in functional roles and responsibilities of the adolescent's experience—from the development of physical and cognitive capabilities needed for assuming more adult roles to the establishment of personal values and identity.

The physical and behavioral manifestations of adolescent development reflect corresponding changes in neural substrates (Blakemore, Burnett, & Dahl, 2010; Forbes & Dahl, 2010). Globally, cortical gray matter tends to peak during adolescence followed by a steady decline that continues into adulthood (Giedd et al., 1999, 2009; Lenroot & Giedd, 2006), whereas white matter increases through adolescence and tends to level out in early adulthood (Giedd et al., 1999, 2009; Gogtay et al., 2004). More important than these gross global measures is the maturation of complementary networks governing cognition and behavior (Casey, 2015; Walhovd et al., 2015). The capacity for self-regulation and inhibitory control attributed to prefrontal brain regions begins to crystalize during adolescence, while at the same time subcortical and limbic regions associated with emotive processes such as reward seeking and motivated behavior mature more rapidly than prefrontal regions, resulting in an imbalance between the circuits (Casey, Jones, & Hare, 2008; Casey, Jones, & Somerville, 2011). Although the characterization of this imbalance (i.e., too much "gas pedal" and not enough "braking") as the driving force behind adolescent behavior is an oversimplification, the heuristic model underscores that the functional manifestations of adolescent development are likely attributable in part to the pace of maturation of underlying brain circuits governing self-regulation, leading adolescence to be a period of both "vulnerabilities and opportunities" (Dahl, 2004). That is, adolescent brain development is characterized by maximum plasticity as neural networks become more efficient through reductions in unnecessary connections and increases in the organization and integrity of neural pathways (Paus et al., 1999).

The changes taking place inside adolescents are only part of the complexity of this period because social and environmental factors evolve nearly as rapidly. Managing social, cognitive, and emotional changes during adolescence poses developmental challenges as youth begin to develop more flexible goals adapted for constantly changing environments and must learn to navigate competing desires (Blakemore & Choudhury, 2006; Choudhury, Blakemore, & Charman, 2006; Crone & Dahl, 2012). Self-regulation, or the ability to control and plan behaviors and to resist impulses that may put one at risk for negative consequences or may favor immediate over longer term rewards, is one of the primary skills developed during adolescence (Brown et al., 2008). Self-regulation of emotion and behavior matures during adolescence, but a propensity for risk-taking behavior exists in the meantime (Chein, Albert, O'Brien, Uckert, & Steinberg, 2011; Steinberg, 2007). Social and emotional engagement increase along with sensitivity to social cues, including rewards and peer responses, which may serve a developmental purpose in developing independence but also carry a very real risk as evidenced by the increase in psychopathology and preventable deaths that occurs among adolescents (Paus, Keshavan, &

Giedd, 2008). Perhaps not surprisingly, the incidence of mood and anxiety disorders also peaks during adolescence (Merikangas et al., 2010).

Characterizing the challenges of adolescence, in which cognitive and corporeal capacity begin to approach adult levels and may outpace the progression of self-regulation, requires researchers to take a multifactorial approach encompassing the full range of development. Only in the past two decades has research begun using large-scale longitudinal studies focused on risk and resilience for substance use problems in adolescents.

PATTERNS OF ADOLESCENT ALCOHOL USE

According to the two largest epidemiological studies of adolescent drinking behaviors—Monitoring the Future (Miech, Johnston, O'Malley, Bachman, & Schulenberg, 2015) and Youth Risk Behavior Surveillance (Kann et al., 2014)—alcohol use among adolescents has declined during the past decades, although it continues to be the substance of choice among youth. Findings from these large studies indicate that two-thirds of adolescents have tried alcohol by 12th grade. Similarly, approximately one-third of 10th graders and half of 12th graders report current (past month) alcohol use (Kann et al., 2014). Also, approximately 30% of 10th graders and 50% of 12th graders report that they drank to the point of intoxication at least once in their lifetime, whereas 11% of 10th graders and 24% of 12th graders endorsed having been drunk in the past month (Miech et al., 2015). Although heavy drinking (i.e., 5 or more drinks for boys and 4 or more drinks for girls) has declined since the 1970s, 13% of 10th graders and 19% of 12th graders endorsed engaging in heavy drinking at least once in the past 2 weeks in 2014 (Miech et al., 2015). Most alarming is the evidence of extreme binge drinking in the past month, wherein approximately 7.9% of 12th graders and 7.8% of 11th graders reported having 10 or more drinks in a row (Kann et al., 2014), and 4.1% of 12th graders endorsed drinking 15 or more drinks in a row (Miech et al., 2015).

Drinking behaviors among adolescents place youth at great risk for a number of alcohol-related consequences. Specifically, drinking behavior differs between adolescents aged 12–20 years, young adults aged 20–25 years, and adults aged 26 years or older. Whereas adolescents report drinking less days per month (5.5) than young adults (7.5) and adults (9.0), adolescents drink more drinks per episode (4.9) compared to young adults (4.0) and adults (2.6) (SAMHSA, 2013).

Gender differences in patterns of drinking begin to emerge in adolescence. Whereas in 8th grade there are little or no differences in patterns of use, by 12th grade male adolescents are more likely to get drunk and report more heavy drinking episodes compared to their female counterparts (Kann et al., 2014; Miech et al., 2015). For example, 12th-grade males report higher incidences of past month heavy drinking (22%) and having been drunk (33%) compared to females (17% and 24%, respectively). Similarly, males (8.0%) report a larger number of extreme binge drinking episodes—10 or more drinks in a row—compared to females (4.2%; Kann et al., 2014). Nevertheless, although the gender difference is consistent across drinking outcomes, the gap between females and males has continued to narrow during the past decades (Kann et al., 2014; Miech et al., 2015).

Differences in alcohol use by ethnic/racial background can also be observed throughout adolescence. Epidemiological studies (Kann et al., 2014; Miech et al., 2015) report the rates of use by the three largest race/ethnic groups in the United States, namely students of non-Hispanic White, African American, and Hispanic ethnicities. In general, African American youth report the lowest rates of use, and White teens exhibit the highest rates of use. Although drinking rates among Hispanic adolescents fall somewhere in between, their patterns of use are closer to those reported by White youth. These racial/ethnic differences tend to vary by age throughout adolescence. For example, according to data from Monitoring the Future (Johnston, O'Malley, Miech, Bachman, & Schulenberg, 2015), Hispanic youth report the highest prevalence of heavy drinking in the past 2 weeks (5.7%) compared to African American (4.4%) and White (4.2%) youth in 8th grade. However, by 12th grade, White youth report the highest prevalence of heavy drinking episodes (24%), followed by Hispanic (20%) and African American youth (11%). Similarly, by 12th grade, White youth (29%) report the highest rates of having been drunk in the past 30 days compared to Hispanic (20%) and African American (15%) teens (Johnston et al., 2015).

Although the prevalence of teen drinking seems to have been decreasing during the past few decades, it remains a major public health problem, due in part to the intensity patterns of youth drinking episodes. As illustrated by the unique patterns of alcohol use among youth described previously, the study of its etiology and the development of interventions should attend to their biopsychosocial developmental needs.

BRIEF OVERVIEW OF COGNITIVE AND PHYSIOLOGICAL RISK AND PROTECTIVE FACTORS

Among adolescents, alcohol outcome expectancies and valuations, drinking motives, and self-regulation processes have been identified as important cognitive determinants of alcohol use. Alcohol expectancies (AEs) are cognitions about the anticipated effects of drinking alcohol (Christiansen, Smith, Roehling, & Goldman, 1989) that can be identified even before drinking begins (Christiansen, Goldman, & Inn, 1982; Dunn & Goldman, 1998). Positive AEs precede earlier initiation of alcohol use, and they are associated with greater number of drinks consumed per drinking episode, higher frequency of drinking occasions, and higher frequency of getting drunk (Cranford, Zucker, Jester, Puttler, & Fitzgerald, 2010; Leigh & Stacy, 2004; Windle et al., 2008). Similarly, valuations of AEs refer to the perceived desirability or undesirability of these anticipated alcohol effects. Although the literature is less clear with respect to the specific associations between valuations and drinking outcomes, desirability of negative AEs has been associated with patterns of drinking (Bacio & Ray, 2016; Zamboanga et al., 2012).

Whereas AEs and associated valuations refer to possible drinking outcomes, drinking motives are a primary cognitive factor involved in adolescents' decision-making processes of whether or not to drink (Anderson, Grunwald, Bekman, Brown, & Grant, 2011; Cooper, 1994). Drinking motives include social facilitation, coping, and enhancement. In addition, the development of self-regulation plays an important role in youth's alcohol involvement because it is directly linked to adolescent drinking. Neurodevelopmental research suggests that the increase in risk behaviors observed in adolescence, including drinking alcohol, is the result of the protracted development of the prefrontal cortex and its connectivity with relatively more mature subcortical limbic areas (Casey et al., 2011; Galvan et al., 2006). That is, the observed increase in risky decision-making among adolescents is at least partially a function of the more slowly developing prefrontal cortex, reducing control over responses when making decisions in potentially rewarding environments (e.g., peer social settings).

Psychophysiological processes provide a unique window into cognitive and physical functioning of youth as well as, perhaps more important, the interaction and communication of brain and body systems in adolescence. For example, cognitive processes indexed by event-related potential (ERP) measures provide evidence of underlying biological development (Brumback, Arbel, Donchin, & Goldman, 2012). ERP measured responses to novel stimuli may be a unique indicator of risk for substance use and externalizing problems (Gilmore, Malone, & Iacono, 2010; Iacono & Malone, 2011) and serve as an endophenotype, reflecting heritable genetic risk (Salvatore, Gottesman, & Dick, 2015).

In addition to these psychophysiological indices of underlying risk, other measures of functioning of the nervous system also reflect self-regulatory responses. The autonomic nervous system feedback loop between the heart and brain, via efferent vagus and parasympathetic nerve signals to the heart and afferent baroreceptor signals to the brain, has been associated with self-regulation of emotional and behavioral systems (Allen, Matthews, & Kenyon, 2000; Segerstrom & Nes, 2007) and susceptibility to behavioral disorders of adolescence including alcohol problems (Beauchaine, 2012; Beauchaine, Gatzke-Kopp, & Mead, 2007).

CONSEQUENCES OF ALCOHOL USE ON THE ADOLESCENT BRAIN

Repeated or protracted exposure to high doses of alcohol, a phenotypic behavior of alcoholism, is associated with functional and structural brain changes (Pfefferbaum et al., 1992; Pfefferbaum, Sullivan, Mathalon, & Lim, 1997). Whereas some changes appear irrevocable, others exhibit recovery with sustained abstinence (Brumback et all., 2015; Crews et al., 2005). Much of the evidence for brain damage related to alcohol use, however, derives from studies of long-term use in adult populations and experimental animal studies. In adolescent populations, research has highlighted a number of differences between heavy alcohol users and non-using controls

in widespread structural features as well as in functional domains (Sullivan et al., 2016).

Several studies have highlighted volume differences in the limbic region, specifically the hippocampus, which is crucial to intact memory functioning and undergoes significant development in adolescence. Hippocampal volume tends to be smaller in adolescents who meet criteria for alcohol use disorders compared to non- or light-drinking controls, and among drinkers, earlier onset of alcohol use is associated with smaller volumes (De Bellis et al., 2000; Medina, Schweinsburg, Cohen-Zion, Nagel, & Tapert, 2007; Nagel, Schweinsburg, Phan, & Tapert, 2005). In laboratory adolescent animal studies, the structure and function of the hippocampus are particularly susceptible to alterations by alcohol administration (Spear & Swartzwelder, 2014).

Prefrontal cortex structures have also been shown to be affected in a dose-dependent manner in alcohol-abusing adolescents, such that more use is associated with lower volumes (De Bellis et al., 2005). Additional studies have highlighted gender differences in both volume and cortical thickness, with heavy drinking males exhibiting thinner cortices with greater volume and heavy drinking females exhibiting thicker cortices with less volume compared to same-sex healthy controls (Medina et al., 2008; Squeglia et al., 2012). These differential effects may reflect underlying differences in brain development trajectories and timing associated with pubertal development (Blakemore et al., 2010). In addition to gray matter structure, white matter integrity, which develops throughout adolescence and is associated with efficiency of communication between brain regions (Lebel et al., 2012), is lower in youth with a history of heavy substance use (Bava, Jacobus, Thayer, & Tapert, 2013; McQueeny et al., 2009). White matter integrity differences appear to persist over time and are associated with both behavioral and neurocognitive functioning (Jacobus, Squeglia, Bava, & Tapert, 2013; Jacobus, Thayer, et al., 2013).

Definitive dose and duration effects of alcohol on adolescent brain development and neurocognitive functioning have been difficult to disentangle and require more substantial longitudinal study. Recent results indicate that heavy drinking adolescents exhibit accelerated reductions in gray matter in frontal regions and attenuated white matter increases compared to non- and light-drinking controls (Squeglia et al., 2014, 2015). These studies are some of the first to examine the effects of onset heavy drinking in adolescents and highlight the need for large-scale longitudinal investigations with sufficient power to detect the neurotoxic effects of alcohol in adolescent brain and cognitive development.

The differences in brain macrostructure and microstructure between adolescents with and those without histories of alcohol use may underlie a number of differences in neurocognitive functioning observed in both cross-sectional and longitudinal studies of youth. Neuropsychological performance deficits in heavy drinking adolescents compared to their non-drinking peers appear across a number of domains, including memory (Brown, Tapert, Granholm, & Delis, 2000), language abilities, (Moss, Kirisci, Gordon, & Tarter, 1994), visuospatial functioning (Hanson, Medina, Padula, Tapert, & Brown, 2011; Sher, Martin, Wood, & Rutledge, 1997), attention and information processing (Tarter, Mezzich, Hsieh, & Parks, 1995), and executive functioning (Moss et al., 1994). Among adolescents who meet criteria for an alcohol use disorder, and those who have engaged in addiction treatment, neuropsychological performance deficits in visuospatial functioning and attention remain and are even exacerbated with continued use (Hanson, Cummins, Tapert, & Brown, 2011; Hanson et al., 2011; Tapert, Granholm, Leedy, & Brown, 2002). The neuropsychological performance deficits are pronounced in heavy drinking adolescents who meet criteria for alcohol disorders with or without concomitant drug use.

A number of cognitive differences have also been observed among school samples of youth with heavy episodic drinking prior to the onset of alcohol disorder. In functional magnetic resonance imaging (fMRI) studies, heavy drinking adolescents have exhibited increased activation in spatial working memory tasks despite similar behavioral task performance as that of non-drinkers (Tapert et al., 2004). Similar effects have been noted in a verbal encoding task, in which binge-drinking adolescents exhibited greater activation in frontal and parietal regions but less activation in occipital regions (Schweinsburg, McQueeny, Nagel, Eyler, & Tapert, 2010; Schweinsburg, Schweinsburg, Nagel, Eyler, & Tapert, 2011), possibly reflecting compensatory responses in binge drinkers to account for reduced activation in other brain regions because the activation differences are not reliably associated with decreases in performance of the tasks (Tapert, Brown, Baratta, & Brown, 2004).

Gender differences in brain structure in relation to alcohol exposure are also evident in neurocognitive and functional measures of brain activation. For example, in a spatial working memory task, female heavy drinkers exhibited less activation compared to female controls, and male drinkers exhibited greater response compared to male controls (Squeglia, Schweinsburg, Pulido, & Tapert, 2011). Gender differences are not surprising considering the differential developmental trajectories and timing for males and females, and they suggest that alcohol's effects depend on the developmental epoch in which alcohol is introduced (Windle et al., 2008; Zucker, Donovan, Masten, Mattson, & Moss, 2008).

Adolescence is a peak period of brain plasticity and may be able to overcome some forms of alcohol-induced brain damage (Hermens et al., 2013). To examine potential recovery from deficits, we studied neurocognitive performance during 4–6 weeks of monitored abstinence in heavy drinking adolescents. Results showed differences in prospective memory, cognitive switching, inhibition, and language and achievement that persisted across the period of abstinence, although abstinent heavy drinkers exhibited recovery on other domains (e.g., in the block design task; Winward, Hanson, Bekman, Tapert, & Brown, 2014). Adolescent heavy drinkers' responses to visual alcohol cues diminished and approached those of controls after 1 month of abstinence (Brumback et al., 2015). Thus, some neurocognitive differences exhibited by heavy drinking adolescents may normalize with abstinence, whereas others may persist or require more extended time for recovery.

NATIONAL CONSORTIUM ON ALCOHOL AND NEURODEVELOPMENT IN ADOLESCENCE

During the past three decades, tremendous strides have been made in research examining the effects of alcohol and other drugs on adolescent development, although central questions remain, including whether reported brain and behavioral abnormalities, and affective and neurocognitive deficits, predate the onset of alcohol use or result from alcohol consumption. In the future, the goal of research in this domain must be to disentangle risk factors for alcohol-related problems from sequelae of alcohol use. Large-scale longitudinal studies are essential to address these remaining questions. The National Consortium on Alcohol and NeuroDevelopment in Adolescence (NCANDA) was designed specifically to examine the developmental impact of alcohol and other drug use on adolescent neuroanatomy, neurocognition, and behavior (Brown et al., 2015). Specifically, the study will capture details of the effects of alcohol dose, duration, age of exposure, and other drug exposure on adolescent development.

NCANDA enrolled 830 adolescents and young adults, aged 12–21 years at baseline, across five sites constituting a sample that is representative of gender, racial, and ethnic patterns in the United States. We oversampled those aged 12–15 years and individuals who carry known risk factors for early alcohol problems (e.g., family history of alcoholism, externalizing disorders, and symptoms of low self-regulation) so that a large portion of the sample is tracked through critical periods of adolescent development and alcohol use initiation risk. We have utilized a multifaceted assessment protocol including clinical interviewing, neuropsychological testing, and structural and functional magnetic resonance brain imaging in an accelerated longitudinal design in which the majority of participants had no experience with alcohol at baseline. Participants and one parent are assessed annually, which provides a dense data set capturing changes in this developmentally sensitive age window, as well as contextual factors at multiple levels in which these changes occur for individuals (e.g., pubertal status and sleep patterns, family composition and socioeconomic status, and features of school and neighborhood) (Brown et al., 2015).

Developmental neuroscience suggests that the manifold influences on brain development in adolescence are reciprocally influenced by the environment to yield the cognitive, affective, and behavioral results portrayed in adolescence (Crone & Dahl, 2012; Dahl, 2004; Dorn et al., 2003; Smith, Chein, & Steinberg, 2013). The wide array of assessments in NCANDA will provide a comprehensive data set from which brain, cognitive, and affective markers of risk for and resilience to alcohol use and misuse as well as other psychopathology can be derived. At baseline, associations between known risk factors and covariates have been demonstrated for clinical factors (Brown et al., 2015), brain macro- and microstructure (Pfefferbaum et al., 2016), and neurocognitive functioning (Sullivan et al., 2016), establishing a promising base from which the continued longitudinal investigation of this sample will build.

APPLYING DEVELOPMENTAL NEUROSCIENCE OF ADDICTION TO EARLY INTERVENTIONS: PROJECT OPTIONS

Developmental Social Informational Processing Model

A remarkably small proportion of youth who experience alcohol-related problems actually receive formal treatment specific to their alcohol use. In fact, traditional treatments do not typically reach adolescents before they experience problems that bring them to the attention of authorities in the criminal justice system (Brown, 1993). In part, this is due to the negative social stereotypes surrounding traditional approaches to formal interventions (D'Amico et al., 2001; Tucker, 1995). Nevertheless, approximately 15–20% of heavy drinking adolescents stop or reduce their alcohol consumption without any formal services (Brown, 2001; Brown et al., 2005). Consequently, services that promote and enhance the change strategies commonly used by adolescent drinkers may be especially valuable in reducing drinking among youth and slowing progression to alcohol disorder.

Normative role or environmental transitions experienced during adolescence (e.g., getting a job, preparing/going to college, changes in peer groups, sports drug testing, and becoming a parent) may explain a portion of the reduction in alcohol involvement among youth. The environmental and socialization processes associated with these role transitions may impact youth decisions regarding frequency and quantity of alcohol consumption (Yamaguchi & Kandel, 1985). In addition, cognitive social learning processes (Bandura, 1986) as applied to adolescent alcohol use (Metrik, McCarthy, Frissell, MacPherson, & Brown, 2004; Smart & Stodutto, 1997) indicate that personal cessation and/or reduction efforts for alcohol use involve cognitive appraisal (i.e., perceived norms) and evaluation (e.g., cessation expectancies; Klingemann, 1991; Metrik et al., 2004). In addition, motivation has been identified as a key component in understanding drinking-related self-change efforts of youth (Bekman et al., 2011; Brown, 2001). Motivation to reduce or stop drinking alcohol among adolescent drinkers may be lower and qualitatively different from that of adults. Youth are more likely to perceive heavy levels of drinking as normal in their environment and the media, and they are less likely to have experienced severe medical or social consequences from drinking that often trigger adult change efforts (Brown et al., 2008). Consequently, purposeful attempts by adolescent drinkers to de-escalate their alcohol use require a perceived need for change (e.g., from external or intrapersonal factors) and may be facilitated by interventions that provide accurate use norms and normalize self-change or regulatory efforts among peers.

Our developmentally informed social information processing model (Brown, 2001; Brown et al., 2005) integrates this health promotion framework and empirical findings to postulate that cognitive appraisal and evaluation processes influence adolescent decisions of whether and how much to drink within a context (e.g., peer drinking) by considering distal factors (e.g., biological risks, cultural experiences, and family risk and resilience factors) with more proximal conditions (e.g., motivational and emotional state, peer use, and cognitive abilities). If individual resources are sufficient, a more automatic processing occurs (to use or not to use). However, if individual resources are limited (e.g., undeveloped executive functioning skills, low efficacy, and poor coping skills) or contextual or personal risks are high (e.g., repeated exposure and depression), then more intentional processing is needed (Brown et al., 2008). In addition, perceived immediate and/or long-term consequences (e.g., role expectations) are integrated into the social cognitions (e.g., expectancies) depending on the neurocognitive skills of each adolescent (e.g., prefrontal and frontal development). Thus, youth may use a variety of self-change strategies across social contexts when purposefully changing their drinking behavior (Brown et al., 2008).

According to our developmental social information processing model, primary and secondary interventions aimed at facilitating self-change efforts regarding alcohol and drug use may benefit from considering normative role and environmental transitions, changes in the level and type of motivation, and the impact of perceived drinking and cessation outcomes. Adolescent self-change efforts involve two phases: initial attempts to stop or reduce alcohol use, followed by efforts to maintain new behavioral responses (Brown et al., 2001; see Figure 11.1 for an illustration). That is, the developmental factors necessary for initial attempts to de-escalate use (i.e.,

coping skills, motivation, and immediate contingencies) are different from the skills required to maintain these behavioral changes (e.g., self-monitoring skills, emotional self-regulation, and available alternative reinforcers).

Application to Intervention Design

Based on our developmentally informed social information model (see Figure 11.1), we designed and tested an intervention for adolescents with the aim to facilitate their self-change efforts in reducing and/or stopping their alcohol use (i.e., Project Options). For most youth with adequate behavioral skills and resources, attention to and motivation for alcohol change should be sufficient to produce youth self-change efforts. Because the majority of heavy episodic drinking youth reduce drinking without intervention, it is assumed that youth change efforts can be successful in eliminating alcohol use, hazardous pattern of alcohol use, and associated problems (Brown, 2001; Brown et al., 2005).

To enhance personal decision-making, Project Options was designed as a voluntary, high school-based intervention. First developed in the San Diego metropolitan area in schools that serve an ethnically and socioeconomically diverse student body (Brown et al., 2005), the intervention focuses primarily on issues identified as important by adolescents (e.g., peer relations and conflicts with parents). Barriers and facilitators to engagement were assessed through surveys and focus groups conducted at all schools, and they were incorporated into the design of the intervention for two primary reasons: (1) Adolescents develop a sense of ownership and receptivity to the intervention by integrating their ideas, and (2) not addressing these factors may result in reduced voluntary engagement in this intervention.

Adolescents identified concerns regarding confidentiality as a primary barrier to participation in alcohol-focused discussion opportunities. Consequently, parental consent is obtained at the onset of each school year for students to potentially participate, but parents are not informed of youth's choice to participate during the year. Intervention facilitators are not associated with the school (e.g., from local schools or colleges). In addition, given that adolescents identified confidentiality as key for self-disclosure, confidentiality is also discussed as an important issue in building trusting relationships. At

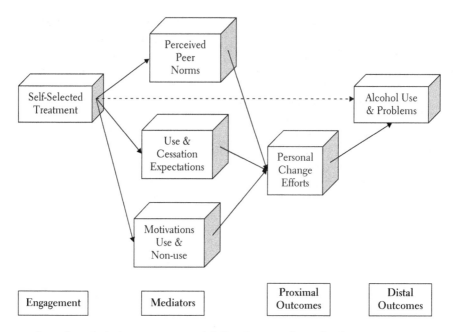

FIGURE 11.1   Secondary alcohol intervention model: Developmental social information processing.

the beginning of each session, the group commits to maintaining confidentiality within the limitations of California law. Intervention content and activities were designed to engage youth in a developmentally and gender-appropriate manner. Importantly, the intervention maximizes access by offering sessions during lunch periods so as to not interfere with instructional time or after-school activities.

The intervention covers distinctive content in the following six different sessions in which participants can rotate in and out at any point (Brown et al., 2005):

1. Norms: Prevalence of alcohol use and causes for overestimation
2. Expectancies and motives: Myths and positive expectancies of alcohol use
3. Self-regulation: Managing stress and temptation without drinking alcohol
4. Building appraisal and evaluation perspective: Evaluating personal effects of alcohol and weighting the advantages and disadvantages of change
5. Building positive lifestyle: Alternative activities/reinforces and how to accomplish these without drinking
6. Self-efficacy and coping: Enhancing skills and resources through social communication

Although a different topic is covered in each session, each contact is intended to (1) motivate participants to evaluate their drinking, (2) provide information about successful self-regulatory and change efforts used by students at their school, and (3) engage and reward participants for attendance. To do so, facilitators use motivational interviewing techniques throughout the intervention. Specifically, a nonconfrontational style is used to respond to information shared by each participant and in turn to discuss common problems among and positive solutions used by peers.

Participants are rewarded for their participation by selecting a small gift card for music, food, clothing, or recreation establishments. They receive these incentives upon completing a questionnaire that assesses their alcohol and drug use, perceived norms, and change efforts at intake and 4 and 12 weeks after their first visit. In addition, during each session, adolescents receive a snack in compliance with state standards for healthy school lunches. Participants also complete a session-specific form after each meeting that provides ratings of the session content, facilitators, and meeting style.

Before implementing the intervention, site tailoring is conducted. First, a youth advisory council representing students from all grades and all schools is formed to refine language and examples used in the intervention (i.e., local language, style, etc.) and generate suggestions for intervention advertisement/promotion. Second, organizational leaders (principals, vice principals, counselors, and key teachers) meet to establish a working alliance, review logistical details, and develop strategies to implement the intervention successfully at each school. Third, each school sends a packet with pertinent information along with consent forms in languages commonly used by parents to each student's home. Presentations at school meetings geared to parents (e.g., parent–teacher–student association and back-to-school night) and focus groups of the protocols and materials provide final feedback for the protocol. Intervention advertisements are tailored to each school and include websites, posters, auditory school announcements, and announcements in student papers.

Project Options: Efficacy Trials

Two efficacy trials of Project Options have been conducted to ascertain adolescent format preferences, assess level of voluntary engagement, and examine intervention proximal and distal outcomes. Project Options was first developed to be delivered in three formats: group sessions, individual discussions, and an interactive website. Offering multiple formats was intended to maximize choice and autonomy of each adolescent. The content of the intervention and incentive options were the same across formats. In addition, the website was available to all participants outside of intervention time. All participants in all formats completed the session rating forms as well as the intake and 4- and 12-week questionnaires. The first trial examined youth voluntary self-selection into Project Options, and the second trial compared self-selection of format type to random assignment to a specific format. Not surprisingly, youth who self-selected their format were more likely to return to treatment and report more satisfaction. Project Options was shown to engage 8–12% of students across schools (D'Amico, McCarthy, Metrik, & Brown, 2004) and attract culturally diverse and high-frequency drinkers (Brown et al., 2005). Findings were in the predicted direction: The intervention was associated with self-change efforts, and heavy drinkers were twice as likely to report quit attempts compared to heavy drinking nonparticipants (Brown et al., 2005). Heavy drinking participants were also shown

to significantly reduce alcohol-related problems. On average, Project Options participants rated the intervention as highly satisfactory regardless of level of drinking experience (Kia-Keating, Brown, Schulte, & Monreal, 2009), and participants in the group and individual formats rated the intervention as more satisfactory compared to participants in the website format (Kia-Keating et al., 2009). Compared to the individual and website formats, the group format was more frequently selected by participants (Brown et al., 2005; D'Amico et al., 2006). Finally, reduction in youth consumption was related to hypothesized mediators (e.g., perceptions of peer use) (Schulte, Monreal, Kia-Keating, & Brown, 2010).

Project Options Multisite Clinical Trial: What Group Process Methods Contribute to Change?

The demonstrated efficacy of Project Options in urban and suburban high schools in San Diego led to the current multisite efficacy/effectiveness clinical trial. Project Options is currently being tested in Miami, Florida (principal investigator [PI]: Erik Wagner); Minneapolis, Minnesota (PI: Ken Winters); and Portland, Oregon (PI: Kristen Anderson). This trial compares the group format of Project Options intervention protocol to an educational format of information delivery. Each site tailored language and examples of the intervention to its school context. Although the intervention content remained the same, feedback was used to update advertisement strategies and incentive options.

The aims of this trial include examining whether and how the motivational interviewing approach facilitates self-change de-escalation efforts among participants by testing the protocol against standard educational intervention approach. Similarly, new method-specific measures will help us identify whether core motivational enhancement processes (i.e., change talk) and group characteristics (e.g., size, gender, and ethnic composition) can predict intervention outcomes. In addition, this trial will allow us to test the purported mechanisms of change proposed by our developmental social cognitive learning model (see Figure 11.1). Importantly, given the sociodemographic diversity of schools at the three sites, this trial will provide rich data to explore how this voluntary school-based intervention not tailored to any specific racial/ethnic group can meet the needs of increasingly diverse student bodies.

Preliminary intervention mechanisms of change data have allowed us to begin to validate the measures developed to examine motivational enhancement processes and explore therapeutic processes. A new measure was developed for independent coders who observe the sessions to code group verbalization and facilitator behavior. Preliminary findings suggest that change talk can be reliably coded via live observation (Ladd, Tomlinson, Myers, & Anderson, 2016). In addition, change talk was associated with participants drinking behavior such that a lower percentage of group-level lifetime alcohol use predicted a greater percentage of "healthy" (reduction/stop-oriented) talk (Ladd et al., 2016). Furthermore, a group actor–partner interdependence model framework (Kenny & Garcia, 2012) was used to examine gender-specific group processes. Results indicated that when groups included girls, both girls and boys reported increased satisfaction as well as satisfaction with and engagement in the group (Garcia, Bacio, Tomlinson, Ladd, & Anderson, 2015). Importantly, group composition (e.g., number of participants and ethnicity/cultural background) was not related to change talk.

CRITICAL QUESTIONS FOR FUTURE STUDY

The future of research on the effects of alcohol and drug use on adolescent development and function is exciting in that significant breakthroughs in understanding causal influences and, in turn, personalized prevention and intervention strategies appear within reach in the coming decades. The belief is that more precise, real-world data collection techniques and superior data sets encompassing a wider array of assessment domains will enable the identification of personal risk and resilience factors that may be time locked to specific developmental epochs. The first step in this process is underway with the collection of large longitudinal studies, such as NCANDA, that utilize multisystem measurement and will form the building blocks of discoveries to come.

As with many of the advances in recent decades, technological advances are a driving force behind the optimism. A multitude of wearable sensors for monitoring behavior, biological systems, and the external environment are already available at the consumer level and can easily be integrated into data collection (Miller, 2012). As these technologies continue to evolve, they will become easier to use, less obtrusive,

less costly, and will provide useful, real-time information (Kim et al., 2011). For example, real-time monitoring of actual timing, content, and level of alcohol consumption using unobtrusive sensors is a realistic vision for replacing self-reported dose and duration of alcohol use in a similar way that glucose or pH levels of skin can be unobtrusively monitored (Bandodkar et al., 2014; Guinovart, Valdés-Ramírez, Windmiller, Andrade, & Wang, 2014). Furthermore, utilizing such passive measurement technology will open the door for real-time prevention and interventions focused on minimizing harm or promoting healthier alternatives (Rahman et al., 2014; Sarker et al., 2014; Vodopivec-Jamsek, de Jongh, Gurol-Urganci, Atun, & Car, 2012). These technologies offer exciting opportunities for data collection, real-time risk prevention, and time-sensitive intervention while simultaneously presenting new challenges in the form of massive data sets.

Collecting and analyzing dense cross-system data sets requires new techniques for data mining and interpretation (Murphy, 2013). Neuroscience has begun to integrate and analyze massive data sets through such efforts as the Human Connectome Project (https://www.neuroscienceblueprint.nih.gov/connectome), and addiction science and psychological science more broadly will need a similar collaborative approach focused on understanding risk and resilience for disorders. However, unlike contemporary projects, we must seek to integrate multiple levels of analysis from the genetic and cellular to the familial and social environment across the developmental trajectory to undercover more specific markers and transition points. In 2015, the National Institutes of Health initiated an ambitious project, the Adolescent Brain Cognitive Development (ABCD) study, which will be the largest study of the effects of drugs on adolescent development (https://addictionresearch.nih.gov/adolescent-brain-cognitive-development-study). This project will study 10,000 children, ages 9 or 10 years, nationwide and follow them for 10 years with neuroimaging, genetic testing, clinical interviewing, and neurocognitive assessments. Similar to the NCANDA project, this endeavor will yield a massive amount of data that can be exploited to move developmental addiction science closer to the goal of understanding risk and resilience factors in order to minimize the acute and long-term harm of alcohol and other drugs in adolescence.

Similarly, finding new and efficient ways to fast track the implementation of prevention and intervention efforts will be crucial in addressing harmful alcohol use among youth. Incorporating new technologies into implementation efforts will indeed create opportunities, from increasing the reach to more youth as they begin using alcohol to improving the monitoring of outcomes. Nevertheless, as the field undertakes this challenge, it will also be critical to address the closing gender gap in alcohol use patterns. In addition, given that ethnic differences in patterns of use begin to emerge during adolescence, researchers must take into consideration the increasing ethnic/racial diversity of youth into research design and implementation efforts.

During the past several decades, advances in understanding and addressing alcohol use patterns among adolescents reflect transformations in behavioral, biomedical, and data analytic technologies. Going forward, re-envisioning prevention and treatment of youth alcohol problems in terms of personalized, real-time prevention and interventions may allow our understanding and efforts to develop as quickly as adolescents develop.

REFERENCES

Allen, M. T., Matthews, K. A., & Kenyon, K. L. (2000). The relationships of resting baroreflex sensitivity, heart rate variability and measures of impulse control in children and adolescents. *International Journal of Psychophysiology*, 37(2), 185–194. doi:10.1016/S0167-8760(00)00089-1

Anderson, K. G., Grunwald, I., Bekman, N., Brown, S. A., & Grant, A. (2011). To drink or not to drink: Motives and expectancies for use and nonuse in adolescence. *Addictive Behaviors*, 36, 972–979.

Bacio, G. A., & Ray, L. A. (2016). Patterns of drinking initiation among Latino youth: Cognitive and contextual explanations of the immigrant paradox. *Journal of Child and Adolescent Substance Abuse*, 25(6), 546–556.

Bandodkar, A. J., Molinnus, D., Mirza, O., Guinovart, T., Windmiller, J. R., Valdés-Ramírez, G., . . . Wang, J. (2014). Epidermal tattoo potentiometric sodium sensors with wireless signal transduction for continuous non-invasive sweat monitoring. *Biosensors and Bioelectronics*, 54, 603–609. doi:10.1016/j.bios.2013.11.039

Bandura, A. (1986). *Social foundations of thought and action: A social cognitive theory*. Englewood Cliffs, NJ: Prentice-Hall.

Bava, S., Jacobus, J., Thayer, R. E., & Tapert, S. F. (2013). Longitudinal changes in white matter integrity among adolescent substance users. *Alcoholism: Clinical and Experimental Research*, 37(Suppl. 1), E181–E189. doi:10.1111/j.1530-0277.2012.01920.x

Beauchaine, T. P. (2012). Physiological markers of emotion and behavioral dysregulation in externalizing psychopathology. *Monographs of the Society for Research in Child Development*, 77(2), 79–86. doi:10.1111/j.1540-5834.2011.00665.x

Beauchaine, T. P., Gatzke-Kopp, L., & Mead, H. K. (2007). Polyvagal theory and developmental psychopathology: Emotion dysregulation and conduct problems from preschool to adolescence. *Biological Psychology*, 74(2), 174–184. doi:10.1016/j.biopsycho.2005.08.008

Bekman, N. M., Anderson, K. G., Metrik, J., Diulio, A. R., Trim, R. S., Myers, M. G., & Brown, S. A. (2011). Thinking and drinking: Alcohol-related cognitions across stages of adolescent alcohol involvement. *Psychology of Addictive Behaviors*, 25(3), 415–425.

Blakemore, S. J., Burnett, S., & Dahl, R. E. (2010). The role of puberty in the developing adolescent brain. *Human Brain Mapping*, 31(6), 926–933. doi:10.1002/hbm.21052

Blakemore, S. J., & Choudhury, S. (2006). Development of the adolescent brain: Implications for executive function and social cognition. *Journal of Child Psychology and Psychiatry*, 47(3–4), 296–312. doi:10.1111/j.1469-7610.2006.01611.x

Brown, S. A. (1993). Recovery patterns in adolescent substance abuse. In J. R. Baer, G. A. Marlatt, & R. J. McMahan (Eds.), *Addictive behaviors across the lifespan: Prevention, treatment, and policy issues*. Beverly Hills, CA: Sage.

Brown, S. A. (2001). Facilitating change for adolescent alcohol problems: A multiple options approach. In E. F. Wagner & H. B. Waldron (Eds.), *Innovations in adolescent substance abuse interventions* (pp. 169–187). Amsterdam, the Netherlands: Pergamon/ Elsevier.

Brown, S. A., Anderson, K., Schulte, M. T., Sintov, N. D., & Frissell, K. C. (2005). Facilitating youth self-change through school-based intervention. *Addictive Behaviors*, 30, 1797–1810.

Brown, S. A., Brumback, T., Tomlinson, K., Cummins, K., Thompson, W. K., Nagel, B. J., . . . Tapert, S. F. (2015). The National Consortium on Alcohol and NeuroDevelopment in Adolescence (NCANDA): A multisite study of adolescent development and substance use. *Journal of Studies on Alcohol and Drugs*, 76(6), 895–908. doi:10.15288/jsad.2015.76.895

Brown, S. A., McGue, M., Maggs, J., Schulenberg, J., Hingson, R., Swartzwelder, S., . . . Murphy, S. (2008). A developmental perspective on alcohol and youths 16 to 20 years of age. *Pediatrics*, *121*(Suppl. 4), S290–S310. doi:10.1542/peds.2007-2243D

Brown, S. A., Tapert, S. F., Granholm, E., & Delis, D. C. (2000). Neurocognitive functioning of adolescents: Effects of protracted alcohol use. *Alcoholism: Clinical and Experimental Research*, *24*(2), 164–171. doi:10.1111/j.1530-0277.2000.tb04586.x

Brumback, T., Arbel, Y., Donchin, E., & Goldman, M. S. (2012). Efficiency of responding to unexpected information varies with sex, age, and pubertal development in early adolescence. *Psychophysiology*, *49*(10), 1330–1339. doi:10.1111/j.1469-8986.2012.01444.x

Brumback, T., Squeglia, L. M., Jacobus, J., Pulido, C., Tapert, S. F., & Brown, S. A. (2015). Adolescent heavy drinkers' amplified brain responses to alcohol cues decrease over one month of abstinence. *Addictive Behaviors*, *46*, 45–52. doi:10.1016/j.addbeh.2015.03.001

Casey, B. J. (2015). Beyond simple models of self-control to circuit-based accounts of adolescent behavior. *Annual Review of Psychology*, *66*(1), 295–319. doi:10.1146/annurev-psych-010814-015156

Casey, B. J., Jones, R. M., & Hare, T. A. (2008). The adolescent brain. *Annals of the New York Academy of Sciences*, *1124*(1), 111–126. doi:10.1196/annals.1440.010

Casey, B. J., Jones, R. M., & Somerville, L. H. (2011). Breaking and accelerating of the adolescent brain. *Journal of Research on Adolescence*, *21*(1), 21–33. doi:10.1111/j.1532-7795.2010.00712.x

Chein, J., Albert, D., O'Brien, L., Uckert, K., & Steinberg, L. (2011). Peers increase adolescent risk taking by enhancing activity in the brain's reward circuitry. *Developmental Science*, *14*(2), F1–F10. doi:10.1111/j.1467-7687.2010.01035.x

Choudhury, S., Blakemore, S. J., & Charman, T. (2006). Social cognitive development during adolescence. *Social Cognitive and Affective Neuroscience*, *1*(3), 165–174. doi:10.1093/scan/nsl024

Christiansen, B. A., Goldman, M. S., & Inn, A. (1982). Development of alcohol-related expectancies in adolescents: Separating pharmacological from social-learning influences. *Journal of Consulting and Clinical Psychology*, *50*(3), 336–344. Retrieved from http://www.ncbi.nlm.nih.gov/pubmed/7096736

Christiansen, B. A., Smith, G. T., Roehling, P. V., & Goldman, M. S. (1989). Using alcohol expectancies

to predict adolescent drinking behavior after one year. *Journal of Consulting and Clinical Psychology*, *57*(1), 93–99. Retrieved from http://www.ncbi.nlm.nih.gov/pubmed/2925979

Cooper, M. L. (1994). Motivations for alcohol use among adolescents: Development and validation of a four-factor model. *Psychological Assessment*, *6*(2), 117–128.

Cranford, J. A., Zucker, R. A., Jester, J. M., Puttler, L. I., & Fitzgerald, H. E. (2010). Parental alcohol involvement and adolescent alcohol expectancies predict alcohol involvement in male adolescents. *Psychology of Addictive Behaviors*, *24*(3), 386–396. Retrieved from http://www.ncbi.nlm.nih.gov/pubmed/20853923

Crews, F. T., Buckley, T., Dodd, P. R., Ende, G., Foley, N., Harper, C., . . . Sullivan, E. V. (2005). Alcoholic neurobiology: Changes in dependence and recovery. *Alcoholism: Clinical and Experimental Research*, *29*(8), 1504–1513. doi:10.1097/01.alc.0000175013.50644.61

Crone, E. A., & Dahl, R. E. (2012). Understanding adolescence as a period of social-affective engagement and goal flexibility. *Nature Reviews: Neuroscience*, *13*(9), 636–650. doi:10.1038/nrn3313

D'Amico, E. J., Anderson, K. G., Metric, J., Frissell, K. C., Ellingstad, T., & Brown, S. A. (2006). Adolescent self-selection of service formats: Implications for secondary interventions targeting alcohol use. *American Journal on Addictions*, *15*, 58–66.

D'Amico, E. J., McCarthy, D. M., Metrik, J., & Brown, S. A. (2004). Alcohol-related services: Prevention, secondary intervention, and treatment preferences of adolescents. *Journal of Child and Adolescent Substance Abuse*, *14*(2), 61–80.

D'Amico, E. J., Metrik, J., McCarthy, D. M., Appelbaum, M., Frissell, K. C., & Brown, S. A. (2001). Progression into and out of binge drinking among high school students. *Psychology of Addictive Behavior*, *15*(4), 341–349.

Dahl, R. E. (2004). Adolescent brain development: A period of vulnerabilities and opportunities. *Annals of the New York Academy of Sciences*, *1021*(1), 1–22. doi:10.1196/annals.1308.001

De Bellis, M. D., Clark, D. B., Beers, S. R., Soloff, P. H., Boring, A. M., Hall, J., . . . Keshavan, M. S. (2000). Hippocampal volume in adolescent-onset alcohol use disorders. *American Journal of Psychiatry*, *157*(5), 737–744. doi:10.1176/appi.ajp.157.5.737

De Bellis, M. D., Narasimhan, A., Thatcher, D. L., Keshavan, M. S., Soloff, P., & Clark, D. B. (2005). Prefrontal cortex, thalamus, and cerebellar volumes in adolescents and young adults with adolescent-onset alcohol use disorders and comorbid mental disorders. *Alcoholism: Clinical and Experimental Research*, 29(9), 1590–1600. doi:10.1097/01.alc.0000179368.87886.76

Dorn, L. D., Dahl, R. E., Williamson, D. E., Birmaher, B., Axelson, D., Perel, J., . . . Ryan, N. D. (2003). Developmental markers in adolescence: Implications for studies of pubertal processes. *Journal of Youth and Adolescence*, 32(5), 315–324. doi:10.1023/a:1024945113763

Dorn, L. D., Dahl, R. E., Woodward, H. R., & Biro, F. (2006). Defining the boundaries of early adolescence: A user's guide to assessing pubertal status and pubertal timing in research with adolescents. *Applied Developmental Science*, 10(1), 30–56. doi:10.1207/s1532480xads1001_3

Dunn, M. E., & Goldman, M. S. (1998). Age and drinking-related differences in the memory organization of alcohol expectancies in 3rd-, 6th-, 9th-, and 12th-grade children. *Journal of Consulting and Clinical Psychology*, 66(3), 579–585. Retrieved from http://www.ncbi.nlm.nih.gov/pubmed/9642899

Forbes, E. E., & Dahl, R. E. (2010). Pubertal development and behavior: Hormonal activation of social and motivational tendencies. *Brain and Cognition*, 72(1), 66–72. doi:10.1016/j.bandc.2009.10.007

Galvan, A., Hare, T. A., Parra, C. E., Penn, J., Voss, H., Glover, G., & Casey, B. J. (2006). Earlier development of the accumbens relative to orbitofrontal cortex might underlie risk-taking behavior in adolescents. *Journal of Neuroscience*, 26(25), 6885–6892.

Garcia, T. A., Bacio, G. A., Tomlinson, K., Ladd, B. O., & Anderson, K. G. (2015). Effects of sex composition on group processes in alcohol prevention groups for teens. *Experimental and Clinical Psychopharmacology*, 4, 275–283.

Giedd, J. N., Blumenthal, J., Jeffries, N. O., Castellanos, F. X., Liu, H., Zijdenbos, A., . . . Rapoport, J. L. (1999). Brain development during childhood and adolescence: A longitudinal MRI study. *Nature Neuroscience*, 2(10), 861–863. doi:10.1038/13158

Giedd, J. N., Lalonde, F. M., Celano, M. J., White, S. L., Wallace, G. L., Lee, N. R., & Lenroot, R. K. (2009). Anatomical brain magnetic resonance imaging of typically developing children and adolescents. *Journal of the American Academy of Child and Adolescent Psychiatry*, 48(5), 465–470. doi:10.1097/CHI.0b013e31819f2715

Gilmore, C., Malone, S., & Iacono, W. (2010). Brain electrophysiological endophenotypes for externalizing psychopathology: A multivariate approach. *Behavior Genetics*, 40(2), 186–200.

Gogtay, N., Giedd, J. N., Lusk, L., Hayashi, K. M., Greenstein, D., Vaituzis, A. C., . . . Thompson, P. M. (2004). Dynamic mapping of human cortical development during childhood through early adulthood. *Proceedings of the National Academy of Sciences of the USA*, 101(21), 8174–8179. doi:10.1073/pnas.0402680101

Guinovart, T., Valdés-Ramírez, G., Windmiller, J. R., Andrade, F. J., & Wang, J. (2014). Bandage-based wearable potentiometric sensor for monitoring wound pH. *Electroanalysis*, 26(6), 1345–1353. doi:10.1002/elan.201300558

Hanson, K. L., Cummins, K., Tapert, S. F., & Brown, S. A. (2011). Changes in neuropsychological functioning over 10 years following adolescent substance abuse treatment. *Psychology of Addictive Behavior*, 25(1), 127–142. doi:10.1037/a0022350

Hanson, K. L., Medina, K. L., Padula, C. B., Tapert, S. F., & Brown, S. A. (2011). Impact of adolescent alcohol and drug use on neuropsychological functioning in young adulthood: 10-Year outcomes. *Journal of Child and Adolescent Substance Abuse*, 20(2), 135–154. doi:10.1080/1067828X.2011.555272

Hermens, D. F., Lagopoulos, J., Tobias-Webb, J., De Regt, T., Dore, G., Juckes, L., . . . Hickie, I. B. (2013). Pathways to alcohol-induced brain impairment in young people: A review. *Cortex*, 49(1), 3–17. doi:10.1016/j.cortex.2012.05.021

Iacono, W. G., & Malone, S. M. (2011). Developmental endophenotypes: Indexing genetic risk for substance abuse with the P300 brain event-related potential. *Child Development Perspectives*, 5(4), 239–247. doi:10.1111/j.1750-8606.2011.00205.x

Jacobus, J., Squeglia, L. M., Bava, S., & Tapert, S. F. (2013). White matter characterization of adolescent binge drinking with and without co-occurring marijuana use: A 3-year investigation. *Psychiatry Research: Neuroimaging*, 214(3), 374–381. doi:http://dx.doi.org/10.1016/j.pscychresns.2013.07.014

Jacobus, J., Thayer, R. E., Trim, R. S., Bava, S., Frank, L. R., & Tapert, S. F. (2013). White matter integrity, substance use, and risk taking in adolescence. *Psychology of Addictive Behaviors*, 27(2), 431–442. doi:http://dx.doi.org/10.1037/a0028235

Johnston, L. D., O'Malley, P. M., Miech, R. A., Bachman, J. G., & Schulenberg, J. E. (2015). *Demographic subgroup trends among adolescents in the use of various licit and illicit drugs, 1975–2014* (Monitoring the Future Occasional Paper No. 83). Ann Arbor, MI: Institute for Social Research, University of Michigan.

Kann, L., Kinchen, S., Shanklin, S., Flint, K. H., Hawkins, J., Harris, W. A., . . . Zaza, S. (2014). *Youth risk behavior surveillance—United States, 2013*. Atlanta, GA: Center for Surveillance,

Epidemiology, and Laboratory Services, Centers for Disease Control and Prevention, US Department of Health and Human Services.

Kenny, D. A., & Garcia, R. L. (2012). Using the actor–partner interdependence model to study the effects of group composition. *Small Group Research*, 43, 468–496.

Kia-Keating, M., Brown, S. A., Schulte, M. T., & Monreal, T. K. (2009). Adolescent satisfaction with brief motivational enhancement for alcohol abuse. *Journal of Behavioral Health Services & Research*, 36(3), 385–395. doi:http://doi.org/10.1007/s11414-008-9127-1

Kim, D.-H., Lu, N., Ma, R., Kim, Y.-S., Kim, R.-H., Wang, S., . . . Rogers, J. A. (2011). Epidermal electronics. *Science*, 333(6044), 838–843. doi:10.1126/science.1206157

Klingemann, H. K. (1991). The motivation for change from problem alcohol and heroin use. *British Journal of Addiction*, 86, 727–744.

Ladd, B. O., Tomlinson, K., Myers, M. G., & Anderson, K. G. (2016). Feasibility and reliability of a coding system to capture in-session group behavior in adolescents. *Prevention Science*, 17, 92–101.

Lebel, C., Gee, M., Camicioli, R., Wieler, M., Martin, W., & Beaulieu, C. (2012). Diffusion tensor imaging of white matter tract evolution over the lifespan. *Neuroimage*, 60(1), 340–352. doi:10.1016/j.neuroimage.2011.11.094

Leigh, B. C., & Stacy, A. W. (2004). Alcohol expectancies and drinking in different age groups. *Addiction*, 99(2), 215–227. Retrieved from http://dx.doi.org/10.1111/j.1360-0443.2003.00641.x

Lenroot, R. K., & Giedd, J. N. (2006). Brain development in children and adolescents: Insights from anatomical magnetic resonance imaging. *Neuroscience & Biobehavioral Reviews*, 30(6), 718–729. doi:10.1016/j.neubiorev.2006.06.001

McQueeny, T., Schweinsburg, B. C., Schweinsburg, A. D., Jacobus, J., Bava, S., Frank, L. R., & Tapert, S. F. (2009). Altered white matter integrity in adolescent binge drinkers. *Alcoholism: Clinical and Experimental Research*, 33(7), 1278–1285. doi:10.1111/j.1530-0277.2009.00953.x

Medina, K. L., McQueeny, T., Nagel, B. J., Hanson, K. L., Schweinsburg, A. D., & Tapert, S. F. (2008). Prefrontal cortex volumes in adolescents with alcohol use disorders: Unique gender effects. *Alcoholism: Clinical and Experimental Research*, 32(3), 386–394. doi:10.1111/j.1530-0277.2007.00602.x

Medina, K. L., Schweinsburg, A. D., Cohen-Zion, M., Nagel, B. J., & Tapert, S. F. (2007). Effects of alcohol and combined marijuana and alcohol use

during adolescence on hippocampal volume and asymmetry. *Neurotoxicology and Teratology*, 29(1), 141–152. doi:10.1016/j.ntt.2006.10.010

Merikangas, K. R., He, J.-p., Burstein, M., Swanson, S. A., Avenevoli, S., Cui, L., . . . Swendsen, J. (2010). Lifetime prevalence of mental disorders in U.S. adolescents: Results from the National Comorbidity Survey Replication–Adolescent Supplement (NCS-A). *Journal of the American Academy of Child & Adolescent Psychiatry*, 49(10), 980–989. doi:10.1016/j.jaac.2010.05.017

Metrik, J., McCarthy, D. M., Frissell, K. C., MacPherson, L., & Brown, S. A. (2004). Adolescent alcohol reduction and cessation expectancies. *Journal of Studies on Alcohol*, 65(2), 217–226.

Miech, R. A., Johnston, L. D., O'Malley, P. M., Bachman, J. G., & Schulenberg, J. E. (2015). *Monitoring the Future national survey results on drug use, 1975–2014: Volume I. Secondary school students*. Ann Arbor, MI: Institute for Social Research, University of Michigan.

Miller, G. (2012). The smartphone psychology manifesto. *Perspectives on Psychological Science*, 7(3), 221–237. doi:10.1177/1745691612441215

Moss, H. B., Kirisci, L., Gordon, H. W., & Tarter, R. E. (1994). A neuropsychologic profile of adolescent alcoholics. *Alcoholism: Clinical and Experimental Research*, 18(1), 159–163. doi:10.1111/j.1530-0277.1994.tb00897.x

Murphy, K. (2013). *From big data to big knowledge*. Paper presented at the Proceedings of the 22nd ACM International Conference on Information & Knowledge Management, San Francisco, CA.

Nagel, B. J., Schweinsburg, A. D., Phan, V., & Tapert, S. F. (2005). Reduced hippocampal volume among adolescents with alcohol use disorders without psychiatric comorbidity. *Psychiatry Research: Neuroimaging*, 139(3), 181–190. doi:10.1016/j.pscychresns.2005.05.008

Paus, T., Keshavan, M., & Giedd, J. N. (2008). Why do many psychiatric disorders emerge during adolescence? *Nature Reviews Neuroscience*, 9(12), 947–957. doi:10.1038/nrn2513

Paus, T., Zijdenbos, A., Worsley, K., Collins, D. L., Blumenthal, J., Giedd, J. N., . . . Evans, A. C. (1999). Structural maturation of neural pathways in children and adolescents: In vivo study. *Science*, 283(5409), 1908–1911. doi:10.1126/science.283.5409.1908

Pfefferbaum, A., Lim, K. O., Zipursky, R. B., Mathalon, D. H., Rosenbloom, M. J., Lane, B., . . . Sullivan, E. V. (1992). Brain gray and white matter volume loss accelerates with aging in chronic alcoholics: A quantitative MRI study. *Alcoholism: Clinical and Experimental Research*, 16(6), 1078–1089.

Pfefferbaum, A., Rohlfing, T., Pohl, K. M., Lane, B., Chu, W., Kwon, D., . . . Sullivan, E. V. (2016). Adolescent development of cortical and white matter structure in the NCANDA sample: Role of sex, ethnicity, puberty, and alcohol drinking. *Cerebral Cortex*, 26(10), 4101–4121. doi:10.1093/cercor/bhv205

Pfefferbaum, A., Sullivan, E. V., Mathalon, D. H., & Lim, K. O. (1997). Frontal lobe volume loss observed with magnetic resonance imaging in older chronic alcoholics. *Alcoholism: Clinical and Experimental Research*, 21(3), 521–529. Retrieved from http://www.ncbi.nlm.nih.gov/pubmed/9161613

Rahman, M., Bari, R., Ali, A. A., Sharmin, M., Raij, A., Hovsepian, K., . . . Kumar, S. (2014). Are we there yet? Feasibility of continuous stress assessment via wireless physiological sensors. *ACM BCB, 2014*, 479–488. doi:10.1145/2649387.2649433

Salvatore, J. E., Gottesman, I. I., & Dick, D. M. (2015). Endophenotypes for alcohol use disorder: An update on the field. *Current Addiction Reports*, 2(1), 76–90. doi:10.1007/s40429-015-0046-y

Sarker, H., Sharmin, M., Ali, A. A., Rahman, M. M., Bari, R., Hossain, S. M., & Kumar, S. (2014). Assessing the availability of users to engage in just-in-time intervention in the natural environment. *Proceedings of the ACM International Conference on Ubiquitous Computing, 2014*, 909–920. doi:10.1145/2632048.2636082

Schulte, M. T., Monreal, T. K., Kia-Keating, M., & Brown, S. A. (2010). Influencing adolescents' social perception of alcohol use to facilitate change through a school-based intervention. *Journal of Child & Adolescent Substance Abuse*, 19(5), 372–390.

Schulz, K. M., Molenda-Figueira, H. A., & Sisk, C. L. (2009). Back to the future: The organizational–activational hypothesis adapted to puberty and adolescence. *Hormones and Behavior*, 55(5), 597–604. doi:10.1016/j.yhbeh.2009.03.010

Schweinsburg, A. D., McQueeny, T., Nagel, B. J., Eyler, L. T., & Tapert, S. F. (2010). A preliminary study of functional magnetic resonance imaging response during verbal encoding among adolescent binge drinkers. *Alcohol*, 44(1), 111–117.

Schweinsburg, A. D., Schweinsburg, B. C., Nagel, B. J., Eyler, L. T., & Tapert, S. F. (2011). Neural correlates of verbal learning in adolescent alcohol and marijuana users. *Addiction*, 106(3), 564–573. doi:10.1111/j.1360-0443.2010.03197.x

Segerstrom, S. C., & Nes, L. S. (2007). Heart rate variability reflects self-regulatory strength, effort, and fatigue. *Psychological Science*, 18(3), 275–281. doi:10.1111/j.1467-9280.2007.01888.x

Sher, K. J., Martin, E. D., Wood, P. K., & Rutledge, P. C. (1997). Alcohol use disorders and neuropsychological functioning in first-year undergraduates. *Experimental and Clinical Psychopharmacology*, 5(3), 304–315. doi:10.1037/1064-1297.5.3.304

Smart, R. G., & Stoduto, G. (1997). Treatment experiences and need for treatment among students with serious alcohol and drug problems. *Journal of Child and Adolescent Substance Abuse*, 7, 63–73.

Smith, A., Chein, J., & Steinberg, L. (2013). Impact of socio-emotional context, brain development, and pubertal maturation on adolescent risk-taking. *Hormones and Behavior*, 64(2), 323–332. doi:10.1016/j.yhbeh.2013.03.006

Spear, L. P. (2000). The adolescent brain and age-related behavioral manifestations. *Neuroscience & Biobehavioral Reviews*, 24(4), 417–463. doi:10.1016/S0149-7634(00)00014-2

Spear, L. P., & Swartzwelder, H. S. (2014). Adolescent alcohol exposure and persistence of adolescent-typical phenotypes into adulthood: A mini-review. *Neuroscience & Biobehavioral Reviews*, 45, 1–8. doi:10.1016/j.neubiorev.2014.04.012

Squeglia, L. M., Rinker, D. A., Bartsch, H., Castro, N., Chung, Y., Dale, A. M., . . . Tapert, S. F. (2014). Brain volume reductions in adolescent heavy drinkers. *Developmental Cognitive Neuroscience*, 9, 117–125. doi:10.1016/j.dcn.2014.02.005

Squeglia, L. M., Schweinsburg, A. D., Pulido, C., & Tapert, S. F. (2011). Adolescent binge drinking linked to abnormal spatial working memory brain activation: Differential gender effects. *Alcoholism: Clinical and Experimental Research*, 35(10), 1831–1841. doi:10.1111/j.1530-0277.2011.01527.x

Squeglia, L. M., Sorg, S. F., Schweinsburg, A. D., Wetherill, R. R., Pulido, C., & Tapert, S. F. (2012). Binge drinking differentially affects adolescent male and female brain morphometry. *Psychopharmacology*, 220(3), 529–539. doi:10.1007/s00213-011-2500-4

Squeglia, L. M., Tapert, S. F., Sullivan, E. V., Jacobus, J., Meloy, M. J., Rohlfing, T., & Pfefferbaum, A. (2015). Brain development in heavy-drinking adolescents. *American Journal of Psychiatry*, 172(6), 531–542. doi:10.1176/appi.ajp.2015.14101249

Steinberg, L. (2007). Risk taking in adolescence. *Current Directions in Psychological Science*, 16(2), 55–59. doi:10.1111/j.1467-8721.2007.00475.x

Substance Abuse and Mental Health Services Administration. (2013). *Report to Congress on the prevention and reduction of underage drinking*.

Washington, DC: US Department of Health and Human Services.

Substance Abuse and Mental Health Services Administration. (2015). *Behavioral health barometer, United States, 2014*. Rockville, MD: Author. Retrieved from http://www.samhsa.gov/data/sites/default/files/National_BHBarometer_2014/National_BHBarometer_2014.pdf

Sullivan, E. V., Brumback, T., Tapert, S. F., Fama, R., Prouty, D., Brown, S. A., . . . Pfefferbaum, A. (2016). Cognitive, emotion control, and motor performance of adolescents in the NCANDA study: Contributions from alcohol consumption, age, sex, ethnicity, and family history of addiction. *Neuropsychology*, 30(4), 449–473. Retrieved from http://dx.doi.org/10.1037/neu0000259

Tapert, S. F., Brown, G. G., Baratta, M. V., & Brown, S. A. (2004). fMRI BOLD response to alcohol stimuli in alcohol dependent young women. *Addictive Behaviors*, 29(1), 33–50.

Tapert, S. F., Granholm, E., Leedy, N. G., & Brown, S. A. (2002). Substance use and withdrawal: Neuropsychological functioning over 8 years in youth. *Journal of the International Neuropsychological Society*, 8(7), 873–883. doi:10.1017/S1355617702870011

Tapert, S. F., Schweinsburg, A. D., Barlett, V. C., Brown, S. A., Frank, L. R., Brown, G. G., & Meloy, M. J. (2004). Blood oxygen level dependent response and spatial working memory in adolescents with alcohol use disorders. *Alcoholism: Clinical and Experimental Research*, 28(10), 1577–1586. doi:10.1097/01.alc.0000141812.81234.a6

Tarter, R. E., Mezzich, A. C., Hsieh, Y.-C., & Parks, S. M. (1995). Cognitive capacity in female adolescent substance abusers. *Drug and Alcohol Dependence*, 39(1), 15–21. doi:10.1016/0376-8716(95)01129-M

Tucker, J. A. (1995). Predictors of help-seeking and the temporal relationship of help to recovery among treated and untreated recovered problem drinkers. *Addiction*, 90(6), 805–809.

Vodopivec-Jamsek, V., de Jongh, T., Gurol-Urganci, I., Atun, R., & Car, J. (2012). Mobile phone messaging for preventive health care. *Cochrane Database of Systematic Reviews*, 12, Cd007457. doi:10.1002/14651858.CD007457.pub2

Walhovd, K. B., Tamnes, C. K., Bjørnerud, A., Due-Tønnessen, P., Holland, D., Dale, A. M., & Fjell, A. M. (2015). Maturation of cortico-subcortical structural networks—Segregation and overlap of medial temporal and fronto-striatal systems in development. *Cerebral Cortex*, 25(7), 1835–1841. doi:10.1093/cercor/bht424

Windle, M., Spear, L. P., Fuligni, A. J., Angold, A., Brown, J. D., Pine, D., . . . Dahl, R. E. (2008). Transitions into underage and problem drinking: Developmental processes and mechanisms between 10 and 15 years of age. *Pediatrics*, 121(Suppl. 4), S273–S289. doi:10.1542/peds.2007-2243C

Winward, J. L., Hanson, K. L., Bekman, N. M., Tapert, S. F., & Brown, S. A. (2014). Adolescent heavy episodic drinking: Neurocognitive functioning during early abstinence. *Journal of the International Neuropsychological Society*, 20(2), 218–229. doi:doi:10.1017/S1355617713001410

Yamaguchi, K., & Kandel, D. (1985). On the resolution of role incompatibility: A life event history analysis of family roles and marijuana use. *American Journal of Sociology*, 90, 1284–1325.

Zamboanga, B. L., Ham, L. S., Olthuis, J. V., Martens, M. P., Grossbard, J. R., & Van Tyne, K. (2012). Alcohol expectancies and risky drinking behaviors among high school athletes: "I'd rather keep my head in the game." *Prevention Science*, 13(2), 140–149. doi:10.1007/s11121-011-0252-3

Zucker, R. A., Donovan, J. E., Masten, A. S., Mattson, M. E., & Moss, H. B. (2008). Early developmental processes and the continuity of risk for underage drinking and problem drinking. *Pediatrics*, 121(Suppl. 4), S252–S272. doi:10.1542/peds.2007-2243B

PART IV

ALCOHOL AND SUBSTANCE USE DISORDERS

Developmental Transitions from Adolescence to Emergent Adulthood

---

OVERVIEW

Adolescence is a time of great diversity with respect to growth spurts, emergence of secondary sexual characteristics, formation of new peer groups, and, increasingly in the United States, exposure to peers from many different socioeconomic and cultural backgrounds. How one negotiates the transition to adolescence will depend in part on the developmental pathways that were constructed from infancy though childhood. There is a tendency for individuals who are risk-taking, or who have risk-filled pathways, to seek out peers with similar pathways, just as there is a tendency for children without such backgrounds to seek out similar peers. Thus, children who are aggressive tend to develop friendships with similarly aggressive peers, whereas those with strong prosocial skills develop friendships with peers with similar skills. Much is the same with respect to ethno-racial, socioeconomic, and other characteristics during early adolescence. Therefore, it should not be surprising that similar distinctions are seen with respect to substance use or abuse.

In Chapter 12, Schulenberg and colleagues describe the demography of adolescent-reported substance use, its heterogeneity, and its embeddedness within the adolescent experience as reported by adolescents in large national surveys. Drawing on survey data, they provide an overview of the context of adolescence and the transition to adulthood, particularly within evidence of continuity, discontinuity, and transitional challenges. Finally, they draw attention to risk and protective factors surrounding substance use during adolescence and emergent adulthood.

The transition from childhood to adolescence is also a time for experimentation with addictive behaviors that often serve as gateways to alcohol consumption. Smoking is an addictive behavior that correlates highly with drinking. Once an issue fairly restricted to cigarette smoking and chewing tobacco, smoking now offers a much more diverse set of options. In Chapter 13, Loukas and Argawal describe a tobacco landscape that includes such alternative tobacco and nicotine produces as hookah, cigarillos, snus, and electronic nicotine delivery systems, also referred to as e-cigarettes. Indeed, the authors note that both e-cigarette and hookah use are now more prevalent than cigarette use among adolescents in the United States. Manufacturers enhance the appeal of these alternative tobacco products by producing them in a wide variety of flavors (e.g., grape, cherry, coffee, rum) and offering them at significantly cheaper prices than cigarettes. As a result, there is currently a tendency for adolescents to perceive these alternative products to be less harmful than cigarettes. Although much is being learned about use of such products, Loukas and Argawal note that research to date is primarily cross-sectional rather than longitudinal. Longitudinal studies are needed to provide new insights into developmental trajectories of use and whether use serves as a gateway to alcohol and other drugs. One such study is described in Chapter 14.

In Chapter 14, Chassin and colleagues summarize findings from their cohort-sequential, multigenerational study of cigarette smoking to illustrate both a developmental approach and a longitudinal method to gain a deeper understanding of (1) pathways of smoking behavior (in relation to other forms of tobacco use noted by Loukas et al. in Chapter 13) and the factors that affect transitions from nonsmoking to smoking, (2) the heterogeneity of pathways with respect to the intergenerational transmission of smoking, (3) the societal and historical influences on developmental pathways, and (4) the influence of family systems and intergenerational family context on developmental pathways. Understanding cigarette smoking during adolescence in this manner is crucial to our ability to provide more effective prevention and intervention programs.

In Chapter 15, Ashenhurst and Fromme focus on a specific population of adolescents/emerging adults—those attending college. College campuses provide settings in which a great deal of drinking occurs, particularly high-risk binge drinking. Twenty-first birthday celebrations, during which the celebrant consumes 21 ounces of alcohol, often result in toxic poisoning and death. Ashenhurst and Fromme report on a long-standing longitudinal study of drinking behavior involving students at the University of Texas at Austin during college and thereafter. They describe general drinking patterns and then highlight heavy episodic drinking (binge drinking) within the context of risk factors for alcohol use. Among the risk factors are demographic characteristic, peer norms, parental monitoring and concern, academic issues, personality, and subjective responses to alcohol. Somewhat consistent with alcohol use disorder (AUD) in general, those at greatest risk are men, those with family wealth, sexual minorities, and Caucasians. Factors such as sensation seeking, impulsive personality, low parental awareness, and higher peer drinking norms contribute to risky drinking in this population. Consequences of AUD are aggression, drinking and driving, and alcohol-induced blackouts. All of these consequences have been linked to "date" rape, death, and antisocial behaviors on campuses throughout the country.

College attendance involves leaving home for extended periods of time, a life course event that may be new for many students. In Chapter 16, Ichiyama and colleagues note that perceptions that parents disconnect from college students when they leave home may be misleading. They report that there is evidence that contemporary parents of college students continue to contribute to maintaining resilience. For example, they note that there is research supporting the continuing protective influence of parents on the drinking behavior of college students. The authors review the literature examining parental influences on college student drinking, touching on such topics as parenting styles, parental monitoring, parent–child communication, parental modeling and attitudes toward drinking, and parental relationship quality. Conclusions based on their review form the basis for recommendations for parents of college-bound children to help reduce the risk for the development of problem drinking during this important developmental transition. A unique feature of this chapter is that all of Professor Ichiyama's co-authors are students.

In Chapter 17, Sher and colleagues discuss relations between personality and AUD. They discuss how personality traits are implicated in etiologic pathways to AUD, including via (1) deviance proneness, (2) pharmacological vulnerability to alcohol effects, (3) affect regulation, and (4) selection into high-risk contexts. A second area explored is research emphasizing movement beyond the static view of personality, recognizing that personality traits are dynamic and change as a function of human development and life transitions. Sher et al. discuss recent findings revealing normative patterns of developmental personality maturation, providing evidence that contextual role effects and personality maturation can perhaps be integrated into a broader model of maturing out of AUD. Finally, the authors provide future directions for research, including those related to (1) genetic and gene-by-environment influences, (2) potential utility of personality-based AUD treatments, and (3) policy strategies for buffering personality-based risk.

12

Substance Use and Abuse During Adolescence and the Transition to Adulthood Are Developmental Phenomena

Conceptual and Empirical Considerations

John Schulenberg

Julie Maslowsky

Justin Jager

During the past several decades, numerous influential scholars, many included in this edited volume, have advocated for a developmental perspective in understanding substance use and addiction. If we were to give an award for excellence in persistence and convincingness to someone within this astute group of scholars, it would surely go to Professor Robert Zucker. In reading his work, listening to him, and watching him in action during the past three decades, we can say that he is always explicitly or implicitly arguing for a developmental perspective, articulating what this means, and making sure that national decision-makers regarding the direction of addiction science understand the beauty and necessity of a broader developmental perspective. Three of his early influential papers were published in the mid- to late 1980s (Zucker, 1986, 1989; Zucker & Gomberg, 1986). In these, he argued for a multilevel consideration of biological, psychological, and social mechanisms, as well as for distinct heterogeneity in the etiology of alcohol use disorder across the life course. This work presaged the gathering prominence of lifespan psychology and developmental science (Lerner, 2006), as well as life course sociology (Elder, Johnson, & Crosnoe, 2003),

all of which were similarly arguing for considerations of multilevel mechanisms and heterogeneity in developmental course. When the first author of this chapter met Professor Zucker during the mid-1990s and, after reading the papers mentioned previously, asked him about his foretelling ability, Professor Zucker shrugged it off and simply said, "These are just scientific directions that are in the air, affecting us all." During the past three decades, we and many others in the field have been trying to breathe the same air as Professor Zucker.

In this chapter, we consider conceptual and empirical issues and implications that follow from taking a developmental perspective on substance use during adolescence and the transition to adulthood. We begin by describing what it means to take a developmental perspective on substance use, followed by a consideration of the developmental and historical context of adolescence and the transition to adulthood. We then summarize key conceptual issues related to developmental continuity, discontinuity, and transitions. Building on these developmental concepts, we examine implications for considerations of risk and protective factors for, and consequences of, substance use during adolescence and the transition to adulthood. We conclude with a discussion of opportunities and challenges for future research.

COMPONENTS OF A DEVELOPMENTAL PERSPECTIVE ON SUBSTANCE USE DURING ADOLESCENCE AND THE TRANSITION TO ADULTHOOD

What it means to take a developmental perspective can cover a myriad of conceptual and empirical ground. Building on the perspective of Schulenberg and colleagues (Schulenberg, Maslowsky, Patrick, & Martz, 2016; Schulenberg, Patrick, Maslowsky, & Maggs, 2014) and of others (Zucker, Hicks, & Heitzeg, 2016), we highlight six interrelated components of a developmental perspective on substance use across adolescence and the transition to adulthood.

Age Curve

First, a developmental perspective means an emphasis on stability and change over time—an emphasis well suited to substance use onset, escalation, and, for many, eventual decline across adolescence and early adulthood. Understanding the normative age curve of substance use is essential for both epidemiological and etiological purposes and helps target prevention and intervention efforts. At the population level, most forms of substance use increase across adolescence and the transition to adulthood and then decline as adult roles are assumed (Bachman et al., 2002; Johnston, O'Malley, Bachman, Schulenberg, & Miech, 2015).

Heterogeneity in the Age Curve

Giving attention to heterogeneity about the age curve is the next component of a developmental perspective—that is, focusing on individual trajectories of substance use that describe intraindividual change as well as interindividual differences in the course of change (Chassin, Colder, Hussong, & Sher, 2016; Schulenberg, Wadsworth, O'Malley, Bachman, & Johnston, 1996). This includes emphasis on different change patterns of substance use that include, for example, persistent heavy use and initial heavy then declining use. This also includes emphasis on age of onset and rate of escalation/decline. Age of onset has

proven to be important in distinguishing more problematic substance use (earlier onset) from more developmentally limited substance use (later onset) (King & Chassin, 2007; Moffitt, 1993; Moffitt & Caspi, 2001; Walters, 2011; Zucker, 1994). Faster increase in use typically reflects more difficulties (Bryant, Schulenberg, O'Malley, Bachman, & Johnston, 2003; D'Amico et al., 2001; Lynne-Landsman, Bradshaw, & Ialongo, 2010; Schulenberg & Maggs, 2001). This focus on heterogeneity suggests the limited utility of measuring substance use at one point in time, making it essential to follow individuals across multiple waves to track individual trajectories of substance use and associated covariates.

Embed in All Else That Is Developing

The third component of taking a developmental perspective concerns viewing substance use trajectories as embedded within all else that is developing and changing in the lives of young people. Nearly every domain of adolescent and early adult development, ranging from neurocognitive changes to changing peer and romantic relations, is connected to substance use. The search for multilevel risk factors, covariates, and consequences of substance use spans the entirety of adolescence and early adulthood. This necessitates an emphasis on the meaning and purpose of substance use for the individual (Schulenberg & Maggs, 2002; Schulenberg, Maslowsky, Patrick, et al., 2016), especially in terms of how substance use relates to various developmental tasks and transitions concurrently and into the future.

Embed in the Larger Social–Cultural Context

The fourth component of a developmental perspective on adolescent and early adult substance use involves attending to the multilevel social–cultural context that structures young people's lives, ranging from sociodemographic characteristics to the broader macrosystem and chronosystem (Bronfenbrenner, 1979; Tomasik & Silbereisen, 2012). There are clear differences in typical substance use trajectories as a function of, for example, gender, race/ethnicity, and historical time; substance use tends to escalate faster among today's young adults (relative to young adults of the past), to start later for Black than White youth, and to escalate faster for boys than girls (Jager, Keyes, & Schulenberg, 2015; Johnston et al., 2015;

Schulenberg et al., 2014). More generally, not only substance use during adolescence and young adulthood but also the broader sociocultural context that structures adolescent and early adult development in general and substance use in particular are best viewed as moving targets. That is, studies of substance use etiology and epidemiology must go hand in hand in order to capture both individual and structural dynamics that contribute to substance use (Compton, Thomas, Conway, & Colliver, 2005; Jager et al., 2015; Maslowsky & Schulenberg, 2013; Schulenberg et al., 2014; Tarter, 2010).

Long-Term Developmental Connections

The fifth component involves embedding substance use trajectories within the full lifespan, giving attention to upstream predictors and downstream consequences. This entails attending to earlier developmental precursors of substance use trajectories across adolescence and the transition to adulthood, as well as the long-term consequences of such trajectories (Brown et al., 2008; Schulenberg et al., 2014; Zucker et al., 2016). This represents a long-term continuity perspective, underscoring the fact that substance use during adolescence and early adulthood is often predictable based on earlier difficulties (Zucker et al., 2016), and in turn, some substance use during this time, especially heavy and long-term use, has later consequences on functioning and adjustment (Maggs et al., 2015; Merline, Jager, & Schulenberg, 2008; Volkow, Baler, Compton, & Weiss, 2014).

Interplay Between Developmentally Distal and Proximal Effects

In contrast to the fifth component, the sixth component gives attention to discontinuity across the lifespan. That is, not all substance use during adolescence and young adulthood has strong roots in childhood and earlier, nor does it always lead to major consequences going forward into adulthood. Especially during adolescence and young adulthood when experimentation in its many forms is common and often functional (Crosnoe, 2011), not all substance use reflects enduring difficulties. Likewise, as discussed later, the many developmental and social context changes during the second and third decades of life can set the stage for turning points, for better and worse, such that developmentally proximal effects

overrule developmentally distal effects. This gives attention to the interplay of developmentally distal and proximal effects, how they comingle to either work together to solidify an ongoing trajectory or work in competition such that distal effects are negated, reversed, or enhanced by more proximal effects (Schulenberg, Maslowsky, Patrick, et al., 2016).

THE DEVELOPMENTAL AND HISTORICAL CONTEXT: ADOLESCENCE AND THE TRANSITION TO ADULTHOOD

One particular challenge in conceptualizing and studying adolescence and the transition to adulthood is that relatively little remains unchanged, both developmentally and historically. Although this can be said about any period in the life course, it is especially true during this period. Individuals enter this period as dependent children located in a few close contexts, and they typically exit it as autonomous and interdependent adults with a life, family, and career of their own located in larger and more complex contexts. Moreover, what adolescence and the transition to adulthood looks like now in terms of timing and content of developmental milestones is quite different from what it looked like just a generation ago (Settersten & Ray, 2010), and it may well look different a generation from now. Thus, adolescence and the transition to adulthood is best conceptualized as a multilevel moving target that is characterized by change at both the developmental (or individual) level and the historical level.

Adolescence and the Transition to Adulthood as Developmental Moving Targets

Across adolescence and the transition to adulthood, individuals undergo profound biological, cognitive, and social change. With the manifestation and progression of puberty come dramatic changes in both physical appearance and internal biological systems. Although child-like at the transition into adolescence, cognition and decision-making capabilities tend to be fully mature by young adulthood (Casey & Jones, 2010; Pfeifer & Allen, 2012; Steinberg, Cauffman, Woolard, Grahman, & Banich, 2009). Moreover, sensation seeking increases in adolescence before decreasing in young adulthood, as does boredom. Self-awareness heightens, along with concerns about concurrent and future identity, gradually dropping off as adult roles are solidified. Meanwhile, relations with parents are renegotiated (Laursen & Collins, 2009), relations with peers evolve and mature (Brown & Larsen, 2009), and romantic relationships are initiated and become more committed and adult-like (Furman & Collibee, 2014). Educational experiences are transformed from the typically cozy context of primary school to the often chaotic, brusque, and consequential context of middle and high school (Eccles & Roeser, 2009) and then college for many. Employment experiences become more demanding and consequential.

Amid these broad developmental and contextual changes, we believe that it is no coincidence that opportunities for substance use as well as actual patterns of use—as indicated by the age curve mentioned previously—are also characterized by dramatic change during this period. Despite the many serious risks involved, alcohol and other drug use can serve numerous positively perceived purposes for some young people. Alcohol and other drug use can be a way to cope with stress; a way to facilitate distance from parents and social integration with peers; and a way to experiment, gather new sensations, and create and manage new self-images (Chassin, Presson, & Sherman, 1989; Crosnoe, 2011; Schulenberg & Maggs, 2002).

Adolescence and the Transition to Adulthood as Historical Moving Targets

Due largely to advances in nutrition and health care during the past 150 years, the average age at which puberty starts has declined sharply within industrialized countries (Susman & Dorn, 2009). Meanwhile, it has become clear that the transition to adulthood has changed in many important ways in recent decades to become, on average, more protracted, more individualized, and less linear than in the past (Bynner, 2005; Institute of Medicine & National Research Council, 2014; Schulenberg & Maggs, 2002; Settersten & Ray, 2010). Thus, the period in between childhood and adulthood has expanded at both ends.

Key indices of health and well-being among adolescents and young adults also show important historical variation, highlighting that in certain respects the experience of this period of life is different for successive generations (Institute of Medicine & National Research Council, 2014). For example, the

rate of adolescent obesity steadily increased during the 1970s–1990s but has since leveled off (Spruijt-Metz, 2011), whereas the percentage of US adolescents regularly getting adequate sleep has steadily declined since the early 1990s (Keyes, Maslowsky, Hamilton, & Schulenberg, 2015). Sensation seeking has increased during the past few decades, especially during the 1990s, finding a "new normal" of higher sensation seeking among US adolescents (Keyes, Jager, et al., 2015).

Likewise, at the population level, rates of and attitudes toward substance use shift historically, with documented wide fluctuations regarding most substances during the past four decades (Johnston et al., 2015; Keyes et al., 2011, 2012). These macro and time-varying trends in behaviors and supporting attitudes set the context for individual substance use trajectories, making some trajectories more or less likely. In the United States, adolescent rates of many substances have declined since the mid- to late 1990s, more so for younger than older students (Johnston et al., 2015). These changes have resulted in a population age curve that now starts later but increases more rapidly across adolescence (Schulenberg et al., 2014). Furthermore, this slower start but faster increase pattern also applies to rates of alcohol and marijuana use across the transition to adulthood, with more recent cohorts showing lower rates in their senior year but rates that rise faster through the mid-20s (Jager, Schulenberg, O'Malley, & Bachman, 2013; Jager et al., 2015). Thus, at the broader sociohistorical level, the normative developmental course of substance use across adolescence and the transition to adulthood appears to be shifting toward later onset but more rapid escalation.

Conceptualizing Developmental and Historical Moving Targets

A viable overarching theoretical framework for the study of adolescence and the transition to adulthood, in general and specifically regarding substance etiology, needs to be multilevel such that it captures both individual and historical change and is capable of connecting the two, as well as tying adolescence and the transition to adulthood into the entire life course. One framework that meets these criteria is life course theory (LCT), an interdisciplinary approach focused on the connection between individual lives and the historical and socioeconomic context in which those lives unfold (Elder et al., 2003; Elder & Shanahan, 2006). Despite the utility and popularity of LCT, a common alternative approach in the psychological literature for examining, in particular, the transition to adulthood is Arnett's (2000, 2007a) theory of emerging adulthood (TEA). The relative merits of these two theoretical approaches have been widely and openly debated (Arnett, 2000, 2007a, 2007b; Bynner 2005; Côté & Bynner, 2008; Hendry & Kloep, 2007). Because this debate is instructive for how best to conceptualize the transition from adolescence to adulthood, we briefly summarize the debate and compare the scientific merits of the two approaches.

First, LCT and TEA converge on a number of key points. Both approaches recognize that (1) the transition to adulthood is now, on average, more protracted, more individualized, and less linear than it was in the past (Arnett, 2007a; Bynner, 2005; Settersten & Ray, 2010); (2) these changes apply primarily to those from middle- to upper-class backgrounds from industrialized countries (Arnett, 2000; Côté & Bynner, 2008); and (3) the transition to adulthood is influenced by both individual agency and social structure, although LCT places greater emphasis on the constraining forces of social structure (Settersten & Gannon, 2005), whereas TEA places greater emphasis on the role of individual agency (Arnett, 2000).

The debate between LCT and TEA currently centers on whether, in its contemporary form, the transition to adulthood amounts to a new developmental period—which Arnett (2000, 2007a) refers to as "emerging adulthood"—that past generations did not experience. Arnett argues that emerging adulthood is indeed a new developmental period because it is lengthy (approximately 7 or 8 years long on average) and because it is distinct in terms of both organization (i.e., density of transitions) and developmental tasks (i.e., identity exploration in areas of romance and work) from the periods of the life course that precede it (adolescence) and follow it (adulthood).

Life course theorists posit that instead of amounting to a new developmental period, what Arnett calls emerging adulthood is simply a modern variant of the transition to adulthood that, for now anyway, is experienced by a particular subpopulation of transitioning adults. Specifically, life course theorists argue that a true developmental period or stage, even if it varies in quality or duration, should still apply broadly; thus, because emerging adulthood does not appear to apply to those from less affluent backgrounds or majority-world countries, it does not constitute a new developmental period (Côté & Bynner, 2008; Hendry & Kloep, 2007). Furthermore, not only is "emerging adulthood" a relatively recent addition to the life course but also it appeared over a relatively brief period of history and could disappear just as quickly—points that Arnett (2000, 2007b) concedes. Life course theorists argue that the existence of a developmental period should not be predicated on relatively short bursts of history (Bynner, 2005; Hendry & Kloep, 2007).

For our purposes, the central question is which theory is better equipped to adequately represent the period between childhood and adulthood, especially as it relates to substance use. LCT is the better equipped theory. Only LCT provides a multilevel framework for explicitly addressing if, how, and why the transition to adulthood is connected to historical change, both past and pending. In contrast, TEA is ahistorical. That is, although TEA recognizes that the transition to adulthood has changed historically, it is ill-equipped to examine why and when it changed and why it only changed for some. A second advantage of LCT is that the transition to adulthood, as conceptualized by LCT, is nearly universal—although its length, timing, and form can certainly vary across culture, class, and historical time. In contrast "emerging adulthood" only generalizes to a specific segment of contemporary transitioning adults, making it less than parsimonious. A third advantage of LCT is that it provides a way to connect the experiences of the transition to adulthood to what happens before and after, making it inherently developmental; in contrast, TEA focuses largely on the 6–8 years it spans. As a result, LCT offers a more useful avenue into understanding how adolescence and the transition to adulthood contributes to continuities and discontinuities across the life course as they relate to substance use etiology.

DEVELOPMENTAL CONCEPTUALIZATIONS: CONTINUITY, DISCONTINUITY, AND TRANSITIONS

Continuity and discontinuity are essential concepts for the understanding of development (Kagan, 1980; Werner, 1957) and, in our view, essential for understanding substance use etiology. Through a series of conceptual papers and chapters, we have elaborated a developmental framework that draws from

LCT (Elder et al., 2003; Elder & Shanahan, 2006), developmental science (Cairns, 2000; Lerner, 2006; Sameroff, 2010), and developmental psychopathology (Cicchetti & Rogosch, 1996, 2002) regarding substance use during adolescence and the transition to adulthood. This framework emphasizes person–context interactions, continuity and discontinuity, as well as developmental transitions, tasks, and trajectories (Maggs & Schulenberg, 2004; Schulenberg & Maggs, 2002; Schulenberg & Maslowsky, 2009; Schulenberg, Maslowsky, Maggs, & Zucker, in press; Schulenberg, Maslowsky, Patrick, et al., 2016; Schulenberg & Patrick, 2012; Schulenberg et al., 2014; Schulenberg, Sameroff, & Cicchetti, 2004). Within this framework, we view individuals and contexts as playing strong, interactive roles in the process of development, highlighting the importance of the person–context match or mismatch—that is, the connection between what the developing individual needs and what the context provides. Individuals select available contexts and activities based on opportunities and personal characteristics. Selected contexts then provide additional opportunities for continued socialization and further selection. This progressive mutual selection and accommodation underscores coherence and continuity in development. However, with dynamic person–context interactions comes the potential for discontinuity such that development does not always follow a smooth and progressive function, and early experiences do not always have strong or lasting effects (Cairns, 2000; Lewis, 1999; Rutter, 1996). Thus, both continuity and discontinuity are expected across the lifespan.

Ontogenetic Continuity and Discontinuity

The concepts of continuity and discontinuity have multiple meanings in the literature. In this chapter, we focus on continuity and discontinuity as they pertain to causative linkages across the lifespan (Lewis, 1999), termed ontogenetic continuity and discontinuity. Ontogenetic continuity reflects progression and individual coherence over time, with earlier developmentally distal events and experiences essentially causing future outcomes (Caspi, 2000). Not surprisingly, ontogenetic continuity is quite common across the life course—a developmental perspective would not be justified if this were not true. Nonetheless, later functioning is not necessarily a direct effect of earlier functioning (Cicchetti & Rogosch, 2002;

Lewis, 1999; Martin & Martin, 2002). Instead, the effects of early experiences may be amplified, neutralized, or reversed by later experiences (Schulenberg & Maggs, 2002; Schulenberg, Maslowsky, Patrick, et al., 2016). Such developmentally proximal influences introduce ontogenetic discontinuity, whereby current functioning and adjustment is due more to recent and current contexts and experiences than to earlier ones (Lewis, 1999).

Similarly, the distinction between ontogenetic continuity and discontinuity is important when examining the etiology of substance use. Much of substance use that occurs during adolescence and the transition to adulthood is appropriately viewed as "the result" of earlier difficulties (Dodge et al., 2009; Zucker et al., 2016), reflecting ontogenetic continuity. Consistent with the concept of ontogenetic continuity, adolescent and young adult substance use can have direct consequences on later functioning and adjustment (Hall, 2014; Volkow et al., 2014; Wilcox, Dekonenko, Mayer, Bogenschutz, & Turner, 2014). In other cases, however, the roots of substance use do not go that far into the past but, rather, are grounded more in current social contexts and developmental tasks and transitions (Schulenberg & Maslowsky, 2009), reflecting ontogenetic discontinuity. Likewise, due to experiences that occur after adolescence and early adulthood that serve to neutralize or even reverse potential consequences of substance use (e.g., marriage and changes in identity and friends), adolescent and early adulthood substance use does not always have long-term consequences (Schulenberg & Maggs, 2002; Schulenberg, Maslowsky, Patrick, et al., 2016). This distinction between ontogenetic continuity and discontinuity regarding the etiology of substance use and related difficulties is consistent with the distinction between life course-persistent and adolescence-limited antisocial behavior (Moffitt, 1993; Moffitt & Caspi, 2001), as well as between developmentally cumulative and developmentally limited alcohol use disorders (Zucker, 1986, 1994; Zucker et al., 2016).

Developmental Transitions

Developmental transitions include transformations in individuals, their contexts, and the relations between individuals and their contexts across the life course (Bronfenbrenner, 1979; Schulenberg & Maggs, 2002). Developmental transitions can be viewed globally, such as the transitions into adolescence and into adulthood; they can also be viewed more specifically in terms of internal, intraindividual transitions (e.g., biological, cognitive, and identity) and external, socially based transitions (e.g., school and work related) (Rutter, 1996). The second and third decades of life are dense with such internally and externally based transitions (Schulenberg & Maggs, 2002; Settersten & Ray, 2010). The power of these interlinked transitions on the course of substance use during adolescence and the transition to adulthood can be understood in relation to the concepts of continuity and discontinuity discussed previously. Schulenberg and colleagues (Schulenberg & Maggs, 2002; Schulenberg, Maslowsky, Maggs, et al., in press; Schulenberg, Maslowsky, Patrick, et al., 2016) summarize numerous ways in which transitions can contribute to substance use onset, escalation, and desistence. For example, multiple transitions can serve to overwhelm coping capacities, resulting in decrements in health and well-being. Transitions can alter the person–context match, resulting in improved or decreased health and well-being. They can also place young people in new contexts, putting them at increased risk for chance events, good or bad, through exposure to new situations and opportunities.

Turning first to the potential impact of transitions on discontinuity, internal and external transitions can have proximal effects on developmental trajectories that counteract developmentally distal effects. Such transitions may introduce ontogenetic discontinuity through the presentation of novel contexts that alter the person–context match. The transitions into middle and high school, for example, constitute important developmental transitions that can have an impact in escalating difficulties including substance use (Eccles & Roeser, 2009; Guo, Collins, Hill, & Hawkins, 2000; Jackson & Schulenberg, 2013). This discontinuity in ongoing trajectories can take the form of turning points or developmental disturbances. Turning points designate "permanent" change that reflects positive or negative long-term changes in course (Elder & Shanahan, 2006; Rutter, 1996). In contrast, developmental disturbances reflect more momentary perturbations (Rauer & Schulenberg, 2017). Once individuals are given time to adjust, they might resume their prior, ongoing trajectory, consistent with the notion of homeorhesis in systems theories of developmental psychopathology (Sameroff, 2010). In such cases, a transition may simply result in short-term deviance (e.g., an escalation in binge

drinking and experimenting with illicit drugs) that subsides and thus may not have long-term effects on developmental course or predict later functioning in adulthood (Rauer & Schulenberg, 2017; Schulenberg & Maggs, 2002; Schulenberg, Maslowsky, Patrick, et al., 2016).

However, developmental transitions do not just contribute to discontinuity—they can also contribute to continuity. Because the notion of ontogenetic continuity is at the foundation of developmental psychology (Cairns, 2000; Lewis, 1999), continuity can be thought of as occurring automatically as an inherent part of development, suggesting that transitions have no part in contributing to continuity. From a person–context interaction perspective, however, continuity is not viewed as so automatic, and transitions are viewed as important mechanisms for both discontinuity and continuity. For example, transitions can contribute to continuity by serving as proving grounds that help consolidate and strengthen ongoing behavioral and adjustment trajectories for better and worse (Schulenberg & Maggs, 2002; Schulenberg, Maslowsky, Patrick, et al., 2016). In novel and ambiguous situations, such as new social contexts, individuals tend to rely on intrinsic tendencies and known behavioral and coping repertoires (Caspi, 2000; Dannefer, 1987), contributing to increased heterogeneity, or fanning, of individual differences in coping. That is, young people already experiencing difficulties prior to a major transition may have trouble negotiating the new transitions and fall further behind their well-functioning peers. In contrast, young people doing well prior to the transition likely have the resources to deal successfully with the new transition and move further ahead of their age mates having difficulties (Schulenberg & Maggs, 2002; Schulenberg, Maslowsky, Patrick, et al., 2016). Thus, during major transitions such as into high school or college, ongoing salutary and deviant trajectories may become more solidified, highlighting the role of transitions in perpetuating ontogenetic continuity.

DEVELOPMENTAL PERSPECTIVE ON RISK AND PROTECTIVE FACTORS

Researchers in the fields of developmental science and addictions have long been aware of the multiple and multilevel risk and protective factors for adolescent and young adult substance use, spanning nearly every aspect of young people's lives and ranging from biological to cultural-level influences (Brown et al., 2008; Hawkins, Catalano, & Miller, 1992; Jessor, 1987; Sloboda, Glantz, & Tarter, 2012; Windle et al., 2008; Zucker et al., 2016). Further advances in understanding substance use etiology are likely to derive from a more complete understanding of how risk and protective factors interrelate, especially across levels of explanation (e.g., biological to cultural) and over time. In this section, we summarize issues and approaches regarding risk and protective factors that follow from taking a developmental perspective.

Interactive Effects

Risk and protective factors are typically viewed in isolation in their relation to substance use outcomes. This "unique effects" approach is clearly important, but it leaves open questions about how risk and protective factors work together and in competition to predict substance use. Across studies, some risk factors show inconsistent associations with substance use, which can be attributed to many methodological sources as well as to failure to consider interactive effects. For example, internalizing symptoms are not consistently related to substance use during adolescence; perhaps this is due to whether other risk factors are considered as moderating the effect of internalizing symptoms. Indeed, research shows that internalizing symptoms relate to substance use under certain conditions, such as when externalizing symptoms (Maslowsky & Schulenberg, 2013) or parent substance abuse (Gorka, Shankman, Seeley, & Lewinsohn, 2013) are also present. Thus, in this case, considerations of interactions can clarify inconsistencies across studies.

As often used in research, protective factors are at the opposite side of the same continuum as risk factors. Experiencing academic difficulties is a risk factor, and academic success is a protective factor. However, as sometimes conceptualized, protective factors come into play only when individuals are otherwise at risk—that is, protective factors only work in interaction with risk factors. In such cases, the term *promotive factor* is used to describe a salutary influence that pertains to all in general, whereas *protective factor* is used to describe a salutary influence that pertains only to those at risk (Gutman, Sameroff, & Cole, 2003). For example, among national samples of 8th and 10th graders, Dever et al. (2012) found that

parental monitoring was both a promotive factor (it predicted lower substance use for all) and a protective factor (it had an especially powerful positive effect for youth at high risk for substance use due to their high levels of sensation seeking). Thus, by considering interactions among risk and protective factors, we can gain needed understanding of resilience mechanisms (Cicchetti & Rogosch, 2002).

An important methodological aspect of highlighting interaction effects among risk and protective factors is the need for large and representative samples. To the extent that given risk and protective factors are moderated by sociodemographic and other risk and protective factors, commensurate sample sizes and representativeness are important considerations. When multiple interactions are anticipated, necessarily sample sizes will be larger than when only main effects are anticipated. Furthermore, when moderation of risk and protective processes by sociodemographic characteristics is anticipated, adequate representation among the given subgroups is needed. Large-scale survey research is well suited to research based on large representative samples.

Of course, survey research by itself cannot get at interactions involving risk and protective factors operating at levels not subject to self-report, including biological and situation-specific factors. For example, in both animal and human models, the adolescent brain differs structurally and functionally from the adult brain (Spear, 2000). Dramatic neural transformations occur in the adolescent brain and continue to shape the brain into early adulthood (Gogtay et al., 2004). According to the differential maturity mismatch hypothesis, the gap that occurs during adolescence between an early maturing, reward-seeking limbic system and a slower maturing cognitive control system in the prefrontal cortex contributes to increased risk-taking (Bava & Tapert, 2010; Casey & Jones, 2010; Steinberg et al., 2006, 2008; but for an alternative view, see Pfeifer & Allen, 2012). Neural changes and risk-taking behaviors may also interact bidirectionally. Not only do characteristics of the developing adolescent brain contribute to susceptibility for risk-taking and substance use but also the use of substances (particularly at high or frequent levels) during adolescence may hinder cognitive functioning and structural neural development (Squeglia, Jacobus, & Tapert, 2009). In addition, hormonal shifts initiated during puberty, and the influence of pubertal hormones on neural circuitry within the adolescent brain, may interact to drive the propensity for risk-taking (Sisk & Zehr, 2005; Spear, 2000; Steinberg et al., 2008). An exciting direction for future research is the combination of survey and laboratory-based techniques, such as in the National Institutes of Health's Adolescent Brain and Cognitive Development study (https://addictionresearch.nih.gov/abcd-study), in order to assess interactions among risk factors measured at multiple levels of analysis, from biological to cultural, and to approach an integrated picture of risk and protective processes for adolescent substance use.

Multiple Pathways

Risk and protective factors are probabilistic in their relations to substance use. For some individuals, having one or even many given risk factors does not make substance use a certainty; for others, it may take having only one given risk factor to set the stage for substance use onset and escalation. This means that there are multiple pathways to substance use, demonstrating the notion of equifinality (Cicchetti & Rogosch, 1996). Equifinality, which describes the presence of several distinct routes to a common outcome, poses many challenges for understanding substance use etiology. For example, when we list all the risk and protective factors for substance use evident across multiple samples, we likely end up with a description of everyone in general and no one in particular. Furthermore, what are found to be risk factors predating substance use for some young people may be correlates or even consequences for others. Whether a construct functions as a risk factor or a consequence may also be a matter of developmental stage. For example, in adolescence, mental health symptoms tend to predate substance use (Kessler et al., 2005; Maslowsky, Schulenberg, & Zucker, 2014), but in young adulthood, the relationship becomes more bidirectional such that substance use also contributes to the development or worsening of mental health problems (Brook, Brook, Zhang, Cohen, & Whiteman, 2002; Needham, 2007).

A developmental perspective can be useful for bringing some order to such seemingly infinite etiologic possibilities by identifying specific, multiple longitudinal trajectories and pathways to substance use. Longitudinal research is a powerful tool for distinguishing developmental timing, ordering, and specificity of risk factors, correlates, and consequences. Although there are multiple pathways into

substance use, it is likely that some pathways are more common than others. For example, Dodge et al. (2009) identified a common pathway into substance use that begins with early childhood factors such as child's temperament and parenting behaviors, progresses into difficulties in childhood behavior and peer relations, and culminates in adolescent behavior problems and deviant peer associations, which are known proximal risk factors for adolescent substance use. Describing and explaining common pathways can capture most, but not all, of the ways adolescents become involved with substance use. This enables a systematic approach to studying multiple pathways into substance use. Those who do not follow a common pathway can then be identified, and their unique pathways into substance use can provide a more nuanced understanding of substance use etiology. For example, although the role of externalizing symptoms as a strong and robust risk factor for later substance use and abuse is well established (Maslowsky, Schulenberg, & Zucker, 2014; Masten, Faden, Zucker, & Spear, 2008; Zucker et al., 2016), Hussong, Jones, Stein, Baucom, and Boeding (2011) have identified a less common but equally important "internalizing pathway" to substance use, consistent with Zucker's (1986, 1994) conceptualizations.

The transition to adulthood constitutes an important potential turning point in substance use trajectories, when pathways are either interrupted or codified. For some young people, the turmoil of adolescence starts to recede. On average, well-being and mental health improve during this period (Galambos, Barker, & Krahn, 2006; Jager, 2011; Schulenberg & Maggs, 2002). Much of the earlier risk-taking behavior and substance use follow a normative developmental progression in which the majority of the behaviors begin to fade across the transition to adulthood. Impulsivity and sensation seeking decline for most during the transition to adulthood, and those individuals who do not experience the normative declines in these traits are those who increase most rapidly in their substance use (Quinn & Harden, 2013). Some types of psychopathology, including conduct disorder, have an adolescence-limited subtype (Moffitt, 1993; Walters, 2011), so their contributions to substance use also decline across the transition to adulthood.

For other youth, however, early adulthood simultaneously presents many new stresses that serve to maintain or exacerbate difficulties. Leaving the family home and taking on new responsibilities and life roles can take its toll. Early life risk factors may continue to exert their influence as some individuals who experienced a number of early childhood risk factors become "snagged" on negative life events in adolescence or early adulthood, such as an unplanned pregnancy or legal trouble (Moffitt et al., 2011). Risk factors may also compound across development to create cumulative risk at each subsequent life stage (Rutter & Garmezy, 1983). Those entering adulthood with an accumulation of risk factors are likely to struggle during this transition (Jager, 2011). Mental health and other adjustment problems that persist into adulthood are likely to be problematic in the long term (Moffit, 1993; Newcomb, Scheier, & Bentler, 1993). The significance of persistent risk behaviors and their underlying motivations may shift as they persist into adulthood. Reasons for using substances shift from socially oriented to coping oriented (Patrick, Schulenberg, O'Malley, Johnston, & Bachman, 2011). As mentioned previously, during the transition to adulthood, mental health problems may start to become more a consequence of substance use rather than a risk factor for it (Marmorstein, Iacono, & Malone, 2010).

Developmental Arrays of Risk and Protective Factors

Building on the interactive characteristics and multiple pathways of risk and protective factors is the fact that risk and protective factors array developmentally. Identifying developmental windows during which key predictors are most influential brings needed insight into the etiology of substance use and possibilities for intervention. There are several ways to consider how developmental arrays work, including cascading effects, in which earlier difficulties in one domain contribute to difficulties in other domains and eventually to substance use (Dodge et al., 2009; Masten et al., 2008; Zucker et al., 2008). Cascades can be used to model heterotypic continuity, which refers to continuity in underlying functions that manifest in different behaviors across development, such as externalizing disorder appearing in different forms during the course of childhood and adolescence. For example, Dodge et al. observed continuity of underlying externalizing difficulties that manifested differently over time, from early childhood difficult behavior to middle childhood peer problems, adolescent behavior problems and affiliations with deviant peers, and ultimately substance use.

The developmental array of risk factors is also important when attempting to distinguish developmentally distal and proximal effects. In general, proximal risk factors are expected to be more powerful because they are temporally closer to the outcome, but central to much developmental meta-theory is the idea of sensitive periods and powerful developmentally distal effects (Lerner, 2006). For example, although temporally distal, early childhood risk factors such as child temperament and family stress can strongly relate to substance use in adolescence (Burk et al., 2011; Dodge et al., 2009). Similarly, early emerging mental health symptoms have been shown to be a stronger risk factor for adolescent substance use than later emerging but more proximal symptoms (Maslowsky, Schulenberg, & Zucker, 2014). Thus, the etiology of adolescent substance use is further specified by the identification of developmental windows—sensitive periods—during which key predictors are most influential on the development of substance use. Describing sensitive periods and the most influential predictors within them is also important for informing the design of developmentally appropriate substance use prevention and intervention programs for adolescents.

Another matter regarding the developmental array of risk and protective factors pertains to the prediction of substance use onset versus substance use escalation (Jackson & Schulenberg, 2013). Studies that predict both the onset and the escalation of substance use often find different effects of risk and protective factors (Capaldi, Stoolmiller, Kim, & Yoerger, 2009; D'Amico & McCarthy, 2006). Initiation and escalation are obviously connected, and in fact, early onset in adolescence contributes to greater subsequent escalation (Lynskey et al., 2003). However, the etiologic processes underlying initiation and escalation are at least partially distinct, with the risk factors associated with onset during adolescence being of different magnitude, and perhaps even different type, compared to risk factors associated with escalating use during adolescence and the transition to adulthood (Donovan, 2004; Schulenberg & Maslowsky, 2009). Understanding the prediction of onset versus escalation brings us to our final subsection concerning risk and protective factors.

Predicting Substance Use over Time

Substance use at one point in time, especially during adolescence and the transition to adulthood, may provide little information about etiology. Studies that focus on a single time point or limited period of time provide little insight into the developmental array of risk factors discussed previously and may not be able to distinguish short-lived versus chronic substance use. Focusing instead on longer term trajectories of substance use can provide some needed leverage on etiologic mechanisms and process. Distinguishing substance use from abuse is a fundamental purpose of etiologic research (Newcomb & Bentler, 1989). Among the many issues involved in defining substance abuse, in contrast to use, is developmental course. A trajectory of earlier and heavier use is likely to reflect abuse, whereas a trajectory of later onset and lighter use is likely to reflect experimental use (Chassin, Pitts, & Prost, 2002; Hill, White, Chung, Hawkins, & Catalano, 2000). Using a developmentally informed study design, one can model trajectories of use; identify the most severe trajectories (in terms of levels of use, abuse, and chronicity); and look backward to identify early predictors of severe use, such as early age of substance use onset, which has been shown to predict a greater likelihood of substance use disorder (Grant & Dawson, 1997; Tarter, 2010; Wagner & Anthony, 2002). Developmentally informed designs also help to contextualize the substance use within the developmental period in which it occurs. Substance use, particularly alcohol use, becomes normative and sometimes functional in later adolescence and early adulthood and thus may be less associated with risk factors. That is, a trajectory of use that reflects a developmental disturbance, described previously as a common period of time-limited deviance, may not be especially predictable in advance.

DEVELOPMENTAL PERSPECTIVE ON CONSEQUENCES OF SUBSTANCE USE

Attempting to isolate consequences of substance use during adolescence and the transition to adulthood on later functioning and adjustment is difficult given that substance use tends to coexist with many other aspects of development. Furthermore, substance use constitutes multiple constructs, and adulthood functioning and adjustment also consists of multiple constructs covering the wide expanse of life domains. Applying the developmental perspective that we have advocated in this chapter can help attend to the various complexities of conceptualizing

and examining long-term connections across the lifespan (Schulenberg & Maggs, 2002; Schulenberg, Maslowsky, Patrick, et al., 2016). In this section, we summarize key issues and approaches regarding substance use consequences that follow from taking a developmental perspective.

Causality and Endogeneity

Questions of causality loom large when attempting to determine consequences of adolescent and young adulthood substance use. One key aspect of attempts to isolate substance use as a causative factor for later functioning and adjustment is the consideration of developmentally distal and contemporaneous characteristics and experiences that contribute to both substance use and later difficulties. Without the possibility of random assignment to or away from substance use, we need to use methods to control for selection effects, wherein individuals who are more prone to experience adolescent and young adult substance use are also more prone to experience later adulthood difficulties. Long-term longitudinal studies are becoming more common. With such data, within-person multilevel longitudinal analyses provide an effective strategy for isolating potential causal effects of substance use (Staff et al., 2010). By controlling for all time-stable individual characteristics (e.g., early life risk factors), within-person techniques can provide some controls for selection effects and show the extent to which within-person changes in substance use are associated with subsequent functioning. Studies employing this method have demonstrated, for example, that within-person increases in symptoms of alcohol abuse and depression contribute to increased likelihood of diagnosis with major depressive disorder (Fergusson, Boden, & Horwood, 2009), and within-person increases in smoking behavior contribute to higher levels of depressive symptoms (Duncan & Rees, 2005). Also useful are propensity score matching analyses, whereby respondents are matched on numerous prior and contemporaneous characteristics with the exception of substance use. This helps control for selection effects and thus can determine the contribution of substance use to later functioning and adjustment. For example, using this type of analysis with Monitoring the Future longitudinal data, Maggs et al. (2015) found that frequent marijuana use in adolescence contributed to lower educational attainment at age 26 years. Finally, instrumental variables help remove endogeneity, or potential reverse causation, within an analytic model so as to clarify the causal direction between variables (Gage, Munafo, & Davey Smith, 2016; Gennetian, Magnuson, & Morris, 2008).

Multiple Outcomes and Multiple Patterns of Use

Multifinality refers to multiple endpoints resulting from the same starting point (Cicchetti & Rogosch, 1996). In the case of adolescent and young adult substance use, the same initial starting point can lead to a full range of negative, null, and sometimes even positive consequences. Substance use is probabilistically related to a range of negative health, social, and achievement consequences, including educational failure, addiction, mental health problems, and chronic disease (Maggs et al., 2015; Moolchan et al., 2007; Reardon & Buka, 2002; Schulenberg et al., 2015). However, only a subset of those who engage in normative and even problematic substance use experience its potential negative consequences. What are the factors that distinguish those whose substance use is less costly from those who develop an addiction, become sick or injured, or experience social and achievement difficulties as a result of their substance use?

First, the trajectory of substance use during adolescence—including timing of onset and escalation—is important in terms of consequences. Early initiation and ongoing use of alcohol and marijuana are well-known predictors of later substance use disorders (Grant & Dawson, 1997; Lynskey et al., 2003; Schulenberg & Patrick, 2012; Wagner & Anthony, 2002). Redirecting risky trajectories by delaying initiation of substance use in adolescence has been shown to reduce problematic substance use in young adulthood (Kellam & Anthony, 1998; Spoth, Trudeau, Guyll, Shin, & Redmond, 2009). However, heavy use over a relatively short period of time, especially during late adolescence and early adulthood, may carry relatively few consequences for some. That is, consistent with the notion of developmental disturbance discussed previously (Rauer & Schulenberg, 2017), some short-term heavy substance use may reflect a temporary deviation from a given individual's ongoing pattern, and such temporary deviations, especially during a time of life when substance use is more normative, may not be predictive of later functioning and adjustment (Schulenberg, Maslowsky, Patrick,

et al., 2016). For example, Newcomb et al. (1993) found that a trajectory of increasing polysubstance use from adolescence into young adulthood predicted serious mental health problems such as psychoticism and suicidality in adulthood, whereas polysubstance use that lasted only during adolescence had no association with adult mental health. Similarly, focusing on college students from the Monitoring the Future study, Schulenberg and Patrick (2012) report that a "fling" pattern of frequent binge drinking (i.e., frequent binge drinking that starts with transition to college and then subsides after a few years) showed no association with a full range of psychosocial outcomes 10–15 years later. A cautionary aspect of this finding, however, is that those who followed the fling pattern, compared to those who followed an "infrequent" pattern, were at heightened risk for an alcohol use disorder at age 35 years. Thus, based on community and national studies, it appears that the consequences of substance use during adolescence and early adulthood depend to some extent on whether substance use continues beyond early adulthood. Of course, at the individual level, any heavy substance use, regardless of ongoing pattern, can increase the likelihood of tragedies such as automobile accidents and criminal offenses that indeed can have long-term consequences (Newcomb & Bentler, 1988; Schulenberg & Maggs, 2002).

Second, the reasons why one uses substances can be important in terms of the consequences of substance use. Self-reported reasons for engaging in substance use reflect the perceived functions of substance use in meeting the individual's needs, or what the individual gains (or expects to gain) from his or her substance use (Boys, Marsden, & Strang, 2001; Cooper, 1994; Cox & Klinger, 1988; Kuntsche, Knibbe, Gmel, & Engels, 2005). The majority of self-reported reasons for using alcohol and marijuana (e.g., to have fun with friends) decrease from adolescence to young adulthood, and some reasons that are less common among adolescents increase with the transition to adulthood (e.g., to relax and using alcohol to aid sleep) (Patrick, Schulenberg, O'Malley, Maggs, et al., 2011). These underlying motives for substance use have implications for current and continued use and consequences of use. Reasons associated with the lowest levels of use during adolescence include a desire to experiment and to fit in with peers (Patrick, Schulenberg, O'Malley, Maggs, et al., 2011). Drinking alcohol to get high and because of boredom are reasons most strongly associated with increases in binge drinking from ages 18 to 22 years. Those who continue to use alcohol to escape their problems are most likely to continue with higher rates of binge drinking after age 22 years (Patrick & Schulenberg, 2011). Adolescents and young adults who use substances to regulate emotions may be at increased risk for adult substance use disorders (Patrick, Schulenberg, O'Malley, Johnston, & Bachman, 2011).

Third, substance use consequences depend to some extent on with what substance use is interacting. Polysubstance use is generally associated with more severe consequences and developmental outcomes compared to use of a single substance (Agrawal, Lynskey, Madden, Bucholz, & Heath, 2007). Indeed, studies have shown that polysubstance use confers elevated risk for a range of adverse health behaviors and conditions in adolescence and adulthood, including risky sexual behavior, addiction, and suicidality (Connell, Gilreath, & Hansen, 2009; Newcomb & Bentler, 1988; Wu, Pilowsky, & Schlenger, 2005). Comorbidity of substance use with mental health problems is another consistent indicator of likelihood of severe and problematic substance use (Jackson, Sher, & Schulenberg, 2008; Maslowsky & Schulenberg, 2013; Maslowsky, Schulenberg, O'Malley, & Kloska, 2014; Stenbacka, 2003). In general, the same attention given to the interaction of risk factors for substance use during adolescence and early adulthood discussed previously should be given to understanding the interaction of substance use with other individual and contextual risk factors in the prediction of adulthood functioning and adjustment.

Distinguishing Short- and Long-Term Effects

Building on the issues of causality and patterns of use, a developmentally informed approach includes an emphasis on both short- and long-term consequences of adolescent and young adult substance use. No doubt, continuities in consequences are to be expected over time. Within a cascading model, short- and long-term consequences of substance use should go hand-in-hand, where initial negative consequences in one domain (e.g., cognitive) cascade into negative consequences in another (e.g., education). However, discontinuities in consequences are also to be expected over time. Just as risk factors temporally closer to the outcome tend to be more powerful than developmentally distal risk factors, it is reasonable to expect that short-term consequences of substance use are more severe than long-term ones. Negative effects of earlier substance use may wear off with age as other experiences and major transitions occur—that is, as the multifinality mentioned previously becomes manifest.

In contrast, there are also reasons to expect that long-term effects would be more powerful than short-term ones. Some effects of substance use may not be apparent initially but only appear as life wears on and there is increased heterogeneity in interindividual differences in the extent to which substance use impacts other life domains (Schulenberg, Maslowsky, Patrick, et al., 2016). For example, substance use may negatively impact work performance or romantic relationships, resulting in immediate job loss or breakup for some but more delayed consequences for others who are able to leverage other abilities to compensate for the negative effects of substance use. Resilience, coping ability, or social integration may suffice as compensatory mechanisms for a period in order to avoid initial negative consequences of substance use (Fergus & Zimmerman, 2005). However, these mechanisms may fade in the face of accumulated health and social effects of earlier substance use. Indeed, given the perceived positive functions of alcohol and other drug use discussed previously in terms of social integration during adolescence and the transition to adulthood, it is possible that there are positive short-term consequences in some domains followed by negative long-term consequences in the same or other domains. Ultimately, how substance use consequences are manifest in the short and long term and whether such consequences take different forms in different developmental periods are empirical questions most appropriately addressed with a developmentally informed approach and long-term longitudinal data.

THEORETICAL, PRACTICAL, AND METHODOLOGICAL CONCLUSIONS AND IMPLICATIONS

In this chapter, we advocate taking a developmental perspective on substance use during adolescence and the transition to adulthood. As we described previously, taking a developmental perspective includes focusing on the age curve of substance use across adolescence and the transition to adulthood as well as on the heterogeneity about the age curve in terms of individual substance use trajectories. It also includes embedding substance use trajectories within the multiple levels of all else that is developing and changing during adolescence and early adulthood—ranging from neurological to social context changes—as well as the larger social–cultural context, including sociodemographic, sociocultural, and historical contexts.

Additional key components of a developmental perspective pertain to developmentally distal and proximal effects on adolescent and early adult substance use. For many young people, substance use reflects a cascading effect whereby earlier difficulties in a variety of domains contribute to substance use onset and escalation, which then cascades into other difficulties (Dodge et al., 2009; Masten et al., 2008). In contrast, partly as a function of the numerous individual and social context transitions during adolescence and the transition to adulthood, this cascading flow can get interrupted or diverted, resulting in ontogenetic discontinuity whereby, for example, substance use and other risky behaviors are more the result of developmentally proximal individual and contextual characteristics than distal ones (Moffitt & Caspi, 2001). In some cases, this discontinuity may prove to be a developmental disturbance (Rauer & Schulenberg, 2017; Schulenberg, Maslowsky, Patrick, et al., 2016), and more salutary behavior trajectories are expected to eventually resume. In other cases, however, this detour is best understood as a turning point—discontinuity that reflects a profound and permanent change in course (Rutter, 1996). Thus, understanding substance use from a developmental perspective requires acknowledging the important transitions in multiple domains of young people's lives.

During the past few decades, the increased emphasis in the literature on the developmental aspects of substance use has resulted in substantial progress in our understanding of distal and proximal risk factors for substance use, developmental specificity of both risks for and consequences of substance use, and important subgroup differences in processes leading up to substance use. We are now soundly situated in an era of interdisciplinary, multilevel, biopsychosocial research on psychopathology, anticipated decades ago by Zucker and Gomberg (1986). New and innovative research emphasizes interconnections among the biological, psychosocial, and contextual

factors affecting development of psychopathology (Burnette & Cicchetti, 2012; Cicchetti & Dawson, 2002). Advances in the neuroscience and genetics of substance use increasingly indicate that biological risk factors are as dynamic and interactive as social and behavioral factors (Sloboda et al., 2012; Zucker et al., 2008). Due to the complexity of neural, biological, psychological, and social aspects of development across adolescence and the transition to adulthood, multidisciplinary collaborations that allow consideration of mechanisms at multiple levels will likely prove most productive in providing a truer view of substance use etiology across the second and third decades of life. Such approaches can be especially useful to gain a better understanding of which multilevel configurations of developmentally distal and proximal risk factors differentiate more experimental use from more chronic use, keeping the emphasis on common and unique trajectories.

New opportunities for better characterizing substance use abound, from the cellular to the population level. Biomarkers present an opportunity to capture risk factors and consequences of substance use operating at levels not always subject to self-report. An exciting direction is the addition of biomarker data to survey research in order to assess interactions among risk factors measured at multiple levels of analysis, from biological to behavioral, and to approach an integrated picture of risk and protective processes for psychopathology and health (McDade & Hayward, 2009). Also crucial for advancing risk factor research will be examination of interactions between multiple established risk and protective factors, as well as moderation of established risk factors by new ones, including those in the biological domain. Much of the innovative new research on psychopathology demonstrates how risk factors interact with each other. The multifinality currently observed with regard to effects of risk factors on later substance use outcomes may be to some extent attributable to missed interactions among multiple risk and protective factors. For example, there is now a robust literature demonstrating the moderating effect of genotype on response to life stress, with effects persisting into adulthood (Brody et al., 2012). Attending to multiple levels of analysis will be key in the examination of interactions in risk factors.

Extending our inquiries downward, to the cellular level, is not the only direction needed in future research. Development is also about heterogeneity of life paths, the fanning of population-level variance in life roles and experiences. Candidate developmental mechanisms underlying mental health and psychopathology in early adulthood should also be examined in large epidemiological samples to study the breadth of their applicability across the population and within key subgroups. Adopting an epidemiological perspective, with attention to the representativeness of our samples and the subsequent generalizability of results, will yield insight into the population-level impact of substance use and abuse. Such attunement to population-level effects is often a necessity for policy relevance of findings. The field of developmental epidemiology has already exemplified this approach in the study of psychopathology in children and adolescents (Costello, Egger, & Angold, 2005; Kershaw et al., 2009). A similar approach is also justified in substance use research in order to describe the wide range of pathways into substance use and consequences of use.

Population-level studies are also necessary to further elucidate the sources of disparities in the development of substance use and associated consequences. There are significant disparities in rates of substance use among some subgroups of young people in the population, including sexual minority youth (D'Avazo et al., 2016; Dermody et al., 2016; Fish & Pasley, 2015); military service members (Golub & Bennett, 2014), rural youth (Evans, Cotter, Rose, & Smokowski, 2016; Monnat & Rigg, 2016), and youth involved with the foster care and justice systems (Braciszewski & Colby, 2015; Welty et al., 2016). Likewise, there are disparities in the consequences of their substance use, with minorities who use substances more likely to experience consequences such as school dropout, substance use disorders, and physical health problems (Moolchan et al., 2007; Reardon & Buka, 2002). Finally, members of many minority groups find it difficult to access treatment, and when they do access treatment, they experience less optimal treatment outcomes (Chan et al., 2016; Mennis & Stahler, 2016). Large-scale longitudinal studies with adequate characterization and representation of these minority groups are necessary to reveal the predictors and consequences of their substance use trajectories, which may differ from those identified in studies of majority youth.

Moving forward, we note the advantages of utilizing the full array of analytical approaches that allow for a more dynamic examination of the course, predictors, and consequences of adolescent and young adult substance use, especially building on latent growth (Muthén & Curran, 1997), latent growth mixture (Muthén & Asparouhov, 2008), and repeated measures latent class analyses (Collins & Lanza, 2013) to identify and predict trajectories both to and from substance use (Schulenberg, Maslowsky, Maggs, et al., in press). With these analytic models, developmentally informed research questions abound. For example, a primary implication of taking the sort of developmental perspective on predictors and consequences we are advocating is to give attention to interactive effects, over and above main effects—such as examining how onset and escalation of substance use interact in contributing to short- and long-term health and well-being outcomes. In this example, the extent to which post-high school substance use escalation contributes to later difficulties may depend on the young person's extent of substance use in high school. This can be examined by including interaction terms of intercepts (starting points) and slopes (rates of escalation) in latent growth models, a powerful approach that is often overlooked in such models. Recent advances in estimating latent variable interactions have made such analyses more accessible (Maslowsky, Jager, & Hemken, 2015). Another important developmental consideration is to determine how ongoing trajectories of substance use are altered by developmental transitions (e.g., transition to college and marriage). Latent change models (e.g., proportional change and dual change models; Dogon, Stockdale, Widaman, & Conger, 2010; Grimm, An, McArdle, Zonderman, & Resnick, 2012) permit identification of predictors and consequences of deviations from one's more generalized trajectory of substance use, and they determine the extent to which such deviations are temporary (i.e., a developmental disturbance) or permanent (i.e., a turning point).

Ultimately, as advocated decades ago by Professor Zucker (Zucker, 1986, 1989; Zucker & Gomberg, 1986), multilevel longitudinal approaches can help to more fully address pressing questions about the extent to which adolescent and young adult substance use and other risky behaviors contribute to difficulties in adulthood functioning and adjustment (Schulenberg & Maslowsky, 2015). That is, for whom and under what conditions do substance use and other experiences of adolescence and early adulthood matter the most in terms of long-term health and well-being? For us, providing answers to this question is the ultimate benefit of taking a developmental perspective on substance use.

ACKNOWLEDGMENTS

Work on this chapter was supported in part by the National Institute on Drug Abuse (grants R01 DA01411 and R01 DA016575). Dr. Maslowsky is a Faculty Research Associate of the Population Research Center at the University of Texas at Austin, which is supported by grant R24 HD042849 from the Eunice Kennedy Shriver National Institute of Child Health and Human Development. The findings and conclusions in this report are those of the authors and do not necessarily represent the views of the sponsors. The authors thank the editors and also Professor Robert Zucker for his enduring support and impact on the field.

REFERENCES

Agrawal, A., Lynskey, M. T., Madden, P. A. F., Bucholz, K. K., & Heath, A. C. (2007). A latent class analysis of illicit drug abuse/dependence: Results from the National Epidemiological Survey on Alcohol and Related Conditions. *Addiction*, *102*(1), 94–104. doi:10.1111/j.1360-0443.2006.01630.x

Arnett, J. J. (2000). Emerging adulthood—A theory of development from the late teens through the twenties. *American Psychologist*, *55*(5), 469–480. doi:10.1037/0003-066X.55.5.469

Arnett, J. J. (2007a). Emerging adulthood: What is it, and what is it good for? *Child Development Perspectives*, *1*(2), 68–73.

Arnett, J. J. (2007b). Emerging adulthood, a 21st century theory: A rejoinder to Hendry and Kloep. *Child Development Perspectives*, *1*(2), 80–82. doi:10.1111/j.1750-8606.2007.00018.x

Bachman, J. G., O'Malley, P. M., Schulenberg, J. E., Johnston, L. D., Bryant, A. L., & Merline, A. C. (2002). *The decline of substance use in young adulthood: Changes in social activities, roles, and beliefs*. Mahwah, NJ: Erlbaum.

Bava, S., & Tapert, S. F. (2010). Adolescent brain development and the risk for alcohol and other drug problems. *Neuropsychology Review*, *20*(4), 398–413. doi:10.1007/s11065-010-9146-6

Boys, A., Marsden, J., & Strang, J. (2001). Understanding reasons for drug use amongst young people: A functional perspective. *Health Education Research*, *16*(4), 457–469. doi:10.1093/her/16.4.457

Braciszewski, J. M., & Colby, S. M. (2015). Tobacco use among foster youth: Evidence of health disparities. *Children and Youth Services Review*, *58*, 142–145. Retrieved from http://doi.org/10.1016/j.childyouth.2015.09.017

Brody, G. H., Chen, Y.-F., Yu, T., Beach, S. R. H., Kogan, S. M., Simons, R. L., . . . Philibert, R. A. (2012). Life stress, the dopamine receptor gene, and emerging adult drug use trajectories: A longitudinal, multilevel, mediated moderation analysis. *Development and Psychopathology*, *24*(3), 941–951. doi:10.1017/s0954579412000466

Bronfenbrenner, U. (1979). *The ecology of human development: Experiments by nature and design*. Cambridge, MA: Harvard University Press.

Brook, D. W., Brook, J. S., Zhang, C., Cohen, P., & Whiteman, M. (2002). Drug use and the risk of major depressive disorder, alcohol dependence and substance use disorders. *Archives of General Psychiatry*, *59*, 1039–1044. doi:10.1001/archpsyc.59.11.1039

Brown, B. B., & Larson, J. (2009). Peer relationships in adolescence. In R. M. Lerner & L. Steinberg (Eds.), *Handbook of adolescent psychology* (3rd ed., Vol. 2, pp. 74–103). Hoboken, NJ: Wiley.

Brown, S. A., McGue, M., Maggs, J., Schulenberg, J., Hingson, R., Swartzwelder, S., . . . Murphy, S. (2008). A developmental perspective on alcohol and youths 16 to 20 years of age. *Pediatrics*, *121*(Suppl. 4), S290–S310. doi:10.1542/peds.2007-2243D

Bryant, A. L., Schulenberg, J. E., O'Malley, P. M., Bachman, J. G., & Johnston, L. D. (2003). How academic achievement, attitudes, and behaviors relate to the course of substance use during adolescence: A 6-year, multiwave national longitudinal study. *Journal of Research on Adolescence*, *13*(3), 361–397. doi:10.1111/1532-7795.1303005

Burk, L. R., Armstrong, J. M., Goldsmith, H. H., Klein, M. H., Strauman, T. J., Costanzo, P., & Essex, M. J. (2011). Sex, temperament, and family context: How the interactions of early factors differentially predict adolescent alcohol use and are mediated by proximal adolescent factors. *Psychology of Addictive Behaviors*, *25*(1), 1–15. doi:10.1037/a0022349

Burnette, M. L., & Cicchetti, D. (2012). Multilevel approaches toward understanding antisocial behavior: Current research and future directions. *Development and Psychopathology*, *24*(3), 703–704. doi:10.1017/s0954579412000314

Bynner, J. M. (2005). Rethinking the youth phase of the life-course: The case for emerging adulthood? *Journal of Youth Studies*, *8*(4), 367–384. doi:10.1080/13676260500431628

Cairns, R. B. (2000). *Developmental science: Three auda-cious implications.* Mahwah, NJ: Erlbaum.

Capaldi, D. M., Stoolmiller, M., Kim, H. K., & Yoerger, K. (2009). Growth in alcohol use in at-risk ado-lescent boys: Two-part random effects prediction models. *Drug and Alcohol Dependence, 105*(1–2), 109–117. doi:10.1016/j.drugalcdep.2009.06.013

Casey, B. J., & Jones, R. M. (2010). Neurobiology of the adolescent brain and behavior: Implications for substance use disorders. *Journal of the American Academy of Child and Adolescent Psychiatry, 49*(12), 1189–1201. doi:10.1016/j.jaac.2010.08.017

Caspi, A. (2000). The child is father of the man: Personality continuities from childhood to adulthood. *Journal of Personality and Social Psychology, 78*(1), 158–172. doi:10.1037/0022-3514.78.1.158

Chan, Y.-F., Lu, S.-E., Howe, B., Tieben, H., Hoeft, T., & Unützer, J. (2016). Screening and follow-up moni-toring for substance use in primary care: An explo-ration of rural–urban variations. *Journal of General Internal Medicine, 31*(2), 215–222. Retrieved from http://doi.org/10.1007/s11606-015-3488-y

Chassin, L., Colder, C. R., Hussong, A., & Sher, K. J. (2016). Substance use and substance use disorders. In D. Cicchetti (Ed.), *Developmental psychopathol-ogy: Volume 3. Maladaptation and psychopathology* (3rd ed., Vol. 3, pp. 833–897). Hoboken, NJ: Wiley.

Chassin, L., Pitts, S. C., & Prost, J. (2002). Binge drink-ing trajectories from adolescence to emerging adulthood in a high-risk sample: Predictors and sub-stance abuse outcomes. *Journal of Consulting and Clinical Psychology, 70*(1), 67–78. doi:10.1037//0022-006x.70.1.67

Chassin, L., Presson, C. C., & Sherman, S. J. (1989). Constructive vs. destructive deviance in adoles-cent health-related behaviors. *Journal of Youth and Adolescence, 18*(3), 245–262.

Cicchetti, D., & Dawson, G. (2002). Editorial: Multiple levels of analysis. *Development and Psychopathology, 14*(3), 417–420. doi:10.1017/S0954579402003012

Cicchetti, D., & Rogosch, F. A. (1996). Equifinality and multifinality in developmental psychopathology. *Development and Psychopathology, 8*(4), 597–600. doi:10.1017/S0954579400007318

Cicchetti, D., & Rogosch, F. A. (2002). A developmen-tal psychopathology perspective on adolescence. *Journal of Consulting and Clinical Psychology, 70*(1), 6–20. doi:10.1037/0022-006X.70.1.6

Collins, L. M., & Lanza, S. T. (2013). *Latent class and latent transition analysis: With applications in the social, behavioral, and health sciences.* Hoboken, NJ: Wiley.

Compton, W. M., Thomas, Y. F., Conway, K. P., & Colliver, J. D. (2005). Developments in the epidemiology of drug use and drug use disorders. *American Journal of Psychiatry, 162*(8), 1494–1502. doi:10.1176/appi.ajp.162.8.1494

Connell, C. M., Gilreath, T. D., & Hansen, N. B. (2009). A multiprocess latent class analysis of the co-occurrence of substance use and sexual risk behavior among adolescents. *Journal of Studies on Alcohol and Drugs, 70*(6), 943–951.

Cooper, M. L. (1994). Motivations for alcohol use among adolescents: Development and validation of a four-factor model. *Psychological Assessment, 6*(2), 117–128. doi:10.1037/1040-3590.6.2.117

Costello, E. J., Egger, H., & Angold, A. (2005). 10-year research update review: The epidemiology of child and adolescent psychiatric disorders: I. Methods and public health burden. *Journal of the American Academy of Child and Adolescent Psychiatry, 44*(10), 972–986. doi:10.1097/01.chi.0000172552.41596.6f

Côté, J., & Bynner, J. M. (2008). Changes in the tran-sition to adulthood in the UK and Canada: The role of structure and agency in emerging adult-hood. *Journal of Youth Studies, 11*(3), 251–268. doi:10.1080/13676260801946464

Cox, W. M., & Klinger, E. (1988). A motivational model of alcohol use. *Journal of Abnormal Psychology, 97*(2), 168–180. doi:10.1037//0021-843x.97.2.168

Crosnoe, R. (2011). *Fitting in, standing out: Navigating the social challenges of high school to get an educa-tion.* New York, NY: Cambridge University Press.

D'Amico, E. J., & McCarthy, D. M. (2006). Escalation and initiation of younger adolescents' substance use: The impact of perceived peer use. *Journal of Adolescent Health, 39*(4), 481–487. doi:10.1016/j.jadohealth.2006.02.010

D'Amico, E. J., Metrik, J., McCarthy, D. M., Frissell, K. C., Appelbaum, M., & Brown, S. A. (2001). Progression into and out of binge drinking among high school students. *Psychology of Addictive Behaviors, 15*(4), 341–349. doi:10.1037/0893-164x.15.4.341

Dannefer, D. (1987). Aging as intracohort differen-tiation: Accentuation, the Matthew effect, and the life course. *Sociological Forum, 2*(2), 211–236. doi:10.1007/BF01124164

Dermody, S. S., Marshal, M. P., Cheong, J., Chung, T., D Stepp, S., & Hipwell, A. (2016). Adolescent sex-ual minority girls are at elevated risk for use of mul-tiple substances. *Substance Use & Misuse, 51*(5), 574–585. Retrieved from http://doi.org/10.3109/10826084.2015.1126743

Dever, B. V., Schulenberg, J. E., Dworkin, J. B., O'Malley, P. M., Kloska, D. D., & Bachman, J. G. (2012). Predicting risk-taking with and without substance use: The effects of parental monitoring, school bonding, and sports participation. *Prevention Science*, *13*(6), 605–615. doi:10.1007/s11121-012-0288-z

Dodge, K. A., Malone, P. S., Lansford, J. E., Miller, S., Pettit, G. S., & Bates, J. E. (2009). A dynamic cascade model of the development of substance-use onset. *Monographs of the Society for Research in Child Development*, *74*(3), vii–119. doi:10.1111/j.1540-5834.2009.00528.x

Dogon, S. J., Stockdale, G. D., Widaman, K. F., & Conger, R. D. (2010). Developmental relations and patterns of change between alcohol use and number of sexual partners from adolescence through adulthood. *Developmental Psychology*, *46*, 1747–1759. doi:10.1037/a0019655

Donovan, J. E. (2004). Adolescent alcohol initiation: A review of psychosocial risk factors. *Journal of Adolescent Health*, *35*(6), 529.e527–e518. doi:10.1016/j.jadohealth.2004.02.003

Duncan, B., & Rees, D. I. (2005). Effect of smoking on depressive symptomatology: A reexamination of data from the national longitudinal study of adolescent health. *American Journal of Epidemiology*, *162*(5), 461–470. doi:10.1093/aje/kwi219

Eccles, J. S., & Roeser, R. W. (2009). Schools, academic motivation, and stage–environment fit. In R. M. Lerner & L. Steinberg (Eds.), *Handbook of adolescent psychology* (3rd ed., Vol. 1, pp. 404–434). Hoboken, NJ: Wiley.

Elder, G. H., Jr., Johnson, M. K., & Crosnoe, R. (2003). The emergence and development of life course theory. In J. T. Mortimer & M. J. Shanahan (Eds.), *Handbook of the life course* (pp. 3–19). New York, NY: Springer.

Elder, G. H., Jr., & Shanahan, M. J. (2006). The life course and human development. In R. M. Lerner (Ed.), *Handbook of child psychology* (6th ed., Vol. 1, pp. 665–715). Hoboken, NJ: Wiley.

Evans, C. B. R., Cotter, K. L., Rose, R. A., & Smokowski, P. R. (2016). Substance use in rural adolescents: The impact of social capital, anti-social capital, and social capital deprivation. *Journal of Addictive Diseases*, *35*(4), 244–257. Retrieved from http://doi.org/10.1080/10550887.2016.1171671

Fergus, S., & Zimmerman, M. A. (2005). Adolescent resilience: A framework for understanding healthy development in the face of risk. *Annual Review of Public Health*, *26*, 399–419. doi:10.1146/annurev.publhealth.26.021304.144357

Fergusson, D. M., Boden, J. M., & Horwood, L. J. (2009). Tests of causal links between alcohol abuse or dependence and major depression. *Archives of General Psychiatry*, *66*(3), 260–266. doi:10.1001/archgenpsychiatry.2008.543

Fish, J. N., & Pasley, K. (2015). Sexual (minority) trajectories, mental health, and alcohol use: A longitudinal study of youth as they transition to adulthood. *Journal of Youth and Adolescence*, *44*(8), 1508–1527. Retrieved from http://doi.org/10.1007/s10964-015-0280-6

Furman, W., & Collibee, C. (2014). A matter of timing: Developmental theories of romantic involvement and psychosocial adjustment. *Development and Psychopathology*, *26*(4), 1149–1160. doi:10.1017/s0954579414000182

Gage, S. H., Munafo, M. R., & Davey Smith, G. (2016). Causal inference in developmental origins of health and disease (DOHaD) research. *Annual Review of Psychology*, *67*, 567–585. doi:10.1146/annurev-psych-122414-033352

Galambos, N., Barker, E., & Krahn, H. (2006). Depression, self-esteem, and anger in emerging adulthood: Seven-year trajectories. *Developmental Psychology*, *42*, 350–365.

Gennetian, L. A., Magnuson, K., & Morris, P. A. (2008). From statistical associations to causation: What developmentalists can learn from instrumental variables techniques coupled with experimental data. *Developmental Psychology*, *44*(2), 381–394. doi:10.1037/0012-1649.44.2.381

Gogtay, N., Giedd, J. N., Lusk, L., Hayashi, K. M., Greenstein, D., Vaituzis, A. C., . . . Thompson, P. M. (2004). Dynamic mapping of human cortical development during childhood through early adulthood. *Proceedings of the National Academy of Sciences of the USA*, *101*(21), 8174–8179. Retrieved from http://doi.org/10.1073/pnas.0402680101

Golub, A., & Bennett, A. S. (2014). Substance use over the military–veteran life course: An analysis of a sample of OEF/OIF veterans returning to low-income predominately minority communities. *Addictive Behaviors*, *39*(2), 449–454. Retrieved from http://doi.org/10.1016/j.addbeh.2013.06.020

Gorka, S. M., Shankman, S. A., Seeley, J. R., & Lewinsohn, P. M. (2013). The moderating effect of parental illicit substance use disorders on the relation between adolescent depression and subsequent illicit substance use disorders. *Drug and Alcohol Dependence*, *128*(1–2), 1–7. doi:10.1016/j.drugalcdep.2012.07.011

Grant, B. F., & Dawson, D. A. (1997). Age at onset of alcohol use and its association with DSM-IV alcohol abuse and dependence: Results from the National Longitudinal Alcohol Epidemiologic Survey. *Journal of Substance Abuse*, *9*, 103–110. doi:10.1016/s0899-3289(97)90009-2

Grimm, K. J., An, A., McArdle, J. J., Zonderman, A. B., & Resnick, S. M. (2012). Recent changes leading to subsequent changes: Extensions of multivariate latent difference score models. *Structural Equation Modeling, 19,* 268–292. doi:10.1080/10705511.2012.659627

Guo, J., Collins, L. M., Hill, K. G., & Hawkins, J. D. (2000). Developmental pathways to alcohol abuse and dependence in young adulthood. *Journal of Studies on Alcohol, 61*(6), 799–808.

Gutman, L. M., Sameroff, A. J., & Cole, R. (2003). Academic growth curve trajectories from 1st grade to 12th grade: Effects of multiple social risk factors and preschool child factors. *Developmental Psychology, 39*(4), 777–790. doi:10.1037/0012-1649.39.4.777

Hall, W. (2014). What has research over the past two decades revealed about the adverse health effects of recreational cannabis use? *Addiction, 110*(1), 19–35. doi:10.1111/add.12703

Hawkins, J. D., Catalano, R. F., & Miller, J. Y. (1992). Risk and protective factors for alcohol and other drug problems in adolescence and early adulthood: Implications for substance abuse prevention. *Psychological Bulletin, 112*(1), 64–105. doi:10.1037/0033-2909.112.1.64

Hendry, L. B., & Kloep, M. (2007). Conceptualizing emerging adulthood: Inspecting the emperor's new clothes? *Child Development Perspectives, 1*(2), 74–79.

Hill, K. G., White, H. R., Chung, I.-J., Hawkins, J. D., & Catalano, R. F. (2000). Early adult outcomes of adolescent binge drinking: Person- and variable-centered analyses of binge drinking trajectories. *Alcoholism: Clinical and Experimental Research, 24*(6), 892–901. doi:10.1111/j.1530-0277.2000.tb02071.x

Hussong, A. M., Jones, D. J., Stein, G. L., Baucom, D. H., & Boeding, S. (2011). An internalizing pathway to alcohol use and disorder. *Psychology of Addictive Behaviors, 25*(3), 390–404. doi:10.1037/a0024519

Institute of Medicine & National Research Council. (2014). *Investing in the health and well-being of young adults.* Washington, DC: National Academies Press. Retrieved from http://www.nationalacademies.org/hmd/Reports/2014/Investing-in-the-Health-and-Well-Being-of-Young-Adults.aspx

Jackson, K. M., & Schulenberg, J. E. (2013). Alcohol use during the transition from middle school to high school: National panel data on prevalence and moderators. *Developmental Psychology, 49*(11), 2147–2158. doi:10.1037/a0031843

Jackson, K. M., Sher, K. J., & Schulenberg, J. E. (2008). Conjoint developmental trajectories of young adult substance use. *Alcoholism: Clinical and Experimental Research, 32*(5), 723–737. doi:10.1111/j.1530-0277.2008.00643.x

Jager, J. (2011). A developmental shift in Black–White differences in depressive affect across adolescence and early-adulthood: The influence of early adult social roles and socio-economic status. *International Journal of Behavioral Development, 35,* 457–469. doi:10.1177/0165025411417504

Jager, J., Keyes, K. M., & Schulenberg, J. E. (2015). Historical variation in young adult binge drinking trajectories and its link to historical variation in social roles and minimum legal drinking age. *Developmental Psychology, 51*(7), 962–974. doi:10.1037/dev0000022

Jager, J., Schulenberg, J. E., O'Malley, P. M., & Bachman, J. G. (2013). Historical variation in drug use trajectories across the transition to adulthood: The trend toward lower intercepts and steeper, ascending slopes. *Development and Psychopathology, 25*(2), 527–543. doi:10.1017/s0954579412001228

Jessor, R. (1987). Problem-behavior theory, psychosocial development, and adolescent problem drinking. *British Journal of Addiction, 82*(4), 331–342.

Johnston, L. D., O'Malley, P. M., Bachman, J. G., Schulenberg, J. E., & Miech, R. A. (2015). *Monitoring the Future national survey results on drug use, 1975–2014: Volume II. College students and adults ages 19–55.* Ann Arbor, MI: Institute for Social Research, University of Michigan.

Kagan, J. (1980). Perspectives on continuity. In J. O. G. Bring & J. Kagan (Eds.), *Constancy and change in human development* (pp. 26–74). Cambridge, MA: Harvard University Press.

Kellam, S. G., & Anthony, J. C. (1998). Targeting early antecedents to prevent tobacco smoking: Findings from an epidemiologically based randomized field trial. *American Journal of Public Health, 88*(10), 1490–1495. doi:10.2105/ajph.88.10.1490

Kershaw, P., Forer, B., Lloyd, J. E. V., Hertzman, C., Boyce, W. T., Zumbo, B. D., . . . Smith, A. (2009). The use of population-level data to advance interdisciplinary methodology: A cell-through-society sampling framework for child development research. *International Journal of Social Research Methodology, 12*(5), 387–403. doi:10.1080/13645570802550257

Kessler, R. C., Berglund, P., Demler, O., Jin, R., Merikangas, K. R., & Walters, E. E. (2005). Lifetime prevalence and age-of-onset distributions of DSM-IV disorders in the National Comorbidity Survey Replication. *Archives of General Psychiatry, 62,* 593–602. doi:10.1001/archpsyc.62.6.593

Keyes, K. M., Jager, J., Hamilton, A., O'Malley, P. M., Miech, R., & Schulenberg, J. E. (2015). National multi-cohort time trends in adolescent risk preference and the relation with substance use and problem behavior from 1976 to 2011. *Drug and Alcohol Dependence*, *155*, 267–274. doi:10.1016/j.drugalcdep.2015.06.031

Keyes, K. M., Maslowsky, J., Hamilton, A., & Schulenberg, J. (2015). The great sleep recession: Changes in sleep duration among U.S. adolescents, 1991–2012. *Pediatrics*, *135*(3), 460–468. doi:10.1542/peds.2014-2707

Keyes, K. M., Schulenberg, J. E., O'Malley, P. M., Johnston, L. D., Bachman, J. G., Li, G. H., & Hasin, D. (2011). The social norms of birth cohorts and adolescent marijuana use in the United States, 1976–2007. *Addiction*, *106*(10), 1790–1800. doi:10.1111/j.1360-0443.2011.03485.x

Keyes, K. M., Schulenberg, J. E., O'Malley, P. M., Johnston, L. D., Bachman, J. G., Li, G. H., & Hasin, D. (2012). Birth cohort effects on adolescent alcohol use: The influence of social norms from 1976 to 2007. *Archives of General Psychiatry*, *69*(12), 1304–1313. doi:10.1001/archgenpsychiatry.2012.787

King, K. M., & Chassin, L. (2007). A prospective study of the effects of age of initiation of alcohol and drug use on young adult substance dependence. *Journal of Studies on Alcohol and Drugs*, *68*(2), 256–265. doi:10.15288/jsad.2007.68.256

Kuntsche, E., Knibbe, R., Gmel, G., & Engels, R. (2005). Why do young people drink? A review of drinking motives. *Clinical Psychology Review*, *25*(7), 841–861. doi:10.1016/j.cpr.2005.06.002

Laursen, B., & Collins, W. A. (2009). Parent–child relationships during adolescence. In R. Lerner & L. Steinberg (Eds.), *Handbook of adolescent psychology* (3rd ed., Vol. 2, pp. 3–42). Hoboken, NJ: Wiley.

Lerner, R. M. (2006). Developmental science, developmental systems, and contemporary theories of human development. In R. M. Lerner (Ed.), *Handbook of child psychology* (6th ed., Vol. 1, pp. 1–17). Hoboken, NJ: Wiley.

Lewis, M. (1999). Contextualism and the issue of continuity. *Infant Behavior & Development*, *22*(4), 431–444. doi:10.1016/s0163-6383(00)00017-5

Lynne-Landsman, S. D., Bradshaw, C. P., & Ialongo, N. S. (2010). Testing a developmental cascade model of adolescent substance use trajectories and young adult adjustment. *Development and Psychopathology*, *22*(4), 933–948. doi:10.1017/s0954579410000556

Lynskey, M. T., Heath, A. C., Bucholz, K. K., Slutske, W. S., Madden, P. A. F., Nelson, E. C., . . . Martin, N. G. (2003). Escalation of drug use in early-onset cannabis users vs. co-twin controls. *Journal of the American Medical Association*, *289*(4), 427–433. doi:10.1001/jama.289.4.427

Maggs, J. L., & Schulenberg, J. E. (2004). Trajectories of alcohol use during the transition to adulthood. *Alcohol Research & Health*, *28*(4), 195–201.

Maggs, J. L., Staff, J., Kloska, D. D., Patrick, M. E., O'Malley, P. M., & Schulenberg, J. (2015). Predicting young adult degree attainment by late adolescent marijuana use. *Journal of Adolescent Health*, *57*(2), 205–211. doi:10.1016/j.jadohealth.2015.04.028

Marmorstein, N. R., Iacono, W. G., & Malone, S. M. (2010). Longitudinal associations between depression and substance dependence from adolescence through early adulthood. *Drug and Alcohol Dependence*, *107*(2–3), 154–160. doi:10.1016/j.drugalcdep.2009.10.002

Martin, P., & Martin, M. (2002). Proximal and distal influences on development: The model of developmental adaptation. *Developmental Review*, *22*(1), 78–96. doi:10.1006/drev.2001.0538

Maslowsky, J., Jager, J., & Hemken, D. (2015). Estimating and interpreting latent variable interactions: A tutorial for applying latent moderated structural equation method. *International Journal of Behavioral Development*, *39*, 87–96. doi:10.1177/0165025414552301

Maslowsky, J., & Schulenberg, J. E. (2013). Interaction matters: Quantifying conduct problem by depressive symptoms interaction and its association with adolescent alcohol, cigarette, and marijuana use in a national sample. *Development and Psychopathology*, *25*(4), 1029–1043. doi:10.1017/S0954579413000357

Maslowsky, J., Schulenberg, J. E., O'Malley, P. M., & Kloska, D. D. (2014). Depressive symptoms, conduct problems, and risk for polysubstance use among adolescents: Results from U.S. national surveys. *Mental Health and Substance Use: Dual Diagnosis*, *7*(2), 157–169. doi:10.1080/17523281.2013.786750

Maslowsky, J., Schulenberg, J. E., & Zucker, R. A. (2014). Influence of conduct problems and depressive symptomatology on adolescent substance use: Developmentally proximal versus distal effects. *Developmental Psychology*, *50*(4), 1179–1189. doi:10.1037/a0035085

Masten, A. S., Faden, V. B., Zucker, R. A., & Spear, L. P. (2008). Underage drinking: A developmental framework. *Pediatrics*, *121*, S235–S251. doi:10.1542/peds.2007-2243A

McDade, T. W., & Hayward, M. D. (2009). Rationale and methodological options for assessing infectious disease and related measures in social science surveys. *Biodemography and Social Biology*, 55(2), 159–177. doi:10.1080/19485560903382478

Mennis, J., & Stahler, G. J. (2016). Racial and ethnic disparities in outpatient substance use disorder treatment episode completion for different substances. *Journal of Substance Abuse Treatment*, 63, 25–33. Retrieved from http://doi.org/10.1016/j.jsat.2015.12.007

Merline, A., Jager, J., & Schulenberg, J. E. (2008). Adolescent risk factors for alcohol use and abuse: Stability and change of predictive value across early and middle adulthood. *Addiction*, 103, 84–99. doi:10.1111/j.1360-0442.2008.02178.x

Moffitt, T. E. (1993). Adolescence-limited and life-course-persistent antisocial behavior: A developmental taxonomy. *Psychological Review*, 100(4), 674–701. doi:10.1037/0033-295X.100.4.674

Moffitt, T. E., Arseneault, L., Belsky, D., Dickson, N., Hancox, R. J., Harrington, H., . . . Caspi, A. (2011). A gradient of childhood self-control predicts health, wealth, and public safety. *Proceedings of the National Academy of Sciences of the USA*, 108(7), 2693–2698. doi:10.1073/pnas.1010076108

Moffitt, T. E., & Caspi, A. (2001). Childhood predictors differentiate life-course persistent and adolescence-limited antisocial pathways among males and females. *Development and Psychopathology*, 13(2), 355–375. doi:10.1017/s0954579401002097

Monnat, S. M., & Rigg, K. K. (2016). Examining rural/urban differences in prescription opioid misuse among US adolescents. *Journal of Rural Health*, 32(2), 204–218. Retrieved from http://doi.org/10.1111/jrh.12141

Moolchan, E. T., Fagan, P., Fernander, A. F., Velicer, W. F., Hayward, M. D., King, G., & Clayton, R. R. (2007). Addressing tobacco-related health disparities. *Addiction*, 102(Suppl. 2), 30–42. doi:10.1111/j.1360-0443.2007.01953.x

Muthén, B. O., & Asparouhov, T. (2008, January 9). Growth mixture modeling: Analysis with non-Gaussian random effects. *Longitudinal Data Analysis*, 143–165.

Muthén, B. O., & Curran, P. J. (1997). General longitudinal modeling of individual differences in experimental designs: A latent variable framework for analysis and power estimation. *Psychological Methods*, 2, 371–402.

Needham, B. L. (2007). Gender differences in trajectories of depressive symptomatology and substance use during the transition from adolescence to young adulthood. *Social Science & Medicine*, 65, 1166–1179. doi:10.1016/j.socscimed.2007.04.037

Newcomb, M. D., & Bentler, P. M. (1988). Impact of adolescent drug use and social support on problems of young adults: A longitudinal study. *Journal of Abnormal Psychology*, 97(1), 64–75. doi:10.1037/0021-843x.97.1.64

Newcomb, M. D., & Bentler, P. M. (1989). Substance use and abuse among children and teenagers. *American Psychologist*, 44(2), 242–248.

Newcomb, M. D., Scheier, L. M., & Bentler, P. M. (1993). Effects of adolescent drug use on adult mental health: A prospective study of a community sample. *Experimental and Clinical Psychopharmacology*, 1(1–4), 215–241. doi:10.1037/1064-1297.1.1-4.215

Patrick, M. E., & Schulenberg, J. E. (2011). How trajectories of reasons for alcohol use relate to trajectories of binge drinking: National panel data spanning late adolescence to early adulthood. *Developmental Psychology*, 47(2), 311–317. doi:10.1037/a0021939

Patrick, M. E., Schulenberg, J. E., O'Malley, P. M., Johnston, L. D., & Bachman, J. G. (2011). Adolescents' reported reasons for alcohol and marijuana use as predictors of substance use and problems in adulthood. *Journal of Studies on Alcohol and Drugs*, 72(1), 106–116.

Patrick, M. E., Schulenberg, J. E., O'Malley, P. M., Maggs, J. L., Kloska, D. D., Johnston, L. D., & Bachman, J. G. (2011). Age-related changes in reasons for using alcohol and marijuana from ages 18 to 30 in a national sample. *Psychology of Addictive Behaviors*, 25(2), 330–339. doi:10.1037/a0022445

Pfeifer, J. H., & Allen, N. B. (2012). Arrested development? Reconsidering dual-systems models of brain function in adolescence and disorders. *Trends in Cognitive Sciences*, 16(6), 322–329. doi:10.1016/j.tics.2012.04.011

Quinn, P. D., & Harden, K. P. (2013). Differential changes in impulsivity and sensation seeking and the escalation of substance use from adolescence to early adulthood. *Development and Psychopathology*, 25, 223–239.

Rauer, A. J., & Schulenberg, J. E. (2017). Developmental disturbances. In M. H. Bornstein, M. Arterberry, K. Fingerman, & J. Lansford (Eds.), *The Sage encyclopedia of lifespan human development*. Thousand Oaks, CA: Sage.

Reardon, S. F., & Buka, S. L. (2002). Differences in onset and persistence of substance abuse and dependence among Whites, Blacks, and Hispanics. *Public Health Reports*, 117(Suppl. 1), S51–S59.

Rutter, M. (1996). Transitions and turning points in developmental psychopathology: As applied to the age span between childhood and mid-adulthood. *International Journal of Behavioral Development*, 19(3), 603–626. doi:10.1177/016502549601900309

Rutter, M., & Garmezy, N. (1983). Developmental psychopathology. In P. H. Mussen & E. M. Hetherington (Eds.), *Handbook of child psychology* (Vol. 4, pp. 775–911). New York, NY: Wiley.

Sameroff, A. (2010). A unified theory of development: A dialectic integration of nature and nurture. *Child Development*, 81(1), 6–22. doi:10.1111/j.1467-8624.2009.01378.x

Schulenberg, J., & Maggs, J. L. (2001). Moving targets: Modeling developmental trajectories of adolescent alcohol misuse, individual and peer risk factors, and intervention effects. *Applied Developmental Science*, 5, 237–253.

Schulenberg, J. E., & Maggs, J. L. (2002, March). A developmental perspective on alcohol use and heavy drinking during adolescence and the transition to young adulthood. *Journal of Studies on Alcohol*, 54–70.

Schulenberg, J. E., & Maslowsky, J. (2009). Taking substance use and development seriously: Developmentally distal and proximal influences on adolescent drug use. *Monographs of the Society for Research in Child Development*, 74(3), 121–130.

Schulenberg, J., & Maslowsky, J. (2015). Contribution of adolescence to the life course: What matters most in the long run? *Research in Human Development*, 12(3–4), 319–326. doi:10.1080/15427609.2015.1068039

Schulenberg, J. E., Maslowsky, J., Maggs, J. L., & Zucker, R. (in press). Development matters: Taking the long view on substance use and abuse during adolescence and the transition to adulthood. In S. M. Colby, T. Tevyaw, & P. M. Monti (Eds.), *Adolescents, alcohol, and substance abuse: Reaching teens through brief intervention* (2nd ed.). New York: Guilford.

Schulenberg, J. E., Maslowsky, J., Patrick, M. E., & Martz, M. E. (2016). Substance use in the context of adolescent and young adult development. In S. Brown & R. A. Zucker (Eds.), *The Oxford handbook of adolescent substance abuse*. New York, NY: Oxford University Press.

Schulenberg, J. E., & Patrick, M. E. (2012). Historical and developmental patterns of alcohol and drug use among college students: Framing the problem. In H. R. White & D. Rabiner (Eds.), *College drinking and drug use* (pp. 13–35). New York, NY: Guilford.

Schulenberg, J. E., Patrick, M. E., Kloska, D. D., Maslowsky, J., Maggs, J. L., & O'Malley, P. M.

(2015). Substance use disorder in early midlife: A national prospective study on health and well-being correlates and long-term predictors. *Substance Abuse*, 9(Suppl. 1), 41–57.

Schulenberg, J. E., Patrick, M. E., Maslowsky, J., & Maggs, J. L. (2014). The epidemiology and etiology of adolescent substance use in the developmental perspective. In M. Lewis & K. Rudolph (Eds.), *Handbook of developmental psychopathology* (3rd ed., pp. 601–620). New York, NY: Springer.

Schulenberg, J. E., Sameroff, A. J., & Cicchetti, D. (2004). The transition to adulthood as a critical juncture in the course of psychopathology and mental health. *Development and Psychopathology*, 16(4), 799–806. doi:10.1017/s0954579404040015

Schulenberg, J., Wadsworth, K. N., O'Malley, P. M., Bachman, J. G., & Johnston, L. D. (1996). Adolescent risk factors for binge drinking during the transition to young adulthood: Variable- and pattern-centered approaches to change. *Developmental Psychology*, 32(4), 659–674. doi:10.1037/0012-1649.32.4.659

Settersten, R. A., & Gannon, L. (2005). Structure, agency, and the space between: On the challenges and contradictions of a blended view of the life course. *Advances in Life Course Research*, 10, 35–55.

Settersten, R. A., Jr., & Ray, B. (2010). What's going on with young people today? The long and twisting path to adulthood. *Future of Children*, 20(1), 19–41.

Sisk, C. L., & Zehr, J. L. (2005). Pubertal hormones organize the adolescent brain and behavior. *Frontiers in Neuroendocrinology*, 26(3–4), 163–174. doi:10.1016/j.yfrne.2005.10.003

Sloboda, Z., Glantz, M. D., & Tarter, R. E. (2012). Revisiting the concepts of risk and protective factors for understanding the etiology and development of substance use and substance use disorders: Implications for prevention. *Substance Use & Misuse*, 47(8–9), 944–962. doi:10.3109/10826084.2012.663280

Spear, L. P. (2000). The adolescent brain and age-related behavioral manifestations. *Neuroscience and Biobehavioral Reviews*, 24(4), 417–463. doi:10.1016/s0149-7634(00)00014-2

Spoth, R., Trudeau, L., Guyll, M., Shin, C., & Redmond, C. (2009). Universal intervention effects on substance use among young adults mediated by delayed adolescent substance initiation. *Journal of Consulting and Clinical Psychology*, 77(4), 620–632. doi:10.1037/a0016029

Spruijt-Metz, D. (2011). Etiology, treatment, and prevention of obesity in childhood and adolescence: A decade in review. *Journal of Research on Adolescence, 21*(1), 129–152. doi:10.1111/j.1532-7795.2010.00719.x

Squeglia, L. M., Jacobus, J., & Tapert, S. F. (2009). The influence of substance use on adolescent brain development. *Clinical EEG and Neuroscience, 40*(1), 31–38.

Staff, J., Schulenberg, J. E., Maslowsky, J., Bachman, J. G., O'Malley, P. M., Maggs, J. L., & Johnston, L. D. (2010). Substance use changes and social role transitions: Proximal developmental effects on ongoing trajectories from late adolescence through early adulthood. *Development and Psychopathology, 22*(4), 917–932. doi:10.1017/S0954579410000544

Steinberg, L., Albert, D., Cauffman, E., Banich, M., Graham, S., & Woolard, J. (2008). Age differences in sensation seeking and impulsivity as indexed by behavior and self-report: Evidence for a dual systems model. *Developmental Psychology, 44*(6), 1764–1778. doi:10.1037/a0012955

Steinberg, L., Cauffman, E., Woolard, J., Graham, S., & Banich, M. (2009). Are adolescents less mature than adults? Minors' access to abortion, the juvenile death penalty, and the alleged APA "flip-flop." *American Psychologist, 64*(7), 583–594. doi:10.1037/a0014763

Steinberg, L., Dahl, R., Keating, D. P., Kupfer, D. J., Masten, A. S., & Pine, D. S. (2006). Psychopathology in adolescence: Integrating affective neuroscience with the study of context. In D. Cicchetti & D. Cohen (Eds.), *Developmental psychopathology* (2nd ed., Vol. 2, pp. 710–741). New York, NY: Wiley.

Stenbacka, M. (2003). Problematic alcohol and cannabis use in adolescence—Risk of serious adult substance abuse? *Drug and Alcohol Review, 22*(3), 277–286. doi:10.1080/0959523031000154418

Susman, E. J., & Dorn, L. D. (2009). Puberty: Its role in development. In R. M. Lerner & L. Steinberg (Eds.), *Handbook of adolescent psychology* (3rd ed., pp. 116–151). Hoboken, NJ: Wiley.

Tarter, R. E. (2010). Etiology of adolescent substance abuse: A developmental perspective. *American Journal on Addictions, 11*(3), 171–191. doi:10.1080/10550490290087965

Tomasik, M. J., & Silbereisen, R. K. (2012). Social change and adolescent developmental tasks: The case of postcommunist Europe. *Child Development Perspectives, 6*(4), 326–334. doi:10.1111/j.1750-8606.2011.00228.x

Volkow, N. D., Baler, R. D., Compton, W. M., & Weiss, S. R. B. (2014). Adverse health effects of marijuana use. *New England Journal of Medicine, 370*(23), 2219–2227. doi:10.1056/NEJMra1402309

Wagner, F. A., & Anthony, J. C. (2002). From first drug use to drug dependence: Developmental periods of risk for dependence upon marijuana, cocaine, and alcohol. *Neuropsychopharmacology, 26*(4), 479–488. doi:10.1038/S0893-133X(01)00367-0

Walters, G. D. (2011). The latent structure of life-course-persistent antisocial behavior: Is Moffitt's developmental taxonomy a true taxonomy? *Journal of Consulting and Clinical Psychology, 79*(1), 96–105. doi:10.1037/a0021519

Welty, L. J., Harrison, A. J., Abram, K. M., Olson, N. D., Aaby, D. A., McCoy, K. P., . . . Teplin, L. A. (2016). Health disparities in drug- and alcohol-use disorders: A 12-year longitudinal study of youths after detention. *American Journal of Public Health, 106*(5), 872–880. Retrieved from http://doi.org/10.2105/AJPH.2015.303032

Werner, H. (1957). The concept of development from a comparative and organismic point of view. In D. B. Harris (Ed.), *The concept of development: An issue in the study of human behavior* (pp. 125–148). Minneapolis, MN: University of Minnesota Press.

Wilcox, C. E., Dekonenko, C. J., Mayer, A. R., Bogenschutz, M. P., & Turner, J. A. (2014). Cognitive control in alcohol use disorder: Deficits and clinical relevance. *Reviews in the Neurosciences, 25*(1), 1–24. doi:10.1515/revneuro-2013-0054

Windle, M., Spear, L. P., Fuligni, A. J., Angold, A., Brown, J. D., Pine, D., . . . Dahl, R. E. (2008). Transitions into underage and problem drinking: Developmental processes and mechanisms between 10 and 15 years of age. *Pediatrics, 121*(Suppl. 4), S273–S289. doi:10.1542/peds.2007-2243C

Wu, L.-T., Pilowsky, D. J., & Schlenger, W. E. (2005). High prevalence of substance use disorders among adolescents who use marijuana and inhalants. *Drug and Alcohol Dependence, 78*(1), 23–32. doi:10.1016/j.drugalcdep.2004.08.025

Zucker, R. A. (1986). The four alcoholisms: A developmental account of the etiologic process. *Nebraska Symposium on Motivation, 34*, 27–83.

Zucker, R. A. (1989). Is risk for alcoholism predictable? A probabilistic approach to a developmental problem. *Drugs and Society, 4*, 69–93.

Zucker, R. A. (1994). Pathways to alcohol problems and alcoholism: A developmental account of the evidence for multiple alcoholisms and for contextual contributions to risk. In R. A. Zucker, J. Howard, & G. M. Boyd (Eds.), *The development of alcohol problems: Exploring the biopsychosocial matrix of risk* (pp. 255–289). Rockville, MD: National Institute of Alcohol Abuse and Alcoholism.

Zucker, R. A., Donovan, J. E., Masten, A. S., Mattson, M. E., & Moss, H. B. (2008). Early developmental processes and the continuity of risk for underage drinking and problem drinking. *Pediatrics, 121*(Suppl. 4), S252–S272. doi:10.1542/peds.2007-2243B

Zucker, R. A., & Gomberg, E. S. L. (1986). Etiology of alcoholism reconsidered: The case for a biopsychosocial process. *American Psychologist, 41*(7), 783–793. doi:10.1037//0003-066x.41.7.783

Zucker, R. A., Hicks, B. M., & Heitzeg, M. H. (2016). Alcohol use and the alcohol use disorders over the life course: A cross-level developmental review. In D. Cicchetti (Ed.), *Developmental psychopathology* (3rd ed., Vol. 3, pp. 793–833). Hoboken, NJ: Wiley.

13

Who Is Using Alternative Tobacco Products and Why?

Research on Adolescents and Young Adults

Alexandra Loukas

Deepti Agarwal

Tobacco use remains the leading cause of preventable disease and death in the United States and worldwide. According to the 2012 Surgeon General's report on adolescent and young adult tobacco use (US Department of Health and Human Services [USDHHS], 2012), each year approximately 480,000 deaths in the United States are attributable to cigarettes and second-hand smoke. Considering that this estimate is limited to cigarettes only, the actual yearly death toll due to all forms of tobacco use is likely much higher. Tobacco has negative physical effects on nearly all organs of the body, with adult tobacco use associated with respiratory problems, cardiovascular disease, and various cancers (USDHHS, 2014). Most notably, approximately 90% of all lung cancers are directly attributable to cigarette use alone. Adolescents and young adults are in no way shielded from the negative consequences of using tobacco. For example, accumulating evidence from animal and limited human studies indicates that compared with older adults, the developing brains of the adolescent and young adult are more vulnerable to the effects of nicotine, the addictive component of tobacco, which may alter brain development and result in subsequent disturbances in emotion and attention regulation (Yuan, Cross, Loughlin, & Leslie, 2015). Additional evidence indicates that compared with their non-smoking peers, 10- to 18-year-old adolescents who smoke five or more cigarettes a day are more likely to have lower levels and slower growth of lung functioning, early indictors of lung disease among adult smokers (Gold et al., 1996). In view of the detrimental health effects of tobacco use, it is estimated that one-third of adolescents who smoke cigarettes and continue to do so into adulthood will die prematurely (USDHHS, 2012).

Adolescence and young adulthood are characterized by transitions in various developmental domains (Arnett, 2015; Schulenberg, Maggs, & Hurrelmann, 1997), including tobacco use. These two developmental periods capture the most significant transitions in tobacco use, namely initiation and progression to regular tobacco use, a precursor to nicotine dependence (Mayhew, Flay, & Mott, 2000). Virtually all tobacco use is initiated and regular tobacco use is established prior to the age of 26 years (Breslau, Johnson, Hiripi, & Kessler, 2001; Chen & Kandel, 1995; USDHHS, 2012). It is commonly acknowledged that the majority of adult tobacco users began using tobacco prior to the age of 18 years. Accordingly, research conducted by Chassin, Presson, Sherman, and Edwards (1990), and described in this volume, indicates that smoking cigarettes at least monthly in adolescence raises the risk for adult smoking by a factor of 16. However, a considerable number of tobacco users also initiate during young adulthood (Chassin, Presson, Sherman, & Edwards, 1991; USDHHS, 2012). Results from one of the few studies examining initiation of not only cigarettes but also various alternative tobacco products, such as hookah, smokeless tobacco, snus, and electronic nicotine delivery systems, commonly referred to as e-cigarettes, indicate that 32% of 18- to 34-year-old ever tobacco users reported tobacco initiation after the age of 18 years. The same study found that 39% of regular tobacco users reported progressing to regular use during young adulthood (Rath, Villanti, Abrams, & Vallone, 2012). Both adolescence and young adulthood therefore represent heightened periods of vulnerability for initiating and potentially sustaining all tobacco use.

INCREASING DIVERSITY OF TOBACCO PRODUCTS

The tobacco products landscape to which today's adolescents and young adults are exposed varies considerably from that to which their parents were exposed, and the diversity of available tobacco products is greater than ever before. Although cigarettes, smokeless tobacco, and traditional cigars have been widely available and used at various times throughout US history, today's adolescents and young adults are exposed to a growing array of alternative tobacco and nicotine products, including hookah/shisha, little cigars and cigarillos, snus, dissolvable tobacco, and e-cigarettes. The ever-changing tobacco landscape underscores the importance of assessing the use of all types of tobacco and nicotine products, not just cigarettes, as well as the concurrent use of more than one product to capture total tobacco use and assess the potential health consequences.

CIGARETTE SMOKING IS DECREASING, BUT ALTERNATIVE TOBACCO PRODUCT USE IS INCREASING

Despite increasing recognition of the diversity of available products, research on tobacco use is focused overwhelmingly on cigarettes, most likely because they continue to be the most common form of tobacco used by adults (Agaku, King, & Dube, 2014). Almost one in five US adults smoke cigarettes (Jamal et al., 2014). However, cigarette use has been declining since 2000, due in large part to public health efforts and the introduction of federal and state policies that mandate increased taxation of cigarettes, comprehensive clean indoor air policies, minimum age laws, and restrictions on cigarette marketing (Agaku et al., 2014;

Centers for Disease Control and Prevention, 2010). At the same time, use of alternative tobacco products has been increasing (Connolly & Alpert, 2008; King, Patel, Nguyen, & Dube, 2015). Young adults have the highest prevalence of alternative tobacco product use (McMillen, Maduka, & Winickoff, 2012), with 22% of 18- to 34-year-olds reporting ever use of at least one noncombustible alternative product (i.e., smokeless tobacco, snus, dissolvable tobacco, and e-cigarettes) and more than half (51.5%) reporting use of at least one combustible alternative (i.e., cigars/little cigars/cigarillos, pipes, bidi, and hookah) (Richardson, Williams, Rath, Villanti, & Vallone, 2014).

Until recently, cigarettes were the most common form of tobacco used by adolescents. However, data from the National Youth Tobacco Survey (NYTS) indicate that adolescents' use of e-cigarettes and hookah surpassed use of cigarettes in 2014 (Arrazola et al., 2015). Whereas 9.2% of high school students used cigarettes in 2014, 13.4% used e-cigarettes and 9.4% used hookah. Middle school students' use of e-cigarettes also surpassed use of cigarettes, with 3.9% of middle school students using e-cigarettes compared with 2.5% using cigarettes. Additional data from the 2014 NYTS indicate that cigarette use decreased from 2011 to 2014 among middle and high school students, but e-cigarette and hookah use increased. Although increasingly more research is focused on the use of alternative tobacco products, there continue to be important gaps in our knowledge regarding who is using these products and why they are being used.

WHO IS USING ALTERNATIVE TOBACCO PRODUCTS?

Use of alternative tobacco products is not equally distributed among all adolescent and young adult populations. Adolescents and young adults who smoke cigarettes are more likely than non-cigarette smokers to use both combustible and noncombustible alternative products (Loukas, Batanova, Fernandez, & Agarwal, 2015). For example, using data from a national study of college students, Jarrett, Blosnich, and Horn (2012) found that 28.5% of current cigarette smokers were current hookah users in comparison with 5.9% of non-cigarette smokers. There are also gender differences in prevalence of alternative tobacco product use within smokers and non-smokers. Thus, a nationally representative study of

14- to 17-year-olds indicated that male current smokers were more likely than their female counterparts to use smokeless tobacco, cigars, and pipes (Saunders & Geletko, 2012). Among non-cigarette smoking adolescents, males were more likely than females to use smokeless tobacco and cigars, but not pipes.

In addition to variability in use of alternative tobacco products by smoking status, evidence indicates that older adolescents and young adults are more likely than younger adolescents to report tobacco use, reflecting an increasing developmental gradient (USDHHS, 2014). Non-Hispanic White adolescents are more likely than adolescents of other races/ethnicities to report smokeless tobacco use. Although there are fewer race/ethnicity differences for other alternative products (Saunders & Geletko, 2012), some studies report that African American adolescents and young adults are more likely than their counterparts to use little cigars and cigarillos (Corey et al., 2014; Sterling, Berg, Thomas, Glantz, & Ahluwalia, 2013). There is also variability in prevalence across gender, with males being more likely than females to report use of alternative products, although differences are not consistent across products or studies (Higgins et al., 2015).

Examination of gender and race/ethnicity differences in use of alternative tobacco products is becoming increasingly important because females and racial/ethnic minorities are targets of alternative tobacco products advertising and promotions. For example, e-cigarette manufacturers are targeting females with products designed specifically for this gender, offering products that are fashionable, slim, and available in colors such as pink and yellow (Yao, Jiang, Grana, Ling, & Glantz, 2016). Similarly, marketing for little cigars and cigarillos has been targeted to African Americans and the communities in which they live. Thus, assessments of neighborhoods with higher percentages of African Americans indicate there are more retail outlets that sell little cigars and cigarillos and more storefront advertisements for such products in these neighborhoods (Cantrell et al., 2013; Roberts, Berman, Slater, Hinton, & Ferketich, 2015). Moreover, little cigars and cigarillos are cheaper at stores located in neighborhoods with more African Americans than in other neighborhoods (Cantrell et al., 2013). Despite targeted marketing, few studies have gone beyond the examination of gender or race/ethnicity differences in prevalence of use of alternative products. Additional research is needed to determine if there are gender or race/ethnicity differences in the role of marketing in use of alternative products and in the reasons for use of these products, expectancies of use, and their associations with progression to regular use of alternative tobacco products.

ALTERNATIVE TOBACCO PRODUCTS APPEAL TO ADOLESCENTS AND YOUNG ADULTS

In addition to characterizing the users of alternative tobacco products, it is important to understand why alternative tobacco products are used by adolescents and young adults. Such information is essential to the development of programs and policies that prevent tobacco initiation and reduce use. Interestingly, much of the research on the appeal of alternative tobacco products is focused on how characteristics, functions, and motives for use vary from those of traditional cigarettes. Indeed, the term *alternative tobacco product* juxtaposes products such as smokeless tobacco, e-cigarettes, and cigars with cigarettes. Consequently, there is little research on the appeal of alternative tobacco products that does not take a comparative approach. Even so, findings from limited studies indicate that alternative tobacco products fulfill important developmental needs, including autonomy, identity exploration, and quality interpersonal relationships and intimacy. The top two reasons given by high school and college students for trying e-cigarettes were curiosity and because friends and family used e-cigarettes (Kong, Morean, Cavallo, Camenga, & Krishnan-Sarin, 2015). Similarly, 18- to 22-year-old cigarette smokers reported that they first tried alternative tobacco products, such as cigars, out of curiosity and/or because a friend or family member was using the product (Richter, Caraballo, Pederson, & Gupta, 2008). Other reasons why alternative tobacco products appeal to adolescents and young adults are that they are cheaper than cigarettes and that noncombustible products, such as smokeless tobacco and snus, are easier to conceal (Lee, Battle, Lipton, & Soller, 2010; Peters, Meshack, Lin, Hill, & Abughosh, 2013).

Flavors and Alternative Tobacco Products

Alternative tobacco products may also appeal to adolescents and young adults because they are available in a variety flavors, such as grape, cherry, coffee, and rum (Kong et al., 2015). An extreme example of flavor offerings is that of e-cigarettes. As of January 2014, e-cigarettes were available in more than 7,500 unique flavors (Zhu et al., 2014). The US Food and Drug Administration's (FDA) 2009 Family Smoking Prevention and Tobacco Control Act banned the addition of flavors to cigarettes, with the exception of menthol, but flavors continue to be available in all alternative tobacco products. Researchers propose that flavors are included in tobacco products to entice adolescents and young adults to initiate and sustain use of these products. Indeed, evidence indicates that adolescents and younger adults (18- to 24-year-olds) are more likely than older adults (25- to 35-year-olds) to use flavored tobacco products (Villanti, Richardson, Vallone, & Rath, 2013). Documents obtained from the tobacco industry confirm that flavors are more appealing to novice and younger smokers than established and older smokers because flavors reduce harshness and enhance aroma and taste, making tobacco products easier to use (Carpenter, Wayne, Pauly, Koh, & Connolly, 2005).

Marketing and Alternative Tobacco Products

Alternative tobacco products may also appeal to adolescents and young adults because of how they are marketed. Billions of dollars are spent each year on advertisements and promotions to sell tobacco products (Federal Trade Commission, 2015a, 2015b; Kim, Arnold, & Makarenko, 2014). Although federal regulations restrict the marketing of tobacco to children and adolescents, young adults have been subject to aggressive tobacco marketing (Carpenter et al., 2005; Ling & Glantz, 2002). The tobacco industry is well aware that young adulthood, with its multiple life transitions including new-found freedom from parents and formation of new social roles, is an ideal period during which tobacco use can be introduced and solidified (Ling & Glantz, 2002). Further recognizing that young adults are their youngest legal targets (18+ years old), the tobacco industry has targeted this segment of the population through various marketing channels. One channel that is particularly advantageous, given restrictions in marketing to youth, is bars, where marketing is largely unregulated. Bars provide a context for direct product advertising (e.g., posters and other ads) and promotion (e.g., coupons for discounted tobacco products and other giveaways),

and they also serve as a means to collect customer (existing and new) contact information, who will then directly receive mail/e-mail advertisements and promotions from the company (Katz & Lavack, 2002).

Federal regulations also ban tobacco advertising on television and radio. However, there is widespread promotion of alternative tobacco products on the Internet and in magazines and newspapers (Freeman, 2012; Kim et al., 2014). Recently, there has been concern about the advertising of e-cigarettes (Kim et al., 2014). Until August 2016, e-cigarettes were not considered tobacco products; therefore, there were no federal regulations regarding e-cigarettes or the marketing of these products. From November to June 2013 alone, e-cigarette companies spent $39 million marketing their products (Legacy, 2014). During this period, more money was spent on television and magazine advertising than on any other channels (Legacy, 2014), with tactics that appeal to younger audiences, such as the use of celebrity endorsements, sexual and romantic appeal, and sponsorship of fashionable events (de Andrade, Hastings, & Angus, 2013; Grana & Ling, 2014). Early advertising of e-cigarettes was conducted primarily on the Internet; however, advertisements for e-cigarettes on television are increasingly prevalent (Duke et al., 2014). The number of e-cigarette advertisements on television to which adolescents were exposed increased by 256% between 2011 and 2013 (Duke et al., 2014). During the same period, young adults' exposure to e-cigarette advertisements on television increased by 321%.

Tobacco marketing aims to influence consumers' behaviors by increasing awareness of a product, highlighting its benefits, and encouraging positive attitudes toward the product (Lovato, Watts, & Stead, 2011). Adolescents and young adults are more receptive to tobacco advertisements and promotions compared to older adults (Biener & Albers, 2004), and receptivity is associated with initiation and future smoking behaviors (Gilpin, White, Messer, & Pierce, 2007; Lovato et al., 2011). There is also evidence for a causal link between exposure to cigarette marketing and adolescent initiation and progression to regular smoking (Biener & Siegel, 2000; DiFranza et al., 2006). Greater exposure to cigarette advertisements and promotions is linked to subsequent initiation and use of cigarettes. Despite increasing prevalence of alternative tobacco products use among adolescents and young adults, most marketing research has been limited to cigarettes, with little known about how marketing influences the use of alternative tobacco products.

Harm Perceptions and Alternative Tobacco Products

Another reason why alternative tobacco products may appeal to adolescents and young adults is that they are perceived to be less harmful than cigarettes (Amrock, Zakhar, Zhou, & Weitzman, 2015; Cohn, Cobb, Niaura, & Richardson, 2015). Adolescent and young adult perceptions of lower harm may be appropriate for noncombustible products, such as smokeless tobacco and snus. Noncombustible products pose fewer health risks than cigarettes because they do not expose the user or those near him or her to the toxins in tobacco smoke, although they are not completely safe and carry some risks, including for oral cancers and cardiovascular disease (O'Connor, 2012). Combustible products (e.g., cigars and hookah), on the other hand, pose many of the same health risks as smoking cigarettes; thus, lower harm perceptions of these products relative to cigarettes are inaccurate. Moreover, all alternative products contain nicotine and, similar to cigarettes, regular use can lead to nicotine dependence (USDHHS, 2012). There is also concern that the flavors added to alternative tobacco products may themselves increase risk for health problems (Barrington-Trimis, Samet, & McConnell, 2014). However, the majority of alternative tobacco products, with the exception of smokeless tobacco, were not regulated by the FDA until August 2016, and thus were not subject to product standards requirements (i.e., product design and safety requirements) or to reporting the constituents of the product. Therefore, significantly less is known about the health risks of noncombustible and combustible alternative products than about cigarettes. Nonetheless, adolescent and young adult perceptions of the harmfulness of tobacco products have consistently been linked to tobacco initiation and use (Agarwal & Loukas, 2015; Amrock et al., 2015; Cohn et al., 2015).

Perhaps one of the most striking findings in the tobacco harm perceptions literature is adolescents' and young adults' misperceptions regarding the harms associated with using hookah, a behavior that is on the rise among adolescents and young adults (Arrazola et al., 2015; Barnett, Forrest, Porter, & Curbow, 2014). Use of this product is especially popular among young adults, in part because it facilitates social interactions with peers (Braun, Glassman, Wohlwend, Whewell, & Reindl, 2012; Sharma, Beck, & Clark, 2013). Hookah is often used in groups with friends at lounges and bars, and it may serve as an alternative to drinking alcohol to enhance social interaction (Sharma et al., 2013). However, hookah contains many of the same toxic chemicals (tar, carbon monoxide, etc.) as cigarettes (Cobb, Shihadeh, Weaver, & Eissenberg, 2011), and use has been linked with similar health outcomes, including various cancers and cardiovascular disease (Kadhum, Sweidan, Jaffery, Al-Saadi, & Madden, 2015). Because one mouth piece is often used by multiple individuals to smoke hookah, hookah use is also associated with elevated risk for infectious diseases, such as herpes and hepatitis (Kadhum et al., 2015). Despite these risks, adolescents and young adults report that hookah use is safer than cigarette use (Heinz et al., 2013). Misperceptions of harm are based in part on hookah's aesthetic appeal—the sweet smell and taste of the flavored tobacco—and on the incorrect belief that the smoke resulting from hookah is safer than cigarette smoke because it is filtered through water (Aljarrah, Ababneh, & Al-Delaimy, 2009; Maziak et al., 2004; Smith-Simone et al., 2008). These misperceptions are concerning because similar to findings for other alternative tobacco products, adolescents and young adults who hold lower harm perceptions regarding hookah are more likely than their peers to use hookah (Chen & Loukas, 2015; Heinz et al., 2013; Minaker, Shuh, Burkhalter, & Manske, 2015).

ALTERNATIVE TOBACCO PRODUCTS USE TRAJECTORIES

Existing studies only begin to scratch the surface of who uses alternative tobacco products and why these products are used by adolescents and young adults. Existing research, most of which is cross-sectional, provides important information on the prevalence and correlates of alternative tobacco products use. Longitudinal research is needed, however, to determine why and how trial of alternative tobacco products potentially progresses to regular use. As described in Chapter 14 of this volume, longitudinal research on cigarette smoking indicates that although there is an overall increasing trajectory of cigarette use from adolescence into adulthood, smokers are a heterogeneous population with several distinct developmental trajectories of smoking behaviors. These developmental trajectories capture the onset, acceleration, and persistence of cigarette use across time, and they are important for understanding both the antecedents and the consequences of alternative tobacco use. Thus, examination of heterogeneity in the developmental trajectories of alternative tobacco products use is needed to ultimately identify adolescents at most risk for regular and sustained tobacco use.

ARE ALTERNATIVE TOBACCO PRODUCTS A GATEWAY TO CIGARETTE USE?

Longitudinal models that map the trajectories and transitions in use of varying types of tobacco products across adolescence and young adulthood are also needed to provide clarity on the potential sequence of product use beginning, for example, with the less harmful noncombustible products and progressing to combustible tobacco products. Such models can address the concerns of researchers who argue that noncombustible products may serve as a "gateway" to more harmful combustible products, particularly cigarettes and particularly by adolescents and young adults. However, the empirical evidence for a causal link from the use of noncombustible products to subsequent combustible product use is conflicting and weak (Kozlowski, O'Connor, Edwards, & Flaherty, 2003; O'Connor, Flaherty, Quinio Edwards, & Kozlowski, 2003; Phillips, 2015).

Claims about noncombustible products as gateways to combustible product use have been based on limited research, some of which includes cross-sectional or short-term longitudinal studies. Although short-term longitudinal studies are able to establish temporality (e.g., hookah use is initiated prior to cigarette use), they do not allow researchers to examine the role of noncombustible products in the regular and sustained use of combustible products. Much of the research on gateway effects also fails to take into account confounding variables that likely contribute to initiation and use of both noncombustible and combustible products (Timberlake, Huh, & Lakon, 2009). For example, Tomar (2003) concluded that smokeless tobacco may be a gateway to cigarette smoking based on findings that 12- to 18-year-old males who never used cigarettes but used smokeless tobacco at baseline were more likely than their counterparts to become cigarette smokers 4 years later. Subsequent

reanalysis of these data indicated that once baseline school performance was taken into consideration, the role of smokeless tobacco use in later smoking disappeared (O'Connor et al., 2003). These findings underscore the importance of considering all other potential causes of tobacco use prior to making claims regarding gateway effects.

Another limitation of the existing research on gateway effects is that the overwhelming majority of studies have been conducted with smokeless tobacco and cigarettes. Because non-Hispanic White males are significantly more likely than racial/ethnic minorities and females to use smokeless tobacco (Higgins et al., 2015), this research has also been limited to White male tobacco use. Relatively few studies have examined the role of other alternative tobacco products in cigarette smoking initiation or in the initiation of other combustible products. An exception is a study indicating that ninth-grade boys and girls who used e-cigarettes but never used any combustible products were more likely than their peers who did not use e-cigarettes to report subsequent use of cigarettes, hookah, and cigars 12 months later (Leventhal et al., 2015). The prospective association was present even after a host of sociodemographic, environmental, and intrapersonal covariates were taken into consideration. Although the authors did not make any claims regarding a causal or gateway effect, their findings provide support for the role of e-cigarettes in the initiation, or at least the trial, of combustible products. The findings do not, however, address the role of e-cigarette use in the progression to regular and sustained use of combustible products. Given these findings and methodological shortcomings of previous studies, additional research that accounts for confounding variables and uses longitudinal data to map the trajectories and transitions of tobacco use is needed to adequately determine the role of alternative tobacco products not only in smoking initiation but also in progression to regular use and ultimately dependence.

ALTERNATIVE TOBACCO PRODUCTS AND HARM REDUCTION

Despite disagreement about the harms associated with some alternative tobacco products and their role as gateway products, tobacco researchers are in agreement that alternative tobacco products and cigarettes should never be promoted to or used by children and adolescents. However, the suitability and usefulness of certain lower risk alternative products, such as smokeless tobacco and e-cigarettes, for adult smokers is a hotly debated topic that has caused a deep rift in the tobacco research community between those who argue for a harm reduction approach (Kozlowski, 2007) and those who question the usefulness of any tobacco or nicotine product for any reason (Tomar, Fox, & Severson, 2009). It is important to recognize that although arguments for harm reduction have been widely accepted for other types of drugs (Toumbourou et al., 2007), this approach has only recently been taken seriously within the tobacco community. Increasing availability, acceptability, and use of e-cigarettes and their promotion as cigarette alternatives have been particularly influential in stimulating arguments both in favor and against harm reduction (Cahn & Siegel, 2011).

Proponents of the harm reduction approach argue that adults who use combustible products, particularly cigarettes, and who cannot or will not quit should be encouraged to switch to noncombustible products (Kiviniemi & Kozlowski, 2015). The basis for the harm reduction argument is that switching to noncombustible products will result not only in lowering individual health risks but also in reducing the burden of disease to society. Alternatively, opponents of the harm reduction approach voice at least two concerns (O'Connor, 2012). First, pointing to the gateway hypothesis, opponents worry that adolescents' entry into tobacco product use will be with the less harmful, cheaper, and easier to conceal noncombustible products, which eventually will be substituted with the more harmful combustible products, namely cigarettes. Opponents note that the resulting increase in the number of new tobacco users, with their increased risk for negative health consequences, will offset the reduced disease burden realized by adult smokers who may switch to noncombustible products to quit smoking. Second, opponents argue that promotion of the harm reduction approach will be detrimental because it may result in an increase in multiple tobacco product users. That is, heeding the harm reduction message, cigarette smokers may begin to use less harmful noncombustible products. Rather than quitting smoking, however, less harmful noncombustible products may be used to supplement cigarettes. As evidence, opponents highlight data indicating that multiple tobacco use impedes cessation

success (Popova & Ling, 2013) and in turn prolongs use and nicotine dependence. Like other research on alternative tobacco products, firm conclusions regarding the harm reduction approach are difficult to draw because of conflicting findings and limited data, much of which focus on the use of cigarettes and smokeless tobacco, to the exclusion of other types of alternative products.

MULTIPLE TOBACCO PRODUCT USE

A discussion of alternative tobacco products would not be complete without examination of multiple tobacco use, a pattern that is now more prevalent among adolescents and young adults than is use of cigarettes alone (Lee, Hebert, Nonnemaker, & Kim, 2014; Richardson et al., 2014; Wills, Knight, Williams, Pagano, & Sargent, 2015). Recent evidence indicates that whereas 6.7% of middle and high school students are current users of only one tobacco or nicotine product, 3.6% are current users of two or more products and 4.3% are current users of three or more products (Lee, Hebert, Nonnemaker, & Kim, 2015). As noted previously, adolescents and young adults who are cigarette smokers are more likely than non-smokers to use alternative tobacco products and thus comprise a considerable portion of the increasing number of multiple tobacco products users (Loukas et al., 2015). Prior to delving further into this research, however, an overview must be provided of how multiple tobacco use is conceptualized and measured.

Multiple tobacco use is generally defined as the concurrent use of more than one tobacco product. To be clear, multiple tobacco use does not refer to using more than one product at the exact same time but, rather, to alternating use of different products. For example, a multiple tobacco product user may use cigarettes at home but smokeless tobacco in a non-smoking workplace. Beyond this basic definition, however, there is considerable variability in the term used to describe the behavior and in measurement of the construct (for a review, see Klesges et al., 2011). Numerous terms are used to describe the concurrent use of multiple tobacco products, including *dual use, poly use, concurrent use,* and *concomitant use.* Similarly, there is variability in what tobacco products (cigarettes, cigars, etc.) are assessed and the frequency of tobacco use (daily, past month, ever use, etc.). Thus, whereas one study defined dual users of e-cigarettes as adolescents who ever used both e-cigarettes and cigarettes (Wills et al., 2015), another defined dual users as adolescents who were current (past 30-day) users of both e-cigarettes and cigarettes (Cooper, Case, Loukas, Creamer, & Perry, 2016). The lack of consistency in terminology and measurement makes comparing results and drawing conclusions difficult. However, evidence indicates that multiple tobacco use is increasingly prevalent, particularly among young adults, who are more likely than older adults to be concurrent users of more than one tobacco product (Kasza et al., 2014; Lee et al., 2014).

Research on multiple tobacco product use is focused primarily on examining differences in sociodemographic characteristics and risk behaviors between exclusive users of one tobacco or nicotine product and users of two or more products. Results from these studies indicate that adolescent and young adult multiple tobacco product users are more likely than their peers to be male, non-Hispanic White, and to report lower individual or parent education (Apelberg et al., 2014; Rath et al., 2012; Wills et al., 2015). Although males are more likely than females to be multiple tobacco users, both genders' use of alternative tobacco products has become increasingly diverse. That is, 72% of girls who reported current tobacco use (i.e., cigarettes, cigars, and smokeless tobacco) in 1999 were exclusive users of cigarettes only, compared with 46% in 2013. Similarly, 27% of current tobacco-using boys in 1999 reported exclusive use of cigarettes, compared with only 16% in 2013 (Creamer, Perry, Harrell, & Diamond, 2015). Research on multiple tobacco use paints a picture of adolescents and young adults who engage in a variety of risk behaviors and affiliate with deviant peers. Thus, results from one study indicate that 12- to 25-year-old polytobacco users (i.e., used at least two of four tobacco products in the past 30 days) were more likely than their peers to report alcohol abuse/dependence, drug abuse/dependence, being arrested, and driving under the influence of alcohol and/or drugs, all within the past 12 months (Fix et al., 2014). Results from a study of 9th- and 10th-grade students indicate that those who were dual users of cigarettes and e-cigarettes were more likely than cigarette-only and non-tobacco users to report lower grades, alcohol and marijuana use, and to have peers who smoke cigarettes (Wills et al., 2015). Taken together, findings indicate that multiple tobacco product use may be part of a constellation of risk behaviors.

In addition to concerns about participation in risk behaviors, multiple tobacco use raises concerns about the amount of tobacco consumed and the potential of this pattern of use to lead to continued multiple tobacco use and nicotine dependence. Limited data indicate that adolescent polytobacco users are more likely than single-product users to use tobacco more frequently (Apelberg et al., 2014) and to follow a trajectory of increased and prolonged tobacco use (Rosendahl, Galanti, & Gilljam, 2008). Dual use is a particularly persistent behavior. One nationally representative study of adolescents showed that the probability of maintaining dual use of cigarettes and smokeless tobacco across a 1-year period was 81% (Kaufman, Land, Parascandola, Augustson, & Backinger, 2015). Adolescent polytobacco users are also more likely than single-product users to report a variety of indicators of nicotine dependence, including strong cravings to use tobacco, feeling irritable or restless when not using tobacco for a while, using tobacco within 30 minutes of waking, and moderate to high levels of loss of autonomy over nicotine (Bombard, Rock, Pederson, & Asman, 2008; Lee et al., 2015). Given these findings, use of multiple tobacco products also raises important questions regarding heterogeneity among users based on patterns of use of various types of tobacco. Additional research is needed to more carefully characterize these patterns and determine if factors contributing to initiation, progression, and even cessation of tobacco use differ across use patterns. Given variations in use of alternative tobacco products by gender and race/ethnicity, additional research is also needed to determine if these patterns and associated predictors vary across males and females and also across non-Hispanic White and non-White adolescents and young adults. Nonetheless, existing evidence underscores the importance of differentiating between single- and multiple-product-using adolescents and young adults, and it also has important implications for prevention and intervention efforts. Different strategies and messages may be necessary to address the needs of these heterogeneous groups, some of which appear to be at considerably higher risk for regular and sustained tobacco use.

CONCLUSIONS AND FUTURE DIRECTIONS

The tobacco landscape is more complex and diverse than it has ever been, with the availability of multiple types of combustible and noncombustible products. Adding to the complexity are the varying levels of harm associated with use of these products and the varying characteristics that make them more or less appealing to adolescents and young adults. Given the known health risks of cigarettes, the growing social disapproval of cigarette smoking, and, in turn, the decline in cigarette use (USDHHS, 2012), it is perhaps not surprising that use of alternative tobacco products is becoming increasingly prevalent. After all, alternative tobacco products are widely advertised and are perceived to be less harmful, cheaper, and easier to conceal and also to taste better than cigarettes. Although research on alternative tobacco product use is increasing, it has not kept pace with this ever-changing landscape. To move the field forward, tobacco researchers will need to use sophisticated analytic approaches to map developmental trajectories and transitions of alternative tobacco product use and, in so doing, pay close attention to characterizing the heterogeneity in patterns of use.

Constructing longitudinal models that map developmental trajectories and transitions of alternative tobacco use will allow researchers to draw more definitive answers to several outstanding questions. First, longitudinal models offer a stronger test of the "gateway" hypothesis and the potential (multiple) transitions across time from one type of tobacco product to another. Second, longitudinal models can be used to identify the individual (e.g., need for belonging) and contextual (e.g., tobacco marketing) factors that either alone or in combination contribute to both the initiation and the progression of alternative tobacco product use. Importantly, such models can also be used to identify level of risk for progression to regular use and subsequent nicotine dependence based on age of tobacco use initiation. Finally, longitudinal models are well suited to mapping the varying patterns of tobacco use and identifying distinct tobacco use trajectories. To date, research on alternative tobacco products has been limited primarily to describing users of the products and differentiating them from non-users, with little effort aimed at understanding the implications for various patterns of use or how these patterns vary across gender and race/ethnicity. Researchers must draw from rich developmental traditions in other areas of substance use (Zucker, Donovan, Masten, Mattson, & Moss, 2008; Zucker, Ellis, Fitzgerald, & Bingham, 1996) to understand why some adolescents and young adults who try alternative tobacco products continue to use those products and possibly also other products.

ACKNOWLEDGMENT

Preparation of this chapter was supported by grant 1 P50 CA180906 from the National Cancer Institute and the US Food and Drug Administration's Center for Tobacco Products. The content is solely the responsibility of the authors and does not necessarily represent the official views of the National Institutes of Health or the US Food and Drug Administration.

REFERENCES

Agaku, I. T., King, B. A., & Dube, S. R. (2014). Current cigarette smoking among adults—United States, 2005–2012. *MMWR Morbidity and Mortality Weekly Report*, 63(2), 29–34. Retrieved from http://www.cdc.gov/MMWR/preview/mmwrhtml/mm6302a2.htm

Agarwal, D., & Loukas, A. (2015). Examining e-cigarette use among college students. *Tobacco Regulatory Science*, 1(2), 166–174.

Aljarrah, K., Ababneh, Z. Q., & Al-Delaimy, W. K. (2009). Perceptions of hookah smoking harmfulness: predictors and characteristics among current hookah users. *Tobacco Induced Diseases*, 5, 16.

Amrock, S. M., Zakhar, J., Zhou, S., & Weitzman, M. (2015). Perception of e-cigarette harm and its correlation with use among U.S. adolescents. *Nicotine & Tobacco Research*, 17(3), 330–336. doi:10.1093/ntr/ntu156

Apelberg, B. J., Corey, C. G., Hoffman, A. C., Schroeder, M. J., Husten, C. G., Caraballo, R. S., & Backinger, C. L. (2014). Symptoms of tobacco dependence among middle and high school tobacco users: Results from the 2012 National Youth Tobacco Survey. *American Journal of Preventive Medicine*, 47(2 Suppl. 1), S4–S14. doi:10.1016/j.amepre.2014.04.013

Arnett, J. J. (2015). *Emerging adulthood: The winding road from the late teens through the twenties* (2nd ed.). New York, NY: Oxford University Press.

Arrazola, R. A., Singh, T., Corey, C. G., Husten, C. G., Neff, L. J., Apelberg, B. J., . . . Caraballo, R. S. (2015). Tobacco use among middle and high school students—United States, 2011–2014. *MMWR Morbidity and Mortality Weekly Report*, 64(14), 381–385.

Barnett, T. E., Forrest, J. R., Porter, L., & Curbow, B. A. (2014). A multiyear assessment of hookah use prevalence among Florida high school students. *Nicotine & Tobacco Research*, 16(3), 373–377. doi:10.1093/ntr/ntt188

Barrington-Trimis, J. L., Samet, J. M., & McConnell, R. (2014). Flavorings in electronic cigarettes: An unrecognized respiratory health hazard? *Journal of the American Medical Association*, 312(23), 2493–2494. doi:10.1001/jama.2014.14830

Biener, L., & Albers, A. B. (2004). Young adults: Vulnerable new targets of tobacco marketing. *American Journal of Public Health*, 94(2), 326–330.

Biener, L., & Siegel, M. (2000). Tobacco marketing and adolescent smoking: More support for a causal inference. *American Journal of Public Health*, 90(3), 407–411.

Bombard, J. M., Rock, V. J., Pederson, L. L., & Asman, K. J. (2008). Monitoring polytobacco use among adolescents: Do cigarette smokers use other forms of tobacco? *Nicotine & Tobacco Research*, 10(11), 1581–1589. doi:10.1080/14622200802412887

Braun, R. E., Glassman, T., Wohlwend, J., Whewell, A., & Reindl, D. M. (2012). Hookah use among college students from a Midwest university. *Journal of Community Health*, 37(2), 294–298. doi:10.1007/s10900-011-9444-9

Breslau, N., Johnson, E. O., Hiripi, E., & Kessler, R. (2001). Nicotine dependence in the United States: Prevalence, trends, and smoking persistence. *Archives of General Psychiatry*, 58(9), 810–816.

Cahn, Z., & Siegel, M. (2011). Electronic cigarettes as a harm reduction strategy for tobacco control: A step forward or a repeat of past mistakes? *Journal of Public Health Policy*, 32(1), 16–31. doi:10.1057/jphp.2010.41

Cantrell, J., Kreslake, J. M., Ganz, O., Pearson, J. L., Vallone, D., Anesetti-Rothermel, A., & Kirchner, T. R. (2013). Marketing little cigars and cigarillos: advertising, price, and associations with neighborhood demographics. *American Journal of Public Health*, 103(10), 1902–1909.

Carpenter, C. M., Wayne, G. F., Pauly, J. L., Koh, H. K., & Connolly, G. N. (2005). New cigarette brands with flavors that appeal to youth: Tobacco marketing strategies. *Health Affairs*, 24(6), 1601–1610. doi:10.1377/hlthaff.24.6.1601

Centers for Disease Control and Prevention. (2010). Tobacco use among middle and high school students—United States, 2000–2009. *MMWR Morbidity and Mortality Weekly Report*, 59(33), 1063–1068.

Chassin, L., Presson, C. C., Sherman, S. J., & Edwards, D. A. (1990). The natural history of cigarette smoking: Predicting young-adult smoking outcomes from adolescent smoking patterns. *Health Psychology*, 9(6), 701–716. doi:10.1037/0278-6133.9.6.701

Chassin, L., Presson, C. C., Sherman, S. J., & Edwards, D. A. (1991). Four pathways to young-adult smoking status: Adolescent social–psychological antecedents in a Midwestern community sample. *Health Psychology*, 10(6), 409–418. doi:10.1037/0278-6133.10.6.409

Chen, K., & Kandel, D. B. (1995). The natural history of drug use from adolescence to the mid-thirties in a general population sample. *American Journal of Public Health*, 85(1), 41–47. doi:10.2105/AJPH.85.1.41

Chen, Y. T., & Loukas, A. (2015). Examining hookah use among US college students. *Health Behavior and Policy Review*, 5, 343–351.

Cobb, C. O., Shihadeh, A., Weaver, M. F., & Eissenberg, T. (2011). Waterpipe tobacco smoking and cigarette smoking: A direct comparison of toxicant exposure and subjective effects. *Nicotine & Tobacco Research*, 13(2), 78–87. doi:10.1093/ntr/ntq212

Cohn, A., Cobb, C. O., Niaura, R. S., & Richardson, A. (2015). The other combustible products: Prevalence and correlates of little cigar/cigarillo use among cigarette smokers. *Nicotine & Tobacco Research*, 17(12), 1473–1481. doi:10.1093/ntr/ntv022

Connolly, G. N., & Alpert, H. R. (2008). Trends in the use of cigarettes and other tobacco products, 2000–2007. *Journal of the American Medical Association*, 299(22), 2629–2630. doi:10.1001/jama.299.22.2629

Cooper, M., Case, K. R., Loukas, A., Creamer, M. R., & Perry, C. L. (2016). E-cigarette dual users, exclusive users and perceptions of tobacco products. *American Journal of Health Behavior*, 40(1), 108–116. doi:10.5993/ajhb.40.1.12

Corey, C. G., Dube, S. R., Ambrose, B. K., King, B. A., Apelberg, B. J., & Husten, C. G. (2014). Cigar smoking among U.S. students: Reported use after adding brands to survey items. *American Journal of Preventive Medicine*, 47(2, Suppl. 1), S28–S35. doi:http://dx.doi.org/10.1016/j.amepre.2014.05.004

Creamer, M. R., Perry, C. L., Harrell, M. H., & Diamond, P. M. (2015). Trends in multiple tobacco product use among high school students. *Tobacco Regulatory Science*, 1(3), 204–214.

de Andrade, M., Hastings, G., & Angus, K. (2013). Promotion of electronic cigarettes: Tobacco marketing reinvented? *BMJ*, 347, f7473. doi:10.1136/bmj.f7473

DiFranza, J. R., Wellman, R. J., Sargent, J. D., Weitzman, M., Hipple, B. J., & Winickoff, J. P. (2006). Tobacco promotion and the initiation of tobacco use: Assessing the evidence for causality. *Pediatrics*, *117*(6), e1237–e1248. doi:10.1542/peds.2005-1817

Duke, J. C., Lee, Y. O., Kim, A. E., Watson, K. A., Arnold, K. Y., Nonnemaker, J. M., & Porter, L. (2014). Exposure to electronic cigarette television advertisements among youth and young adults. *Pediatrics*, *134*(1), e29–e36. doi:10.1542/peds.2014-0269

Federal Trade Commission. (2015a). *Federal Trade Commission cigarette report for 2012*. Retrieved from https://www.ftc.gov/system/files/documents/reports/federal-trade-commission-cigarette-report-2012/150327-2012cigaretterpt.pdf

Federal Trade Commission. (2015b). *Federal Trade Commission smokeless tobacco report for 2012*. Retrieved from https://www.ftc.gov/system/files/documents/reports/federal-trade-commission-smokeless-tobacco-report-2012/150327-2012smokelesstobaccorpt.pdf

Fix, B. V., O'Connor, R. J., Vogl, L., Smith, D., Bansal-Travers, M., Conway, K. P., . . . Hyland, A. (2014). Patterns and correlates of polytobacco use in the United States over a decade: NSDUH 2002–2011. *Addictive Behaviors*, *39*(4), 768–781. doi:10.1016/j.addbeh.2013.12.015

Freeman, B. (2012). New media and tobacco control. *Tobacco Control*, *21*(2), 139–144. doi:10.1136/tobaccocontrol-2011-050193

Gilpin, E. A., White, M. M., Messer, K., & Pierce, J. P. (2007). Receptivity to tobacco advertising and promotions among young adolescents as a predictor of established smoking in young adulthood. *American Journal of Public Health*, *97*(8), 1489–1495. doi:10.2105/ajph.2005.070359

Gold, D. R., Wang, X., Wypij, D., Speizer, F. E., Ware, J. H., & Dockery, D. W. (1996). Effects of cigarette smoking on lung function in adolescent boys and girls. *New England Journal of Medicine*, *335*(13), 931–937. doi:10.1056/nejm199609263351304

Grana, R. A., & Ling, P. M. (2014). "Smoking revolution": A content analysis of electronic cigarette retail websites. *American Journal of Preventive Medicine*, *46*(4), 395–403. doi:10.1016/j.amepre.2013.12.010

Heinz, A. J., Giedgowd, G. E., Crane, N. A., Veilleux, J. C., Conrad, M., Braun, A. R., . . . Kassel, J. D. (2013). A comprehensive examination of hookah smoking in college students: Use patterns and contexts, social norms and attitudes, harm perception, psychological correlates and co-occurring substance use. *Addictive Behaviors*, *38*(11), 2751–2760. doi:10.1016/j.addbeh.2013.07.009

Higgins, S. T., Kurti, A. N., Redner, R., White, T. J., Gaalema, D. E., Roberts, M. E., . . . Atwood, G. S. (2015). A literature review on prevalence of gender differences and intersections with other vulnerabilities to tobacco use in the United States, 2004–2014. *Preventive Medicine*, *80*, 89–100. doi:10.1016/j.ypmed.2015.06.009

Jamal, A., Agaku, I. T., O'Connor, E., King, B. A., Kenemer, J. B., & Neff, L. (2014). Current cigarette smoking among adults—United States, 2005–2013. MMWR *Morbidity and Mortality Weekly Report*, *63*(47), 1108–1112.

Jarrett, T., Blosnich, J., Tworek, C., & Horn, K. (2012). Hookah use among U.S. college students: Results from the National College Health Assessment II. *Nicotine & Tobacco Research*, *14*(10), 1145–1153. doi:10.1093/ntr/nts003

Kadhum, M., Sweidan, A., Jaffery, A. E., Al-Saadi, A., & Madden, B. (2015). A review of the health effects of smoking shisha. *Clinical Medicine*, *15*(3), 263–266. doi:10.7861/clinmedicine.15-3-263

Kasza, K. A., Bansal-Travers, M., O'Connor, R. J., Compton, W. M., Kettermann, A., Borek, N., . . . Hyland, A. J. (2014). Cigarette smokers' use of unconventional tobacco products and associations with quitting activity: Findings from the ITC-4 U.S. cohort. *Nicotine & Tobacco Research*, *16*(6), 672–681. doi:10.1093/ntr/ntt212

Katz, S. K., & Lavack, A. M. (2002). Tobacco related bar promotions: Insights from tobacco industry documents. *Tobacco Control*, *11*(Suppl. 1), I92–101. Retrieved from http://www.ncbi.nlm.nih.gov/pubmed/11893819

Kaufman, A. R., Land, S., Parascandola, M., Augustson, E., & Backinger, C. L. (2015). Tobacco use transitions in the United States: The National Longitudinal Study of Adolescent Health. *Preventive Medicine*, *81*, 251–257. doi:10.1016/j.ypmed.2015.08.026

Kim, A. E., Arnold, K. Y., & Makarenko, O. (2014). E-cigarette advertising expenditures in the U.S., 2011–2012. *American Journal of Preventive Medicine*, *46*(4), 409–412. doi:10.1016/j.amepre.2013.11.003

King, B. A., Patel, R., Nguyen, K. H., & Dube, S. R. (2015). Trends in awareness and use of electronic cigarettes among US adults, 2010–2013. *Nicotine & Tobacco Research*, *17*(2), 219–227. doi:10.1093/ntr/ntu191

Kiviniemi, M. T., & Kozlowski, L. T. (2015). Deficiencies in public understanding about tobacco harm reduction: Results from a United States national survey. *Harm Reduction Journal*, *12*, 21. doi:10.1186/s12954-015-0055-0

Klesges, R. C., Ebbert, J. O., Morgan, G. D., Sherrill-Mittleman, D., Asfar, T., Talcott, W. G., & DeBon, M. (2011). Impact of differing definitions of dual tobacco use: Implications for studying dual use and a call for operational definitions. *Nicotine & Tobacco Research*, 13(7), 523–531. doi:10.1093/ntr/ntr032

Kong, G., Morean, M. E., Cavallo, D. A., Camenga, D. R., & Krishnan-Sarin, S. (2015). Reasons for electronic cigarette experimentation and discontinuation among adolescents and young adults. *Nicotine & Tobacco Research*, 17(7), 847–854. doi:10.1093/ntr/ntu257

Kozlowski, L. T. (2007). Effect of smokeless tobacco product marketing and use on population harm from tobacco use policy perspective for tobacco-risk reduction. *American Journal of Preventive Medicine*, 33(6 Suppl.), S379–S386. doi:10.1016/j.amepre.2007.09.015

Kozlowski, L. T., O'Connor, R. J., Edwards, B. Q., & Flaherty, B. P. (2003). Most smokeless tobacco use is not a causal gateway to cigarettes: Using order of product use to evaluate causation in a national US sample. *Addiction*, 98(8), 1077–1085. doi:460 [pii]

Lee, J. P., Battle, R. S., Lipton, R., & Soller, B. (2010). "Smoking": Use of cigarettes, cigars and blunts among Southeast Asian American youth and young adults. *Health Education Research*, 25(1), 83–96. doi:10.1093/her/cyp066

Lee, Y. O., Hebert, C. J., Nonnemaker, J. M., & Kim, A. E. (2014). Multiple tobacco product use among adults in the United States: Cigarettes, cigars, electronic cigarettes, hookah, smokeless tobacco, and snus. *Preventive Medicine*, 62, 14–19. doi:10.1016/j.ypmed.2014.01.014

Lee, Y. O., Hebert, C. J., Nonnemaker, J. M., & Kim, A. E. (2015). Youth tobacco product use in the United States. *Pediatrics*, 135(3), 409–415. doi:10.1542/peds.2014-3202

Legacy. (2014). *Vaporized: E-cigarettes, advertising, and youth*. Retrieved from https://truthinitiative.org/sites/default/files/Vaporized_E-cigarettes_Advertising_and_Youth_May2014.pdf

Leventhal, A. M., Strong, D. R., Kirkpatrick, M. G., Unger, J. B., Sussman, S., Riggs, N. R., . . . Audrain-McGovern, J. (2015). Association of electronic cigarette use with initiation of combustible tobacco product smoking in early adolescence. *Journal of the American Medical Association*, 314(7), 700–707. doi:10.1001/jama.2015.8950

Ling, P. M., & Glantz, S. A. (2002). Why and how the tobacco industry sells cigarettes to young adults: Evidence from industry documents. *American Journal of Public Health*, 92(6), 908–916.

Loukas, A., Batanova, M., Fernandez, A., & Agarwal, D. (2015). Changes in use of cigarettes and non-cigarette alternative products among college students. *Addictive Behaviors*, 49, 46–51. doi:10.1016/j.addbeh.2015.05.005

Lovato, C., Watts, A., & Stead, L. F. (2011). Impact of tobacco advertising and promotion on increasing adolescent smoking behaviours. *Cochrane Database System Review*, 2011(10), CD003439. doi:10.1002/14651858.CD003439.pub2

Mayhew, K. P., Flay, B. R., & Mott, J. A. (2000). Stages in the development of adolescent smoking. *Drug & Alcohol Dependence*, 59(Suppl. 1), S61–S81.

McMillen, R., Maduka, J., & Winickoff, J. (2012). Use of emerging tobacco products in the United States. *Journal of Environmental Public Health*, 2012, 989474. doi:10.1155/2012/989474

Minaker, L. M., Shuh, A., Burkhalter, R. J., & Manske, S. R. (2015). Hookah use prevalence, predictors, and perceptions among Canadian youth: Findings from the 2012/2013 Youth Smoking Survey. *Cancer Causes & Control*, 26(6), 831–838. doi:10.1007/s10552-015-0556-x

O'Connor, R. J. (2012). Non-cigarette tobacco products: What have we learnt and where are we headed? *Tobacco Control*, 21(2), 181–190. doi:10.1136/tobaccocontrol-2011-050281

O'Connor, R. J., Flaherty, B. P., Quinio Edwards, B., & Kozlowski, L. T. (2003). Regular smokeless tobacco use is not a reliable predictor of smoking onset when psychosocial predictors are included in the model. *Nicotine & Tobacco Research*, 5(4), 535–543. doi:W1MJG9PHGF6DYK38 [pii]

Peters, R. J., Jr., Meshack, A., Lin, M. T., Hill, M., & Abughosh, S. (2013). The social norms and beliefs of teenage male electronic cigarette use. *Journal of Ethnicity in Substance Abuse*, 12(4), 300–307. doi:10.1080/15332640.2013.819310

Phillips, C. V. (2015). Gateway effects: Why the cited evidence does not support their existence for low-risk tobacco products (and what evidence would). *International Journal of Environmental Research & Public Health*, 12(5), 5439–5464. doi:10.3390/ijerph120505439

Popova, L., & Ling, P. M. (2013). Alternative tobacco product use and smoking cessation: A national study. *American Journal of Public Health*, 103(5), 923–930. doi:10.2105/ajph.2012.301070

Maziak, W., Eissenberg, T., Rastam, S., Hammal, F., Asfar, T., Bachir, M. E., et al. (2004). Beliefs and attitudes related to narghile (waterpipe) smoking among university students in Syria. *Annals of Epidemiology*, 14(9), 646–654.

Rath, J. M., Villanti, A. C., Abrams, D. B., & Vallone, D. M. (2012). Patterns of tobacco use and dual use in US young adults: The missing link between youth prevention and adult cessation. *Journal of Environmental Public Health, 2012*, 679134. doi:10.1155/2012/679134

Richardson, A., Williams, V., Rath, J., Villanti, A. C., & Vallone, D. (2014). The next generation of users: Prevalence and longitudinal patterns of tobacco use among US young adults. *American Journal of Public Health, 104*(8), 1429–1436. doi:10.2105/ajph.2013.301802

Richter, P., Caraballo, R., Pederson, L. L., & Gupta, N. (2008). Exploring use of nontraditional tobacco products through focus groups with young adult smokers, 2002. *Preventing Chronic Disease, 5*(3), A87.

Roberts, M. E., Berman, M. L., Slater, M. D., Hinton, A., & Ferketich, A. K. (2015). Point-of-sale tobacco marketing in rural and urban Ohio: Could the new landscape of tobacco products widen inequalities? *Preventive Medicine, 81*, 232–235.

Rosendahl, K. I., Galanti, M. R., & Gilljam, H. (2008). Trajectories of smokeless tobacco use and of cigarette smoking in a cohort of Swedish adolescents: Differences and implications. *Nicotine & Tobacco Research, 10*(6), 1021–1027. doi:10.1080/14622200802097522

Saunders, C., & Geletko, K. (2012). Adolescent cigarette smokers' and non-cigarette smokers' use of alternative tobacco products. *Nicotine & Tobacco Research, 14*(8), 977–985. doi:10.1093/ntr/ntr323

Schulenberg, J., Maggs, J. L., & Hurrelmann, K. (1997). Negotiating developmental transitions during adolescence and young adulthood: Health risks and opportunities. In J. Schulenberg, J. L. Maggs, & K. Hurrelmann (Eds.), *Health risks and developmental transitions during adolescence.* (pp. 1–19). New York, NY: Cambridge University Press.

Sharma, E., Beck, K. H., & Clark, P. I. (2013). Social context of smoking hookah among college students: Scale development and validation. *Journal of American College Health, 61*(4), 204–211. doi:10.1080/07448481.2013.787621

Smith-Simone, S., Maziak, W., Ward, K. D., & Eissenberg, T. (2008). Waterpipe tobacco smoking: knowledge, attitudes, beliefs, and behavior in two US samples. *Nicotine & Tobacco Research, 10*(2), 393–398.

Sterling, K., Berg, C. J., Thomas, A. N., Glantz, S. A., & Ahluwalia, J. S. (2013). Factors associated with small cigar use among college students. *American Journal of Health Behavior, 37*(3), 325–333.

Timberlake, D. S., Huh, J., & Lakon, C. M. (2009). Use of propensity score matching in evaluating smokeless tobacco as a gateway to smoking. *Nicotine & Tobacco Research, 11*(4), 455–462. doi:10.1093/ntr/ntp008

Tomar, S. L. (2003). Is use of smokeless tobacco a risk factor for cigarette smoking? The U.S. experience. *Nicotine & Tobacco Research, 5*(4), 561–569.

Tomar, S. L., Fox, B. J., & Severson, H. H. (2009). Is smokeless tobacco use an appropriate public health strategy for reducing societal harm from cigarette smoking? *International Journal of Environmental Research & Public Health, 6*(1), 10–24. doi:10.3390/ijerph6010010

Toumbourou, J. W., Stockwell, T., Neighbors, C., Marlatt, G. A., Sturge, J., & Rehm, J. (2007). Interventions to reduce harm associated with adolescent substance use. *Lancet, 369*(9570), 1391–1401. doi:10.1016/s0140-6736(07)60369-9

US Department of Health and Human Services. (2012). *Preventing tobacco use among youth and young adults: A report of the Surgeon General.* Atlanta, GA: US Department of Health and Human Services, Centers for Disease Control and Prevention, National Center for Chronic Disease Prevention and Health Promotion, Office on Smoking and Health.

US Department of Health and Human Services. (2014). *The health consequences of smoking—50 years of progress: A report of the Surgeon General.* Washington, DC: US Department of Health and Human Services, Centers for Disease Control and Prevention, National Center for Chronic Disease Prevention and Health Promotion, Office on Smoking and Health.

Villanti, A. C., Richardson, A., Vallone, D. M., & Rath, J. M. (2013). Flavored tobacco product use among U.S. young adults. *American Journal of Preventive Medicine, 44*(4), 388–391. doi:10.1016/j.amepre.2012.11.031

Wills, T. A., Knight, R., Williams, R. J., Pagano, I., & Sargent, J. D. (2015). Risk factors for exclusive e-cigarette use and dual e-cigarette use and tobacco use in adolescents. *Pediatrics, 135*(1), e43–e51. doi:10.1542/peds.2014-0760

Yao, T., Jiang, N., Grana, R., Ling, P. M., & Glantz, S. A. (2016). A content analysis of electronic cigarette manufacturer websites in China. *Tobacco Control, 25*, 188–194. doi:10.1136/tobaccocontrol-2014-051840

Yuan, M., Cross, S. J., Loughlin, S. E., & Leslie, F. M. (2015). Nicotine and the adolescent brain. *Journal of Physiology, 593*(16), 3397–3412. doi:10.1113/jp270492

Zhu, S. H., Sun, J. Y., Bonnevie, E., Cummins, S. E., Gamst, A., Yin, L., & Lee, M. (2014). Four hundred and sixty brands of e-cigarettes and counting: Implications for product regulation. *Tobacco Control*, 23(Suppl. 3), iii3–iii9. doi:10.1136/tobaccocontrol-2014-051670

Zucker, R. A., Donovan, J. E., Masten, A. S., Mattson, M. E., & Moss, H. B. (2008). Early developmental processes and the continuity of risk for underage drinking and problem drinking. *Pediatrics*, 121(Suppl. 4), S252–S272. doi:10.1542/peds.2007-2243B

Zucker, R. A., Ellis, D. A., Fitzgerald, H. E., & Bingham, C. R. (1996). Other evidence for at least two alcoholisms II. Life course variation in antisociality and heterogeneity of alcoholic outcome. *Development and Psychopathology*, 8(4), 831–848. doi:10.1017/S0954579400007458

14

Cigarette Smoking from Adolescence to Adulthood

Findings from the Indiana University Smoking Survey

Laurie Chassin

Clark C. Presson

Jonathan T. Macy

Steven J. Sherman

Despite substantial declines in smoking prevalence in recent decades, almost one in five adults in the United States are current smokers, and cigarette smoking remains the single largest cause of preventable mortality and morbidity in the United States (US Department of Health and Human Services, 2014). When the Indiana University Smoking Survey began in 1980, the existing research literature largely consisted of cross-sectional studies of demographic correlates of smoking. Our project applies a developmental perspective to cigarette smoking, and it uses theories and methods from social psychology and developmental psychology to understand smoking behavior. Throughout the years, with funding from the National Institute of Child Health and Human Development, the National Institute on Drug Abuse, the National Cancer Institute, and the US Food and Drug Administration (FDA), we have applied a developmental perspective to track the natural history of cigarette smoking from adolescence to midlife and to examine mechanisms of its intergenerational transmission. This chapter provides an overview of our project findings. Although it is not possible to describe all our studies, we have selected those that are most relevant and illustrative of our developmental perspective.

METHODOLOGY AND PARTICIPANTS

Our project is best described as a long-term longitudinal study with a cohort-sequential design, combined with embedded substudies that are either laboratory based or web based. Data collection for the longitudinal study began in 1980. The original participants were all of the 6th to 12th graders in a Midwestern county school system who were present in school on the day of testing at annual intervals between 1980 and 1983 (creating 10 cohorts of graduating classes with a total sample size of more than 8,400). These participants were followed annually between 1980 and 1983 and then at approximately 5- or 6-year intervals, with the most recent survey conducted in 2010. Retention rates have averaged 70% or higher, and the smoking rate was 19% at the most recent follow-up. As participants aged and had children of their own, we began a series of family-based studies to test mechanisms of intergenerational transmission, and we also began a series of web-based studies of implicit attitudes toward smoking, including attempts to manipulate those attitudes using approach–avoidance practice interventions, public service announcements, and exposure to graphic warning labels.

HETEROGENEITY IN SMOKING TRAJECTORIES

Our early work documented changes in smoking status from high school to adulthood, noting that regular (at least monthly) smoking in adolescence raised the risk for adult smoking by a factor of 16 and that a pattern of early onset and stable smoking carried the greatest risk (Chassin, Presson, Sherman, & Edwards, 1990). However, we also found that there was appreciable onset of smoking after the high school years, and this "late-onset" smoking had not been widely recognized (Chassin, Presson, Sherman, & Edwards, 1991). These findings suggested the possibility that smoking transitions might have different determinants at different ages and there might be multiple developmental pathways leading to smoking behavior (i.e., equifinality). Indeed, we found that beliefs about the negative consequences of smoking for social success, academic success, and independence were significantly related to adolescent but not young adult smoking (Chassin et al., 1991). Findings also suggested that the post-high school years might be an underappreciated developmental period to target for smoking prevention.

Tracking participants into adulthood, we found that the overall trajectory showed a significant increase in smoking from adolescence to adulthood and a nonsignificant decline after the mid-20s. This stability after the mid-20s differs from the "maturing out" that is seen for other forms of substance use (Chen & Kandel, 1995) and may reflect the high addictive potential of cigarette smoking. However, this apparent stability also masked appreciable cessation and relapse (Chassin, Presson, Rose, & Sherman, 1996). Similar to other addictive behaviors and problem behaviors, smoking cessation in adulthood was related to the assumption of adult social roles (Chassin et al., 1996).

It is important to note that within this overall group trajectory, there was substantial heterogeneity. With advances in quantitative methods, we used mixture modeling to empirically identify multiple trajectories of smoking from ages 11 to 31 years, publishing the first demonstration of these multiple trajectories in the literature (Chassin, Presson, Pitts, & Sherman, 2000). We established two groups a priori—that is, lifelong abstainers and "erratics" who showed complex trajectories that reflected multiple periods of relapse and remission from smoking. Our empirically identified trajectory groups included an early stable group who began to smoke at an early age, escalated steeply, and remained smoking through early adulthood, whereas a late-onset group began to smoke after the high school years and smoked at lower levels. We also identified an "experimenter group," whose smoking never reached heavy levels and did not persist into adulthood, and a "quitter" group, who successfully quit smoking.

Illustrating the importance of applying a developmental perspective to understanding smoking behavior, these groups showed different antecedents and consequences. The early stable smokers and the erratic smokers were the least socially conventional as adolescents. They showed high tolerance for deviance, had lower levels of parental support, and reported the most positive beliefs about smoking. They had the most smoking in their social environments and were the least likely to attend college. Most important, in a later extension of this work using our family-based data, we showed that it was the early stable group whose smoking was transmitted to the next generation, and this effect was significant over and above parents' current smoking behavior and educational attainment (Chassin et al., 2008). These findings suggest that a developmental trajectory characterized by early onset, steep acceleration, and persistence might be an endophenotype of interest in studying the intergenerational transmission of smoking. Given the heterogeneity of smoking behavior and the differential heritability that is found when studying behavior at different ages, such developmental trajectories may be helpful in illuminating the genetic underpinnings of smoking behavior (Chassin, Curran, Presson, Wirth, & Sherman, 2009).

In contrast to early onset stable smokers, we also identified a group of adolescents who experimented with smoking but who did not become persistent, regular smokers. These experimenters showed a profile of psychosocial antecedents that reflected some adolescent rebellion in having friends who smoke, tolerance for deviant behavior, and relatively pro-smoking beliefs (Chassin et al., 2000). Interestingly, however, experimenters had somewhat stronger ties to conventional institutions that were reflected in higher rates of college attendance and somewhat higher parent support. These stronger ties to parents and to higher education might have helped keep smoking behavior more developmentally limited. Because experimenters were also less likely to have parents who smoked, they might also have less genetic risk for smoking behavior.

As with our earlier analyses, the mixture model also identified a late-onset group of smokers who established their regular smoking relatively late (after the high school years), who maintained as regular smokers, but who never achieved the same high levels of smoking as the early stable group. As noted previously, late-onset smoking has not been widely recognized or targeted for smoking prevention. As adolescents, the late-onset smokers had few indications of smoking risk. They had few friends or parents who were smokers, and their beliefs about smoking were relatively negative. Members of this group may have been less likely to establish regular smoking in adolescence because of their social conventionality. However, as they age into adulthood, smoking becomes less socially deviant because of its age-graded nature, and after leaving the parental home, these individuals are no longer regulated by parental supervision. College attendance was relatively common in this group, and this was the age at which their smoking became regular. It is possible that late-onset smokers were responding to a new college social environment in which some cigarette smoking was more acceptable.

Another trajectory that we identified was individuals who established regular smoking but who successfully quit. Similar to findings for other forms of substance use, these quitters began their decline in cigarette smoking after age 22 years, when individuals are taking on adult roles and responsibilities (Yamaguchi & Kandel, 1985). The size of this group was relatively small, which is consistent with other findings that cigarette smoking is more stable compared to other forms of substance use (Chassin et al., 1996; Chen & Kandel, 1995). The relative stability of cigarette smoking from adolescence through the third decade of life is likely due to a combination of factors, including the fact that it is legal and available, addictive, and does not produce intoxication, which minimizes impairment in role performance due to smoking. For those who did successfully quit, their relatively negative beliefs about the health and psychological consequences of smoking may have aided in this effort.

In summary, an important contribution of our project was the first empirical demonstration of heterogeneity in the developmental trajectories of smoking behavior. Our findings suggest that this heterogeneity is important for understanding the causes of cigarette smoking and transitions in smoking status as well as for understanding how smoking is transmitted across generations. That is, we found that variability in age of onset, steepness of acceleration to high levels of smoking, and persistence over time were systematically related to different predictors and consequences of smoking. The early onset persistent subgroup was of particular public health significance because of its members' high levels of smoking and because they pass this risk to the next generation. Methodologically, it is important to note that this heterogeneity in age of onset, steepness of acceleration, and persistence over time is not captured in typical cross-sectional measures of smoking. For this reason, any single cross-sectional measure (other than retrospections about trajectories) will produce a heterogeneous group of smokers. This will obscure potentially important subgroups that have different risk factors. Consistent with the developmental psychopathology perspective, a clearer understanding of the processes underlying smoking behavior might be produced by using developmental trajectories of smoking as the "phenotypes" of interest (Chassin et al., 2009).

DUAL TRAJECTORIES OF CIGARETTE SMOKING AND SMOKELESS TOBACCO USE

Another trajectory study of tobacco use that we conducted with our longitudinal data explored dual trajectories of cigarette smoking and smokeless tobacco from 1987 to 2011 among the males in our sample (Macy, Li, Xun, Presson, & Chassin, 2016). Although our project was unable to assess multiple forms of substance use, we did assess multiple forms of tobacco use, and it is important to consider whether other tobacco products can substitute for or promote cigarette smoking. For example, smokeless tobacco use has been promoted as a safer and convenient alternative to smoking in places where smoking is prohibited (e.g., "Take a pouch instead of a puff") (Severson, Lichtenstein, & Gallison, 1985). However, longitudinal research on trajectories of smokeless tobacco and dual use of smokeless tobacco and cigarettes has been very limited, and ours was the first study to empirically identify trajectories of cigarette smoking and smokeless tobacco among men from adolescence to midlife.

In these analyses, we identified five smoking trajectory groups: (1) consistent abstinence from cigarettes;

(2) late-onset intermittent smoking, then cessation; (3) early onset regular smoking, then cessation; (4) delayed-onset regular smoking, then cessation; and (5) consistent regular smoking. Four smokeless tobacco trajectory groups were identified: (1) early onset use, then cessation; (2) consistent abstinence from smokeless tobacco; (3) late onset, escalating use; and (4) consistent regular use. The prevalence of dual use of cigarettes and smokeless tobacco was low, and there was little evidence to suggest switching between tobacco products. Finally, we tested correlates of membership in the trajectory groups and found that participants who held more positive beliefs about smoking and smokeless tobacco as adolescents were more likely to be consistent regular users of cigarettes and smokeless tobacco into adulthood. Given the lack of evidence for switching between cigarette smoking and smokeless tobacco use, these findings support the use of product-specific messaging in prevention and cessation interventions.

DEVELOPMENTAL CHANGES IN SOCIAL INFLUENCES ON CIGARETTE SMOKING

One common view of the development of adolescence is that the relative importance of peers sharply increases during adolescence and that peers replace parents as the strongest influence. We used our longitudinal data to examine the relative importance of peer and parent influences on smoking transitions at different ages. Importantly, the pattern of findings that we observed depended almost completely on whether the data were analyzed longitudinally or cross-sectionally.

We included a wide range of factors associated with potential peer and parent influence, including peer and parent smoking and the levels of expectation, strictness, and supportiveness that our participants reported receiving from their friends and their parents. When we tested these parent and peer variables as prospective predictors of smoking transitions 1 year later (from never smoker to experimental smoker, or from trier to regular smoker), both parent and peer influences were consistent, significant predictors of those transitions, and there were virtually no interactions with grade. Thus, our longitudinal findings showed no evidence of age-related differences in the importance of peer and parent influences, at least on cigarette smoking (Chassin, Presson, Sherman, Montello, & McGrew, 1986).

These findings contrasted to those reported by others who had used cross-sectional analyses predicting smoking status from peer and parent variables. For example, Krosnick and Judd (1982) found that peer factors were more strongly related to smoking status for older adolescents than for younger ones and that there was some decline in the relation of smoking to parent variables. When we reanalyzed our data using cross-sectional analysis at each time of measurement, we found the same pattern reported by Krosnick and Judd, with a stronger relation between peer variables and smoking for the older adolescents than for younger ones and the reverse for many of the parent variables. These findings support the importance of longitudinal designs in understanding developmental processes because longitudinal designs can separate the antecedents and consequences of behavioral transitions. As our data have shown, changes in the perceived social environment both precede and follow from smoking transitions (Chassin, Presson, & Sherman, 1984), so age differences in social influences cannot be properly tested with cross-sectional designs.

Although not explicitly testing age differences in social influence, our data have also shown the importance of social image factors in adolescents' intentions to smoke cigarettes. Behaviors can be adopted in part to express or affirm an existing self-image and also to enhance self-image or favorably impress others, and such social image factors should theoretically be particularly salient in adolescence. We investigated the role of social image factors in two studies. One study used relatively direct measurement, asking adolescents in early high school to use bipolar adjective scales to describe themselves, their ideal selves, their ideal date, as well as the kind of boy and girl who smokes cigarettes (Chassin, Presson, Sherman, Corty, & Olshavsky, 1981). In the second study, we examined the social image of the adolescent smoker using more indirect measurement, with adolescents assigned randomly to conditions to rate their first impression of adolescents in photographs. The adolescent targets were posed either holding cigarettes or with the cigarettes air-brushed out (Barton, Chassin, Presson, & Sherman, 1982). In both of these studies, we found that the social image associated with smoking cigarettes was an ambivalent one. Smoking was associated with several negative characteristics such as poor health, disobedience, and being poor at schoolwork. However, smoking was also associated with characteristics such as being tough, sociable, and interested in the opposite sex. These characteristics are likely to be desirable to adolescents, and they may be particularly desirable to adolescents who are susceptible to risk-taking. Most important, these social image factors were related to smoking behavior and intentions. Adolescents whose self-concepts were consistent with the stereotypic smoker were more likely to themselves smoke and, among non-smokers, were more likely to intend to smoke in the future (Barton et al., 1982; Chassin et al., 1981). Furthermore, non-smoking adolescents whose ideal self-ratings were closer to the image of a smoker were also more likely to intend to smoke in the future.

DEVELOPMENTAL CHANGE WITHIN HISTORICAL CONTEXT

Paralleling age-related changes in actual smoking behavior, we also modeled age-related changing in smoking-related beliefs from adolescence to adulthood (ages 12–37 years; Chassin, Presson, Rose, & Sherman, 2001). We found that beliefs about the personalized risk of smoking declined in adolescence, whereas beliefs in potential psychological benefits increased. However, after adolescence, beliefs in the personalized risks of smoking increased with age, as did the value that participants placed on having good health. A greater sense of personalized risk in adulthood may be part of the broader personality change that occurs at this time — for example, adult increases in conscientiousness and decreases in impulsivity (Littlefield, Sher, & Wood, 2010). These age-related changes in attitudes and beliefs may support changes in smoking behavior.

It is important to remember that these age-related trajectories of smoking behavior and smoking-related beliefs unfold within a particular cultural–historical context. In the United States, there has been rapid social change in the acceptability of smoking reflected in policy changes such as restrictions on smoking in public places. Indeed, the Monitoring the Future study, a national epidemiological study of adolescent substance use, has reported cohort effects for adolescent cigarette smoking, with successive cohorts smoking less (O'Malley, Bachman, & Johnston, 1984).

To examine cultural–historical changes in smoking and smoking-related beliefs, we retested the middle school and high school students in the same schools as those in our original study using the same survey instrument, but 20 years later, and compared the data from 1980 to those from 2001 (Chassin, Presson, Sherman, & Kim, 2003). Smoking was less prevalent in 2001 than in 1980, with a large drop in the number of experimental smokers and smaller decreases in regular smokers. As might be expected from this drop in smoking prevalence, adolescents in 2001 were also more negative in their beliefs about smoking compared to adolescents in 1980. Specifically, adolescents in 2001 viewed smoking as being more addictive, less socially desirable, and having more negative consequences compared to adolescents in 1980.

Of course, one possible interpretation of these changes is that rather than reflecting historical change, they reflect changes in the demographic composition of the community. Indeed, the community was more ethnically diverse in 2001 than in 1980. To help separate changes in the demographics of the community from cultural–historical change, we matched data from a subsample of adolescents in 2001 with data from their parents who we had assessed (as adolescents) in our original surveys (from 1980 to 1983). Findings within these adolescent–parent matched pairs confirmed the findings from the larger sample, suggesting that more negative smoking-related beliefs were due to cultural–historical changes rather than to demographic differences in the community over time.

One of the interesting reconceptualizations of smoking that has occurred since 1980 is the shift from viewing smoking as a "problem behavior" to an "addictive behavior." Indeed, the US Surgeon General's report formally labeled smoking as "addictive" in 1988 (U.S. Department of Health and Human Services, 1988). This reframing of cigarette smoking as addictive may have helped lower the prevalence of adolescent smoking behavior (shown in our cultural–historical change data; Chassin et al., 2003). However, little is known about how adolescents understand the concept of addiction, and we should not assume that they conceptualize addiction in the same way as do adults. We explored this question by asking adolescents and their parents to rate the importance of 17 items as indicators that someone was "addicted" (Chassin, Presson, Rose, & Sherman, 2007). Items included both appetitive aspects of dependence (e.g., "getting high") and compulsive aspects (e.g., "not being able to control the behavior"). The factor structure of the ratings showed that both parents and adolescents viewed addiction as having multiple dimensions, but for adults the compulsive aspects were more important, whereas for the adolescents the two dimensions were equally important in the definition. These differences were also seen when we used the dimensional scores to predict the perceived addictiveness of cigarette smoking. For adolescents, the appetitive dimension significantly predicted the ratings of cigarette addictiveness, whereas for the adults, the compulsive factor was the one that predicted ratings of cigarette addictiveness. These findings suggest that messages about the "addictiveness" of smoking may have different meanings for adolescents and adults.

The most obvious influences of cultural–historical context on smoking behavior have been the societal declines in the acceptability of smoking and in its reframing as an addictive behavior. However, societal influences on smoking behavior can also be indirect through changes in social conditions or roles. For example, our data tracked smoking behavior before and after the 2008 economic downturn and found that financial strain predicted change in adult cigarette smoking, above and beyond demographic covariates (Macy, Chassin, & Presson, 2013).

A particularly interesting example of social change that affects health behaviors and cigarette smoking is the increase in "sandwich generation" families, in which parents (most often mothers) provide caretaking to both their children and their parents. A combination of social trends, including longer life expectancy, delayed marriage and childbearing, and more adult children returning home after divorce, has led to an increase in multigenerational caregiving (Hamill & Goldberg, 1997). Just as social change has influenced adolescent cigarette smoking, the increase in multigenerational caregiving influences the challenges of midlife development, which may in turn influence adult cigarette smoking. The stress of role demands may increase cigarette smoking and erode health behaviors in general, or the added role responsibilities may increase adults' commitment to health goals in order to successfully meet these responsibilities. Our data provided an opportunity to test these predictions in a rigorous way by controlling for a variety of potentially confounding demographic variables in addition to controlling for initial levels of these health behaviors. Results showed that "sandwich generation" membership was generally predictive of poorer health behavior, including marginally higher levels of cigarette smoking. Although the actual mechanism for these effects is unclear, effects were not due

to the number of hours spent in caregiving and might instead reflect the influence of stress, perhaps reducing the salience of personal health goals (Chassin, Macy, Seo, Presson, & Sherman, 2010). Considering the effects of societal change on both adolescents and their parents presents particularly interesting opportunities for developmental scientists. That is, developmentalists typically consider adolescence and midlife separately, but it is important to recognize that the conditions and challenges of midlife development that impinge on parents' behaviors (including parents' own cigarette smoking) will also influence their adolescent children, and cultural–historical effects on adolescents will also show reciprocal effects on parents. Thus, it is important to recognize that development unfolds not only in a cultural–historical perspective but also within family systems.

PARENTING AND INTERGENERATIONAL TRANSMISSION

Recognizing the importance of family systems as well as the importance of adolescence as a developmental period during which risk behavior in general and cigarette smoking in particular are common, we studied parenting practices and parent–child relationships as potentially important etiological influences on cigarette smoking. As our participants aged, we recruited their adolescent children into multigenerational studies of parenting influences and of the intergenerational transmission of smoking behavior (Chassin et al., 2005). As mentioned previously, one predictor of intergenerational transmission was the parent's developmental trajectory of smoking, with trajectories characterized by early onset, steep acceleration, and stability showing the greatest transmission across generations.

Drawing on the broader literature on parent socialization and adolescent risk behaviors, we distinguished between general parent socialization and parent practices that were specific to their adolescent's smoking behavior. For general parenting, we studied parental warmth (nurturance and attachment) and control (monitoring and consistent discipline). As described by Baumrind (1991), these dimensions produce four general parenting styles: authoritative (high levels of warmth and control), authoritarian (high level of control but low level of warmth), permissive (high level of warmth but low level of control), and disengaged (low levels of both warmth and control). To examine the role of smoking-specific parenting practices, we assessed reports of smoking-specific discussions (e.g., parents explaining why their adolescent should not smoke) and smoking-specific punishment (e.g., removing a privilege). Importantly, we found that general parenting had strong effects in prospectively predicting later smoking among adolescents who were initially non-smokers.

We then prospectively predicted smoking initiation (18 months later) from both general parenting and smoking-specific parenting. Consistent with previous literature, we found that adolescents who received low levels of parental warmth and control (i.e., who had disengaged parents) were most likely to initiate smoking. The effect of general parenting was unique, over and above the effects of parental smoking, parental education, and family structure. In addition, the relations were strongest when adolescent, rather than parental, perceptions of general parenting were considered (Chassin et al., 2005).

Although general parenting style significantly prospectively predicted adolescent smoking onset, smoking-specific parenting practices also added significant predictive value. These results have implications for family-based preventive interventions in that it may be insufficient to focus only on either modifying general parenting or modifying parents' smoking-specific socialization. We suggest that both general and smoking-specific parental socialization practices need to be considered.

We also found a significant interaction between smoking-significant parenting and parent smoking, such that the effects of smoking-specific parenting were confined to families with non-smoking parents. This suggests that when there is a discrepancy between messages conveyed by parents' smoking behavior and their socialization attempts (e.g., in a situation of "do as I say and not as I do"), parents' specific attempts to deter their adolescents' cigarette smoking may not succeed. Perhaps smoking parents inadvertently communicate subtle messages that undermine their smoking-specific parenting.

One way to understand the messages that smoking parents may transmit to their children is to examine parents' implicit attitudes toward smoking. Most early research that explored the role of attitudes in predicting smoking behavior employed explicit measures of these attitudes, such as semantic differential or Likert scales. Such explicit measures, especially for socially relevant behaviors, are subject to social norms and concerns about social desirability. Cigarette smoking is a behavior that has very strong social norms and concerns about social desirability. Thus, explicit measures of smoking often poorly predict smoking-relevant behaviors. In response to this issue, psychologists have developed a variety of implicit measures of attitudes. Because implicit attitudes operate below the level of awareness and because they are difficult to control, implicit measures are not subject to issues of social norms or social desirability. Thus, these measures are ideal for assessing attitudes toward smoking and for exploring the relation between these attitudes and smoking-related behaviors and smoking transitions.

We used the Implicit Association Test (Greenwald, McGhee, & Schwartz, 1998) to assess implicit attitudes toward smoking by considering the relative reaction time to pair smoking-related pictures and abstract line drawings with positive and negative words. We also measured explicit attitudes toward smoking with a semantic differential. Findings showed that implicit and explicit attitudes toward smoking were weakly related to each other. Most important, mothers with more positive implicit attitudes toward smoking had children with more positive implicit attitudes, and these implicit attitudes prospectively predicted adolescent smoking initiation (Sherman, Chassin, Presson, Seo, & Macy, 2009). These intergenerational effects were unique, over and above explicit attitudes. This study was the first to show intergenerational transmission of implicit attitudes toward smoking and provided the first evidence that the intergenerational transmission of implicit attitudes could serve as a pathway underlying the intergenerational transmission of cigarette smoking. The findings suggest that smoking parents may transmit subtle messages about cigarette smoking to their children that might even be outside of their awareness. They also suggest that prevention programs might need to consider techniques that have been useful for modifying implicit attitudes.

THE ROLE OF IMPLICIT ATTITUDES IN THE INITIATION AND CHANGE OF SMOKING BEHAVIOR

As described previously, studying implicit attitudes toward smoking can be a useful method because smoking is a socially undesirable behavior, creating bias in explicitly reported attitude measures. In one of the first studies of implicit attitudes toward cigarette smoking, we investigated the effects of context and motivational state on implicit measures of attitudes (Sherman, Rose, Koch, Presson, & Chassin; 2003). Although implicit attitudes were originally thought to be extremely stable and difficult to change, we found that both contextual and motivational factors could change these implicit attitudes. Because implicit attitudes are predictive of both smoking initiation and cessation, the fact that these attitudes can be changed by applying the appropriate techniques is very important.

Specifically in this research, we first manipulated the salience of different aspects of smoking. In one condition, we measured implicit attitudes toward smoking while participants who smoked were exposed either to pictures highlighting the sensory aspects of smoking (e.g., cigarettes burning in an ashtray) or to pictures highlighting the economic and health aspects of smoking (e.g., a carton of cigarettes in a grocery store with the warning label visible). We found that the implicit attitudes of smokers varied greatly as a function of the highlighted aspects of smoking. Their implicit attitudes toward smoking were significantly more positive in the sensory aspects condition than in the packaging condition, illustrating context dependency in these implicit attitudes.

In a second study, we varied the motivational states of smokers. One group was deprived of nicotine for at least 4 hours. The other group smoked a cigarette immediately before the experimental session and was thus was dosed with nicotine. We also included a non-smoking comparison group. When smokers were nicotine deprived, their implicit attitudes toward smoking were extremely positive. When they were nicotine loaded, however, their implicit attitudes were quite negative—even more negative than the implicit attitudes of non-smokers. There were no differences in the explicit attitudes of deprived and nicotine-loaded participants. In a more recent study (Rydell, Sherman, Boucher, & Macy, 2012), we found that after nicotine loading, smokers' implicit evaluations of cigarettes became more negative when they were exposed to a strong anti-smoking persuasive message.

This sensitivity of the implicit attitudes of smokers to contextual and motivational factors is extremely important. Inducing negative implicit attitudes in smokers is likely to increase the probability of quitting, and inducing negative implicit attitudes in non-smokers is likely to decrease the probability of their smoking initiation.

In an 18-month longitudinal study, we explored the role of implicit and explicit attitudes in predicting smoking cessation (Chassin, Presson, Sherman, Seo, & Macy, 2010). Results showed that the effects of these attitudes varied with levels of past experience to control smoking and with the development of specific plans to quit. Explicit attitudes predicted smoking cessation 18 months later for smokers who had little previous failure to control smoking. On the other hand, implicit attitudes predicted later successful cessation for smokers who had a good deal of previous experience with failures to control smoking, but only if they had a specific plan to quit. These results indicate that smoking cessation involves both controlled processes (as captured by explicit measures) and automatic processes (as captured by implicit measures). We suggest that interventions designed to bring about smoking cessation consider a focus on changing both explicit and implicit attitudes. Changing implicit versus explicit attitudes requires very different approaches (Rydell & McConnell, 2006). For changing implicit attitudes toward smoking, interventions might include creating new associations in memory, retraining attention, and/or using practice to change controlled processes into automatized processes (Wiers & Stacy, 2006). For changing explicit attitudes, persuasive messages that focus on social norms or the social desirability of not smoking should be very useful.

Given the importance of implicit attitudes in predicting future smoking behavior (both initiation and cessation), our most recent work has focused on testing interventions designed to make implicit attitudes toward smoking more negative. One intervention strategy that has demonstrated some utility is approach–avoidance practice. It is based on theories of cognitive embodiment, which have demonstrated the effects of motor actions on attitudes (Neumann, Förster, & Strack, 2003). Studies of early applications of this strategy showed that simple movements involving "pulling toward" and "pushing away" pictures of target objects affected both implicit attitudes and social behavior with regard to racism (Kawakami, Phills, Steele, & Dovidio, 2007) and math among women (Kawakami, Steele, Cifa, Phills, & Dovidio, 2008). More recently, this intervention strategy has been successfully applied to an addictive behavior. Studies showed that approach–avoidance practice changed automatic cognitive biases among heavy drinkers (Wiers, Rinck, Kordts, Houben, & Strack, 2010) and alcoholics (Eberl et al., 2013; Wiers, Eberl, Rinck, Becker, & Lindenmeyer, 2011). We applied this same strategy to the behavior of cigarette smoking and tested whether approach–avoidance practice changed smokers' implicit attitudes toward smoking (Macy, Chassin, Presson, & Sherman, 2015). We randomly assigned smokers to complete a push–pull approach–avoidance task or a side-to-side control task, in which participants used a computer mouse to move pictures of cigarettes on the computer screen. Our results suggest that the approach–avoidance practice task may be able to make some smokers' implicit attitudes toward smoking more negative. First, the intervention may be able to make implicit attitudes toward smoking more negative for smokers with low levels of educational attainment. Importantly, this is the group that is at highest risk for heavy smoking and smoking-related morbidity and mortality (Hiscock, Bauld, Amos, Fidler, & Munafò, 2012). It is also a group that has been reported to be difficult to influence through traditional interventions such as media campaigns that target explicit outcomes (Niederdeppe, Fiore, Backer, & Smith, 2008). Second, smokers who reported having plans to quit smoking at baseline and completed the push–pull practice task were found to have more negative implicit attitudes toward smoking at follow-up.

We have also tested how implicit attitudes toward smoking can be influenced by exposure to graphic health warnings on cigarette packages. The Family Smoking Prevention and Tobacco Control Act of 2009 required that large health warning labels appear on tobacco packages in the United States (Deyton, Sharfstein, & Hamburg, 2010). However, the requirement was not implemented due to legal action taken by the tobacco industry. To bolster the evidence base on the effectiveness of graphic health warnings on influencing smoking behavior, considerable research is ongoing. We tested the effects of exposure to the proposed graphic warning labels on the implicit attitudes of young adults (Macy, Yeung, Presson, & Chassin, 2016). We found that young adult smokers exposed to packages with the graphic health warnings demonstrated more negative implicit attitudes compared to those exposed to packages with large text warnings only or with the current Surgeon General's warnings on the side of the package. Given the role that implicit attitudes play in predicting future smoking behavior, this finding is important as the US government

continues to determine how to implement cigarette package labeling policies.

LIMITATIONS

Although our project has made many important contributions to the understanding of smoking behavior, from adolescence to adulthood, there are also limitations that need to be acknowledged. First, given the importance of cultural and social influences, our early data may lack generalizability to more recent cohorts. Second, although our sample is representative of its community, and although the smoking rates in our sample have consistently been higher than the national prevalence, the community itself is predominantly White and relatively well-educated. Thus, our findings may be limited in generalizability to more racially and ethnically diverse populations. Finally, because of our lengthy and comprehensive assessment of tobacco-related variables, our protocols were not able to include assessments of other forms of substance use. Thus, we cannot assess the extent to which our findings would apply in a broader context of substance use behaviors.

CONCLUSIONS AND FUTURE DIRECTIONS

In this chapter, we hope to have communicated several themes that illustrate our application of a developmental approach to cigarette smoking from adolescence to adulthood and the benefits of taking this approach. First, it is important to consider developmental trajectories of smoking behavior and to understand the conditions and challenges of the developmental periods that show transitions in smoking status, particularly adolescent smoking onset and midlife challenges when parents are caring for adolescent children.

Second, it is important to understand heterogeneity in these trajectories. We have shown both differential antecedents and consequences of this heterogeneity such that differing trajectories may have different etiological underpinnings as well as different implications for intergenerational transmission of smoking.

Third, it is important to recognize that development unfolds within the larger context of societal and historical change. This has been particularly important in the study of cigarette smoking, which has undergone considerable societal reconceptualization in recent decades, such that adolescent smoking is now at the lowest rate since the Monitoring the Future study began national surveillance in the 1970s (Johnston, O'Malley, Miech, Bachman, & Schulenberg, 2015). In particular, we showed that there was a substantial reduction in adolescent smoking in the community that we studied between 1980 and 2001 and also that increasing beliefs that cigarette smoking was addictive and socially undesirable were related to that reduction in prevalence. Moreover, in addition to direct societal reframing of cigarette smoking, it is important to recognize that societal change can indirectly affect outcomes. For example, our data suggest that changes in family conditions (i.e., the increase in multigenerational caretaking) and financial stress might influence smoking among adults.

In addition to emphasizing the importance of heterogeneity in developmental trajectories that unfold within the context of cultural–historical change, we have also highlighted the importance of considering development within a family systems and multigenerational context. For example, adolescent development and midlife development are inextricably tied together when midlife parents are providing general and smoking-specific socialization to their adolescent children and possibly also modeling cigarette smoking behavior. Moreover, in studying intergenerational transmission, we have shown that both explicit attitudes and implicit attitudes that may be outside of conscious awareness can be transmitted from parent to children and that both are important for intergenerational transmission of smoking behavior.

Finally, we have illustrated the importance of considering cigarette smoking within the context of multiple forms of tobacco use. Although our findings did not suggest substantial switching between cigarette smoking and smokeless tobacco use, the possibility that one form of tobacco use might influence the development of another is a particularly important future direction given the many new tobacco products that have been introduced. In this regard, it is particularly striking that more adolescents now use e-cigarettes than smoke traditional cigarettes (Johnston et al., 2015). Currently, it is unclear whether e-cigarettes may be an effective form of harm reduction, which facilitates adult smoking cessation or reduces harm among smokers who switch to e-cigarettes, or whether e-cigarettes are a risk factor for adolescent initiation of cigarette smoking (or both). This is an important future research direction.

In terms of other future directions, the FDA mission to regulate tobacco products has created a need for a tobacco regulatory science agenda. One part of this agenda that may be of particular relevance for developmental scientists concerns the need to inform the public about the effects of tobacco products. Given our findings that adolescents may understand the concept of addiction differently than do adults, empirical studies may help guide FDA communication programs across the lifespan. Developmental appropriateness of interventions including media campaigns and warning labels can be useful in this regard. Other future research directions involve family-based intervention. Findings that smoking-specific socialization practices are less effective when a parent smokes suggest that these families may need additional attention. Moreover, although there are evidence-based family interventions that reduce adolescent substance use (Institute of Medicine, 2009), evidence-based interventions are rarely implemented in practice, and there is an important research agenda in the implementation science necessary to place empirically based family interventions into natural settings (Spoth et al., 2013). Finally, both our etiological models and intervention studies can be conducted with innovative use of measures at multiple levels of analysis. For example, gene by prevention program interactions have been reported for adolescent smoking outcomes (Vandenbergh et al., 2016), and neural-level data have been shown to significantly add to self-report data in predicting smoking outcomes after exposure to anti-smoking messages (Falk, Berkman, Whalen, & Lieberman, 2011). Such multilevel studies are an important future direction.

ACKNOWLEDGMENTS

Preparation of this chapter was supported by grant DA013555 from the National Institute on Drug Abuse. We thank the participants in the Indiana University Smoking Survey and the participating Monroe County schools for their support.

REFERENCES

Barton, J., Chassin, L., Presson, C. C., & Sherman, S. J. (1982). Social image factors as motivators of smoking initiation in early and middle adolescents. *Child Development, 53,* 1499–1511.

Baumrind, D. (1991). The influence of parenting style on adolescent competence and substance use. *Journal of Early Adolescence, 11,* 56–95.

Chassin, L., Curran, P., Presson, C., Wirth, R. J., & Sherman, S. J. (2009). Trajectories of adolescent smoking: Conceptual issues and an empirical example. In G. Swain (Ed.), *Phenotypes and endophenotypes: Foundations for genetic studies of nicotine use and dependence* (Tobacco Control Monograph No. 20, NIH Publication No. 08–6366). Bethesda, MD: US Department of Health and Human Services, National Institutes of Health, National Cancer Institute.

Chassin, L., Macy, J. T., Seo, D.-C., Presson, C. C., & Sherman, S. J. (2010). The association between membership in the sandwich generation and health behaviors: A longitudinal study. *Journal of Applied Developmental Psychology, 31,* 38–46.

Chassin, L., Presson, C. C., Pitts, S. C., & Sherman, S. J. (2000). The natural history of cigarette smoking from adolescence to adulthood in a Midwestern community sample: Multiple trajectories and their psychosocial correlates. *Health Psychology, 19,* 223–231.

Chassin, L., Presson, C. C., Rose, J. S., & Sherman, S. J. (1996). The natural history of cigarette smoking from adolescence to adulthood: Demographic predictors of continuity and change. *Health Psychology, 15,* 478–484.

Chassin, L., Presson, C. C., Rose, J., & Sherman, S. J. (2001). From adolescence to adulthood: Age-related changes in beliefs about cigarette smoking in a Midwestern community sample. *Health Psychology, 20,* 377–386.

Chassin, L., Presson, C. C., Rose, J., & Sherman, S. J. (2007). What is "addiction"? Age-related differences in the meaning of addiction. Views of adolescents and their parents. *Drug and Alcohol Dependence, 7,* 30–38.

Chassin, L., Presson, C. C., Rose, J., Sherman, S. J., Davis, M. J., & Gonzalez, J. L. (2005). Parenting style and smoking-specific parenting practices as predictors of adolescent smoking onset. *Journal of Pediatric Psychology, 30,* 333–344.

Chassin, L., Presson, C. C., Seo, D. C., Sherman, S. J., Macy, J., Wirth, R. J., & Curran, P. (2008). Multiple trajectories of cigarette smoking and the intergenerational transmission of smoking: A multigenerational longitudinal study of a Midwestern community sample. *Health Psychology, 27,* 819–828.

Chassin, L., Presson, C. C., & Sherman, S. J. (1984). Cigarette smoking and adolescent psychosocial development. *Basic & Applied Social Psychology, 5,* 295–315.

Chassin, L., Presson, C. C., Sherman, S. J., Corty, E., & Olshavsky, R. (1981). Self-images and cigarette smoking in adolescents. *Personality and Social Psychology Bulletin, 7,* 670–676.

Chassin, L., Presson, C. C., Sherman, S. J., & Edwards, D. A. (1990). The natural history of cigarette smoking: Predicting young-adult smoking outcomes from adolescent smoking patterns. *Health Psychology, 9,* 701–716.

Chassin, L., Presson, C. C., Sherman, S. J., & Edwards, D. A. (1991). Four pathways to young-adult smoking status: Adolescent social psychological antecedents in a Midwestern community sample. *Health Psychology, 10,* 409–418.

Chassin, L., Presson, C. C., Sherman, S. J., & Kim, K. (2003). Historical changes in cigarette smoking and smoking-related beliefs over two decades in a Midwestern community. *Health Psychology, 22,* 347–353.

Chassin, L., Presson, C. C., Sherman, S. J., Montello, D., & McGrew, J. (1986). Changes in peer and parent influence during adolescence: Longitudinal versus cross-sectional perspectives on smoking initiation. *Developmental Psychology, 22,* 327–334.

Chassin, L., Presson, C., Sherman, S. J., Seo, D.-C., & Macy, J. (2010). Implicit and explicit attitudes predict smoking cessation: Moderating effects of experienced failure to control smoking and plans to quit. *Psychology of Addictive Behaviors, 24,* 670–679.

Chen, K., & Kandel, D. B. (1995). The natural history of drug use from adolescence to the mid-thirties in a general population sample. *American Journal of Public Health, 85,* 41–47.

Deyton, L., Sharfstein, J., & Hamburg, M. (2010). Tobacco product regulation—A public health approach. *New England Journal of Medicine, 362,* 1753–1756.

Eberl, C., Wiers, R. W., Pawelczack, S., Rinck, M., Becker, E., & Lindenmeyer, J. (2013). Approach bias modification in alcohol dependence: Do clinical effects replicate and for whom does it work best? *Developmental Cognitive Neuroscience, 4,* 38–51.

Falk, E. B., Berkman, E. T., Whalen, D., & Lieberman, M. D. (2011). Neural activity during health messaging predicts reductions in smoking above and beyond self-report. *Health Psychology, 30,* 177–185.

Greenwald, A. G., McGhee, D. E., & Schwartz, J. L. (1998). Measuring individual differences in implicit cognition: The implicit association test. *Journal of Personality and Social Psychology, 74,* 1464–1480.

Hamill, S., & Goldberg, W. (1997). Between adolescents and aging grandparents: Midlife concerns of adults in the "sandwich generation." *Journal of Adult Development, 4,* 135–147.

Hiscock, R., Bauld, L., Amos, A., Fidler, J. A., & Munafò, M. (2012). Socioeconomic status and smoking: A review. *Annals of the New York Academy of Sciences, 1248*, 107–123.

Institute of Medicine. (2009). *Preventing mental, emotional, and behavioral disorders among young people: Progress and possibilities.* Washington, DC: National Academies Press.

Johnston, L. D., O'Malley, P. M., Miech, R. A., Bachman, J. G., & Schulenberg, J. E. (2015). *Monitoring the Future national results on adolescent drug use: Overview of key findings, 2014.* Ann Arbor, MI: Institute for Social Research, University of Michigan.

Kawakami, K., Phills, C., Steele, J., & Dovidio, J. (2007). (Close) distance makes the heart grow fonder: Improving implicit racial attitudes and interracial interactions through approach behaviors. *Journal of Personality and Social Psychology, 92*, 957–971.

Kawakami, K., Steele, J., Cifa, C., Phills, C., & Dovidio, J. (2008). Approaching math increases math=me and math=pleasant. *Journal of Experimental Social Psychology, 44*, 818–825.

Krosnick, J. A., & Judd, C. M. (1982). Transitions in social influence at adolescence: Who induces cigarette smoking? *Developmental Psychology, 18*, 359–368.

Littlefield, A. K., Sher, K. J., & Wood, P. K. (2010). A personality-based description of maturing out of alcohol problems: Extension with a five-factor model and robustness to modeling challenges. *Addictive Behaviors, 35*, 948–954.

Macy, J. T., Chassin, L., & Presson, C. C. (2013). Predictors of health behaviors after the economic downturn: A longitudinal study. *Social Science and Medicine, 89*, 8–15.

Macy, J. T., Chassin, L., Presson, C. C., & Sherman, J. W. (2015). Changing implicit attitudes toward smoking: Results from a web-based approach–avoidance practice intervention. *Journal of Behavioral Medicine, 38*, 143–152.

Macy, J. T., Li, J., Xun, P., Presson, C. C., & Chassin, L. (2016). Dual trajectories of cigarette smoking and smokeless tobacco use from adolescence to midlife among males in a Midwestern U.S. community sample. *Nicotine and Tobacco Research, 18*(2), 186–195. doi:10.1093/ntr/ntv070

Macy, J. T., Yeung, E., Presson, C. C., & Chassin, L. (2016). Exposure to graphic warning labels on cigarette packages: Effects on implicit and explicit attitudes toward smoking among young adults. *Psychology and Health, 31*(3), 349–363.

Neumann, R., Förster, J., & Strack, F. (2003). Motor compatibility: The bidirectional link between behavior

and evaluation. In J. Musch & K. C. Klauer (Eds.), *The psychology of evaluation: Affective processes in cognition and emotion* (pp. 371–391). Mahwah, NJ: Erlbaum.

Niederdeppe, J., Fiore, M. C., Baker, T. B., & Smith, S. S. (2008). Smoking-cessation media campaigns and their effectiveness among socioeconomically advantaged and disadvantaged populations. *American Journal of Public Health, 98*, 916–924.

O'Malley, P. M., Bachman, J. G., & Johnson, L. D. (1984). Period, age, and cohort effects on substance use among American youth, 1976–1982. *American Journal of Public Health, 74*, 682–688.

Rydell, R. J., & McConnell, A. R. (2006). Understanding implicit and explicit attitude change: A systems of reasoning analysis. *Journal of Personality and Social Psychology, 91*, 995–1008.

Rydell, R. J., Sherman, S. J., Boucher, K. L., & Macy, J. T. (2012). The role of motivational and persuasive message factors in changing implicit attitudes toward smoking. *Basic and Applied Social Psychology, 34*, 1–7.

Severson, H., Lichtenstein, E., & Gallison, C. (1985). A pinch or a pouch instead of a puff? Implications of chewing tobacco for addictive processes. *Bulletin of the Society of Psychologists in Addictive Behaviors, 4*(2), 85–92.

Sherman, S. J., Chassin, L., Presson, C., Seo, D.-C., & Macy, J. T. (2009). The intergenerational transmission of implicit and explicit attitudes toward smoking. *Journal of Experimental Social Psychology, 45*, 313–328.

Sherman, S. J., Rose, J. S., Koch, K., Presson, C. C., & Chassin, L. (2003). Implicit and explicit attitudes toward cigarette smoking: The effects of context and motivation. *Journal of Social and Clinical Psychology, 22*, 13–39.

Spoth, R., Rohrbach, L. A., Greenberg, M., Leaf, P., Brown, C. H., Fagan, A., . . . Hawkins, J. D.; Society for Prevention Research Type 2 Translational Task Force Members and Contributing Authors. (2013). Addressing core challenges for the next generation of type 2 translation research and systems: The Translation Science to Population Impact (TSci Impact) framework. *Prevention Science, 14*, 319–351

US Department of Health and Human Services. (1988). *The health consequences of smoking–nicotine addiction: A report of the Surgeon General.* Atlanta, GA: US Department of Health and Human Services, Centers for Disease Control and Prevention, National Center for Chronic Disease Prevention and Health Promotion, Office on Smoking and Health.

US Department of Health and Human Services. (2014). *The health consequences of smoking—50 years of progress: A report of the Surgeon General.* Atlanta, GA: US Department of Health and Human Services, Centers for Disease Control and Prevention, National Center for Chronic Disease Prevention and Health Promotion, Office on Smoking and Health.

Vandenbergh, D. H., Schlomer, G. L., Cleveland, H. H., Schink, A. E., Hair, K. L., Feinberg, M. E., . . . Redmond, C. (2016). An adolescent substance prevention model blocks the effect of CHRNA5 genotype on smoking during high school. *Nicotine and Tobacco Research, 18*(2), 212–220.

Wiers, R. W., Eberl, C., Rinck, M., Becker, E. S., & Lindenmeyer, J. (2011). Retraining automatic action tendencies changes alcoholic patients' approach bias for alcohol and improves treatment outcome. *Psychological Science, 22,* 490–497.

Wiers, R. W., Rinck, M., Kordts, R., Houben, K., & Strack, F. (2010). Retraining automatic action-tendencies to approach alcohol in hazardous drinkers. *Addiction, 105,* 279–287.

Wiers, R. W., & Stacy, A. W. (2006). *Handbook of implicit cognition and addiction.* Thousand Oaks, CA: Sage.

Yamaguchi, K., & Kandel, D. (1985). Patterns of drug abuse from adolescence to young adulthood: II. Sequences of progression. *American Journal of Public Health, 74,* 668–672.

15

Alcohol Use and Consequences Across Developmental Transitions During College and Beyond

James R. Ashenhurst

Kim Fromme

Emerging adulthood, the developmental period after adolescence commonly defined as from 18 to 25 years of age (Arnett, 2000), is a common period of transition out of the home of one's parents and toward independence. This age span is also characterized by heavier drug and alcohol use compared to other periods of life (Bachman, Wadsworth, O' Malley, Johnston, & Schulenberg, 1997), and the incidence of alcohol dependence is approximately twice that of the general population (Esser et al., 2014; Grant et al., 2004; Knight et al., 2002). Hazardous alcohol use often occurs in the context of post-secondary educational institutions, such as colleges and universities. In the United States in 2012, approximately 41% of 18- to 24-year-olds were enrolled in some form of post-secondary education, including both 2- and 4-year institutions (National Center for Education Statistics, 2013).

Being a student may itself be a risk factor for heavy drinking. Alcohol use is slightly more prevalent among college students than among their non-enrolled peers (Bachman et al., 1997; Dawson, Grant, Stinson, & Chou, 2004; O'Malley & Johnston, 2002; Quinn & Fromme, 2011a; Slutske et al., 2004; White, Fleming, Kim, Catalano, & McMorris, 2008). Although the differences in alcohol consumption between age-matched peers who do and those who do not attend college are often small, the most prominent difference appears to be specific to heavy episodic drinking (Slutske et al., 2004). This hazardous pattern of consumption is sometimes termed "binge

drinking," and it was initially defined as consumption of four drinks on one occasion for women and five drinks on one occasion for men. This definition has since been revised to specify a 2-hour duration of drinking (National Institute of Alcohol Abuse and Alcoholism [NIAAA], 2004). In 2014, approximately 35% of US college students reported heavy episodic drinking versus 31% of non-college peers (Johnston, O'Malley, Bachman, Schulenberg, & Miech, 2015). Evidence suggests that the true magnitude of the difference between college students and their non-college peers may be partially masked by protective factors more prevalent among those who attend college, such as greater self-regulation and lower sensation-seeking personality (Quinn & Fromme, 2011a). As such, the college environment appears to foster heavy drinking during an age span already characterized by relatively heavy substance use.

The consequences of alcohol use among college students are manifold, including drunk driving, memory loss, property damage, assault, academic problems, or unplanned sex (Wechsler, Davenport, Dowdall, Moeykens, & Castillo, 1994; White & Hingson, 2013). In order to address this public health and legal burden, understanding the factors and mechanisms that contribute to risk for hazardous alcohol use and the resulting consequences during college is crucial.

In the following sections, we first provide an overview of the large multiyear study conducted by our research group from which many of our reported findings are drawn. We then describe overall patterns of alcohol use across college and review well-studied risk factors for and consequences of alcohol use across the college experience. Specific objective consequences that we highlight are aggression and dating violence, drinking and driving, and alcohol-induced blackouts. Whereas the overall focus is on the college years in general, within each section we highlight aspects unique to either the transition into college or the transition out of college, especially where individual differences in risk factors moderate or mediate alcohol use only during specific periods. We then describe findings on special events common to the college experience during which heavy drinking is prominent: 21st birthdays and football games or other sporting events. The concluding section summarizes our findings and explores gaps in the literature and likely fruitful avenues for future research.

THE UT EXPERIENCE STUDY

Many of the findings discussed in this chapter are drawn from a large 6-year research study—called the "UT Experience!" (UTE)—conducted by our group at the University of Texas at Austin between 2004 and 2009 (Ashenhurst, Harden, Corbin, & Fromme, 2015; Fromme, Corbin, & Kruse, 2008; Stappenbeck, Quinn, Wetherill, & Fromme, 2010). At recruitment, this sample consisted of unmarried first-time college students who had gained admission to the university ($N = 4,832$). These potential respondents were randomized to three arms of the study. Participants in one arm received surveys during their high school summer and year 4 of the study ($n = 426$), whereas those in another arm consented during high school summer but only provided data during year 4 ($n = 421$). Finally, the largest longitudinal sample was followed prospectively over 10 waves of web-based surveys semi-annually (years 1–3) or annually (years 4–6), beginning the summer prior to matriculation on campus ($n = 2,245$). At each wave, respondents provided information about their behavior during the previous 3 months. In addition, longitudinal participants also completed web-based daily monitoring surveys over 30 days during a randomly selected month during each of the first 4 years. This addition to the study design allows for event-level analyses, whereby both intra- and interindividual differences are examined

at a more fine-grained level compared to the past 3-month survey data.

Our study included many measures of substance use, social risk factors, and other behavioral risks that were repeated over time, allowing us to trace individual differences in alcohol use across many years. Importantly, we captured several indices of drinking behavior, including typical quantities and frequencies as well as heavy episodic drinking. Additional drinking measures captured subjective components of alcohol use, such as the number of times an individual felt "drunk" during the past 3 months. Depending on the research question being addressed, some analyses included different sets of measures, with many using an "alcohol use" composite score (Fromme et al., 2008) derived from a combination of both objective (e.g., number of drinks) and subjective items (e.g., times "drunk"). Alcohol researchers are well aware of the difficulties of integrating findings across multiple studies from diverse research groups that use different alcohol use indicators (Mun et al., 2015) because effects can be present for some aspects of drinking but not for others. Among the kinds of measures used across the research field, it appears that the many different ways of assessing heavy episodic drinking (e.g., asking about past 2 weeks vs. past month or defining the number of drinks constituting a "binge") are the least harmonized across the field (Mun et al., 2015). With this in mind, we have taken care to be specific about which alcohol measure is under examination throughout this review.

OVERARCHING TRAJECTORIES OF ALCOHOL USE

The Transition into College

A majority of college-bound high school students— approximately 60%—begin college in the fall semester after completing high school (Arnett, 2004). This move to post-secondary education often means leaving the home of one's parents and living more independently in a dormitory or apartment. As such, many young people find themselves without parental supervision and with increased opportunity to engage in a variety of behavioral risks, including heavy drinking (Fromme et al., 2008; O'Malley & Johnston, 2002; Slutske et al., 2004). As should be expected, the quantity of alcohol use in high school prospectively predicts freshman year quantities consumed, and levels of consumption generally increase (Sher & Rutledge, 2007; Stappenbeck et al., 2010).

Nonetheless, despite mean-level increases in drinking in terms of quantity, frequency, times drunk, and heavy episodic drinking (Fromme et al., 2008) and some interindividual stability (Stappenbeck et al., 2010), there are considerable individual differences across the transition to college life; the response to new freedoms is not uniform. Indeed, a number of factors, such as demographics, personality, academic and social motives, parental relationships, and social norms, associate with changes in drinking across this transition and with the incidence of related negative consequences (Corbin, Vaughan, & Fromme, 2008; Fromme et al., 2008; Hatzenbuehler, Corbin, & Fromme, 2008; Quinn & Fromme, 2011d; Sher & Rutledge, 2007; Stappenbeck et al., 2010). Many prevention/intervention programs are delivered to new freshman upon arrival to campus, so identification of specific mechanisms that confer risk to target groups may enhance the efficacy of such programs.

The Duration of College

Previous studies using large cohorts of emerging adults (e.g., the Monitoring the Future project) have used latent class growth analysis techniques in order to identify prototypic categories of alcohol use over time (Schulenberg, O'Malley, Bachman, Wadsworth, & Johnston, 1996). This technique usually identifies groups that maintain high or low levels of alcohol use and groups that increase or decrease over time, resulting in a "cat's cradle" configuration (Sher, Jackson, & Steinley, 2011).

We conducted one such analysis of heavy episodic drinking (HED) across the entire UTE study and identified seven kinds of trajectories (Ashenhurst et al., 2015). Four of the groups maintained low levels of HED across time, with at most approximately one HED episode per month. Importantly, a substantial portion, the "Rare" drinking group (22.3%), endorsed nearly no HED across all of college. Two other groups had higher levels of HED, with those in the "moderate" category (19.5%) reporting approximately two HED episodes per month and those in the "frequent" group (10.7%) reporting more than six HED episodes per month at their peak of drinking. Both of these groups showed an inverted U curve pattern

of drinking, with the peak corresponding to approximately the spring of junior year. The final group, the "increasers" (8.2%), reported little or no HED freshman year, but by senior year fall, their drinking was comparable to that of the moderate group.

The trajectory groups found in the UTE sample generally resemble those identified among emerging adults in general, except for the absence of a group that decreases from rather high to low levels of HED shown by Schulenberg and colleagues (1996). The heterogeneity among the trajectories of HED provides compelling evidence that there is not one alcohol-related "college experience" but instead many and also that a substantial minority of students rarely drink heavily.

The Transition out of College

Patterns of alcohol use change considerably across the transition away from campus toward the acquisition of new adult roles and responsibilities such as marriage, children, and jobs (Jochman & Fromme, 2010; Tucker, 2003; Watson & Sher, 1998), largely explained by personality change toward greater self-regulation (Littlefield, Sher, & Wood, 2009). Many studies have reported decreases in frequency or quantity of alcohol consumption, heavy episodic drinking, and times drunk across this transition (Boyd, Corbin, & Fromme, 2014; Gotham, Sher, & Wood, 1997; Schulenberg et al., 1996; White, Labouvie, & Papadaratsakis, 2005). Researchers have termed this process, for both alcohol and other drug use, "maturing out" (Donovan, Jessor, & Jessor, 1983; Littlefield et al., 2009; Winick, 1962).

Despite mean-level decreases in alcohol use, some individuals maintain or increase levels of use across this transition (Ashenhurst et al., 2015; Jackson, Sher, Gotham, & Wood, 2001). In particular, our identified "increasers" group reported a further increase in HED across this transition. Members of the other heavier drinking groups (moderate and frequent) decreased frequency of HED to the levels they initially reported when they were seniors in high school (Ashenhurst et al., 2015). The various factors associated with individual differences across this transition, such as personality, peers, and adult roles (Ashenhurst et al., 2015; Bachman et al., 2002; Gotham et al., 1997; Littlefield et al., 2009), are likely important etiologic considerations in the development and maintenance of lifelong alcohol use disorders.

RISK FACTORS FOR ALCOHOL USE IN COLLEGE

The UTE study has provided an excellent opportunity to investigate individual differences that associate with the degree of alcohol use across the transitions into college, over the duration of college, and out of college into early adulthood. The following sections focus on specific domains of factors examined in the UTE study that contribute to individual risk for alcohol use. We first highlight demographic factors, followed by psychosocial elements (parents and peers) and, finally, personal factors such as personality, motives, and subjective intoxication.

Demographics

Gender

Overall, heavy episodic drinking is more frequent among college males (approximately 40%) than females (approximately 30%) (Johnston et al., 2015). Across the college years, it appears that men increase heavy episodic drinking more than do women, who often decrease by senior year compared to freshman year (McCabe, 2002). Men overall drink more heavily in terms of quantity (total drinks per week) than do women across the transition out of high school to college. We found that men increased from 3.49 to 6.72 drinks per week, whereas women increased from 2.61 to 4.82 drinks per week on average. This is a difference of 3.23 and 2.21 drinks, respectively (Stappenbeck et al., 2010).

Results differ, however, when using a more holistic composite measure of alcohol use that includes the number of drinking days, the number of drinks per drinking day, the frequency of being "drunk," and the frequency of heavy episodic drinking. When assessed as a broader construct, change across the transition to college does not appear to significantly differ by sex (Fromme et al., 2008; Vaughan, Corbin, & Fromme, 2009). These findings suggest that whereas specific aspects of drinking behavior may change uniquely by sex, on the whole men and women report similar increases in alcohol involvement across this transition. Similarly, respondent sex was not a significant predictor of being in any given class versus the rare class among the trajectory classes describing HED across college that were discussed previously (Ashenhurst et al., 2015). There are sex differences found among

the mechanisms of risk for college drinking, however, and these are described later.

Sex differences have also been described for some drinking measures across the transition out of college, with men overall drinking more in terms of quantity or frequency (Gotham et al., 1997; Wilhite & Fromme, 2015). There is little evidence, however, for differences in rate of change between men and women across this transition. A prospective study reported no differences in rates of change by biological sex using mixed models (Gotham et al., 1997), and we found that men and women were equally likely to be in a class of individuals who increased heavy episodic drinking versus those who maintained low levels across the transition (Ashenhurst et al., 2015). Thus, biological sex alone does not appear to moderate change in alcohol involvement after leaving campus.

Ancestral Background

Individuals from different ethnic or racial backgrounds often show differences in alcohol use across the transition to college (Fromme et al., 2008) and beyond (O'Hare, 1990; O'Malley & Johnston, 2002). In the UTE sample, relative to Caucasian students, those of Asian, African American, or Hispanic/Latino heritage reported lower levels of drinking in the summer before arriving on campus (Corbin, Vaughan, et al., 2008; Fromme et al., 2008), a difference that was maintained across the transition (Fromme et al., 2008).

Across the entire span of the UTE study (approximately ages 18–24 years), our latent class trajectory analyses of HED (Ashenhurst et al., 2015) showed that Asian and African American students were much less likely (vs. Caucasians) to be in any class other than one that reported rare (i.e., less than monthly) drinking episodes. There were fewer differences between Caucasian and Latino students, with Latinos being less represented in the most frequent HED class only. These results are consistent with data from samples gathered at other colleges/universities and during different decades (O'Hare, 1990; O'Malley & Johnston, 2002; Wechsler, Dowdall, Davenport, & Castillo, 1995), indicating that Caucasian students are the persistently highest risk demographic group.

Whereas many studies have noted these demographic differences, fewer have examined mechanistic explanations between or within ethnic groups. For example, we found apparent sex differences across the transition to college within ethnic groups (Corbin, Vaughan, et al., 2008). African American and Latina women reported less drinking than their male counterparts, but there was no difference by sex among Caucasian or Asian students. Multigroup mediation models by ethnicity indicated that Latino individuals are more influenced by family drinking patterns, with Latina women having a more pronounced protective effect. In contrast, perceived peer drinking is more related to individual alcohol use among Caucasians than Latino individuals (Corbin, Gearhardt, & Fromme, 2008). These results indicate that differences in social and cultural factors likely underlie some of the observed differences by ethnic group.

Although mean-level statistics indicate that Asian heritage is protective against heavy episodic drinking (Ashenhurst et al., 2015; O'Hare, 1990), there are, of course, notable individual differences among Asian students as well. Our research group identified three trajectories of heavy episodic drinking across time among Asian American students: abstainers, low increasers, and high increasers (Iwamoto, Corbin, & Fromme, 2010). Many characteristics that associate with HED generally were also markers of risk in this more racially homogeneous sample. Permissive drinking values, more positive alcohol expectancies, and higher quality peer relationships predicted membership in the drinking classes versus abstainers, but parental communication and parental awareness and caring did not (Iwamoto et al., 2010). Overall, considering differing risk levels and mechanistic associations by ethnic background, culturally/ethnically congruent intervention efforts upon arrival to campus are warranted (Corbin, Vaughan, et al., 2008).

Socioeconomic Status

Whereas the relations between economic resources and alcohol use are frequently explored in the broader literature in an attempt to understand health disparities related to risk behaviors among adolescents and adults (Hanson & Chen, 2007a; van Oers, Bongers, van de Goor, & Garretsen, 1999), there has been less focus specifically on socioeconomic status (SES) in college populations. We found that those from backgrounds of greater wealth and parental education (a composite SES score) drank more during the summer after high school (Corbin, Vaughan, et al., 2008), although literature reviews indicate mixed findings about SES among adolescents (Hanson &

Chen, 2007a, 2007b). We also found that despite differences in high school (Corbin, Vaughan, et al., 2008), individuals of different SES did not appear to differ in growth of alcohol involvement across the transition (composite score; Fromme et al., 2008). Somewhat similarly, greater family income was not associated with a specific trajectory of HED across the span of the UTE study but instead with membership in any class other than the rare class (Ashenhurst et al., 2015). These results may reflect greater resources available for purchasing alcohol among those from a wealthier background, or perhaps wealthier students have more available time for heavy drinking than do students balancing both schoolwork and employment.

Sexual Orientation

Sexual minority status is an additional demographic component that is important to consider in the development of alcohol use across the transition to college and beyond. When considering sexuality, it is important to keep in mind that orientation is commonly defined by three correlated but not fully overlapping components: identity, attraction, and behavior (Savin-Williams, 2006). In the general population of adolescents from 7th to 12th grade, lesbian, gay, and bisexual individuals show steeper increasing trajectories of alcohol use than do their heterosexual peers when defined by either identity or behavior but not by attraction (Marshal, Friedman, Stall, & Thompson, 2009). By emerging adulthood, lesbian or bisexual women appear to be the most at-risk group in terms of heavy drinking (Eisenberg & Wechsler, 2003) or related consequences (McCabe, Boyd, Hughes, & d'Arcy, 2003).

In our UTE sample (Hatzenbuehler et al., 2008), we replicated this finding, showing that sexual minority women (defined by combination of identity and behavior) had the highest levels of alcohol use in terms of frequency, quantity, and heavy episodic drinking measures the summer after high school. There were no such differences in high school between heterosexual and sexual minority men. Sexual minority women did not differ from other groups, however, in terms of growth of drinking across transition to college. Instead, sexual minority men showed a significantly greater increase in drinking across the transition to college compared to heterosexual men (Hatzenbuehler et al., 2008).

We further examined mechanisms that might explain these differences. We found that the sexual orientation effects (both in high school and change across the transition) were mediated by individual differences in alcohol expectancies and social norms (Hatzenbuehler et al., 2008). In other words, sexual minority women had greater levels of positive alcohol expectancies and were subject to a greater degree of peer influence that explained the elevated drinking in high school. Similarly, a greater increase in both positive alcohol expectancies and injunctive norms (beliefs about the acceptability of alcohol use) partially explained the larger increase in drinking observed among sexual minority men. As such, these differences between heterosexual and non-heterosexual peers are explained to some degree by social–cognitive mechanisms not unique to sexual minority populations.

Nevertheless, residual unexplained variance may be due to additional factors such as minority stress load (Meyer, 2003). That is, differences in drinking behaviors and outcomes attributed to sexual orientation may also be driven by the additional stressors commonly experienced by sexual minority students facing prejudice and discrimination. Indeed, later waves of data collection in the UTE sample included measures of discrimination and coping motives for drinking, allowing for multivariate mediation models. We showed that negative affect and coping motives mediated the indirect effect between perceived discrimination and alcohol-related problems among minority students (including among sexual minority students and ethnic minorities) (Hatzenbuehler, Corbin, & Fromme, 2011). Thus, elevated alcohol use observed between sexual minority students versus their heterosexual peers is partially explained by coping motives in response to perceived discrimination. Finally, initial findings focusing on dating violence outcomes indicate that discrimination plays an important mediating role in explaining disparities between sexual minority and heterosexual individuals, especially for bisexual women (Martin-Storey & Fromme, 2016).

College Residence

Comprehensive literature reviews indicate that being in a fraternity or sorority is associated with greater drinking in terms of both typical quantity and heavy episodic drinking, explained in part by social norms

of heavy drinking and reduced perceptions of risk (Barry, 2007). In our UTE sample, we also found that freshman year campus housing choice associated with both high school levels of drinking and change across the transition (composite score), with those choosing private dorms being initially heavier drinkers who also increased drinking more steeply compared to those in university-owned dorms or those continuing to live with parents (Fromme et al., 2008). This is indicative of both selection and socialization effects of residential environment. Overall, campus residence is a clear risk factor for alcohol involvement, with students participating in Greek organizations being an extreme risk group who endure significant negative consequences (Barry, 2007).

Parental Awareness and Caring

The degree to which parents have knowledge about their child's alcohol use and the provision of support or care are important predictors of adolescent alcohol use (Barnes & Farrell, 1992; Kerr & Stattin, 2000). Across the transition to college, parents are typically less able to directly monitor their child's use of alcohol and have less knowledge about their child's on-campus activities. There are, of course, considerable individual differences between families, with some parents serving as protective factors against hazardous drinking.

In order to assess this construct, we developed a "parental awareness and caring" (PAC) inventory (Wetherill & Fromme, 2007) that is a combination of indices of both parental support (Barnes, Reifman, Farrell, & Dintcheff, 2000) and monitoring (Kerr & Stattin, 2000). As expected, higher PAC during high school and the first year of college predicted lower quantity and frequency of alcohol consumption during the same time points, with a smaller relation freshman year (Wetherill & Fromme, 2007). Prospectively, high school PAC associates with freshman year quantity but not frequency of alcohol consumed. Quite interestingly, our data also show that PAC during high school constrains drinking, especially among individuals with trait risk factors, such as sensation-seeking personality (Quinn & Fromme, 2011d). Across the transition to campus, parents are less able to monitor their children, and thus high sensation seekers who had high PAC during high school showed more rapid increases in alcohol use once on campus.

Peers Norms, Selection, and Socialization

Perceptions of peer drinking are consistently strong correlates of individual drinking behavior in college students (Neighbors, Lee, Lewis, Fossos, & Larimer, 2007). Norms are often conceptualized as being either descriptive, meaning the perceived pervasiveness of drinking, or injunctive, meaning perceived acceptability of drinking behavior. The movement of individuals into social groups that have matching drinking behavior reflects peer group selection, whereas the effects of peer group drinking on individual behavior are indicative of peer socialization. Both can contribute to observed increases in individual drinking behavior, especially with regard to selection into formal social groups such as fraternities and sororities (Park, Sher, & Krull, 2009).

For the UTE study, we asked high school seniors to describe their perceived descriptive norms for typical student drinking on UT's campus. In these initial and subsequent surveys, we also asked respondents about their descriptive norms of their actual social group, defined as the principal group of friends with whom respondents interacted and spent time. We asked respondents to provide estimates of drinking for male and female friends separately, and analyses focused on descriptive norms for same-gendered peers only because same-gender norms are stronger predictors of personal alcohol use than are opposite-gender norms (Lewis & Neighbors, 2004). Our results showed that across the subsequent transition to campus, "typical student" descriptive norms prospectively predicted alcohol use (total drinks per week) for men but not women and for Caucasian and Hispanic students but not Asian students (Stappenbeck et al., 2010). In other words, young men (especially Caucasians) who believed that typical college students drank more heavily were likely to go on to drink more heavily themselves, but this was not the case for women. High school social group norms predicted freshman year alcohol use for both men and women overall but only for Caucasian students when examined separately by ethnicity. Thus, across this transition, Asian students were especially resistant to socialization effects of high school peers. Peer selection, however, was present for all groups examined.

As expected during later periods of college, descriptive norms continued to be robust correlates of individual alcohol use cross-sectionally and prospectively (Corbin, Iwamoto, & Fromme, 2011b; Hatzenbuehler

et al., 2008). Furthermore, cross-lagged analyses demonstrated that both selection and socialization processes continue to occur across college (Stappenbeck et al., 2010); that is, freshman year alcohol use predicts sophomore year social group norms, and freshman social group norms predict sophomore year alcohol use. Thus, during college, students continue to self-select into groups with similar levels of drinking, and drinking within these social groups further influences individual future drinking behavior.

Upon graduation, many students experience a shift in their peer affiliation not unlike that experienced in the transition from high school into college. As such, behavior across this transitional period may also be associated with peer influences. When examined prospectively from senior year to 1 and 2 years after graduation (Boyd et al., 2014), social group descriptive norms do not predict personal alcohol use (composite score) 1 year after graduation. In contrast, descriptive norms at 1 year out predict personal drinking 2 years out. Personal drinking predicted norms across both years. Thus, peer selection continued to occur beyond college, but socialization did not appear to occur across the immediate transition off of campus. There were also differences between ethnic groups, such that peer selection was stronger among minority students than among Caucasians from 1 year after graduation to 2 years post-graduation (Boyd et al., 2014).

Academic and Social Motives

Students must balance potentially competing motives in guiding their alcohol use behavior on campus. Pursuing a college degree is not only a new academic goal but also marks an important social transition for many students, some of whom seek out exciting and new social experiences among their new peers. Social motives, as opposed to academic motives, are goals or desires for social activity and popularity. Whereas academic motives (i.e., motivation to obtain a degree with good academic standing) are protective against drinking and other risk behaviors that might compromise achievement (Bryant, Schulenberg, O'Malley, Bachman, & Johnston, 2003; Vaughan et al., 2009), high social motives associate with heavy drinking among college students (Corbin et al., 2011b; Rhoades & Maggs, 2006). Individual differences are apparent prior to the move to campus among college-bound high school seniors: Greater academic motivation is associated with diminished plans for on-campus drinking, but those with greater social motives plan to drink more (Rhoades & Maggs, 2006).

In order to determine whether these intentions in high school persist across the transition to college, our UTE survey included questions about how important it was for a respondent to do well in courses and succeed academically or to achieve popularity and an active social life. We found that greater academic motives were protective against drinking in both high school and the first years of college (Vaughan et al., 2009), but the duration of this effect may differ by sex. Women with greater academic motives were protected against alcohol use across the transition, whereas academic motives protected men only in high school (Vaughan et al., 2009).

Further investigation of data spanning high school to senior year revealed important mediators between social motives and alcohol use and problems toward the end of college (Corbin et al., 2011b). Personal drinking values, descriptive norms of peer behavior, and alcohol expectancies (assessed sophomore year) partially mediated the relation between high school social motives and alcohol use (composite scores). In other words, those with greater social motives in high school may be more likely to self-select into social groups whose members they perceive as heavier drinkers, and in turn this peer behavior reinforces or passively influences individual drinking.

The effects mediated through values and alcohol expectancies suggest that social motives encourage the development of positive alcohol-related cognitions, resulting in increases in alcohol use and negative consequences (Corbin et al., 2011b). The direct path between high school social motives and alcohol use remained significant even when including mediators, demonstrating that this fairly simple assessment of motives in high school had predictive power for alcohol use years later. There was no such direct path between high school social motives and senior year alcohol problems, however, because personal values, descriptive norms, and alcohol expectances fully mediated this relation. Thus, intervention efforts targeting perceived drinking norms on campus and positive expectancies about drinking may be particularly fruitful in diminishing problems later (Corbin et al., 2011b).

Personality

Of the many facets of personality, two of the most studied in the context of drinking in general and in college

samples are sensation seeking and impulsivity (Hittner & Swickert, 2006; Jentsch et al., 2014). Sensation seeking refers to having a preference for exciting or new activities or experiences (Hittner & Swickert, 2006), whereas impulsivity is broadly defined as having a diminished ability to withhold prepotent responses, to make and follow plans, and to give immediate consequences much more weight than distal consequences (Dick et al., 2010). Furthermore, some conceptualize impulsive phenotypes as being either impulsive actions or impulsive choices (Jentsch et al., 2014). It is clear that in general, individuals who are relatively more sensation seeking and/or impulsive tend to drink more heavily (Dick et al., 2010; Hittner & Swickert, 2006; Jentsch et al., 2014; Whiteside & Lynam, 2001). The normative pattern of development out of adolescence and across emerging adulthood is reductions in both of these traits (Johnson, Hicks, McGue, & Iacono, 2007; Roberts, Walton, & Viechtbauer, 2006). However, those with more shallow declines in impulsivity and sensation seeking from ages 15 to 26 years endorse more rapidly increasing alcohol use (Quinn & Harden, 2013).

Within the UTE sample, we were able to demonstrate a transactional relationship between these dimensions of personality and alcohol use from high school to senior year (Quinn, Stappenbeck, & Fromme, 2011), such that personality change predicted change in alcohol use over time and vice versa. These findings are consistent with the "corresponsive" principle of personality change, which holds that life experiences are most likely to reinforce changes in the specific dimensions of personality that confer risk for preferring those experiences in the first place (Caspi, Roberts, & Shiner, 2005). A transactional relation also supports the idea that use of drugs of abuse may actually cause changes in impulsive temperament (Jentsch et al., 2014). Quite importantly, social factors, like drinking norms, did not account for our observed changes in personality, whereas alcohol consumption did so (Quinn et al., 2011).

Further analysis of heavy episodic drinking across the span of the UTE study, including data across the transition out of college, identified specific at-risk groups with atypical growth in impulsivity/sensation seeking (Ashenhurst et al., 2015). We used latent class growth analyses to identify distinct trajectories of HED and then quantified personality change within each of these classes of drinkers (Figure 15.1). Of the seven classes identified, several maintained low levels

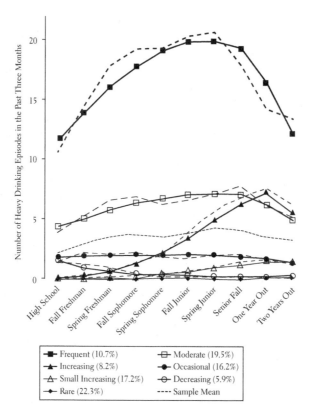

FIGURE 15.1 Trajectories of heavy episodic drinking across emerging adulthood. Trajectory analyses of heavy episodic (or "binge") drinking identified seven classes in the UT Experience study. The solid lines are model-implied values, and the dotted lines trace observed values. The fine-dotted black line shows the full sample means across time. The proportions of the full sample in each trajectory class are provided in the legend.

Source: Adapted with permission from Ashenhurst, J. R., Harden, K. P., Corbin, W. R., & Fromme, K. (2015). Trajectories of binge drinking and personality change across emerging adulthood. *Psychology of Addictive Behaviors, 29*(4), 978–991, published by the American Psychological Association.

of HED across the entire study, and two ("frequent" and "moderate") showed elevated levels of HED that began in high school, increased to a peak during college, and diminished across the transition out. As should be expected, these groups also had the highest overall levels of sensation seeking/impulsivity, with a peak in these traits corresponding to the same time as the heaviest period of drinking.

Quite interestingly, one group, termed the "increasing" class (approximately 8% of the sample), drank very little in high school (almost zero instances of HED) but endorsed just over two instances of HED per month by senior year, commensurate with the "moderate" class of heavy episodic drinkers. Unlike every other group, "increasing" individuals showed a significant rise in sensation seeking between

high school and senior year. Furthermore, this class showed a significant increase in impulsivity across the transition out of college, a rather atypical trend. Overall, more impulsive/sensation-seeking high school students are identifiably at risk for HED across the duration of college, but a select group increases in HED despite not appearing to be particularly at risk in high school. This group of "late bloomers" has atypical growth in both sensation seeking and impulsivity that may be caused, in part, by their increasing alcohol consumption.

The Acquired Preparedness Model

Some have suggested that the relationship between impulsive/sensation-seeking personality and heavy drinking is mediated by positive alcohol expectancies, a theory known as the acquired preparedness model (Anderson, Smith, & Fischer, 2003; Barnow et al., 2004). This model suggests that those who are more disinhibited attend more to positive aspects of alcohol consumption and fail to learn in response to negative consequences, resulting in positively biased alcohol expectancies that in turn drive greater consumption (Corbin, Iwamoto, & Fromme, 2011a). The UTE study allowed our group to directly test this theory in a longitudinal framework, which allows for directional tests to be made over time; cross-sectional analyses cannot assume temporal precedence between measurements, but prospective or cross-lagged models can do so. We tested a model whereby high school impulsive/sensation-seeking personality predicted freshman year positive and negative alcohol expectancies and senior year alcohol use (composite) and problems. Results showed that indeed, freshman year positive alcohol expectancies significantly mediated the path between high school impulsive/sensation-seeking personality and both alcohol use and problems, whereas negative alcohol expectancies were not a significant mediator. Our findings are consistent with the acquired preparedness model, and they indicate that interventions that challenge positive alcohol expectancies for those high in trait disinhibition may reduce alcohol use and problems later in college (Corbin et al., 2011a).

Subjective Response to Alcohol Intoxication

People respond differently to the same level of blood alcohol concentration, a phenomenon conceptualized as subjective response to alcohol (Quinn & Fromme, 2011c). Individual differences in subjective response, which is often distinguished into stimulation versus sedation domains, are thought to be an important etiologic factor driving alcohol consumption and alcohol use disorders (Quinn & Fromme, 2011c; Ray, Bujarski, & Roche, 2016; Ray, Mackillop, & Monti, 2010). One model, the low level of response (LLR) model (Schuckit, 1994), suggests that individuals with innate tolerance to the effects of alcohol drink more in order to achieve the desired effects, resulting in greater liability for alcohol dependence and problems. A competing model called the differentiator model holds that those who have low levels of sedative response but higher levels of stimulation response

are at greatest risk (Newlin & Thomson, 1990). Laboratory-based alcohol administration studies have provided supporting evidence for the differentiator model both cross-sectionally and prospectively (King, de Wit, McNamara, & Cao, 2011; King, Houle, de Wit, Holdstock, & Schuster, 2002).

Our daily monitoring data allowed us to examine individual differences in subjective intoxication (using a measure most related to sedative response) among students while accounting for estimated blood alcohol concentration (eBAC). In partial support of the LLR model, we found that students who generally drank more reported lower levels of subjective intoxication, whereas men and those with a positive family history of alcohol problems endorsed higher subjective intoxication (Quinn & Fromme, 2011b). Many studies of subjective intoxication have employed laboratory administration paradigms (as reviewed in Quinn & Fromme, 2011c), which suffer from low ecological validity and the obvious ethical limitations on providing students with high doses of alcohol. To address this, we conducted in-depth structured interviews in a subsample of students with respect to their 21st birthday drinking that had occurred in the natural environment (Wetherill & Fromme, 2009). These retrospective reports included both stimulating and sedative response measures. Results indicated that individual differences in the stimulating, but not the sedative, effects at the midpoint of alcohol consumption predicted the final eBAC achieved during the event. Overall, our data from the UTE sample indicate that greater stimulation response may drive increases in drinking, but among those who tend to drink more heavily, sedative responses are generally lower.

ALCOHOL-RELATED PROBLEMS AND CONSEQUENCES IN COLLEGE

Many, but not all, of the factors associated with risk for alcohol use are also associated with alcohol problems and consequences, both general and specific. This section examines factors that differentially predict alcohol problems across the transition to college in terms of general measures of alcohol problems, as well as specific objective consequences such as alcohol-induced memory impairment (blackouts), drinking and driving, aggression, and sexual assault.

General Measures

One commonly used index of general alcohol-related problems is the Rutgers Alcohol Problem Index (RAPI; White & Labouvie, 1989), which we included in the UTE study. This inventory addresses a variety of problems, including both the subjective (e.g., had a bad time) and the objective (e.g., missed school or work, had a fight, or neglected responsibilities due to alcohol) consequences. Consistent with other investigations (Baer, Kivlahan, & Marlatt, 1995; White et al., 2005), we found that overall, RAPI scores increase across the transition to college. It is unsurprising that greater rates of alcohol problems should accompany greater levels of alcohol use. Whereas some reports have found sex differences in the severity of alcohol problems across the transition to college, with men scoring higher (White et al., 2005), we found that both level and growth of problems do not differ by sex (Vaughan et al., 2009). Regarding ethnicity, levels of alcohol did differ in high school (intercept in the model, Latinos and Asian students having fewer problems than their Caucasian peers), but growth in problems was not related to ethnicity.

As with drinking, individual differences in a number of key factors associate with likelihood of experiencing more problems. These factors include earlier age of onset of drinking, having a positive family history of alcohol problems, and higher trait impulsivity (Morean, Corbin, & Fromme, 2012). Academic motives are protective against problems due to alcohol, but stronger social motives associate with greater alcohol problems (Vaughan et al., 2009). Although those with an earlier age of onset show more problems overall, *growth* in problems is associated with a later age of onset of use, indicative of "catching up" with early onset drinkers (Morean et al., 2012). Overall, it is clear that many of the personal and contextual factors associated with heavy drinking also associate with problems due to drinking.

Objective Consequences

Behavioral Risks

Many risky behaviors are known to accompany alcohol use among emerging adults and college students specifically. Examined among freshman, a variety of behavioral risks associate with alcohol use at both the global level and the event level (Neal & Fromme, 2007a). That is, when monitored over 30 days, differences in between-person eBAC are associated with increased incidence of illicit drug use, drinking and driving, committing aggressive acts, gambling, engaging in sexual behavior, and being the victim or perpetrator of coerced sex. Some risks varied by gender, such as women being more likely than men to engage in any sex. These *between-person* results indicate that heavier drinkers are overall more likely to engage in these behaviors, a finding consistent with problem behavior theory (Donovan & Jessor, 1985; Jessor & Jessor, 1977), which holds that individuals who exhibit one kind of "problem behavior" are also likely to exhibit other forms of socially undesirable or health-compromising behavior. Individual differences in behavioral risks are not merely associated with overall level of drinking but are also attributable to subjective intoxication (controlling for eBAC). We observed that students who reported greater average subjective intoxication at a given level of eBAC were more likely to co-use illicit drugs, to commit aggressive acts or property crime, and to endorse having unsafe sex (Quinn & Fromme, 2011b).

Event-level data can also be used to assess the degree to which deviation from a person's average eBAC predicts these risk behaviors, a *within-person* comparison. Our within-person analyses indicated a more narrow set of behavioral risks. Specifically, the more a freshman individual drank above his or her own average, the more likely he or she would be to have unsafe sex, be a victim or perpetrator of sexual coercion, to exhibit aggressive behavior, or to commit vandalism (Neal & Fromme, 2007a). Furthermore, within-person increases in subjective intoxication were associated only with greater odds of illicit drug use and unsafe sex (Quinn & Fromme, 2011b).

Aggression

Laboratory-based studies have shown that acute alcohol intoxication increases aggressive behavior (in aggression task paradigms), with stronger effects for men than women (Giancola et al., 2009). Our daily monitoring data set also included event-level information about aggression (both verbal and physical) in the context of drinking, allowing us to test if alcohol increased the likelihood of aggressive behavior in the natural environment. We found that on days when a college student drank more than was typical (assessed in terms of eBAC), aggression was more likely to occur (Quinn, Stappenbeck, & Fromme, 2013). Furthermore, there was a stronger effect for men than women and also for those who reported greater levels of subjective intoxication controlling for eBAC. The magnitude of the sex effect was such that drinking to 0.08 g/dL predicted an approximately 44% increase in the likelihood of aggression for college women but a 90% increase for college men (Quinn et al., 2013). Thus, our event-level findings from the natural environment support results found in laboratory analog studies of aggression (Giancola et al., 2009).

Our study also examined specific forms of aggression, such as physical violence occurring in romantic relationships and sexual assault. We found a greater reported frequency of physical dating violence among women than men (Stappenbeck & Fromme, 2010a), and approximately 5.6% of the sample endorsed perpetrating sexual aggression during the summer after high school (Stappenbeck & Fromme, 2010b). When examined prospectively, heavy drinking (composite score) during sophomore year predicted dating violence during junior year for women but not men. There was no such prospective relation for men, who instead showed a concurrent correlation between heavy drinking and dating violence during freshman year only (Stappenbeck & Fromme, 2010a). These results may be due to selection of heavy drinking male partners among heavy drinking women, a phenomenon observed in new marriages (Leonard & Das Eiden, 1999; Leonard & Mudar, 2003), which might increase the likelihood of future dating aggression within the relationship.

Alcohol-Induced Blackouts

Alcohol-induced blackouts, defined as having difficulty remembering events (in part or in whole) that occurred while intoxicated, are thought to stem from impairments in the transfer of short-term memories into long-term, consolidated forms (White, 2003). Previous studies have focused mostly on the incidence of blackouts among those with alcohol use disorders rather than the general population, and they have generally conceptualized blackouts as indicative or related to alcoholism and more severe problems (Goodwin, Crane, & Guze, 1969; Tarter & Schneider, 1976) rather than being something commonly experienced. Our data (Wetherill & Fromme, 2009; Wilhite & Fromme, 2015) and those of others (White, Jamieson-Drake, & Swartzwelder,

2002) clearly demonstrate that blackouts are common among those who may not meet criteria for an alcohol use disorder. Indeed, approximately 50% of college students report experiencing alcohol-induced blackouts (White et al., 2002). We found that approximately 47% of men and 33% of women reported experiencing blackouts on their 21st birthday (Wetherill & Fromme, 2009), and during the last years of college, just over half of drinkers in the UTE sample reported having experienced blackouts (Wilhite & Fromme, 2015). Unlike during 21st birthdays, there was overall greater frequency among college women (67%) than men (33%) (Wilhite & Fromme, 2015). Despite a decrease in alcohol quantity consumed across the transition out of college, the frequency of blackouts actually increased (Marino & Fromme, 2015; Wilhite & Fromme, 2015).

In terms of risk factors, we found that family background (a history of alcohol problems within the family), age of onset, and subjective response patterns are all significant predictors of blackout vulnerability in college. Specifically, those with a family history of alcohol problems have a greater probability of experiencing a blackout, with men who have a maternal history of alcohol problems being more susceptible to blackouts compared to women (Marino & Fromme, 2015). Similarly, an earlier age of onset for alcohol use prospectively predicted the overall frequency (but not growth) of blackouts in the later years of college (Marino & Fromme, 2016). Our 21st birthday data also showed that both greater stimulation and sedation subjective responses associated with incidence of blackouts even when controlling for eBAC (Wetherill & Fromme, 2009). Considering the prevalence of alcohol-induced blackouts, continued research on these and other potential risk factors is strongly warranted in order to understand and prevent negative consequences.

Because blackouts were previously studied as a phenomenon related to alcohol dependence (Goodwin, Crane, & Guze, 1969), they were mostly studied in the context of severe, dependence-like symptoms. Because they are commonly experienced, however, it may be that blackouts are also associated with less severe consequences among emerging adults. Having a blackout might mean a failure to remember a variety of previous actions (White, 2003), such as conversations or aggressive behavior, and as a result, less severe consequences might be common (i.e., embarrassment and social or emotional consequences). We used a cross-lagged model across the transition out of college to test for prospective associations between blackouts and future dependence-like symptoms versus social/emotional consequences. We found that blackouts predicted future social/emotional consequences in addition to senior year social/emotional consequences and alcohol use (quantity) but that blackouts *did not* predict future alcohol dependence-like symptoms (Wilhite & Fromme, 2015). We concluded that among emerging adults generally, blackouts may not be a prognostic indicator of alcohol dependence, but across the transition out of college, blackouts do prospectively predict less severe kinds of consequences. In our recent review of the blackout literature (Wetherill & Fromme, 2016), we indicate the strong need for further research to better understand the potential individual and genetic risk factors that confer vulnerability for blackouts.

Drinking and Driving

Far too many college students drive after consuming unsafe amounts of alcohol, with as many as 41% reporting drinking and driving in the past 30 days (Hingson, Heeren, Zakocs, Winter, & Wechsler, 2003). Our event-level data showed increases in the frequency of drinking and driving after age 21 years, perhaps due to greater autonomy in purchasing alcohol and changes in location of drinking from house parties to bars and clubs (Fromme, Wetherill, & Neal, 2010). This increase in frequency of drinking and driving was related to growth in frequency of heavy episodic drinking (Quinn & Fromme, 2012b). Furthermore, male students and those with earlier onset of drinking had steeper increases in drinking and driving. Sensation-seeking personality, however, was not associated with level or growth of drinking and driving over time, whereas residence on campus was a protective factor (Quinn & Fromme, 2012b). Last, the difference between objective and subjective intoxication is also an important predictor of likelihood of driving drunk. Our event-level data showed that drinking and driving was most likely when students felt subjectively less intoxicated despite being at a high level of eBAC (Quinn & Fromme, 2012a). Thus, a discrepancy between feelings of intoxication and actual intoxication promotes very risky driving, even at levels greater than the legal limit of intoxication. Interventions that include education about within-person variability of subjective intoxication

may help students better identify when they should avoid driving.

HIGH-RISK EVENTS

Twenty-First Birthdays

Many college students reach the milestone of their 21st birthday during the course of college. Being the age of legal alcohol consumption in the United States, 21st birthday celebrations are often extreme drinking events. Indeed, between 80% and 90% of students report drinking to celebrate their 21st birthday, with consumption levels being between approximately 7 and 13 drinks, sometimes resulting in dangerously high blood alcohol content (Brister, Sher, & Fromme, 2011; Brister, Wetherill, & Fromme, 2010; Fromme et al., 2010; Neighbors et al., 2011; Neighbors, Oster-Aaland, Bergstrom, & Lewis, 2006; Rutledge, Park, & Sher, 2008; Wetherill & Fromme, 2009). Indeed, one study of a large college sample found that 12% of both men and women endorsed consuming 21 drinks, evidence of the "21 for 21" drinking phenomenon (Rutledge et al., 2008).

Compared to other holidays and events during which drinking commonly occurs, such as New Year's Eve or St. Patrick's Day, the 21st birthday celebration ranks as the most extreme drinking event (Neighbors et al., 2011), during which students drink approximately three drinks more than anticipated (Brister et al., 2010). Our event-level data showed that drinking was substantially higher during the birthday week than during the weeks surrounding the event (Fromme et al., 2010). Estimated BAC achieved during 21st birthdays was in hazardous territory. We calculated that experienced drinkers achieve higher eBAC (approximately 0.21 g/dL) than do naive drinkers (approximately 0.08 g/dL; Brister et al., 2011). The following are common consequences of this extreme drinking: Approximately 40% of celebrants report alcohol-induced blackouts (Wetherill & Fromme, 2009), 35% report vomiting (Brister et al., 2011), and 17% report missing work or school because of drinking. Students who consume extreme amounts of alcohol on these occasions may reach levels of intoxication that result in hypothermia, coma, or death (NIAAA, 2015). Although there is currently no central data collection mechanism for reporting the number of deaths that occur due to excessive 21st birthday celebrations specifically, popular media outlets report on such deaths periodically (Zernike, 2005). Researchers have estimated that there are approximately 1,700 college student alcohol-related deaths annually (Hingson, Heeren, Winter, & Wechsler, 2005), and it is possible that some of these deaths occur in the context of 21st birthdays.

Several demographic and individual factors associate with different levels of consumption and the resulting consequences of 21st birthday celebrations. As expected, those with a past history of heavier drinking and men report consuming more alcohol during these events than do women (Brister et al., 2011; Rutledge et al., 2008), although the resulting BAC achieved may be comparable across the sexes (Wetherill & Fromme, 2009). Men also underestimate their anticipated drinking to a greater degree than do women (Brister et al., 2010). Curiously, whereas students underestimate their own drinking (Brister et al., 2010), students tend to overestimate peer drinking at these events, with greater overestimation predicting heavier drinking at one's own 21st birthday (Neighbors et al., 2006). In addition, a greater stimulation response to alcohol predicts a higher BAC achieved, whereas sedation response does not associate with BAC during 21st birthdays (Wetherill & Fromme, 2009).

Those who drink more heavily on their 21st birthday than is typical are more likely to encounter negative consequences as a result (Lewis, Lindgren, Fossos, Neighbors, & Oster-Aaland, 2009). Participation in drinking games during 21st birthdays is associated with heavier drinking and greater incidence of negative consequences, with a stronger association for men (Neighbors et al., 2014). In summary, 21st birthday celebrations represent the most extreme drinking occasions in student life and result in heavy safety and health burdens for the campus community. These findings indicate that interventions targeting drinking during this specific event are strongly warranted, perhaps including strategies such as normative feedback (Neighbors et al., 2006) or education about protective behavioral strategies (Martens et al., 2005, 2007).

Sporting Events

Heavy episodic drinking is also associated with campus sporting events, often in the form of tailgating, drinking in the stadium, or drinking at house parties. Indeed, college football fans drink more on game days

(approximately 5.6 drinks) than on other typical party/drinking days (approximately 4.86 drinks) (Glassman, Werch, Jobli, & Bian, 2007). Although this effect is greater for men than women, prior research has not shown a significant difference between students and non-students participating in watching college sporting events (Glassman et al., 2007). Nonetheless, given that football games are a central social event on many campuses (including the University of Texas) with significant student participation, these events represent significant drinking events in student life.

Overall, perceptions of alcohol consumption at games do not match reality: Students underestimate the proportion of students who drink at games, but they overestimate the levels of alcohol consumption (Neighbors et al., 2006). Men and those who overestimate the typical quantity consumed tend to drink more themselves and are more likely to report alcohol-related negative consequences, including both personal (e.g., headache and hangover) and behavioral (e.g., getting into fights) (Neighbors et al., 2006). Our event-level data from the UTE study found significantly more drinking on game-day Saturdays (an increase of approximately 1.93 drinks) than on typical Saturdays (Neal & Fromme, 2007b). Both home- and away-game Saturdays associated with greater than usual drinking for men but not women. There was an interaction, however, such that women who were heavier drinkers consumed significantly more on away-game Saturdays than on typical Saturdays. Among light drinkers, there was a greater probability of behavioral risks on away-game days than on typical Saturdays or home-game Saturdays, whereas no differences were found among heavier drinkers. Although drinking during sporting games may not be as extreme as that during 21st birthday celebrations, the greater frequency and broad participation mark sporting events as an impactful source of hazards and risk for college students.

CONCLUSIONS AND FUTURE DIRECTIONS

The college years are clearly an important time in the lives of many emerging adults, but this period is also demonstrably marked by risky alcohol use that can result in serious social, physical, or legal consequences. Our UTE project and the resulting research on the traits and factors associated with drinking have illuminated various mechanisms of risk, some of which are indicated for specific populations. Demographic factors provide important information about who might most benefit from prematriculation or on-campus interventions: particularly men, those with greater family wealth, sexual minorities, and Caucasian students. Nonetheless, we note that mechanisms that contribute to risk across the population in general also operate within otherwise low-risk categories. We have shown that several psychosocial factors, such as social or academic motives, parental awareness and caring, and beliefs about peer norms, are clear correlates of risky alcohol use. Personal factors such as sensation seeking/impulsive personality and one's subjective experience of intoxication further elaborated our understanding of who is at elevated risk. Many of the factors that predict hazardous drinking also confer risk for experiencing negative consequences of use, but not all do so in all circumstances. For example, we found that men increase their quantity of alcohol consumed across the transition to campus compared to women (Stappenbeck et al., 2010) but also that growth and level of alcohol-related problems across this transition are not related to gender (Vaughan et al., 2009).

Last, our data, and those of others, clearly show that 21st birthdays represent an alcohol consumption outlier in the lives of many young adults in the United States (Brister et al., 2011; Neighbors et al., 2006). Drinking can be hazardously extreme, with negative physical consequences being rather prevalent. Although football games, another example of an event that is often centered around alcohol, may not be as extreme as 21st birthdays with regard to alcohol consumption (Neal & Fromme, 2007b; Neighbors et al., 2006), the broad participation on many campuses implicates that targeting hazardous drinking at football games may have a substantial impact on improving safety on campus.

Although much of the focus of the UTE project has been on dissecting psychosocial and demographic indicators of risk, researchers have long understood that there are important biological or genetic factors to consider as well (Schuckit, 2009). In particular, the segregation of alcohol use disorders within families (Cotton, 1979) provides evidence for familial/genetic causes of problematic drinking behavior, a finding generally replicated within our studies. For example, positive family history of alcohol problems predicted a greater likelihood of experiencing blackouts (Marino & Fromme, 2015) and was associated with greater levels of subjective intoxication (Quinn & Fromme, 2011b) and with

higher RAPI scores (Morean et al., 2012). A meta-analysis of family history studies within college populations indicates that having a positive family history of alcohol problems is not strongly linked with alcohol consumption per se but that it is associated with both greater odds of consequences and alcohol use disorder symptoms (Elliott, Carey, & Bonafide, 2012). Our current project, called the Genes and New Experiences Study (GENES), extends the UTE project into new territory: molecular genetic analyses. Data collection remains ongoing, but the goal of the project is to discover or confirm associations between specific genetic single nucleotide polymorphisms (SNPs) or sets of SNPs (from an available set of hundreds of thousands of SNPs per respondent) and longitudinal and multivariate models derived from UTE data. These data will allow for investigations of the molecular genetic architecture of alcohol use on campus—an exciting direction for future research.

One final, and related, avenue for future research is continued examination of the shared variability between alcohol use and other risky or problem behaviors, such as illicit drug use, truancy, vandalism, risky sex, and tobacco use. As discussed previously, problem behavior theory (Donovan & Jessor, 1985; Jessor & Jessor, 1977) suggests that many of these risky behaviors co-occur, and twin studies have indicated that these behaviors likely also share a common genetic etiology (Krueger et al., 2002). These findings call into question the specificity of the path between genetic risk and hazardous or problematic alcohol use. Instead, it may be that much of the genetic vulnerability thought to contribute exclusively to alcohol problems actually confers risk for a broad spectrum of health-compromising or "problem behaviors." The combination of comprehensive longitudinal data on these behaviors in the UTE sample with the massive genetic data available from the GENES extension will likely yield important answers to these and other questions. Given the variety of psychosocial or environmental variables also available, we are also poised to detect any moderation of genetic effects by components of the measured college environment.

ACKNOWLEDGMENTS

We thank the many contributors to the UTE and GENES projects, including Elise Marino, Emily

Wilhite, Patrick Quinn, Cynthia Stappenbeck, William Corbin, Paige Harden, Stephen Boyd, Meghan Morean, Reagan Wetherill, Heather Brister, Mark Hatzenbuehler, Derek Iwamoto, Dan Neal, Ellen Vaughan, Marc Kruse, and Alexa Martin-Storey. This work was supported by NIAAA grants 5T32 AA7471-28 (R. Gonzales), R01 AA013967 (K. Fromme), and R01 AA020637 (K. Fromme) and by the Waggoner Center for Alcohol & Addiction Research.

REFERENCES

Anderson, K. G., Smith, G. T., & Fischer, S. F. (2003). Women and acquired preparedness: Personality and learning implications for alcohol use. *Journal of Studies on Alcohol, 64*(3), 384–392.

Arnett, J. J. (2000). Emerging adulthood: A theory of development from the late teens through the twenties. *American Psychologist, 55*(5), 469.

Arnett, J. J. (2004). The road to college: Twists and turns. In J. J. Arnett (Ed.), *Emerging adulthood: The winding road from the late teens through the twenties* (pp. 119–141). New York, NY: Oxford University Press.

Ashenhurst, J. R., Harden, K. P., Corbin, W. R., & Fromme, K. (2015). Trajectories of binge drinking and personality change across emerging adulthood. *Psychology of Addictive Behaviors, 29*(4), 978–991. doi:10.1037/adb0000116

Bachman, J. G., O'Malley, P. M., Schulenberg, J. E., Johnston, L. D., Bryant, A. L., & Merline, A. C. (2002). *The decline of substance use in young adulthood: Changes in social activities, roles, and beliefs.* Mahwah, NJ: Erlbaum.

Bachman, J. G., Wadsworth, K. N., O'Malley, P. M., Johnston, L. D., & Schulenberg, J. E. (1997). *Smoking, drinking, and drug use in young adulthood: The impacts of new freedoms and new responsibilities.* Mahway, NJ: Erlbaum.

Baer, J. S., Kivlahan, D. R., & Marlatt, G. A. (1995). High-risk drinking across the transition from high school to college. *Alcoholism: Clinical and Experimental Research, 19*(1), 54–58.

Barnes, G. M., & Farrell, M. P. (1992). Parental support and control as predictors of adolescent drinking, delinquency, and related problem behaviors. *Journal of Marriage and Family, 54*(4), 763–776.

Barnes, G. M., Reifman, A. S., Farrell, M. P., & Dintcheff, B. A. (2000). The effects of parenting on the development of adolescent alcohol misuse: A Six-Wave latent growth model. *Journal of Marriage and Family, 62*(1), 175–186.

Barnow, S., Schultz, G., Lucht, M., Ulrich, I., Preuss, U. W., & Freyberger, H. J. (2004). Do alcohol expectancies and peer delinquency/substance use mediate the relationship between impulsivity and drinking behaviour in adolescence? *Alcohol and Alcoholism, 39*(3), 213–219.

Barry, A. E. (2007). Using theory-based constructs to explore the impact of Greek membership on alcohol-related beliefs and behaviors: A systematic literature review. *Journal of American College Health, 56*(3), 307–315. doi:10.3200/JACH.56.3.307–316

Boyd, S. J., Corbin, W. R., & Fromme, K. (2014). Parental and peer influences on alcohol use during the transition out of college. *Psychology of Addictive Behaviors, 28*(4), 960–968. doi:10.1037/a0037782

Brister, H. A., Sher, K. J., & Fromme, K. (2011). 21st birthday drinking and associated physical consequences and behavioral risks. *Psychology of Addictive Behaviors, 25*(4), 573–582. doi:10.1037/a0025209

Brister, H. A., Wetherill, R. R., & Fromme, K. (2010). Anticipated versus actual alcohol consumption during 21st birthday celebrations. *Journal of Studies on Alcohol and Drugs, 71*(2), 180–183.

Bryant, A. L., Schulenberg, J. E., O'Malley, P. M., Bachman, J. G., & Johnston, L. D. (2003). How academic achievement, attitudes, and behaviors relate to the course of substance use during adolescence: A 6-year, multiwave national longitudinal study. *Journal of Research on Adolescence, 13*(3), 361–397.

Caspi, A., Roberts, B. W., & Shiner, R. L. (2005). Personality development: Stability and change. *Annual Reviews of Psychology, 56*, 453–484. doi:10.1146/annurev.psych.55.090902.141913

Corbin, W. R., Gearhardt, A., & Fromme, K. (2008). Stimulant alcohol effects prime within session drinking behavior. *Psychopharmacology, 197*(2), 327–337. doi:10.1007/s00213-007-1039-x

Corbin, W. R., Iwamoto, D. K., & Fromme, K. (2011a). A comprehensive longitudinal test of the acquired preparedness model for alcohol use and related problems. *Journal of Studies on Alcohol and Drugs, 72*(4), 602–610.

Corbin, W. R., Iwamoto, D. K., & Fromme, K. (2011b). Broad social motives, alcohol use, and related problems: Mechanisms of risk from high school through college. *Addictive Behaviors, 36*(3), 222–230. doi:10.1016/j.addbeh.2010.11.004

Corbin, W. R., Vaughan, E. L., & Fromme, K. (2008). Ethnic differences and the closing of the sex gap in alcohol use among college-bound students. *Psychology of Addictive Behaviors, 22*(2), 240–248. doi:10.1037/0893-164X.22.2.240

Cotton, N. S. (1979). The familial incidence of alcoholism: A review. *Journal of Studies on Alcohol, 40*(1), 89–116.

Dawson, D. A., Grant, B. F., Stinson, F. S., & Chou, P. S. (2004). Another look at heavy episodic drinking and alcohol use disorders among college and non-college youth. *Journal of Studies on Alcohol and Drugs, 65*(4), 477–488.

Dick, D. M., Smith, G., Olausson, P., Mitchell, S. H., Leeman, R. F., O'Malley, S. S., & Sher, K. (2010). Understanding the construct of impulsivity and its relationship to alcohol use disorders. *Addiction Biology, 15*(2), 217–226. doi:10.1111/j.1369-1600.2009.00190.x

Donovan, J. E., & Jessor, R. (1985). Structure of problem behavior in adolescence and young adulthood. *Journal of Consulting and Clinical Psychology, 53*(6), 890–904.

Donovan, J. E., Jessor, R., & Jessor, L. (1983). Problem drinking in adolescence and young adulthood: A follow-up study. *Journal of Studies on Alcohol and Drugs, 44*(1), 109–137.

Eisenberg, M., & Wechsler, H. (2003). Substance use behaviors among college students with same-sex and opposite-sex experience: Results from a national study. *Addictive Behaviors, 28*(5), 899–913.

Elliott, J. C., Carey, K. B., & Bonafide, K. E. (2012). Does family history of alcohol problems influence college and university drinking or substance use? A meta-analytical review. *Addiction, 107*(10), 1774–1785. doi:10.1111/j.1360-0443.2012.03903.x

Esser, M. B., Hedden, S. L., Kanny, D., Brewer, R. D., Gfroerer, J. C., & Naimi, T. S. (2014). Prevalence of alcohol dependence among US adult drinkers, 2009–2011. *Preventing Chronic Disease, 11*, E206. doi:10.5888/pcd11.140329

Fromme, K., Corbin, W. R., & Kruse, M. I. (2008). Behavioral risks during the transition from high school to college. *Developmental Psychology, 44*(5), 1497–1504. doi:10.1037/a0012614

Fromme, K., Wetherill, R. R., & Neal, D. J. (2010). Turning 21 and the associated changes in drinking and driving after drinking among college students. *Journal of American College Health, 59*(1), 21–27. doi:10.1080/07448481.2010.483706

Giancola, P. R., Levinson, C. A., Corman, M. D., Godlaski, A. J., Morris, D. H., Phillips, J. P., & Holt, J. C. (2009). Men and women, alcohol and aggression. *Experimental and Clinical Psychopharmacology, 17*(3), 154–164. doi:10.1037/a0016385

Glassman, T., Werch, C. E., Jobli, E., & Bian, H. (2007). Alcohol-related fan behavior on college football game day. *Journal of American College Health, 56*(3), 255–260. doi:10.3200/JACH.56.3.255–260

Goodwin, D. W., Crane, J. B., & Guze, S. B. (1969). Alcoholic "blackouts": A review and clinical study of 100 alcoholics. *American Journal of Psychiatry, 126*(2), 191–198. doi:10.1176/ajp.126.2.191

Gotham, H. J., Sher, K. J., & Wood, P. K. (1997). Predicting stability and change in frequency of intoxication from the college years to beyond: Individual-difference and role transition variables. *Journal of Abnormal Psychology, 106*(4), 619–629.

Grant, B. F., Dawson, D. A., Stinson, F. S., Chou, S. P., Dufour, M. C., & Pickering, R. P. (2004). The 12-month prevalence and trends in DSM-IV alcohol abuse and dependence: United States, 1991–1992 and 2001–2002. *Drug and Alcohol Dependence, 74*(3), 223–234. doi:10.1016/j.drugalcdep.2004.02.004

Hanson, M. D., & Chen, E. (2007a). Socioeconomic status and health behaviors in adolescence: A review of the literature. *Journal of Behavioral Medicine, 30*(3), 263–285. doi:10.1007/s10865-007-9098-3

Hanson, M. D., & Chen, E. (2007b). Socioeconomic status and substance use behaviors in adolescents: The role of family resources versus family social status. *Journal of Health Psychology, 12*(1), 32–35. doi:10.1177/1359105306069073

Hatzenbuehler, M. L., Corbin, W. R., & Fromme, K. (2008). Trajectories and determinants of alcohol use among LGB young adults and their heterosexual peers: Results from a prospective study. *Developmental Psychology, 44*(1), 81–90. doi:10.1037/0012-1649.44.1.81

Hatzenbuehler, M. L., Corbin, W. R., & Fromme, K. (2011). Discrimination and alcohol-related problems among college students: A prospective examination of mediating effects. *Drug and Alcohol Dependence, 115*(3), 213–220. doi:10.1016/j.drugalcdep.2010.11.002

Hingson, R., Heeren, T., Winter, M., & Wechsler, H. (2005). Magnitude of alcohol-related mortality and morbidity among U.S. college students ages 18–24: Changes from 1998 to 2001. *Annual Reviews of Public Health, 26*, 259–279. doi:10.1146/annurev.publhealth.26.021304.144652

Hingson, R., Heeren, T., Zakocs, R., Winter, M., & Wechsler, H. (2003). Age of first intoxication, heavy drinking, driving after drinking and risk of unintentional injury among U.S. college students. *Journal of Studies on Alcohol, 64*(1), 23–31.

Hittner, J. B., & Swickert, R. (2006). Sensation seeking and alcohol use: A meta-analytic review. *Addictive*

Behaviors, 31(8), 1383–1401. doi:10.1016/j.addbeh.2005.11.004

Iwamoto, D. K., Corbin, W., & Fromme, K. (2010). Trajectory classes of heavy episodic drinking among Asian American college students. *Addiction*, 105(11), 1912–1920. doi:10.1111/j.1360-0443.2010.03019.x

Jackson, K. M., Sher, K. J., Gotham, H. J., & Wood, P. K. (2001). Transitioning into and out of large-effect drinking in young adulthood. *Journal of Abnormal Psychology*, 110(3), 378–391.

Jentsch, J. D., Ashenhurst, J. R., Cervantes, M. C., Groman, S. M., James, A. S., & Pennington, Z. T. (2014). Dissecting impulsivity and its relationships to drug addictions. *Annals of the New York Academy of Sciences*, 1327(1), 1–26. doi:10.1111/nyas.12388

Jessor, R., & Jessor, S. L. (1977). *Problem behavior and psychosocial development: A longitudinal study of youth.* New York, NY: Academic Press.

Jochman, K., & Fromme, K. (2010). Maturing out of substance use: The other side of etiology. In L. Scheier (Ed.), *Handbook of drug use etiology: Theory, methods, and empirical findings* (pp. 565–578). Washington, DC: American Psychological Association.

Johnson, W., Hicks, B. M., McGue, M., & Iacono, W. G. (2007). Most of the girls are alright, but some aren't: Personality trajectory groups from ages 14 to 24 and some associations with outcomes. *Journal of Personality and Social Psychology*, 93(2), 266–284. doi:10.1037/0022-3514.93.2.266

Johnston, L. D., O'Malley, P. M., Bachman, J. G., Schulenberg, J. E., & Miech, R. A. (2015). *Monitoring the Future national survey results on drug use, 1975–2014: Volume 2. College students and adults ages 19–55.* Ann Arbor, MI: Institute for Social Research, University of Michigan.

Kerr, M., & Stattin, H. (2000). What parents know, how they know it, and several forms of adolescent adjustment: Further support for a reinterpretation of monitoring. *Developmental Psychology*, 36(3), 366–380.

King, A. C., de Wit, H., McNamara, P. J., & Cao, D. (2011). Rewarding, stimulant, and sedative alcohol responses and relationship to future binge drinking. *Archives of General Psychiatry*, 68(4), 389–399. doi:10.1001/archgenpsychiatry.2011.26

King, A. C., Houle, T., de Wit, H., Holdstock, L., & Schuster, A. (2002). Biphasic alcohol response differs in heavy versus light drinkers. *Alcoholism: Clinical and Experimental Research*, 26(6), 827–835.

Knight, J. R., Wechsler, H., Kuo, M., Seibring, M., Weitzman, E. R., & Schuckit, M. A. (2002). Alcohol abuse and dependence among U.S. college students. *Journal of Studies on Alcohol and Drugs*, 63(3), 263–270.

Krueger, R. F., Hicks, B. M., Patrick, C. J., Carlson, S. R., Iacono, W. G., & McGue, M. (2002). Etiologic connections among substance dependence, antisocial behavior, and personality: Modeling the externalizing spectrum. *Journal of Abnormal Psychology*, 111(3), 411–424.

Leonard, K. E., & Das Eiden, R. (1999). Husband's and wife's drinking: Unilateral or bilateral influences among newlyweds in a general population sample. *Journal of Studies on Alcohol Supplement* 13, 130–138.

Leonard, K. E., & Mudar, P. (2003). Peer and partner drinking and the transition to marriage: A longitudinal examination of selection and influence processes. *Psychology of Addictive Behaviors*, 17(2), 115–125.

Lewis, M. A., Lindgren, K. P., Fossos, N., Neighbors, C., & Oster-Aaland, L. (2009). Examining the relationship between typical drinking behavior and 21st birthday drinking behavior among college students: Implications for event-specific prevention. *Addiction*, 104(5), 760–767. doi:10.1111/j.1360-0443.2009.02518.x

Lewis, M. A., & Neighbors, C. (2004). Gender-specific misperceptions of college student drinking norms. *Psychology of Addictive Behaviors*, 18(4), 334–339. doi:10.1037/0893-164X.18.4.334

Littlefield, A. K., Sher, K. J., & Wood, P. K. (2009). Is "maturing out" of problematic alcohol involvement related to personality change? *Journal of Abnormal Psychology*, 118(2), 360–374. doi:10.1037/a0015125

Marino, E. N., & Fromme, K. (2015). Alcohol-induced blackouts and maternal family history of problematic alcohol use. *Addictive Behaviors*, 45, 201–206. doi:10.1016/j.addbeh.2015.01.043

Marino, E. N., & Fromme, K. (2016). Early onset drinking predicts greater level but not growth of alcohol-induced blackouts beyond the effect of binge drinking during emerging adulthood. *Alcoholism: Clinical and Experimental Research*, 40(3), 599–605. doi:10.1111/acer.12981

Marshal, M. P., Friedman, M. S., Stall, R., & Thompson, A. L. (2009). Individual trajectories of substance use in lesbian, gay and bisexual youth and heterosexual youth. *Addiction*, 104(6), 974–981. doi:10.1111/j.1360-0443.2009.02531.x

Martens, M. P., Cimini, M. D., Barr, A. R., Rivero, E. M., Vellis, P. A., Desemone, G. A., & Horner, K. J. (2007). Implementing a screening and brief intervention for high-risk drinking in university-based health and mental health care settings: Reductions in alcohol use and correlates of success. *Addictive Behaviors*, 32(11), 2563–2572. doi:10.1016/j.addbeh.2007.05.005

Martens, M. P., Ferrier, A. G., Sheehy, M. J., Corbett, K., Anderson, D. A., & Simmons, A. (2005). Development of the Protective Behavioral Strategies Survey. *Journal of Studies on Alcohol*, 66(5), 698–705.

Martin-Storey, A., & Fromme, K. (2016). Trajectories of dating violence: differences by sexual minority status and gender. *Journal of Adolescence*, 49, 28–37.

McCabe, S. E. (2002). Gender differences in collegiate risk factors for heavy episodic drinking. *Journal of Studies on Alcohol*, 63(1), 49–56.

McCabe, S. E., Boyd, C., Hughes, T. L., & d'Arcy, H. (2003). Sexual identity and substance use among undergraduate students. *Substance Abuse*, 24(2), 77–91.

Meyer, I. H. (2003). Prejudice, social stress, and mental health in lesbian, gay, and bisexual populations: Conceptual issues and research evidence. *Psychological Bulletin*, 129(5), 674–697. doi:10.1037/0033-2909.129.5.674

Morean, M. E., Corbin, W. R., & Fromme, K. (2012). Age of first use and delay to first intoxication in relation to trajectories of heavy drinking and alcohol-related problems during emerging adulthood. *Alcoholism: Clinical and Experimental Research*, 36(11), 1991–1999. doi:10.1111/j.1530-0277.2012.01812.x

Mun, E. Y., de la Torre, J., Atkins, D. C., White, H. R., Ray, A. E., Kim, S. Y., . . . Team, P. I. (2015). Project INTEGRATE: An integrative study of brief alcohol interventions for college students. *Psychology of Addictive Behaviors*, 29(1), 34–48. doi:10.1037/adb0000047

National Center for Education Statistics. (2013). Percentage of 18- to 24-year-olds enrolled in degree-granting institutions, by level of institution and sex and race/ethnicity of student: 1967 through 2012. *Digest of Education Statistics*. Retrieved from https://nces.ed.gov/programs/digest/d13/tables/dt13_302.60.asp

National Institute of Alcohol Abuse and Alcoholism. (2004, Winter). National Institute of Alcohol Abuse and Alcoholism Council approves definition of binge drinking. *NIAAA Newsletter*. Retrieved from http://pubs.niaaa.nih.gov/publications/Newsletter/winter2004/Newsletter_Number3.pdf

National Institute of Alcohol Abuse and Alcoholism. (2015). *Alcohol overdose: The dangers of drinking too much*. Retrieved from http://pubs.niaaa.nih.gov/publications/AlcoholOverdoseFactsheet/Overdosefact.htm

Neal, D. J., & Fromme, K. (2007a). Event-level covariation of alcohol intoxication and behavioral risks during the first year of college. *Journal of Consulting and Clinical Psychology*, 75(2), 294–306. doi:10.1037/0022-006X.75.2.294

Neal, D. J., & Fromme, K. (2007b). Hook 'em horns and heavy drinking: Alcohol use and collegiate sports. *Addictive Behaviors*, 32(11), 2681–2693. doi:10.1016/j.addbeh.2007.06.020

Neighbors, C., Atkins, D. C., Lewis, M. A., Lee, C. M., Kaysen, D., Mittmann, A., . . . Rodriguez, L. M. (2011). Event-specific drinking among college students. *Psychology of Addictive Behaviors*, 25(4), 702–707. doi:10.1037/a0024051

Neighbors, C., Lee, C. M., Lewis, M. A., Fossos, N., & Larimer, M. E. (2007). Are social norms the best predictor of outcomes among heavy-drinking college students? *Journal of Studies on Alcohol and Drugs*, 68(4), 556–565.

Neighbors, C., Oster-Aaland, L., Bergstrom, R. L., & Lewis, M. A. (2006). Event- and context-specific normative misperceptions and high-risk drinking: 21st birthday celebrations and football tailgating. *Journal of Studies on Alcohol*, 67(2), 282–289.

Neighbors, C., Rodriguez, L. M., Rinker, D. V., DiBello, A. M., Young, C. M., & Chen, C. H. (2014). Drinking games and contextual factors of 21st birthday drinking. *American Journal of Drug and Alcohol Abuse*, 40(5), 380–387. doi:10.3109/00952990.2014.918623

Newlin, D. B., & Thomson, J. B. (1990). Alcohol challenge with sons of alcoholics: A critical review and analysis. *Psychological Bulletin*, 108(3), 383–402.

O'Hare, T. M. (1990). Drinking in college: Consumption patterns, problems, sex differences and legal drinking age. *Journal of Studies on Alcohol*, 51(6), 536–541.

O'Malley, P. M., & Johnston, L. D. (2002). Epidemiology of alcohol and other drug use among American college students. *Journal of Studies on Alcohol and Drugs Supplement* (14), 23–39.

Park, A., Sher, K. J., & Krull, J. L. (2009). Selection and socialization of risky drinking during the college transition: The importance of microenvironments associated with specific living units. *Psychology of Addictive Behaviors*, 23(3), 404–414. doi:10.1037/a0016293

Quinn, P. D., & Fromme, K. (2011a). Alcohol use and related problems among college students and their noncollege peers: The competing roles of personality and peer influence. *Journal of Studies on Alcohol and Drugs*, 72(4), 622–632.

Quinn, P. D., & Fromme, K. (2011b). Predictors and outcomes of variability in subjective alcohol intoxication among college students: An event-level analysis across 4 years. *Alcoholism: Clinical and Experimental Research*, 35(3), 484–495. doi:10.1111/j.1530-0277.2010.01365.x

Quinn, P. D., & Fromme, K. (2011c). Subjective response to alcohol challenge: A quantitative review. *Alcoholism: Clinical and Experimental Research*, 35(10), 1759–1770. doi:10.1111/j.1530-0277.2011.01521.x

Quinn, P. D., & Fromme, K. (2011d). The role of person–environment interactions in increased alcohol use in the transition to college. *Addiction*, 106(6), 1104–1113. doi:10.1111/j.1360-0443.2011.03411.x

Quinn, P. D., & Fromme, K. (2012a). Event-level associations between objective and subjective alcohol intoxication and driving after drinking across the college years. *Psychology of Addictive Behaviors*, 26(3), 384–392. doi:10.1037/a0024275

Quinn, P. D., & Fromme, K. (2012b). Personal and contextual factors in the escalation of driving after drinking across the college years. *Psychology of Addictive Behaviors*, 26(4), 714–723. doi:10.1037/a0026819

Quinn, P. D., & Harden, K. P. (2013). Differential changes in impulsivity and sensation seeking and the escalation of substance use from adolescence to early adulthood. *Developmental Psychopathology*, 25(1), 223–239. doi:10.1017/S0954579412000284

Quinn, P. D., Stappenbeck, C. A., & Fromme, K. (2011). Collegiate heavy drinking prospectively predicts change in sensation seeking and impulsivity. *Journal of Abnormal Psychology*, 120(3), 543–556. doi:10.1037/a0023159

Quinn, P. D., Stappenbeck, C. A., & Fromme, K. (2013). An event-level examination of sex differences and subjective intoxication in alcohol-related aggression. *Experimental and Clinical Psychopharmacology*, 21(2), 93–102. doi:10.1037/a0031552

Ray, L. A., Bujarski, S., & Roche, D. J. (2016). Subjective response to alcohol as a research domain criterion. *Alcoholism: Clinical and Experimental Research*, 40(1), 6–17. doi:10.1111/acer.12927

Ray, L. A., Mackillop, J., & Monti, P. M. (2010). Subjective responses to alcohol consumption as endophenotypes: Advancing behavioral genetics in etiological and treatment models of alcoholism. *Substance Use & Misuse*, 45(11), 1742–1765. doi:10.3109/10826084.2010.482427

Rhoades, B. L., & Maggs, J. L. (2006). Do academic and social goals predict planned alcohol use among college-bound high school graduates? *Journal of Youth and Adolescence*, 35(6), 913–923.

Roberts, B. W., Walton, K. E., & Viechtbauer, W. (2006). Patterns of mean-level change in personality traits across the life course: A meta-analysis of longitudinal studies. *Psychological Bulletin*, 132(1), 1–25. doi:10.1037/0033-2909.132.1.1

Rutledge, P. C., Park, A., & Sher, K. J. (2008). 21st birthday drinking: Extremely extreme. *Journal of Consulting and Clinical Psychology*, 76(3), 511–516. doi:10.1037/0022-006X.76.3.511

Savin-Williams, R. C. (2006). Who's gay? Does it matter? *Current Directions in Psychological Science*, 15(1), 40–44.

Schuckit, M. A. (1994). Low level of response to alcohol as a predictor of future alcoholism. *American Journal of Psychiatry*, 151(2), 184–189. doi:10.1176/ajp.151.2.184

Schuckit, M. A. (2009). An overview of genetic influences in alcoholism. *Journal of Substance Abuse Treatment*, 36(1), S5–S14.

Schulenberg, J., O'Malley, P. M., Bachman, J. G., Wadsworth, K. N., & Johnston, L. D. (1996). Getting drunk and growing up: Trajectories of frequent binge drinking during the transition to young adulthood. *Journal of Studies on Alcohol and Drugs*, 57(3), 289–304.

Sher, K. J., Jackson, K. M., & Steinley, D. (2011). Alcohol use trajectories and the ubiquitous cat's cradle: Cause for concern? *Journal of Abnormal Psychology*, 120(2), 322–335. doi:10.1037/a0021813

Sher, K. J., & Rutledge, P. C. (2007). Heavy drinking across the transition to college: Predicting first-semester heavy drinking from precollege variables. *Addictive Behaviors*, 32(4), 819–835. doi:10.1016/j.addbeh.2006.06.024

Slutske, W. S., Hunt-Carter, E. E., Nabors-Oberg, R. E., Sher, K. J., Bucholz, K. K., Madden, P. A., ... Heath, A. C. (2004). Do college students drink more than their non-college-attending peers? Evidence from a population-based longitudinal female twin study. *Journal of Abnormal Psychology*, 113(4), 530–540. doi:10.1037/0021-843X.113.4.530

Stappenbeck, C. A., & Fromme, K. (2010a). A longitudinal investigation of heavy drinking and physical dating violence in men and women. *Addictive Behaviors*, 35(5), 479–485. doi:10.1016/j.addbeh.2009.12.027

Stappenbeck, C. A., & Fromme, K. (2010b). Alcohol use and perceived social and emotional consequences among perpetrators of general and sexual aggression. *Journal of Interpersonal Violence*, 25(4), 699–715. doi:10.1177/0886260509334399

Stappenbeck, C. A., Quinn, P. D., Wetherill, R. R., & Fromme, K. (2010). Perceived norms for drinking in the transition from high school to college and beyond. *Journal of Studies on Alcohol and Drugs*, 71(6), 895–903.

Tarter, R. E., & Schneider, D. U. (1976). Blackouts: Relationship with memory capacity and alcoholism history. *Archives of General Psychiatry*, 33(12), 1492–1496.

Tucker, J. A. (2003). Natural resolution of alcohol-related problems. *Recent Developments in Alcoholism*, 16, 77–90.

van Oers, J. A., Bongers, I. M., van de Goor, L. A., & Garretsen, H. F. (1999). Alcohol consumption, alcohol-related problems, problem drinking, and socioeconomic status. *Alcohol and Alcoholism*, 34(1), 78–88.

Vaughan, E. L., Corbin, W. R., & Fromme, K. (2009). Academic and social motives and drinking behavior. *Psychology of Addictive Behaviors*, 23(4), 564–576. doi:10.1037/a0017331

Watson, A. L., & Sher, K. J. (1998). Resolution of alcohol problems without treatment: Methodological issues and future directions of natural recovery research. *Clinical Psychology: Science and Practice*, 5(1), 1–18.

Wechsler, H., Davenport, A., Dowdall, G., Moeykens, B., & Castillo, S. (1994). Health and behavioral consequences of binge drinking in college: A national survey of students at 140 campuses. *Journal of the American Medical Association*, 272(21), 1672–1677.

Wechsler, H., Dowdall, G. W., Davenport, A., & Castillo, S. (1995). Correlates of college student binge drinking. *American Journal of Public Health*, 85(7), 921–926.

Wetherill, R. R., & Fromme, K. (2007). Perceived awareness and caring influences alcohol use by high school and college students. *Psychology of Addictive Behaviors*, 21(2), 147.

Wetherill, R. R., & Fromme, K. (2009). Subjective responses to alcohol prime event-specific alcohol consumption and predict blackouts and hangover. *Journal of Studies on Alcohol and Drugs*, 70(4), 593–600.

Wetherill, R. R., & Fromme, K. (2016). Alcohol-induced blackouts: A review of recent clinical research with practical implications and recommendations for future studies. *Alcoholism: Clinical and Experimental Research*, 40(5), 922–935.

White, A. M. (2003). What happened? Alcohol, memory blackouts, and the brain. *Alcohol Research & Health*, 27(2), 186–196.

White, A. M., & Hingson, R. (2013). The burden of alcohol use: Excessive alcohol consumption and related consequences among college students. *Alcoholism Research*, 35(2), 201–218.

White, A. M., Jamieson-Drake, D. W., & Swartzwelder, H. S. (2002). Prevalence and correlates of alcohol-induced blackouts among college students: Results of an e-mail survey. *Journal of American College Health*, 51(3), 117–119, 122–131. doi:10.1080/07448480209596339

White, H. R., Fleming, C. B., Kim, M. J., Catalano, R. F., & McMorris, B. J. (2008). Identifying two potential mechanisms for changes in alcohol use among college-attending and non-college-attending emerging adults. *Developmental Psychology*, 44(6), 1625–1639. doi:10.1037/a0013855

White, H. R., & Labouvie, E. W. (1989). Towards the assessment of adolescent problem drinking. *Journal of Studies on Alcohol*, 50(1), 30–37.

White, H. R., Labouvie, E. W., & Papadaratsakis, V. (2005). Changes in substance use during the transition to adulthood: A comparison of college students and their noncollege age peers. *Journal of Drug Issues*, 35(2), 281–306.

Whiteside, S. P., & Lynam, D. R. (2001). The five factor model and impulsivity: Using a structural model of personality to understand impulsivity. *Personality and Individual Differences*, 30(4), 669–689.

Wilhite, E. R., & Fromme, K. (2015). Alcohol-induced blackouts and other negative outcomes during the transition out of college. *Journal of Studies on Alcohol and Drugs*, 76(4), 516–524.

Winick, C. (1962). Maturing out of narcotic addiction. *Bulletin on Narcotics*, 14(1), 1–7.

Zernike, K. (2005, March 12). A 21st birthday drinking game can be a deadly rite Of passage. *The New York Times*, p. A1.

16

Developmental Transitions and College Student Drinking

Why Parents Still Matter

Michael Ichiyama

Annie Wescott

Kayla Swart

Sarah Harrison

Kelly Birch

College student alcohol abuse is a significant and enduring public health concern facing colleges and universities throughout the United States. Compared to other age cohorts, the college student age group (18–24 years) has the highest rates of both alcohol use disorders and prevalence of past year alcohol dependence (Johnston, O'Malley, Bachman, & Schulenberg, 2013). This cohort has been found to consume alcohol on fewer occasions but to drink more per occasion compared to older adults. Heavy episodic alcohol consumption (i.e., binge drinking) is particularly prevalent among college students, with an estimated 40–50% of students reporting consuming five or more drinks in a row during the past month (Wechsler & Nelson, 2008). Although college students are less likely to binge drink prior to attending college, compared to their non-college peers, they are more likely to binge drink once they attend college (Timberlake et al., 2007). University and college students are also more likely to drink and drive than are their non-college peers (Hingson, Zha, & Weitzman, 2009). The wide array of negative consequences associated with alcohol misuse among college students is well documented and includes academic problems,

health concerns, legal issues, sexual and physical assaults, unprotected sex, unintentional injury, driving under the influence, and even death (Hingson, 2010; White et al., 2006).

Zucker (1994) articulated the importance of incorporating a developmental perspective in the conceptualization of alcohol abuse and dependence. Zucker's conceptual model illustrated the importance of how the relative influences of biological, psychological, social, and sociocultural factors that shape us will wax and wane as a function of where we are in our developmental trajectory. This developmental perspective is especially important to our understanding of college age drinking.

The entry into college represents a significant developmental milestone in the lives of a large number of young adults and their parents throughout the United States. The transition to college is well recognized as a high-risk period for the initiation and continuation of problem drinking and alcohol-related problems among young adults (Sher & Rutledge, 2007), and it has been the subject of important federal initiatives (National Institute of Alcohol Abuse and Alcoholism, 2007). The transition to college from high school frequently involves moving away from home and is accompanied by increased autonomy and independence coupled with decreased parental contact and direct parental influence. The decrease in direct parental involvement can be a significant factor contributing to increased risk for problem behaviors because colleges and universities often do not have the resources and support staff needed to manage the volume of student-related substance abuse and mental health-related issues that emerge. This makes monitoring student behavior a difficult challenge for both parents and institutional support staff. Therefore, the transition to college represents a significant developmental event in the lives of many young adults and their parents (Sher & Rutledge, 2007).

Regarding the emergence of alcohol-related problems among college students, the developmental perspective highlights the importance of predisposing risk factors associated with this cohort. Some of the predisposing risk factors associated with an increased probability of alcohol use problems among college students include earlier initiation of alcohol use, a positive family history of alcoholism, the presence of behavioral undercontrol (a propensity linked to aggressiveness, externalizing behavior, sensation seeking, and disinhibition), high levels of parental conflict, exposure to spousal violence, parental divorce, and parental modeling of drinking (Windle & Zucker, 2010).

Although the significance of parental influence on younger children is unquestioned, there has been debate about the continued influence of parents on the behavior of college students (Ham & Hope, 2003; Kandel & Andrews, 1987; Wood, Read, Palfai, & Stevenson, 2001). Some of the literature in this area has presumed that the impact of socialization agents over the course of adolescence to young adulthood shifts, with parental influences weakening and peer influences strengthening over the course of this developmental transition (Harris, 1998). These assertions may have contributed to the relative neglect of alcohol prevention strategies focusing on parental involvement with college students (Ichiyama et al., 2009). However, in contrast to the arguments of diminished influence of parents on college students' drinking behavior, there is a growing body of research providing evidence in support of continued parental influence related to reductions in problem drinking among college students.

In this chapter, we review and summarize recent studies investigating parental influences on college student alcohol use and misuse. We review studies that focus on parental influence variables that serve as risk or protective factors relating to college student drinking. The efficacy of parent-based intervention strategies for the prevention and reduction of problem drinking among college students is also reviewed. For reader clarity, we categorized the reviewed studies on parent influence variables on college alcohol use with full awareness of the substantial overlap across concepts. We conclude with a summary of recommendations and future directions for parent-based research and intervention strategies.

PARENTING STYLES

Baumrind (1971) identified four parenting styles characterized by differences in levels of parental control and warmth: permissive (low control, high warmth), authoritarian (high control, low warmth), authoritative (high control, high warmth), and uninvolved (low control, low warmth). A number of studies have examined the effects of parenting styles (as conceptualized by Baumrind) and related parenting typologies on college student drinking behaviors.

Although the authoritative parenting style (control with warmth) has shown the most consistent negative association with heavy drinking in adolescence and young adults (Bahr & Hoffman, 2010), studies by Patock-Peckham and Morgan-Lopez (2006, 2007, 2009a&b) and Hartman and colleagues (2015) have shed light on the complexities underlying the relationship between parenting styles and college alcohol use. These complexities illustrate the roles of moderator and mediator variables in empirical research. Other studies reviewed later in this chapter also involve these concepts. For reader clarity, we provide a brief description of the moderator and mediator variable distinction.

A moderator variable changes the strength of a relationship between two variables. A given moderator variable may increase or decrease the strength of the relationship. For example, disagreements with friends are associated with more drinking for college students who report they drink to forget about their problems, but friend disagreements are not related to increased drinking for those students who report they do not drink to forget about their problems. In this example, drinking to forget about problems moderates the relationship between friend disagreements and drinking (Mohr et al., 2005).

Mediator variables, on the other hand, help to specify how a particular relationship between two (or more) variables might operate. Mediators usually involve internal psychological processes that occur to help explain the relationship. As a hypothetical example, a student's academic overload (taking too many classes) will increase test anxiety, which in turn leads to increased drinking. In this example, test anxiety is a mediator that explains how academic overload may lead to increased drinking. For a more detailed reference on this topic, see the classic article by Baron and Kenny (1986).

The importance of parent–child gender match illustrates some of the complexities underlying the relationship between parenting style and college drinking. The parenting style of the same gender parent as the college student was found to exert the greatest influence on college students' alcohol use. Whereas trait impulsivity mediated the effects of a permissive parenting style across genders (the more permissive the parents, the more impulsive were their daughters and sons), Patock-Peckham and Morgan-Lopez (2006) found that a more authoritative parenting style on the part of fathers was related to decreased impulsivity on the part of their sons, whereas when mothers showed a more authoritarian parenting style, this was related to an increase in daughters' impulsivity. Thus, when fathers exerted a parenting style combining control with warm support (authoritative), this was related to less impulsiveness in their sons. However, when mothers exerted a controlling parenting style in the absence of warmth (authoritarian), this was related to greater impulsiveness among their daughters. Greater impulsivity was related to higher levels of drinking, and less impulsivity was linked to lower levels of drinking.

In a study of alcohol-consuming college students, a positive paternal bond mediated the effects of an authoritative paternal parenting style on depression and related alcohol use problems. Among female drinkers, a negative paternal bond significantly increased the effect of an authoritarian paternal parenting style on depression and alcohol use problems (Patock-Peckham & Morgan-Lopez, 2007). In this study, the effects of a parenting style characterized by control with warmth among fathers (paternal authoritativeness) on student depression and alcohol-related

problems were mediated by positive relationship quality between the student and the father (paternal bond), whereas among female alcohol-consuming students, the effects of a controlling parenting style by fathers (paternal authoritarianism) on their daughters' depression and alcohol problems were related to a more negative relationship quality between the father and the daughter. Patock-Peckham and Morgan-Lopez (2009) also found that among college males, the perception of having an authoritarian father was positively linked to an increased desire to use alcohol, whereas among females, the perception of having a permissive father was shown to be a risk factor for increased alcohol use.

In another study on college student drinkers, Hartman and colleagues (2015) found that higher levels of maternal authoritarianism were linked to higher alcohol use and more alcohol-related problems through the mediating influence of high self-concealment (the tendency to keep secrets) (Larson & Chastain, 1990), whereas higher levels of paternal authoritativeness were indirectly linked to lower levels of drinking and alcohol problems through lower levels of self-concealment and less impaired control over drinking. In Hartman et al.'s study, a controlling parenting style by mothers (authoritarian) was associated with more student alcohol problems when the students showed a high tendency to inhibit and keep secrets (relating to a tendency to not disclose personal information), whereas a style of warm control (authoritative) among fathers was associated with decreased alcohol problems when students showed lower tendencies to inhibit.

A study by Mallett and colleagues (2011) on matriculating first-year college athletes examined parenting styles within the moderating context of the parent-based intervention (PBI) created by Turrisi, Taki, Dunnam, Jaccard, and Grimes (2001). Briefly, Turrisi's PBI is a parent training method designed to help parents communicate effectively with their college-bound child to develop strategies to reduce the risks associated with heavy drinking. The PBI approach is based on the dissemination of an informational handbook to parents prior to their child's college matriculation (Turrisi's PBI method is described in depth later). Mallett et al. found that first-year college athletes with authoritarian parents who did not receive the PBI were at highest risk for heavy drinking during the first year of college, and participants with both authoritarian and permissive style parents who received a combination of PBI and peer-based interventions reduced their alcohol consumption during the first year of college.

Summary

The studies we reviewed provide strong empirical evidence that parenting styles influence college alcohol use generally, but the pathways through which they appear to operate are complex (Fromme, 2006). The magnitude of effect of parenting styles on college drinking appears to be mediated and moderated by psychological and interpersonal processes (trait impulsivity, self-concealment, and parental bond are some of the variables that have been investigated), and the specific pathways through which particular parenting styles exert influence on college drinking depend on the gender of both the child and the parent (parent–child gender matching studies). Taken together, the general indications of the studies reviewed previously suggest that (1) the parenting style that combines structure/control with warmth/support (authoritative style) appears most effective overall, (2) parental warmth in the absence of maintaining structure/control (permissive style) is the least effective approach and associated with increased risk for problem drinking, and (3) the parenting styles of both mothers and fathers are significant factors that affect the alcohol use of their college-bound sons and daughters. These findings point to the importance of parents maintaining active involvement in the lives of their college student child, which can be challenging when one's child is no longer residing in the home. In the following sections, we discuss studies examining the effects of parental involvement variables on college student drinking.

PARENTAL MONITORING

Parental monitoring in reference to teenagers and young adults has been conceptualized as parental knowledge of a teen's activities, peer relationships, and behaviors (Bailey, Hill, Oesterle, & Hawkins, 2009). Among college students, higher levels of parental monitoring are associated with decreased alcohol consumption (Abar &Turrisi, 2008), and low levels of parental monitoring are associated with an increased probability of developing alcohol dependence during the first year of college (Arria et al., 2008). In studies

of parenting types that include parental monitoring, higher levels of perceived parental monitoring were associated with a lower likelihood of engaging in heavy drinking and experiencing negative alcohol-related consequences (Varvil-Weld, Scaglione, et al., 2014; Walls, Fairlie, & Wood, 2009), whereas low parental monitoring was associated with an increased likelihood of engaging in high-risk drinking practices (Abar, 2012).

The association between parental monitoring and alcohol-related behaviors among college students can be complex. Varvil-Weld, Turrisi, Scaglione, Mallett, and Ray (2013) found that parents of incoming first-year college students reported significantly higher levels of parental monitoring than did their student children (i.e., parents believed they knew more about their college student's activities than they actually did know). Another study found that (1) college students' approval of their own drinking (i.e., holding more favorable attitudes toward drinking) mediated the association between perceived parental knowledge and actual student drinking and (2) perceived parental approval of drinking (i.e., students' beliefs of whether their parents view drinking positively or negatively) was found to moderate the association between perceived parental knowledge and student approval of drinking (Hummer, LaBrie, & Ehret, 2013). Arria and colleagues (2008) showed that higher levels of parental monitoring were related to lower alcohol consumption at both high school and college levels, but the association between parental monitoring of college drinking was not significant once high school drinking was accounted for. In their study, parental monitoring appeared to indirectly influence college drinking through reductions in high school drinking. Similarly, Kaynak and colleagues (2013) found that parental monitoring during high school significantly reduced the risk of alcohol dependence in college. Turrisi and Ray (2010) showed parental monitoring (among other parent variables) that was sustained from pre-college to mid-semester of the first year of college was linked to lower levels of high-risk drinking tendencies.

Summary

Our review of parental monitoring studies indicates that (1) in general, higher levels of parental monitoring are associated with decreases in college student drinking overall, and lower levels of monitoring are associated with increased risk of alcohol abuse among college students; (2) parental monitoring appears most effective as an established pattern that begins prior to the student entering college and is sustained through the college years; (3) the magnitude of effects of parental monitoring on college drinking appears to be mediated and moderated by the students' level of approval of their own drinking behavior and the students' perceptions of parental approval of drinking; and (4) parents appear to believe they know more about their college student's activities in college than they actually do know. These conclusions highlight the importance of both sustained parental involvement and parent–child communication processes, a topic we turn to next.

PARENT–CHILD COMMUNICATION

A number of recent studies have examined the role of both the quality and the frequency of general and alcohol-specific communication processes between parents and their college student children and its associations with college student drinking. The majority of studies in this area have focused on general non-alcohol-specific communication processes among matriculating first-year college students.

Abar, Fernandes, and Wood (2011) showed that greater frequency and openness in parent–teen communication was linked to lower levels of alcohol use, greater parental monitoring, and enhanced parent–teen relationship satisfaction among matriculating first-year college students. In two studies on parenting types, the parenting profile involving high levels of positive parent–child communication was associated with a lower likelihood of high-risk drinking among incoming college freshmen (Varvil-Weld, Scaglione, et al., 2014), and the parent profile containing negative and conflictual communication with the father was linked to increased likelihood of high-risk drinking (Varvil-Weld, Mallett, Turrisi, & Abar, 2012). Among incoming first-year college Latina/o students, greater mother–child communication was linked to lower levels of alcohol-related consequences (Varvil-Weld, Turrisi, Hospital, Mallett, & Bámaca-Colbert, 2014).

Other studies in this area have examined various factors that may affect parent–child communication processes. Parents who participated in a web-based intervention about college alcohol use were found to communicate more with their college student children about protective strategies related to drinking compared to parents who did not participate in the intervention (Donovan, Wood, Frayjo, Black, & Surette, 2012). Napper, Hummer, Lac, and LaBrie (2014) found that among college undergraduates and their parents, parents overestimated how much other parents talked to their college student children about the frequency and quantity of the students' alcohol use generally, but they underestimated how often other parents actually initiated conversations with their child about alcohol. These findings suggest that parental levels of alcohol-specific communication are related to misperceptions of how often other parents actually initiate and talk about alcohol use with their college student child. Such misperceptions could mitigate the potentially protective influence of alcohol-specific parent–child communications. In a subsequent study by Napper, Grimaldi, and LaBrie (2015), greater levels of parental intent to communicate with their college student children were associated with higher rates of past parent–child communication, greater perceived likelihood of alcohol-related risk on the part of their child, and more knowledge of their child's alcohol use. Thus, parents who believed their child was more likely to experience alcohol problems and were more open in their knowledge of the student's alcohol-related behavior were more motivated to talk to their child about alcohol. Finally, Abar, Abar, Turrisi, and Belden (2013) assessed multiple modalities of communication among first-year college students and their parents. Most students used multiple modes of communication with their parents (e.g., cell phone, e-mail, and text messaging), and being female and having higher socioeconomic status were associated with greater context frequency with parents. Increased knowledge of contemporary forms of technological communication most often used by college students and their parents has implications for future research in this area.

Summary

The studies reviewed on parent–child communication suggest that (1) higher frequency of parent–child communication generally is associated with decreased risk for college alcohol misuse; (2) not surprisingly, the decreased risk for alcohol misuse is more likely when the parent–child communication quality is positive rather than negative and conflicted; (3) higher frequency of alcohol-specific parent–child communication (talking to college student child about his or her alcohol use) is associated with greater parent–child communication frequency generally and whether parents believe or know their college student child is drinking or at risk for alcohol misuse; and (4) students use multiple modes of technological communication with their parents, and females generally communicate more frequently with their parents while in college compared to males. The findings on alcohol-specific communication suggest that parents are more likely to initiate conversations about alcohol use with their college student children reactively (when drinking risk or use is perceived). The efficacy of preventive strategies for enhancing parent–child communication about college alcohol use is described later. These findings also highlight the importance of student and parental attitudes toward drinking.

PARENTAL MODELING AND ATTITUDES REGARDING ALCOHOL

Recent studies of the effects of parent behaviors regarding alcohol use on their college student children typically involved perceived parental approval of alcohol use, perceived parental permissiveness of drinking, and parental modeling of drinking behavior. Among first-year college students, higher perceived parental approval of alcohol was linked to increased likelihood of college students engaging in high-risk drinking (Abar, 2012), lower perceived parental approval of drinking was linked to a decrease in alcohol use frequency (Messler, Quevillon, & Simons, 2014), and higher levels of perceived parental permissiveness of drinking were associated with greater alcohol use and alcohol-related consequences (Varvil-Weld, Crowley, Turrisi, Greenberg, & Mallett, 2014; Walls et al., 2009). In a study of incoming first-year college students, Fairlie, Wood, and Laird (2012) found that prematriculation parental drinking permissiveness was associated with higher prematriculation levels of heavy episodic drinking. College students who believed their parents would greatly disapprove of their heavy drinking were significantly less likely to engage in weekly drinking and heavy episodic drinking, and they reported fewer negative alcohol-related consequences (Walls et al., 2009). Parents of first-year college students who did not allow any drinking in high school had college-bound teens who drank less

on weekends and had lower peak drinking (heavy single-episode drinking), lower frequency of reported drunkenness, and fewer negative alcohol-related consequences (Abar, Abar, & Turrisi, 2009). In a study of college student light drinkers, LaBrie, Boyle, and Napper (2015) found that compared to students who received harm reduction messages from their parents, light drinkers who received more abstinence communications from their parents reported less frequent alcohol use, lower peak alcohol consumption, and greater use of protective drinking strategies.

A pair of studies examined disparities in perceived parental approval of drinking between parents and their college student children and between parents and peers. Varvil-Weld and colleagues (2013) found that parents reported lower levels of permissibility regarding alcohol and lower approval of moderate and heavy drinking compared to their student children. In their study, student-reported data were found to be more reliably associated with college drinking behaviors compared to parent-reported information. Cail and LaBrie (2010) found greater disparities between perceived approval of alcohol among parents and friends to be significantly associated with greater student drinking and alcohol-related consequences. Compared to females, the male college students in this study experienced significantly greater disparities between their beliefs and those of their parents and peers.

In a study examining trajectories of different parenting profiles and their linkages to first-year college student alcohol use, the parenting profile associated with higher levels of parental modeling of drinking and parental approval of drinking had the highest levels of heavy drinking among students (Abar, Turrisi, & Mallett, 2014). Glanton and Wulfert (2013) found that higher levels of perceived paternal alcohol use were associated with more positive alcohol expectancies, lower perceived efficacy to refuse drinking, and greater intention for future alcohol use among college students. Perceived parental alcohol-related problems were associated with alcohol use problems among college students (Fischer, Forthun, Pidcock, & Dowd, 2007).

Summary

Our review of studies on parental modeling attitudes toward alcohol suggests the following: (1) The more that students perceive their parents approve or condone their drinking, the greater the risk for alcohol-related problems in college, whereas perceived parental disapproval of drinking is associated with lower rates of heavy drinking in college; (2) abstinence messages appear to be more effective in reducing high-risk drinking in college compared to harm reduction messaging (drinking in moderation); (3) greater disparities between perceived parental approval of drinking and actual parental approval of drinking (when students believe their parents approve of their drinking more than they actually do so) are associated with higher alcohol consumption and alcohol-related problems, especially among college males; and (4) higher levels of parental drinking (modeling), especially paternal drinking, are associated with higher risk drinking behaviors among college students.

PARENTAL RELATIONSHIP QUALITY

The strength of the parent–child bond has been shown to be directly or indirectly linked to alcohol use problems among college students. Backer-Fulghum, Patock-Peckham, King, Roufa, and Hagen (2012) showed that higher perceived parental neglect was indirectly linked to more frequent alcohol-related problems via stress and pathological reasons for drinking mediators, and higher levels of paternal rejection were associated with increased risk of problem drinking via low self-esteem and stress mediators (with the opposite effect found for maternal care). Perceived awareness and caring of parents have also been found to be linked to lower quantity of alcohol consumed per drinking episode among first-year college students (Wetherill & Fromme, 2007). In a longitudinal study of first-year college students, greater attachment to the mother was associated with lower alcohol risk, and weaker attachment to the mother was related to increased drinking and alcohol-related consequences at the 6-month follow-up (LaBrie & Sessoms, 2012). In this study, first-year college males with weaker maternal attachments reported experiencing more alcohol-related consequences compared to females or male counterparts who reported strong attachments with their mothers. The study by LaBrie and Sessoms identified male first-year college students with low maternal attachments as a potentially high-risk student group. A previously noted study by Patock-Peckham and Morgan-Lopez (2007) found

that a positive paternal bond mediated the effects of an authoritative paternal parenting style on alcohol use problems via depression, and among females, a negative paternal bond significantly increased the effect of an authoritarian paternal parenting style on alcohol use problems.

Summary

Overall, the studies on parental relationship quality suggest that (1) perceived parental neglect and rejection (particularly from the father) are associated with greater risk for college student alcohol abuse and (2) strong and positive parental bonding and attachment with both mothers and fathers are associated with lower risk for alcohol use problems.

PARENT-BASED INTERVENTIONS

Parent-based interventions have been developed to help prevent and reduce problem drinking among college students. The earliest and most researched PBI was developed by Rob Turrisi and colleagues (2001). Turrisi's PBI involves the administration of a 35-page parent handbook titled "A Parent Handbook for Talking with College Students About Alcohol" (for a detailed description of the handbook's content and evaluation, see Turrisi et al., 2001). Subsequent evaluation studies of Turrisi's PBI have elaborated on the basic handbook administration method.

The initial study of Turrisi's PBI approach was conducted on 154 matriculating first-year college students. Students in the PBI treatment group reported less frequency of drunkenness, less favorable perceived approval of drinking by parents, and more negative perceptions regarding drinking activities (Turrisi et al., 2001). On a larger first-year college student sample, compared to a non-intervention comparison group, the PBI intervention was associated with lower frequency of weekend drinking and lower frequency of heavy episodic drinking (Turrisi, Abar, Mallett, & Jaccard, 2010). Based on a sample of first-year college student athletes, Cleveland, Lanza, Ray, and Mallett (2012) found the PBI to be most effective at keeping baseline non-drinkers from subsequently becoming heavy drinkers once they entered college. In another study of first-year college students, heavy drinkers were found to be more likely to transition out of the heavy drinking pattern trajectory when their parents received the PBI during pre-college matriculation (Turrisi et al., 2013). In a randomized longitudinal trial of the PBI on incoming first-year college students, Ichiyama and colleagues (2009) found that compared to students in an intervention-as-usual condition, students receiving the PBI were significantly less likely to transition from non-drinker to drinker status and showed less growth in drinking during the first year in college. However, the direct PBI effect of significantly reducing growth in drinking applied only to the women in the PBI condition. Doumas, Turrisi, Ray, Esp, and Curtis-Schaeffer (2013) examined the effectiveness of the PBI alone and with brochure boosters on multiple measures of drinking. The PBI with brochure boosters was linked to significantly lower levels of reported drinking to intoxication during the past month and single night peak drinking. In a study of 978 incoming first-year college women, those in an enhanced PBI condition (e.g., administered supplementary materials on sexual assertiveness) were significantly less likely to report involvement in an intoxicated sexual assault relative to females in a non-intervention control group (Testa, Hoffman, Livingston, & Turrisi, 2010). In this study, mother–daughter communication mediated the effects of the PBI on heavy episodic drinking.

Reviews of college alcohol intervention studies by Cronce and Larimar (2011) and Larimar and Cronce (2002, 2007) strongly supported the efficacy of individual-focused intervention approaches and pointed to the need for college campuses to develop comprehensive prevention and intervention programs. Several recent studies have examined the efficacy of the PBI as both a stand-alone and a combined intervention approach. Grossbard and colleagues (2010) assessed the effects of the PBI alone, Brief Alcohol Screening and Intervention for College Students (BASICS) alone, and PBI–BASICS combined on alcohol and other substance use during the past 30 days. The combined condition was related to significant reductions in marijuana use, but there were no significant differences of intervention type on alcohol use. In a study of incoming first-year college athletes, the effects of the PBI alone, BASICS alone, and PBI–BASICS were compared (Turrisi et al., 2009). Students in the combined PBI–BASICS intervention group reported significantly fewer alcohol-related consequences and lower levels of alcohol consumption. In a subsequent study on the same sample of incoming first-year college athletes,

the effectiveness of the PBI alone, Brief Motivational Interviewing (BMI) alone, and PBI–BMI combined on college drinking was assessed (Mallett et al., 2010). Student athletes who had the earliest age of onset of drinking were found to respond best to the combined PBI–BMI intervention.

Donovan and colleagues (2012) examined the efficacy of a web-based parent intervention in enhancing parent–child communication about alcohol-related behavior. Parents who participated in the intervention reported more communication about protective behavioral strategies regarding alcohol use compared to parents in a non-intervention control group. However, there were no significant reductions in reported heavy episodic drinking as a result of the intervention. The study by Donovan et al. and the body of work investigating the efficacy of Turrisi's handbook PBI methodology in reducing overall alcohol consumption levels among college students share a common limitation—the relative inability of their PBIs to reduce heavy episodic drinking behavior (LaBrie, Napper, & Hummer, 2014).

A pair of recent studies by LaBrie and colleagues (2014) and Earle and LaBrie (2016) examined the effects of an innovative parent-based normative feedback intervention designed to correct misperceptions of student alcohol use and parental approval of drinking. Parent FITSTART (Feedback Intervention Targeting Student Transitions and Alcohol Related Trajectories) is an interactive normative feedback intervention designed to correct normative misperceptions held by parents of matriculating college undergraduates. The hour-long group sessions conducted during college orientation utilized a wireless interactive polling platform to provide immediate normative feedback to groups of parents. The FITSTART intervention resulted in parents (1) reporting significant increases in their intentions to talk to students about alcohol use, (2) reporting less confidence in what they knew about their child's alcohol use in college based on the feedback they received from the intervention, (3) showing increased accuracy in their estimates of how much students actually drank, and (4) reporting an increased likelihood that they would discuss alcohol use with their child. In addition, students whose parents received FITSTART (1) consumed less alcohol overall, (2) were less likely to engage in heavy episodic drinking, (3) were less likely to initiate drinking (among high school non-drinkers), and (4) reported fewer alcohol-related consequences overall (among high school drinkers). Significantly, FITSTART is the first PBI methodology using a randomized controlled trial with a 4-month follow-up to demonstrate reductions in the most high-risk form of college student alcohol consumption, heavy episodic drinking (LaBrie et al., 2014).

Summary

The general conclusions based on our review of studies examining the efficacy of parent-based interventions suggest that in general, Turrisi's PBI approach has been shown to be effective in reducing overall college student alcohol consumption, decreasing the risk for initiating and continuing drinking once in college, and reducing the frequency of subsequent alcohol-related problems. Combined campus intervention strategies (e.g., PBI combined with BASICS and/or BMI) appear to be more efficacious at reducing college alcohol risk compared to using the PBI as a stand-alone intervention. Importantly, the initial success of an innovative normative feedback intervention (FITSTART) appears promising, particularly in its efficacy for reducing heavy episodic drinking among college students.

CONCLUSIONS AND FUTURE DIRECTIONS

Our review of recent studies of parental influences on college student drinking has revealed nine consistent general findings, which are presented here. The research conclusions are accompanied by recommendations for parents. Finally, the parental influence literature is summarized with considerations for future research. The nine consistent general findings and recommendations for parents are as follows:

1. The parenting style characterized by a combination of control and warmth/support (the authoritative parenting style) was found to be associated with lower levels of college student drinking problems.

   Takeaway for parents: Being warm and supportive is not enough. Your child also needs continued structure and clear expectations to be known even when he or she is no longer in the home.

2. Higher levels of parental knowledge of a child's activities and peer relationships (parental monitoring) were associated with reductions in high-risk drinking behaviors, whereas low parental monitoring was linked to increased probability of developing problem drinking behaviors.

   Takeaway for parents: As much as possible, keep involved and aware of your child's day-to-day activities (without hovering; it shows that you care).

3. More frequent and positive parent–child communication processes were associated with lower levels of drinking, and negative communication processes were linked to increased risk of problem alcohol consumption.

   Takeaway for parents: It is important to be positive, supportive, and maintain consistent contact with your child while he or she is in college.

4. Greater perceived parental permissiveness and approval of alcohol use were associated with higher alcohol consumption and more alcohol-related problems.

   Takeaway for parents: What you say (or do not say) to your child about drinking alcohol conveys a message. Be clear and open about your attitudes toward their drinking.

5. Higher perceived alcohol use on the part of parents (parental modeling) was linked to greater risk of problem drinking among college students.

   Takeaway for parents: What you do (and not just what you say) about alcohol use is also important. Children pay attention to how their parents use alcohol and will often follow their lead.

6. Abstinence messaging (vs. harm reduction messaging) from parents was associated with a lower frequency of alcohol use.

   Takeaway for parents: Parents who discourage using alcohol versus parents who approve of drinking even in moderation reduce their child's risk of drinking in college.

7. Strong parental bonding and attachment were found to be protective factors against the development of problem drinking behaviors for some college students.

   Takeaway for parents: Maintain warm and supportive contact with your college student child. Do not hesitate to use modern forms of technological communication.

8. Parent-based interventions were shown to be efficacious in producing reductions in problem drinking among college students and promoting protective alcohol-related behaviors among parents.

    Takeaway for parents: When you have the opportunity to participate in any parent-based research initiatives at your child's college/university, do so.

9. The involvement and influence of fathers as well as mothers are important protective factors in reducing problem drinking risk among college students.

    Takeaway for parents: College students appear to be at higher risk for problem drinking when their fathers are perceived as uninvolved or neglectful. Typically, it is the mother who maintains the most consistent contact with the college-bound child. However, the evidence is clear: In the lives of their college student children, fathers are still important. Stay involved.

Although the general findings uncovered in our review helped to demonstrate the important role parents play in influencing college student alcohol use, more research is needed to help gain a better understanding of the complex mechanisms underlying how parental influence variables actually impact college student drinking behavior. For example, the pathways through which parenting styles are linked to reductions in alcohol consumption have been shown to be mediated by variables such as depression, trait impulsivity, parental bond, and self-concealment. In addition, the specific impact of parenting style on college student drinking appears to vary as a function of gender and parent–child gender matching. The effects of parenting styles on college drinking clearly operate in a more complex manner that goes beyond the general conclusion of a protective influence on college drinking through adopting an authoritative parenting style.

Although positive and frequent parent–child communication processes have been associated with greater parental monitoring and enhanced parent–child relationship satisfaction, the precise pathways through which parent–child communication influences college student drinking behavior are not well understood and are in need of future study. How disparities in parent and child perceptions related to alcohol use and related behaviors develop needs further elucidation through research. Although there is an overall paucity of research on alcohol-specific parent–child communication processes, a significant finding that emerged was that increased parental intention to talk to their child about alcohol was linked to whether or not the parents believed their child was more likely to experience alcohol-related problems in college. Future research in this area may seek to find avenues through which parents increase their likelihood of engaging in alcohol-specific communication with their child whether or not their child is perceived as being at high risk for college alcohol-related problems.

Future research in this area would also benefit from longitudinal designs that could trace the sustained influence of parent variables prior to and throughout the college years. The impact of parental influence on college student drinking can be affected based on when it is initiated and whether it is sustained over time.

The incorporation of parents in campus intervention programs to reduce college student alcohol abuse is a promising venture in need of further development and research. The large majority of research in this area has centered on Turrisi's handbook version of the PBI. Since the initial study of Turrisi's PBI, a now sizeable body of research has supported its effectiveness in reducing problem drinking and alcohol-related problems, particularly among matriculating college students. On the other hand, relatively little is known about the sustained impact of the PBI beyond the first year of college, further emphasizing the need for longitudinal studies in this area. However, the handbook PBI methodology has shown limited success in reducing heavy episodic drinking. A recently developed PBI known as FITSTART is an innovative normative feedback parent intervention method that has been shown to be effective in reducing the most high-risk form of college alcohol abuse (heavy episodic drinking or "binge drinking). The development of parent-based interventions is in its early stages, but these interventions show promise as an integral component of alcohol prevention programming on college campuses.

The now substantial body of research that has accumulated on college student drinking and seeks to understand its causes and develop effective prevention strategies is a testament to its relevance as a national public health concern (Hingson, 2010). Within this larger realm of study, the role of parents as crucial influence agents in the reduction and prevention of problem drinking among college students has been the target of increased research activity. We believe the substantial number of recent empirical studies we reviewed that specifically focus on the influence of parents on college student drinking provide compelling evidence of the ongoing relevance of parents in the lives of their college-bound children. In our view, the question of parental influence on college student drinking behavior can be put to rest. Parents still matter.

REFERENCES

Abar, C. (2012). Examining the relationship between parenting types and patterns of student alcohol-related behavior during the transition to college. *Psychology of Addictive Behaviors, 26*(1), 20–29.

Abar, C., Abar, B., & Turrisi, R. (2009). The impact of parental modeling and permissibility on alcohol use and experienced negative drinking consequences in college. *Addictive Behaviors, 34*, 542–547.

Abar, C., Abar, B., Turrisi, R., & Belden, C. (2013). Communication technology used among parents and their college teens: Implications for college health promotion and risk prevention programs. *Journal of the First-Year Experience & Students in Transition, 25*(1), 61–76.

Abar, C., Fernandes, A., & Wood, M. (2011). Parent–teen communication and pre-college alcohol involvement: A latent class analysis. *Addictive Behavior, 36*, 1357–1360.

Abar, C., & Turrisi, R. (2008). How important are parents during the college years? A longitudinal perspective of indirect influences parents yield on their college teens' alcohol use. *Addictive Behaviors, 33*, 1360–1368.

Abar, C., Turrisi, R., & Mallett, K. (2014). Differential trajectories of alcohol-related behaviors across the first year of college by parenting profiles. *Psychology of Addictive Behaviors, 28*(1), 53–61.

Arria, A. M., Kuhn, V., Caldeira, K. M., O'Grady, K. E., Vincent, K. B., & Wish, E. D. (2008). High school drinking mediates the relationship between parental monitoring and college drinking: A longitudinal analysis. *Substance Abuse Treatment, Prevention, and Policy, 3*, 6.

Backer-Fulghum, L. M., Patock-Peckham, J. A., King, K. M., Roufa, L., & Hagen, L. (2012). The stress–response dampening hypothesis: How self-esteem and stress act as mechanisms between negative parental bonds and alcohol-related problems in emerging adulthood. *Addictive Behaviors, 37*, 477–484.

Bahr, S. J., & Hoffman, J. P. (2010). Parenting style, religiosity, peers, and adolescent heavy drinking. *Journal of Studies on Alcohol and Drugs, 71*, 539–543.

Bailey, J. A., Hill, K. G., Oesterle, S., & Hawkins, J. D. (2009). Parenting practices and problem behavior across three generations: Monitoring, harsh discipline, and drug use in the intergenerational transmission of externalizing behavior. *Developmental Psychology, 45*, 1214–1226.

Baron, R., & Kenny, D. (1986). The moderator–mediator variable distinction in social psychological research: Conceptual, strategic, and statistical considerations. *Journal of Personality and Social Psychology, 51*, 1173–1182.

Baumrind, D. (1971). Current patterns of parental authority. *Developmental Psychology, 4*(1), 1–103.

Cail, J., & LaBrie, J. W. (2010). Disparity between the perceived alcohol-related attitudes of parents and peers increases alcohol risk in college students. *Addictive Behaviors, 35*, 135–139.

Cleveland, M. J., Lanza, S. T., Ray, A. E., & Mallett, K. A. (2012). Transitions in first-year college students drinking behaviors: Does pre-college drinking moderate the effects of parent- and peer-based intervention components? *Psychology of Addictive Behaviors, 26*(3), 440–450.

Cronce, J. M., & Larimer, M. E. (2011). Individual-focused approaches to the prevention of college student drinking. *Alcohol Research & Health, 34*(2), 210–221.

Donovan, E., Wood, M., Frayjo, K., Black, R. A., & Surette, D. A. (2012). A randomized, controlled trial to test the efficacy of an online, parent-based intervention for reducing the risks associated with college-student alcohol use. *Addictive Behaviors, 37*, 25–35.

Doumas, D. M., Turrisi, R., Ray, A. E., Esp, S. M., & Curtis-Schaeffer, A. K. (2013). A randomized trial evaluating a parent based intervention to reduce college drinking. *Journal of Substance Abuse Treatment, 45*(1), 31–37.

Earle, A. M., & LaBrie, J. W. (2016). The upside of helicopter parenting: Engaging parents to reduce first-year student drinking. *Journal of Student Affairs Research and Practice, 53*(3), 319–330.

Fairlie, A. M., Wood, M. D., & Laird, R. D. (2012). Prospective protective effect of parents on peer influences and college alcohol involvement. *Psychology of Addictive Behaviors, 26*(1), 30–41.

Fischer, J. L., Forthun, L. F., Pidcock, B. W., & Dowd, D. A. (2007). Parent relationships, emotion regulation, psychosocial maturity and college student alcohol use problems. *Journal of Youth & Adolescence, 36*(7), 912–926.

Fromme, K. (2006). Parenting and other influences on the alcohol use and emotional adjustment of children, adolescents, and emerging adults. *Psychology of Addictive Behaviors, 20*(2), 138–139.

Glanton, C. F., & Wulfert, E. (2013). The relationship between parental alcohol use and college students' alcohol related cognitions. *Addictive Behaviors, 38,* 2761–2767.

Grossbard, J. R., Mastroleo, N. R., Kilmer, J. R., Lee, C. M., Turrisi, R., Larimer, M. E., & Ray, A. (2010). Substance use patterns among first-year college students: Secondary effects of a combined alcohol intervention. *Journal of Substance Abuse Treatment, 39,* 384–390.

Ham, L. S., & Hope, D. A. (2003). College students and problematic drinking: A review of the literature. *Clinical Psychology Review, 23,* 719–759.

Harris, J. R. (1998). *The nurture assumption: Why children turn out the way that they do.* New York, NY: Free Press.

Hartman, J. D., Patock-Peckham, J. A., Corbin, W. R., Gates, J. R., Leeman, R. F., Luk, J. W., & King, K. M. (2015). Direct and indirect links between parenting styles, self-concealment (secrets), impaired control over drinking and alcohol-related outcomes. *Addictive Behaviors, 40,* 102–108.

Hingson, R. W. (2010). Focus on: College drinking and related problems. Magnitude and prevention of college drinking and related problems. *Alcohol Research & Health, 33*(1), 45–54.

Hingson, R. W., Zha, W., & Weitzman, E. R. (2009). Magnitude of and trends in alcohol-related mortality and morbidity among U.S. college students ages 18–24, 1998–2005. *Journal of Studies on Alcohol and Drugs Supplement, 16,* 12–20.

Hummer, J. F., LaBrie, J. W., & Ehret, P. J. (2013). Do as I say, not as you perceive: Examining the roles of perceived parental knowledge and perceived parental approval in college students' alcohol-related approval and behavior. *Parenting: Science & Practice, 13*(3), 196–212.

Ichiyama, M. A., Fairlie, A. M., Wood, M. D., Turrisi, R., Francis, D. P., Ray, A. E., & Stanger, L. A. (2009). A randomized trial of a parent-based intervention on drinking behavior among incoming college freshmen. *Journal of Studies on Alcohol and Drugs, 16,* 67–76.

Johnston, L. D., O'Malley, P. M., Bachman, J. G., & Schulenberg, J. E., (2013). Prevalence of drug use among college students. In Monitoring the Future national survey results on drug use, 1975–2012: Volume 2, College students and adults ages 19–50

(pp. 364–375). Ann Arbor: Institute for Social Research, The University of Michigan.

Kandel, D. B., & Andrews, K. (1987). Processes of adolescent socialization by parents and peers. *International Journal of the Addictions, 22,* 319–342.

Kaynak, O., Meyers, K., Caldeira, K. M., Vincent, K. B., Winters, K. C., & Arria, A. M. (2013). Relationships among parental monitoring and sensation seeking on the development of substance use disorder among college students. *Addictive Behaviors, 38,* 1457–1463.

LaBrie, J. W., Boyle, S. C., & Napper, L. E. (2015). Alcohol abstinence or harm reduction? Parental messages for college-bound light drinkers. *Addictive Behaviors, 46,* 10–13.

LaBrie, J. W., Napper, L. E., & Hummer, J. F. (2014). Normative feedback for parents of college students: Piloting a parent based intervention to correct misperceptions of students' alcohol use and other parents' approval of drinking. *Addictive Behaviors 39,* 107–113.

LaBrie, J. W., & Sessoms, A. E. (2012). Parents still matter: The role of parental attachment in risky drinking among college students. *Journal of Child & Adolescent Substance Abuse, 21*(1), 91–104.

Larson, D. G., & Chastain, R. L. (1990). Self-concealment: Conceptualization, measurement, and health implications. *Journal of Social and Clinical Psychology, 9*(4), 439–455.

Mallett, K. A., Ray, A. E., Turrisi, R., Belden, C. Bachrach, R. L., & Larimer, M. E. (2010). Age of drinking onset as a moderator of the efficacy of parent-based, brief motivational, and combined intervention approaches to reduce drinking and consequences among college students. *Alcoholism: Clinical and Experimental Research, 34*(7), 1–8.

Mallett, K. A., Turrisi, R., Ray, A. E., Stapleton, J., Abar, C., Mastroleo, N. R., & Larimer, M. E. (2011). Do parents know best? Examining the relationship between parenting profiles, prevention efforts, and peak drinking in college students. *Journal of Applied Social Psychology, 41*(12), 2904–2927.

Messler, E. C., Quevillon, R. P., & Simons, J. S. (2014). The effect of perceived parental approval of drinking on alcohol use and problems. *Journal of Alcohol & Drug Education, 58*(1), 44–59.

Mohr, C. D., Armeli, S., Tennen, H., Todd, M., Clark, J., & Carney, M. A. (2005). Moving beyond the key party: A daily process study of college student drinking motivations. *Psychology of Addictive Behaviors, 19*(4), 392–403.

Napper, L. E., Grimaldi, E. M., & LaBrie, J. W. (2015). Parents' and students' perceptions of college alcohol risk: The role of parental risk perception in intentions to communicate about alcohol. *Addictive Behaviors, 42,* 114–118.

Napper, L. E., Hummer, J. F., Lac, A., & LaBrie, J. W. (2014). What are other parents saying? Perceived parental communication norms and the relationship between alcohol-specific parental communication and college student drinking. *Psychology of Addictive Behaviors, 28*(1), 31–41.

National Institute of Alcohol Abuse and Alcoholism. (2007). *What colleges need to know now: An update on college drinking research* (NIH Publication No. 07-5010). Bethesda, MD: National Institutes of Health.

Patock-Peckham, J. A., & Morgan-Lopez, A. A. (2006). College drinking behaviors: Mediational links between parenting styles, impulse control, and alcohol-related outcomes. *Psychology of Addictive Behaviors, 20*(2), 117–125.

Patock-Peckham, J. A., & Morgan-Lopez, A. A. (2007). College drinking behaviors: Mediational links between parenting styles, parental bonds, depression, and alcohol problems. *Psychology of Addictive Behaviors, 21*(3), 297–306.

Patock-Peckham, J. A., & Morgan-Lopez, A. A. (2009a, March). Mediational links among parenting Styles, Perceptions of Parental Confidence, Self-Esteem, and Depression on Alcohol-Related Problems in Emerging Adulthood. *Journal of Studies on Alcohol and Drugs, 70*(2), 215–226.

Patock-Peckham, J. A., & Morgan-Lopez, A. A. (2009b, March). The gender specific mediational pathways between parenting styles, neuroticism, pathological reasons for drinking, and alcohol-related problems in emerging adulthood. *Addictive Behaviors, 34,* 312–315.

Sher, K. J., & Rutledge, P. C. (2007). Heavy drinking across the transition to college: Predicting first-semester heavy drinking from precollege variables. *Addictive Behavior, 32,* 819–835.

Testa, M., Hoffman, J. H., Livingston, J. A., & Turrisi, R. (2010). Preventing college women's sexual victimization through parent based intervention: A randomized controlled trial. *Prevention Science, 11*(3), 308–318.

Timberlake, D. S., Hopfer, S. H. R., Rhee, S. H., Friedman, N. P., Haberstick, B. C., Lessem, J. M., & Hewitt, J. K. (2007). College attendance and its effects on drinking behaviors in a longitudinal study of adolescents. *Alcoholism: Clinical Experimental Research, 31,* 1020–1030.

Turrisi, R., Abar, C., Mallett, K. A., & Jaccard, J. (2010). An examination of the mediational effects of cognitive and attitudinal factors of a parent intervention to reduce college drinking. *Journal of Applied Social Psychology, 40*(10), 2500–2526.

Turrisi, R., Larimer, M. E., Mallett, K. A., Kilmer, J. R., Ray, A. E., Mastroleo, N. R., & Montoya, H. (2009). A randomized clinical trial evaluating a combined alcohol intervention for high-risk college students. *Journal of Studies on Alcohol and Drugs, 70,* 555–567.

Turrisi, R., Mallett, K. A., Cleveland, M., Varvil-Weld, L., Abar, C., Scaglione, N., & Hultgren, B. (2013). An evaluation of timing and dosage of a parent based intervention to minimize college students' alcohol consumption. *Journal of Studies on Alcohol and Drugs, 74*(1), 30–40.

Turrisi, R., & Ray, A. E. (2010). Sustained parenting and college drinking in first-year students. *Developmental Psychobiology, 52,* 286–294.

Turrisi, R., Taki, R., Dunnam, H., Jaccard, J., & Grimes, J. (2001). Examination of the short-term efficacy of a parent intervention to reduce college student drinking tendencies. *Psychology of Addictive Behavior, 15*(4), 366–372.

Varvil-Weld, L., Crowley, D. M., Turrisi, R., Greenberg, M. T., & Mallett, K. A. (2014). Hurting, helping, or neutral? The effects of parental permissiveness toward adolescent drinking on college student alcohol use and problems. *Prevention Science, 15*(5), 716–724.

Varvil-Weld, L., Mallett, K. A., Turrisi, R., & Abar, C. C. (2012). Using parental profiles to predict membership in a subset of college students experiencing excessive alcohol consequences: Findings from a longitudinal study. *Journal of Studies on Alcohol and Drugs, 73,* 434–443.

Varvil-Weld, L., Scaglione, N., Cleveland, M., Mallett, K., Turrisi, R., & Abar, C. (2014). Optimizing timing and dosage: Does parent type moderate the effects of variations of a parent-based intervention to reduce college student drinking? *Prevention Science, 15*(1), 94–102.

Varvil-Weld, L., Turrisi, R., Hospital, M. M., Mallett, K. A., & Bámaca-Colbert, M. Y. (2014). Maternal and peer influences on drinking among Latino college students. *Addictive Behaviors, 39,* 246–252.

Varvil-Weld, L., Turrisi, R., Scaglione, N., Mallett, K. A., & Ray, A. E. (2013). Parents' and students' reports of parenting: Which are more reliably associated with college student drinking? *Addictive Behaviors, 38,* 1699–1703.

Walls, T. A., Fairlie, A. M, & Wood, M. D. (2009). Parents do matter: A longitudinal two-part mixed model of early college alcohol participation and intensity. *Journal of Studies on Alcohol and Drugs, 70,* 908–918.

Wechsler, H., & Nelson, T. F. (2008). What we have learned from the Harvard School of Public Health

College Alcohol Study: Focusing attention on college student alcohol consumption and the environmental conditions that promote it. *Journal of Studies on Alcohol and Drugs, 69,* 481–490.

Wetherill, R. R., & Fromme, K. (2007). Perceived awareness and caring influences alcohol use by high school and college students. *Psychology of Addictive Behaviors, 21*(2), 147–154.

White, H. R., McMorris, B. J., Catalano, R. F., Fleming, C. B., Haggerty, K. P., & Abbott, R. D. (2006). Increases in alcohol and marijuana use during the transition out of high school into emerging adulthood: The effects of leaving home, going to college, and high school protective factors. *Journal of Studies on Alcohol and Drugs, 67,* 810–822.

Windle, M., & Zucker, R. A. (2010). Reducing underage and young adult drinking: How to address critical drinking problems during this developmental period. *Alcohol Research & Health, 33*(1), 29–44.

Wood, M. D., Read, J. P., Palfai, T., & Stevenson, J. (2001). Social influence processes and college student drinking: The mediational role of alcohol outcome expectancies. *Journal of Studies on Alcohol and Drugs, 62,* 32–43.

Zucker, R. A. (1994). Pathways to alcohol problems and alcoholism: A developmental account of the evidence for multiple alcoholisms and for contextual contributions to risk. In J. Howard, G. M. Boyd, & R. A. Zucker (Eds.). *The development of alcohol problems: Exploring the biopsychosocial matrix of risk* (pp. 255–289). Rockville, MD: US Department of Health and Human Services.

17

Personality Processes Related to the Development and Resolution of Alcohol Use Disorders

Kenneth J. Sher

Andrew Littlefield

Matthew Lee

There is a long history of theorizing about the relation between "alcoholism" (now subsumed under the formal DSM-5 diagnosis of alcohol use disorder [AUD]; American Psychiatric Association, 2013) and personality, in which personality is thought to play a pivotal role in the development of this disorder. Indeed, concepts such as "alcoholic personality" and "addictive personality" are common parlance despite the fact that decades of research reveals no unique constellation of traits that characterizes individuals prone to develop an AUD.

Although a global concept of "alcoholic" personality can be discarded, considerable evidence exists to demonstrate that specific personality traits are associated, to varying degrees, with both risk for AUD and the subsequent course of AUD among those who are affected. Rather than provide a simple listing of traits that have been correlated both cross-sectionally and prospectively with AUD and related indices of problematic alcohol involvement (e.g., frequency of heavy drinking), which have been covered in prior reviews (and also see the meta-analytic studies by Kotov, Gamez, Schmidt, and Watson [2010] and Malouff, Thorsteinsson, Rooke, and Schutte [2007]), in this chapter we focus on two major areas of contemporary research on the relation between personality and AUD.

The first of these is that personality traits are implicated in multiple pathways associated with the development and course of AUDs. Consequently, a comprehensive understanding of the personality–AUD relation provides a broad perspective on AUD etiology more generally. For example, although it has been well established from twin studies that AUDs show relatively high heritability, there are several lines of evidence suggesting the genetic diathesis for AUDs can be, in part, attributed to genetic influences on specific personality traits. First proposed by Cloninger (1987), strong evidence for the genetic correlation between personality and AUDs was first demonstrated by Slutske et al. (2002), who found that genetic variance in behavioral undercontrol (i.e., traits related to impulsiveness, novelty seeking, nonconformity, and aggressiveness; Sher, 1991) accounted for approximately 40% of the genetic variation in alcohol dependence. In contrast, genetic variation in negative emotionality only accounted for a modest (although significant) 4% of genetic variation in alcohol dependence in men and failed to account for a significant portion of alcohol dependence in women. These findings suggest that genetic-based explanations of AUD etiology are likely to overlap with personality-based explanations and, furthermore, personality can provide a foundation for understanding the frequently observed observation of comorbidity among AUDs and other externalizing conditions sharing common personality features (Kendler, Prescott, Myers, & Neale, 2003; Krueger, Markon, Patrick, & Iacono, 2005).

However, even if we know that (1) personality and AUD and related disorders are correlated phenomena, (2) a significant proportion of this overlap can be attributed to additive genetic influences, and (3) these findings provide insight into the phenotypic manifestation of risk, this level of understanding fails to illuminate the *specific* mechanisms linking personality to AUD. At a general level, there are a number of distinct ways that personality traits and psychological disorders can be related (Durbin & Hicks, 2014). For example, we can think of personality as serving as a predisposition to developing a disorder, as a modulator of the expression of disorder, as a part of the same underlying spectrum giving rise to the disorder, or as a consequence (either acute or chronic) of an episode of disorder. Notably, these various descriptions are not exhaustive nor mutually exclusive. For instance, someone who is higher in impulsigenic traits (i.e., "traits that are manifested in impulsive behavior"; Sharma, Kohl, Morgan, & Clark, 2013) in early adolescence may be more prone to engage in early and problematic drinking, which in turn may further enhance levels of impulsigenic traits across development. Furthermore, not all of these possible models of personality and problem drinking have been tested empirically. Regardless, these varied possibilities highlight the fact that simply noting an association between two constructs tells us little about their functional relation.

The second major area of contemporary research regarding the personality–alcohol relation moves beyond conceptualizing personality as a static, relatively inflexible "trait" (e.g., that may be cross-sectionally related to AUD or prospectively predict the subsequent likelihood of an AUD). This burgeoning area of research explicitly recognizes that personality traits should be viewed as dynamic constructs that change as a function of human development and in response to changing life circumstances. If one is to understand factors such as "maturing out" or "recovery" (either natural recovery or treatment-related recovery), it is important to understand the dynamic interplay of personality and pathological alcohol involvement over time.

It is worth highlighting that interest in the relation between personality and psychopathology more generally has increased sharply in recent years. Although personality theory was intimately linked to psychopathology by psychologists (and others) in the first half of the 20th century, as evidenced by intense interest

in both projective and objective personality testing as part of clinical assessment, the behavioral revolution in clinical psychology tended to discount explanations rooted in personality theory. To the behaviorists of the mid-20th century, personality-based explanations were viewed as problematic on two fronts. First, influential scholars described generally low correlations between personality traits and a range of outcomes (Mischel, 1968), suggesting that these were not useful constructs for understanding behavior (but for an opposing view, see Epstein, 1979). Second, behaviorally oriented clinicians argued that intervening variables such as personality traits are largely irrelevant to assessing and treating individuals with mental disorders of all kinds, whereas direct assessment of behaviors of interest and their antecedents and consequences is a more fruitful approach to inform the implementation of appropriately targeted treatments and to assess clinical progress (Goldfried & Kent, 1972).

For a number of reasons, there has been a resurgence of interest in personality in recent years, with leading theorists proposing that not only is personality relevant for understanding psychopathology in general but also such understanding should be a top priority for contemporary research in psychopathology. For example, Kotov et al. (2010) noted in their meta-analysis that "it is clear from the present results that no model of anxiety, depressive, or substance use disorders will be complete without some consideration of these [personality] traits" (p. 207). In his review of the physical and mental health consequences of neuroticism, Lahey (2009) noted, "Achieving a full understanding of the nature and origins of neuroticism, and the mechanisms through which neuroticism is linked to mental and physical disorders, should be a top priority for research" (p. 241). Focusing primarily on internalizing disorders, Barlow, Sauer-Zavala, Carl, Bullis, and Ellard (2014) argue for moving away from the symptom-specific characterization of mood and anxiety disorders toward focusing on "higher order temperamental factors that may be a more appropriate target for assessment and intervention than symptom-level manifestations of these traits" (p. 344). Recently, novel interventions for AUDs have been developed that are matched with specific personality traits associated with risk for AUDs such as "impulsivity," sensation seeking, anxiety sensitivity, and hopelessness, with these intervention approaches showing promising results (Conrod, Castellanos-Ryan, & Strang,

2010). In summary, interest in the personality–AUD relation extends to both psychopathologists and intervention researchers, and attention toward this topic appears to be increasing.

WHAT IS PERSONALITY?

Although there is no universally agreed upon definition of personality (Wrosch & Scheier, 2003), many definitions overlap to varying degrees. For example, Watson, Clark, and Harkness (1994) defined personality as "internal, organized, and characteristic of an individual over time and situations . . . [and having] motivational and adaptive significance" (p. 18). Similarly, Roberts, Caspi, and Moffitt (2001) defined personality as "individual differences in the tendency to behave, think, and feel in certain consistent ways" (p. 670). Although typically conceived as highly stable over time and situations, recent theorists have highlighted developmental changes in personality (Roberts, Wood, & Caspi, 2008) as well as within-person variation in the expression of personality traits across situations (Fleeson, 2004). For the purposes of this chapter, we conceptualize personality broadly as referring to coherent individual differences in thought, behavior, and affect that demonstrate both stability and variability across situations and time.

There are multiple frameworks for identifying, defining, and organizing personality traits. For example, "general factor models" attempt to inclusively define and measure the major dimensions of adult personality (Watson et al., 1994). These models typically include either three (Big Three) or five major dimensions (Big Five). Within Big Three models, the major traits typically refer to neuroticism/negative emotionality, impulsivity/disinhibition, and extraversion/sociability (Sher, Trull, Bartholow, & Vieth, 1999). As we have noted elsewhere (Littlefield & Sher, 2014), neuroticism/negative emotionality is a broad-band measure that includes facets such as anxiety, depression, emotionality, guilt, and stress reactivity. Extraversion/sociability includes liveliness, social closeness, and surgency. Impulsivity/disinhibition includes embracing risk, nontraditionalism, and impulsigenic traits. Within the AUD literature, traits related to "impulsivity" and disinhibition are sometimes referred to as "behavioral undercontrol" or poor "self-control" more generally. Big Five models typically refer to systems organized by traits such as

openness to experience (O) (paralleling "intellect" in Goldberg's [1990] model), conscientiousness (C), extraversion (E), agreeableness (A), and neuroticism (N) (Digman, 1990). Although extraversion and neuroticism correspond to the similarly named traits in most Big Three systems, agreeableness includes altruism, compliance, and modesty. Conscientiousness, broadly similar to (reverse-scored) impulsivity/disinhibition in Big Three systems, includes achievement striving, competence, and deliberation. The Big Three and Big Five models of personality can be integrated to some degree (Watson et al., 1994; Zuckerman, Kuhlman, Joireman, Teta, & Kraft, 1993) and appear to represent replicable structures of personality across diverse cultures (McCrae & Allik, 2002). These personality typologies provide utility to examinations of the relation between personality and AUDs as well as other substance use disorders (SUDs; Littlefield & Sher, 2014; Sher et al., 1999).

It is important to note that other approaches to personality measurement have also been theoretically and empirically linked with AUDs (e.g., private self-consciousness; Hull, 1987). In addition, traits reflecting different aspects of "impulsivity" (Cyders & Smith, 2008; Whiteside & Lynam, 2001) appear to be distributed across Big Five factors (Whiteside & Lynam, 2001) and are differentially correlated with AUDs and associated problems (for an alternative conceptualization of distinct impulsive traits, see Sharma, Markon, & Clark, 2014). That is, some common, broad terms for important traits (e.g., impulsivity) obscure important heterogeneity among more nuanced personality facets (e.g., sensation seeking and lack of planning), and this heterogeneity does not simply reflect subfactors of a single higher order factor (Sharma et al., 2014; Whiteside & Lynam, 2001). Unfortunately, a consequence of this is that much of the earlier existing research literature blurs many potential distinctions that more recent research indicates are important. Despite this limitation, which is inevitable in a cumulative area of science, we can still learn much from the existing literature.

IS PERSONALITY RELATED TO ALCOHOL USE DISORDERS?

As noted previously, the answer to this simple question is a simple "yes." In a previous review (Littlefield & Sher, 2014), various aspects of alcohol use and its consequences were related to each of the Big Three and Big Five personality factors just described. However, it appears that the factors most associated with alcohol involvement in the literature are conscientiousness (low), agreeableness (low), and neuroticism (high) (Malouff et al., 2007)—a pattern of findings that is consistent across a range of both internalizing- and externalizing-disorder outcomes (Kotov et al., 2010; Trull & Sher, 1994).

Currently, there is little debate that personality traits are associated contemporaneously with manifest "alcoholism" and premorbidly with future "alcoholism." Indeed, in two influential and comprehensive literature reviews performed more than 30 years ago, Gordon Barnes (1979, 1983) reviewed evidence suggesting a strong association between personality and AUD and made the important distinction between "clinical alcoholic" traits and "prealcoholic" traits. These traits shared overlapping characteristics, such that both are associated with externalizing traits such as low socialization and "impulsivity." However, these traits were also somewhat distinct, such that clinical alcoholism more strongly associated with negative affectivity compared to prealcoholism. In rereading Barnes' reviews in the present day, one cannot help but be impressed with the scope of his narrative research synthesis. His work not only highlighted the objective personality test approach that is commonly employed today but also drew from approaches that are rarely considered in modern-day research (at least in many research areas), including projective assessment (e.g., Rorschach and Thematic Apperception Test) and so-called "perceptual" assessment approaches (e.g., Field Dependency and Stimulus Intensity Modulation). At the time of Barnes' writing, there were limited prospective or follow-back studies but sufficient data to allow him to distinguish prealcoholic and clinical alcoholic traits.

This distinction is prophetic, in a sense, in that it presaged current-day interest in the question of the mutability of personality and how personality changes over the course of an AUD and development more generally. Later reviewers (Malouff et al., 2007; Sher et al., 1999) arrived at similar conclusions to those of Barnes, but they did so with the benefit of a much stronger evidence base supported by a myriad of prospective studies, conducted subsequent to Barnes' reviews, that utilized more consistent measurements of key constructs. Perhaps most critically, later research did not only address the issue of whether

there was a general association and "*What* specific traits?" are most strongly associated with AUDs but also attempted to address the question of "*How* might these personality traits be related to personality?"

IN WHAT WAYS IS PERSONALITY RELATED TO ALCOHOL USE DISORDERS?

Personality appears to be associated with the development of AUDs in multiple ways. For the purposes of this review, we focus on four major, conceptually distinct yet overlapping classes of mechanisms: (1) deviance proneness, (2) pharmacological vulnerability to the reinforcing and disinhibiting effects of ethanol, (3) affect regulation, and (4) selection of high-risk drinking exposures.

Deviance Proneness

Rather than indicating that problematic alcohol use is the result of psychological or psychobiological risk factors, the deviance proneness model (Sher et al., 1999) presupposes that substance use represents a facet of a broad pattern of deviant behaviors that are thought to emerge in childhood as a result of deficient socialization and genetic vulnerability. In this framework, these deficits are not specific to substance use but also are associated with a number of other problematic outcomes, including association with deviant peers, childhood achievement problems, and delinquent behaviors. That is, the deviance proneness model posits that problematic alcohol use is one of several characteristics that are reflective of general deviance. Providing empirical support for this perspective, Cooper, Wood, Orcutt, and Albino (2003) demonstrated that the relations among educational underachievement, delinquent behavior, substance use, and sexual behavior could be adequately modeled as a single higher order factor and that avoidance coping and "impulsivity" were risk factors for engaging in these behaviors. Factor analytic models also suggest that alcohol dependence, reverse-scored constraint (a construct sometimes operationalized to assess "impulsivity"), drug dependence, conduct disorder, and antisocial behavior appear to be well represented by an "externalizing" factor (i.e., latent variable), providing evidence that both personality and substance use should be viewed along the same externalizing continuum (Krueger et al., 2005).

Rather than highlighting deficient socialization processes per se, these models suggest that the overlap between alcohol dependence, constraint, and other externalizing behaviors is due largely to genetic factors (as alluded to previously) and, to a lesser extent, environmental influences (Krueger et al., 2005).

There are a number of alternative, although not incompatible, theories regarding the role of personality in the deviance proneness model. For example, long-term socialization processes, such as those created through parents and community institutions (e.g., schools), are thought to be influenced by personality (Sher et al., 1999). Contrastingly, other theories hypothesize that "risky" personality characteristics act proximally to influence problematic substance use through impulsive decision-making styles. Thus, under the deviance proneness model, personality could influence substance use both distally (e.g., through peer group norms) and proximally (e.g., "risky" decision-making).

Personality and Vulnerability to the Pharmacological Effects of Ethanol

Broadly, the pharmacological vulnerability model (Sher, 1991) suggests that individuals have differential responses to the acute and/or chronic effects of alcohol. That is, there are significant individual differences regarding the extent to which individuals are sensitive to the reinforcing (both positive and negative) and punishing effects of alcohol, and these individual differences are related to personality characteristics (for more details, see Sher et al., 1999). William McDougall (1929), one of the preeminent psychologists in the first half of the 20th century, described this notion more than 85 years ago:

> I *have observed* [emphasis added] . . . that the markedly extroverted personality is very susceptible to the influence of alcohol. A very small dose deprives him of normal self-restraint and control and brings on the symptoms of intoxication, all of which are essentially expressions of diminished cortical control over the lower brain-levels. (p. 301)

The basic premise that personality was intimately linked to drug effects gave rise to a number of influential research programs by leading British psychologists. Specifically, work conducted by Eysenck (1963)

and Claridge (1970) focused on the behavioral correlates of personality (especially extraversion and neuroticism) with respect to the effects of both depressant and stimulant drugs sedation thresholds, learning, and performance on a number of behavioral measures. At that time, the concept of extraversion incorporated elements of both sociability (how we tend to think of extraversion today) and inhibition. Indeed, McDougall (1929) described the extravert as follows:

> The man who . . . does not suffer in the same degree the inhibition of all emotional expressions that characterizes the introvert. Every affect, every emotional-conative excitement, readily flows out from the subcortical levels into outward expression, instead of being largely drained off to and absorbed into the cortex. His emotional stirrings find immediate expression in action, save only on the occasions when some real difficulty or problem compels him to stop to think, or when he makes a voluntary effort to deliberate before action. (p. 300)

In ensuing years, the general premise that those who are initially low in self-control are likely to show more florid disinhibition after alcohol consumption appears to have become widely accepted. In enumerating his well-known criteria for diagnosing psychopathy, Cleckley (1941) noted that psychopathic personalities exhibited "fantastic and uninviting behavior after drink . . . and sometimes without" (p. 184).

These general observations from theorists and clinicians such as McDougall and Cleckley regarding personality-based individual differences in alcohol effects have garnered empirical support in controlled laboratory research. For example, laboratory studies examining individual differences in the stress-dampening effects of alcohol (Levenson, Oyama, & Meek, 1987; Sher & Levenson, 1982) found that individuals characterized by aggressive, antisocial, impulsive, and outgoing characteristics had pronounced stress-response-dampening effects from alcohol, suggesting that these individuals may find alcohol consumption to be especially reinforcing. Similarly, individuals high in anxiety sensitivity, a "cognitive, individual difference variable characterized by a fear of arousal-related bodily sensations such as dizziness, trembling, and racing heartbeat" (Stewart & Kushner, 2001, p. 775), also demonstrate marked anxiolytic effects from alcohol (Conrod, Pihl, & Vassileva, 1998; see also Stewart & Kushner, 2001).

Furthermore, diagnosis of AUDs is determined, in part, by the consequences that follow consumption. Traits ranging from empathy (Giancola, 2003) to those related to hostility (Giancola, 2002) and behavioral measures of self-regulation (Giancola, 2004) are associated with experimentally provoked alcohol-related aggression. Indeed, alcohol is generally associated with impaired inhibition, which can itself promote further drinking (Fillmore & Weafer, 2013). Such findings demonstrate that independent of the link between personality and the "reinforcing" or "punishing" effects of alcohol, personality also appears to influence the nature of drunken comportment and the acute consequences of alcohol intoxication. This suggests that part of the correlation between personality traits and AUD may reflect mere personality expression during periods of intoxication. Thus, disentangling the influences of alcohol use and personality traits on ostensible alcohol consequences that are key to diagnosing AUDs is not straightforward (Martin, Langenbucher, Chung, & Sher, 2014). For example, given Cleckley's (1941) observation that "fantastic and uninviting behavior" is sometimes exhibited "without drink" (p. 184), seemingly difficult or obnoxious intoxicated drinkers may display similar characteristics while sober. This potentiality dampens confidence in the extent to which current diagnostic criteria truly reflect "alcohol use disorder" as opposed to a personality disorder, which notably was the nosological location of alcoholism in pre-1980 versions of the DSM (American Psychiatric Association, 1968). Although this potentially artifactual contribution to the personality–AUD association cannot be ruled out, laboratory studies suggest that personality effects on individual differences in alcohol response are relevant to both etiological processes and consequences of drinking, thus providing strong evidence of a causal association.

Several limitations regarding personality as a moderator of the pharmacological effects of alcohol (at least regarding response to stress) must be noted. Not all laboratory-based findings have been consistent with this notion (Sher & Walitzer, 1986; see also Sher & Wood, 2005), and many of the studies in this area did not utilize more structured and empirically verified measures of personality (e.g., five-factor measures of personality; Costa & McCrae, 1992) or more nuanced measures of "impulsivity" (Cyders & Smith,

2008; Whiteside & Lynam, 2001). Thus, integrating these initial findings into more contemporary models of personality is somewhat difficult. Research using within-person, process-oriented methodology (e.g., daily-diary data) and five-factor measures of personality (e.g., NEO–PI–R; Costa & McCrae, 1992) has also produced inconsistent findings regarding personality as a moderator of the alcohol–stress relationship. For example, Armeli et al. (2003) hypothesized that the stress-response-dampening effects of alcohol should be stronger for participants high in extraversion, neuroticism, and self-consciousness. Although there was some support for hypotheses involving extraversion and self-consciousness, results were inconsistent across the five moods assessed in the study (i.e., sad, nervous, relaxed, happy, and angry). In summary, pharmacological vulnerability models of personality are conceptually important, although empirical support for these models appears to vary as a function of measurement and research paradigm.

Affect Regulation

There is little doubt that individuals use substances for various reasons, including the regulation of both positive and negative emotions. Based on the work of previous theorists (Cox & Klinger, 1990), Cooper (1994) developed and validated a four-factor model for drinking motivations. In this model, drinking motives are characterized as a function of two underlying dimensions reflecting the source (internal or external) and the valence (positive or negative) of the outcomes an individual seeks to attain by drinking. Crossing these two dimensions constructs four motivational classes: (1) intrinsic, positive reinforcement ("enhancement"); (2) extrinsic, positive reinforcement for social rewards ("social"); (3) intrinsic, negative reinforcement ("coping"); and (4) extrinsic, negative reinforcement to avoid social disapproval ("conformity").

Given that personality traits are thought to generally influence the motivation of behavior, they are also assumed to relate to specific alcohol-related motivations, particularly motives that are directly related to internal affect regulation (i.e., enhancement and coping). Accordingly, several theorists have presupposed that the distal influences of personality on substance use are mediated by more proximal alcohol-related motivations (Cooper, Frone, Russell, & Mudar, 1995; Cox & Klinger, 1990; see also Sher et al., 1999).

Indeed, based on the review of more than 80 scientific papers that focused on drinking motives of people aged 10–25 years, Kuntsche, Knibbe, Gmel, and Engels (2006) determined there was a robust positive relation between neuroticism and coping motives (i.e., drinking to alleviate negative emotional states). Furthermore, their review found that enhancement motives (i.e., drinking to enhance positive emotional state) have been primarily linked to extraversion, "impulsivity," low inhibitory control, and sensation seeking.

In addition, coping and enhancement motives exhibit robust relations with alcohol involvement and have been shown to mediate the influence of personality on alcohol outcomes (Cooper et al., 1995; see also Kuntsche, Knibbe, Gmel, & Engels, 2005; Kuntsche et al., 2006). As reviewed by Kuntsche et al., enhancement motives are linked to heavy drinking, whereas coping motives appear to be related to both heavy drinking and alcohol-related problems.

Despite these findings, several issues concerning the relation between personality and drinking motives must be highlighted. First, personality traits do not necessarily explain a substantial proportion of observed variance in drinking motives. For example, several studies show small to medium effect sizes for the relation between sensation seeking and enhancement motives (e.g., $r = .20$ [Cooper et al., 1995] and $r = .18$ [Comeau, Stewart, & Loba, 2001]). Second, the influence of personality on alcohol involvement often remains even when adjusting for drinking motives, indicating that other variables may serve as important mechanisms of the personality–alcohol involvement relation. Third, the specificity between personality traits and motives may be overstated to some degree. Although the review by Kuntsche et al. (2006) concluded that adolescents and young adults who drink for enhancement rather than coping motives tend to be "impulsive," "impulsivity" exhibited similar correlations with enhancement ($r = .19$) and coping ($r = .21$) motives in the study by Cooper, Agocha, and Sheldon (2000). Indeed, Cooper et al. posited that impulsivity may be linked with both enhancement and coping motives (a notion supported by developmental findings in Littlefield, Sher, & Wood [2010a] and discussed later), noting that individuals high in impulsivity may engage in risky behaviors associated with immediate rewards that can be positively or negatively reinforcing. Furthermore, "impulsivity" failed to be a significant predictor of enhancement motives

when simultaneously adjusting for neuroticism and extraversion, indicating the relation between "impulsivity" and enhancement motives is at least partially accounted for by other personality traits (Cooper et al., 2000; Kuntsche et al., 2006).

Other models also highlight the use of alcohol as a means to regulate affect. For example, the self-awareness model of alcohol use (Hull, 1987) posits that painful affective states are mediated by a state of self-awareness. Thus, alcohol is thought to reduce distress by disrupting psychological mechanisms that are foundational to self-awareness. High private self-consciousness (i.e., the corresponding trait of the state of self-awareness) is thought to enhance the relation between exposures to negative information about the self and negative affect. Thus, individuals high in private self-consciousness may be more likely to attempt amelioration of negative affect via the use of substances (e.g., alcohol) that interrupt processes that contribute to self-awareness. Indeed, Park, Sher, and Krull (2006) found that sorority members increased their drinking as private self-consciousness increased, suggesting that their experience of self-consciousness-related emotional distress may have prompted their heavy drinking as a coping strategy.

Personality and Environmental Selection

The notion that individuals tend to self-select into personality-compatible environments, typically referred to as *selection* process or niche seeking (Buss, 1987; see also Caspi & Bem, 1990; Scarr & McCartney, 1983), is evidenced in several areas of human behavior (e.g., peer relationships; Caspi, Roberts, & Shiner, 2005). Given that individuals are inclined to act on the basis of their existing characteristics, personality-influenced selection processes may be particularly likely during periods of transitions that involve a range of choices (Caspi & Bem, 1990).

In a prospective study of more than 3,000 undergraduates, Park, Sher, Krull, and Wood (2009) found that individuals high on "impulsivity"/novelty seeking, which relates to heavier alcohol consumption, appeared to select into Greek societies (i.e., college fraternities/sororities) because of the heavy drinking environment associated with these organizations. This is an important finding for understanding why fraternity and sorority members tend to drink heavily because it indicates that many of these individuals possessed characteristics related to heavy drinking and engaged in heavy drinking prior to Greek membership. Perhaps more intriguing, however, Park et al. also found that individuals high in extraversion selected into the Greek system despite not being particularly heavy drinkers prior to affiliation with a fraternity or sorority. Ostensibly, extraverted students may opt into the Greek system as a means to enhance positive emotions by meeting their higher affiliative and other social needs. In turn, Greek affiliation placed members at risk for heavy drinking, even after taking these selection processes into account. That is, the extravert might be attracted to Greek life for interests that could be viewed as prosocial and beneficial to the person (and society) but then get caught up in a heavy drinking culture. Given this heavy drinking culture is not only incidental to but also potentially inconsistent with the motivation for affiliation, this scenario arguably reflects a type of "social trap" (Platt, 1973). Thus, personality appears to contribute to AUDs through self-selection into risky environments that promote drinking through later socialization processes *even if drinking was not a primary motive for self-selection into a heavy drinking environment.* Importantly, this observation also sheds light on other empirical findings. For example, Grekin, Sher, and Wood (2006) found that alcohol dependence was associated with extraversion but not dependence on illicit drugs or tobacco in their college student sample. These findings may reflect, in part, the selection of extraverted students into an environment that differentially promoted alcohol use over other substance use.

Summary of Proposed Mechanisms Underlying the Relation Between Personality and Drinking (and Its Consequences)

The mechanisms relating personality to drinking and AUDs are diverse, including (1) individual differences in very basic psychopharmacological effects of ethanol, (2) propensity to seek out desired psychological states associated with both positive reinforcement (i.e., enhancement motives) and negative reinforcement (i.e., coping motives), (3) general deviance associated with deficient socialization and lower likelihood of social and cultural norms controlling use, and (4) selection of high-risk drinking environments (even if selection into these environments is based on non-drinking aspects of such environments). An important implication of the heterogeneity of mechanisms is that it provides multiple targets for both

preventing and treating alcohol excess and, more fundamentally, understanding why some individuals drink too much or are disproportionately influenced by a given amount of alcohol.

HOW PERSONALITY AND ALCOHOL USE DISORDERS CHANGE OVER THE LIFE COURSE

In examining the age–prevalence curve of AUDs and age-related trends in personality traits, it is striking how much parallel there is between the function relating age with AUD prevalence and the functions relating age and major personality traits (but especially neuroticism/negative affectivity and conscientiousness/impulsivity), at least from late adolescence through adulthood. The high prevalence of AUD during late adolescence and emerging adulthood has been noted for many years and has even led us to label AUD as largely "a developmental disorder of young adulthood" (Sher & Gotham, 1999, p. 933).

Figure 17.1 shows the age–prevalence curve of AUD from the National Epidemiologic Survey on Alcohol and Related Conditions (NESARC; Grant, Kaplan, & Stinson, 2005), a large epidemiological study of AUDs, SUDs, and other psychological disorders in the general population of the United States. These cross-sectional data portray an exceptionally high prevalence at approximately ages 18–25 years that then drops off precipitously during the latter part of the third decade of life and steadily declines thereafter. Of course, such cross-sectional data must be interpreted with caution, given that differential mortality of those suffering from AUDs and secular changes in the prevalence of AUD could conspire to artifactually contribute to the appearance of developmental changes in prevalence. However, it is unlikely that these other factors could plausibly explain the magnitude of the dramatic changes evident in the third decade of life, given the somewhat limited extent of overall mortality and secular variation.

This decline in prevalence of alcohol use and associated problems as individuals grow older following the peak prevalence of AUDs in the early 20s is referred to as "maturing out" of problematic alcohol involvement (Winick, 1962; for a review, see Littlefield & Winograd, 2013). Much of this decline in prevalence of excessive alcohol use and AUDs is thought to be associated with the assumption of adult

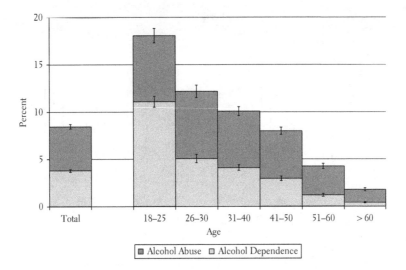

FIGURE 17.1 Prevalence of past-year alcohol use disorders within different age ranges of the US nationally representative NESARC sample (N = 43,093; Grant et al., 2005).

roles (Jessor, Donovan, & Costa, 1991; Yamaguchi & Kandel, 1985; see also O'Malley, 2004/2005), a hypothesis that has garnered considerable empirical support (Bachman et al., 2002; Gotham, Sher, & Wood, 2003; Lee, Chassin, & MacKinnon, 2015; Leonard & Rothbard, 1999).

Calling into question, at least to some extent, this notion of widespread maturing out due to assumption of adult roles in the third decade of life, our analyses on the age–prevalence of alcohol dependence (Vergés et al., 2012) suggest that rates of desistance are relatively stable throughout adulthood (although slightly higher during the third decade of life than at later ages; Figure 17.2, top). Furthermore, these results suggest that much of the dramatic reduction in prevalence of alcohol dependence with age is attributable to large age-graded decreases in rates of both new onsets and recurrences (Figure 17.2, middle and bottom). From the perspective of this type of analysis, maturing out is a lifelong process, not one limited to early adulthood. Furthermore, in addition to desistance, developmental decreases in risk for problem drinking onset and escalation are a key, yet often overlooked, aspect of this phenomenon. This does not undermine the importance of the phenomenon itself. However, it does suggest that similar developmental processes may be related to desistance over the entire life course.

Relative to drinking-related age–prevalence curves, the phenomenon of age-graded changes in personality has been more slowly recognized.

Traditionally, personality traits have been perceived as stable internal dispositions (McCrae et al., 2000; but see Costa & McCrae, 2006). However, several studies have documented systematic patterns of marked mean-level change in specific personality traits, especially during emerging and young adulthood (Caspi et al., 2005; McCrae et al., 1999; Roberts, Walton, & Viechtbauer, 2006). As shown in Roberts et al.'s meta-analysis of prospective studies of personality, the overall levels of change are fairly dramatic and, normatively, in the direction of increasing psychological maturity across the lifespan (e.g., increased self-control and decreased neuroticism). Figure 17.3 shows some of Roberts et al.'s major findings, illustrating both the life course pattern of change and how it seems to be more pronounced during the same life stage in which the prevalence of AUD is dramatically decreasing.

The *maturity principle* (Caspi et al., 2005) refers to the normative trend toward personality configurations that reflect greater agreeableness, emotional stability (i.e., lower neuroticism), self-control, and risk avoidance (i.e., lower impulsivity/behavioral undercontrol) as people reach adulthood. In line with the *social investment hypothesis* (Roberts, Wood, & Smith, 2005), this trend has been empirically linked to adult role transitions such as marriage and parenthood as well as to positive aspects of such roles (e.g., role-related satisfaction and emotional security; see Roberts & Mroczek, 2008). That is, events and life

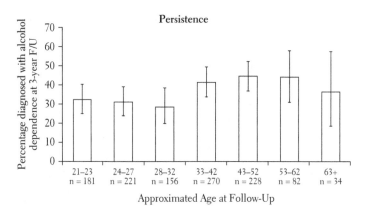

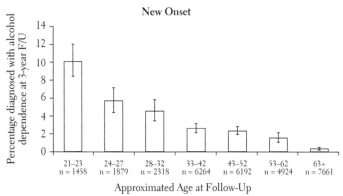

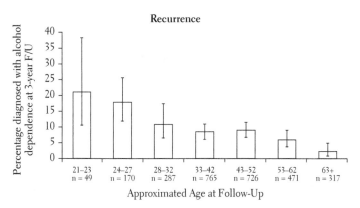

FIGURE 17.2 Alcohol dependence persistence (i.e., non-desistance; top), new onset (middle), and recurrence (bottom) as three distinct contributors to overall age-related reductions in the prevalence of alcohol dependence. Rates of persistence, new onset, and recurrence during a 3-year period are depicted within different age groups of the US nationally representative NESARC sample (N = 43,093; Grant et al., 2005). Persistence rate was defines as the percentage of participants with a past-year alcohol dependence diagnosis at the baseline wave who also had a past-year alcohol dependence diagnosis at the 3-year follow-up (F/U) wave. New-onset rate was defines as the percentage of participant with no lifetime history of alcohol dependence at baseline who had a diagnosis of past-year alcohol dependence at the 3-year follow-up wave. Recurrence rate was defines as the percentage of participants with lifetime but not past-year alcohol dependence at the baseline wave who had a diagnosis of past-year alcohol dependence by the 3-year follow-up wave. Brackets represent 95% confidence intervals around means.

Source: Vergés, A., Jackson, K. M., Bucholz, K. K., Grant, J. D., Trull, T. J., Wood, P. K., & Sher, K. J. (2012). Deconstructing the age–prevalence curve of alcohol dependence: Why "maturing out" is only a small piece of the puzzle. *Journal of Abnormal Psychology, 121*(2), 511–523. Reprinted with permission from the American Psychological Association.

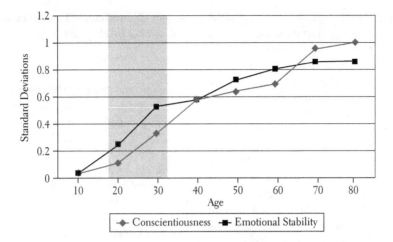

FIGURE 17.3 Results from Roberts et al.'s (2006) meta-analysis characterizing developmental changes in personality across the lifespan. The shaded area highlights that personality maturation appears most pronounced in the 20s and 30s, the period during which reductions in AUD prevalence are also particularly dramatic.

Source: Adapted from Roberts, B. W., Walton, K. E., & Viechtbauer, W. (2006). Patterns of mean-level change in personality traits across the life course: A meta-analysis of longitudinal studies. *Psychological Bulletin, 132,* 1–25, with permission from the American Psychological Association.

circumstances associated with maturing out of problematic alcohol involvement are highly overlapping with those associated with increases in psychological maturity, suggesting a possible relation between personality change and changes in alcohol consumption. Research has only recently begun to consider personality–maturation in the context of the normative drinking-related reductions that are typically attributed to adult role transitions.

Correlated Change in Personality and Drinking

Recently, changes in personality were linked to changes in alcohol problems across late adolescence into early adulthood (i.e., ages 18–35 years). Individuals who demonstrated steeper increases in conscientiousness and steeper decreases in neuroticism and "impulsivity" (using an impulsivity measure generally reflecting "lack of planning"; Littlefield, Sher, & Wood, 2010b) across these age periods also tended to display sharper decreases in alcohol problems (Littlefield, Sher, & Wood, 2009, 2010b). Other related work has addressed recent measurement advances noted previously indicating a multidimensional structure of impulsivity (Cyders & Smith, 2008). This work suggests that across adolescence and young adulthood, developmental reductions in sensation seeking relate more closely to decreases

in drinking quantity, whereas developmental reductions in lack of perseverance relate more closely to decreases in drinking consequences (Thompson, Roemer, & Leadbeater, 2015).

Individual differences in developmental changes in drinking motives appear to be an important mechanism through which changes in both impulsivity and neuroticism influence changes in alcohol problems. Littlefield, Sher, and Wood (2010a) provided evidence that changes in neuroticism and impulsivity appear to influence changes in coping motives, such that individuals who decreased in these respective personality constructs also tended to show more pronounced decreases in coping motives. In turn, steeper decreases in coping motives related to sharper decreases in alcohol problems. These findings suggest that changes in coping motives largely mediate the relation between changes in personality and alcohol problems and that these constructs should be integrated within the same developmental framework.

Despite normative trends, some individuals do not undergo presumably adaptive changes in personality (Johnson, Hicks, McGue, & Iacono, 2007) or alcohol involvement. Thus, some studies have characterized subgroups displaying different developmental trajectories of change. Littlefield, Sher, and Steinley (2010) demonstrated that distinct impulsivity trajectory groups demonstrated differential changes in alcohol involvement, especially from ages 18 to 25 years (using the same sample and across the same time span as used by Littlefield et al. [2009], again utilizing an "impulsivity" measure generally reflecting lack of planning). That is, individuals in a trajectory group characterized by substantial decreases in impulsivity from ages 18 to 25 years were more likely to exhibit significant decreases in several alcohol-related indices (including consumption and consequence measures) across this period compared to other trajectory groups. These findings indicate that individuals high and comparatively stable in impulsivity are at an increased risk for maintaining elevated levels of problematic alcohol involvement during emerging adulthood. In a different study focusing on heterogeneity of drinking trajectories rather than heterogeneity of personality trajectories, Ashenhurst, Harden, Corbin, and Fromme (2015) identified distinct binge-drinking trajectory groups spanning from late adolescence to emerging adulthood. They found that changes in sensation seeking and impulsivity (the latter largely reflecting a "lack of premeditation"; Ashenhurst et al., 2015) tended to parallel the drinking changes occurring within each binge-drinking trajectory group. The authors emphasized that their classification approach revealed a subgroup characterized by a late-college onset of binge drinking and a non-normative trajectory of impulsivity with continuing increases beyond college graduation.

Studies such as these investigating concurrent changes in personality and drinking over a given time span leave questions regarding directionality of effects. However, Littlefield et al. (2010) noted an aspect of their trajectory classification findings that provides a clue toward delineating the functional form of these relations and thereby providing a more refined picture of the dynamic relations between impulsivity and alcohol involvement. Specifically, their pattern of covariation among constructs showed that alcohol use and other drinking-related outcomes appeared to be trailing indicators (i.e., a consequence) of impulsivity development (as opposed to leading, apparent etiologic predictors of the developmental course of impulsivity; see Littlefield et al., 2010; Sher, Gotham, & Watson, 2004). However, they also noted that their data are still correlational in nature and thus that causal relations between impulsivity and alcohol cannot be completely determined.

Studies of Directional Effects Between Personality and Alcohol Involvement

Using the same sample as that described previously in Littlefield's work (e.g., Littlefield, 2009), Lee, Ellingson, and Sher (2015) estimated a cross-lag model characterizing prospective effects among personality and problem drinking spanning emerging adulthood to early midlife. Their results showed directional effects of impulsivity and conscientiousness on subsequent problem drinking, with these effects being specific to the later developmental period of their analysis that spanned from late young adulthood to early midlife (using a similar impulsivity measure as in Littlefield's work [e.g., 2009], again largely reflecting lack of planning). In contrast, regarding the opposite potential direction of effect, they found no evidence for effects of problem drinking on subsequent impulsivity or conscientiousness. For neuroticism and problem drinking, they concluded that despite confirming contemporaneous correlation as was shown by Littlefield et al. (2009, 2010b), neuroticism did not prospectively predict problem drinking nor vice versa.

Other studies have investigated directionality of effects between alcohol involvement and personality change in the earlier developmental period of adolescence, with results yielding mixed conclusions. Using latent difference score models (McArdle, 2009), Quinn, Stappenbeck, and Fromme (2011) concluded that heavy drinking during the sophomore year of college prospectively predicted change in sensation seeking and impulsivity between high school and senior year of college. Based on these findings, Quinn et al. concluded that their models provide evidence for a directional transactional relation (i.e., personality influences drinking, and drinking in turn influences change in personality) between heavy alcohol use and subsequent personality, suggesting that such transactional relations may underlie prior findings demonstrating correlated changes among these constructs (Littlefield et al., 2009). Further supporting the possibility of reciprocal, transactional effects, Hicks, Durbin, Blonigen, Iacono, and McGue (2012) found that behavioral disinhibition and negative emotionality at age 11 years predicted greater onset and chronicity of alcohol disorder during adolescence, which in turn predicted less maturation in behavioral disinhibition and negative emotionality from adolescence to emerging adulthood.

However, other studies of adolescents have shown only effects of early alcohol involvement on subsequent personality change rather than the transactional relationships. Chassin et al. (2010) found that from age 15 to age 21 years, higher alcohol use predicted a significant decline 6 months later in psychosocial maturity (a construct similar to the personality trait conscientiousness), although with a small effect size. In contrast, they did not find psychosocial maturity to significantly predict analogous changes in alcohol use. Similarly, Blonigen et al., (2015) found that age of alcohol use initiation predicted greater subsequent increases in negative emotionality and greater subsequent decreases in positive emotionality and behavioral constraint.

In contrast, using data from Littlefield et al. (2009), Littlefield, Vergés, Wood, and Sher (2012) found no evidence that heavy drinking or alcohol-related problems predicted subsequent changes in personality. Furthermore, analyses conducted in another large prospective sample focusing on changes in alcohol involvement and novelty seeking across the college years found no evidence for significant transactional pathways when parallel assessments were used. However, when a more proximal measure of heavy drinking was incorporated into the model, significant transactional pathways emerged. These findings are consistent with the extant literature that suggests proximal, but not necessarily distal, alcohol use influences subsequent changes in personality (Chassin et al., 2010; Quinn et al., 2011, footnote 2). When using parallel assessments across a longer time frame using a subsample of participants from these data, there was no evidence that heavy drinking significantly predicted change in personality, although personality at age 21 years appeared to predict changes in heavy drinking from age 21 to age 25 years. Despite a general lack of evidence of problematic alcohol involvement predicting personality change, there was consistent evidence of correlated changes between alcohol involvement and personality across the two samples (Littlefield et al., 2012). Notably, structural equation models cannot delineate among various causal and noncausal models (for a review, see Tomarken & Waller, 2003). Thus, other methodologies will need to be employed to make firmer conclusions regarding the functional relations between changes in alcohol involvement and personality (Littlefield & Alquist, 2014).

Regarding opposite effects of personality on drinking-related changes, the inconsistent evidence for these effects, as presented in the studies reviewed previously, may be partially clarified by recent evidence suggesting personality influences problem drinking only among certain individuals and/or during certain critical periods. Adams, Milich, Lynam, and Charnigo (2013) found that during the critical transition to the college environment, effects of pre-college negative urgency (i.e., negative emotion-based rash action; Cyders & Smith, 2008) on college drinking were strongest among moderate pre-college drinkers. Thus, contextual transitions may sometimes activate the expression of intrapersonal drinking-related liabilities such as impulsivity. A different type of moderation was shown by Ellingson, Fleming, Vergés, Bartholow, and Sher (2014), with prospective effects of impulsivity on college student alcohol use and consequences exacerbated among those with poorer working memory. The authors suggest that the working memory of impulsive individuals may be differentially devoted to reward-oriented information and that a scarcity of working memory resources may further limit consideration of other pertinent information.

In summary, despite consistent evidence of correlated developmental change between personality and problem drinking, evidence is mixed regarding the nature of transactional influences between them that may unfold over development. Future research may establish more firmly that this depends on a number of factors, including the developmental period and duration of effects (e.g., one vs. many years) under investigation.

Integrating Adult Role Transition Effects into Models of Developmental Personality Maturation and Drinking Reductions

As noted previously, adult role transitions (e.g., marriage and parenthood) represent another key empirically supported influence on developmental reductions in problem drinking. With regard to considering such role transitions in the context of the previously discussed work on age-related changes in personality and drinking problems, it is noteworthy that Littlefield et al.'s (2009, 2010b) demonstration of correlated change in personality and problem drinking was found after adjusting for influences of adult role statuses. This provides evidence that personality maturation and familial role transitions *uniquely* influence age-related drinking reductions. Beyond this, however, very little has been done to investigate how these two unique influences on drinking-related changes operate within the context of one another.

Lee, Ellingson, et al. (2015) characterized prospective and mediational effects among personality, role transitions, and problem drinking. Consistent with the notion of personality-based social selection (noted previously with regard to college student Greek affiliation), emerging adult personality maturity reflected by higher conscientiousness and lower impulsivity (again, with a measure largely reflecting lack of planning) was found to predict transitions into marriage or parenthood by young adulthood. In turn, these young adult familial role transitions were found to predict problem drinking reductions between young adulthood and early midlife, suggesting young adult familial role transitions mediated the relation between personality change and change in drinking problems.

In contrast, personality maturation was not found to mediate role transition effects on problem drinking reductions. The authors noted that much of the past work showing role effects on personality maturation has emphasized positive role characteristics (e.g., support and security) rather than role transitions per se, so focusing future work on such positive role characteristics may help reveal how adult role transitions can spur personality-mediated drinking reductions. For instance, Bogg, Finn, and Monsey (2012) found that greater college-student investment in the student role predicted greater subsequent self-control, with self-control in turn predicting reduced subsequent alcohol consumption. Indeed, in discussing their findings, the authors emphasized the importance of considering role qualities (e.g., investment) in addition to mere role occupancy (e.g., college student status) toward better understanding interrelations among social roles, personality change, and risky behaviors.

Summary of Personality Change and the Course of Alcohol Problems During Adulthood

As noted previously, characterization of the well-established phenomenon of maturing out and the mechanisms underlying it has progressed in recent years in two critical ways: (1) Maturing out may be viewed as more of a lifelong process and not one limited to emerging and early adulthood, and (2) desistance from problematic alcohol involvement during adulthood is associated with changes in

critical personality traits in addition to its association with adoption of adult roles. However, this work is still in its early stages. Still to be resolved are issues surrounding (1) the directions of effect among drinking, role adoption/loss, and personality; (2) how the structure of these relations changes over the course of development and the severity of the drinking problem; (3) the specificity of the processes to specific traits; and (4) generalization to other substances. Despite the extent of these unresolved issues, findings to date indicate that charting the dynamic interplay of drinking, social roles, and personality change is fundamental to understanding the developmental course of drinking problems and AUD in adulthood.

CONCLUSIONS AND FUTURE DIRECTIONS

Clearly, personality is associated with multiple pathways to excessive drinking, alcohol problems, and AUDs, including individual differences in the rewarding and disinhibiting effects of alcohol, the various reasons why people drink (and drink to excess), the likelihood of adopting a deviant lifestyle associated with non-normative alcohol use, and the likelihood of seeking out (and subsequently being influenced by) environments conducive to excessive alcohol use. Although the parameters of these pathways require additional specifications requiring further experimental and longitudinal research, a number of implications can be drawn from what is currently known.

Implications for Research

As discussed previously, prior research has noted a relatively strong genetic association between alcohol dependence and certain personality traits. This suggests that understanding genetic risk likely involves identifying genes related to the general liability to misuse alcohol (and other substances) associated with personality traits as well as genes that might be unrelated to personality variation but, perhaps, related to neuroadaptation or other effects of alcohol on the organism. This could be achieved by subtyping, as proposed by Cloninger (1987) and others, or, alternatively, by decomposing the broad phenotype into component parts that statistically control for the other components. For example, genes associated with withdrawal liability might be directly related to withdrawal conditional upon a given level of ethanol exposure. However, genes related to personality might also be related to withdrawal but only in an *indirect* way—that is, by goading levels of exposure necessary for withdrawal development. The genetic distinctiveness of different groups of alcohol dependence criteria (Kendler, Aggen, Prescott, Crabbe, & Neale, 2012) indicate that such an approach might be especially fruitful and serve to refine those aspects of the AUD phenotype that are part of the externalizing spectrum (Krueger et al., 2005) and those aspects that might be unique to AUD likely resulting from epigenetic changes in the alcoholic brain induced by chronic ethanol consumption (Wong, Mill, & Fernandes, 2011).

In addition, understanding the mechanisms of how high-risk drinking environments generate risk could be aided by more carefully analyzing personality × situation interactions on drinking. Clearly, some individuals are relatively immune to the pathogenic effects of some environments, such as collegiate Greek organizations on alcohol excess (Park et al., 2006) or aggressive provocation on the expression of hostility (Giancola, 2003). Understanding the critical personality × situation interactions not only helps to identify vulnerable populations but also helps to resolve the underlying mechanisms responsible for the effects of interest (Giancola, 2002).

Another important research implication is that if we want to understand personality risk, we need to track it developmentally. Traditionally, because of the assumption that personality was relatively immutable and unlikely to change, many longitudinal studies treated personality variables as fixed covariates and did not assess them repeatedly over time. Currently, research suggests a reconceptionalization of personality as having time-varying components, and to understand personality-based risk, we need to chart its course over time and consider both individual and normative developmental changes in updating risk profiles.

Implications for Clinical Practice

There are a number of intriguing implications of the personality–AUD association for interventions. The first and most obvious is the potential importance of targeting personality traits for modification, presumably along with more symptomatic approaches to reducing drinking and associated harms. Such a view is currently being promoted in the treatment of internalizing disorders in that targeting personality holds potential for more wide-ranging effects compared to traditional, disorder-focused treatments (Barlow et al., 2014). This approach also holds promise in the context of treatments for AUD and other substance-use problems. In addition to directly targeting personality change, it is possible to adopt treatment approaches to "work with" predominant personality traits in order to maximize more targeted coping skills related to drinking (Conrod et al., 2010). In addition, to the extent that treatment of any type is effective, tracking personality over time in individuals who are "recovering" could be evaluated to determine the extent to which symptom change without concomitant (or even delayed) personality change presages a poorer long-term outcome or relapse/recurrence relative to outcomes that show positive changes in both drinking and personality.

Environmental Design/Prevention

To the extent that part of the personality-based risk for excessive drinking and AUDs is based on environmental selection, one could conceive of constructing safer environments that meet personality-based motives (e.g., for "enhancement" or social engagement) that are largely incompatible with drinking. For example, extending the hours of operation of athletic facilities (for competitive sports, weight training, endurance sports, yoga practice, etc.) to compete with the hours of operation of bars and night clubs could be evaluated to determine if availability of venues to "see and be seen" and interact in a stimulating environment with potential intimate partners might lead to reduced bar or club hopping. That is, "wet environments" often are associated with a range of reinforcements; creating compelling "dry environments" (or making existing ones able to compete) could represent a strategy for creating settings that meet personality needs currently met by heavy drinking environments.

The previously discussed examples are meant to be illustrative of the wide-ranging implications for understanding the role of personality in AUDs and should not be taken as exhaustive or, necessarily, the most critical implications. If our knowledge in this area is to progress, we need to be more precise in our assessment of both personality traits and alcohol-related phenotypes, and we need to recognize that both are dynamic constructs that interact with both the imposed and the selected environment.

REFERENCES

Adams, Z. W., Milich, R., Lynam, D. R., & Charnigo, R. J. (2013). Interactive effects of drinking history and impulsivity on college drinking. *Addictive Behaviors*, 38(12), 2860–2867.

American Psychiatric Association. (1968). *Diagnostic and statistical manual of mental disorders* (2nd ed.). Washington, DC: Author.

American Psychiatric Association. (2013). *Diagnostic and statistical manual of mental disorders* (5th ed.). Arlington, VA: American Psychiatric Publishing.

Armeli, S., Tennen, H., Todd, M., Carney, M. A., Mohr, C., Affleck, G., & Hromi, A. (2003). A daily process examination of the stress-response dampening effects of alcohol consumption. *Psychology of Addictive Behaviors*, 17, 266–276.

Ashenhurst, J. R., Harden, K. P., Corbin, W. R., & Fromme, K. (2015). Trajectories of binge drinking and personality change across emerging adulthood. *Psychology of Addictive Behaviors*, 29(4), 978–991. Retrieved from http://doi.org/10.1037/adb0000116

Bachman, J. G., O'Malley, P. M., Schulenberg, J. E., Johnston, L. D., Bryant, A. L., & Merline, A. C. (2002). *The decline of substance use in young adulthood: Changes in social activities, roles, and beliefs.* Mahwah, NJ: Erlbaum.

Barlow, D. H., Sauer-Zavala, S., Carl, J. R., Bullis, J. R., & Ellard, K. K. (2014). The nature, diagnosis, and treatment of neuroticism back to the future. *Clinical Psychological Science*, 2(3), 344–365.

Barnes, G. E. (1979). The alcoholic personality: A reanalysis of the literature. *Journal of Studies on Alcohol*, 40, 571–633.

Barnes, G. E. (1983). Clinical and prealcoholic personality characteristics. In *The biology of alcoholism* (pp. 113–195). New York, NY: Springer.

Blonigen, D. M., Durbin, C. E., Hicks, B. M., Johnson, W., McGue, M., & Iacono, W. G. (2015). Alcohol use initiation is associated with changes in personality trait trajectories from early adolescence to young adulthood. *Alcoholism: Clinical and Experimental Research*, 39(11), 2163–2170. Retrieved from http://doi.org/10.1111/acer.12878

Bogg, T., Finn, P. R., & Monsey, K. E. (2012). A year in the college life: Evidence for the social investment hypothesis via trait self-control and alcohol consumption. *Journal of Research in Personality*, 46(6), 694–699. Retrieved from http://doi.org/10.1016/j.jrp.2012.08.004

Buss, D. M. (1987). Selection, evocation and manipulation. *Journal of Personality and Social Psychology*, 53, 1214–1221.

Caspi, A., & Bem, D. J. (1990). Personality continuity and change across the life course. In L. Pervin (Ed.), *Handbook of personality: Theory and research* (pp. 549–575). New York: Guilford.

Caspi, A., Roberts, B. W., & Shiner, R. L. (2005). Personality development: Stability and change. *Annual Review of Psychology*, 56, 453–484.

Chassin, L., Dmitrieva, J., Modecki, K., Steinberg, L., Cauffman, E., Piquero, A. R., & Losoya, S. H. (2010). Does adolescent alcohol and marijuana use predict suppressed growth in psychosocial maturity among male juvenile offenders? *Psychology of Addictive Behaviors*, 24, 48–60. doi:10.1037/a0017692

Claridge, G. (1970). *Drugs and human behavior.* London, UK: Praeger.

Cleckley, H. M. (1941). *The mask of sanity: An attempt to reinterpret the so-called psychopathic personality.* Oxford, UK: Mosby.

Cloninger, C. R. (1987). Neurogenetic adaptive mechanisms in alcoholism. *Science*, 236, 410–416.

Comeau, M. N., Stewart, S. H., & Loba, P. (2001). The relations of anxiety sensitivity, trait anxiety, and sensation seeking to adolescents' motivations for alcohol, cigarette, and marijuana use. *Addictive Behaviors*, 26, 803–825.

Conrod, P. J., Castellanos-Ryan, N., & Strang, J. (2010). Brief, personality-targeted coping skills interventions and survival as a non–drug user over a 2-year period during adolescence. *Archives of General Psychiatry*, 67(1), 85–93.

Conrod, P. J., Pihl, R. O., & Vassileva, J. (1998). Differential sensitivity to alcohol reinforcement in groups of men at risk for distinct alcoholism syndromes. *Alcoholism: Clinical and Experimental Research*, 22, 585–597.

Cooper, M. L. (1994). Motivations for alcohol use among adolescents: Development and validation of a four-factor model. *Psychological Assessments*, 6, 117–128.

Cooper, M. L., Agocha, V. B., & Sheldon, M. S. (2000). A motivational perspective on risky behaviors: The role of personality and affect regulatory processes. *Journal of Personality*, 68, 1059–1088.

Cooper, M. L., Frone, M. R., Russell, M., & Mudar, P. (1995). Drinking to regulate positive and negative emotions: A motivational model of alcohol use. *Journal of Personality and Social Psychology*, 69, 990–1005.

Cooper, M. L., Wood, P. K., Orcutt, H. K., & Albino, A. (2003). Personality and the predisposition to engage in risky or problem behaviors during adolescence. *Journal of Personality and Social Psychology*, 84, 390–410.

Costa, P. T., Jr., & McCrae, R. R. (1992). *The NEO Personality Inventory professional manual*. Odessa, FL: Psychological Assessment Resources.

Costa, P. T., Jr., & McCrae, R. R. (2006). Age changes in personality and their origins: Comment on Roberts, Walton, and Viechtbauer (2006). *Psychological Bulletin, 132*, 28–30.

Cox, W. M., & Klinger, E. (1990). Incentive motivation, affective change and alcohol use: A model. In *Why people drink: Parameters of alcohol as a reinforcer* (pp. 291–314). New York, NY: Gardner.

Cyders, M. A., & Smith, G. T. (2008). Emotion-based dispositions to rash action: Positive and negative urgency. *Psychological Bulletin, 134*(6), 807–828.

Digman, J. M. (1990). Personality structure: Emergence of the five-factor model. *Annual Review of Psychology, 41*(1), 417–440.

Durbin, C. E., & Hicks, B. M. (2014). Personality and psychopathology: A stagnant field in need of development. *European Journal of Personality, 28*(4), 362–386.

Ellingson, J. M., Fleming, K. A., Vergés, A., Bartholow, B. D., & Sher, K. J. (2014). Working memory as a moderator of impulsivity and alcohol involvement: Testing the cognitive–motivational theory of alcohol use with prospective and working memory updating data. *Addictive Behaviors, 39*(11), 1622–1631. Retrieved from http://doi.org/10.1016/j.addbeh.2014.01.004

Epstein, S. (1979). The stability of behavior: I. On predicting most of the people much of the time. *Journal of Personality and Social Psychology, 37*(7), 1097–1126.

Eysenck, H. J. (1963). *Experiments with drugs*. Oxford, UK: Macmillan.

Fillmore, M. T., & Weafer, J. (2013). Behavioral inhibition and alcohol. In J. MacKillop & H. de Wit (Eds.), *The Wiley–Blackwell handbook of addiction psychopharmacology* (pp. 135–164). West Sussex, UK: Wiley.

Fleeson, W. (2004). Moving personality beyond the person–situation debate: The challenge and the opportunity of within-person variability. *Current Directions in Psychological Science, 13*(2), 83–87.

Giancola, P. R. (2002). Alcohol-related aggression in men and women: The influence of dispositional aggressivity. *Journal of Studies on Alcohol, 63*, 696–708.

Giancola, P. R. (2003). The moderating effects of dispositional empathy on alcohol-related aggression in men and women. *Journal of Abnormal Psychology, 112*(2), 275–281.

Giancola, P. R. (2004). Executive functioning and alcohol-related aggression. *Journal of Abnormal Psychology, 113*(4), 541–555.

Goldberg, L. R. (1990). An alternative "description of personality": The big-5 factor structure. *Journal of Personality and Social Psychology, 59*, 1216–1229.

Goldfried, M. R., & Kent, R. N. (1972). Traditional versus behavioral personality assessment: A comparison of methodological and theoretical assumptions. *Psychological Bulletin, 77*(6), 409.

Gotham, H. J., Sher, K. J., & Wood, P. K. (2003). Alcohol involvement and developmental task completion during young adulthood. *Journal of Studies on Alcohol, 64*, 32–42.

Grant, B. F., Kaplan, K. K., & Stinson, F. S. (2005). Source and accuracy statement for *the Wave 2 National Epidemiologic Survey on Alcohol and Related Conditions*. Bethesda, MD: National Institute on Alcohol Abuse and Alcoholism.

Grekin, E. R., Sher, K. J., & Wood, P. K. (2006). Personality and substance dependence symptoms: Modeling substance-specific traits. *Psychology of Addictive Behavior, 20*, 415–424.

Hicks, B. M., Durbin, C. E., Blonigen, D. M., Iacono, W. G., & McGue, M. (2012). Relationship between personality change and the onset and course of alcohol dependence in young adulthood. *Addiction, 107*(3), 540–548.

Hull, J. G. (1987). Self-awareness model. In H. T. Blane & K. E. Leonard (Eds.), *Psychological theories of drinking and alcoholism* (pp. 272–301). New York, NY: Guilford.

Jessor, R., Donovan, J. E., & Costa, F. M. (1991). *Beyond adolescence: Problem behavior and young adult development*. New York, NY: Cambridge University Press.

Johnson, W., Hicks, B., McGue, M., & Iacono, W. G. (2007). Most of the girls are alright, but some aren't: Personality trajectory groups from ages 14 to 24 and some associations with outcomes. *Journal of Personality and Social Psychology, 93*, 266–284.

Kendler, K. S., Aggen, S. H., Prescott, C. A., Crabbe, J., & Neale, M. C. (2012). Evidence for multiple genetic factors underlying the DSM-IV criteria for alcohol dependence. *Molecular Psychiatry, 17*(12), 1306–1315.

Kendler, K. S., Prescott, C. A., Myers, J., & Neale, M. C. (2003). The structure of genetic and environmental risk factors for common psychiatric and substance use disorders in men and women. *Archives of General Psychiatry, 60*, 929–937.

Kotov, R., Gamez, W., Schmidt, F., & Watson, D. (2010). Linking "big" personality traits to anxiety, depressive, and substance use disorders: A meta-analysis. *Psychological Bulletin, 136*(5), 768.

Krueger, R. F., Markon, K. E., Patrick, C. J., & Iacono, W. G. (2005). Externalizing psychopathology in adulthood: A dimensional-spectrum conceptualization and its implications for DSM-V. *Journal of Abnormal Psychology, 114*, 537–550.

Kuntsche, E. N., Knibbe, R., Gmel, G., & Engels, R. (2005). Why do young people drink? A review of drinking motives. *Clinical Psychology Review, 25*, 841–861.

Kuntsche, E. N., Knibbe, R., Gmel, G., & Engels, R. (2006). Who drinks and why? A review of sociodemographic, personality, and contextual issues behind the drinking motives in young people. *Psychology of Addictive Behaviors, 31*, 1844–1857.

Lahey, B. (2009). Public health significance of neuroticism. *American Psychologist, 64*, 241–256.

Lee, M. R., Chassin, L., & MacKinnon, D. (2015). Role transitions and young adult maturing out of heavy drinking: Evidence for larger effects of marriage among more severe pre-marriage problem drinkers. *Alcoholism: Clinical and Experimental Research, 39*(6), 1064–1074. doi:10.1111/acer.12715

Lee, M. R., Ellingson, J. M., & Sher, K. J. (2015). Integrating social–contextual and intrapersonal mechanisms of "maturing out": Joint influences of familial role transitions and personality maturation on problem drinking reductions. *Alcoholism: Clinical and Experimental Research, 39*(9), 1775–1787.

Leonard, K. E., & Rothbard, J. C. (1999). Alcohol and the marriage effect. *Journal of Studies on Alcohol, 13*, 139–146.

Levenson, R. W., Oyama, O. N., & Meek, P. S. (1987). Greater reinforcement from alcohol for those at risk: Parental risk, personality risk, and sex. *Journal of Abnormal Psychology, 96*(3), 242–253.

Littlefield, A. K., & Alquist, J. L. (2014). Greater clarity with consilience: Testing causal models across methodological approaches. *European Journal of Personality, 28*, 394–395.

Littlefield, A. K., & Sher, K. J. (2016). Personality and substance use disorders. In K. J. Sher (Ed.), *Handbook of Substance Use and Substance Use Disorders* (Vol. 1, pp. 351–374). New York: Oxford University Press.

Littlefield, A. K., Sher, K. J., & Steinley, D. (2010). Developmental trajectories of impulsivity and their association with alcohol use and related outcomes during emerging and young adulthood I. *Alcoholism: Clinical and Experimental Research, 34*, 1409–1416.

Littlefield, A. K., Sher, K. J., & Wood, P. K. (2009). Is "maturing out" of problematic alcohol involvement related to personality change? *Journal of Abnormal Psychology, 118*, 360–374.

Littlefield, A. K., Sher, K. J., & Wood, P. K. (2010a). Do changes in drinking motives mediate the relation between personality change and "maturing out" of problem drinking? *Journal of Abnormal Psychology, 119*, 93–105.

Littlefield, A. K., Sher, K. J., & Wood, P. K. (2010b). A personality-based description of maturing out of alcohol problems: Extension with a five-factor model and robustness to modeling challenges. *Addictive Behaviors, 35*, 948–954.

Littlefield, A. K., Vergés, A., Wood, P. K., & Sher, K. J. (2012). Transactional models between personality and alcohol involvement: A further examination. *Journal of Abnormal Psychology, 121*(3), 778–783.

Littlefield, A., & Winograd, R. (2013). Maturing out. In *Principles of addiction: Comprehensive addictive behaviors and disorders* (pp. 363–370). San Diego, CA: Elsevier.

Malouff, J., Thorsteinsson, E., Rooke, S., & Schutte, N. (2007). Alcohol involvement and the five factor model of personality: A meta-analysis. *Journal of Drug Education, 37*, 277–294.

Martin, C. S., Langenbucher, J. W., Chung, T., & Sher, K. J. (2014). Truth or consequences in the diagnosis of substance use disorders. *Addiction, 109*(11), 1773–1778.

McArdle, J. J. (2009). Latent variable modeling of differences and changes with longitudinal data. *Annual Review of Psychology, 60*, 577–605. doi:10.1146/annurev.psych.60.110707.163612

McCrae, R. R., & Allik, J. (Eds.). (2002). *The five-factor model of personality across cultures.* New York, NY: Kluwer.

McCrae, R. R., Costa, P. T., Jr., Lima, M. P., Simoes, A., Ostendorf, F., Angleitner, A., . . . Piedmont, R. L. (1999). Age differences in personality across the adult life span: Parallels in five countries. *Developmental Psychology, 35*, 466–477.

McCrae, R. R., Costa, P. T., Jr., Ostendorf, F., Angleitner, A., Hrebickova, M., Avia, M. D., . . . Smith, P. B. (2000). Nature over nurture: Temperament, personality, and life span development. *Journal of Personality and Social Psychology, 78*, 173–186.

McDougall, W. (1929). The chemical theory of temperament applied to introversion and extroversion. *Journal of Abnormal and Social Psychology, 24*, 293–309.

Mischel, V. W. (1968). *Personality and assessment.* New York, NY: Wiley.

O'Malley, P. (2004/2005). Maturing out of problematic alcohol use. *Alcohol Research and Health, 28*, 202–204.

Park, A., Sher, K. J., & Krull, J. (2006). Individual differences in the Greek effect on risky drinking: The role of self-consciousness. *Psychology of Addictive Behaviors, 20*, 85–90.

Park, A., Sher, K. J., Krull, J. L., & Wood, P. K. (2009). Dual mechanisms underlying accentuation of risky drinking via fraternity/sorority affiliation: The role of personality, peer norms, and alcohol availability. *Journal of Abnormal Psychology*, 118, 241–245.

Platt, J. (1973). Social traps. *American Psychologist*, 28(8), 641–651.

Quinn, P. D., Stappenbeck, C. A., & Fromme, K. (2011). Collegiate heavy drinking prospectively predicts change in sensation seeking and impulsivity. *Journal of Abnormal Psychology*, 120, 543–556. doi:10.1037/a0023159

Roberts, B. W., Caspi, A., & Moffitt, T. E. (2001). The kids are alright: Growth and stability in personality development from adolescence to adulthood. *Journal of Personality and Social Psychology*, 81, 582–893.

Roberts, B. W., & Mroczek, D. K. (2008). Personality trait stability and change. *Current Directions in Psychological Science*, 17, 31–35.

Roberts, B. W., Walton, K. E., & Viechtbauer, W. (2006). Patterns of mean-level change in personality traits across the life course: A meta-analysis of longitudinal studies. *Psychological Bulletin*, 132, 1–25.

Roberts, B. W., Wood, D., & Caspi, A. (2008). The development of personality traits in adulthood. In O. P. John, R. W. Robins, & L. A. Pervin (Eds.), *Handbook of personality: Theory and research* (3rd ed., pp. 375–398). New York, NY: Guilford.

Roberts, B. W., Wood, D., & Smith, J. L. (2005). Evaluating five factor theory and social investment perspectives on personality trait development. *Journal of Research in Personality*, 39(1), 166–184.

Scarr, S., & McCartney, J. (1983). How people make their own environment: A theory of genotype greater than environmental effects. *Child Development*, 54, 424–435.

Sharma, L., Kohl, K., Morgan, T. A., & Clark, L. A. (2013). "Impulsivity": Relations between self-report and behavior. *Journal of Personality and Social Psychology*, 104(3), 559–575.

Sharma, L., Markon, K. E., & Clark, L. A. (2014). Toward a theory of distinct types of "impulsive" behaviors: A meta-analysis of self-report and behavioral measures. *Psychological Bulletin*, 140(2), 374–408.

Sher, K. J. (1991). *Children of alcoholics: A critical appraisal of theory and research*. A volume in the John D. and Catherine T. MacArthur Foundation Series on Mental Health and Development. Chicago, IL: University of Chicago Press.

Sher, K. J., & Gotham, H. J. (1999). Pathological alcohol involvement: A developmental disorder of young adulthood. *Development and Psychopathology*, 11(04), 933–956.

Sher, K. J., Gotham, H. J., & Watson, A. (2004). Trajectories of dynamic predictors of disorder: Their meanings and implications. *Development and Psychopathology*, 16, 825–856.

Sher, K. J., & Levenson, R. W. (1982). Risk for alcoholism and individual differences in the stress-response-dampening effect of alcohol. *Journal of Abnormal Psychology*, 91(5), 350–367.

Sher, K. J., Trull, T. J., Bartholow, B., & Vieth, A. (1999). Personality and alcoholism: Issues, methods, and etiological processes. In H. Blane & K. Leonard (Eds.), *Psychological theories of drinking and alcoholism* (2nd ed., pp. 55–105). New York, NY: Plenum.

Sher, K. J., & Walitzer, K. S. (1986). Individual differences in the stress-response-dampening effect of alcohol: A dose–response study. *Journal of Abnormal Psychology*, 95(2), 159–167.

Sher, K. J., & Wood, M. D. (2005). Subjective effects of alcohol II: Individual differences. In M. Earleywine (Ed.), *Mind altering drugs: Scientific evidence for subjective experience* (pp. 135–153). New York, NY: Oxford University Press.

Slutske, W. S., Heath, A. C., Madden, P. A. F., Bucholz, K. K., Statham, D. J., & Martin, N. G. (2002). Personality and the genetic risk for alcohol dependence. *Journal of Abnormal Psychology*, 111, 124–133.

Stewart, S. H., & Kushner, M. G. (2001). Introduction to the special issue on anxiety sensitivity and addictive behaviors. *Addictive Behaviors*, 26, 775–785.

Thompson, K., Roemer, A., & Leadbeater, B. (2015). Impulsive personality, parental monitoring, and alcohol outcomes from adolescence through young adulthood. *Journal of Adolescent Health*, 57(3), 320–326.

Tomarken, A. J., & Waller, N. G. (2003). Potential problems with "well fitting" models. *Journal of Abnormal Psychology*, 112, 578–598.

Trull, T. J., & Sher, K. J. (1994). Relationship between the five-factor model of personality and Axis I disorders in a nonclinical sample. *Journal of Abnormal Psychology*, 103, 350–360.

Vergés, A., Jackson, K. M., Bucholz, K. K., Grant, J. D., Trull, T. J., Wood, P. K., & Sher, K. J. (2012). Deconstructing the age–prevalence curve of alcohol dependence: Why "maturing out" is only a small piece of the puzzle. *Journal of Abnormal Psychology*, 121(2), 511–523.

Watson, D., Clark, L. A., & Harkness, A. R. (1994). Structures of personality and their relevance to psychopathology. *Journal of Abnormal Psychology*, 103, 18–31.

Whiteside, S. P., & Lynam, D. R. (2001). The five factor model and impulsivity: Using a structural model of personality to understand impulsivity. *Personality and Individual Differences, 30,* 669–689.

Winick, C. (1962). Maturing out of narcotic addiction. *Bulletin on Narcotics, 14,* 1–7.

Wong, C. C., Mill, J., & Fernandes, C. (2011). Drugs and addiction: An introduction to epigenetics. *Addiction, 106*(3), 480–489.

Wrosch, C., & Scheier, M. F. (2003). Personality and quality of life: The importance of optimism and goal adjustment. *Quality of Life Research, 12,* 59–72.

Yamaguchi, K., & Kandel, D. (1985). On the resolution of role incompatibility: Life event history analysis of family roles and marijuana use. *American Journal of Sociology, 90,* 1284–1325.

Zuckerman, M., Kuhlman, D. M., Joireman, J., Teta, P., & Kraft, M. (1993). A comparison of three structural models for personality: The Big Three, the Big Five, and the Alternative Five. *Journal of Personality and Social Psychology, 65,* 757–768.

PART V

ALCOHOL USE DISORDERS AND MARITAL RELATIONSHIPS

OVERVIEW

Keeping our developmental systems approach and continuing our exploration into developmental transitions, Part V focuses on the marital relationship and its impact on alcohol use disorders. Already explored in previous chapters are some of the multifactorial and bidirectional influences of alcohol consumption and alcohol-related problems during transitions from infancy to college age. For example, according to Sacks, Murphey, and Moore (2014), 28% of 15- to 17-year-olds in the United States experience parental separation or divorce, 12% experience family mental illness, and 10% witness domestic violence—all childhood adverse experiences that predict poor developmental outcomes, including those that relate to intimate relationships. The development of intimate relationships, often leading to marriage (or a civil well-established relationship), and the early years of that relationship represent a potentially critical period for studying risk for excessive drinking and alcohol use disorders. Significant changes in social relationships occur during this important time frame as new influences impact individuals and the couple and other influences are reshaped. In addition, the impact of alcohol use on later marital dissolution is an important area to understand.

In Chapter 18, Levitt and Leonard focus on alcohol use and problems that occur during the transition to and throughout the early years of marriage and also the impact of the marital partner and the broader social environment on the development of alcohol use disorders. The "marriage effect," the finding that married individuals are less likely to have alcohol problems than single or divorced individual, is first explored in the chapter. Drawing primarily from

results of longitudinal studies on newlywed couples, the authors then describe how relationship factors impact alcohol use and alcohol problems and subsequently how drinking in the relationship impacts the relationship. Throughout this discussion, mediation and moderating variables are identified, along with bidirectional effects. A heuristic model of alcohol use and marital development during emerging adulthood is laid out with research supporting and providing evidence for each aspect of the model. Finally, the authors provide future directions, including the need for more research on longer term couples, a greater focus on cultural diversity, research exploring transitions during the relationship such as the birth of a child, and research on the drinking motives of the individuals. Included are suggestions about how research findings can be applied to prevention and intervention efforts.

In Chapter 19, Cranford and Fairbarn continue the focus on dyads and the marital relationship, examining more closely marital dissolution as a result of alcohol involvement. They describe an emerging theoretical framework for research on substance use and marriage based on social psychology, relationship science, and developmental science that (1) includes both spouses and focuses on the dyad as the unit of analysis to explicitly test for husband and wife differences and dyadic patterns of alcohol involvement and (2) assesses core constructs across multiple timescales, with a focus on daily processes as potential linkages between real-time marital interactions and outcomes that unfold over longer timescales. Their framework strengthens connections between social psychological and developmental theory, informing basic research on alcohol and social interaction processes, which it is hoped will enhance prevention and treatment efforts by identifying the mechanisms underlying the associations between alcohol involvement and negative marital outcomes. These authors also provide future directions for research, suggesting the importance of examining the reinforcement properties of alcohol within the marital relationship, as well as the need to examine genetic influences on the covariation between alcohol use and problems and also the frequency of romantic conflict and warmth, on which some initial work is currently being done. Finally, simultaneous monitoring of brain functioning of the couple while interacting is also suggested as a future area of exploration.

REFERENCE

Sacks, V. H., Murphey, D., & Moore, K. (2014). *Adverse childhood experiences: National and state level prevalence*. Washington, DC: Child Trends.

18

Developmental Transitions and Emergent Causative Influences

Intimacy, Influence, and Alcohol Problems During the Early Years of Marriage

Ash Levitt

Kenneth E. Leonard

In the late 1960s and throughout the 1970s, researchers concerned with the behavioral characteristics of alcoholism began to challenge the simple disease model of alcoholism. Some of the earliest challenges focused on whether alcoholics could return to moderate drinking and whether that could be maintained (Davies, 1962; Fox, 1967). Others challenged whether the development of alcohol problems was uniform or progressive (Clark & Cahalan, 1976). Perhaps the most critical challenges involved the presumed physiological primacy of alcoholism, with demonstrations that the "loss of control" that occurred among alcoholics after one or two drinks also occurred when they received a placebo with no alcoholic content (Marlatt, Deming, & Reid, 1973).

As the simple physiological primacy models of alcoholism were challenged, models that emphasized person–environment interactions and highlighted the importance of developmental changes were proposed (Jessor & Jessor, 1977). Within this evolving perspective, Zucker (1979) developed a heuristic model that identified the key sources of influence on the development of alcoholism, how these sources were interrelated, and how they changed over time. Specifically, this model described four general sources of influences: sociocultural/community, family, peer, and intraindividual. *Sociocultural/community influences* encompassed the impact of neighborhood factors

(e.g., community norms with respect to drinking and neighborhood stress or disorganization) as well as social geographic factors (e.g., alcohol outlets and availability of alternative activities). Other sociocultural/community influences would include religious and cultural factors as well as socioeconomic status and poverty of the community. *Family influences* focused primarily on factors within the family of origin and included both alcohol-specific factors, such as parents' drinking patterns and attitudes about alcohol, and nonspecific factors, such as parenting practices, sibling behaviors, and the behavior of other family members. *Peer influences* focused on peers' drinking patterns and attitudes about alcohol as well as interpersonal processes that might occur, such as peer pressure. The final general source was *intraindividual influences*. From a functional perspective, the intraindividual influences were viewed as the proximal factors leading to drinking behavior throughout adolescence and adulthood. These influences included genetic factors and other nongenetic biological factors (prenatal alcohol exposure) but would also include psychosocial factors such as individual difference factors (e.g., personality, socialization, and self-efficacy) and alcohol constructs (e.g., norms and expectancies). The impact of sociocultural/community, family, and peer factors on drinking was seen as mediated through the intraindividual factors.

Moreover, Zucker's (1979) approach suggested that intraindividual factors could impact the other sources of influence and that, in fact, all of the sources had the potential to influence the other sources of influence. In this sense, this model was both interactional (person–environment) and bidirectional. One of the key aspects of Zucker's approach was that the sources of influence and their role in the model changed over development.

Understanding the development of alcohol use and alcohol use disorders from this developmental perspective presents a number of challenges. These risk factors can remain stable over long periods of development, change at different times for different individuals, and have a very rapid impact. In describing the implications of the approach, Zucker, Fitzgerald, and Moses (1995) write that "within such a framework, one can conceive of risk as a fluid characteristic which increases or decreases depending on the interplay of ongoing trajectory and the influence of new external and internal (stage triggered) causative agents" (p. 686). The implication of this is clear: One way to clarify the factors impacting the development of substance use is to focus on transitional periods or events, particularly those that introduce, remove, or reorganize the biological, psychological, and social influences on drinking.

From this perspective, the development of intimate relationships, the transitional event of marriage, and the early years of marriage represent a potentially very critical period for studying risk for excessive drinking and alcohol use disorders. Although the prevalence of marriage has declined, it remains the case that nearly 85% of both men and women will marry at some point in their lives (Copen, Daniels, Vespa, & Mosher, 2012). This prevalence exceeds the proportion of individuals who graduate from high school (Stillwell & Sable, 2013), and therefore the proportion who go to college, and it is roughly equal to the proportion who will have children (Livingston & Cohn, 2010). In addition, marriage, and the processes surrounding marriage, introduces, removes, and reorganizes many psychological and social influences. Moreover, the role of spouse provides a new set of normative expectations and behavioral contingencies regarding interdependence, responsibility, and risk-taking. Addressing these expectations often involves an accommodation to one's spouse's expectations and behaviors while similarly addressing the expectations of friends and family. The outcome of

this process is the potential for significant levels of partner influence on behavior, a potential shift in the social network toward partner and family and away from peers (Kearns & Leonard, 2004), and an emergent role for factors within the relationship (e.g., intimacy or conflict) to impact behavior. In the context of alcohol consumption, Zucker (1979) recognized this shift, stating

> the phenomenon that marks the break [between heavy drinking and social drinking] is marriage and its related values for increased interdependence, achievement, and prosocial activity. I hypothesize that the presumed developmental transition away from drinking is related to this significant psychological and social-structural event. (p. 131)

This chapter focuses first on the impact of marriage on drinking, a phenomenon that has come to be known as "the marriage effect." In subsequent sections, we introduce an expanded version of Zucker's developmental-probabilistic model as it applies to the early years of marriage, and we present work from our ongoing studies of newlywed couples, as well as that of others who have examined the interface between intimate partner relationships and alcohol use, that addresses different aspects of this model. In the final section, we address the implications of these findings for prevention, treatment, and future areas of research.

THE MARRIAGE EFFECT

It is has been recognized since the early 1940s that married individuals are less likely to have alcohol problems compared to single or divorced individuals (Bacon, 1944). This was substantiated in the first nationally representative study of drinking practices conducted by Cahalan, Cisin, and Crossley (1969), and it has been supported multiple times since then (Clark & Midanik, 1982; Hasin, Stinson, Ogburn, & Grant, 2007; Hilton, 1991). Recent research suggests that these lower rates of heavy drinking and alcohol disorders may also apply to same-sex marriages (Reczek, Liu, & Spiker, 2014). Although some of this seemingly protective effect may be accounted for by developmental changes and less risky individuals being preferentially "selected into" marriage, fairly consistent findings from longitudinal studies suggest that the process of marriage initiates reductions in alcohol use, the use of other substances, as well as antisocial behaviors.

The first demonstration of the longitudinal impact of marriage on heavy drinking was reported by Miller-Tutzauer, Leonard, and Windle (1991). Using data from the National Longitudinal Survey of Youth for 1984, 1985, and 1986, they examined heavy drinking among stably married and stably single couples and contrasted this with the heavy drinking of couples who transitioned from single to married during one of those years. Their results clearly indicated that heavy drinking declined from the previous year among both men and women who transitioned to marriage in that year. However, two other findings were of interest. First, individuals who would marry in 1986 evidenced reduced drinking in 1985, suggesting either that processes immediately preceding marriage, such as a formal engagement, also impacted drinking or that the reduction in drinking facilitated the subsequent transition to marriage. Second, once the transition to marriage occurred, couples experiencing the transition drank at the same level as those who had been stably married for 3 years, suggesting that most of the change in drinking occurred quite rapidly. A number of additional studies have similarly demonstrated an effect of marriage on drinking as well as other behaviors. Perhaps the most persuasive evidence was based on the Monitoring the Future project (Bachman, Wadsworth, O'Malley, Johnston, & Schulenberg, 1997), which collected nationally representative samples of high school seniors from 1975 through 1994 and reassessed them every 2 years. This study found evidence for a marital effect, controlling for a variety of other transitions that occur during this developmental period. The marital effect was observed for drinking, heavy drinking, as well as the use of tobacco, marijuana, and cocaine. In addition, they identified a reduction in drinking prior to marriage but only among individuals who reported being engaged, supporting the findings of Miller-Tutzauer et al.'s (1991) study. In support of a socialization effect as opposed to a selection effect, Lee, Chassin, and MacKinnon (2010) found that the marriage effect on reduced heavy drinking was mediated through reductions in social activities.

The potential clinical significance of the marital effect has been demonstrated in several studies. Lee, Chassin, and MacKinnon (2015) found that the drinking reduction that occurs with marriage was stronger for those with more severe drinking problems prior to marriage. In an earlier study, Chilcoat and Breslau (1996) found that marriage was associated with a reduced likelihood of an onset of an alcohol diagnosis and an increased likelihood of remission of a previous alcohol diagnosis. Similarly, Verges et al. (2012) could not find specific effects for onset of a new diagnosis, remission from a current diagnosis, or recurrence of a previous diagnosis, but they did find evidence for a marital effect for decreases in alcohol diagnoses across all of these specific effects.

A Heuristic Model of Alcohol Use in Marriage

The transition to marriage entails a shift in the locus of influence for individuals. Although the family of origin and peers are likely to continue to exert some influence, the fundamental shift that occurs with marriage is the impact of the partner and the marital relationship. A heuristic model displaying this influence is shown in Figure 18.1. We view influence arising in four primary domains, with the influence of the first three being substantially the same as that in Zucker's model: sociocultural/community, peer, and intraindividual. However, the unique elements of the marital relationship lead us to differentiate this from peer as well as from family of origin influences. For the sake of simplicity, and because little research has examined family of origin influences in early adulthood, Figure 18.1 does not include family of origin. These sources of influence can impact each other. Moreover, this model includes the possibility of bidirectional influences between drinking/drinking consequences and marital, peer, and intraindividual factors. It also allows for intraindividual factors to serve as moderating influences on the bidirectional associations with alcohol use and consequences (dashed lines in Figure 18.1) as well as mediating influences. In the following sections, we describe first how relationship factors impact alcohol use and alcohol problems and subsequently how drinking in the relationship impacts the relationship.

Much of the research we discuss is drawn from our longitudinal studies of newlywed couples. The most extensive of these studies was the Adult Development Study (ADS; Leonard & Mudar, 2003), which began with the recruitment of couples as they applied for their marriage license. We focused on couples who were entering their first marriage, and we assessed them at the time of marriage and also at their first, second, fourth, seventh, and ninth anniversaries. Couples

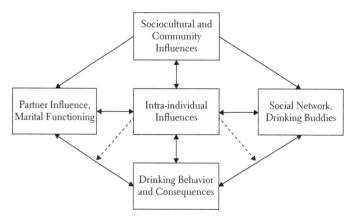

FIGURE 18.1 Heuristic model of alcohol use and marital development in emerging adulthood.

completed questionnaires at home that assessed personality, alcohol factors, relationship factors, and family/peer factors. Prior to the ADS, we conducted the Buffalo Newlywed Study (BNS; Leonard & Senchak, 1993), which included couples in which the husband was between ages 18 and 30 years and which assessed couples at the time of marriage and also at their first and third anniversaries.

The selection criteria for other studies reviewed in this chapter were restricted, considering the large amount of variation across studies examining alcohol use in romantic relationships (for reviews, see Fischer & Wiersma, 2012; Leonard & Eiden, 2007; Marshal, 2003; Roberts & Linney, 2000; Rodriguez, Neighbors, & Knee, 2014), especially pertaining to relationship status and study methodology. Therefore, we primarily focused on studies that examined temporal or causal inferences (i.e., longitudinal, daily diary, or laboratory studies), used reports from both couple members, and/or included relationship-specific assessments of alcohol use-related variables (as opposed to general assessments). We also attempted to focus primarily on married couples, although some research reviewed involved mixed samples (i.e., both married and nonmarried couples) or, where appropriate, only nonmarried or cohabiting couples in committed relationships.

THE INFLUENCE OF INTIMATE PARTNERS IN ALCOHOL USE AND ALCOHOL PROBLEMS

The similarity between husband and wife drinking is often cast as the result of selection or influence,

with the possibility of common life events sometimes being included as a third option. As noted previously, mate selection reflects a series of processes that culminate in the mutual commitment of marriage. These processes include gaining access to a specific pool of potential mates, pursuing and/or accepting pursuit by some of these potential mates, and mutually evaluating the benefits and costs of a continued relationship. Because we rarely evaluate the relationship between husband and wife alcohol use prior to their relationship, it is difficult to know how much of the similarity they exhibit reflects selection versus influence.

Some sense of role of selection can be seen in a study by Ask, Rognmo, Torvik, Roysamb, and Tambs (2012). This study successfully assessed 75% of the entire population older than age 20 years of a Norwegian town in 1984–1986 with respect to their current alcohol use. For couples who were married or cohabiting, Ask et al. recorded how long they had been doing so. They then examined records from 1992–2000 and determined whether any two individuals whom they had assessed had married during that time and how long after the assessment they had married. They also determined whether two individuals whom they had assessed were cohabiting and for how long (this is present in public files but only if the couple had children). Ask et al. were then able to correlate the drinking of the members of the married/cohabiting couples and chart and model the change in that correlation as a function of how long after marriage or how long prior to marriage the drinking assessment occurred. This model indicated that at 12 years prior to marriage, when couples were unlikely to have been involved with each other, the correlation was .26. This correlation gradually increased for couples who were closer to marriage, with an estimated correlation of .48 if they had been assessed for drinking in the year they were married, at which point they had undoubtedly known each other for some longer period of time. Thus, the study suggested a minimum level of selection (correlation of .26) and a convergence of husband–wife drinking as they approached marriage. However, this convergence does not necessarily reflect only selection factors. The possibility of partners influencing each other prior to marriage is very real, even if rarely acknowledged. In fact, Mushquash et al. (2013) found that one's heavy drinking over a month-long period was predicted by the heavy drinking of one's dating partner. This influence was observed for both men and women.

Although it is not exactly clear how much selection and influence contribute independently, it is clear that at the time of marriage, couples are similar with respect to patterns of alcohol use. In the BNS, the alcohol involvement factor (a composite including average daily consumption, frequency of intoxication, and frequency of drinking six or more drinks at one time) of husbands and wives was correlated .45 in a structural equation model (Leonard & Eiden, 1999). In the ADS, the correlation between partners was .46 (Leonard & Mudar, 2003). From this baseline similarity (which, as previously noted, may reflect selection, influence, and third-variable processes), both of these studies then examined the extent to which one partner's drinking during the year before marriage predicted the other partner's drinking during the first year of marriage. In both studies, husband's drinking was a significant longitudinal predictor of wife's drinking, whereas wife's drinking was not a significant predictor of husband's drinking.

Although we have found this asymmetric pattern of husband-to-wife influence in two studies of the transition to marriage, this pattern does not seem to persist beyond this transition. From the first to the second year of marriage in the ADS, there was a reversal of this pattern, with a significant wife-to-husband influence but no significant husband-to-wife influence (Leonard & Mudar, 2004). However, when we examine the influence patterns during the first 4 years of marriage, both husbands and wives appear to significantly influence each other (Leonard & Homish, 2008). This influence is observed both with respect to heavy drinking as well as alcohol problems and after controlling for individual factors, relationship factors, and social network factors.

Our perspective on partner influence in the context of marriage is that there is probably both husband-to-wife and wife-to-husband influence and that this influence occurs throughout relationship development and into marriage. Research among older adults suggests that partner influence continues throughout marriage and is evident in both social drinkers and problem drinkers (Lemke, Brennan, Schutte, & Moos, 2007). There may be specific periods in which there is more influence from one partner than the other. The transition to marriage may be one of those periods in which the influence is more strongly husband to wife, but there may be other periods in which the influence is more strongly wife to husband. In the context of a relationship with stable drinking patterns, factors that result in dramatic shifts in one partner's drinking may have an impact on the other partner's drinking. For example, the impact of pregnancy has a rather dramatic influence on women's drinking, an effect that might lead to reductions in their husbands' drinking. However, although this influence continues throughout adulthood, there are other influences as well. Thus, although the correlation between husband and wife drinking does not increase dramatically after marriage, this may reflect the erratic and variable impact of other influences on each of their drinking rather than a reduction in partner influence.

In order to understand why we might observe husband-to-wife influence over the transition to marriage but not wife-to-husband influence, we explored several potential moderating factors. Based on theories of gender and interdependence, Leonard and Mudar (2004) hypothesized that during the transition to marriage, women, more so than men, would be likely to accommodate and change their behavior in the direction of their husbands' behavior in order to enhance the relationship. This was described as a relationship motivation model of partner drinking. As such, several constructs were hypothesized to enhance this effect. Women with high levels of dependence were hypothesized to be more influenced by their partner's behavior. Similarly, we thought that women who reported fewer friends, were more satisfied with their marriage, and expected alcohol to enhance the relationship with their partner would be more influenced than women without these characteristics. The results supported the hypotheses of the relationship motivation model for three of the four constructs. Dependency, number of friends, and expectations of intimacy moderated the longitudinal pathway from husband to wife heavy drinking. However, it only strengthened this path during the transition to marriage and did not impact influence from the first to the second anniversary.

The Role of the Social Network in Alcohol Use During the Early Years of Marriage

Research on drinking and drinking problems among adolescents has historically focused on the impact of peers. However, few studies have addressed the potential impact of peers or the social network among young adults. As with spouses, any relationship may reflect selection or influence processes. Several cross-sectional studies have found a relationship between one's drinking and the drinking behaviors among one's adult peers (Aspler & Blackman, 1979; Fromme & Ruela, 1994). Also, two longitudinal studies have found evidence for selection (one's drinking predicted changes in the drinking status of peers) but no evidence for peer influence (Bullers, Cooper, & Russell, 2001; Labouvie, 1996). However, both of these studies examined the relationship over a fairly lengthy time frame (3 and 7 years, respectively). This raises the possibility as to whether these results would be similar over shorter periods of time and over the early years of marriage, particularly given the expected reduction in peer influence among married couples.

In our cross-sectional analyses of newlyweds, we found that both husband and wife heavy drinking were associated with the presence of heavy drinking peers in each of their social networks. Of interest, husband and wife drinking also correlated with the drinking of their partner's peers. Unsurprising, the drinking of husbands' peers was also correlated with the drinking of wives' peers (Leonard & Mudar, 2000). One might wonder whether these relationships occur because husbands and wives have some overlap among members of their social networks and therefore are sometimes reporting on the same people. However, at the time of marriage, the overlap between husbands' and wives' peers was only 16%, increasing to 23% in the first year of marriage.

During the transition to marriage, Leonard and Mudar (2003) examined both spousal influence, as described previously, and peer influence versus selection. Interestingly, there was no evidence for peer influence during this time frame for either husband or wife. However, there was strong evidence for peer selection. One aspect of this peer selection was that

husband's premarital heavy drinking was longitudinally predictive of the extent of heavy drinking in his peer network. A second, rather unexpected, aspect of this selection was that husbands' premarital heavy drinking also predicted the extent of heavy drinking among wives' peer networks in the first year of marriage, which in turn was associated with wives' drinking. This suggests that heavy drinking husbands can influence their wives' drinking directly as well as indirectly by reshaping the characteristics of wives' social networks.

Although our initial analyses did not support the expectation that the larger social network influenced the drinking of husbands and wives, we wondered, given the reshaping of the social networks by the first anniversary, whether the new network composition might influence drinking as the marriage progressed. The drinking characteristics of the social network across the transition to marriage did show some stability, but it was only modest. In the Leonard and Homish (2008) study, we included peer network characteristics along with individual, partner, and relationship characteristics as prospective predictors of heavy drinking and alcohol problems. The number of drinking buddies in one's social network predicted heavy drinking and alcohol problems for both husbands and wives, whereas the number of heavy drinkers in the network independently influenced husbands' alcohol problems and wives' heavy drinking.

In a separate examination of the first four waves of the ADS, Lau-Barraco, Braitman, Leonard, and Padilla (2012) found evidence that the number of drinking buddies husbands and wives had in their social networks continued to influence their drinking outcomes over time. Drinking buddies continued to have a direct effect on both typical drinking and heavy drinking over time, with partial mediation through social facilitation expectancies, and these effects did not differ between husbands and wives. However, the effect of drinking buddies on alcohol problems was fully mediated through social facilitation expectancies and was only found for husbands. In addition, comparisons of temporally lagged correlations between drinking buddies and alcohol variables did not distinguish between socialization and selection interpretations of effects. Despite the fact that these analyses suggest that drinking buddies continue to influence husbands' and wives' drinking in adulthood, and that the process involves social facilitation effects and expectancies, more research is needed to examine these influences and to determine the extent to which other aspects of the model (e.g., intraindividual factors and marital factors) are involved.

As suggested in our heuristic model, many of the domains influence each other, as well as drinking. Given the role of peers' alcohol use, it is worth considering factors that modify the drinking characteristics of the social network. Using data from the ADS, Homish and Leonard (2008) examined the extent to which husbands' and wives' drinking, individual factors, and marital satisfaction prospectively predicted the drinking characteristics of the social network during the first 4 years of marriage. For both husbands and wives, the personality characteristic of extroversion and the expectancy that alcohol enhanced social relationships were longitudinal predictors of the number of drinking buddies. In addition, heavy drinking in individuals was predictive of increased peer drinking in their own and their partner's networks. This was true for both husbands and wives. Interestingly, marital satisfaction was complexly related to changes in peer drinking. For both husbands and wives, marital satisfaction was associated with less drinking in one's own social network and more drinking in the partner's social network. One's own sense of marital satisfaction may reduce peer contact, particularly with peers whose behavior is at odds with the normative expectations of married individuals. On the other hand, the marital satisfaction of one's partner may enable a belief that one can have this level and kind of peer relationships without risking ones' relationship.

Bidirectional Associations Between Marital Functioning and Alcohol Use

As mentioned previously, the processes linking marital functioning and alcohol use and consequences are theoretically presumed to be bidirectional (see Figure 18.1). In other words, there is dynamic interplay over time in marriage in which marital functioning predicts subsequent alcohol use and consequences, which in turn predict subsequent marital functioning. Broadly, these reciprocal processes can be partially addressed by theories such as social learning theory (Bandura, 1971; in both directions) and alcohol myopia theory (Steele & Josephs, 1990; in the direction of alcohol use predicting marital functioning). However, theoretical perspectives such as these do not always

converge to directly address factors and processes that are specific to alcohol use in romantic relationships, such as interdependence between couple members' behaviors and experiences (Rodriguez, Neighbors, et al., 2014). Furthermore, the literature as a whole has predominantly focused on adverse relationship outcomes as a function of problematic levels of drinking, particularly among alcohol-dependent husbands, while ignoring alcohol use among wives (Marshal, 2003; Roberts & Linney, 2000). Relatively recently, there has been a call for research to specifically situate relationship drinking in its interpersonal relationship context, to examine bidirectional associations between relationship functioning and alcohol use among both partners, and to acknowledge that alcohol use processes can be both adaptive and maladaptive for relationships over time (Fischer & Wiersma, 2012; Levitt & Cooper, 2010; Rodriguez, Neighbors, et al., 2014). We define adaptive (vs. maladaptive) processes as being beneficial (vs. detrimental), either immediately or over time, to the psychological and/or physical well-being of the couple members or to the state of the relationship itself (e.g., relationship maintenance and survival vs. dissolution). This distinction is fundamental to understanding how alcohol use behaviors develop in marriage and, consequently, why individuals continue to be motivated to engage in drinking behaviors over time. Thus, this section reviews research on these bidirectional associations by examining (1) how marital functioning predicts alcohol use and consequences, (2) how alcohol use and consequences in turn predict marital functioning, (3) key emerging factors that establish when and how these processes are either adaptive or maladaptive, and (4) whether and how intraindividual influences serve as both mediating and moderating mechanisms in these associations.

Marital Functioning Predicting Alcohol Use

According to our model, marital functioning predicts subsequent alcohol use in relationships, although this temporal direction has received overall less attention in the literature compared to its opposite direction. Research in this direction has primarily focused on mechanisms of maladaptive processes in which poor relationship functioning predicts problematic alcohol use and consequences. However, theory and some limited research suggest that these processes can be adaptive as well, in that positive relationship functioning can be protective against problematic alcohol use.

Drinking in Response to Relationship Distress

Previous cross-sectional research in the BNS (Leonard & Senchak, 1993) has shown that marital dissatisfaction is associated with greater rates of heavy drinking in both individuals and their spouses. One interpretation of these associations is that individuals drink to cope in response to poor relationship functioning or distress in their relationships. Drinking to cope with or reduce negative emotions is considered to be a maladaptive drinking motive because it is associated with problematic drinking-related consequences beyond other motives and amount consumed (Cooper, Frone, Russell, & Mudar, 1995; Cooper, Kuntsche, Levitt, Barber, & Wolf, 2016). Recent research suggests that drinking to cope with relationship distress is similarly maladaptive and that it is characterized by unique features that are specific to the relationship. For instance, Rodriguez, Knee, and Neighbors (2014) have shown that relationship-contingent self-esteem (RCSE)—how much one's self-worth is tied to the ups and downs of relationship events—is an important factor in predicting drinking to cope and drinking problems in relationships. In nonmarried and married couples, experiencing poor relationship functioning predicted greater drinking problems, mediated through greater drinking to cope. For men, however, the effects of poor relationship functioning were moderated by RCSE, such that those whose self-esteem was highly dependent on the relationship reported greater drinking to cope and drinking problems at low levels of relationship functioning compared to those low in RCSE. DiBello, Rodriguez, Hadden, and Neighbors (2015) also showed in a sample of nonmarried and married individuals that one mechanism through which RCSE may operate in predicting drinking to cope and drinking problems in relationships is through experiencing cognitive jealousy. In line with this research, Levitt and Leonard (2015) used the ADS data set to examine drinking to cope that is specific to a stressful relationship problem, and they hypothesized that anxiously attached individuals would drink with their partner more to cope with relationship stressors, whereas avoidantly attached individuals would drink apart from their partner more to cope. Relationship-specific drinking to cope mediated the effects of attachment anxiety

to predict greater frequencies of drinking apart from the partner, counter to expectation, and greater rates of marital alcohol problems, as expected, during the first 9 years of marriage. These effects did not differ by gender, and no effects were found for attachment avoidance. As a whole, these studies illustrate the maladaptive nature of drinking to cope with relationship distress, and they highlight relationship-specific variables that can be further explored in future research on relationship drinking processes.

Drinking in Response to Relationship Dissolution

Limited research has examined alcohol use as a consequence of relationship dissolution over time. However, that which has suggests that relationship dissolution can be a unique, double-edged sword for alcohol use outcomes. Using data from the National Epidemiologic Survey on Alcohol and Related Conditions (NESARC), Smith, Homish, Leonard, and Cornelius (2012) found that women drank more heavily and drank more frequently over time following the dissolution of a relationship with a non-problem drinker. In contrast, among women in relationships with a problem-drinking partner, relationship dissolution predicted decreases in their heavy drinking over time. This suggests that in some cases, women may use alcohol problematically to cope with relationship dissolution, whereas in other cases, adverse partner influence on heavy drinking may be reversed once that influence is removed.

Drinking in Response to Positive Relationship Functioning

Drinking in response to positive relationship functioning can take one of two divergent paths: (1) In an effort to maintain or enhance existing levels of positive relationship functioning (e.g., feelings of intimacy and marital satisfaction), couple members may increase their drinking, or (2) positive relationship functioning may exert a protective effect and reduce drinking, particularly heavy or problematic drinking. Little attention has been given to directly testing the first possibility. Nevertheless, among nonclinical couples, non-problematic drinking can theoretically be a normative result of approach motives for positive affect enhancement (Cooper et al., 2016) that may be desired by couple members to achieve relationship-specific effects. Couple members, especially women, may drink with their partner to restore feelings of intimacy in the relationship (Levitt & Cooper, 2010) or to maintain already existing positive relationship functioning (as opposed to drinking for reparative reasons) (Covington & Surrey, 1997). However, it is not clear what kinds of consequences might be associated with drinking for reparative versus maintenance or enhancement reasons. Future research is needed to examine these differences, particularly in nonclinical couples.

In contrast, there is considerably more evidence supporting the second possibility that positive relationship functioning is protective against problematic alcohol use. In the ADS, we examined the role of self and partner marital satisfaction as longitudinal predictors of heavy drinking and alcohol problems (Leonard & Homish, 2008). For wives, their own marital satisfaction was predictive of less heavy drinking and lower alcohol problems. However, their partner's marital satisfaction was not related to their drinking or alcohol problems. For husbands, their own marital satisfaction was predictive of less alcohol problems, but their partner's marital satisfaction was not predictive. It was interesting that the protective effect of marital satisfaction was stronger for alcohol problems than for heavy drinking. This raises the possibility that marital satisfaction may predict changes in the context of drinking or in protective behavioral strategies when drinking rather than strictly reduced drinking. Cranford, Tennen, and Zucker (2015) showed supporting evidence in a diary study of individuals in treatment for an alcohol use disorder (AUD) and their spouses that daily positive marital behaviors by husbands predicted a decreased likelihood of wives' drinking the following day. One specific mechanism that may explain these effects that has recently been examined is that of perceived partner regard, which is longitudinally predictive of marital satisfaction (Derrick, Leonard, & Homish, 2012). Although it is not yet clear how perceived partner regard directly affects alcohol use, it has been shown to predict decreases in cigarette smoking during the first 9 years of marriage (Derrick, Leonard, & Homish, 2013), suggesting that a similar protective effect might occur for problematic alcohol use.

Alcohol Use Predicting Marital Functioning

Main effects of alcohol use, particularly heavy or problematic alcohol use, tend to predict negative linear declines in marital satisfaction and relationship functioning, although evidence exists that drinking at low to moderate levels can predict positive relationship outcomes, particularly enhanced intimacy, as well (Fischer & Wiersma, 2012; Levitt & Cooper, 2010; Marshal, 2003; Roberts & Linney, 2000). However, research is now clear that the effects an individual's drinking has on the relationship are dependent primarily on the interaction with the partner's drinking and on the context in which relationship drinking occurs.

Concordant Versus Discordant Consumption

Historically, research on marital alcohol use has largely only examined an individual's own effects of drinking on his or her own marital functioning (Marshal, 2003; Roberts & Linney, 2000). In essence, this approach treats an individual's alcohol use in marriage as a behavior that occurs in a vacuum because it ignores interactions with the partner's alcohol consumption. In reality, marital alcohol use is a dynamic, interdependent phenomenon that involves both partners. That is, an individual's marital functioning is affected by both his or her own alcohol use and that of his or her partner, particularly in the unique configuration of use between the two. Relationship consequences of marital alcohol use are dependent on differences in these configurations. Specifically, recent research suggests that concordant versus discordant patterns of partners' alcohol consumption is one factor at the core of whether alcohol use has adaptive versus maladaptive effects on subsequent marital functioning. Longitudinal and daily diary studies reliably show that discordant drinking—when one partner drinks heavily and the other partner drinks lightly or abstains—is decidedly more maladaptive for subsequent marital functioning compared to concordant drinking—when couple members drink similar amounts—which is relatively more adaptive. In a programmatic series of studies examining concordance in couple members' alcohol and substance use using the ADS, a reliable pattern of results suggests that discordant use predicts lower marital satisfaction over time. Mudar, Leonard, and Soltysinski (2001) found that in the first year of marriage, discordant heavy alcohol use and drug use predicted lower marital satisfaction relative to concordant use. Extending these analyses across multiple time points in the same sample, Homish and Leonard (2007) found that discordant consumption predicted lower marital satisfaction for both husbands and wives during the first 3 years of marriage, whereas concordant consumption predicted relatively high levels of marital satisfaction, controlling for heavy drinking and demographic factors. Furthermore, discordance in comorbid alcohol and cigarette use predicted the greatest decreases in marital satisfaction during the first 7 years of marriage compared to discordance in the use of only one substance or concordance in use (Homish, Leonard, Kozlowski, & Cornelius, 2009). These results as a whole suggest that dissimilarity in other substance use in addition to discordant alcohol use could contribute additive strain to marital functioning.

Levitt and Cooper (2010) have shown similar results in a daily diary study of both nonmarried and married couples. They found that on days in which one couple member drank relatively more heavily compared to their partner, couple members reported greater next-day relationship problems and lower next-day intimacy. This pattern was also stronger for women, suggesting that women significantly outdrinking their male partners, as opposed to the reverse, may violate gender norms or expectations as to what is appropriate for women's drinking that hinders adaptive relationship functioning. Another explanation may be that women in discordant heavy drinking couples have lower expectations for intimacy enhancement effects when drinking with their partner compared to women in concordant heavy drinking couples (Derrick et al., 2010).

The maladaptive nature of discordant drinking may also ultimately lead to relationship dissolution. Although one study found that the highest rates of relationship dissolution were associated with concordant heavy drinking couples compared to other couples (Wiersma & Fischer, 2014), the vast majority of studies reviewed here show strong and consistent evidence that the highest rates of relationship dissolution across studies and stages of development are associated with discordant drinking patterns compared to concordant. In a sample of older adults (aged 51–61 years at baseline), Ostermann, Sloan, and Taylor (2005) showed proportionally higher rates of divorce during the next 8 years among couples with discordant drinking patterns compared to concordant light and concordant heavy drinking couples. Leonard, Smith, and Homish (2014) also provide evidence that discordant heavy alcohol use operates differently for marital dissolution compared to discordant tobacco or

marijuana use. In the ADS, concordant or discordant tobacco use or marijuana use were not associated with marital dissolution after controlling for heavy alcohol use and other substance use, sociodemographic factors, and personality factors. Only discordant heavy alcohol use was directly associated with marital dissolution after controlling for other variables, whereas concordant heavy alcohol use was not. This study also suggests that discordance in substance use processes might operate differently for couples that dissolve compared to those that remain together but still experience additive relationship strain from multiple substance use discrepancies (Homish et al., 2009).

Substantial research also exists suggesting that effects of discordant alcohol use on relationship dissolution vary by gender. In a large-scale longitudinal sample of Norwegian couples, Torvik, Roysamb, Gustavson, Idstad, and Tambs (2013) showed that discordant drinking couples with one heavy drinker predicted higher hazard ratios for divorce 15 years later compared to light-drinking discordant couples or concordant drinking couples. The highest risk for divorce—three times higher than that for other couples—was found for couples in which the wife drank heavily and the husband did not. Similarly, Keenan, Kenward, Grundy, and Leon (2013) reported that the highest odds for divorce in a longitudinal Russian sample were among couples in which wives drank more frequently than their husbands, although the interaction between husbands' and wives' drinking was not significant. Wives' binge drinking in that sample also predicted significantly higher odds of divorce over time, whereas husbands' binge drinking did not. These findings corroborate those of Levitt and Cooper (2010) at the daily level, showing greater adverse impact on daily relationship functioning when women outdrank their male partners compared to other drinking configurations.

Although not examining drinking concordance between partners directly, further evidence exists supporting the studies reviewed previously. Longitudinal research examining clinically problematic levels of drinking in marriage shows that diagnoses of an AUD predict lower marital satisfaction over time when the wife has the AUD diagnosis instead of the husband (Cranford, Floyd, Schulenberg, & Zucker, 2011). Furthermore, AUDs in either husbands or wives predict greater rates of relationship dissolution over time (Cranford, 2014; Waldron et al., 2011). These results provide further indirect support that discordant drinking (i.e., one partner meeting criteria for an AUD but presumably not the other) is maladaptive for marital functioning and that effects may be worse among women than men.

Similar to the research reviewed previously on perceived partner regard and responsiveness, a promising new direction for relationship drinking research that may help shed light on the gender differences found in the previously mentioned studies is in the examination of partner perceptions. In a short-term longitudinal study of married couples, Rodriguez and Neighbors (2015) found that husbands of heavy drinking wives only experienced declines in marital adjustment when they perceived their wives to have a drinking problem. The association between perceiving one's partner to have a drinking problem and lower relationship satisfaction also appears to be mediated through other intraindividual influences, such as maladaptive punishment and reward strategies for dealing with one's partner (Rodriguez, DiBello, & Neighbors, 2013).

Relationship Drinking Contexts

The context in which relationship drinking occurs is also emerging as a reliable and important factor in determining whether alcohol's effects are adaptive versus maladaptive. Drinking with one's partner appears to be adaptive for relationship functioning outcomes, whereas drinking apart from one's partner appears to be maladaptive. In the ADS, Homish and Leonard (2005) found that wives who frequently drank with their partner had higher rates of marital satisfaction during the first 2 years of marriage compared to those who frequently drank apart from their partner and non-drinkers. Levitt and Cooper (2010) found a similar set of results at the daily level, such that drinking with (vs. apart from) one's partner on a given day predicted greater next-day intimacy and fewer next-day relationship problems. Furthermore, the effects for intimacy were stronger for women even when consuming heavier amounts. Women's next-day intimacy declined as a function of heavier drinking if they drank apart from their partner. However, those who drank with their partner did not experience these declines in intimacy.

Drinking contexts in marriage also appear to be dynamically and reciprocally associated with relationship-specific alcohol expectancies. Levitt and Leonard (2013) found that during the first 9 years of marriage, drinking with one's partner was associated with greater subsequent expectancies for intimacy and social enhancement effects, which in turn predicted subsequently more frequent drinking together. Given the results of Homish and Leonard (2005) and Levitt and Cooper (2010), this process appears to be adaptive for marriages. In contrast, drinking apart was associated with greater subsequent expectancies for power and assertiveness effects, which in turn predicted subsequently more frequent drinking apart. In line with other results reviewed for drinking apart, this process appears to be maladaptive for marital functioning. Another way that drinking apart may be maladaptive for daily relationship functioning is that is does not allow individuals who hold strong expectancies for intimacy enhancement effects to realize those effects when drinking apart from their partner (Levitt, Derrick, & Testa, 2014).

CONCLUSIONS AND FUTURE DIRECTIONS

The determinants and consequences of alcohol use over time in marriage are dynamic, nuanced, and complex. Alcohol use as an outcome depends on critical developmental transitions including the period leading into marriage, shifts in partner influence, changes in the social network of drinking peers, and variations in relationship functioning as the marriage develops. These associations are also bidirectional such that alcohol use, in turn, predicts subsequent changes in the social network of drinking peers and relationship functioning over time. Furthermore, a host of intraindividual influences, from personality variables to alcohol expectancies and motives, have the potential to mediate and moderate all these associations. Our heuristic model incorporates all these associations into a framework that can be easily and immediately applied to model and hypothesis testing while also being broad and flexible enough to allow for exploration of additional mechanisms and variables in future research. The research that we reviewed in this chapter supports and provides evidence for each aspect of this model.

Furthermore, it is impressive that many of the effects discussed exist robustly and consistently across stages of relationship development, study methodologies, and different levels of examination. Like a photographer using a camera's zoom lens, we are able to zoom in and out from daily processes to yearly processes in the research reviewed to get a better understanding of how these processes develop over time in marriage. As a whole, the evidence suggests that these varying perspectives are not only consistent with one another but also complementary and that it is therefore important for future research to continue to use a breadth of perspectives. However, it is also important for future research to extend beyond the methods and developmental stages previously examined. At a more proximal level, it is still largely unknown how these processes operate momentarily. Studies using ecological momentary assessment or naturalistic observation methods can help illuminate how these processes unfold in real time to better inform our understanding of the momentary antecedents and consequences of relationship drinking. Research is also relatively lacking on relationships at more advanced stages of development. Much of the research examined is on the transition into marriage and the early years of marriage, usually in emerging adult or young adult couples, which is important considering that this is the period in which relationship processes solidify as couple members converge as a dyad. Although some research suggests that partner influence continues throughout adulthood (Lemke et al., 2007), less is known overall about how these processes operate in older couples in long-standing relationships compared to younger couples. It is possible that some couples reach a stasis in their relationship alcohol use, whereas others may continue to experience variation in their use, potentially as a result of significant life events. In addition, future research should strive to examine the potential role of cultural diversity as an influence on these processes. Some of the studies have utilized heterogeneous samples but have not explicitly examined whether the processes differed among the different groups in their samples. Other studies have used relatively homogeneous samples. Consequently, there is little empirical or theoretical knowledge regarding how diverse cultural influences may impact marriage and alcohol use processes.

Some of the research reviewed in this chapter directly tested mechanisms of alcohol use processes in marriage. However, there is still much to learn about other potential mechanisms of interest. One mechanism that may impact longitudinal changes in marital alcohol use, particularly in shifts in partner influence during the early years of marriage (Leonard & Homish, 2008), is that of pregnancy and having children. Children represent a major life event that causes a shift in relationship roles (Lawrence, Rothman, Cobb, Rothman, & Bradbury, 2008) and ultimately may affect alcohol use through changes in the social network and changes in partner influence, particularly in husbands' influence on wives' drinking during the first year of marriage (Leonard & Mudar, 2004). Furthermore, these influences almost certainly change over time as children age and leave the home, although how such changes influence alcohol-related behaviors requires future research. In addition to children, other major developmental influences may affect alcohol and other substance use, such as changes in employment, caregiving for a spouse or other family member, or shifts in relationship roles. These developmental markers are certainly in line with Zucker et al.'s (1995) conceptualization of stage-triggered causative events, and they are as potentially impactful on changes to alcohol and other substance use as the transition to marriage. It is important for future research to parse out effects of developmental shifts within the relationship from changes in partner influence.

Another critical set of mechanisms in relationship alcohol use that needs further investigation is that of motives. Drinking motives are considered to be the final causal pathway between expectancies and other distal individual differences and alcohol use outcomes (Cooper et al., 2016). Much of the research reviewed, particularly studies examining relationship-specific alcohol expectancies (Derrick et al., 2010; Levitt & Leonard, 2013; Levitt et al., 2014), at least implicitly suggests that couple members are motivated to drink in their relationship for various reasons. For example, couple members appear to be motivated to drink to improve their feelings of intimacy (Levitt & Cooper, 2010; Levitt & Leonard, 2013), to be more social with their partner (Levitt & Leonard, 2013), to cope with relationship distress (Levitt & Leonard, 2015; Rodriguez, Neighbors, et al., 2014), and to assert power in the relationship (Levitt & Leonard, 2013). However, research is still lacking on both expectancies and motives as mechanisms of relationship drinking. The currently available measure of relationship-specific alcohol expectancies (Leonard & Mudar, 2004) is limited in that it assesses only four relationship domains: intimacy, social, sexual, and power enhancement. Similarly, the only known relationship-specific assessment of drinking motives is limited to drinking to cope with a stressful relationship problem

(Levitt & Leonard, 2015). Furthermore, it is currently impossible to directly test theoretical associations between corresponding expectancies and motives sets with these assessments considering they do not overlap in their relationship domains. Therefore, future research is needed to examine a broader, more exhaustive set of both relationship-specific expectancies and motives for drinking. We are currently developing a new measure of relationship-specific drinking motives that taps a number of relationship domains.

Beyond expectancies and motives for drinking, researchers should also consider other sets of motives that pertain directly to achieving relationship goals. For example, some couple members might be motivated simply to attend to their partner's needs or to be more responsive in the relationship. Such relationship motives do not directly pertain to alcohol use but may impact alcohol use behaviors indirectly. This type of indirect influence might underlie partner influence processes (Leonard & Homish, 2008) at a more proximal level. Like other processes discussed in this chapter, couple members' pursuits of relationship goals are also theoretically interdependent (Fitzsimmons, Finkel, & vanDellen, 2015). Future research is needed to examine how and when these interdependencies converge to predict relationship-motivated drinking, as well as situations in which alcohol use might prevent achievement of other pro-relationship goals.

Future research should also explore other factors that may moderate marital alcohol use associations over time. Our heuristic model allows for intraindividual variables to moderate the bidirectional associations to and from marital alcohol use as an alternative to mediation. Some of the studies we reviewed have examined moderating intraindividual influences such as relationship-specific alcohol expectancies (Levitt et al., 2014) and personality variables (Leonard & Mudar, 2004). However, there is still much to be explored concerning moderating influences, including more complex tests of moderated mediation of the pathways in our model (not shown).

Although all of the associations in our model are theorized to be bidirectional, not all of the research reviewed equally represents tests of bidirectionality. In particular, more research is needed to examine alcohol use and consequences as an outcome of relationship functioning, especially among couple members who are motivated to drink to enhance or maintain adaptive relationship functioning. More research is

also needed to examine changes in social networks of drinking peers as a function of relationship behaviors (e.g., spending more time with one's partner during the early years of marriage) compared to couple members' drinking behaviors.

We view our model as being applicable to other substances besides alcohol. Although some of the research reviewed accounted for multiple substances, such as alcohol, marijuana, and tobacco use (Leonard, Smith, & Homish, 2014), it is unclear how other substance use develops over time in marriage compared to alcohol use. For instance, it is unknown whether bidirectional influences between couple members and their social network of substance-using peers operate similarly for marijuana use as they do for alcohol use (Lau et al., 2012). Similarly, it is not clear whether couple members' marijuana use is associated with different contexts of use (e.g., with vs. apart from partner) or different sets of relationship-specific expectancies over time (Levitt & Leonard, 2013). These questions are of immediate interest to marijuana and relationship researchers given recent policy changes toward the legalization and use of marijuana. These processes are also of immediate interest to researchers of cigarette smoking. The work by Derrick et al. (2013) showing smoking reductions as a function of perceived partner responsiveness importantly highlights how relationship functioning can have a beneficial impact on the health behaviors of couple members.

Our review also has implications for future clinical research and practice. Given the interdependence between relationship functioning and alcohol use, clinicians and researchers should target relationship functioning variables as potential sources of impact in prevention and intervention efforts as much as the drinking behavior itself. As reviewed, daily positive marital functioning has a protective effect in reducing drinking among individuals with an AUD (Cranford et al., 2015). These findings are in line with previous research showing that alcoholism treatments that focus on improving marital functioning are more effective than those that do not (McCrady et al., 1986; O'Farrell, Cutter, & Floyd, 1985). Furthermore, considering that behavioral and cognitive therapies are also preferred over other therapies (for a review, see Leonard & Eiden, 2007), clinicians could target specific positive marital behaviors and cognitions (e.g., perceived partner regard; Derrick et al., 2012, 2013) in efforts to reduce problematic relationship drinking. Targeting of behavioral and cognitive variables can also extend to maladaptive alcohol use processes examined, such as discordant heavy drinking and drinking apart from one's partner. As suggested previously, adverse effects associated with these processes may be due to a lack of communication between couple members regarding expectations surrounding appropriate levels of drinking and related behavior, which clinicians could focus on in treatment efforts.

In summary, research on alcohol use in romantic relationships is thriving. There is much that we know and are learning, but there is also much yet to discover. By examining alcohol use processes among both couple members using a relational lens, and also how drinking, relationship factors, and relationship-specific intraindividual factors mutually influence each other, every new result opens the door to other avenues of exploration.

ACKNOWLEDGMENTS

This work was supported by National Alcohol Abuse and Alcoholism grant K01-AA021769 awarded to Ash Levitt and grants R01-AA07183, R37-AA09922, and R01-AA016829 awarded to Kenneth E. Leonard.

REFERENCES

Ask, H., Rognmo, K., Torvik, F. A., Roysamb, E., & Tambs, K. (2012). Non-random mating and convergence over time for alcohol consumption, smoking, and exercise: The Nord–Trondelag Health Study. *Behavior Genetics*, 42, 354–365. doi:10.1007/s10519-011-9509-7

Aspler, R., & Blackman, C. (1979). Adults' drug use: Relationship to perceived drug use of parents, friends while growing up, and present friends. *American Journal of Drug and Alcohol Abuse*, 6, 291–300.

Bachman, J. G., Wadsworth, K. N., O'Malley, P. M., Johnston, L. D., & Schulenberg, J. E. (1997). *Smoking, drinking, and drug use in young adulthood.* Mahwah, NJ: Erlbaum.

Bacon, S. D. (1944). Inebriety, social integration, and marriage. *Quarterly Journal of Studies on Alcohol*, 5, 86–125.

Bandura, A. (1971). *Social learning theory.* New York, NY: General Learning Press.

Bullers, S., Cooper, M. L., & Russell, M. (2001). Social network drinking and adult alcohol involvement: A longitudinal exploration of the direction of influence. *Addictive Behaviors*, 26, 181–199.

Cahalan, D., Cisin, I. H., & Crossley, H. M. (1969). *American drinking practices: A national study of drinking behaviors and attitudes.* New Brunswick, NJ: Rutgers Center of Alcohol Studies.

Chilcoat, H. D., & Breslau, N. (1996). Alcohol disorders in young adulthood: Effects of transitions into adult roles. *Journal of Health and Social Behavior*, 37, 339–349.

Clark, W. B., & Cahalan, D. (1976). Changes in problem drinking over a 4-year span. *Addictive Behaviors*, 1, 251–259.

Clark, W. B., & Midanik, L. (1982). Alcohol use and alcohol problems among U.S. adults: Results of the 1979 national survey. In *Alcohol consumption and related problems* (National Institute on Alcohol Abuse and Alcoholism, Alcohol and Health Monograph No. 1, DHHS Publication No. ADM 82-1190). Washington, DC: US Government Printing Office.

Cooper, M. L., Frone, M. R., Russell, M., & Mudar, P. (1995). Drinking to regulate positive and negative emotions: A motivational model of alcohol use. *Journal of Personality and Social Psychology*, 69, 990–1005.

Cooper, M. L., Kuntsche, E., Levitt, A., Barber, L. L., & Wolf, S. T. (2016). Motivational models of substance use: A review of theory and research on motives for using alcohol, marijuana, and tobacco. In K. J. Sher (Ed.), *The Oxford handbook of substance use disorders* (Vol. 1, pp. 375–421). New York, NY: Oxford University Press. doi:10.1093/oxfordhb/9780199381678.013.017

Copen, C. E., Daniels, K., Vespa, J., & Mosher, W. D. (2012, March 22). First marriages in the United States: Data from the 2006–2010 National Survey of Family Growth. *National Health Statistics Report*, No. 49, 1–21.

Covington, S. S., & Surrey, J. L. (1997). The relational model of women's psychological development: Implications for substance use. In S. Wilsnack & R. Wilsnack (Eds.), *Gender and alcohol: Individual and social perspectives* (pp. 335–351). New Brunswick, NJ: Rutgers Center of Alcohol Studies.

Cranford, J. A. (2014). DSM-IV alcohol dependence and marital dissolution: Evidence from the National Epidemiologic Survey on Alcohol and Related Conditions. *Journal of Studies on Alcohol and Drugs*, 75, 520–529.

Cranford, J. A., Floyd, F. J., Schulenberg, J. E., & Zucker, R. A. (2011). Husbands' and wives' alcohol use disorders and marital interactions as longitudinal predictors of marital adjustment. *Journal of Abnormal Psychology, 120,* 210–222.

Cranford, J. A., Tennen, H., & Zucker, R. A. (2015). Using multiple methods to examine gender differences in alcohol involvement and marital interactions in alcoholic probands. *Addictive Behaviors, 41,* 192–198.

Davies, D. L. (1962). Normal drinking in recovered alcohol addicts. *Quarterly Journal of Studies on Alcohol, 23,* 94–104.

Derrick, J. L., Leonard, K. E., & Homish, G. G. (2012). Dependence regulation in newlywed couples: A prospective examination. *Personal Relationships, 19,* 644–662.

Derrick, J. L., Leonard, K. E., & Homish, G. G. (2013). Perceived partner responsiveness predicts decreases in smoking during the first nine years of marriage. *Nicotine & Tobacco Research, 15,* 1528–1536.

Derrick, J. L., Leonard, K. E., Quigley, B. M., Houston, R. J., Testa, M., & Kubiak, A. (2010). Relationship-specific alcohol expectancies in couples with concordant and discrepant drinking patterns. *Journal of Studies on Alcohol and Drugs, 71,* 761–768.

DiBello, A. M., Rodriguez, L. M., Hadden, B. W., & Neighbors, C. (2015). The green eyed monster in the bottle: Relationship contingent self-esteem, romantic jealousy, and alcohol-related problems. *Addictive Behaviors, 49,* 52–58.

Fischer, J. L., & Wiersma, J. D. (2012). Romantic relationships and alcohol use. *Current Drug Abuse Reviews, 5,* 98–116.

Fitzsimmons, G. M., Finkel, E. J., & vanDellen, M. R. (2015). Transactive goal dynamics. *Psychological Review, 122,* 648–673.

Fox, R. (1967). A multidisciplinary approach to treatment of alcoholism. *American Journal of Psychiatry, 123,* 769–778.

Fromme, K., & Ruela, A. (1994). Mediators and moderators of young adults' drinking. *Addiction, 89,* 63–71.

Hasin, D. S., Stinson, F. S., Ogburn, E., & Grant, B. F. (2007). Prevalence, correlates, disability, and comorbidity of DSM-IV alcohol abuse and dependence in the United States: Results from the National Epidemiologic Survey on Alcohol and Related Conditions. *Archives of General Psychiatry, 64,* 830–842.

Hilton, M. E. (1991). The demographic distribution of drinking patterns in 1984. In W. B. Clark & M. E. Hilton (Eds.), *Alcohol in America: Drinking practices and problems* (pp. 73–86). Albany, NY: State University of New York Press.

Homish, G. G., & Leonard, K. E. (2005). Marital quality and congruent drinking. *Journal of Studies on Alcohol, 66,* 488–496.

Homish, G. G., & Leonard, K. E. (2007). The drinking partnership and marital satisfaction: The longitudinal influence of discrepant drinking. *Journal of Consulting and Clinical Psychology, 75,* 43–51.

Homish, G. G., & Leonard, K. E. (2008). The social network and alcohol use. *Journal of Studies on Alcohol and Drugs, 69,* 906–914.

Homish, G. G., Leonard, K. E., Kozlowski, L. T., & Cornelius, J. R. (2009). The longitudinal association between multiple substance use discrepancies and marital satisfaction. *Addiction, 104,* 1201–1209.

Jessor, R., & Jessor, S. (1977). *Problem behavior and psychological development: A longitudinal study of youth.* New York, NY: Academic Press.

Kearns, J. N., & Leonard, K. E. (2004). The impact of changes in social network involvement on marital quality over the transition to marriage. *Journal of Family Psychology, 18,* 383–395.

Keenan, K., Kenward, M. G., Grundy, E., & Leon, D. A. (2013). Longitudinal prediction of divorce in Russia: The role of individual and couple drinking patterns. *Alcohol and Alcoholism, 48,* 737–742.

Labouvie, E. (1996). Maturing out of substance use: Selection and self-correction. *Journal of Drug Issues, 26,* 457–476.

Lau-Barraco, C., Braitman, A. L., Leonard, K. E., & Padilla, M. (2012). Drinking buddies and their prospective influence on alcohol outcomes: Alcohol expectancies as a mediator. *Psychology of Addictive Behaviors, 26,* 747–758.

Lawrence, E., Rothman, A. D., Cobb, R. J., Rothman, M. T., & Bradbury, T. N. (2008). Marital satisfaction across the transition to parenthood. *Journal of Family Psychology, 22,* 41–50.

Lee, M. R., Chassin, L., & MacKinnon, D. (2010). The effect of marriage on young adult heavy drinking and its mediators: Results from two methods of adjusting for selection into marriage. *Psychology of Addictive Behaviors, 24,* 712–718.

Lee, M. R., Chassin, L., & MacKinnon, D. P. (2015). Role transitions and young adult maturing out of heavy drinking: Evidence for larger effects of marriage among more severe premarriage problem drinkers. *Alcoholism: Clinical and Experimental Research, 39,* 1064–1074.

Lemke, S., Brennan, P. L., Schutte, K. K., & Moos, R. H. (2007). Upward pressures on drinking: Exposure and reactivity in adulthood. *Journal of Studies on Alcohol and Drugs, 68,* 437–445.

Leonard, K. E., & Eiden, R. D. (1999). Husband's and wive's drinking: Unilateral or bilateral influences among newlyweds in a general population sample. *Journal of Studies on Alcohol Supplement, 13,* 130–138.

Leonard, K. E., & Eiden, R. D. (2007). Marital and family processes in the context of alcohol use and alcohol disorders. *Annual Review of Clinical Psychology,* 3, 285–310.

Leonard, K. E., & Homish, G. G. (2008). Predictors of heavy drinking and drinking problems over the first 4 years of marriage. *Psychology of Addictive Behaviors,* 22, 25–35.

Leonard, K. E., & Mudar, P. (2000). Alcohol use in the year before marriage: Alcohol expectancies, peer and partner drinking as proximal influences on husband and wife alcohol involvement. *Alcoholism: Clinical and Experimental Research,* 24, 1666–1679.

Leonard, K. E., & Mudar, P. (2003). Peer and partner drinking and the transition to marriage: A longitudinal examination of selection and influence processes. *Psychology of Addictive Behaviors,* 17, 115–125.

Leonard, K. E., & Mudar, P. (2004). Husbands' influence on wives' drinking: Testing a relationship motivation model in the early years of marriage. *Psychology of Addictive Behaviors,* 18, 340–349.

Leonard, K. E., & Senchak, M. (1993). Alcohol and premarital aggression among newlywed couples. *Journal of Studies on Alcohol Supplement,* 11, 96–108.

Leonard, K. E., Smith, P. H., & Homish, G. G. (2014). Concordant and discordant alcohol, tobacco, and marijuana use as predictors of marital dissolution. *Psychology of Addictive Behaviors,* 28, 780–789.

Levitt, A., & Cooper, M. L. (2010). Daily alcohol use and romantic relationship functioning: Evidence of bidirectional, gender- and context-specific effects. *Personality and Social Psychology Bulletin,* 36, 1706–1722. doi:10.1177/0146167210388420

Levitt, A., Derrick, J. L., & Testa, M. (2014). Relationship-specific alcohol expectancies moderate the effects of relationship-drinking contexts on daily relationship functioning. *Journal of Studies on Alcohol and Drugs,* 75, 269–278. PMCID:PMC3965681

Levitt, A., & Leonard, K. E. (2013). Relationship-specific alcohol expectancies and relationship-drinking contexts: Reciprocal influence and gender-specific effects over the first 9 years of marriage. *Psychology of Addictive Behaviors,* 27, 986–996. PMCID:PMC3855643

Levitt, A., & Leonard, K. E. (2015). Insecure attachment styles, relationship-drinking contexts, and marital alcohol problems: Testing the mediating role of relationship-specific drinking-to-cope motives. *Psychology of Addictive Behaviors,* 29(3), 696–705.

Livingston, G., & Cohn, D. (2010, June 25). *Childlessness up among all women; Down among women with advanced degrees.* Pew Research Center, Social & Demographic Trends Report.

Marlatt, G. A., Demming, B., & Reid, J. B. (1973). Loss of control drinking in alcoholics: Experimental analog. *Journal of Abnormal Psychology,* 81, 233–241.

Marshal, M. P. (2003). For better or worse? The effects of alcohol use on marital functioning. *Clinical Psychology Review,* 23, 959–997.

McCrady, B. S., Noel, N. E., Abrans, D. B., Stout, R. L., Nelson, H. F., & Hay, W. M. (1986). Comparative effectiveness of three types of spouse involvement in outpatient behavioral alcoholism treatment. *Journal of Studies on Alcohol,* 47, 459–467.

Miller-Tutzauer, C., Leonard, K. E., & Windle, M. (1991). Marriage and alcohol use: A longitudinal study of "maturing out." *Journal of Studies on Alcohol,* 52, 434–440.

Mudar, P., Leonard, K. E., & Soltysinski, K. (2001). Discrepant substance use and marital functioning in newlywed couples. *Journal of Consulting and Clinical Psychology,* 69, 130–134.

Mushquash, A. R., Stewart, S. H., Sherry, S. B., Mackinnon, S. P., Antony, M. M., & Sherry, D. L. (2013). Heavy episodic drinking among dating partners: A longitudinal actor–partner interdependence model. *Psychology of Addictive Behaviors,* 27, 178–183.

O'Farrell, T. J., Cutter, H. S., & Floyd, F. J. (1985). Evaluating behavioral marital therapy for male alcoholics: Effects on marital adjustment and communication from before to after treatment. *Behavior Therapy,* 16, 147–167.

Ostermann, J., Sloan, F. A., & Taylor, D. H. (2005). Heavy alcohol use and marital dissolution in the USA. *Social Science & Medicine,* 61, 2304–2316.

Reczek, C., Liu, H., & Spiker, R. (2014). A population-based study of alcohol use in same-sex and different-sex unions. *Journal of Marriage and Family,* 76, 557–572.

Roberts, L. J., & Linney, K. D. (2000). Alcohol problems and couples: Drinking in an intimate relational context. In K. B. Schmaling & T. G. Sher (Eds.), *The psychology of couples and illness: Theory, research, and practice* (pp. 269–310). Washington, DC: American Psychological Association.

Rodriguez, L. M., DiBello, A. M., & Neighbors, C. (2013). Perceptions of partner drinking problems, regulation strategies and relationship outcomes. *Addictive Behaviors,* 38, 2949–2957.

Rodriguez, L. M., Knee, C. R., & Neighbors, C. (2014). Relationships can drive some to drink: Relationship-contingent self-esteem and drinking problems. *Journal of Social and Personal Relationships,* 31, 270–290.

Rodriguez, L. M., & Neighbors, C. (2015). An interdependent look at perceptions of spousal drinking problems and marital outcomes. *Alcohol, 49*, 597–605.

Rodriguez, L. M., Neighbors, C., & Knee, C. R. (2014). Problematic alcohol use and marital distress: An interdependence theory perspective. *Addiction Research and Theory, 22*, 294–312.

Smith, P. H., Homish, G. G., Leonard, K. E., & Cornelius, J. R. (2012). Women ending marriage to a problem drinking partner decrease their own risk for problem drinking. *Addiction, 107*, 1453–1461.

Steele, C. M., & Josephs, R. A. (1990). Alcohol myopia: Its prized and dangerous effects. *American Psychologist, 45*, 921–933.

Stillwell, R., & Stable, J. (2013). *Public school graduates and dropouts from the Common Core of Data: School year 2009–10: First look (provisional data)* (NCES 2013-309 rev.). Washington, DC: US Department of Education, National Center for Education Statistics. Retrieved from http://nces.ed.gov/pubsearch

Torvik, F. A., Roysamb, E., Gustavson, K., Idstad, M., & Tambs, K. (2013). Discordant and concordant alcohol use in spouses as predictors of marital dissolution in the general population: Results from the Hunt Study. *Alcoholism: Clinical and Experimental Research, 37*, 877–884.

Verges, A., Jackson, K. M., Bucholz, K. K., Grant, J. D., Trull, T. J., Wood, P. K., & Sher, K. J. (2012). Deconstructing the age–prevalence curve of alcohol dependence: Why "maturing out" is only a small piece of the puzzle. *Journal of Abnormal Psychology, 121*, 511–523.

Waldron, M., Heath, A. C., Lynskey, M. T., Bucholz, K. K., Madden, P. A. F., & Martin, N. G. (2011). Alcoholic marriage: Later start, sooner end. *Alcoholism: Clinical and Experimental Research, 35*, 632–642.

Wiersma, J. D., & Fischer, J. L. (2014). Young adult drinking partnerships: Alcohol-related consequences and relationship problems six years later. *Journal of Studies on Alcohol and Drugs, 75*, 704–712.

Zucker, R. A. (1979). Developmental aspects of drinking through the young adult years. In H. T. Blane & M. E. Chafetz (Eds.), *Youth, alcohol, & social policy* (pp. 91–146). New York, NY: Plenum.

Zucker, R. A., Fitzgerald, H. E., & Moses, H. D. (1995). Emergence of alcohol problems and the several alcoholisms: A developmental perspective on etiologic theory and life course trajectory. In D. Cicchetti & D. J. Cohen (Eds.), *Developmental psychopathology: Vol. 2. Risk, disorder, and adaptation* (Wiley Series on Personality Processes, pp. 677–711). Oxford, UK: Wiley.

19

Social Psychology of Alcohol Involvement, Marital Dissolution, and Marital Interaction Processes Across Multiple Timescales

James A. Cranford

Catharine E. Fairbairn

The Michigan Longitudinal Study (MLS; Zucker, 2014) was among the first studies to collect data from multiple informants within the same family via multiple methods to examine associations between alcohol involvement and social interaction processes across multiple timescales. These methodological innovations were informed by an evolving developmental psychopathology conceptual framework that focused on risk aggregation as an organizing construct for understanding the developmental course of alcoholism. Results from the MLS and other projects (Leonard & Eiden, 2007; Leonard & Rothbard, 1999) have also illuminated some of the dyadic associations between alcohol involvement and marital interaction processes across different timescales. This chapter reviews research on the association between alcohol involvement and marital dissolution. We describe an emerging theoretical framework for research on substance use and marriage based on social psychology, relationship science, and developmental science that (1) includes both spouses and focuses on the dyad as the unit of analysis to explicitly test for husband and wife differences and dyadic patterns of alcohol involvement and (2) assesses core constructs across multiple timescales, with a focus on daily processes as potential linkages between real-time marital interactions and outcomes that unfold over longer timescales. This framework can strengthen connections between social

psychological and developmental theory, inform basic research on alcohol and social interaction processes, and potentially enhance prevention and treatment efforts by identifying the mechanisms underlying the associations between alcohol involvement and negative marital outcomes.

ALCOHOL INVOLVEMENT AND MARITAL DISSOLUTION

A substantial body of evidence shows that alcohol involvement is associated with negative marital outcomes, including marital dissatisfaction (Leonard & Eiden, 2007; Marshal, 2003) and marital violence (Capaldi, Knoble, Shortt, & Kim, 2012; Devries et al., 2014). At the turn of the 21st century, Leonard and Rothbard (1999) noted that "perhaps because of the commonsense appeal that drinking causes marital problems and divorce, few studies have systematically addressed this issue" (p. 143). Although systematic investigation of this association is relatively recent, there is clear historical evidence for a relationship between alcohol involvement and marital dissolution. For example, prior to the 19th century, adultery and desertion were legally valid grounds for divorce in the United States (Bishop, 1852; Loomis, 1866). In the 19th century, some states included "habitual drunkenness," habitual intemperance," and "gross and confirmed habits of drunkenness" as legal grounds for divorce (Amato & Irving, 2006; Woolsey, 1869). The first US government report related to marriage and divorce, published in 1889, estimated that "drunkenness or intemperance" was a direct or indirect cause of approximately 20.1% of all divorces granted in the United States between 1867 and 1886 (US Department of Labor, 1889; see also US Department of Health, Education, and Welfare, 1973). Similarly, "intemperance" was a direct or indirect cause of 19.5% of all divorces granted in the United States between 1887 and 1906 (US Department of Commerce and Labor, 1909).

Evidence for a relationship between alcohol involvement and marital dissolution continued to accumulate during the 20th century (Bacon, 1944; Heron, 1912; Kephart, 1954; Rosenbaum, 1958; Straus & Bacon, 1951; for a review of early studies on alcoholism and marriage, see Bailey, 1961). Paolino, McCrady, and Diamond (1978) reviewed studies from the 1940s through the 1970s showing higher rates of marital problems among those with alcohol use disorders (AUDs) or alcohol problems. In approximately the past 25 years, results from several large-scale epidemiological studies using cross-sectional and longitudinal designs supported the hypothesized association between alcohol involvement and marital dissolution (Amato & Previti, 2003; Amato & Rogers, 1997; Chilcoat & Breslau, 1996; Kessler, Walters, & Forthofer, 1998; Leonard & Roberts, 1998 [cited in Roberts & Linney, 2000]; Power & Estaugh, 1990; Prescott & Kendler, 2001; Smith, Homish, Leonard, & Cornelius, 2012; Waldron, Bucholz, Lynskey, Madden, & Heath, 2013; Waldron et al., 2011; Wilsnack & Wilsnack, 1991). For example, results from the National Epidemiologic Survey on Alcohol and Related Conditions (NESARC) indicated that (1) almost half (48.3%) of those with a lifetime AUD also reported lifetime marital dissolution; and (2) past 12-months AUD predicted marital dissolution 3 years later independently of marital history, stressful life events, other substance use disorders, mood and anxiety disorders, and personality disorders (Cranford, 2014). In one of the few longitudinal studies that assessed both partners, Leonard, Smith, and Homish (2014) analyzed data from 634 couples over 9 years and found that the odds of divorce were significantly higher among discrepant drinking couples (i.e.,

couples in which the wife was a heavy drinker but the husband was not).

Some evidence suggested that AUDs have specific effects on marital outcomes (Malzberg, 1947; Wolf, 1958). For example, Collins, Ellickson, and Klein (2007) showed that frequency of intoxication (but not frequency of marijuana use, frequency of cigarette smoking, or any hard drug use) was longitudinally associated with divorce. Determining the relative importance of alcohol involvement as a predictor of marital dissolution is difficult (1) due to high rates of comorbidity between AUDs and other psychological disorders that are associated with negative marital outcomes (e.g., depression and antisocial personality disorder; Cranford, Nolen-Hoeksema, & Zucker, 2011; Floyd, Cranford, Daugherty, Fitzgerald, & Zucker, 2006) and (2) because heavy alcohol use and AUDs are associated with numerous demographic and behavioral correlates of divorce (e.g., marital aggression and infidelity; Amato, 2010). However, at least two longitudinal studies found that alcohol involvement predicted subsequent marital dissolution when comorbid depression and antisocial personality disorder were statistically controlled (Cranford, 2014; Leonard et al., 2014).

Although a great deal of evidence indicated linkages between alcohol involvement and marital dissolution, some longitudinal studies have yielded inconsistent results. For example, Fu and Goldman (2000) did not find the hypothesized association between alcohol involvement and marital dissolution in a longitudinal study. Indeed, their results showed that moderate alcohol use among men was associated with *lower* risk of divorce. Several other studies also reported nonsignificant associations between alcohol involvement and marital outcomes (Bruce, 1998; Locke & Newcomb, 2003; Power, Rodgers, & Hope, 1999; Sanchez & Gager, 2000). In the following sections, we describe a model of marital interaction based on social psychological theory that (1) specifies pathways between alcohol involvement and marital outcomes that emphasize marital interactions, (2) highlights the importance of studying both members of the couple to examine husband–wife differences and spousal concordance, and (3) assesses core constructs across multiple timescales to examine the connections between real-time marital interactions and marital outcomes over longer developmental timespans.

SOCIAL PSYCHOLOGICAL MODELS OF MARITAL INTERACTION PROCESSES AND OUTCOMES

Social psychology has been defined as "the scientific study of how people think about, influence, and relate to one another" (Myers, 2013). However, despite social psychology's status as the scientific discipline that studies social interaction, social psychological theory and research on marriage were relatively rare until the late 20th century (Levinger, 1976, 1980). *Interdependence theory* (Kelley et al., 1983; Thibaut & Kelley, 1959), one of the oldest theories of interpersonal relations in social psychology, explicitly focused on social interaction and defined *interdependence* as the causal connections between the thoughts, feelings, and behaviors of two people as their interaction unfolds over time. Early social psychologists such as Lewin (1936) suggested the equation $B = f(P, E)$ (i.e., behavior is a function of the person and the environment), and Kelley et al. (2003) adapted this equation based on interdependence theory to define the interaction between two people, Person A and Person B: $I = f(S, A, B)$—that is, interaction is a function of the situation, Person A, and Person B.

Subsequent work applied interdependence theory to the study of marriage in the form of social exchange and behavioral theory (Levinger, 1965, 1976, 1980; Levinger & Huston, 1990). In an extensive review of theory and research on the longitudinal course of marital quality and stability, Karney and Bradbury (1995) integrated elements of social exchange, behavioral, attachment, and crisis theory to advance a vulnerability–stress–adaptation model (VSAM) of marriage. The VSAM includes three broad classes of variables that are hypothesized to influence marital outcomes: (1) *enduring vulnerabilities* (stable personal characteristics, such as lifetime AUD), (2) *stressful events* (acute and chronic stressors that couples face, such as financial strain), and (3) *adaptive processes* (the behaviors that spouses exchange, such as marital interactions that involve problem-solving or provision of social support). According to the VSAM, enduring vulnerabilities and stressful events may have independent effects on marital satisfaction, and these effects are mediated by marital interactions. As noted by Karney and Bradbury, the hypothesized mediational role of marital interaction is based on the idea that "any variable that affects a close relationship can do so only through its influence on ongoing interaction" (p. 23).

In addition to organizing theory and research on marital dissolution, the Karney and Bradbury (1995) review advanced two additional suggestions that are particularly relevant to the study of alcohol involvement and marriage: (1) assessing both members of the couple and (2) assessing core constructs over multiple timescales. Next, we describe how these theory-based methodological innovations can inform research on alcohol involvement and marital outcomes.

Assessing Both Spouses: Behavioral Observation Studies of Alcoholic Couples

Karney and Bradbury (1995) noted that 43% of the samples included in the 115 studies they reviewed were based on data from one spouse, and they observed that data from both partners are needed for examination of within- and between-couple processes (Capaldi et al., 2012; Whisman, Uebelacker, & Weinstock, 2004). Early studies using behavioral observation methods anticipated this suggestion and examined associations between alcohol involvement and real-time interactions between spouses. To our knowledge, the first studies to use behavioral observation methods with videotaped recordings of marital interactions of alcoholic couples (i.e., couples in which one or both partners have an AUD) were conducted in the early 1970s (Eisler, Hersen, & Agras, 1973; Hersen, Miller, & Eisler, 1973). Although there are some exceptions (Becker & Miller, 1976), the available evidence from early behavioral observation studies generally showed that compared to non-alcoholic (NALC) couples, alcoholic (ALC) couples displayed (1) higher levels of negative marital interaction (Billings, Kessler, Gomberg, & Weiner, 1979; Frankenstein, Hay, & Nathan, 1985; Haber & Jacob, 1997; Jacob, Ritchey, Cvitkovic, & Blane, 1981), (2) lower levels of positive marital interaction (Frankenstein et al., 1985; Haber & Jacob, 1997; Jacob et al., 1981; Jacob, Leonard, & Haber, 2001), and (3) fewer problem-solving behaviors in marital interaction (Billings et al., 1979; for a review, see McCrady & Epstein, 1995).

Some researchers incorporated experimental drinking conditions into their behavioral observational studies of ALC and NALC couples and used versions of the Marital Interaction Coding System (MICS; see Heyman, 2004) to code behaviors during marital problem-solving interactions. For example, Billings et al. (1979) found no differences in the marital interaction behaviors of ALC couples who consumed alcohol in a laboratory session and those who did not (see also Frankenstein et al., 1985). By contrast, Jacob and Leonard (1988) observed increases in negative interaction and decreases in problem-solving interaction among ALC couples (with an episodic ALC husband) in "drink" compared to "no drink" conditions (see also Jacob et al., 1981, 2001). Other behavioral observation studies using alcohol administration showed that higher levels of negativity in ALC compared to NALC depressed and nondistressed couples emerged only when spouses had consumed alcohol (Jacob & Krahn, 1988), but these differences were not as strong when sequential interactions were examined (Jacob & Leonard, 1992).

Taken as a whole, results from these behavioral observation studies indicated some differences in the real-time marital interactions of ALC compared to NALC couples but few differences between ALC and distressed NALC couples (Marshal, 2003). Relatively recently, our team analyzed data from the MLS and found elevated levels of hostile behavior in couples with an antisocial alcoholic husband (Floyd et al., 2006). To our knowledge, the largest behavioral observation study of marital conflict and alcohol was conducted by Testa, Crane, Quigley, Levitt, and Leonard (2014). Adding to the complexity of this literature, they found that actor's alcohol use was associated with higher levels of positive and lower levels of negative behavior when partners did *not* consume alcohol; alcohol did not have any effects on behavior when both partners consumed it (Testa & Derrick, 2014).

The available evidence from behavioral observation studies provided some clues about the potential mechanisms underlying the alcohol involvement–marital dissolution association, but results have not been consistent. As noted by Marshal (2003), there is considerable variability across studies in terms of the system used to code the behaviors, and "inconsistent coding and operational definitions of the various behavioral interaction categories across studies limits our ability to draw strong, substantive conclusions regarding the effects of alcohol use on marital interaction" (p. 978; see also Floyd, O'Farrell, & Goldberg, 1987). In addition, questions have been raised about the reliability and validity of marital interaction measures based on manual coding (Floyd, 1989). Substantively, there is evidence that marital conflict may not be as important as originally believed (Fincham, Stanley, & Beach, 2007). As a result of these challenges, "routine use of empirically

based couple assessment using ABO in clinical settings remains elusive" (Snyder, Heyman, & Haynes, 2005, p. 298), and it is unclear how real-time marital interactions translate into marital outcomes over longer timespans.

Assessing Both Spouses: Husband–Wife Differences and Concordance

Including both spouses also allows for specific tests of hypotheses based on dyadic models. Reis, Collins, and Berscheid (2000) suggested that the relatively new field of relationship science required a move away from a focus on individuals toward a dyadic, systems science perspective to better understand the developmental context of relationships. Consistent with this suggestion, there are now many models that explicitly focus on the dyad as the unit of analysis when studying marriage (Berg & Upchurch, 2007; Birditt, Newton, Cranford, & Ryan, 2016).

Although dyadic models in social psychology are not new (Sears, 1951), the development of appropriate statistical methods to test them (e.g., the Actor–Partner Interdependence Model [APIM]; Kenny, Kashy, & Cook, 2006) is relatively recent. For example, our team (Cranford, Floyd, Schulenberg, & Zucker, 2011) used the APIM to test hypotheses about the longitudinal association between husbands' and wives' AUD, martial interactions, and marital adjustment using data from Zucker's (2014) MLS. Husbands' AUD predicted a lower ratio of positive to negative behaviors (P:N ratio) among wives 3 years later but was not associated with their own marital behavior, nor was it associated with their own or their wives' marital adjustment 9 years later. By contrast, wives' AUD and P:N ratio were independently associated with their own and their husbands' marital adjustment. These findings suggested that marital adjustment in ALC couples may be driven more by the wives' than the husbands' AUD and marital behaviors (Rodriguez & Neighbors, 2015). In general, results highlighted the importance of assessing both partners over time to better understand the effects of AUDs on marriage (see also Testa et al., 2014).

Collecting data from both spouses is also important because gender "permeates social interaction throughout life" (Reis et al., 2000, p. 862), and this is a particularly important consideration in studies of alcohol and marriage because of consistent gender differences in alcohol involvement. The majority of studies of alcohol and marriage have focused on couples with an ALC husband and a NALC wife (McCrady & Epstein, 1995), due in part to the fact that in the population as a whole, and in the population of married and cohabiting adults age 18 years or older, male ALCs outnumber female ALCs by a ratio of almost 2:1 (Grant et al., 2015; see also Nolen-Hoeksema & Hilt, 2006). A smaller set of studies have examined the associations of wives' alcohol involvement and marital outcomes. Earlier research showed that alcoholic women had higher rates of marital disruption compared to non-alcoholic women (Lisansky, 1957; Rosenbaum, 1958), and longitudinal research indicated that heavy drinking among women predicted later marital separation and divorce (Wilsnack & Wilsnack, 1991). Subsequent studies have yielded inconsistent findings. For example, Dumka and Roosa (1993) found no direct associations between husbands' or wives' problem drinking and wives' marital satisfaction. By contrast, Noel, McCrady, Stout, and Fisher-Nelson (1991) reported that female alcoholics and their husbands reported *higher* marital satisfaction compared to a sample of male alcoholics and their wives.

Recently, our team used behavioral observation and daily process methods to assess gender differences in a small sample of male and female alcoholic probands (Cranford, Tennen, & Zucker, 2015). We found that female probands and male spouses generally reported higher levels of negative marital interaction during the past 1 month and during the 14-day diary period compared to male probands/female spouses. Results also showed that during a 15-minute behavioral observation task, female probands displayed less humor, a lower positive-to-negative ratio of positive to negative behaviors, and more negative reciprocity. Taken together, results showed that marital conflict, assessed via multiple methods over multiple timescales, was higher in female proband/male spouse couples.

Another reason why assessing both partners is important for understanding the association of alcohol involvement with marital dissolution stems from the observation of consistent differences in marital outcomes based on *concordance* between spouses on AUD and drinking behaviors (as well as other health behaviors). A substantial body of evidence indicates that the pattern of husbands' and wives' alcohol involvement has implications for marital outcomes (Homish & Leonard, 2005, 2007; Homish, Leonard,

Kozlowski, & Cornelius, 2009; Leonard et al., 2014; Mudar, Leonard, & Soltysinski, 2001; Ostermann, Sloan, & Taylor, 2005; Quigley & Leonard, 2000; for reviews, see Leonard & Eiden, 2007; Marshal, 2003). For example, results from the MLS (Floyd et al., 2006) showed that the ratio of positive to negative behaviors during a marital interaction (as a dyad-level variable) was lower among couples that included an alcoholic husband/non-alcoholic wife compared to couples with either (1) a non-alcoholic husband and wife or (2) an alcoholic husband and wife. In a subsequent paper (Cranford, Floyd, et al., 2011), we found that dyadic adjustment was lower among wives but not husbands in couples with discordant lifetime AUD status, regardless of the nature of the discordance (i.e., husband yes AUD/wife no AUD and husband no AUD/wife yes AUD). The previously described study by Leonard et al. (2014) showed that discrepant drinking was associated with subsequent marital dissolution. However, concordance effects are not always observed (Testa et al., 2012), and sometimes the pattern of results is contrary to prediction (Testa et al., 2014).

Assessing Core Constructs over Multiple Timescales

Relatively few behavioral observation studies of alcoholic couples have examined the longer term implications of real-time marital interactions. Although interdependence theory acknowledged the importance of time and the temporal structure of situations, it did not explicitly identify the timescale of social interaction or incorporate a developmental focus (Karney & Bradbury, 1995). In later writings, Kelley (1997) noted the complexity of defining the temporal flow of social interaction sequences. However, relationship science maintains that "relationships are . . . inherently temporal in nature" (Reis et al., 2000, p. 845), and early social psychological theory on marital interaction made gross distinctions between "short-term interaction," as reflected in "sequences and cycles that last seconds, minutes, or hours," and "long-term interdependence," defined as "developmental changes which endure days, months, or many years in the life of a relationship" (Levinger, 1980, p. 519).

A more explicit consideration of the conceptual and empirical utility of multiple timescales is provided by approaches based on complex nonlinear dynamic systems and general systems theories. In social and personality psychology, this framework is sometimes referred to as *the dynamical approach* or *dynamical social psychology* (Vallacher, Read, & Nowak, 2002; Wiese, Vallacher, & Strawinska, 2010). Based on nonlinear dynamic systems models in the mathematical and physical sciences, this approach has found application across a range of disciplines and subdisciplines, including developmental psychopathology (Granic & Hollenstein, 2003), marriage (Boker & Laurenceau, 2006; Gottman, Swanson, & Swanson, 2002), and alcohol involvement (Witkiewitz & Marlatt, 2007). Indeed, early work used a general systems approach with a developmental focus to interpret the influence of alcohol involvement on marital interaction patterns (Steinglass, Davis, & Berenson, 1977; for a review, see Jacob, Favorini, Meisel, & Anderson, 1978).

Relatively recently, dynamic systems approaches have explored the connections between real-time (i.e., moment-to-moment, "microsocial") and developmental time (i.e., "macrosocial") processes (Granic & Patterson, 2006). As noted by Molenaar, Sinclair, Rovine, Ram, and Corneal (2009), one goal of dynamic systems theory is "to model the interplay between short-term observations and long-term trajectories" (p. 261). Similarly, Gerstorf, Hoppmann, and Ram (2014) reviewed research on adult cognitive functioning and noted that

> there are well-replicated and conceptually meaningful associations between micro time-scale variability and macro time-scale development [in cognitive functioning], but the more intermediate mechanisms remain uncharted territory (e.g., what connects the micro and macro time-scales and which kinds of meso time-scales are operating). (p. 77)

The gap between real time and developmental time was also noted in the marital literature (Huston, 2000; Larson & Almeida, 1999). Similarly, the research we reviewed on alcohol involvement and marital outcomes includes a considerable number of behavioral observation studies of real-time processes and also prospective panel studies of processes over years and decades (Cranford, Nolen-Hoeksema, et al., 2011). As described next, using multiple timescales can potentially link "micro" and "macro" levels of analysis and also connect social psychological theories on alcohol and marriage with developmental theory.

LINKING REAL-TIME AND DEVELOPMENTAL TIME DYADIC PROCESSES WITH INTENSIVE LONGITUDINAL METHODS

It has been asserted that concepts based on dynamic systems theory "provide the bridge between real-time and longer term patterns of couple relationship" (Howe, 2007, p. 302). In addition, Kelley (1997) suggested daily diary and ecological momentary assessment (EMA) methods for testing hypotheses based on interdependence theory. *Daily process designs*, also known as *diary methods* (Bolger, Davis, & Rafaeli, 2003), involve the assessment of variables that "are thought to change in *meaningful* ways from day to day (or within a day) and are measured *prospectively* at daily (or within-day) intervals" (Affleck, Zautra, Tennen, & Armeli, 1999, p. 747). Similarly, as defined by Stone, Shiffman, Atienza, and Nebeling (2007), "EMA methods are characterized by the repeated collection of real-time data on participants' momentary states in the natural environment" (p. 3). We further suggest that the use of daily process and EMA methods (referred to collectively as "intensive longitudinal methods"; Bolger & Laurenceau, 2013) may yield insights into the linkages between real-time and developmental time marital interaction processes and outcomes in ALC couples (Cranford, Tennen, & Zucker, 2010). For example, as described previously, our team recently used behavioral observation and daily process methods to examine gender differences in marital interactions as a function of alcohol involvement (Cranford et al., 2015), and results also showed that daily urge to drink was predictive of depressive symptoms 6 months later (Yang, Cranford, Li, & Buu, 2015).

Using intensive longitudinal methods to assess constructs across multiple timescales might also inform substance use treatment. A large body of evidence showed that substance use disorders (SUDs), defined as "a cluster of cognitive, behavioral, and physiological symptoms indicating that the individual continues using the substance despite significant substance-related problems" (American Psychiatric Association, 2013, p. 483), are major public health problems that impose an enormous burden on individuals, families, and communities (Whiteford et al., 2013). The substantial burden of alcohol and other SUDs highlights the importance of effective interventions and treatment, and there is good evidence that relationship factors are important predictors of treatment outcomes among adults with alcohol and other SUDs (McCrady, Epstein, Cook, Jensen, & Hildebrandt, 2009; for a review, see O'Farrell, 2015). In addition, evidence showed that couple-level interventions reduced alcohol involvement and marital violence and increased marital satisfaction (for reviews, see Epstein & McCrady, 1998; O'Farrell & Fals-Stewart, 2003). There is strong evidence that couples-oriented alcoholism treatment has beneficial effects on individual-level drinking and marital quality (McCrady, Hayaki, Epstein, & Hirsch, 2002), and a relatively recent paper reviewed evidence for couple-based interventions for a wide range of psychiatric disorders (Baucom, Belus, Adelman, Fischer, & Paprocki, 2014). The approach described here has the potential to advance our understanding of the specific marital interactions that increase the risk of short- and long-term marital- and individual-level outcomes in ALC and NALC couples, and it may inform couples-focused therapeutic efforts designed to reduce the risk of negative marital and individual-level outcomes (Bamberger, 2016).

CONCLUSIONS AND FUTURE DIRECTIONS

This chapter reviewed evidence showing that alcohol involvement has relatively consistent associations with marital dissolution. However, there are several studies that did not support this prediction. Differences in methodology across studies could be one reason for the disparity in results. Thus, we described a framework for marriage and close relationships based on social psychological theory that highlights the importance of (1) including both spouses and focusing on the dyad as the unit of analysis and (2) assessing core constructs over multiple timescales, and we argued that the use of intensive longitudinal methods may provide an important bridge between real time and developmental timescales. This in turn could facilitate linkages between social psychology and dynamic systems approaches to substance use and marriage. Greater attention to the developmental context of substance use and marriage can in turn enhance prevention and treatment efforts that target the marital dyad.

Here, we briefly note several promising directions for future work. Consistent with the suggestion to assess core constructs across multiple timescales, there is an extensive body of literature on the examination of the association between substance use and marriage at multiple levels of analysis. For example, emerging evidence indicates genetic influences on marriage and divorce (Jerskey et al., 2010; Spotts & Ganiban, 2015), and recent work has revealed genetic influences on the covariation between alcohol use and problems and the frequency of romantic conflict and warmth (Salvatore, Prom-Wormley, Prescott, & Kendler, 2015; for reviews, see Reiss, 2010; Robinson, Fernald, & Clayton, 2008). From social neuroscience, there has been considerable interest in the influence of oxytocin on social behavior in general (Love, 2014) and marital interaction in particular (Ditzen et al., 2009; Gouin et al., 2010). In addition, a developing area variously referred to as "two-person neuroscience" (Hari, Henriksson, Malinen, & Parkkonen, 2015), "two-body neuroscience" (Dumas, 2011), or "second-person neuroscience" (Dumas, Kelso, & Nadel, 2014) has developed methods to simultaneously monitor brain function in two people as they interact in order to determine function relations between two brains (for a review, see Kasai, Fukuda, Yahata, Morita, & Fujii, 2015). To our knowledge, this methodology has not yet been used to study marital interactions and could be an interesting avenue of exploration.

In addition to exploring how alcohol use might influence marital functioning, recent work has examined how processes observed in close relationships might influence alcohol use outcomes (Fairbairn & Sayette, 2014; Leonard & Eiden, 2007). Results of longitudinal studies suggest that indexes of marital quality and marital satisfaction predict prospectively to drinking outcomes (Leonard & Homish, 2008; Whisman, Uebelacker, & Bruce, 2006), and individuals in recovery from AUD indicate spousal factors as a primary contributor to relapse (Maisto, McKay, & O'Farrell, 1995). As noted previously, interventions aimed primarily at improving marital quality have been shown to decrease problematic drinking (O'Farrell, 2015). Thus, an understanding of the processes involved in close relationships is highly relevant to the understanding of the initiation and progression of AUD.

In ongoing research exploring this question, we incorporate alcohol-administration methods, examining the reinforcement that people get from alcohol within the context of marital interactions. The vast majority of alcohol is consumed within the context of social interaction (Fairbairn & Sayette, 2014), and the reward that people get from drinking in these contexts may be highly relevant for understanding vulnerability for AUD (Fairbairn, Sayette, Aalen, & Frigessi, 2015; Fairbairn, Sayette, Wright, et al., 2015; Sayette, Reichle, & Schooler, 2009). In particular, we have been examining the social and emotional rewards that people gain from drinking within the context of social interactions as a way to understand AUD risk. This line of research has explored several questions, including the following: (1) Might alcohol reinforcement differ depending on whether drinkers consume alcohol within the context of interactions with close others versus interactions involving lessor acquaintances or strangers? and (2) When alcohol is consumed within the context of close relationships, might the quality of these relationships determine the extent to which alcohol is experienced as reinforcing?

With respect to the former of these questions, we conducted a comprehensive review of the alcohol-administration literature and, on the basis of this review, formulated a social-attributional model of alcohol reinforcement (Fairbairn & Sayette, 2014). This model predicts that the degree of alcohol reinforcement will vary depending on whether alcohol is consumed together with close family and friends or whether it is consumed within the context of interactions with lessor acquaintances. For example, in a recent examination of the couples involved in Testa et al.'s (2014) large-scale alcohol-administration study, which explored alcohol's effects within the context of marital interaction, we found that the degree of reinforcement participants gained from alcohol differed significantly depending on how satisfied they were in their intimate partnerships (Fairbairn & Testa, 2017). Specifically, we found that alcohol consumption reduced negative behaviors, reduced negative reciprocity, and increased self-reported reward selectively among couples who were dissatisfied with their relationships. In contrast, alcohol had comparatively little reinforcing effect when individuals were already happy in their relationships. Because alcohol may often be consumed within the context of couples interactions, these results indicate acute alcohol reinforcement as one mechanism explaining prospective links between marital distress and alcohol problems (Fairbairn & Cranford, 2016; Leonard & Homish, 2008; Whisman et al., 2006).

In summary, more than 40 years ago, Orford (1975) argued against specialism in research on alcohol involvement and marriage and cited interdependence theory (Levinger, 1976) as a potentially useful theoretical framework. The research on alcohol involvement and marital dissolution reviewed in this chapter supports Orford's suggestion that social psychological theory could potentially provide "guidelines for the development of a more truly social–psychological theory of alcoholism and marriage" (p. 1558). We believe that the field will continue to move forward by further integration of concepts and methods from the growing areas of relationship science, developmental science, and dynamic systems theories. Along with these conceptual and theoretical additions, we believe that a theoretical framework that focuses on marital interaction as the unit of analysis and that assesses core constructs over multiple timescales will advance our understanding of the developmental dynamics of alcohol involvement and marriage and maximize the impact of prevention and treatment efforts.

REFERENCES

Affleck, G., Zautra, A., Tennen, H., & Armeli, S. (1999). Multilevel daily process designs for consulting and clinical psychology: A preface for the perplexed. *Journal of Consulting and Clinical Psychology, 67*(5), 746–754. doi:10.1037/0022-006X.67.5.746

Amato, P. R. (2010). Research on divorce: Continuing trends and new developments. *Journal of Marriage and Family, 72*(3), 650–666. doi:10.1111/j.1741-3737.2010.00723.x

Amato, P. R., & Irving, S. (2006). Historical trends in divorce in the United States. In M. A. Fine & J. H. Harvey (Eds.), *Handbook of divorce and relationship dissolution* (pp. 41–57). Mahwah, NJ: Erlbaum.

Amato, P. R., & Previti, D. (2003). People's reasons for divorcing: Gender, social class, the life course, and adjustment. *Journal of Family Issues, 24*(5), 602–626.

Amato, P. R., & Rogers, S. J. (1997). A longitudinal study of marital problems and subsequent divorce. *Journal of Marriage and Family, 59*(3), 612–624.

American Psychiatric Association. (2013). *The diagnostic and statistical manual of mental disorders* (5th ed.). Arlington, VA: American Psychiatric Publishing.

Bacon, S. D. (1944). Inebriety, social integration, and marriage. *Quarterly Journal of Studies on Alcohol, 5*, 86–125.

Bailey, M. B. (1961). Alcoholism and marriage: A review of research and professional literature. *Quarterly Journal of Studies on Alcohol, 22*, 81–97.

Bamberger, K. T. (2016). The application of intensive longitudinal methods to investigate change: Stimulating the field of applied family research. *Clinical Child and Family Psychology Review*, 19(1), 21–38. doi:10.1007/s10567-015-0194-6

Baucom, D. H., Belus, J. M., Adelman, C. B., Fischer, M. S., & Paprocki, C. (2014). Couple-based interventions for psychopathology: A renewed direction for the field. *Family Process*, 53(3), 445–461.

Becker, J. V., & Miller, P. M. (1976). Verbal and nonverbal marital interaction patterns of alcoholics and nonalcoholics. *Journal of Studies on Alcohol*, 37, 1616–1624.

Berg, C. A., & Upchurch, R. (2007). A developmental–contextual model of couples coping with chronic illness across the adult life span. *Psychological Bulletin*, 133(6), 920–954.

Billings, A. G., Kessler, M., Gomberg, C. A., & Weiner, S. (1979). Marital conflict resolution of alcoholic and nonalcoholic couples during drinking and nondrinking sessions. *Journal of Studies on Alcohol*, 40(3), 183–195.

Birditt, K. S., Newton, N. J., Cranford, J. A., & Ryan, L. H. (2016). Stress and negative relationship quality among older couples: Implications for blood pressure. *Journals of Gerontology Series B: Psychological Sciences and Social Sciences*, 71(5), 775–785.

Bishop, J. P. (1852). *Commentaries on the law of marriage and divorce, and evidence in matrimonial suits.* Boston, MA: Little, Brown.

Boker, S. M., & Laurenceau, J.-P. (2006). Dynamical systems modeling: An application to the regulation of intimacy and disclosure in marriage. In T. A. Walls & J. L. Schafer (Eds.), *Models for intensive longitudinal data* (pp. 195–218). New York, NY: Oxford University Press.

Bolger, N., Davis, A., & Rafaeli, E. (2003). Diary methods: Capturing life as it is lived. *Annual Review of Psychology*, 54, 579–616.

Bolger, N., & Laurenceau, J.-P. (2013). *Intensive longitudinal methods: An introduction to diary and experience sampling research.* New York, NY: Guilford.

Bruce, M. L. (1998). Divorce and psychopathology. In B. P. Dohrenwend (Ed.), *Adversity, stress, and psychopathology* (pp. 219–232). New York, NY: Oxford University Press.

Capaldi, D. M., Knoble, N. B., Shortt, J. W., & Kim, H. K. (2012). A systematic review of risk factors for intimate partner violence. *Partner Abuse*, 3(2), 231–280.

Chilcoat, H. D., & Breslau, N. (1996). Alcohol disorders in young adulthood: Effects of transitions into adult roles. *Journal of Health and Social Behavior*, 37(4), 339–349.

Collins, R. L., Ellickson, P. L., & Klein, D. J. (2007). The role of substance use in young adult divorce. *Addiction*, 102(5), 786–794.

Cranford, J. A. (2014). DSM-IV alcohol dependence and marital dissolution: Evidence from the National Epidemiologic Survey on Alcohol and Related Conditions. *Journal of Studies on Alcohol and Drugs*, 75(3), 520–529.

Cranford, J. A., Floyd, F. J., Schulenberg, J. E., & Zucker, R. A. (2011). Husbands' and wives' alcohol use disorders and marital interactions as longitudinal predictors of marital adjustment. *Journal of Abnormal Psychology*, 120(1), 210–222. doi:10.1037/a0021349

Cranford, J. A., Nolen-Hoeksema, S., & Zucker, R. A. (2011). Alcohol involvement as a function of co-occurring alcohol use disorders and major depressive episode: Evidence from the National Epidemiologic Survey on Alcohol and Related Conditions. *Drug and Alcohol Dependence*, 117(2–3), 145–151.

Cranford, J. A., Tennen, H., & Zucker, R. A. (2010). Feasibility of using interactive voice response to monitor daily drinking, moods, and relationship processes on a daily basis in alcoholic couples. *Alcoholism: Clinical and Experimental Research*, 34, 499–508.

Cranford, J. A., Tennen, H., & Zucker, R. A. (2015). Using multiple methods to examine gender differences in alcohol involvement and marital interactions in alcoholic probands. *Addictive Behaviors*, 41, 192–198. http://dx.doi.org/10.1016/j.addbeh.2014.10.009

Devries, K. M., Child, J. C., Bacchus, L. J., Mak, J., Falder, G., Graham, K., . . . Heise, L. (2014). Intimate partner violence victimization and alcohol consumption in women: A systematic review and meta-analysis. *Addiction*, 109(3), 379–391. doi:10.1111/add.12393

Ditzen, B., Schaer, M., Gabriel, B., Bodenmann, G., Ehlert, U., & Heinrichs, M. (2009). Intranasal oxytocin increases positive communication and reduces cortisol levels during couple conflict. *Biological Psychiatry*, 65(9), 728–731.

Dumas, G. (2011). Towards a two-body neuroscience. *Communicative and Integrative Biology*, 4(3), 349–352. doi:10.4161/cib.4.3.15110

Dumas, G., Kelso, J. A. S., & Nadel, J. (2014). Tackling the social cognition paradox through multi-scale approaches. *Frontiers in Psychology*, 5, 882.

Dumka, L. E., & Roosa, M. W. (1993). Factors mediating problem drinking and mothers' personal adjustment. *Journal of Family Psychology*, 7(3), 333–343.

Eisler, R. M., Hersen, M., & Agras, W. S. (1973). Videotape: A method for the controlled observation of nonverbal interpersonal behavior. *Behavior Therapy, 4*(3), 420–425.

Epstein, E. E., & McCrady, B. S. (1998). Behavioral couples treatment of alcohol and drug use disorders: Current status and innovations. *Clinical Psychology Review, 18*, 689–711.

Fairbairn, C. E., & Cranford, J. A. (2016). A multimethod examination of negative behaviors during couples interactions and problem drinking trajectories. *Journal of Abnormal Psychology, 125*(6), 805–810. doi:10.1037/abn0000186. and 10.1037/abn0000186.supp (Supplemental)

Fairbairn, C. E., & Sayette, M. A. (2014). A social-attributional analysis of alcohol response. *Psychological Bulletin, 140*(5), 1361–1382. doi:10.1037/a0037563

Fairbairn, C. E., Sayette, M. A., Aalen, O. O., & Frigessi, A. (2015). Alcohol and emotional contagion: An examination of the spreading of smiles in male and female drinking groups. *Clinical Psychological Science, 3*(5), 686–701. doi:10.1177/2167702614548892

Fairbairn, C. E., Sayette, M. A., Wright, A. G. C., Levine, J. M., Cohn, J. F., & Creswell, K. G. (2015). Extraversion and the rewarding effects of alcohol in a social context. *Journal of Abnormal Psychology, 124*(3), 660–673. doi:10.1037/abn0000024

Fairbairn, C. E., & Testa, M. (2017). Relationship quality and alcohol-related social reinforcement during couples interaction. *Clinical Psychological Science, 5*(1), 74–84. doi:doi:10.1177/2167702616649365

Fincham, F. D., Stanley, S. M., & Beach, S. R. H. (2007). Transformative processes in marriage: An analysis of emerging trends. *Journal of Marriage and Family, 69*(2), 275–292.

Floyd, F. J. (1989). Segmenting interactions: Coding units for assessing marital and family behaviors. *Behavioral Assessment, 11*(1), 13–29.

Floyd, F. J., Cranford, J. A., Daugherty, M. K., Fitzgerald, H. E., & Zucker, R. A. (2006). Marital interaction in alcoholic and nonalcoholic couples: Alcoholic subtype variations and wives' alcoholism status. *Journal of Abnormal Psychology, 115*(1), 121–130.

Floyd, F. J., O'Farrell, T. J., & Goldberg, M. (1987). Comparison of marital observational measures: The Marital Interaction Coding System and the Communication Skills Test. *Journal of Consulting and Clinical Psychology, 55*(3), 423–429.

Frankenstein, W., Hay, W. M., & Nathan, P. E. (1985). Effects of intoxication on alcoholics' marital communication and problem solving. *Journal of Studies on Alcohol, 46*, 1–6.

Fu, H., & Goldman, N. (2000). The association between health-related behaviours and the risk of divorce in the USA. *Journal of Biosocial Science, 32*(1), 63–88.

Gerstorf, D., Hoppmann, C. A., & Ram, N. (2014). The promise and challenges of integrating multiple time-scales in adult developmental inquiry. *Research in Human Development, 11*(2), 75–90.

Gottman, J., Swanson, C., & Swanson, K. (2002). A general systems theory of marriage: Nonlinear difference equation modeling of marital interaction. *Personality and Social Psychology Review, 6*(4), 326–340.

Gouin, J.-P., Carter, C. S., Pournajafi-Nazarloo, H., Glaser, R., Malarkey, W. B., Loving, T. J., . . . Kiecolt-Glaser, J. K. (2010). Marital behavior, oxytocin, vasopressin, and wound healing. *Psychoneuroendocrinology, 35*(7), 1082–1090.

Granic, I., & Hollenstein, T. (2003). Dynamic systems methods for models of developmental psychopathology. *Development and Psychopathology, 15*(3), 641–669.

Granic, I., & Patterson, G. R. (2006). Toward a comprehensive model of antisocial development: A dynamic systems approach. *Psychological Review, 113*(1), 101–131.

Grant, B. F., Goldstein, R. B., Saha, T. D., Chou, S. P., Jung, J., Zhang, H., . . . Huang, B. (2015). Epidemiology of DSM-5 alcohol use disorder: Results from the National Epidemiologic Survey on Alcohol and Related Conditions III. *JAMA Psychiatry, 72*(8), 757–766.

Haber, J. R., & Jacob, T. (1997). Marital interactions of male versus female alcoholics. *Family Process, 36*(4), 385–402.

Hari, R., Henriksson, L., Malinen, S., & Parkkonen, L. (2015). Centrality of social interaction in human brain function. *Neuron, 88*(1), 181–193.

Heron, D. (1912). A second study of extreme alcoholism in adults, with special reference to the Home Office Inebriate Reformatory data. *Eugenics Laboratory Memoirs, 17*, 1–95.

Hersen, M., Miller, P. M., & Eisler, R. M. (1973). Interactions between alcoholics and their wives: A descriptive analysis of verbal and nonverbal behavior. *Quarterly Journal of Studies on Alcohol, 34*(2), 516–520.

Heyman, R. E. (2004). Rapid Marital Interaction Coding System (RMICS). In P. K. Kerig & D. H. Baucom (Eds.), *Couple observation coding systems* (pp. 67–93). Mahwah, NJ: Erlbaum.

Homish, G. G., & Leonard, K. E. (2005). Marital quality and congruent drinking. *Journal of Studies on Alcohol, 66*(4), 488–496.

Homish, G. G., & Leonard, K. E. (2007). The drinking partnership and marital satisfaction: The longitudinal influence of discrepant drinking. *Journal of Consulting and Clinical Psychology, 75*(1), 43–51.

Homish, G. G., Leonard, K. E., Kozlowski, L. T., & Cornelius, J. R. (2009). The longitudinal association between multiple substance use discrepancies and marital satisfaction. *Addiction, 104*(7), 1201–1209.

Howe, G. W. (2007). Socially situated cognition and the couple as a dynamic system: A commentary. *Journal of Marriage and Family, 69*(2), 299–304.

Huston, T. L. (2000). The social ecology of marriage and other intimate unions. *Journal of Marriage and Family, 62*(2), 298–320.

Jacob, T., Favorini, A., Meisel, S. S., & Anderson, C. M. (1978). The alcoholic's spouse, children and family interactions: Substantive findings and methodological issues. *Journal of Studies on Alcohol, 39*, 1231–1251.

Jacob, T., & Krahn, G. L. (1988). Marital interactions of alcoholic couples: Comparison with depressed and nondistressed couples. *Journal of Consulting and Clinical Psychology, 56*, 73–79.

Jacob, T., & Leonard, K. E. (1988). Alcoholic–spouse interaction as a function of alcoholism subtype and alcohol consumption interaction. *Journal of Abnormal Psychology, 97*, 231–237.

Jacob, T., & Leonard, K. E. (1992). Sequential analysis of marital interactions involving alcoholic, depressed, and nondistressed men. *Journal of Abnormal Psychology, 101*, 647–656.

Jacob, T., Leonard, K. E., & Haber, J. R. (2001). Family interactions of alcoholics as related to alcoholism type and drinking condition. *Alcoholism: Clinical and Experimental Research, 25*(6), 835–843.

Jacob, T., Ritchey, D., Cvitkovic, J. F., & Blane, H. T. (1981). Communication styles of alcoholic and nonalcoholic families when drinking and not drinking. *Journal of Studies on Alcohol, 42*(5), 466–482.

Jerskey, B. A., Panizzon, M. S., Jacobson, K. C., Neale, M. C., Grant, M. D., Schultz, M., . . . Lyons, M. J. (2010). Marriage and divorce: A genetic perspective. *Personality and Individual Differences, 49*(5), 473–478.

Karney, B. R., & Bradbury, T. N. (1995). The longitudinal course of marital quality and stability: A review of theory, method, and research. *Psychological Bulletin, 118*(1), 3–34.

Kasai, K., Fukuda, M., Yahata, N., Morita, K., & Fujii, N. (2015). The future of real-world neuroscience: Imaging techniques to assess active brains in social environments. *Neuroscience Research, 90*, 65–71.

Kelley, H. H. (1997). The "stimulus field" for interpersonal phenomena: The source of language and thought about interpersonal events. *Personality and Social Psychology Review, 1*(2), 140–169.

Kelley, H. H., Berscheid, E., Christensen, A., Harvey, J. H., Huston, T. L., Levinger, G., . . . Peterson, D. R. (1983). *Close relationships.* New York, NY: Freeman.

Kelley, H. H., Holmes, J. G., Kerr, N. L., Reis, H. T., Rusbult, C. E., & Van Lange, P. A. M. (2003). *An atlas of interpersonal situations.* New York, NY: Cambridge University Press.

Kenny, D. A., Kashy, D. A., & Cook, W. L. (2006). *Dyadic data analysis.* New York, NY: Guilford.

Kephart, W. M. (1954). Drinking and marital disruption: A research note. *Quarterly Journal of Studies on Alcohol, 15*(1), 63–73.

Kessler, R. C., Walters, E. E., & Forthofer, M. S. (1998). The social consequences of psychiatric disorders: III. Probability of marital stability. *American Journal of Psychiatry, 155*(8), 1092–1096.

Larson, R. W., & Almeida, D. M. (1999). Emotional transmission in the daily lives of families: A new paradigm for studying family process. *Journal of Marriage and the Family, 61*, 5–20.

Leonard, K. E., & Eiden, R. D. (2007). Marital and family processes in the context of alcohol use and alcohol disorders. *Annual Review of Clinical Psychology, 3*, 285–310.

Leonard, K. E., & Homish, G. G. (2008). Predictors of heavy drinking and drinking problems over the first 4 years of marriage. *Psychology of Addictive Behaviors, 22*(1), 25–35.

Leonard, K. E., & Roberts, L. J. (1998). The effects of alcohol on the marital interactions of aggressive and nonaggressive husbands and their wives. *Journal of Abnormal Psychology, 107*, 602–615.

Leonard, K. E., & Rothbard, J. C. (1999). Alcohol and the marriage effect. *Journal of Studies on Alcohol, 13*, 139–146.

Leonard, K. E., Smith, P. H., & Homish, G. G. (2014). Concordant and discordant alcohol, tobacco, and marijuana use as predictors of marital dissolution. *Psychology of Addictive Behaviors, 28*(3), 780–789.

Levinger, G. (1965). Marital cohesiveness and dissolution: An integrative review. *Journal of Marriage and Family, 27*(1), 19–28. doi:10.2307/349801

Levinger, G. (1976). A social psychological perspective on marital dissolution. *Journal of Social Issues, 32*(1), 21–47.

Levinger, G. (1980). Toward the analysis of close relationships. *Journal of Experimental Social Psychology, 16*(6), 510–544.

Levinger, G., & Huston, T. L. (1990). The social psychology of marriage. In F. D. Fincham & T. N. Bradbury (Eds.), *The psychology of marriage: Basic issues and applications* (pp. 19–58). New York, NY: Guilford.

Lewin, K. (1936). *Principles of topological psychology* (F. Heider & G. M. Heider, Trans.). New York, NY: McGraw-Hill.

Lisansky, E. S. (1957). Alcoholism in women: Social and psychological concomitants: I. Social history data. *Quarterly Journal of Studies on Alcohol, 18,* 588–623.

Locke, T. F., & Newcomb, M. D. (2003). Psychosocial outcomes of alcohol involvement and dysphoria in women: A 16-year prospective community study. *Journal of Studies on Alcohol, 64,* 531–546.

Loomis, H., Jr. (1866). Divorce legislation in Connecticut. *The New Englander, 25,* 436–454.

Love, T. M. (2014). Oxytocin, motivation and the role of dopamine. *Pharmacology Biochemistry and Behavior, 119,* 49–60.

Maisto, S. A., McKay, J. R., & O'Farrell, T. J. (1995). Relapse precipitants and behavioral marital therapy. *Addictive Behaviors, 20*(3), 383–393.

Malzberg, B. (1947). A study of first admissions with alcoholic psychoses in New York State, 1943–1944. *Quarterly Journal of Studies on Alcohol, 8*(2), 274.

Marshal, M. P. (2003). For better or for worse? The effects of alcohol use on marital functioning. *Clinical Psychology Review, 23,* 959–997.

McCrady, B. S., & Epstein, E. E. (1995). Directions for research on alcoholic relationships: Marital- and individual-based models of heterogeneity. *Psychology of Addictive Behaviors, 9*(3), 157–166.

McCrady, B. S., Epstein, E. E., Cook, S., Jensen, N., & Hildebrandt, T. (2009). A randomized trial of individual and couple behavioral alcohol treatment for women. *Journal of Consulting and Clinical Psychology, 77*(2), 243–256.

McCrady, B. S., Hayaki, J., Epstein, E. E., & Hirsch, L. S. (2002). Testing hypothesized predictors of change in conjoint behavioral alcoholism treatment for men. *Alcoholism: Clinical and Experimental Research, 26,* 463–470.

Molenaar, P. C. M., Sinclair, K. O., Rovine, M. J., Ram, N., & Corneal, S. E. (2009). Analyzing developmental processes on an individual level using nonstationary time series modeling. *Developmental Psychology, 45*(1), 260–271.

Mudar, P., Leonard, K. E., & Soltysinski, K. (2001). Discrepant substance use and marital functioning in newlywed couples. *Journal of Consulting and Clinical Psychology, 69,* 130–134.

Myers, D. G. (2013). *Social psychology* (11th ed.). New York, NY: McGraw-Hill.

Noel, N. E., McCrady, B. S., Stout, R. L., & Fisher-Nelson, H. (1991). Gender differences in marital functioning of male and female alcoholics. *Family Dynamics of Addiction Quarterly, 1*(4), 31–38.

Nolen-Hoeksema, S., & Hilt, L. (2006). Possible contributors to the gender differences in alcohol use and problems. *Journal of General Psychology, 133*(4), 357–374.

O'Farrell, T. J. (2015). Couples therapy in treatment of alcoholism and drug abuse. In N. el-Guebaly, G. Carrà, & M. Galanter (Eds.), *Textbook of addiction treatment: International perspectives* (pp. 907–925). New York, NY: Springer.

O'Farrell, T. J., & Fals-Stewart, W. (2003). Alcohol abuse. *Journal of Marital and Family Therapy, 29,* 121–146.

Orford, J. (1975). Alcoholism and marriage: The argument against specialism. *Journal of Studies on Alcohol, 36*(11), 1537–1563.

Ostermann, J., Sloan, F. A., & Taylor, D. H. (2005). Heavy alcohol use and marital dissolution in the USA. *Social Science and Medicine, 61,* 2304–2316.

Paolino, T. J., McCrady, B. S., & Diamond, S. (1978). Statistics on alcoholic marriages: An overview. *International Journal of the Addictions, 13*(8), 1285–1293.

Power, C., & Estaugh, V. (1990). The role of family formation and dissolution in shaping drinking behavior in early adulthood. *British Journal of Addiction, 85,* 521–530.

Power, C., Rodgers, B., & Hope, S. (1999). Heavy alcohol consumption and marital status: Disentangling the relationship in a national study of young adults. *Addiction, 94*(10), 1477–1487.

Prescott, C. A., & Kendler, K. S. (2001). Associations between marital status and alcohol consumption in a longitudinal study of female twins. *Journal of Studies on Alcohol, 62*(5), 589–604.

Quigley, B. M., & Leonard, K. E. (2000). Alcohol and the continuation of early marital aggression. *Alcoholism: Clinical and Experimental Research, 24,* 1003–1010.

Reis, H. T., Collins, W. A., & Berscheid, E. (2000). The relationship context of human behavior and development. *Psychological Bulletin, 126*(6), 844–872.

Reiss, D. (2010). Genetic thinking in the study of social relationships: Five points of entry. *Perspectives on Psychological Science, 5*(5), 502–515.

Roberts, L. J., & Linney, K. D. (2000). Alcohol problems and couples: Drinking in an intimate relational context. In K. B. Schmaling & T. G. Sher (Eds.), *The psychology of couples and illness: Theory, research, & practice.* (pp. 269–310). Washington, DC: American Psychological Association.

Robinson, G. E., Fernald, R. D., & Clayton, D. F. (2008). Genes and social behavior. *Science, 322*(5903), 896–900.

Rodriguez, L. M., & Neighbors, C. (2015). An interdependent look at perceptions of spousal drinking problems and marital outcomes. *Alcohol, 49*(6), 597–605.

Rosenbaum, B. (1958). Married women alcoholics at the Washingtonian Hospital. *Quarterly Journal of Studies on Alcohol, 19*(1), 79–89.

Salvatore, J. E., Prom-Wormley, E., Prescott, C. A., & Kendler, K. S. (2015). Overlapping genetic and environmental influences among men's alcohol consumption and problems, romantic quality and social support. *Psychological Medicine, 45*(11), 2353–2364.

Sanchez, L., & Gager, C. T. (2000). Hard living, perceived entitlement to a great marriage, and marital dissolution. *Journal of Marriage and Family, 62*(3), 708–722.

Sayette, M. A., Reichle, E. D., & Schooler, J. W. (2009). Lost in the sauce: The effects of alcohol on mind wandering. *Psychological Science, 20*(6), 747–752. doi:10.1111/j.1467-9280.2009.02351.x

Sears, R. R. (1951). A theoretical framework for personality and social behavior. *American Psychologist, 6*(9), 476–482.

Smith, P. H., Homish, G. G., Leonard, K. E., & Cornelius, J. R. (2012). Intimate partner violence and specific substance use disorders: Findings from the National Epidemiologic Survey on Alcohol and Related Conditions. *Psychology of Addictive Behaviors, 26*(2), 236–245.

Snyder, D. K., Heyman, R. E., & Haynes, S. N. (2005). Evidence-based approaches to assessing couple distress. *Psychological Assessment, 17*(3), 288–307.

Spotts, E. L., & Ganiban, J. M. (2015). Spouse, parent, and co-workers: Relationships and roles during adulthood. In B. N. Horwitz & J. M. Neiderhiser (Eds.), *Gene–environment interplay in interpersonal relationships across the lifespan* (Vol. 3, pp. 171–202). New York, NY: Springer.

Steinglass, P., Davis, D. I., & Berenson, D. (1977). Observations of conjointly hospitalized "alcoholic couples" during sobriety and intoxication: Implications for theory and therapy. *Family Process, 16*(1), 1–16.

Stone, A. A., Shiffman, S., Atienza, A. A., & Nebeling, L. (2007). Historical roots and rationale of ecological momentary assessment (EMA). In A. A. Stone, S. Shiffman, A. A. Atienza, & L. Nebeling (Eds.), *The science of real-time data capture: Self-reports in health research* (pp. 3–10). New York, NY: Oxford University Press.

Straus, R., & Bacon, S. D. (1951). Alcoholism and social stability: A study of occupational integration in 2,023 male clinic patients. *Quarterly Journal of Studies on Alcohol, 12*(2), 231–260.

Testa, M., Crane, C. A., Quigley, B. M., Levitt, A., & Leonard, K. E. (2014). Effects of administered alcohol on intimate partner interactions in a conflict resolution paradigm. *Journal of Studies on Alcohol and Drugs, 75*(2), 249–258.

Testa, M., & Derrick, J. L. (2014). A daily process examination of the temporal association between alcohol use and verbal and physical aggression in community couples. *Psychology of Addictive Behaviors, 28*(1), 127–138.

Testa, M., Kubiak, A., Quigley, B. M., Houston, R. J., Derrick, J. L., Levitt, A., . . . Leonard, K. E. (2012). Husband and wife alcohol use as independent or interactive predictors of intimate partner violence. *Journal of Studies on Alcohol and Drugs, 73*(2), 268–276.

Thibaut, J. W., & Kelley, H. H. (1959). *The social psychology of groups.* New York, NY: Wiley.

US Department of Commerce and Labor, Bureau of the Census. (1909). *Marriage and divorce, 1867–1906: Part I. Summary, laws, foreign statistics.* Washington, DC: Government Printing Office.

US Department of Health, Education, and Welfare. (1973). *100 years of marriage and divorce statistics, United States, 1867 to 1967* (DHEW Publication No. 74-1902). Rockville, MD: National Center for Health Statistics.

US Department of Labor. (1889). *A report on marriage and divorce in the United States, 1867 to 1886.* Washington, DC: Government Printing Office.

Vallacher, R. R., Read, S. J., & Nowak, A. (2002). The dynamical perspective in personality and social psychology. *Personality and Social Psychology Review, 6*(4), 264–273.

Waldron, M., Bucholz, K. K., Lynskey, M. T., Madden, P. A., & Heath, A. C. (2013). Alcoholism and timing of separation in parents: Findings in a Midwestern birth cohort. *Journal of Studies on Alcohol and Drugs, 74*(2), 337–348.

Waldron, M., Heath, A. C., Lynskey, M. T., Bucholz, K. K., Madden, P. A. F., & Martin, N. G. (2011). Alcoholic marriage: Later start, sooner end. *Alcoholism: Clinical and Experimental Research*, 35(4), 632–642.

Whisman, M. A., Uebelacker, L. A., & Bruce, M. L. (2006). Longitudinal association between marital dissatisfaction and alcohol use disorders in a community sample. *Journal of Family Psychology*, 20(1), 164–167.

Whisman, M. A., Uebelacker, L. A., & Weinstock, L. M. (2004). Psychopathology and marital satisfaction: The importance of evaluating both partners. *Journal of Consulting and Clinical Psychology*, 72(5), 830–838.

Whiteford, H. A., Degenhardt, L., Rehm, J., Baxter, A. J., Ferrari, A. J., Erskine, H. E., . . . Vos, T. (2013). Global burden of disease attributable to mental and substance use disorders: Findings from the Global Burden of Disease Study 2010. *Lancet*, 382(9904), 1575–1586.

Wiese, S. L., Vallacher, R. R., & Strawinska, U. (2010). Dynamical social psychology: Complexity and coherence in human experience. *Social and Personality Psychology Compass*, 4(11), 1018–1030.

Wilsnack, S. C., & Wilsnack, R. W. (1991). Epidemiology of women's drinking. *Journal of Substance Abuse*, 3(2), 133–157.

Witkiewitz, K., & Marlatt, G. A. (2007). Modeling the complexity of post-treatment drinking: It's a rocky road to relapse. *Clinical Psychology Review*, 27(6), 724–738.

Wolf, I. (1958). Alcoholism and marriage. *Quarterly Journal of Studies on Alcohol*, 19(3), 511–513.

Woolsey, T. D. (1869). *Essay on divorce and divorce legislation, with special reference to the United States*. New York, NY: Scribner.

Yang, H., Cranford, J. A., Li, R., & Buu, A. (2015). Two-stage model for time-varying effects of discrete longitudinal covariates with applications in analysis of daily process data. *Statistics in Medicine*, 34(4), 571–581.

Zucker, R. A. (2014). Genes, brain, behavior, and context: The developmental matrix of addictive behavior. In S. F. Stoltenberg (Ed.), *Genes and the motivation to use substances* (Vol. 61, pp. 51–69). New York, NY: Springer.

PART VI

METHODOLOGICAL AND STATISTICAL INNOVATIONS

OVERVIEW

As evidenced by the chapters presented previously in this volume, there have been many interesting findings and conclusions regarding alcohol use disorder and other substance use disorders. However, to continue to make progress in the field, especially due to the complexity of the problem and the variables that need to be explored, it is incumbent on researchers to be aware of recent methodological and statistical advancements in other fields in order to research the complex issues of the development of alcohol use disorder and to continue to improve our knowledge about it. It is important to note that not so many years ago, we did not have analytic techniques such as cluster analysis, survival analysis, latent trajectory class analysis, unconditional growth mixture models analysis, or hierarchical linear modeling to guide analyses of longitudinal data. It is also the case that not so many years ago a meta-analysis consisted of a detailed verbal integrative paper assessing commonalities and differences between published research. Today, meta-analysis is a quantitative anchored assessment of a carefully prescribed set of studies. However, another approach has emerged in which data from independent longitudinal studies are integrated into one "new" longitudinal data set that includes individual data. This new approach is referred to as integrative data analysis (Curran & Hussong, 2009; Curran et al., 2008, 2014).

In Chapter 20, Mun and Ray introduce integrative data analysis (IDA) as a promising new approach aimed at providing a larger unifying research synthesis framework. The conceptualization of IDA related to other similar research synthesis methods may be helpful for better understanding the approach and for better utilization of this emerging approach in the field. Major advantages of IDA of individual participant-level data include better and more flexible ways to examine subgroups, model complex relationships, deal with methodological and clinical heterogeneity, and examine infrequently occurring behaviors. However, Mun and Ray note that based on their work on the Project INTEGRATE data set, which combined individual participant-level data from 24 independent college brief alcohol intervention studies, IDA investigations require a wide range of expertise and considerable resources. They call for development of minimum standards for reporting IDA studies in order to improve transparency and quality of evidence.

In Chapter 21, Buu and Li provide a nontechnical review of new statistical methodology for longitudinal data analysis. The methodology has applications in four important areas: (1) conducting variable selection among many highly correlated risk factors when the outcome measure is zero-inflated count, (2) characterizing developmental trajectories of symptomatology using regression splines, (3) modeling the longitudinal association between risk factors and substance use outcomes as time-varying effects, and (4) testing measurement reactivity and predictive validity using daily process data. The excellent statistical properties of the methods introduced have been supported by simulation studies. The applications in alcohol and substance abuse research have also been demonstrated by graphs on real longitudinal data.

REFERENCES

Curran, P. J., & Hussong, A. M. (2009). Integrative data analysis: The simultaneous analysis of multiple data sets. *Psychometric Methods, 14,* 81–100.

Curran, P. J., Hussong, A. M., Cai, L., Huang, W., Chassin, L., Sher, K. J., & Zucker, R. A. (2008). Pooling data from multiple longitudinal studies: The role of item response theory in integrative data analysis. *Developmental Psychology, 44,* 365–380.

Curran, P. J., McGinley, J. S., Bauer, D. J., Hussong, A. M., Burns, A., Chassin, L., . . . Zucker, R. A. (2014). A moderated nonlinear factor model for the development of commensurate measures in integrative data analysis. *Multivariate Behavioral Research, 49,* 214–231.

20

Integrative Data Analysis from a Unifying Research Synthesis Perspective

Eun-Young Mun

Anne E. Ray

The purpose of this chapter is to present a broader unified framework for integrative data analysis (IDA; Curran & Hussong, 2009; Hussong, Curran, & Bauer, 2013) and to provide an overview of the strengths of IDA as well as future directions for IDA. IDA, defined as "the statistical analysis of a single data set that consists of two or more separate samples that have been pooled into one" (Curran & Hussong, 2009, p. 82), is a newly emerging set of advanced analytic techniques aimed at synthesizing large-scale evidence. IDA offers specific advantages, as well as incurs certain challenges, compared to single studies. The advantages of IDA are that it (1) provides a built-in replication mechanism across independent studies and tests between-study heterogeneity; (2) has better statistical power, greater diversity in sample, and an extended duration of observations; (3) provides a broader psychometric assessment approach to key constructs; (4) handles low base-rate behaviors better; and (5) maximizes limited resources for research (Curran & Hussong, 2009). However, these advantages are not unique to IDA. Meta-analysis using aggregate data (e.g., means, standard deviations, or effect size estimates) shares many of these advantages in common with IDA. Instead, what is unique and innovative about IDA may be best attributed to its use of individual participant-level (patient-level) data in generating large-scale evidence.

Based on our experience of conducting a large-scale IDA study of brief motivational interventions aimed at reducing alcohol use among college students (Project INTEGRATE; Mun, de la Torre, et al., 2015), this chapter intends to broaden the scope of

IDA and, consequently, its utilities for future IDA investigations. Toward this goal, we place IDA in the context of other related approaches and methods that have been developed in other disciplines, highlight relatively less-known challenges of IDA, and underscore the promise of IDA in the current research environment. Table 20.1 provides a brief summary of the promise of, common misconceptions about, and requirements for IDA.

INTEGRATIVE DATA ANALYSIS AS ONE APPROACH TO RESEARCH SYNTHESIS

Broadly, IDA can be viewed as a special case of the large-scale research synthesis methods (or meta-analysis methods), in which individual participant data from multiple sources are analyzed together in a single, one-stage analysis. Placing IDA within a broad research synthesis framework may be helpful for several reasons. This broad perspective allows one to take advantage of a large pool of available methodological approaches to IDA, depending on the specific data characteristics, challenges, and goals of each project.

Figures 20.1–20.4 graphically show various research synthesis approaches, including IDA. Figure 20.1 shows a typical meta-analysis using aggregate data in which a single coefficient (e.g., an estimate of the standardized mean difference) is obtained per study and the obtained estimates from multiple studies are combined across studies. Figure 20.2 shows a different approach in which individual participant data are used to directly derive the needed estimate per study

TABLE 20.1 Integrative Data Analysis (IDA) from a Unifying Research Synthesis Perspective

Promise of Integrative Data Analysis
- IDA may be considered as a quantitative research synthesis approach to large-scale existing data from multiple sources.
- IDA provides large-scale robust evidence.
- Study- and participant-level effects, as well as their cross-level effects, can be examined systematically.
- IDA offers modeling flexibility and better capacity to handle low base rate behaviors, including rare adverse events from treatment studies.
- More advanced research synthesis approaches (e.g., multivariate meta-analysis) are possible with individual participant data.
- IDA meets two major demands of the current research environment: (1) scientific rigor and reproducibility and (2) data sharing and collaboration.

Less-Known Aspects of Integrative Data Analysis
- IDA is not a single-entity analytic method. IDA is an inclusive term referring to a series of data handling and decision making in addition to analyzing measurement models, analytical models, and synthesis models.
- IDA approaches need to be tailored to meet the specific challenges of each IDA study.
- IDA requires a wide range of substantive and methodological expertise and skills and considerable resources. A team science approach is appropriate for IDA.

What to Consider When Planning Integrative Data Analysis
- Specific research questions for IDA and the study inclusion and exclusion criteria should be set clearly.
- Data should be pooled only from sufficiently similar studies.
- Overlap across studies in participants, measures, designs, treatment/control groups, and settings is needed to draw combined inference.
- Data collection and checking processes should be carefully documented.
- Study-level missing data and unexplained between-study heterogeneity are major challenges.

in the first stage and the resulting estimates are combined in the next stage. The two-stage approach to individual participant data illustrated in Figure 20.2 has been, by far, the most common way individual participant data have been utilized in research synthesis (Simmonds et al., 2005). Although individual participant data are reduced to aggregate data in the first stage, it is still more advantageous than the typical meta-analysis of aggregate data illustrated in Figure 20.1 because researchers can check and correct data and also because estimates can be derived from the same model across studies. More important, this approach can accommodate necessary extensions and adaptations when the number of studies included in research synthesis increases or when more complex models are needed to adequately fit data. For example, the two-stage approach can be extended to multivariate meta-analysis for multiple related parameters (Cheung, 2015; Gasparrini, Armstrong, & Kenward, 2012; Jackson & Riley, 2014; Jackson, Riley, & White, 2011; Jiao, Mun, & Xie, 2017) and to complex synthesis combining both individual participant data and aggregate data (Donegan, Williamson, D'Alessandro, Garner, & Smith, 2013; Riley et al., 2008).

In contrast, Figures 20.3 and 20.4 both show the one-stage approach to individual participant data with one difference. The IDA approach illustrated in Figure 20.3 assumes that outcome measures hold the same interpretation across studies. Certain outcome

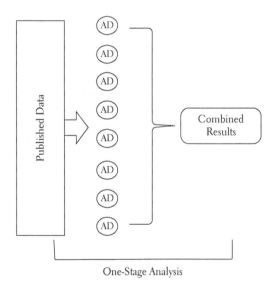

One-Stage Analysis

FIGURE 20.1 Traditional univariate meta-analysis using published data. AD, aggregate data.

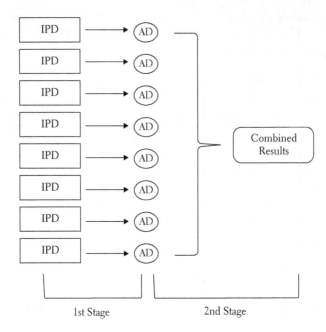

FIGURE 20.2 Univariate meta-analysis using aggregate data (AD) derived from individual participant data (IPD).

measures, such as survival/death, the number of drinks per week, and the percentage of disposable income allocated to drinking, may satisfy this assumption, especially if data were originally collected from

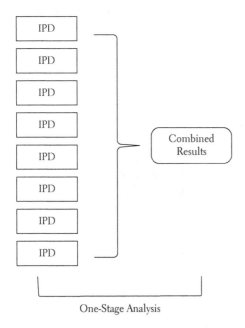

FIGURE 20.3 Integrative data analysis using individual participant data (IPD).

sufficiently similar samples and across similar settings. In all other cases, IDA involves prerequisite steps (Figure 20.4) to establish measurement equivalence across studies by harmonizing and linking different measures and using advanced analytical models to derive commensurate trait scores for participants from different studies (for application examples of this IDA approach, see Huh et al., 2015; Hussong et al., 2007).

The broader research synthesis framework presented in this chapter is intended for expanding the utilities of valuable individual participant data from multiple studies so that when one approach is not feasible, researchers can still proceed with alternative approaches, including the multivariate and mixed-evidence approaches shown in Figures 20.5 and 20.6. In this way, embarking on an IDA study does not necessarily become an "all-or-nothing" proposition. In addition, researchers can make the most out of valuable individual participant data.

MAJOR SOURCES OF HETEROGENEITY ACROSS DIFFERENT STUDIES

As shown graphically in Figures 20.3 and 20.4, for IDA to be feasible, there is a need to establish measurement equivalence across different studies as

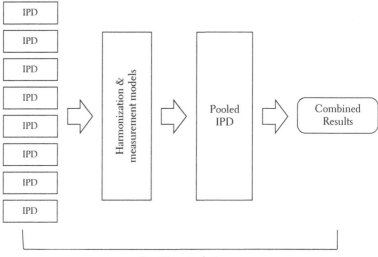

FIGURE 20.4 Integrative data analysis using individual participant data (IPD) with an intermediate measurement model.

part of IDA methodologies (Curran et al., 2008). Measurement heterogeneity is an important source of between-study heterogeneity, which needs to be resolved. A number of different methodological approaches have been proposed and studied (Bauer & Hussong, 2009; Curran et al., 2008, 2014; Huo et al., 2015; McArdle, Grimm, Hamagami, Bowles, & Meredith, 2009). However, in addition to dealing with different measures across different studies, there are other challenges associated with between-study heterogeneity. Measurement heterogeneity, although important, represents only one aspect of the populations that vary across studies. In other words, for IDA studies to provide built-in replications and large-scale

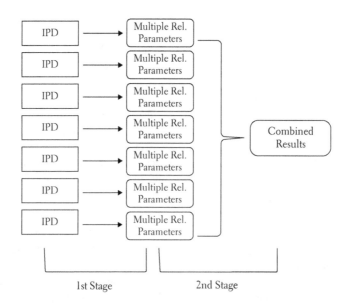

FIGURE 20.5 Multivariate meta-analysis using individual participant data (IPD).

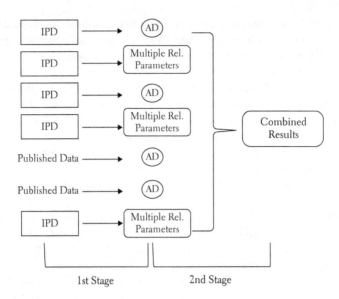

FIGURE 20.6 Mixed-evidence multivariate meta-analysis using both aggregate data (AD) and individual participant data (IPD).

robust evidence (Curran & Hussong, 2009), one needs to consider several population boundaries to which inference is made. Cronbach (1982), for example, identified four major domains of populations to which we attempt to draw inference: unit of analysis (U; participants), treatments (T; a targeted effect), outcome measures (O), and settings (S) in which a treatment takes place. These multiple domains of populations suggest that even if outcome measures are comparable for one of the population domains across studies, there are other important sources of heterogeneity across studies that need to be carefully considered or controlled. In addition to the UTOS variations, there are design differences, such as between-study differences in the inclusion of key covariates or timing of follow-up assessments.

Some of the variations (e.g., assessment timing) across studies may be easily accommodated in a model. Others may be more difficult to take into account (e.g., unassessed covariates) or to justify that they merely represent random variations. For example, when individual participant data are combined from multiple studies, study-level missing data can easily result in situations in which no studies have all covariates included in the model to adequately fit data (Jiao et al., 2017). One outcome of study-level missing covariates is that those studies are by default excluded in analysis. This problem becomes more

serious as the dimensions of the data analyzed (i.e., number of covariates and studies) increase. However, the need to overcome study-level missing data or other sources of between-study variation has not been thoroughly highlighted in the IDA literature, relative to the attention focused on measures across studies. These complex challenges may help explain the existing gap between the potential utilities and modeling flexibilities of individual participant data (Brown et al., 2013; Sutton & Higgins, 2008) and the actual applications (Simmonds et al., 2005). However, recent methodological advances have been made for complex synthesis methods, especially those utilizing individual participant data in statistics and biostatistics. Accordingly, we can tap into these emerging approaches for the analysis of individual participant data in research synthesis, such as combining the confidence density functions to accommodate study-level missing data under a general likelihood inference framework (Liu, Liu, & Xie, 2015).

INTEGRATIVE DATA ANALYSIS CHALLENGES AND MISCONCEPTIONS

The first step to IDA may be to understand the specific challenges of each IDA study and appropriately address them. Some may think that IDA is a well-defined analysis with established routines, such as latent curve models, so that its implementation may be similar across IDA studies. There may also be a notion that IDA is a single-entity analytic technique or is essentially a method to establish measurement equivalence. In reality, IDA involves a complex series of steps, including data handling, decision-making, and utilizing available measurement and statistical models to combine and analyze multiple data sets that were independently designed and collected. Accordingly, how IDA should be executed may be different across studies. The major considerations needed for an IDA study in which data are combined from randomized clinical trials would be different from those of a study in which data are combined from longitudinal family studies. Even within the pool of randomized clinical trials, key challenges may be different depending on the specific goals and characteristics of IDA studies. Therefore, IDA studies may require unique solutions because the nature of the specific challenges will likely be different for different studies. Consequently, there can be as many different IDA approaches as the number of IDA studies. In that sense, there are no exact recipes to follow from one IDA study to the next.

Relatedly, the level of expertise and resources required for IDA studies can be equivalent to what is required for launching a new data collection project (Hussong et al., 2013). IDA studies require a wide range of substantive, as well as methodological, expertise and skill sets to successfully implement. Thus, a team science approach would be generally more appropriate for conducting an IDA study. Project INTEGRATE (Mun, de la Torre, et al., 2015), for example, has experts in the areas of individual-focused brief alcohol interventions for college students, alcohol-related measurement construction, alcohol etiology and prevention across the lifespan, psychometrics, biostatistics, and theoretical and mathematical statistics. Although Project INTEGRATE is the largest IDA study in alcohol research to date and, hence, the needed range of expertise may have been greater than usual, our experience suggests that a wide range of expertise is generally necessary to successfully navigate an IDA study.

IDA is sometimes referred to as secondary data analysis of existing data. In the sense that de-identified data from individual studies are combined, IDA does not involve any direct contacts with human subjects. Consequently, IDA does not pose any additional risks to human subjects. Beyond that, however, IDA digresses from secondary data analysis. The notion that IDA is "secondary data analysis" obscures the fact that IDA is a major undertaking. In an IDA study, all key aspects of studies should be examined, both individually and in connection with other studies, to be able to integrate and synthesize data across studies. This process can be quite arduous—a fact that may be lost when labeled as secondary data analysis.

In addition, there is a limit to the principle that increased heterogeneity in participant samples, measures, settings, and study designs via pooling data from multiple sources is an asset. Individual studies included in research synthesis should be "sufficiently similar" to be combined. In other words, there is an underlying assumption that studies should not be meaningfully different from one another and should have sufficient overlap. That is, important key covariates should be similarly distributed and have similar meanings across studies. This is the "similarity assumption" in network meta-analysis or meta-regression (Jansen et al., 2011). For example, if a treatment modifier (a moderator) exists, this modifier should not be confounded with the effect under investigation.

In larger IDA studies, heterogeneity in effect size estimates may be better quantified and subsequently examined. However, in small IDA studies, variability or heterogeneity in estimates may be more difficult to probe, even if they can be detected. Therefore, it is important to be aware that heterogeneous studies cannot be pooled without careful considerations and that sufficiently similar studies should be combined based on the predefined inclusion criteria. This recommendation is quite typical for meta-analysis and also applicable for IDA.

BETWEEN-STUDY HETEROGENEITY AND THE UNDERLYING ASSUMPTIONS OF META-ANALYSIS MODELS

As briefly discussed previously, there is a need to differentiate between-study heterogeneity that improves diversity and broadens population representation from heterogeneity that diminishes the validity of combining data from different studies (for further discussion on between-study heterogeneity, see Mun, Atkins, & Walters, 2015; Mun, Jiao, & Xie, 2016). When combining data across multiple studies, we typically use a random effects meta-analysis model. The random effects meta-analysis model assumes that there are study-specific effect sizes drawn from a superpopulation with a common true effect and between-study variability surrounding the common effect size. Therefore, the variability surrounding effect sizes can be decomposed to within-study and between-study variability. In a fixed effect meta-analysis model, in contrast, all studies are assumed to have the same true effect size and hence no between-study variability. The assumptions involved in the random effects meta-analysis model are more reasonable than those in the fixed effects meta-analysis model, although these assumptions are difficult to check in reality (Mun et al., 2016; see also Normand, 1999).

Increased heterogeneity by pooling data from multiple studies improves population representation only if it can reasonably be assumed that all the study-specific effects included in analysis are related and stem from the same underlying superpopulation. If this assumption is reasonable, within-study and between-study variability can be quantified and accordingly attributed to observed and unobserved factors at the participant and study level. However, if this assumption is unreasonable, combining data from heterogeneous studies would be like mixing apples, berries, and melons when attempting to make an apple pie. Using the same analogy, apple pies can be made using different apple varieties but using more or less the same recipe (i.e., generalizable and robust). In reality, however, the underlying assumption is difficult to verify. Therefore, any research synthesis project should have clear research goals and prespecified inclusion criteria. Following screening, one needs to select eligible studies that can be broadly representative. The population representativeness issue has been raised before (Curran & Hussong, 2009, p. 88), and we have faced these questions when publishing studies from Project INTEGRATE (Mun, de la Torre, et al., 2015). Because of the limited availability of individual participant data in the psychological literature, IDA studies tend to have convenience samples. With more individual participant data expected to become accessible and searchable in the future, there is a greater need to justify the inclusion criteria and sampling of eligible studies for IDA and to characterize how the pooled sample can be viewed in relation to broader populations.

In terms of achieving population representation as well as examining potential subgroups, note

that a larger IDA study is needed. It is difficult to derive a rule of thumb about the number of studies. Nonetheless, 5 or fewer studies may be considered too small (Borenstein, Hedges, Higgins, & Rothstein, 2009, p. 163). Some investigators have indicated that at least 10 or 20 studies may be needed (Hussong et al., 2013, p. 68). Also note that the level of difficulty increases considerably as the number of studies to be combined increases, especially for a one-stage simultaneous analysis of individual participant data. However, if individual studies are conducted in a highly standardized manner, it may be possible to combine data from just a few studies to determine how strong the effect of interest is in its magnitude and how consistent it is across studies.

TACKLING OTHER SOURCES OF BETWEEN-STUDY HETEROGENEITY

Similar to other well-known analyses, such as analysis of covariance or regression analysis, it is important to identify the sources of variability in data and reduce their influence when conducting IDA with individual participant data. One of the sources in intervention and prevention research may stem from different intervention groups sharing the same brand names across studies or, alternatively, from similar intervention groups holding different labels. Namely, intervention groups may not be equivalent across different studies despite similar labels.

For example, Project INTEGRATE (Mun, de la Torre, et al., 2015) obtained all intervention materials from individual studies (for descriptions of coding, see Ray et al., 2014). There were a total of 67 groups across 24 studies. These groups were created by crossing sample characteristics (e.g., volunteer vs. mandated within studies) with intervention conditions (e.g., feedback intervention vs. control). There were a total of 12 control groups across studies. We examined a total of seven intervention coding variables that had some variability across studies for principal component analysis (PCA). These variables were as follows:

1. The total number of content areas covered
2. The level of personalization of the content
3. Whether the intervention was delivered in person
4. Whether a personalized feedback profile was given

5. Whether motivational interviewing was incorporated
6. The number of intervention sessions
7. The duration of the total sessions in minutes

These variables were chosen because they represented important substantive distinctions but also because their values showed variability across studies. For example, whether interventions included content about alcohol use would not be a good variable to consider (and impossible to include in any analysis) because no variability existed among interventions.

PCA results indicated that two principal components explained 83% of the total variance. We utilized a varimax rotation method for better interpretation. Based on the PCA result, we discussed the nature of one group (18.30 in Figure 20.7) that was originally labeled "Education" but was subsequently relabeled as a control. In addition, group 9.10 was originally

labeled as "Alcohol Edu," which is generally regarded as an education condition. However, there are many different versions of this intervention because it has been updated over time. Upon further discussion, we obtained the closest version available to the one given to participants at the time of intervention and recoded its content. The number of content areas covered was subsequently changed from 7 to 13. The reanalysis result was largely the same (not shown); the position of the Alcohol Edu on the y-axis moved up but remained below zero. Overall, the results showed that there were different degrees of similarity among interventions sharing the same name. For example, the group Education appears to be more heterogeneous than other intervention groups. In contrast, brief alcohol interventions utilizing an in-person motivational interviewing style combined with normative feedback were quite similar to one another. The purpose of reviewing this analysis is to show that intervention

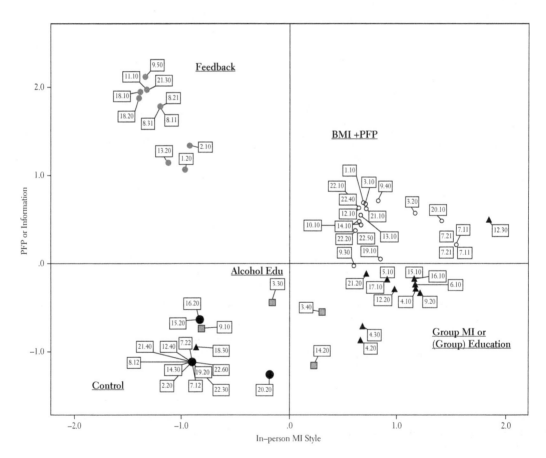

FIGURE 20.7 Intervention groups examined (and subsequently re-evaluated). MI, motivational interviewing. BMI, Brief motivational intervention. PFP, Personalized feedback profile.

characteristics and modalities can be dismantled and numerically coded. Any irregularities can then be brought to attention for necessary follow-up actions. Furthermore, one can assess the extent of heterogeneity within similar interventions and across different types of interventions.

PROMISE OF INDIVIDUAL PARTICIPANT DATA IN QUANTITATIVE RESEARCH SYNTHESIS

Despite the noted complexities of pooling and analyzing individual participant data in research synthesis, it remains an important lure that we can better examine subgroups using individual participant data (Borenstein & Higgins, 2013). The lack of consistency of the overall (combined) estimate across studies, which suggests the presence of subgroups, is just as important as the estimate itself in research synthesis. In the context of interventions, these subgroups can indicate that intervention/treatment effect modifiers or moderators exist, which widely encompass different types of interventions, delivery settings, participant characteristics (high-risk vs. low-risk drinkers), and post-intervention responses (immediate response, sustained benefits, sleeper effects, etc.). Although some of these potential modifiers (e.g., study-level variables such as intervention modality) can be examined in an analysis using study-level aggregate data, it is much more advantageous to analyze individual participant data when the effect in question may vary across individual-level variables. In addition, inference from individual participant data analysis is less susceptible to ecological bias compared to that from the analysis of aggregate data. Ecological bias or fallacy refers to incorrectly drawing inference about a phenomenon at the lower level from the analysis with the higher level data structure (e.g., inference about within-person change made from between-individual data).

Furthermore, the analysis of individual participant data allows better modeling flexibility. Whereas the analysis of aggregate data has a well-established set of analytic techniques, for analytical models, there are no limits as to how individual participant data can be analyzed. In addition to testing whether an overall effect exists and whether the effect differs across studies in subsequent subgroup analysis, discovery-oriented investigations are possible because individual participant data from multiple sources represent a larger and more diverse sample than those from single studies. This modeling flexibility encompasses the capacity to use more advanced techniques to address questions previously unanswered or to address new questions, better tackle or reduce methodological and clinical heterogeneity across studies, and benefit from greater power when examining subgroups.

In line with modeling flexibility, another important benefit of obtaining individual participant data is that more advanced research synthesis approaches are possible. For example, multivariate meta-analysis is feasible with individual participant data. Multivariate meta-analysis (Jackson et al., 2011) is a method that combines related data, such as multiple related outcomes (also called multiple endpoints; e.g., any survival and disease-specific survival, and heavy drinking and alcohol-related consequences) and multiple related interventions (e.g., multiple competing interventions in a trial). This approach borrows strength from within-study correlations, which reduces standard errors of overall effect estimates (increased precision) and mean-square error (between-study variance; for a simulation study, see Riley, 2009), thus resulting in more desirable estimates. It is possible to conduct multivariate meta-analysis using aggregate data, as long as the correlations between related conditions are known. However, they are typically unreported in published studies and are subsequently more difficult to obtain. In contrast, with individual participant data, any necessary information can be derived directly from the data in the first stage and then combined in the second stage for multivariate meta-analysis.

The modeling flexibility of individual participant data also applies when included studies in IDA provide limited overlap in measures, participants, observed time periods, and any other design aspects, which renders IDA not feasible. The principle of chaining or linking across studies is based on the availability of sufficient overlap across sufficiently similar studies. Whether sufficient overlap exists across studies can be difficult to ascertain prior to embarking on an IDA study because necessary information is not always available based on published studies alone. When individual studies cannot reasonably be linked, however, one can still check and correct data and derive equivalent estimates from each study and also combine the resulting estimates across studies for their overall magnitude and consistency.

In addition, rare adverse effects or infrequent behaviors can be better examined by using individual participant data. Infrequent low base-rate behaviors tend to be unreported in individual studies. Thus, when collecting individual participant data from individual studies, individual participant data provide unique opportunities to reasonably approach these understudied behaviors. Even when no available statistical procedures are available, a rarely observed behavior or no such behavior from a sample of 10,000 carries a different meaning than that from a sample of 500. Even for relatively more frequent behaviors, when the extent or severity of these behaviors provides additional substantive implications, a large-scale data set would provide an opportunity to test the robustness of the results from existing studies in the literature.

CONCLUSIONS AND FUTURE DIRECTIONS

The current discussion on IDA is timely because the number of funded IDA studies from the National Institute on Alcohol Abuse and Alcoholism (NIAAA), the National Institute on Drug Abuse (NIDA), and the National Institute of Mental Health (NIMH) has steadily increased each year for the past 5 years (Figure 20.8) (National Institutes of Health, 2015), but IDA as a method is relatively novel in the psychology literature. The understanding that individual participant data can be utilized in several ways can save one from labor-intensive, unsuccessful efforts to analyze individual participant data in a one-stage analysis by taking alternative routes when they are called for. The current chapter highlights various approaches to individual participant data in the context of a more unified research synthesis framework. Depending on the purpose of research and features of individual participant data at hand, the most appropriate approaches can be selected to provide large-scale evidence for more robust inference. IDA is quite challenging but has the potential to facilitate new discoveries, strengthen large-scale inference, and shore up current research practice.

Despite the noted challenges in this chapter, IDA is very promising given the current research environment. First, the current research environment increasingly emphasizes data sharing and collaboration for faster access to clinical findings. For example, the 21st Century Cures Act enacted into law in 2016 is intended to speed up access to clinical data and promote data sharing. Similarly, the Precision Medicine Initiative announced by President Obama during the 2015 State of the Union Address has been shaped by the availability of large-scale data and computing innovation to enable individualized treatment strategies (Collins & Varmus, 2015). A better understanding of what works for whom, under what circumstances, and how is a necessary condition for developing individualized treatment strategies, which can be fulfilled by large-scale IDA investigations. Second, the scientific community has increasingly been concerned about improving reproducibility or replicability (Collins & Tabak, 2014). IDA or research synthesis approaches are aimed at meeting both of these demands.

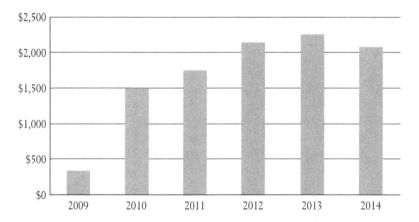

FIGURE 20.8 Total funding for IDA studies. Cumulatively, a total of 42 projects were funded by NIAAA, NIDA, and NIMH for fiscal years 2009 through 2014. Y-axis dollars are in thousands. Search keywords = "integrative data analysis" or "a multi-sample analysis."

Given the promise of IDA, it seems critical to develop some reporting guidelines to ensure the growth of IDA as a method in the field. There is a new guideline for a systematic review and meta-analysis of individual participant data (Stewart et al., 2015) based on the Preferred Reporting Items for Systematic Reviews and Meta-Analysis (PRISMA; Moher et al., 2009) of randomized controlled trials. This guideline can be extended or adapted for other types of IDA investigations. Similarly, there is a need to discuss what should be reported in IDA studies to improve transparency of such studies and to evaluate the quality of evidence resulting from IDA studies. Given the flexibility of this approach and potentially far-reaching applications, it may not be easy to establish specific standards. Nonetheless, this is necessary so that the field can develop consensus about how IDA investigations may be best reported.

Based on the discussion in this chapter, we may start by including the keywords *IDA (meta-analysis)* and *individual participant data* in the title or abstract of studies that utilize IDA for better identification and discoverability. This can be followed by a description about research goals, inclusion criteria, search and selection of eligible studies, and the representation of the combined sample in relation to broader populations. In addition, the measurement approach and missing data should be explained in sufficient detail. Also, it is recommended to include a description of how individual participant data from studies were combined, namely how between-study differences were examined and incorporated in analytical models. Finally, any challenges or issues should be clearly discussed. With continued discussions about how IDA may be best utilized to answer new questions and improve our research practice, methodological innovation is likely to follow to meet new challenges in the field.

IDA is a promising new research direction that will be called upon more frequently in the existing research environment (Hussong et al., 2013). The integration of IDA methodologies into the broader research synthesis framework may spur a wide range of new IDA investigations in the addiction field, as well as new methodological advances needed for addiction research. To maximally benefit from this approach, it is important that investigators who seek to conduct an IDA study understand that it is not a one-size-fits-all methodology. Accordingly, decisions regarding how to apply IDA to a given research question should take into account the considerations outlined in this chapter.

ACKNOWLEDGMENTS

We thank the following contributors to Project INTEGRATE in alphabetical order: David Atkins, Department of Psychiatry and Behavioral Sciences, University of Washington; John S. Baer, Department of Psychology, University of Washington, and Veterans' Affairs Puget Sound Health Care System; Nancy P. Barnett, Center for Alcohol and Addiction Studies, Brown University; M. Dolores Cimini, University Counseling Center, University at Albany, State University of New York; William R. Corbin, Department of Psychology, Arizona State University; Jimmy de la Torre, Department of Educational Psychology, Rutgers, The State University of New Jersey; Kim Fromme, Department of Psychology, The University of Texas at Austin; Joseph W. LaBrie, Department of Psychology, Loyola Marymount University; Mary E. Larimer, Department of Psychiatry and Behavioral Sciences, University of Washington; Matthew P. Martens, Department of Educational, School, and Counseling Psychology, University of Missouri; James G. Murphy, Department of Psychology, University of Memphis; Scott T. Walters, Department of Behavioral and Community Health, University of North Texas Health Science Center; Helene R. White, Center of Alcohol Studies, Rutgers, The State University of New Jersey; and the late Mark D. Wood, Department of Psychology, University of Rhode Island.

The project described was supported by Award No. R01 AA019511 from the National Institute on Alcohol Abuse and Alcoholism (NIAAA). The content is solely the responsibility of the authors and does not necessarily represent the official views of the NIAAA or the National Institutes of Health.

REFERENCES

Bauer, D. J., & Hussong, A. M. (2009). Psychometric approaches for developing commensurate measures across independent studies: Traditional and new models. *Psychological Methods, 14*(2), 101–125. doi:10.1037/a0015583

Borenstein, M., Hedges, L. V., Higgins, J. P. T., & Rothstein, H. R. (2009). *Introduction to meta-analysis*. West Sussex, UK: Wiley.

Borenstein, M., & Higgins, J. P. T. (2013). Meta-analysis and subgroups. *Prevention Science, 14*(2), 134–143. doi:10.1007/s11121-013-0377-7

Brown, C. H., Sloboda, Z., Faggiano, F., Teasdale, B., Keller, F., Burkhart, G., . . . Perrino, T. (2013). Methods for synthesizing findings on moderation effects across multiple randomized trials. *Prevention Science, 14*(2), 144–156. doi:10.1007/s11121-011-0207-8

Cheung, M. W.-L. (2015). *Meta-analysis: A structural equation modeling approach*. New York, NY: Wiley.

Collins, F. S., & Tabak, L. A. (2014). NIH plans to enhance reproducibility. *Nature, 505*, 612–613.

Collins, F. S., & Varmus, H. (2015). A new initiative on precision medicine. *New England Journal of Medicine, 372*(9), 793–795. doi:10.1056/NEJMp1500523

Cronbach, L. J. (1982). *Designing evaluations of educational and social programs*. San Francisco, CA: Jossey-Bass.

Curran, P. J., & Hussong, A. M. (2009). Integrative data analysis: The simultaneous analysis of multiple data sets. *Psychological Methods, 14*(2), 81–100. doi:10.1037/a0015914

Curran, P. J., Hussong, A. M., Cai, L., Huang, W., Chassin, L., Sher, K. J., & Zucker, R. A. (2008). Pooling data from multiple longitudinal studies: The role of item response theory in integrative data analysis. *Developmental Psychology, 44*(2), 365–380. doi:10.1037/0012-1649.44.2.365

Curran, P. J., McGinley, J. S., Bauer, D. J., Hussong, A. M., Burns, A., Chassin, L., . . . Zucker, R. (2014). A moderated nonlinear factor model for the development of commensurate measures in integrative data analysis. *Multivariate Behavioral Research, 49*(3), 214–231. doi:10.1080/00273171.2014.889594

Donegan, S., Williamson, P., D'Alessandro, U., Garner, P., & Smith, C. T. (2013). Combining individual patient data and aggregate data in mixed treatment comparison meta-analysis: Individual patient data may be beneficial if only for a subset of trials. *Statistics in Medicine, 32*(6), 914–930. doi:10.1002/sim.5584

Gasparrini, A., Armstrong, B., & Kenward, M. G. (2012). Multivariate meta-analysis for non-linear and other multi-parameter associations. *Statistics in Medicine, 31*(29), 3821–3839. doi:10.1002/sim.5471

Huh, D., Mun, E.-Y., Larimer, M. E., White, H. R., Ray, A. E., Rhew, I. C., . . . Atkins, D. C. (2015). Brief motivational interventions for college student drinking may not be as powerful as we think: An individual participant-level data meta-analysis.

Alcoholism: Clinical and Experimental Research, 39(5), 919–931. doi:10.1111/acer.12714

Huo, Y., de la Torre, J., Mun, E.-Y., Kim, S.-Y., Ray, A. E., Jiao, Y., & White, H. R. (2015). A hierarchical multi-unidimensional IRT approach for analyzing sparse, multi-group data for integrative data analysis. *Psychometrika, 80*(3), 834–855. doi:10.1007/s11336-014-9420-2

Hussong, A. M., Curran, P. J., & Bauer, D. J. (2013). Integrative data analysis in clinical psychology research. *Annual Review of Clinical Psychology, 9*(1), 61–89. doi:10.1146/annurev-clinpsy-050212-185522

Hussong, A. M., Wirth, R. J., Edwards, M. C., Curran, P. J., Chassin, L. A., & Zucker, R. A. (2007). Externalizing symptoms among children of alcoholic parents: Entry points for an antisocial pathway to alcoholism. *Journal of Abnormal Psychology, 116*(3), 529–542. doi:10.1037/0021-843X.116.3.529

Jackson, D., & Riley, R. D. (2014). A refined method for multivariate meta-analysis and meta-regression. *Statistics in Medicine, 33*(4), 541–554. doi:10.1002/sim.5957

Jackson, D., Riley, R., & White, I. R. (2011). Multivariate meta-analysis: Potential and promise. *Statistics in Medicine, 30*(20), 2481–2498. doi:10.1002/sim.4172

Jansen, J. P., Fleurence, R., Devine, B., Itzler, R., Barrett, A., Hawkins, N., . . . Cappelleri, J. C. (2011). Interpreting indirect treatment comparisons and network meta-analysis for health-care decision making: Report of the ISPOR Task Force on indirect treatment comparisons good research practices: Part 1. *Value in Health, 14*(4), 417–428. doi:10.1016/j.jval.2011.04.002

Jiao, Y., Mun, E.-Y., & Xie, M. (2017). *Multivariate random-effects meta-analysis of individual participant data from clinical trials with heterogeneous designs and partial information*. Manuscript submitted for publication.

Liu, D., Liu, R. Y., & Xie, M. (2015). Multivariate meta-analysis of heterogeneous studies using only summary statistics: Efficiency and robustness. *Journal of the American Statistical Association, 110*, 326–340. doi:10.1080/01621459.2014.899235

McArdle, J. J., Grimm, K. J., Hamagami, F., Bowles, R. P., & Meredith, W. (2009). Modeling life-span growth curves of cognition using longitudinal data with multiple samples and changing scales of measurement. *Psychological Methods, 14*(2), 126–149. doi:10.1037/a0015857

Moher, D., Liberati, A., Tetzlaff, J., Altman, D. G., & The PRISMA Group. (2009). Preferred reporting items for systematic reviews and meta-analyses: The

PRISMA statement. *PLoS Med, 6*(7), e1000097. doi:10.1371/journal.pmed.1000097

Mun, E.-Y., Atkins, D. C., & Walters, S. T. (2015). Is motivational interviewing effective at reducing alcohol misuse in young adults? A critical review of Foxcroft et al. (2014). *Psychology of Addictive Behaviors, 29*(4), 836–846. doi:10.1037/adb0000100

Mun, E.-Y., de la Torre, J., Atkins, D. C., White, H. R., Ray, A. E., Kim, S.-Y., . . . Huh, D. (2015). Project INTEGRATE: An integrative study of brief alcohol interventions for college students. *Psychology of Addictive Behaviors, 29*(1), 34–48. doi:10.1037/adb0000047

Mun, E.-Y., Jiao, Y., & Xie, M. (2016). Integrative data analysis for research in developmental psychopathology. In D. Cicchetti (Ed.), *Developmental psychopathology* (3rd ed.). New York, NY: Wiley.

National Institutes of Health. (2015). *NIH RePORTER* (Version 7.2.0) [software]. Retrieved from https://projectreporter.nih.gov/reporter.cfm

Normand, S.-L. T. (1999). Meta-analysis: Formulating, evaluating, combining, and reporting. *Statistics in Medicine, 18*(3), 321–359. doi:10.1002/(sici)1097-0258(19990215)18:3<321::aid-sim28>3.0.co;2-p

Ray, A. E., Kim, S.-Y., White, H. R., Larimer, M. E., Mun, E.-Y., Clarke, N., . . . Huh, D. (2014). When less is more and more is mess in brief motivational interventions: Characteristics of intervention content and their associations with drinking outcomes.

Psychology of Addictive Behaviors, 28, 1026–1040. doi:10.1037/a0036593

Riley, R. D. (2009). Multivariate meta-analysis: The effect of ignoring within-study correlation. *Journal of the Royal Statistical Society: Series A, 172*(4), 789–811. doi:10.1111/j.1467-985X.2008.00593.x

Riley, R. D., Lambert, P. C., Staessen, J. A., Wang, J., Gueyffier, F., Thijs, L., & Boutitie, F. (2008). Meta-analysis of continuous outcomes combining individual patient data and aggregate data. *Statistics in Medicine, 27*(11), 1870–1893. doi:10.1002/sim.3165

Simmonds, M. C., Higginsa, J. P. T., Stewartb, L. A., Tierneyb, J. F., Clarke, M. J., & Thompson, S. G. (2005). Meta-analysis of individual patient data from randomized trials: A review of methods used in practice. *Clinical Trials, 2*(3), 209–217. doi:10.1191/1740774505cn087oa

Stewart, L. A., Clarke, M., Rovers, M., Riley, R. D., Simmonds, M., Stewart, G., Tierney, J. F.; PRISMA-IPD Development Group. (2015). Preferred reporting items for a systematic review and meta-analysis of individual participant data: The PRISMA-IPD statement. *Journal of the American Medical Association, 313*(16), 1657–1665. doi:10.1001/jama.2015.3656

Sutton, A. J., & Higgins, J. P. T. (2008). Recent developments in meta-analysis. *Statistics in Medicine, 27*(5), 625–650. doi:10.1002/sim.2934

21

New Statistical Methods Inspired by Data Collected from Alcohol and Substance Abuse Research

Anne Buu

Runze Li

As we celebrate Robert A. Zucker's wonderful career in the alcohol and substance abuse field, we highlight one of his great contributions that is often overlooked: quantitative methodology. Zucker's vision for studying the etiology of alcoholism by following high-risk youth prospectively from early childhood to adulthood in the context of multiple levels of influence (individual, family, and neighborhood) creates tremendous opportunities for not only prevention scientists but also quantitative methodologists. The rich multiwave data collected from his well-known Michigan Longitudinal Study (MLS; Zucker et al., 2000) have made it possible to study childhood risk factors that predict later development of substance use disorders (Buu et al., 2009; Buu, Li, Tan, & Zucker, 2012) and to characterize the developmental trajectories of substance use-related symptomatology across different developmental stages (Buu et al., 2014; Buu, Wang, et al., 2012).

Despite the opportunities reviewed previously, the MLS data have unavoidably brought major challenges to data analysts. First, although the MLS protocol requires extensive in-home assessments at 3-year intervals and annual assessments during the critical developmental period of alcohol use (adolescence to emerging adulthood), unavailability or schedule difficulty at some waves tends to result in variable numbers of waves or assessment schedules across all participants. Classical repeated measure methods require a fixed data collection timeline and, thus, do not apply to these kinds of data. Second, a long-term study such as the MLS tends to have many more time points than those in a typical longitudinal study (less than five), so the commonly adopted growth curve modeling that prespecifies a simple shape for developmental trajectories such as linear or quadratic may not characterize the real trajectories well. Particularly, alcoholism and substance use disorders are relapsing–remitting in nature; the disease course manifests itself clinically by nondeterministic fluctuations between periods of worsening symptoms and periods of improvement. These kinds of trajectories can hardly be characterized by involving polynomial functions (i.e., employing intercept, slope, and curvature) because they have all orders of derivatives everywhere, polynomial degree cannot be controlled continuously, and further individual observations can have a large influence on remote parts of the curve (Fan & Gijbels, 1996). Third, substance use behaviors are mostly self-reported and thus are subject to measurement errors due to recall bias and social embarrassment (Tourangeau & Yan, 2007). Modern statistical techniques such as regression calibration and joint likelihood are often needed to handle these kinds of measurement errors (Bhadra, Daniels, Kim, Ghosh, & Mukherjee, 2012; Zhang, Lin, & Sowers, 2007). However, these techniques are not incorporated into commercial statistical software and thus are not accessible to prevention scientists. Fourth, substance use variables tend to be categorical instead of continuous. Particularly, they are often ordinal or zero-inflated count measurements (Buu, Johnson, Li,

& Tan, 2011; Dziak, Li, Zimmerman, & Buu, 2014). Classical regression methods that rely on the normality assumption or the generalized linear model framework (McCullagh & Nelder, 1989) are unsuitable in modeling these kinds of measurement scales. Thus, special modeling approaches such as the hurdle model (Mullahy, 1986) or the zero-inflated Poisson model (Lamber, 1992) should be adopted to deal with them.

In this chapter, we introduce some of the statistical methods that our team developed in recent years for use by prevention scientists. These methods were all inspired by data collected from the alcohol and substance abuse field, such as those from the MLS. Although they have been published in statistical journals (Buu et al., 2011; Buu, Li, et al., 2012; Dziak et al., 2014; Yang, Cranford, Li, & Buu, 2015), most prevention scientists are unaware of them and their potential wide range of applications. The purpose of this chapter is to fill this important gap of knowledge. We organize the rest of the chapter in terms of the application areas of our methodological work: (1) variable selection, (2) characterization of developmental trajectories, (3) time-varying effect modeling, and (4) psychometrics.

VARIABLE SELECTION

Many risk factors involving the neighborhood environment, such as high poverty rate and unemployment rate, have been found to be associated with residents' alcohol or other substance use (Buu et al., 2009; Cerda, Sanchez, Galea, Tracy, & Buka, 2008; Luthar & Cushing, 1999; Saxe et al., 2001; Tarter, et al., 2009). The neighborhood environment is usually characterized by descriptive statistics at the census tract level. Through geocoding, study participants' alcohol or substance use data and potential individual and familial risk factors can be merged with potential risk factors at the neighborhood level (i.e., the census tract level). However, there are many candidate variables in the census data, and some of them are highly correlated. Our methodological work was motivated by the need to select a subset of important neighborhood risk factors for alcohol use disorder (AUD) symptomatology that can be used for model-building purposes.

The number of DSM-IV (American Psychiatric Association [APA], 1994) symptom criteria for AUD

met by the participant is a commonly adopted measure for AUD severity (range, 0–11). This measure, however, tends to have a high frequency of zero values when data are collected from the general population or a community sample such as the MLS participants. Because zero-inflated count data are very common in the alcohol and substance abuse field, a variable selection method that can handle such highly skewed discrete distributions is very desirable in practice. Traditional variable selection procedures such as stepwise and best subset selection are, however, unstable—that is, small changes in the data may result in very different models (Breiman, 1995). Furthermore, when the pool of candidate variables is large, the best subset selection procedure becomes infeasible because it is computationally expensive.

Variable selection has been an active research area in the relatively recent statistical literature. The least absolute shrinkage and selection operator (LASSO; Tibshirani, 1996) and the smoothly clipped absolute deviation penalty (SCAD; Fan & Li, 2001) are two well-known variable selection procedures developed in the past few decades. Both methods have desirable properties, and both have been extended to generalized linear models that can handle binary, categorical, and count data (Park & Hastie, 2007; Zou & Li, 2008). Our team developed new variable selection procedures for zero-inflated count data using LASSO and one-step SCAD techniques (Buu et al., 2011). We adopted the zero-inflated Poisson (ZIP) model (Lambert, 1992), which employs a finite mixture of zero and a Poisson distribution to model a group of people who can *only* have zero symptoms (e.g., non-drinkers) and another group who *may* have zero symptoms (e.g., drinkers), respectively. The major strength of the ZIP model is that it can *simultaneously* accommodate one set of factors that contribute to the zero component and another set of factors that contribute to the Poisson component. Thus, our variable selection procedures involve maximizing the penalized likelihood function of the ZIP model with the LASSO or SCAD penalty function.

In order to better assess the applicability of these variable selection methods in the area of alcohol and substance abuse research, we conducted simulations to evaluate their performance based on the data features of the 2000 US census and the National Epidemiologic Survey on Alcohol and Related Conditions (NESARC; Grant et al., 2004). We also demonstrated the application of our methodology by analyzing data from the MLS. Based on the results of our simulation on the national data, we recommend the use of SCAD because (1) it can maintain both specificity and sensitivity at the highest level (mostly >.90), (2) it has the greatest accuracy of parameter estimation, and (3) it has the highest value of exact fit. In addition, it demonstrates such excellent performance not only in the Poisson component but also in the zero component. In general, its performance improves as the sample size increases, the correlation between covariates decreases, the proportion of non-zero coefficients decreases, and the proportion of zero outcome decreases.

CHARACTERIZATION OF DEVELOPMENTAL TRAJECTORIES

Measuring AUD symptomatology longitudinally can provide useful data for assessing disease progression or evaluating long-term effects of treatment or intervention. Particularly, characterizing the developmental trajectory of AUD symptomatology in a high-risk sample such as the MLS participants can identify critical developmental periods for intervention. As indicated in our introductory comments, the disease course of substance use disorders can hardly be delineated by growth curve modeling. Other important methodological challenges include excess zero values in the symptom count data and large individual differences in developmental trajectories. Our team conducted a comprehensive review and comparison of two competing models for zero-inflated count data—the ZIP model and the hurdle model—in the setting of longitudinal data analysis, which involves regression splines for modeling longitudinal trajectories and random effects for handling within-subject correlation and between-subject heterogeneity (Buu, Li, et al., 2012). We demonstrated the applications of these models by fitting them on the MLS data. We also conducted simulations to evaluate the performance of these models based on the data features of the MLS.

The ZIP model, a finite mixture of zero and a Poisson distribution, was originally proposed to model the number of defects on an item in a manufacturing process that is assumed to move randomly back and forth between a perfect state and an imperfect state (Lambert, 1992). It can simultaneously accommodate one set of factors that make the perfect state more likely and another set of factors that contribute

to fewer defects in the imperfect state. The hurdle model is an alternative model for handling zero-inflated count data that has mostly been adopted to conduct economic analysis of health care utilization (Mullahy, 1986). The model postulates a two-stage decision structure in the demand process: The first stage involves the decision to seek care; the second stage determines how much care is demanded among the subgroup of users for whom the hurdle is crossed. Like the ZIP model, the hurdle model can simultaneously accommodate two sets of factors that contribute to separate stages. Although the ZIP and hurdle models are both finite mixture models, the ZIP mixes zero and a regular Poisson, whereas the hurdle mixes zero and a truncated Poisson.

Conceptually, the ZIP model is more intuitive when the population consists of a group of people who are at risk for a disease and another group who are not at risk (e.g., women are not at risk for prostate cancer), whereas the hurdle model is more appropriate when all people in the population are considered at risk of an event and the realization of the event represents a hurdle that has been crossed (Rose, Martin, Wannemuehler, & Plikaytis, 2006). In substance abuse research, either way of conceptualization makes sense. For example, the ZIP model is applicable when we divide the population into non-drinkers who can *only* have zero alcohol-related symptoms and drinkers who *may* have zero symptoms. As another example, the hurdle model is appropriate if every person in the population is considered at risk for alcohol dependence but only some people meet at least one symptom criterion. For longitudinal studies on high-risk youth such as the MLS, people are assumed to be at different levels of risk for alcohol-related symptoms at different ages. People also change from non-drinkers to drinkers or vice versa across time. The hurdle model tends to have reasonable grounds for such settings.

The major strength of the hurdle model is that it can handle not only zero-inflated data but also zero-deflated data, whereas the ZIP model can only deal with zero-inflated data (Min & Agresti, 2005). Although this strength makes the hurdle model more applicable in general settings, it is less relevant for substance abuse data because zero-inflated count data are typically the norm, whereas zero-deflated count data are extremely rare in the field. Symptom count data collected from the general population or a community sample tend to be zero-inflated because

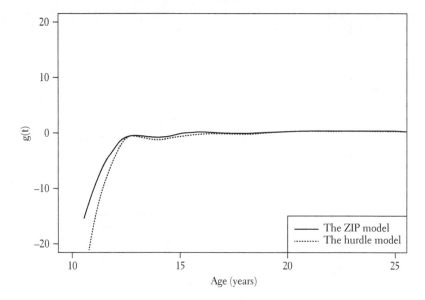

FIGURE 21.1 The developmental trajectories for the severity of AUD symptomatology (the Poisson component) based on the MLS data.

Source: Buu, A., Li, R., Tan, X., & Zucker, R. A. (2012). Statistical models for longitudinal zero-inflated count data with applications to the substance abuse field. *Statistics in Medicine, 31,* 4074–4086. doi:10.1002/sim.5510. Reprinted with permission from John Wiley and Sons.

many participants are non-drinkers or drinkers who have not yet developed symptomatology.

Even when we collect symptom count data from a treatment sample such as patients with alcohol dependence, we are likely to observe many participants having only the minimum number of symptoms (e.g., the DSM-IV [APA, 1994] requires at least three out of seven possible symptoms to meet an alcohol dependence diagnosis). The resultant data can again be analyzed by the hurdle or ZIP model with a shift on the location.

Another strength of the hurdle model is its computational simplicity. When there is no random effect, it is shown that the log-likelihood function of the hurdle model can be factored into two terms, with one involving the effect of the factors contributing to the severity of symptomatology and another involving the effect of the factors accounting for the probability of being symptom-free (Min & Agresti, 2005). Thus, one can obtain maximum likelihood estimates by *separately* maximizing the two terms. For the ZIP model, however, the model components must be fitted *simultaneously* so the computation is more complex. Nevertheless, when random effects are included, as in the longitudinal models proposed in our paper (Buu, Li, et al., 2012), this strength may disappear due to the

fact that the model components must be fit simultaneously for both models because the random effects have to be integrated out in the optimization process.

We applied both models to the longitudinal data on DSM-IV AUD symptom counts collected from the high-risk youth in the MLS, and the fitted developmental trajectories are shown in Figures 21.1 and 21.2. The developmental trajectories in the Poisson component generated by the two models look very similar—the severity level of AUD symptomatology increases rapidly from age 10 to 13 years and stays at the same high level throughout early adulthood (see Figure 21.1). On the other hand, Figure 21.2 shows that the two models produce very different developmental trajectories in the zero component during early adolescence. The ZIP model indicates that the probability of being a non-drinker increases from age 10 to 13 years, whereas the hurdle model delineates that the probability of being symptom-free decreases rapidly during the same period. Both models demonstrate that the corresponding probability gradually decreases year by year from age 13 years to the early 20s and afterwards stays relatively flat.

The developmental trajectories of AUD symptomatology under the hurdle model are more legitimate because the youth in this high-risk sample tend to start

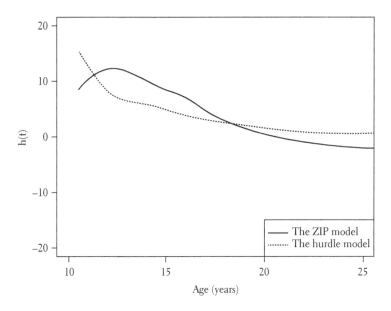

FIGURE 21.2 The developmental trajectories for the probability of being a non-drinker or symptom-free (the zero component) based on the MLS data.

Source: Buu, A., Li, R., Tan, X., & Zucker, R. A. (2012). Statistical models for longitudinal zero-inflated count data with applications to the substance abuse field. *Statistics in Medicine, 31*, 4074–4086. doi:10.1002/sim.5510. Reprinted with permission from John Wiley and Sons.

drinking earlier and thus are more likely to develop alcohol-related symptoms quickly in early adolescence. Furthermore, for longitudinal studies such as the MLS, people are assumed to be at different levels of risk for alcohol-related symptoms at different ages. People also change from non-drinkers to drinkers or vice versa across time. The logic behind the hurdle model thus tends to have reasonable grounds in such a setting. For these reasons, we designated the hurdle model as the *true model* in the simulation study.

We filled in the current knowledge gaps by conducting simulations based on the data features of the MLS to (1) investigate the consequences of using the ZIP model when the hurdle model is more natural under the conceptual framework of the data; (2) evaluate the performance under different sample sizes, proportions of missing data, and correlations between covariates; and (3) compare the computational time consumed by the two models. Our simulation results demonstrate the disadvantage of using the Poisson regression model to analyze longitudinal count data when excess zeros exist in the data: The model tends to produce much higher mean squared error (MSE) compared to the hurdle and ZIP models. Based on both the simulations and empirical analysis of real data, when the hurdle model is more natural under

the conceptual framework of the data, the ZIP model tends to result in relatively high MSE, particularly in the zero component. Moreover, the performance of the models improves with a larger sample size, lower proportion of missing data, and lower correlation between covariates. The simulation also shows that the computational strength of the hurdle model disappears when random effects are included in the model.

TIME-VARYING EFFECT MODELING

The convention of treating the association between an outcome of interest and a covariate as constant across time (i.e., time-invariant effect) has been challenged in recent years because there are many practical settings in which the phenomenon of time-varying associations exists (Walls & Schafer, 2006). For example, a smoking-cessation study found that the effect of negative affect on urge to smoke changed in a complex and dynamic way during various stages of the smoking-cessation process (Li, Root, & Shiffman, 2006). Tan et al. (2012) introduced a time-varying effect model (TVEM) for longitudinal data with continuous responses to social and behavioral science researchers. They also developed a SAS macro to implement a P-spline approach to estimating TVEM using SAS PROC MIXED. Although this macro was later extended to handle binary, count, and zero-inflated count responses (Yang, Tan, Li, & Wagner, 2012), it was not able to handle ordinal responses.

Substance use outcomes are often ordinal in nature, with participants classified in terms of degrees of use (Hedeker & Mermelstein, 2000). An important feature of this type of data is that they tend to be skewed to the right due to high frequencies at the lower end. Although it is common practice to use linear models (for continuous responses) to analyze ordinal responses with several categories, such practice has been shown to produce misleading results, especially when the response only had a few categories (less than seven) or was not distributed like a bell shape (Bauer & Sterba, 2011; Hastie, Botha, & Schnitzler, 1989). Our recent work contributed to the field by extending the TVEM to handle ordinal responses and conducting a simulation study to examine the consequences of fitting the linear TVEM to ordinal responses (Dziak et al., 2014). We also evaluated the performance of the proposed TVEM model when the number of levels on the ordinal scale, the sample size, the number of waves, and the distribution shape were varied.

We adopted the proportional odds model (Agresti, 2002) to handle the ordinal response, ensuring the proper order among the cumulative probabilities and providing simple interpretation of the effects of covariates. We also employed time-varying coefficients for the covariates whose relationships with the response are assumed to vary across time. The time-varying coefficients were treated as nonparametric functions and were approximated by the B-spline basis, which can be easily implemented in most commonly used statistical software packages such as SAS and R.

The proposed model was applied to analyze longitudinal data from the participants of the Flint Adolescent Study, an ongoing longitudinal study aiming to investigate both risk and protective factors for health risk behaviors from adolescence to adulthood (Zimmerman & Schmeelk-Cone, 2003). In general, the impact of peer factors is hypothesized to become stronger during the course of adolescence and into early adulthood, as the youth gradually establishes his or her own social network outside the home. However, few studies have found that the developmental change in this effect may be nonlinear, with

the effect being nonsignificant at some points of time (Cleveland, Feinberg, & Jones, 2012; Dishion & Owen, 2002; Van Ryzin, Fosco, & Dishion, 2012). Our investigation thus aimed to characterize the time-varying effect of negative peer influences (NPI) on alcohol use across this critical period of human development. The outcome variable was alcohol use in the past 30 days, with a 0–6 ordinal scale. The risk factor, NPI, was measured by the mean score of 13 items about how many of the participant's friends were involved in delinquent or violent behaviors, and it was treated as a continuous variable. The fitted functions for the linear TVEM are plotted in the top two panels of Figure 21.3. Dotted lines represent estimated 95% pointwise confidence intervals. The fitted functions for proportional odds TVEM are plotted in the bottom two panels of Figure 21.3. Comparison between panels b and d demonstrates different time-varying effects of NPI on drinking as characterized by the two models. The different magnitudes of the coefficients are not inherently of interest because they represent different models. However, the shapes of the coefficients differ. In particular, the linear TVEM suggests that the time of greatest peer influence is approximately age 22 years, whereas the proportional odds TVEM suggests that the time of greatest peer influence is approximately age 17 years. The later result is more consistent with the findings of existing studies (Cleveland et al., 2012; Dishion et al., 2002; Van Ryzin et al., 2012). Thus, this fitted proportional odds TVEM model was adopted as the true model to generate data in the simulation study.

The simulation study shows that the proposed model, in general, produces very small biases across different numbers of levels on the ordinal scale, sample sizes, numbers of waves, and distribution shapes, although there is a tendency for some slight bias to be found in more skewed distributions with fewer levels. Furthermore, the MSE tends to be higher in scenarios in which skewness is greater or when the number of subjects, waves, or response levels is smaller. Our simulation also shows that fitting the linear TVEM to ordinal responses is particularly problematic when the ordinal scale is highly skewed. Contrary to a common assumption that an ordinal scale with several levels can be treated as a continuous scale, our results indicate that it is not so much the number of levels on the ordinal scale but, rather, the skewness of the distribution that makes a difference on relative performance of linear versus ordinal models.

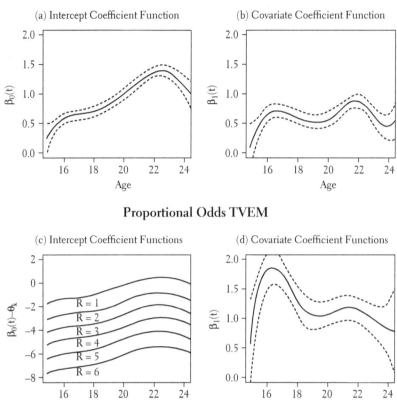

FIGURE 21.3 The fitted time-varying effect model (TVEM) on the Flint Adolescent Study data.

Source: Dziak, J. J., Li, R., Zimmerman, M. A., & Buu, A. (2014). Time-varying effect models for ordinal responses with applications in substance abuse research. *Statistics in Medicine, 33,* 5126–5137. doi:10.1002/sim.6303. Reprinted with permission from John Wiley and Sons.

PSYCHOMETRICS

Daily patterns of health risk behaviors such as substance use can be used to assess the risk of developing health problems (Mundt, Perrine, Searles, & Walter, 1995) and to examine the dynamics of intervention effects over time (Gwaltney et al., 2011). The advancement of new telecommunication technology such as the interactive voice response (IVR) has made it possible to collect this type of data *prospectively*. Prospective daily data collection using the IVR has the advantages of reducing costs of staff time as well as minimizing recall bias and the tendency to underreport socially undesirable behaviors (Bardone, Krahn, Goodman, & Searles, 2000). However, it unavoidably involves self-monitoring of the target behavior, which is an active component of some cognitive–behavioral interventions for

substance use disorders (Simpson, Kivlahan, Bush, & McFall, 2005). The potential *measurement reactivity* (defined as reducing the target behavior due to self-awareness) is undesirable for those studies that aim to investigate the association between the target behavior and its precursor or consequence. On the other hand, for those applications aiming to facilitate behavior changes, such an effect can be used to boost or extend intervention effects (Tucker, Blum, Xie, Roth, & Simpson, 2012). Thus, verifying measurement reactivity is an important psychometric issue, especially given that existing empirical investigations are few and have produced mixed results (Barta, Tennen, & Litt, 2012; Stritzke, Dandy, Durkin, & Houghton, 2005).

Another important psychometric issue associated with the IVR assessment is its *predictive validity*, which refers to the utility of the pattern of changes in these repeated measures for predicting a short-term or long-term health outcome. For example, an alcohol study may examine whether the pattern of daily alcohol consumption over a period of time is predictive of alcohol-related problems or symptoms at a later time point. In order to evaluate the effect of longitudinal patterns of health risk behaviors on a health outcome, some methodological challenges must be overcome. First, the covariate is measured at many time points but the outcome is collected at one future time point, so standard longitudinal methods that were designed for longitudinal outcomes are not applicable in this setting. Second, the effect of longitudinal patterns of health risk behaviors on a future health outcome may be a complex function of time. For example, those periods with frequent occurrence of binge drinking (defined as consuming more than five standard alcohol drinks in one episode) tend to have higher negative effects on alcohol-related problems. Third, health risk behaviors are most often self-reported and thus subject to measurement errors due to recall bias or social embarrassment (Tourangeau & Yan, 2007). Fourth, the between-subject and within-subject variability tends to be large in this kind of data, especially for studies on high-risk youth who have not yet developed regular patterns of health risk behaviors (Collins, Kashdan, Koutsky, Morsheimer, & Vetter, 2008).

In a recent study (Yang et al., 2015), we provided a statistical model that can be used to characterize the individual trajectory of the health risk behaviors collected through the IVR and examine the hypothesis of measurement reactivity. The proposed statistical model can also address all the methodological challenges associated with predictive validity. Our model involves two stages: Stage 1 estimates the smooth latent individual trajectory based on the observed longitudinal covariate process (e.g., the IVR data), which tends to contain measurement errors; Stage 2 estimates the smooth function for the time-varying effect of longitudinal patterns of health risk behaviors on a later outcome, based on the latent trajectory estimated in Stage 1 and the outcome. In the estimation procedure, we approximated the nonparametric functions corresponding to the latent trajectory and its time-varying effect by employing the natural cubic spline (Green & Silverman, 1994).

To demonstrate applications of the proposed model, we conducted statistical analysis on the real data of a study on the feasibility of using IVR technology to collect daily diary data from alcoholic couples for 14 consecutive days (Cranford, Tennen, & Zucker, 2010). We applied the proposed method to characterize the overall change in self-reported urge to drink (a binary covariate) during the 14 days of IVR assessment. Urge to drink refers to a broad range of thoughts, physical sensations, or emotions that tempt someone to drink, even though he or she has at least some desire not to do so. A decreasing trajectory of urge to drink would be evidence to support the theory of measurement reactivity. We also modeled the time-varying effect of urge to drink on a continuous scale of depression (the Beck Depression Inventory; Beck, Steer, & Brown, 1996) that was measured 6 months after the IVR assessment. This set of analysis allows us to investigate the predictive validity of the daily patterns of urge to drink.

Figure 21.4 characterizes the overall covariate trajectory and the time-varying effect. The left panel indicates that although participants' urge to drink showed a systematic decrease in the first week of IVR assessment, it rebounded during the second week. This implies that the effect of measurement reactivity was only short term. The right panel indicates that the initial level of urge to drink (i.e., before measurement reactivity took effect) was more predictive of the depression level 6 months later because the time-varying effect of urge to drink on depression was only significantly positive in the first few days of the IVR assessment.

We conducted a simulation study based on the data features of the study on alcoholic couples. The results show that the performance improves with larger sample sizes, more time points, and smaller proportions of zeros in the binary longitudinal covariate. We also evaluated the performance of the proposed method by comparing the estimated curves of the overall covariate trajectory across all subjects and the time-varying effect with the true curves in each setting. The results indicate that our proposed method estimates these curves well with relatively small bias, and the true functions are covered by 95% pointwise empirical confidence intervals in all settings.

CONCLUSIONS AND FUTURE DIRECTIONS

The methodology work by our team presented in this chapter demonstrates that empirical data collected from the alcohol and substance abuse field have special features that are often challenging analytically.

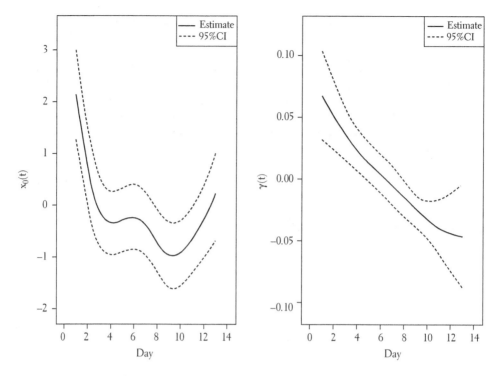

FIGURE 21.4 Trajectories of the longitudinal covariate (left) and its time-varying effect (right) based on the study on alcoholic couples. CI, confidence interval.

Source: Yang, H., Cranford, J. A., Li, R., & Buu, A. (2015). Two-stage model for time-varying effects of discrete longitudinal covariates with applications in analysis of daily process data. *Statistics in Medicine, 34,* 571–581. doi:10.1002/sim.6368. Reprinted with permission from John Wiley and Sons.

Thus, in many practical settings, the one-size-fits-all approach may produce misleading results or eliminate crucial information in the rich data. Therefore, stronger collaborations between prevention scientists and quantitative methodologists are needed to better inform future prevention and intervention work based on the data. Our joint research work with Dr. Zucker in the past few years shows the great potential of this kind of interdisciplinary collaborations.

The methodological work reviewed in this chapter may be further extended through ongoing and future collaborations between quantitative methodologists and prevention scientists so that the statistical methods can have broader applications (Yang, Li, Zucker, & Buu, 2016). Because intensive data collection methods (e.g., ecological momentary assessment and daily diaries) have been adopted more frequently for studying patterns of health behaviors, the number of relevant psychometric issues has been increasing in recent years. For example, the field needs more flexible statistical models (e.g.,

nonparametric regression) to better characterize the daily patterns of health risk behaviors in distinct groups (e.g., gender groups) and to conduct hypothesis testing for group differences (Yang, Cranford, Li, Zucker, & Buu, 2015). As another example, a new correlation measure designed for a pair of functional data needs to be developed to better study how well the retrospective timeline followback data capture the daily patterns of health risk behaviors reported in prospective diary data. Furthermore, in recent years, increasingly more longitudinal studies such as the MLS have incorporated genetic data collection in their protocols. Thus, sophisticated statistical methodology and efficient computational algorithms are becoming highly desirable in order to elucidate the complex interplay of genetic and environmental factors in developmental trajectories of substance use disorders and comorbid conditions. We are hopeful that future interdisciplinary collaborations in this exciting area of research will be fruitful.

ACKNOWLEDGMENT

This work was supported by the National Institutes of Health (NIH) (grants K01 AA016591 and R01 DA035183 to Anne Buu; grants P50 DA010075, P50 DA036107, and R01 CA168676 to Runze Li). The content is solely the responsibility of the authors and does not necessarily represent the official view of the NIH.

REFERENCES

Agresti, A. (2002). *Categorical data analysis* (2nd ed.). New York, NY: Wiley.

American Psychiatric Association. (1994). *Diagnostic and statistical manual of mental disorders* (4th ed.). Washington, DC: American Psychiatric Association.

Bardone, A. M., Krahn, D. D., Goodman, B. M., & Searles, J. S. (2000). Using interactive voice response technology and timeline follow-back methodology in studying binge eating and drinking behavior: Different answers to different forms of the same question? *Addictive Behaviors, 25*, 1–11. doi:10.1016/S0306-4603(99)00031-3

Barta, W. D., Tennen, H., & Litt, M. D. (2012). Measurement reactivity in diary research. In M. R. Mehl & T. S. Conner (Eds.), *Handbook of research methods for studying daily life* (pp. 108–123). New York, NY: Guilford.

Bauer, D. J., & Sterba, S. K. (2011). Fitting multilevel models with ordinal outcomes: Performance of alternative specifications and methods of estimation. *Psychological Methods, 16*, 373–390. doi:10.1037/a0025813

Beck, A. T., Steer, R. A., & Brown, G. K. (1996). *Manual for Beck Depression Inventory-II*. San Antonio, TX: Psychological Corporation.

Bhadra, D., Daniels, M. J., Kim, S., Ghosh, M., & Mukherjee, B. (2012). A Bayesian semiparametric approach for incorporating longitudinal information on exposure history for inference in case–control studies. *Biometrics, 68*, 361–370. doi:10.1111/j.1541-0420.2011.01686.x

Breiman, L. (1995). Better subset regression using the nonnegative garrote. *Technometrics, 37*, 373–384. doi:10.2307/1269730

Buu, A., Dabrowska, A., Mygrants, M., Puttler, L. I., Jester, J. M., & Zucker, R. A. (2014). Gender differences in the developmental risk for onset of alcohol, nicotine, and marijuana use and the effects of nicotine and marijuana use on alcohol outcomes. *Journal of Studies on Alcohol and Drugs, 75*, 850–858.

Buu, A., DiPiazza, C., Wang, J., Puttler, L. I., Fitzgerald, H. E., & Zucker, R. A. (2009). Parent, family, and neighborhood effects on the development of child substance use and other psychopathology from preschool to the start of adulthood. *Journal of Studies on Alcohol and Drugs, 70*, 489–498.

Buu, A., Johnson, N. J., Li, R., & Tan, X. (2011). New variable selection methods for zero-inflated count data with applications to the substance abuse field. *Statistics in Medicine, 30*, 2326–2340. doi:10.1002/sim.4268

Buu, A., Li, R., Tan, X., & Zucker, R. A. (2012). Statistical models for longitudinal zero-inflated count data with applications to the substance abuse field. *Statistics in Medicine, 31*, 4074–4086. doi:10.1002/sim.5510

Buu, A., Wang, W., Schroder, S. A., Kalaida, N. L., Puttler, L. I., & Zucker, R. A. (2012). Developmental emergence of alcohol use disorder symptoms and their potential as early indicators for progression to alcohol dependence in a high risk sample: A longitudinal study from childhood to early adulthood. *Journal of Abnormal Psychology, 121*, 897–908. doi:10.1037/a0024926

Cerda, M., Sanchez, B. N., Galea, S., Tracy, M., & Buka, S. L. (2008). Estimating co-occurring behavioral trajectories within a neighborhood context. *American Journal of Epidemiology, 168*, 1190–1203. doi:10.1093/aje/kwn241

Cleveland, M. J., Feinberg, M. E., & Jones, D. E. (2012). Predicting alcohol use across adolescence: Relative strength of individual, family, peer, and contextual risk and protective factors. *Psychology of Addictive Behaviors, 26*, 703–713. doi:10.1037/a0027583

Collins, L. R., Kashdan, T. B., Koutsky, J. R., Morsheimer, E. T., & Vetter, C. J. (2008). A self-administered timeline followback to measure variations in underage drinkers' alcohol intake and binge drinking. *Addictive Behaviors, 33*, 196–200. doi:10.1016/j.addbeh.2007.07.001

Cranford, J. A., Tennen, H., & Zucker, R. A. (2010). Feasibility of using interactive voice response to monitor daily drinking, moods, and relationship processes on a daily basis in alcoholic couples. *Alcoholism: Clinical and Experimental Research, 34*, 499–508. doi:10.1111/j.1530-0277.2009.01115.x

Dishion, T. J., & Owen, L. D. (2002). A longitudinal analysis of friendships and substance use: Bidirectional influence from adolescence to adulthood. *Developmental Psychology, 38*, 480–491. doi:10.1037/0012-1649.38.4.480

Dziak, J. J., Li, R., Zimmerman, M. A., & Buu, A. (2014). Time-varying effect models for ordinal responses with applications in substance abuse research. *Statistics in Medicine, 33,* 5126–5137. doi:10.1002/sim.6303

Fan, J., & Gijbels, I. (1996). *Local polynomial modeling and its applications.* London, UK: Chapman & Hall.

Fan, J., & Li, R. (2001). Variable selection via nonconcave penalized likelihood and its oracle properties. *Journal of American Statistical Association, 96,* 1348–1360. doi:10.1198/016214501753382273

Grant, B. F., Stinson, F. S., Dawson, D. A., Chou, S. P., Dufour, M. C., Compton, W., . . . Kaplan, K. (2004). Prevalence and co-occurrence of substance use disorders and independent mood and anxiety disorders: Results from the National Epidemiologic Survey on Alcohol and Related Conditions. *Archives of General Psychiatry, 61,* 807–816. doi:10.1001/archpsyc.61.8.807

Green, P. J., & Silverman, B. W. (1994). *Nonparametric regression and generalized linear models.* London, UK: Chapman & Hall.

Gwaltney, C. J., Magill, M., Barnett, N. P., Apodaca, T. R., Colby, S. M., & Monti, P. M. (2011). Using daily drinking data to characterize the effects of a brief alcohol intervention in an emergency room. *Addictive Behaviors, 36,* 248–250. doi:10.1016/j.addbeh.2010.10.010

Hastie, T. J., Botha, J. L., & Schnitzler, C. M. (1989). Regression with an ordered categorical response. *Statistics in Medicine, 8,* 785–794. doi:10.1002/sim.4780080703

Hedeker, D., & Mermelstein, R. J. (2000). Analysis of longitudinal substance use outcomes using ordinal random-effects regression models. *Addiction, 95,* S381–S394. doi:10.1080/09652140020004296

Lambert, D. (1992). Zero-inflated Poisson regression, with an application to defects in manufacturing. *Technometrics, 34,* 1–13. doi:10.2307/1269547

Li, R., Root, T. L., & Shiffman, S. (2006). A local linear estimation procedure for functional multilevel modeling. In T. A. Walls & J. L. Schafer (Eds.), *Models for intensive longitudinal data* (pp. 63–83). New York, NY: Oxford University Press.

Luthar, S. S., & Cushing, G. (1999). Neighborhood influences and child development: A prospective study of substance abusers' offspring. *Development and Psychopathology, 11,* 763–784. doi:10.1017/S095457949900231X

McCullagh, P., & Nelder, J. A. (1989). *Generalized linear models.* London, UK: Chapman & Hall.

Min, Y., & Agresti, A. (2005). Random effect models for repeated measures of zero-inflated count data. *Statistical Modeling, 5,* 1–19. doi:10.1191/1471082X05st084oa

Mullahy, J. (1986). Specification and testing of some modified count data models. *Journal of Econometrics, 33,* 341–365. doi:10.1016/0304-4076(86)90002-3

Mundt, J. C., Perrine, M. W., Searles, J. S., & Walter, D. (1995). An application of interactive voice response (IVR) technology to longitudinal studies of daily behavior. *Behavior Research Methods, Instruments, & Computers, 27,* 351–357. doi:10.3758/BF03200429

Park, M. Y., & Hastie, T. (2007). L1-regularization path algorithm for generalized linear models. *Journal of Royal Statistical Society B, 69,* 659–677. doi:10.1111/j.1467-9868.2007.00607.x

Rose, C. E., Martin, S. W., Wannemuehler, K. A., & Plikaytis, B. D. (2006). On the use of zero-inflated and hurdle models for modeling vaccine adverse event count data. *Journal of Biopharmaceutical Statistics, 16,* 463–481. doi:10.1080/10543400600719384

Saxe, L., Kadushin, C., Beveridge, A., Livert, D., Tighe, E., Rindskopf, D., . . . Brodky, A. (2001). The visibility of illicit drugs: Implications for community-based drug control strategies. *American Journal of Public Health, 91,* 1987–1994. doi:10.2105/AJPH.91.12.1987

Simpson, T. L., Kivlahan, D. R., Bush, K. R., & McFall, M. E. (2005). Telephone self-monitoring among alcohol use disorder patients in early recovery: A randomized study of feasibility and measurement reactivity. *Drug and Alcohol Dependence, 79,* 241–250. doi:10.1016/j.drugalcdep.2005.02.001

Stritzke, W. G. K., Dandy, J., Durkin, K., & Houghton, S. (2005). Use of interactive voice response (IVR) technology in health research with children. *Behavior Research Methods, 37,* 119–126. doi:10.3758/BF03206405

Tan, X., Shiyko, M. P., Li, R., Li, Y., & Dierker, L. (2012). A time-varying effect model for intensive longitudinal data. *Psychological Methods, 17,* 61–77. doi:10.1037/a0025814

Tarter, R. E., Kirisci, L., Gavaler, J. S., Reynolds, M., Kirillova, G., Clark, D. B., . . . Vanyukov, M. (2009). Prospective study of the association between abandoned dwellings and testosterone level on the development of behaviors leading to cannabis use disorder in boys. *Biological Psychiatry, 65,* 116–121. doi:10.1016/j.biopsych.2008.08.032

Tibshirani, R. J. (1996). Regression shrinkage and selection via the LASSO. *Journal of Royal Statistical Society B, 58,* 267–288.

Tourangeau, R., & Yan, T. (2007). Sensitive questions in surveys. *Psychological Bulletin, 133,* 859–883. doi:10.1037/0033-2909.133.5.859

Tucker, J. A., Blum, E. R., Xie, L., Roth, D. L., & Simpson, C. A. (2012). Interactive voice response self-monitoring to assess risk behaviors in rural substance users living with HIV/AIDS. *AIDS and Behavior, 16,* 432–440. doi:10.1007/s10461-011-9889-y

Van Ryzin, M. J., Fosco, G. M., & Dishion, T. J. (2012). Family and peer predictors of substance use from early adolescence to early adulthood: An 11-year prospective analysis. *Addictive Behaviors, 37,* 1314–1324. doi:10.1016/j.addbeh.2012.06.020

Walls, T. A., & Schafer, J. L. (Eds.). (2006). *Models for intensive longitudinal data.* New York, NY: Oxford University Press.

Yang, H., Cranford, J. A., Li, R., & Buu, A. (2015). Two-stage model for time-varying effects of discrete longitudinal covariates with applications in analysis of daily process data. *Statistics in Medicine, 34,* 571–581. doi:10.1002/sim.6368

Yang, H., Li, R., Zucker, R. A., & Buu, A. (2016). Two-stage model for time-varying effects of zero-inflated count longitudinal covariates with applications in health behavior research. *Journal of the Royal Statistical Society Series C, 65*(3), 431–444.

Yang, S., Cranford, J. A., Li, R., Zucker, R. A., & Buu, A. (2015). A time-varying effect model for studying gender differences in health behavior. *Statistical Methods in Medical Research.* Epub ahead of print.

Yang, J., Tan, X., Li, R., & Wagner, A. (2012). *TVEM (time-varying effect model) SAS macro suite users' guide* (Version 2.1.0). University Park, PA: The Methodology Center, Pennsylvania State University. Retrieved from https://methodology.psu.edu

Zhang, D., Lin, X., & Sowers, M. F. (2007). Two-stage functional mixed models for evaluating the effect of longitudinal covariate profiles on a scalar outcome. *Biometrics, 63,* 351–362. doi:10.1111/j.1541-0420.2006.00713.x

Zimmerman, M. A., & Schmeelk-Cone, K. H. (2003). A longitudinal analysis of adolescent substance use and school motivation among African American youth. *Journal of Research on Adolescence, 13,* 185–210. doi:10.1111/1532-7795.1302003

Zou, H., & Li, R. (2008). One-step sparse estimates in nonconcave penalized likelihood models (with discussion). *Annals of Statistics, 36,* 1509–1566. doi:10.1214/009053607000000802

Zucker, R. A., Fitzgerald, H. E., Refior, S. K., Puttler, L. I., Pallas, D. M., & Ellis, D. A. (2000). The clinical and social ecology of childhood for children of alcoholics: Description of a study and implications for a differentiated social policy. In H. E. Fitzgerald, B. M. Lester, & B. S. Zuckerman (Eds.), *Children of addiction* (pp. 109–142). New York, NY: Garland.

Index